# THE LITTLE, BROWN READER

# THE LITTLE, BROWN READER

*Third Edition*

*Edited by*

MARCIA STUBBS
*Wellesley College*

SYLVAN BARNET
*Tufts University*

**Little, Brown and Company**
*Boston Toronto*

Library of Congress Cataloging in Publication Data
Main entry under title:

The Little, Brown reader.

Includes index.
1. College readers. I. Stubbs, Marcia. II. Barnet, Sylvan.
PE1122.L56 1982 808'.0427 82-20812
ISBN 0-316-82005-9



Library of Congress Catalog Card Number 82-20812

ISBN 0-316-82005-9

9 8 7 6 5 4 3 2 1

MV

Published simultaneously in Canada
by Little, Brown & Company (Canada) Limited

Printed in the United States of America

Produced by Ron Newcomer & Associates

## ACKNOWLEDGMENTS

Maya Angelou, "Graduation" from *I Know Why The Caged Bird Sings,* by Maya Angelou. Copyright © 1969 by Maya Angelou. Reprinted by permission of Random House, Inc.

Anonymous, "Confessions of an Erstwhile Child" from *The New Republic,* June 15, 1974. Reprinted by permission of *The New Republic,* © 1974, The New Republic, Inc.

Anonymous Japanese, "Muddy Road" from *Zen Flesh, Zen Bones* compiled by Paul Reps. Copyright © 1957 by Charles E. Tuttle Co., Inc. Reprinted by permission of Charles E. Tuttle Co., Inc., Tokyo, Japan.

(*continued on page 650*)

# PREFACE

Books have been put to all sorts of unexpected uses. Tolstoy used Tatishef's dictionaries as a test of physical endurance, holding them in his outstretched hand for five minutes, enduring "terrible pain." Books (especially pocket-sized Bibles) have served as armor by deflecting bullets. And they have served as weapons: two hundred years ago the formidable Dr. Johnson knocked a man down with a large book. In this volume you may read of a book hurled at the head of a bigot, with salutary results.

In a course in expository writing, what is the proper use of the book in hand? This anthology contains some eighty essays, together with a few poems, stories, and fables, and numerous paragraphs and aphorisms. But these readings are not the subject matter of the course; writing courses (notoriously) have no subject matter except the essays that the students themselves produce. The responsibilities we felt as editors, then, were to include selections that encourage and enable students to write well, and to exclude selections that do not.

To talk of "enabling" first: students, like all other writers, write best when they write on fairly specific topics that can come within their experience and within their command in the week or so they are given to write an essay. A glance at the first four sections of our table of contents will reveal the general areas within which, we believe, students can find topics they have already given some thought to and are likely to be encountering in other courses as well: family relationships, love and courtship; food and diet, clothing, buildings and neighborhoods; schools; work, sports, and play. Although the next two sections ("Messages" and "Networks") are also on familiar subjects—language, including body language, and popular culture—the selections offer ways of thinking about them that may be less familiar. Television commercials and films, for example, can be thought of as networks that articulate and transmit values implicit in a culture. The last three sections are about areas of experience that, while hardly remote from students' interests, are perhaps more difficult for all of us to grasp concretely: the roots of aggression and alienation; the tension between civil rights and liberties and the need for law and order; the memories, passions, and myths that shape or embody our personal values, our identities, and our being. In these last sections, therefore, we have taken particular care to exclude writing that is, for our purposes, too abstract, or too technical, or too elaborate.

This returns us to the need we felt as editors to think carefully about whether selections we were inclined to use—because they were beautifully written or on a stimulating topic—would encourage students to write. Such encouragement does not come, we feel, solely from the subject of an essay or from its excellence; it comes when the essay engenders in the reader a confidence in the writing process itself. No one quality in essays automatically teaches such confidence: not length or brevity, not difficulty or simplicity, not necessarily clarity, and almost certainly not brilliance. But essays that teach writing demonstrate, in some way, that the writers had some stake in what they were saying, took some pains to say what they meant, and took pleasure in having said it. The selections we include vary in length, complexity, subtlety, tone, and purpose. Most were written by our contemporaries, but not all. The authors include historians, sociologists, architects, scientists, saints, and philosophers, as well as journalists and other professional writers. And we have included some pictures in each section. But we hope everything here will allow students, including those who have previously read very little, to establish helpful connections between the activities that produced the words (and pictures) in these pages and their own work in putting critical responses to them on paper.

Although any arrangement of the selections—thematic, rhetorical, alphabetical, chronological, or random—would have suited our purposes, we preferred the thematic arrangement. For one thing, by narrowing our choices it helped us to make decisions. But more important, we know that in the real world what people write about is subjects, and we didn't want to miss any opportunity to suggest that what goes on in writing courses is something like what goes on outside. The thematic categories are not intended to be rigid, however, and they do not pretend to be comprehensive; some of the questions following the selections suggest that leaping across boundaries is permitted, even encouraged. And, for instructors who prefer to organize their writing courses rhetorically, we have added a selective table of contents organized rhetorically. Finally, we append a glossary of terms for students of writing, a brief essay on reading and writing about essays and another on looking and writing about pictures. The pictures (beautiful things in themselves, we think), like the essays, stories, and poems, suggest or provide immediate or nearly immediate experiences for students to write about.

As usual, we are indebted to readers-in-residence. Morton Berman, William Burto, and Judith Stubbs have often read our material and then told us what we wanted to hear.

While we were selecting the essays, we received helpful advice from Eric D. Brown, Jay Cantor, Kenneth Cooney, William Devlin, George D. Haich, Ruth C. Hege, William E. Lucas, William Lutz, Mary Shesgreen, Judith Stanford, Michael West and Harvey Vetstein.

We thank those instructors who generously offered suggestions based on their classroom experience with the first edition: Kenneth Alrutz, Lloyd Becker, Frank Bidart, Anne Burley, Lillian Broderick, Ruth Brown, John Clifford, Ann Connor, Anne Cooney, Kenneth Cooney, Marion Copeland, Fiona Emde, Robert Erickson, Richard Fahey, Michael Feehan, Gretchen Fillmore, Sister Jeremy Finnegan, Martha Flint, William Ford, James French, Charles Frey, Steven Harvey, Mal Haslett, George Hayhoe, John Howe, William Howrath, Michael Kalter, George Miller, John Milstead, John Nesselhof, Robert Ohafson, Richard Priebe, Phyllis Reed, Duncan Rollo, Harriet Rosenblum, Ronald Ruland, Ralph St. Louis, Emerson Shuck, Carol Sicherman, Mark Smith, Harry Solomon, John Stahl, David Templeman, Robert Thompson, Anthony Vital, and Lyn Yonack.

We owe a special debt to Professor John Harwood and other teachers in the composition program at Pennsylvania State University for suggesting ways in which *The Little, Brown Reader* can be used in a course that emphasizes persuasive writing.

We also thank those instructors who generously offered suggestions based on their classroom experience with the second edition: Bonnie Alexander, Norman Sidney Ashbridge, Andrew Aung, Donald Babcock, Jean Young Brunk, Beth Burch, Debra L. Burgauet, J. V. Chambers, Anne W. Cooney, Robert Cosgrove, John A. R. Dick, Evelyn Farbman, Linda Feldmeier, Kathleen P. Flint, Joseph S. Frany, Yvonne Frey, Hymen H. Hart, Pat Hart, Stephen Hathaway, Mark Hawkins, Zelda Hedden-Sellman, Dr. Elbert R. Hill, Maureen Hoal, Kathryn Holms, Morris Husted, Lois B. Janzer, F. A. Kachur, Walt Klarner, Robert Knox, Sandra M. Lee, Dorinda Lemaire, Claudia Limbert, Joyce D. Lipkis, Marie M. McAllister, Gary Merritt, Mary

F. Minton, Chris M. Mott, Jewyl Pallette, Karyn Riedell, Carole Starikoff, William B. Stone, William L. Stull, Tereatha Taylor, Dr. Lorraine Viscardi, Mark Wenz, and Lee Yosha.

People at Little, Brown have been unfailingly helpful; we would especially like to thank Sarah Clark, Wayne Ellis, Donna McCormick, Carolyn Potts, and Julie Winston.

## *A Note on the Third Edition*

"Never read a book that is not old." Thus Emerson. It's good advice but we are of course pleased that when *The Little, Brown Reader* was published it immediately found a receptive audience. A second edition allowed us to strengthen the book by adding some recent essays, and now the publisher has asked for a third edition, in order to meet the needs of instructors who wish to continue to use the book but who also want something new. William Hazlitt, Emerson's older contemporary, said that he always read an old book when a new one was published; we hope that this new edition allows instructors to read both at once, for although we have added many fresh essays throughout and an entire new section ("Law and Order"), we have also tried to preserve the character of the original book.

# CONTENTS

## 1 ALL IN THE FAMILY

*Denotes fiction.

**Denotes poetry.

## 4 WORK AND PLAY

## 6 NETWORKS

# RHETORICAL GUIDE

## Analogy

Hasidic Tale
Plato, *The Myth of the Cave, Crito*
Wu-Tsu Fa-Yen, *Zen and the Art of Burglary*
Lewis Thoms, *On Committees*
Louis D. Brandeis, *Short View*
"Analogy" in *A Writer's Glossary*

## Analysis or Classification

Jane Howard, *All Happy Clans Are Alike: In Search of the Good Family*
Peter Singer, *Animal Liberation*
Peter Farb and George Armelagos, *The Patterns of Eating*
Ruth Gay, *Fear of Food*
Paul Goldberger, *Quick! Before It Crumbles!*
Robert Sommer, *Hard Architecture*
Neil Postman, *Order in the Classroom*
Bertrand Russell, *Work*
W. H. Auden, *Work, Labor, and Play*
Jeff Greenfield, *The Black and White Truth About Basketball*
Gilbert Highet, *The Gettysburg Address*
Edward T. Hall, *Proxemics in the Arab World*
Stanley Milgram, *Confessions of a News Addict*
Lewis Thomas, *On Committees*
Mark Stevens, *Goya's* Third of May, 1808
Desmond Morris, *Altruistic Behavior*
Martin Luther King, Jr., *Nonviolent Resistance*
Plato, *Crito*
Jacques Barzun, *In Favor of Capital Punishment*

Henry Schwarzschild, *In Opposition to Death Penalty Legislation*
E. M. Forster, *My Wood*
*Reading (and Writing About) Pictures*
"Analysis" in *A Writer's Glossary*

## Argument
(See *Persuasion*)

## Autobiography
(See *Journal and Personal Report*)

## Cause and Effect

Ruth Gay, *Fear of Food*
Paul B. Diederich, *Short View*
Neil Postman, *Order in the Classroom*
Paul Goodman, *A Proposal to Abolish Grading*
Virginia Woolf, *Professions for Women*
Marya Mannes, *Television Advertising: The Splitting Image*
Thomas Hobbes, *Of the Natural Condition of Mankind*
Lewis Thomas, *The Iks*
Desmond Morris, *Altruistic Behavior*
Louis D. Brandeis, *Short View*
Thomas Jefferson, *The Declaration of Independence*
E. M. Forster, *My Wood*
Henry Schwarzchild, *In Opposition to Death Penalty Legislation*

## Comparison and Contrast

Paul Goldberger, *Quick! Before It Crumbles!*
Anne Hollander, *Clothes Make the Man—Uneasy*
Robert Sommer, *Hard Architecture*
E. B. White, *Education*
Paul Robinson, *TV Can't Educate*
W. H. Auden, *Work, Labor, and Play*
Jeff Greenfield, *The Black and White Truth About Basketball*
Edward T. Hall, *Proxemics in the Arab World*
Joseph Wood Krutch, *Short View*

## Definition



## Description



## Diction

## Examples, Illustrations



## Evaluation



## Exposition

## Irony
(See also *Parody* and *Persuasion*)



## Journal and Personal Report

John R. Coleman, *Blue-Collar Journal*
Studs Terkel, *Three Workers*
Black Elk, *War Games*
John Updike, *The Playground*
Richard A. Hawley, *Television and Adolescents: A Teacher's View*
Stanley Milgram, *Confessions of a News Addict*
E. M. Forster, *My Wood*
William Butler Yeats, *Remembering "The Lake Isle of Innisfree"*
Vladimir Nabokov, *Speak, Memory*
Joan Didion, *On Going Home*
May Sarton, *The Rewards of Living a Solitary Life*

## Narration

Laura Cunningham, *The Girls' Room*
Black Elk, *High Horse's Courting*
Maya Angelou, *Graduation*
Wu-tsu Fa-yen, *Zen and the Art of Burglary*
Nakajima Atushi, *The Expert*
Arturo Vivante, *The Orchard*
Malcolm X, *The Shoeshine Boy*
Richard A. Hawley, *Television and Adolescents: A Teacher's View*
James Baldwin, *Stranger in the Village*
George Orwell, *Shooting an Elephant*
Luke, *Parable of the Prodigal Son*
Luke, *Parable of the Good Samaritan*
John, *The Woman Taken in Adultery*
Anonymous Japanese, *Muddy Road*
Chewing Blackbones, *Old Man and Old Woman*
"Narration," "Parable" in *A Writer's Glossary*

## Parody

W. S. Merwin, *Make This Simple Test*
Oliver Jensen, *The Gettysburg Address in Eisenhowese*
C. S. Lewis, *Xmas and Christmas*
"Parody" in *A Writer's Glossary*

## Persuasion

Anonymous, *Confessions of an Erstwhile Child*
Peter Singer, *Animal Liberation*
Robert Sommer, *Hard Architecture*
Plato, *The Myth of the Cave*
E. B. White, *Education*
Neil Postman, *Order in the Classroom*
John Holt, *The Right to Control One's Learning*
Paul Goodman, *A Proposal to Abolish Grading*
Paul Robinson, *TV Can't Educate*
Thomas More, *Work and Play in Utopia*
C. S. Lewis, *Xmas and Christmas*
Thomas Hobbes, *Of the Natural Condition of Mankind*
Martin Luther King, Jr., *Nonviolent Resistance*
Plato, *Crito*
Thomas Jefferson, *The Declaration of Independence*
Rosika Schwimmer, *Court Record of Petition for Naturalization*
Pierce Butler, *Opinion of the Supreme Court, in* U.S. *v.* Rosika Schwimmer
Oliver Wendell Holmes, *Dissent in the Rosika Schwimmer Case*
Jacques Barzun, *In Favor of Capital Punishment*
Henry Schwarzschild, *In Opposition to Death Penalty Legislation*
C. S. Lewis, *We Have No "Right to Happiness"*
"Analogy," "Argument," "Deduction," "Generalization," "Induction," "Persuasion" in *A Writer's Glossary*

## Style

Henry David Thoreau, *As for Clothing*
E. B. White, *Education*
Arturo Vivante, *The Orchard*
Abraham Lincoln, *Address at the Dedication of the Gettysburg National Cemetery*
Gilbert Highet, *The Gettysburg Address*
Oliver Jensen, *The Gettysburg Address in Eisenhowese*
Lewis Thomas, *The Iks*
Martin Luther King, Jr., *Nonviolent Resistance*
Thomas Jefferson, *The Declaration of Independence*
Vladimir Nabokov, *Speak, Memory*
E. M. Forster, *My Wood*
"Style" in *A Writer's Glossary*

# THE LITTLE, BROWN READER

# 1

# ALL IN THE FAMILY

*Outside a Bistro, France*
**Henri Cartier-Bresson, 1968–1969**

**Magnum**

*Sonia*
**Joanne Leonard, 1966**

Woodfin Camp and Associates

*The Acrobat's Family with a Monkey*
**Pablo Picasso, 1905**

Courtesy of the Göteborgs Konstmuseum

*Feeding Time*
**Paul Martin, 1892**

Courtesy of Anthony D'Offay

# Short Views

After a certain age, the more one becomes oneself, the more obvious one's family traits become.

**Marcel Proust**

All happy families resemble one another; every unhappy family is unhappy in its own fashion.

**Leo Tolstoy, *Anna Karenina***

On Tuesday, March 31, he and I dined at General Paoli's. A question was started, whether the state of marriage was natural to man. Johnson. "Sir, it is so far from being natural for a man and woman to live in a state of marriage, that we find all the motives which they have for remaining in that connection, and the restraints which civilized society imposes to prevent separation, are hardly sufficient to keep them together." The General said, that in a state of nature a man and woman uniting together would form a strong and constant affection, by the mutual pleasure each would receive; and that the same causes of dissension would not arise between them, as occur between husband and wife in a civilized state. Johnson. "Sir, they would have dissensions enough, though of another kind. One would choose to go a hunting in this wood, the other in that; one would choose to go a fishing in this lake, the other in that; or, perhaps, one would choose to go a hunting, when the other would choose to go a fishing; and so they would part. Besides, Sir, a savage man and a savage woman meet by chance; and when the man sees another woman that pleases him better, he will leave the first." . . .

**James Boswell**

Marriage is the best of human statuses and the worst, and it will continue to be. And that is why, though its future in some form or other is as assured as anything can be, this future is as equivocal as its past. The demands that men and women make on marriage will never be fully met; they cannot be.

**Jessie Bernard**

The basis of the family is, of course, the fact that parents feel a special kind of affection towards their own children, different from that which they feel towards each other or towards other children. It is true that some parents feel little or no parental affection, and it is also true that some women are capable of feeling an affection for children not their own almost as strong as that which they could feel for their own. Nevertheless the broad fact remains, that parental affection is a special kind of feeling which the normal human being experiences towards his or her own children, but not towards any other human being. This emotion is one which we inherit from our animal ancestors. In this respect Freud seems to me not sufficiently biological in his outlook, for anyone who will observe an animal mother with her young can see that her behavior towards them follows an entirely different pattern from her behavior towards the male with whom she has sex relations. And this same different and instinctive pattern, though in a modified and less definite form, exists among human beings. If it were not for this special emotion there would be almost nothing to be said for the family as an institution, since children might equally well be left to the care of professionals. As things are, however, the special affection which parents have for children, provided their instincts are not atrophied, is of value both to the parents themselves and to the children. The value of parental affection to children lies largely in the fact that it is more reliable than any other affection. One's friends like one for one's merits, one's lovers for one's charms; if the merits or the charms diminish, friends and lovers may vanish. But it is in times of misfortune that parents are most to be relied upon, in illness, and even in disgrace if the parents are of the right sort. We all feel pleasure when we are admired for our merits, but most of us are sufficiently modest at heart to feel that such admiration is precarious. Our parents love us because we are their children and this is an unalterable fact, so that we feel more safe with them than with anyone else. In times of success this may seem unimportant, but in times of failure it affords a consolation and a security not to be found elsewhere.

**Bertrand Russell**

A slavish bondage to parents cramps every faculty of the mind; and Mr. Locke very judiciously observes, that "if the mind be curbed and humbled too much in children; if their spirits be abased and broken much by too strict an hand over them; they lose all their vigour and industry." This strict hand may in some degree account for the weakness of women; for girls, from various causes, are more kept down by their parents, in every sense of the word, than boys. The duty expected from them is, like all the duties arbitrarily imposed on women, more from a sense of propriety, more out of respect for decorum, than reason; and thus taught slavishly to submit to their parents, they are prepared for the slavery of marriage. I may be told that a number of women are not slaves in the marriage state. True, but they then become tyrants; for it is not rational freedom, but a lawless kind of power resembling the authority exercised by the favourites of absolute monarchs, which they obtain by debasing means.

**Mary Wollstonecraft**

Twenty years from now humanity will be in the midst of one of its most painful and difficult social changes. This century will be the last in which families of more than two children can be tolerated; everyone knows this, and the only argument is over the means of achieving the goal. But there is another aspect of the matter which is seldom given much serious consideration.

The two-child family is not large enough to generate the interactions that develop a good personality; this is why single children are often monsters. Probably the optimum number of siblings is four or five—twice the permissible quota. This means that, somehow, several families must be psychologically fused together for the health of the child, and of society. Working out ways of doing this will raise the blood pressure of a whole generation of lawyers and moralists.

**Arthur C. Clarke**

Nobody who has not been in the interior of a family can say what the difficulties of any individual of that family may be.

**Jane Austen, *Emma***

Lewis Coser

# The Family

Following the French anthropologist Claude Lévi-Strauss, we can define the family as a group manifesting these characteristics: it finds its origin in marriage; it consists of husband, wife and children born in their wedlock—though other relatives may find their place close to that nuclear group; and the members of the group are united by moral, legal, economic, religious, and social rights and obligations. These include a network of sexual rights and prohibitions and a variety of socially patterned feelings such as love, attraction, piety, awe, and so on.

The family is among the few universal institutions of mankind. No known society lacks small kinship groups of parents and children related through the process of reproduction. But recognition of the universality of this institution must immediately be followed by the acknowledgment that its forms are exceedingly varied. The fact that many family organizations are not monogamic, as in the West, led many nineteenth-century observers to the erroneous conclusion that in "early" stages of evolution there existed no families, and that "group marriage," institutionalized promiscuity, prevailed. This is emphatically not the case; even though patterned wife-lending shocked the sensibilities of Victorian anthropologists, such an institution is evidently predicated on the fact that men have wives in the first place. No matter what their specific forms, families in all known societies have performed major social functions—reproduction, maintenance, socialization, and social placement of the young.

Families may be monogamous or polygamous—there are systems where one man is entitled to several wives and others where several husbands share one wife. A society may recognize primarily the small nuclear conjugal unit of husband and wife with their immediate descendants or it may institutionalize the large extended family linking several generations and emphasizing consanguinity more

Lewis Coser, born in Berlin, in 1913, was educated at the Sorbonne in Paris and at Columbia University, where he received a Ph.D. in sociology in 1954. He now teaches at the State University of New York, Stony Brook, and holds the title Distinguished Professor.

than the conjugal bond. Residence after marriage may be matrilocal, patrilocal or neolocal; exchanges of goods and services between families at the time of marriage may be based on bride price, groom price or an equal exchange; endogamous or exogamous regulations may indicate who is and who is not eligible for marriage; the choice of a mate may be controlled by parents or it may be left in large measure to the young persons concerned. These are but a few of the many differences which characterize family structures in variant societies.

## Questions

1. At the end of his second paragraph, Coser writes: "No matter what their specific forms, families in all known societies have performed major social functions—reproduction, maintenance, socialization, and social placement of the young." What does "socialization of the young" mean? How does it differ from "social placement of the young"? What specific forms does each take in our society?
2. Can you give examples of "moral, legal, economic, religious, and social rights and obligations" (page 9) that unite members of a family?
3. Compare Coser and Plumb (pages 10–14) on the social functions of the family. According to Plumb, what responsibility does the family in our society have in performing the social functions Coser lists? How do other institutions compete with the family in performing some of these functions?

J. H. Plumb

# The Dying Family

I was rather astonished when a minibus drove up to my house and out poured ten children. They had with them two parents, but not one child had them both in common as mother and father,

J[ohn] H[arold] Plumb, born in England in 1911, was professor of modern English history at the University of Cambridge until his retirement. He also taught at universities in the United States.

and two of them belonged to neither parent, but to a former husband of the wife who had died. Both parents, well into middle age, had just embarked, one on his fourth, the other on her third marriage. The children, who came in all sizes, and ranged from blonde nordic to jet-haired Greek, bounded around the garden, young and old as happy as any children that I have seen. To them, as Californians, their situation was not particularly odd; most of their friends had multiple parents. Indeed to them perhaps the odd family was the one which Western culture has held up as a model for two thousand years or more—the lifelong union of man and wife. But it took me a very long time to believe that they could be either happy or adjusted. And yet, were they a sign of the future, a way the world was going?

Unlike anthropologists or sociologists, historians have not studied family life very closely. Until recently we knew very little of the age at which people married in Western Europe in the centuries earlier than the nineteenth or how many children they had, or what the rates of illegitimacy might be or whether, newly wed, they lived with their parents or set up a house of their own. Few of these questions can be answered with exactitude even now, but we can make better guesses. We know even less, however, of the detailed sexual practices that marriage covered: indeed this is a subject to which historians are only just turning their attention. But we do know much more of the function of family life—its social role—particularly if we turn from the centuries to the millennia and pay attention to the broad similarities rather than the fascinating differences between one region and another: and, if we do, we realize that the family has changed far more profoundly than even the bus load of Californians might lead us to expect.

Basically the family has fulfilled three social functions—to provide a basic labor force, to transmit property and to educate and train children not only into an accepted social pattern, but also in the work skills upon which their future subsistence would depend. Until very recent times, the vast majority of children never went to any school: their school was the family, where they learned to dig and sow and reap and herd their animals, or they learned their father's craft of smith or carpenter or potter. The unitary family was particularly good at coping with the small peasant holdings which covered most of the world's fertile regions from China to Peru. In the primitive peasant world a child of four or five could begin to earn its keep in the fields, as they still can in India and Africa: and whether Moslem, Hindu, Inca or Christian, one wife at a time was all that the bulk of the world's population could support, even though their religion permitted them more. Indeed, it was the primitive nature of peasant economy which gave the family, as we know it, its wide diffusion and its remarkable continuity.

Whether or not it existed before the neolithic revolution we shall never know, but certainly it must have gained in strength as families became rooted to the soil. Many very primitive people who live in a pre-agrarian society of hunting and food-gathering often tend to have a looser structure of marriage and the women a far greater freedom of choice and easier divorce, as with the Esquimaux, than is permitted in peasant societies. There can be little doubt that the neolithic revolution created new opportunities for the family as we know it, partly because this revolution created new property relations. More importantly it created great masses of property, beyond anything earlier societies had known. True, there were a few hunting peoples, such as the Kwakiutl Indians, who had considerable possessions—complex lodges, great pieces of copper and piles of fibre blankets, which periodically they destroyed in great battles of raging pride—but the property, personal or communal, of most primitive hunting people is usually trivial.

After the revolution in agriculture, property and its transmission lay at the very heart of social relations and possessed an actuality which we find hard to grasp. Although we are much richer, possessions are more anonymous, often little more than marks in a ledger, and what we own constantly changes. Whereas for the majority of mankind over this last seven thousand years property has been deeply personal and familial: a plot of land, if not absolute ownership over it, then valuable rights in it; sometimes a house, even though it be a hovel by our standards; perhaps no more than the tools and materials of a craft, yet these possessions were the route both to survival and to betterment. Hence they were endowed with manna, bound up with the deepest roots of personality. In all societies the question of property became embedded in every aspect of family life, particularly marriage and the succession and rights of children. Because of property's vital importance, subservience of women and children to the will of the father, limited only by social custom, became the pattern of most great peasant societies. Marriage was sanctified not only by the rites of religion, but by the transmission of property. Few societies could tolerate freedom of choice in marriage—too much vital to the success or failure of a family depended on it: an ugly girl with five cows was a far fairer prospect than a pretty girl with one. And because of the sexual drives of frail human nature, the customs of marriage and of family relationships needed to be rigorously enforced. Tradition sanctified them; religion blessed them. Some societies reversed the sexually restrictive nature of permanent marriage and permitted additional wives, but such permission was meaningless to the mass of the peasantry who fought a desperate battle to support a single family. And, as we shall see, the patterns of family life were always looser for the rich and the favored.

But a family was always more than property expressed clearly and visibly in real goods; it was for thousands of years both a school and a tribunal, the basic unit of social organization whose function in modern society has been very largely taken over by the state. In most peasant societies, life is regulated by the village community, by the patriarchs of the village, and the only officer of the central government these villagers see with any regularity is the tax-gatherer; but in societies that have grown more complex, and this is particularly true of the West during the last four hundred years, life has become regulated by the nation state or by the growth in power and importance of more generalized local communities—the town or county.

This has naturally weakened the authority of heads of families, a fact that can be symbolically illustrated by change in social custom. No child in Western Europe would sit unbidden in the presence of its parents until the eighteenth century: if it did it could be sure of rebuke and punishment. No head of a household would have thought twice about beating a recalcitrant young servant or apprentice before the end of the nineteenth century. For a younger brother to marry without the consent of his eldest brother would have been regarded as a social enormity; and sisters were disposable property. All of this power has vanished. Indeed the family ties of all of us have been so loosened that we find it hard to grasp the intensity of family relationships or their complexity, they have disintegrated so rapidly this last hundred years. Now nearly every child in the Western world, male or female, is educated outside the family from five years of age. The skills they learn are rarely, if ever, transmitted by parents: and what is more they learn about the nature of their own world, its social structure and its relationships in time outside the family. For millennia the family was the great transmitter and formulator of social custom; but it now only retains a shadow of this function, usually for very young children only.

Although the economic and education functions of the family have declined, most of us feel that it provides the most satisfactory emotional basis for human beings; that a secure family life breeds stability, a capacity not only for happiness, but also to adjust to society's demands. This, too, may be based on misjudgment, for family life in the past was not remarkable for its happiness. We get few glimpses into the private lives of men and women long dead, but when we do we often find strain, frustration, petty tyranny. For so many human beings family life was a prison from which they could not escape. And although it might create deep satisfactions here and there, the majority of the rich and affluent classes of the last four hundred years in Western Europe created for themselves a double standard, particularly as far as sex was concerned. In a few cities such as Calvin's Geneva, the purity of family life might be maintained, but the aristocracies of France, Italy and Britain tolerated, without undue concern, adultery, homosexuality and that sexual freedom which, for better or worse, we consider the hallmark of modern life. Indeed the family as the basic social group began firstly to fail, except in its property relations, amongst the aristocracy.

But what we think of as a social crisis of this generation—the rapid growth of divorce, the emancipation of women and adolescents, the sexual and educational revolutions, even the revolution in eating which is undermining the family as the basis of nourishment, for over a hundred years ago the majority of Europeans never ate in public in their lives—all of these things, which are steadily making the family weaker and weaker, are the inexorable result of the changes in society itself. The family as a unit of social organization was remarkably appropriate for a less complex world of agriculture and craftsmanship, a world which stretches back some seven thousand years, but ever since industry and highly urbanized societies began to take its place, the social functions of the family have steadily weakened—and this is a process that is unlikely to be halted. And there is no historical reason to believe that human beings could be less or more happy, less or more stable. Like any other human institution the family has always been molded by the changing needs of society, sometimes slowly, sometimes fast. And that bus load of children does no more than symbolize the failure, not of marriage, but the role of the old-fashioned family unit in a modern, urbanized, scientific and affluent society.

## Questions

1. On page 11 Plumb uses the term "unitary family," but he does not define it. How might it be defined? Explain how you arrived at your definition.
2. Paraphrase the sentence (on page 12): "Hence they were endowed with manna, bound up with the deepest roots of personality."
3. Plumb says (page 14) that "the revolution in eating" is "undermining the family as the basis of nourishment." Explain. To what extent do you agree that a family's eating habits reveal its stability?

**Laura Cunningham**

# The Girls' Room

When I heard she was coming to stay with us I was pleased. At age 8 I thought of "grandmother" as a generic brand. My friends had grandmothers who seemed permanently bent over cookie racks. They were a source of constant treats and sweets. They were pinchers of cheeks, huggers and kissers. My own grandmother had always lived in a distant state; I had no memory of her when she decided to join the household recently established for me by my two uncles.

But with the example of my friends' grandmothers before me, I could hardly wait to have a grandmother of my own—and the cookies would be nice too. For while my uncles provided a cuisine that ranged from tuna croquettes to Swedish meatballs, they showed no signs of baking anything more elegant than a potato.

My main concern on the day of my grandmother's arrival was: How soon would she start the cookies? I remember her arrival, my uncles flanking her as they walked down the apartment corridor. She wore a hat, a tailored navy blue suit, an ermine stole. She held, tucked

Laura Cunningham was born in 1947. Orphaned at the age of eight, she was brought up by two unmarried uncles, both of whom were writers. She says that she became a writer because she didn't know that one could become anything else. Had she known of other possibilities, she says, she would have become a ballerina.

under her arm, the purple leather folder that contained her work in progress, a manuscript entitled "Philosophy for Women." She was preceded by her custom-made white trunk packed with purses, necklaces, earrings, dresses and more purple-inked pages that stress "the spiritual above the material."

She was small—at 5 feet 1 inch not much taller than I was—thin and straight, with a pug nose, one brown eye (the good eye) and one blue eye (the bad eye, frosted by cataracts). Her name was "Esther in Hebrew, Edna in English and Etka in Russian." She preferred the Russian, referring to herself as "Etka from Minsk." It was not at once apparent that she was deaf in her left ear (the bad ear) but could hear with the right (the good ear). Because her good ear happened to be on the opposite side from the good eye, anyone who spoke to her had to run around her in circles, or sway to and fro, if eye contact and audibility were to be achieved simultaneously.

Etka from Minsk had arrived not directly from Minsk, as the black-eyed ermine stole seemed to suggest, but after many moves. She entered with the draft of family scandal at her back, blown out of her daughter's home after assaults upon her dignity. She held the evidence: an empty-socketed peacock pin. My cousin, an 11-year-old boy, had surgically plucked out the rhinestone eyes. She could not be expected to stay where such acts occurred. She had to be among "human beings," among "real people" who could understand. We seemed to understand. We—my two uncles and I—encircled her, studied her vandalized peacock pin and vowed that such things would never happen with "us."

She patted my head—a good sign—and asked me to sing the Israeli national anthem. I did, and she handed me a dollar. My uncles went off to their jobs, leaving me alone with my grandmother for the first time. I looked at her, expecting her to start rolling out the cookie dough. Instead she suggested: "Now maybe you could fix me some lunch?"

It wasn't supposed to be this way, I thought, as I took her order: "toasted cheese and a sliced orange." Neither was she supposed to share my pink and orange bedroom, but she did. The bedroom soon exhibited a dual character—stuffed animals on one side, a hospital bed on the other. Within the household this chamber was soon referred to as "the girls' room." The name, given by Uncle Abe, who saw no incongruity, only the affinity of sex, turned out to be apt, for what went on in the girls' room could easily have been labeled sibling rivalry if she had not been 80 and I 8. I soon found that I had acquired not a traditional grandmother but an aged kid sister.

The theft and rivalry began within days. My grandmother had given me her most cherished possession, a violet beaded bag. In return I gave her my heart-shaped "ivory" pin and matching earrings. That night she stole back the purse but insisted on keeping the pin and earrings. I turned to my uncles for mediation and ran up against unforseen resistance. They thought my grandmother should keep the beaded bag; they didn't want to upset her.

I burned at the injustice of it and felt the heat of an uncomfortable truth: where I once had my uncles' undivided indulgence, they were now split as my grandmother and I vied for their attention. The household, formerly geared to my little-girl needs, was rearranged to accommodate hers. I suffered serious affronts—my grandmother, in a fit of frugality, scissored all the household blankets, including what a psychiatrist would have dubbed my "security" blanket, in half. "Now," she said, her good eye gleaming, "we have twice as many." I lay under my narrow slice of blanket and stared hopelessly up at the ceiling. I thought evilly of ways of getting my grandmother out of the apartment.

Matters worsened, as more and more of my trinkets disappeared. One afternoon I came home from school to find her squeezed into my unbuttoned favorite blouse. Rouged and beribboned, she insisted that the size 3 blouse was hers. Meanwhile, I was forced to adapt to her idiosyncracies: she covered everything black—from the dog to the telephone—with white doilies. She left saucers balanced on top of glasses. She sang nonstop. She tried to lock my dog out of the apartment.

The word that explained her behavior was "arteriosclerosis." She had forgotten so much that sometimes she would greet me with "You look familiar." At other times she'd ask, "What hotel is this?" My answer, shouted in her good ear, was: "We're not in a hotel! This is our apartment!" The response would be a hoot of laughter: "Then why are we in the ballroom?"

Finally we fought: arm-to-arm combat. I was shocked at her grip, steely as the bars that locked her into bed at night. Her good eye burned into mine and she said, "I'll tell." And she did. For the first time I was scolded. She had turned their love to disapproval, I thought, and how it chafed.

Eventually our rivalry mellowed into conspiracy. Within months we found we had uses for each other. I provided the lunches and secret, forbidden ice cream sundaes. She rewarded me with cold cash. She continued to take my clothes; I charged her competitive prices. I hated school; she paid me not to go. When I came home for lunch I usually stayed.

Our household endured the status quo for eight years: my uncles, my grandmother and I. Within the foursome rivalries and alliances shifted. I became my grandmother's friend and she became mine. We were the source of all the family comedy. When she said she wanted a college diploma we gave her one—with tinfoil stars and a "magna magna summa summa cum laude" inscription. We sang and performed skits. We talcum-powdered hair and wearing one of her old dresses, I would appear as her "long-lost friend." We had other themes, including a pen pal, "The Professor."

Of course, living with an elderly person had its raw aspects. When she was ill our girls' room took on the stark aura of a geriatrics ward. I imagined, to my shame, that neighbors could stare in through curtainless windows as I tended to my grandmother's most personal needs.

Yet, in these times of age segregation, with grandmothers sent off to impersonal places, I wonder if the love and the comedy weren't worth the intermittent difficulties? Certainly I learned what it might be to become old. And I took as much comfort as my grandmother did in a nightly exchange of Russian endearments—"Ya tebya lyublyu," "Ya tebya tozhe lyublyu"—"I love you," "I love you, too."

If I sold my grandmother blouses and baubles, maybe she gave me the truth in exchange. Once, when we were alone in the girls' room, she turned to me, suddenly lucid, her good eye as bright as it would ever be—a look I somehow recognized as her "real" gaze—and said, "My life passes like a dream."

## Questions

1. What does the second sentence mean: What, that is, is "a generic brand"?
2. What is the title of Esther's manuscript? What is it about? Do you detect any irony in the way Cunningham conveys this information? Explain.
3. In the second sentence of the fourth paragraph, what is conveyed by putting the names within quotation marks?

4. Is the fourth paragraph—about Esther's physical disabilities—in bad taste? Explain.
5. In the last paragraph Cunningham says that perhaps her grandmother gave her "the truth." What does she mean?
6. "I burned at the injustice of it and felt the heat of an uncomfortable truth." Where in the narrative does Cunningham say this? What was the "truth"? If you remember a similar experience, write a narrative that discloses both the experience and the truth on which it was based. Or, write an essay of 500 words on your own most potent experience of living with or near an elderly person.

## Lionel Tiger

# Omnigamy

### The New Kinship System

A hapless British cabinet minister responsible for the hapless UK telephone system once complained that the more phones installed in his country, the more there were to call, and so the demand for phones increased: supply creates demand. Somewhat the same thing is happening with marriage in America. The more divorces there are, the more experienced marriers exist, ready to remarry—and many do. The divorce rate has jumped 250 percent in the past 21 years; about 80 percent of the formerly married remarry. With each new marriage, the parents and children involved acquire a whole new set of relatives, friends, and associations—in effect, they stretch their kinship system. Many people are married to people who have been married to other people who are now married to still others to whom the first parties may not have been married, but to whom somebody has likely been married. Our society, once based on the principle of solid monogamy until death do us part, has shifted

Lionel Tiger, born in 1937, is the director of graduate programs in anthropology at Rutgers University. His most recent book is *Optimism: The Biology of Hope.*

toward a pattern of serial polygamy, in which people experience more than one spouse, if only one at a time. Thus we appear to be moving to a new and imprecise system we might call omnigamy, in which each will be married to all.

People keep marrying, even though happy marriages are regarded as surprising and much-envied occurrences. The not-so-stately pageant of marriage goes on, heedless of the cautionary cries of pain and the clenched question: Why? Various responsible estimators expect that from a third to a half of the marriages formed in this decade will end in divorce sometime. That is astonishing. It is also astonishing that, under the circumstances, marriage is still legally allowed. If nearly half of anything else ended so disastrously, the government would surely ban it immediately. If half the tacos served in restaurants caused dysentery, if half the people learning karate broke their palms, if only 6 percent of people who went on roller-coasters damaged their middle ears, the public would be clamoring for action. Yet the most intimate of disasters—with consequences that may last a lifetime for both adults and children—happens over and over again. Marriage has not yet gone underground.

To an anthropologist, the emergence of a new kinship system should be as exciting as the discovery of a new comet to an astronomer. But in the case of omnigamy, the developing pattern is still unclear, the forces shaping it unanalyzed, the final structure difficult to predict. We know the numbers of marriages and remarriages, but what about the apparent acceleration of the process? The new system permits—perhaps even demands—that its members repair themselves quickly after crises of vast personal proportion. In the slap-dash, overpraised, and sentimental film *An Unmarried Woman,* Jill Clayburgh explains to her (quite nauseating) therapist how agonizing and lonely it was when her husband of umpteen years left her, and how she has been without sexual congress for such a long, long time. When the therapist hears this dreadful fact, she earnestly recommends that this casualty of a massive private accident return immediately to the sexual fray. It has, after all, been *seven weeks.*

The heroine subsequently decides to reject an offer to join an attractive and apparently quite suitable artist. Instead she chooses to lead an independent life as a part-time secretary in a SoHo art gallery, which makes her somewhat radical with respect to the omnigamous system. For her obligation seems clear: she must form some sturdy response, one way or the other, to the ambient fact of marriage and remarriage. To remain haunted by grief and inhibited by a sense of failure is taken as a mere expression of cowardice or restlessness. When anthropology first started out, the difficult trick in studying any culture was to discover just what the kinship system was—who was married to whom, and why, and what connections counted for inheritance, status, and authority. We found that marriage was the instrument for creating the extended family, which provided for most human needs in the tribal societies. If an anthropologist from the Trobriand Islands came here now, he or she could well conclude that by stimulating further marriages, divorce has come to be an important organizing principle in our society, since kinship alliances among divorced people are so extensive and complex.

When parents divorce and remarry, the new family connections extend the reach of family life to dimensions a Baganda or Trobriander or Hopi could well understand. Take an example: after the divorce of A and B, siblings A1 and B1 live with A and her new husband, C, but visit B and his new wife, D, on weekends. C's children, C1, C2, and C3, like to go to basketball games with A1 and B1. D's children by her first marriage also enjoy the company of A1 and B1, and take them along on visits to their father, E, a former star athlete who becomes an important hero and role model to the children of A, who has never met him and probably never will.

Nor is it only marriage that binds. In a world where all Mom and Dad's companions are potential mates, Dad's live-in girl friend may turn up for parents' night at school when he's out of town. She also may have a brother—a kind of stepuncle to the kids—with a 40-foot sloop. (The spreading network can put children in touch with a dislocating variety of styles.)

What this means for children, and how it affects their sense of what is stable, what is optional, what is fast, slow, brisk, or stately, is, of course, difficult to say. The generation of children spawned by the Age of Omnigamy has not yet made its mark on the social system in any clear way; we cannot know whether they are immune, immunized, or carriers of the bug across generational lines. In the old days, people were titillated by the polygamous habits of Hollywood celebrities, but few were tempted to emulate them. Parents, grandparents, aunts, and uncles seem to be more important role models for children. When they keep changing partners, it will likely increase the child's sense of the tentativeness in all relations that the new system reflects.

While I am not implying that omnigamous parents set a bad

example, they surely set some example. The consequences for their own children and for those others with whom they come in contact must be considerable. Divorce as a recurrent aspect of life may make it relatively easier for children to accept when they are young, but harder to avoid when they become adults. And who has calculated the effect of omnigamy on grandparents, whose connections with their grandchildren suddenly come to be mediated by strangers—stepparents who might even move them to some distant city?

I do not mean to be alarmist and implacably negative about all this. The existence of relatively civilized divorce options is as much a sign of human freedom as it is of sanctioned personal confusion and pain. Who, after all, would wish to confirm in their desperate plight the countless real-world descendants of Madame Bovary?

Surely, too, there is a value in the extension of personal experience to wider circles of people than strict and permanent monogamy permits. And there is presumably an enhancement of personal vividness, which the new, relatively unstructured world permits—if not coerces.

Omnigamy may have interesting economic implications as well. Adrienne Harris of York University in Toronto has pointed out that each marital separation stimulates the repurchase of those items left in one household and needed in the next. Like amoebas splitting, one dishwasher becomes two, one vacuum cleaner becomes two, one television becomes two; domestic purchases even become impetuous ("Why shouldn't I have my Cuisinart to do my fish mousse when he/she has *our* Cuisinart for hers/his?"). One can't help speculating that the rapid increase in retail outlets selling cooking equipment reflects the doubled demands of the new kinship system.

And where would the real estate market be without house sales to accommodate people who can no longer accommodate each other? And has anyone wondered why the garage sale has recently become so common? The economic shifts that depend on the breakup and re-forming of marital units are a form of internal colonialism: at the same time that the United States can no longer control foreign markets, it is expanding its internal ones. The family system, which both Engels and Marx saw as the stimulus for the development of capitalism, may even, in the new form, turn out to be one of its props. As with all colonialisms, however, many people come to be exploited. Taking up the options omnigamy offers strains the financial and emotional resources both.

Can it be said that these comments apply mostly to a small group of self-involved persons inhabiting the Upper East and West Sides of Manhattan, where the production of novels and articles about marriage and anguished personal failure is a major cottage industry? No. If the divorce rates persist and cities continue to export their social patterns, as in the past, other communities still complacently conventional and relatively monogamous will make a gradual but perceptual shift to omnigamy. The pattern will broaden unless there is soon—and there could be—a renewed commitment to monogamous fidelity, and possibly even to the importance of virginity as a factor in marital choice (this possibility seems rather remote). What does seem clear is that many changes will derive from these many changes, perhaps even a return to notions of marriage based on economic convenience and an agreement to mount a common assault on loneliness. Marriage could be on its way to becoming a generalized corporate, if small-scale, experience capable of providing some sense of community and some prospect of continuity. But it may also become a relatively planless arrangement and rearrangement of fickle magnets inexplicably and episodically drawn into each other's orbits for varying purposes and periods.

## Questions

1. In the first sentence, speaking of the United Kingdom, Tiger uses the adjective "hapless" twice. What does "hapless" mean? Why does he repeat the word? Does the analogy that Tiger makes between telephones and marriages have a point? If so, what is it? Where else does Tiger use comparisons? How effective are they? Do you see any patterns in his use of them?
2. Describe the construction of the sentence, in the first paragraph, beginning "Many people are married to people who have been married. . . ." How would you characterize the tone of this sentence? And how would you characterize the tone of the last sentence in the first paragraph?
3. In the second paragraph Tiger says, "People keep marrying." Does he suggest why they do? Or why they should not?
4. At the end of the third paragraph, why does Tiger italicize *seven weeks*?
5. On page 21, in the paragraph beginning "What this means," Tiger claims that it is "difficult to say" what effect the spreading network of kinship alliances will have on children. Perhaps it is. In the course of his

essay he does nevertheless imply some effects. What are they? How does he imply them?

6. On page 22 Tiger begins a paragraph by saying: "I do not mean to be alarmist and implacably negative about all this." In the next few paragraphs what benefits from "omnigamy" does he foresee? Are they in fact benefits? To whom?
7. On the whole is "Omnigamy: The New Kinship System" more persuasive about the benefits or about the harms of "serial polygamy"?
8. If you have read Plumb's "The Dying Family" (page 10), do you think that Plumb would agree with Tiger about a trend towards "omnigamy"? Does either essayist suggest a cause behind this trend? Can you explain it?

**Jane Howard**

# All Happy Clans Are Alike

## In Search of the Good Family

Call it a clan, call it a network, call it a tribe, call it a family. Whatever you call it, whoever you are, you need one. You need one because you are human. You didn't come from nowhere. Before you, around you, and presumably after you, too, there are others. Some of these others must matter a lot—to you, and if you are very lucky, to one another. Their welfare must be nearly as important to you as your own. Even if you live alone, even if your solitude is elected and ebullient, you still cannot do without a clan or a tribe.

The trouble with the clans and tribes many of us were born into is not that they consist of meddlesome ogres but that they are too far away. In emergencies we rush across continents and if need be oceans to their sides, as they do to ours. Maybe we even make a habit of

Jane Howard, born in Springfield, Illinois, in 1935, was educated at the University of Michigan. She served as reporter, writer, and editor for *Life* magazine, and she is the author of several books.

seeing them, once or twice a year, for the sheer pleasure of it. But blood ties seldom dictate our addresses. Our blood kin are often too remote to ease us from our Tuesdays to our Wednesdays. For this we must rely on our families of friends. If our relatives are not, do not wish to be, or for whatever reasons cannot be our friends, then by some complex alchemy we must try to transform our friends into our relatives. If blood and roots don't do the job, then we must look to water and branches, and sort ourselves into new constellations, new families.

These new families, to borrow the terminology of an African tribe (the Bangwa of the Cameroons), may consist either of friends of the road, ascribed by chance, or friends of the heart, achieved by choice. Ascribed friends are those we happen to go to school with, work with, or live near. They know where we went last weekend and whether we still have a cold. Just being around gives them a provisional importance in our lives, and us in theirs. Maybe they will still matter to us when we or they move away; quite likely they won't. Six months or two years will probably erase us from each other's thoughts, unless by some chance they and we have become friends of the heart.

Wishing to be friends, as Aristotle wrote, is quick work, but friendship is a slowly ripening fruit. An ancient proverb he quotes in his *Ethics* had it that you cannot know a man until you and he together have eaten a peck of salt. Now a peck, a quarter of a bushel, is quite a lot of salt—more, perhaps, than most pairs of people ever have occasion to share. We must try though. We must sit together at as many tables as we can. We must steer each other through enough seasons and weathers so that sooner or later it crosses our minds that one of us, God knows which or with what sorrow, must one day mourn the other.

We must devise new ways, or revive old ones, to equip ourselves with kinfolk. Maybe such an impulse prompted whoever ordered the cake I saw in my neighborhood bakery to have it frosted to say "HAPPY BIRTHDAY SURROGATE." I like to think that this cake was decorated not for a judge but for someone's surrogate mother or surrogate brother: Loathsome jargon, but admirable sentiment. If you didn't conceive me or if we didn't grow up in the same house, we can still be related, if we decide we ought to be. It is never too late, I like to hope, to augment our families in ways nature neglected to do. It is never too late to choose new clans.

The best-chosen clans, like the best friendships and the best blood families, endure by accumulating a history solid enough to suggest a future. But clans that don't last have merit too. We can lament them but we shouldn't deride them. Better an ephemeral clan or tribe than none at all. A few of my life's most tribally joyous times, in fact, have been spent with people whom I have yet to see again. This saddens me, as it may them too, but dwelling overlong on such sadness does no good. A more fertile exercise is to think back on those times and try to figure out what made them, for all their brevity, so stirring. What can such times teach us about forming new and more lasting tribes in the future?

New tribes and clans can no more be willed into existence, of course, than any other good thing can. We keep trying, though. To try, with gritted teeth and girded loins, is after all American. That is what the two Helens and I were talking about the day we had lunch in a room up in a high-rise motel near the Kansas City airport. We had lunch there at the end of a two-day conference on families. The two Helens were social scientists, but I liked them even so, among other reasons because they both objected to that motel's coffee shop even more than I did. One of the Helens, from Virginia, disliked it so much that she had brought along homemade whole wheat bread, sesame butter, and honey from her parents' farm in South Dakota, where she had visited before the conference. Her picnic was the best thing that happened, to me at least, those whole two days.

"If you're voluntarily childless and alone," said the other Helen, who was from Pennsylvania by way of Puerto Rico, "it gets harder and harder with the passage of time. It's stressful. That's why you need support systems." I had been hearing quite a bit of talk about "support systems." The term is not among my favorites, but I can understand its currency. Whatever "support systems" may be, the need for them is clearly urgent, and not just in this country. Are there not thriving "megafamilies" of as many as three hundred people in Scandinavia? Have not the Japanese for years had an honored, enduring—if perhaps by our standards rather rigid—custom of adopting nonrelatives to fill gaps in their families? Should we not applaud and maybe imitate such ingenuity?

And consider our own Unitarians. From Santa Barbara to Boston they have been earnestly dividing their congregations into arbitrary "extended families" whose members are bound to act like each other's relatives. Kurt Vonnegut, Jr., plays with a similar train of thought in his fictional *Slapstick.* In that book every newborn baby is assigned a randomly chosen middle name, like Uranium or Daffodil or Raspberry. These middle names are connected with hyphens to numbers between one and twenty, and any two people who have the same middle name are automatically related. This is all to the good, the author thinks, because "human beings need all the relatives they can get—as possible donors or receivers not of love but of common decency." He envisions these extended families as "one of the four greatest inventions by Americans," the others being *Robert's Rules of Order,* the Bill of Rights, and the principles of Alcoholics Anonymous.

This charming notion might even work, if it weren't so arbitrary. Already each of us is born into one family not of our choosing. If we're going to devise new ones, we might as well have the luxury of picking the members ourselves. Clever picking might result in new families whose benefits would surpass or at least equal those of the old. As a member in reasonable standing of six or seven tribes in addition to the one I was born to, I have been trying to figure which characteristics are common to both kinds of families.

1. Good families have a chief, or a heroine, or a founder—someone around whom others cluster, whose achievements, as the Yiddish word has it, let them *kvell,* and whose example spurs them on to like feats. Some blood dynasties produce such figures regularly; others languish for as many as five generations between demigods, wondering with each new pregnancy whether this, at last, might be the messianic baby who will redeem them. Look, is there not something gubernatorial about her footstep, or musical about the way he bangs with his spoon on his cup? All clans, of all kinds, need such a figure now and then. Sometimes clans based on water rather than blood harbor several such personages at one time. The Bloomsbury Group in London six decades ago was not much hampered by its lack of a temporal history.

2. Good families have a switchboard operator—someone who cannot help but keep track of what all the others are up to, who plays Houston Mission Control to everyone else's Apollo. This role is assumed rather than assigned. The person who volunteers for it often has the instincts of an archivist, and feels driven to keep scrapbooks and photograph albums up to date, so that the clan can see proof of its own continuity.

3. Good families are much to all their members, but everything to none. Good families are fortresses with many windows and doors

to the outer world. The blood clans I feel most drawn to were founded by parents who are nearly as devoted to what they do outside as they are to each other and their children. Their curiosity and passion are contagious. Everbody, where they live, is busy. Paint is spattered on eyeglasses. Mud lurks under fingernails. Person-to-person calls come in the middle of the night from Tokyo and Brussels. Catcher's mitts, ballet slippers, overdue library books, and other signs of extrafamilial concerns are everywhere.

4. Good families are hospitable. Knowing that hosts need guests as much as guests need hosts, they are generous with honorary memberships for friends, whom they urge to come early and often and to stay late. Such clans exude a vivid sense of surrounding rings of relatives, neighbors, teachers, students, and godparents, any of whom at any time might break or slide into the inner circle. Inside that circle a wholesome, tacit emotional feudalism develops: you give me protection, I'll give you fealty. Such pacts begin with, but soon go far beyond, the jolly exchange of pie at Thanksgiving or cake on a birthday. They mean that you can ask me to supervise your children for the fortnight you will be in the hospital, and that however inconvenient this might be for me, I shall manage to do so. It means I can phone you on what for me is a dreary, wretched Sunday afternoon and for you is the eve of a deadline, knowing you will tell me to come right over, if only to watch you type. It means we need not dissemble. ("To yield to seeming," as Martin Buber wrote, "is man's essential cowardice, to resist it is his essential courage . . . one must at times pay dearly for life lived from the being, but it is never too dear.")

5. Good families deal squarely with direness. Pity the tribe that doesn't have, and cherish, at least one flamboyant eccentric. Pity too the one that supposes it can avoid for long the woes to which all flesh is heir. Lunacy, bankruptcy, suicide, and other unthinkable fates sooner or later afflict the noblest of clans with an undertow of gloom. Family life is a set of givens, someone once told me, and it takes courage to see certain givens as blessings rather than as curses. It surely does. Contradictions and inconsistencies are givens, too. So is the battle against what the Oregon patriarch Kenneth Babbs calls malarkey. "There's always malarkey lurking, bubbles in the cesspool, fetid bubbles that pop and smell. But I don't put up with malarkey, between my stepkids and my natural ones or anywhere else in the family."

6. Good families prize their rituals. Nothing welds a family more

than these. Rituals are vital especially for clans without histories, because they evoke a past, imply a future, and hint at continuity. No line in the seder service at Passover reassures more than the last: "Next year in Jerusalem!" A clan becomes more of a clan each time it gathers to observe a fixed ritual (Christmas, birthdays, Thanksgiving, and so on), grieves at a funeral (anyone may come to most funerals; those who do declare their tribalness), and devises a new rite of its own. Equinox breakfasts can be at least as welding as Memorial Day parades. Several of my colleagues and I used to meet for lunch every Pearl Harbor Day, preferably to eat some politically neutral fare like smorgasbord, to "forgive" our only ancestrally Japanese friend, Irene Kubota Neves. For that and other things we became, and remain, a sort of family.

"Rituals," a California friend of mind said, "aren't just externals and holidays. They are the performances of our lives. They are a kind of shorthand. They can't be decreed. My mother used to try to decree them. She'd make such a goddamn fuss over what we talked about at dinner, aiming at Topics of Common Interest, topics that celebrated our cohesion as a family. These performances were always hollow, because the phenomenology of the moment got sacrificed for the *idea* of the moment. Real rituals are discovered in retrospect. They emerge around constitutive moments, moments that only happen once, around whose memory meanings cluster. You don't choose those moments. They choose themselves." A lucky clan includes a born mythologizer, like my blood sister, who has the gift for apprehending such a moment when she sees it, and who cannot help but invent new rituals everywhere she goes.

7. Good families are affectionate. This of course is a matter of style. I know clans whose members greet each other with gingerly handshakes or, in what pass for kisses, with hurried brushes of jawbones, as if the object were to touch not the lips but the ears. I don't see how such people manage. "The tribe that does not hug," as someone who has been part of many *ad hoc* families recently wrote to me, "is no tribe at all. More and more I realize that everybody, regardless of age, needs to be hugged and comforted in a brotherly or sisterly way now and then. Preferably now."

8. Good families have a sense of place, which these days is not achieved easily. As Susanne Langer wrote in 1957, "Most people have no home that is a symbol of their childhood, not even a definite memory of one place to serve that purpose . . . all the old symbols are gone." Once I asked a roomful of supper guests if anyone felt a strong

pull to any certain spot on the face of the earth. Everyone was silent, except for a visitor from Bavaria. The rest of us seemed to know all too well what Walker Percy means in *The Moviegoer* when he tells of the "genie-soul of a place, which every place has or else is not a place [and which] wherever you go, you must meet and master or else be met and mastered." All that meeting and mastering saps plenty of strength. It also underscores our need for tribal bases of the sort which soaring real estate taxes and splintering families have made all but obsolete.

So what are we to do, those of us whose habit and pleasure and doom is our tendency, as a Georgia lady put it, to "fly off at every other whipstich?" Think in terms of movable feasts, that's what. Live here, wherever here may be, as if we were going to belong here for the rest of our lives. Learn to hallow whatever ground we happen to stand on or land on. Like medieval knights who took their tapestries along on Crusades, like modern Afghanis with their yurts, we must pack such totems and icons as we can to make short-term quarters feel like home. Pillows, small rugs, watercolors can dispel much of the chilling anonymity of a motel room or sublet apartment. When we can, we should live in rooms with stoves or fireplaces or at least candelight. The ancient saying is still true: Extinguished hearth, extinguished family.

Round tables help too, and as a friend of mine once put it, so do "too many comfortable chairs, with surfaces to put feet on, arranged so as to encourage a maximum of eye contact." Such rooms inspire good talk, of which good clans can never have enough.

9. Good families, not just the blood kind, find some way to connect with posterity. "To forge a link in the humble chain of being, encircling heirs to ancestors," as Michael Novak has written, "is to walk within a circle of magic as primitive as humans knew in caves." He is talking of course about babies, feeling them leap in wombs, giving them suck. Parenthood, however, is a state which some miss by chance and others by design, and a vocation to which not all are called. Some of us, like the novelist Richard P. Brickner, look on as others "name their children and their children in turn name their own lives, devising their own flags from their parents' cloth." What are we who lack children to do? Build houses? Plant trees? Write books or symphonies or laws? Perhaps, but even if we do these things, there should be children on the sidelines if not at the center of our lives.

It is a sadly impoverished tribe that does not allow access to, and make much of, some children. Not too much, of course; it has truly been said that never in history have so many educated people devoted so much attention to so few children. Attention, in excess, can turn to fawning, which isn't much better than neglect. Still, if we don't regularly see and talk to and laugh with people who can expect to outlive us by twenty years or so, we had better get busy and find some.

10. Good families also honor their elders. The wider the age range, the stronger the tribe. Jean-Paul Sartre and Margaret Mead, to name two spectacularly confident former children, have both remarked on the central importance of grandparents in their own early lives. Grandparents are now in much more abundant supply than they were a generation or two ago, when old age was more rare. If actual grandparents are not at hand, no family should have too hard a time finding substitute ones to whom to pay unfeigned homage. The Soviet Union's enchantment with day-care centers, I have heard, stems at least in part from the state's eagerness to keep children away from their presumably subversive grandparents. Let that be a lesson to clans based on interest as well as to those based on genes.

Of course there are elders and elders. Most people in America, as David T. Bazelon has written, haven't the slightest idea of what to do with the extra thirty years they have been given to live. Few are as briskly secure as Alice Roosevelt Longworth, who once, when I visited her for tea, showed a recent photograph and asked whether I didn't think it made her look like "a malevolent Eurasian concubine —an *aged* malevolent Eurasian concubine." I admitted that it did, which was just what she wanted to hear. But those of us whose fathers weren't Presidents may not grow old, if at all, with such style.

Sad stories abound. The mother of one friend of mine languished for years, never far from a coma, in a nursing home. Only when her husband and children sang one of her favorite old songs, such as "Lord Jeffrey Amherst," would a smile fleet across her face. But a man I know of in New Jersey, who couldn't stand the state of Iowa or babies, changed his mind on both counts when his daughter, who lived in Iowa, had a baby. Suddenly he took to inventing business trips to St. Louis, by way of Cedar Rapids, phoning to say he would be at the airport there at 11:31 P.M., and "Be sure to bring Jake!" That cheers me. So did part of a talk I had with a woman in Albuquerque, whom I hadn't seen since a trip some years before to the Soviet Union.

"Honey," she said when I phoned her during a short stopover

and asked how she was, "if I were any better I'd blow up and *bust!* I can't *tell* you how *neat* it is to put some age on! A lot of it, of course, has to do with going to the shrink, getting uncorked, and of course it doesn't hurt to have money—no, we *don't* have a ranch; it's only 900 acres, so we call it a farm. But every year, as far as age is concerned, I seem to get better, doing more and more stuff I love to do. The only thing I've ever wanted and don't have is a good marriage. Nothing I do ever pleases the men I marry. The only reason I'm still married now is it's too much trouble not to be. But my girls are growing up to be just *neat* humans, and the men they're sharing their lives with are too. They pick nice guys, my girls. I wish I could say the same. But I'm a lot better off than many women my age. I go to parties where sixty-year-olds with blue bouffant hairdos are still telling the same jokes they told twenty-five or thirty years ago. Complacent? No, that's not it, exactly. What they are is sad—sad as the dickens. They don't seem to be *connected.*"

Some days my handwriting resembles my mother's, slanting hopefully and a bit extravagantly eastward. Other days it looks more like my father's: resolute, vertical, guardedly free of loops. Both my parents will remain in my nerves and muscles and mind until the day I die, and so will my sister, but they aren't the only ones. If I were to die tomorrow, the obituary would note that my father and sister survived me. True, but not true enough. Like most official lists of survivors, this one would be incomplete.

Several of the most affecting relationships I have ever known of, or been part of, have sprung not from genes or contracts but from serendipitous, uncanny bonds of choice. I don't think enough can be said for the fierce tenderness such bonds can generate. Maybe the best thing to say is nothing at all, or very little. Midwestern preachers used to hold that "a heavy rain doesn't seep into the ground but rolls off—when you preach to farmers, your sermon should be a drizzle instead of a downpour." So too with any cause that matters: shouting and lapel-grabbing and institutionalizing can do more harm than good. A quiet approach works better.

"I wish it would hurry up and get colder," I said one warm afternoon several Octobers ago to a black man with whom I was walking in a park.

"Don't worry," he told me. "Like my grandmother used to say when I was a boy, 'Hawk'll be here soon enough.' "

"What did she mean by 'hawk'?"

"Hawk meant winter, cold, trouble. And she was right: the hawk always came."

With regard to families, many would say that the hawk has long been here, hovering. "I'd rather put up with being lonely now than have to put up with being still more lonely in the future," says a character in Natsume Soseki's novel *Kokoro.* "We live in an age of freedom, independence, and the self, and I imagine this loneliness is the price we have to pay for it." Seven decades earlier, in *Either/Or,* Sören Kierkegaard had written, "Our age has lost all the substantial categories of family, state, and race. It must leave the individual entirely to himself, so that in a stricter sense he becomes his own creator."

If it is true that we must create ourselves, maybe while we are about it we can also devise some new kinds of families, new connections to supplement the old ones. The second verse of a hymn by James Russell Lowell says,

> New occasions bring new duties;
> Time makes ancient good uncouth.

Surely one outworn "good" is the maxim that blood relatives are the only ones who can or should greatly matter. Or look at it another way: go back six generations, and each one of us has sixty-four direct ancestors. Go back twenty—only four or five centuries, not such a big chunk of human history—and we each have more than a million. Does it not stand to reason, since the world population was then so much smaller, that we all have a lot more cousins—though admittedly distant ones—than we were brought up to suspect? And don't these cousins deserve our attention?

One day after lunch at a friend's apartment I waited in his lobby while he collected his mail. Out of the elevator came two nurses supporting a wizened, staring woman who couldn't have weighed much more than seventy pounds. It was all the woman could do to make her way down the three steps to the sidewalk and the curb where a car was waiting. Those steps must have been to that woman what a steep mountain trail would be to me. The nurses guided her down them with infinite patience.

"Easy, darlin'," one nurse said to the woman.

"That's a good girl," said the other. The woman, my friend's doorman told us, was ninety. That morning she had fallen and hurt herself. On her forehead was something which, had it not been a bruise, we might have thought beautiful: a marvel of mauve and lavender and magenta. This woman, who was then being taken to a nursing home, had lived in my friend's apartment building for forty years. All her relatives were dead, and her few surviving friends no longer chose to see her.

"But how can that be?" I asked my friend. "*We* could never be that alone, could we?"

"Don't be so sure," said my friend, who knows more of such matters than I do. "Even if we were to end up in the same nursing home, if I was in markedly worse shape than you were, you might not want to see me, either."

"But I can't imagine not wanting to see you."

"It happens," my friend said.

Maybe we can keep it from happening. Maybe the hawk can be kept at bay, if we give more thought to our tribes and our clans and our several kinds of families. No aim seems to me more urgent, nor any achievement more worthy of a psalm. So *hosanna in excelsis,* and blest be the tie that binds. And please pass the salt.

## Questions

1. On page 26 Howard begins a paragraph by saying: "New tribes and clans can no more be willed into existence, of course, than any other good thing can." What other passages in the essay support this view? What passages contradict it? Does Howard succeed in reconciling the contradiction?
2. In her last paragraph Howard suggests that we might prevent loneliness by giving "more thought to our tribes and our clans and our several kinds of families." How might Lionel Tiger (pages 19–23) respond to her suggestion? Did either Howard's or Tiger's essay stimulate your thoughts on families? Which did you find more useful in thinking about family relationships?

Black Elk

# High Horse's Courting

You know, in the old days, it was not very easy to get a girl when you wanted to be married. Sometimes it was hard work for a young man and he had to stand a great deal. Say I am a young man and I have seen a young girl who looks so beautiful to me that I feel all sick when I think about her. I cannot just go and tell her about it and then get married if she is willing. I have to be a very sneaky fellow to talk to her at all, and after I have managed to talk to her, that is only the beginning.

Probably for a long time I have been feeling sick about a certain girl because I love her so much, but she will not even look at me, and her parents keep a good watch over her. But I keep feeling worse and worse all the time; so maybe I sneak up to her tepee in the dark and wait until she comes out. Maybe I just wait there all night and don't get any sleep at all and she does not come out. Then I feel sicker than ever about her.

Maybe I hide in the brush by a spring where she sometimes goes to get water, and when she comes by, if nobody is looking, then I jump out and hold her and just make her listen to me. If she likes me too, I can tell that from the way she acts, for she is very bashful and maybe will not say a word or even look at me the first time. So I let her go, and then maybe I sneak around until I can see her father alone, and I tell him how many horses I can give him for his beautiful girl, and by now I am feeling so sick that maybe I would give him all the horses in the world if I had them.

Well, this young man I am telling about was called High Horse, and there was a girl in the village who looked so beautiful to him that he was just sick all over from thinking about her so much and he was getting sicker all the time. The girl was very shy, and her parents

---

Black Elk, a *wichasha wakon* (holy man) of the Oglala Sioux, as a small boy witnessed the battle of the Little Bighorn (1876). He lived to see his people all but annihilated and his hopes for them extinguished. In 1931, toward the end of his life, he told his life story to the poet and scholar John G. Neihardt to preserve a sacred vision given him.

"High Horse's Courting" is a comic interlude in *Black Elk Speaks,* a predominantly tragic memoir.

thought a great deal of her because they were not young any more and this was the only child they had. So they watched her all day long, and they fixed it so that she would be safe at night too when they were asleep. They thought so much of her that they had made a rawhide bed for her to sleep in, and after they knew that High Horse was sneaking around after her, they took rawhide thongs and tied the girl in bed at night so that nobody could steal her when they were asleep, for they were not sure but that their girl might really want to be stolen.

Well, after High Horse had been sneaking around a good while and hiding and waiting for the girl and getting sicker all the time, he finally caught her alone and made her talk to him. Then he found out that she liked him maybe a little. Of course this did not make him feel well. It made him sicker than ever, but now he felt as brave as a bison bull, and so he went right to her father and said he loved the girl so much that he would give two good horses for her—one of them young and the other one not so very old.

But the old man just waved his hand, meaning for High Horse to go away and quit talking foolishness like that.

High Horse was feeling sicker than ever about it; but there was another young fellow who said he would loan High Horse two ponies and when he got some more horses, why, he could just give them back for the ones he had borrowed.

Then High Horse went back to the old man and said he would give four horses for the girl—two of them young and the other two not hardly old at all. But the old man just waved his hand and would not say anything.

So High Horse sneaked around until he could talk to the girl again, and he asked her to run away with him. He told her he thought he would just fall over and die if she did not. But she said she would not do that; she wanted to be bought like a fine woman. You see she thought a great deal of herself too.

That made High Horse feel so very sick that he could not eat a bite, and he went around with his head hanging down as though he might just fall down and die any time.

Red Deer was another young fellow, and he and High Horse were great comrades, always doing things together. Red Deer saw how High Horse was acting, and he said: "Cousin, what is the matter? Are you sick in the belly? You look as though you were going to die."

Then High Horse told Red Deer how it was, and said he thought he could not stay alive much longer if he could not marry the girl pretty quick.

Red Deer thought awhile about it, and then he said: "Cousin, I have a plan, and if you are man enough to do as I tell you, then everything will be all right. She will not run away with you; her old man will not take four horses; and four horses are all you can get. You must steal her and run away with her. Then afterwhile you can come back and the old man cannot do anything because she will be your woman. Probably she wants you to steal her anyway."

So they planned what High Horse had to do, and he said he loved the girl so much that he was man enough to do anything Red Deer or anybody else could think up. So this is what they did.

That night late they sneaked up to the girl's tepee and waited unitl it sounded inside as though the old man and the old woman and the girl were sound asleep. Then High Horse crawled under the tepee with a knife. He had to cut the rawhide thongs first, and then Red Deer, who was pulling up the stakes around that side of the tepee, was going to help drag the girl outside and gag her. After that, High Horse could put her across his pony in front of him and hurry out of there and be happy all the rest of his life.

When High Horse had crawled inside, he felt so nervous that he could hear his heart drumming, and it seemed so loud he felt sure it would 'waken the old folks. But it did not, and afterwhile he began cutting the thongs. Every time he cut one it made a pop and nearly scared him to death. But he was getting along all right and all the thongs were cut down as far as the girl's thighs, when he became so nervous that his knife slipped and stuck the girl. She gave a big, loud yell. Then the old folks jumped up and yelled too. By this time High Horse was outside, and he and Red Deer were running away like antelope. The old man and some other people chased the young men but they got away in the dark and nobody knew who it was.

Well, if you ever wanted a beautiful girl you will know how sick High Horse was now. It was very bad the way he felt, and it looked as though he would starve even if he did not drop over dead sometime.

Red Deer kept thinking about this, and after a few days he went to High Horse and said: "Cousin, take courage! I have another plan, and I am sure, if you are man enough, we can steal her this time." And High Horse said: "I am man enough to do anything anybody can think up, if I can only get that girl."

So this is what they did.

They went away from the village alone, and Red Deer made High Horse strip naked. Then he painted High Horse solid white all over, and after that he painted black stripes all over the white and put black rings around High Horse's eyes. High Horse looked terrible. He looked so terrible that when Red Deer was through painting and took a good look at what he had done, he said it scared even him a little.

"Now," Red Deer said, "if you get caught again, everybody will be so scared they will think you are a bad spirit and will be afraid to chase you."

So when the night was getting old and everybody was sound asleep, they sneaked back to the girl's tepee. High Horse crawled in with his knife, as before, and Red Deer waited outside, ready to drag the girl out and gag her when High Horse had all the thongs cut.

High Horse crept up by the girl's bed and began cutting at the thongs. But he kept thinking, "If they see me they will shoot me because I look so terrible." The girl was restless and kept squirming around in bed, and when a thong was cut, it popped. So High Horse worked very slowly and carefully.

But he must have made some noise, for suddenly the old woman awoke and said to her old man: "Old Man, wake up! There is somebody in this tepee!" But the old man was sleepy and didn't want to be bothered. He said: "Of course there is somebody in this tepee. Go to sleep and don't bother me." Then he snored some more.

But High Horse was so scared by now that he lay very still and as flat to the ground as he could. Now, you see, he had not been sleeping very well for a long time because he was so sick about the girl. And while he was lying there waiting for the old woman to snore, he just forgot everything, even how beautiful the girl was. Red Deer who was lying outside ready to do his part, wondered and wondered what had happened in there, but he did not dare call out to High Horse.

Afterwhile the day began to break and Red Deer had to leave with the two ponies he had staked there for his comrade and girl, or somebody would see him.

So he left.

Now when it was getting light in the tepee, the girl awoke and the first thing she saw was a terrible animal, all white with black stripes on it, lying asleep beside her bed. So she screamed, and then the old woman screamed and the old man yelled. High Horse jumped up, scared almost to death, and he nearly knocked the tepee down getting out of there.

People were coming running from all over the village with guns and bows and axes, and everybody was yelling.

By now High Horse was running so fast that he hardly touched the ground at all, and he looked so terrible that the people fled from him and let him run. Some braves wanted to shoot at him, but the others said he might be some sacred being and it would bring bad trouble to kill him.

High Horse made for the river that was near, and in among the brush he found a hollow tree and dived into it. Afterwhile some braves came there and he could hear them saying that it was some bad spirit that had come out of the water and gone back in again.

That morning the people were ordered to break camp and move away from there. So they did, while High Horse was hiding in his hollow tree.

Now Red Deer had been watching all this from his own tepee and trying to look as though he were as much surprised and scared as all the others. So when the camp moved, he sneaked back to where he had seen his comrade disappear. When he was down there in the brush, he called, and High Horse answered, because he knew his friend's voice. They washed off the paint from High Horse and sat down on the river bank to talk about their troubles.

High Horse said he never would go back to the village as long as he lived and he did not care what happened to him now. He said he was going to go on the war-path all by himself. Red Deer said: "No, cousin, you are not going on the war-path alone, because I am going with you."

So Red Deer got everything ready, and at night they started out on the warpath all alone. After several days they came to a Crow camp just about sundown, and when it was dark they sneaked up to where the Crow horses were grazing, killed the horse guard, who was not thinking about enemies because he thought all the Lakotas were far away, and drove off about a hundred horses.

They got a big start because all the Crow horses stampeded and it was probably morning before the Crow warriors could catch any horses to ride. Red Deer and High Horse fled with their herd three days and nights before they reached the village of their people. Then they drove the whole herd right into the village and up in front of the girl's tepee. The old man was there, and High Horse called out to him and asked if he thought maybe that would be enough horses for his girl. The old man did not wave him away that time. It was not the horses that he wanted. What he wanted was a son who was a real man and good for something.

So High Horse got his girl after all, and I think he deserved her.

## Questions

Although High Horse's behavior is amusing and at times ridiculous, how does Black Elk make it clear that he is not ridiculing the young man, but is instead in sympathy with him? Consider the following questions:

1. What is the effect of the first three paragraphs? Think about the first two sentences, and then the passage beginning "Say I am a young man . . ." and ending ". . . I would give him all the horses in the world if I had them."
2. Describe the behavior of the young girl, and of her father and mother. How do they contribute to the comedy? How does their behavior affect your understanding of Black Elk's attitude toward High Horse?
3. What is the function of Red Deer?
4. The narrative consists of several episodes. List them in the order in which they occur, and then describe the narrative's structure. How does this structure affect the tone?

Judy Syfers

# Why I Want a Wife

I belong to that classification of people known as wives. I am A Wife. And, not altogether incidentally, I am a mother.

Not too long ago a male friend of mine appeared on the scene fresh from a recent divorce. He had one child, who is, of course, with his ex-wife. He is looking for another wife. As I thought about him while I was ironing one evening, it suddenly occurred to me that I, too, would like to have a wife. Why do I want a wife?

I would like to go back to school so that I can become economically independent, support myself, and, if need be, support those dependent upon me. I want a wife who will work and send me to school. And while I am going to school I want a wife to take care of

Judy Syfers was born in San Francisco in 1937. She received a bachelor's degree from the University of Iowa in 1960 and wanted to do the graduate work that would qualify her for teaching in a university; she was dissuaded by her male teachers. "Why I Want a Wife" originally appeared in the first issue of *Ms.*

my children. I want a wife to keep track of the children's doctor and dentist appointments. And to keep track of mine, too. I want a wife to make sure my children eat properly and are kept clean. I want a wife who will wash the children's clothes and keep them mended. I want a wife who is a good nurturant attendant to my children, who arranges for their schooling, makes sure that they have an adequate social life with their peers, takes them to the park, the zoo, etc. I want a wife who takes care of the children when they are sick, a wife who arranges to be around when the children need special care, because, of course, I cannot miss classes at school. My wife must arrange to lose time at work and not lose the job. It may mean a small cut in my wife's income from time to time, but I guess I can tolerate that. Needless to say, my wife will arrange and pay for the care of the children while my wife is working.

I want a wife who will take care of *my* physical needs. I want a wife who will keep my house clean. A wife who will pick up after my children, a wife who will pick up after me. I want a wife who will keep my clothes clean, ironed, mended, replaced when need be, and who will see to it that my personal things are kept in their proper place so that I can find what I need the minute I need it. I want a wife who cooks the meals, a wife who is a *good* cook. I want a wife who will plan the menus, do the necessary grocery shopping, prepare the meals, serve them pleasantly, and then do the cleaning up while I do my studying. I want a wife who will care for me when I am sick and sympathize with my pain and loss of time from school. I want a wife to go along when our family takes a vacation so that someone can continue to care for me and my children when I need a rest and change of scene.

I want a wife who will not bother me with rambling complaints about a wife's duties. But I want a wife who will listen to me when I feel the need to explain a rather difficult point I have come across in my course of studies. And I want a wife who will type my papers for me when I have written them.

I want a wife who will take care of the details of my social life. When my wife and I are invited out by my friends, I want a wife who will take care of the babysitting arrangements. When I meet people at school that I like and want to entertain, I want a wife who will have the house clean, will prepare a special meal, serve it to me and my friends, and not interrupt when I talk about things that interest me and my friends. I want a wife who will have arranged that the children are fed and ready for bed before my guests arrive so that the children do not bother us. I want a wife who takes care of the needs of my guests so that they feel comfortable, who makes sure that they have an ashtray, that they are passed the hors d'oeuvres, that they are offered a second helping of the food, that their wine glasses are replenished when necessary, that their coffee is served to them as they like it. And I want a wife who knows that sometimes I need a night out by myself.

I want a wife who is sensitive to my sexual needs, a wife who makes love passionately and eagerly when I feel like it, a wife who makes sure that I am satisfied. And, of course, I want a wife who will not demand sexual attention when I am not in the mood for it. I want a wife who assumes the complete responsibility for birth control, because I do not want more children. I want a wife who will remain sexually faithful to me so that I do not have to clutter up my intellectual life with jealousies. And I want a wife who understands that *my* sexual needs may entail more than strict adherence to monogamy. I must, after all, be able to relate to people as fully as possible.

If, by chance, I find another person more suitable as a wife than the wife I already have, I want the liberty to replace my present wife with another one. Naturally, I will expect a fresh, new life; my wife will take the children and be solely responsible for them so that I am left free.

When I am through with school and have a job, I want my wife to quit working and remain at home so that my wife can more fully and completely take care of a wife's duties.

My God, who *wouldn't* want a wife?

## Questions

1. Does the second sentence of the essay mean anything different from the first? If so, what? If not, why is it there?
2. Describing a recently divorced man, Syfers says in the second paragraph: "He had one child, who is, of course, with his ex-wife." What information does "of course" convey? What attitude or tone?
3. If the constant repetition of "I want a wife who . . ." is not boring, what keeps it from being boring?
4. Syfers is attacking sexual stereotyping. Do you find in her essay any assumptions or details that limit the stereotyping to an economic class, or to an ethnic or racial group? Explain.

## Anonymous

# Confessions of an Erstwhile Child

Some years ago I attempted to introduce a class of Upward Bound students to political theory via More's *Utopia.* It was a mistake: I taught precious little theory and earned More a class full of undying enemies on account of two of his ideas. The first, that all members of a Utopian family were subject to the lifelong authority of its eldest male. The second, the Utopian provision that should a child wish to follow a profession different from that of his family, he could be transferred by adoption to a family that practiced the desired trade. My students were not impressed with my claim that the one provision softened the other and made for a fair compromise — for what causes most of our quarrels with our parents but our choice of life-patterns, of occupation? In objecting to the first provision my students were picturing themselves as children, subject to an unyielding authority. But on the second provision they surprised me by taking the parents' role and arguing that this form of ad lib adoption denied them a fundamental right of ownership over their children. It occurred to me that these reactions were two parts of the same pathology: having suffered the discipline of unreasonable parents, one has earned the right to be unreasonable in turn to one's children. The phenomenon has well-known parallels, such as frantic martinets who have risen from the ranks. Having served time as property, my Upward Bound students wanted theirs back as proprietors. I shuddered. It hardly takes an advanced course in Freudian psychology to realize that the perpetuation, generation after generation, of psychic lesions must go right to this source, the philosophically dubious notion that children are the property of their biological parents, compounded with the unphilosophic certitude so many parents harbor, that their children must serve an apprenticeship as like their own as they can manage.

---

The anonymous author of this essay has revealed only that he is forty, married, and the father of three children.

The idea of the child as property has always bothered me, for personal reasons I shall outline. I lack the feeling that I own my children and I have always scoffed at the idea that what they are and do is a continuation or a rejection of my being. I like them, I sympathize with them, I acknowledge the obligation to support them for a term of years—but I am not so fond or foolish as to regard a biological tie as a lien on their loyalty or respect, nor to imagine that I am equipped with preternatural powers of guidance as to their success and happiness. Beyond inculcating some of the obvious social protocols required in civilized life, who am I to pronounce on what makes for a happy or successful life? How many of us can say that we have successfully managed our own lives? Can we do better with our children? I am unimpressed, to say no more, with parents who have no great track record, presuming to oracular powers in regard to their children's lives.

The current debate over the Equal Rights Amendment frequently turns to custody questions. Opponents of ERA have made the horrifying discovery that ERA will spell the end of the mother's presumed rights of custody in divorce or separation cases, and that fathers may begin getting custody rights. Indeed a few odd cases have been so settled recently in anticipation of the ratification of ERA. If ratified, ERA would be an extremely blunt instrument for calling the whole idea of custody into question, but I for one will applaud anything that serves to begin debate. As important as equal rights between adults may be, I think that the rights of children are a far more serious and unattended need. To me, custody by natural parents, far from being a presumed right only re-examined in case of collapsing marriages, should be viewed as a privilege.

At this point I have to explain why I can so calmly contemplate the denial of so-called parental rights.

I am the only child of two harsh and combative personalities who married, seemingly, in order to have a sparring partner always at hand. My parents have had no other consistent or lasting aim in life but to win out over each other in a contest of wills. They still live, vigorous and angry septuagenarians, their ferocity little blunted by age or human respect. My earliest memories—almost my sole memories—are of unending combat, in which I was sometimes an appalled spectator, more often a hopeless negotiator in a war of no quarter, and most often a bystander accused of covert belligerency on behalf of one side or the other, and frequently of both! I grew up with two supposed adults who were absorbed in their hatreds and recriminations to the exclusion of almost all other reality. Not only did I pass by almost unnoticed in their struggle, the Depression and World War II passed them by equally unnoticed. I figured mainly as a practice target for sarcasm and invective, and occasionally as the ultimate culprit responsible for their unhappiness. ("If it weren't for you," my mother would sometimes say, "I could leave that SOB," a remark belied by her refusal to leave the SOB during these 20 long years since I left their "shelter.")

The reader may ask, "How did you survive if your parents' house was all that bad?" I have three answers. First, I survived by the moral equivalent of running away to sea or the circus, i.e., by burying myself in books and study, especially in the history of faraway and (I thought) more idealistic times than our own, and by consciously shaping my life and tastes to be as different as possible from those of my parents (this was a reproach to them, they knew, and it formed the basis of a whole secondary area of conflict and misunderstanding). Second, I survived because statistically most people "survive" horrible families, but survival can be a qualified term, as it is in my case by a permanently impaired digestive system and an unnatural sensitivity to raised voices. And third, though I found solace in schooling and the rationality, cooperation and basic fairness in teachers that I missed in my parents, I must now question whether it is healthy for a child to count so heavily on schooling for the love and approval that he deserves from his home and family. Even if schooling can do this well, in later life it means that one is loyal and affectionate toward schooling, not toward parents, who may in some sense need affection even if they don't "deserve" it. I am not unaware that however fair and rational I may be in reaction to my parents' counter-examples, I am a very cold-hearted man. I might have done better transferred to a new family, not just by receiving love, but through learning to give it—a lack I mourn as much or more than my failure to receive it.

It is little wonder then that I have an acquired immunity to the notion that parental custody is by and large a preferable thing. In my case, almost anything else would have been preferable, including even a rather callously run orphanage—anything for a little peace and quiet. Some people are simply unfit, under any conditions, to be parents, even if, indeed especially if, they maintain the charade of a viable marriage. My parents had no moral right to custody of children, and I cannot believe that my experience is unique or particularly isolated. There are all too many such marriages, in which some form of horror, congenial enough to adults too sick or crazed to recognize it, works its daily ruination on children. Surely thousands of children conclude at age 10 or 11, as I did, that marriage is simply an institution in which people are free to be as beastly as they have a mind to, which may lead either to a rejection of marriage or to a decision to reduplicate a sick marriage a second time, with another generation of victims. It is time to consider the rights of the victims.

How to implement a nascent theory of justice for children is difficult to say. One cannot imagine taking the word of a five-year-old against his parents, but what about a 10- or 12-year-old? At *some* point, children should have the right to escape the dominance of impossible parents. The matter used to be easier than it has been since World War I. The time-honored solution—for boys—of running away from home has been made infeasible by economic conditions, fingerprints, social security and minimum wage laws. No apprenticeship system exists any more, much less its upper-class medieval version—with required exchange of boys at puberty among noble families to serve as pages and so forth. The adoption system contemplated in More's *Utopia* is a half-remembered echo of medieval life, in which society, wiser than its theory, decreed a general exchange of children at or just before puberty, whether through apprenticeship or page-service, or more informal arrangements, like going to a university at 14 or running away with troubadors or gypsies.

Exchanging children is a wisely conceived safety valve against a too traumatic involvement between the biological parent and the child. Children need an alternative to living all their formative life in the same biological unit. They should have the right to petition for release from some sorts of families, to join other families, or to engage in other sorts of relationships that may provide equivalent service but may not be organized as a family. The nuclear family, after all, is not such an old or proven vehicle. Phillippe Aries' book, *Centuries of Childhood,* made the important point that the idea of helpless childhood is itself a notion of recent origin, that grew up simultaneously in the 16th and 17th centuries with the small and tight-knit nuclear family, sealed off from the world by another recent invention, "privacy." The older *extended* family (which is the kind More knew about) was probably more authoritarian on paper but much less productive of dependency in actual operation. There ought to be more than one way a youngster can enter adult society with more than half of his sanity left. At least no one should be forced to remain in a no-win game against a couple of crazy parents for 15–18 years. At 10 or 12, children in really messy situations should have the legal right to petition for removal from impossible families, and those rights should be reasonably easy to exercise. (This goes on de facto among the poor, of course, but it is not legal, and usually carries both stigma and danger.) The minimum wage laws should be modified to exempt such persons, especially if they wish to continue their education, working perhaps for public agencies, if they have no other means of support. If their parents can support them, then the equivalent of child support should be charged them to maintain their children, not in luxury, but adequately. Adoption of older children should be facilitated by easing of legal procedures (designed mainly to govern the adoption of *infants*) plus tax advantages for those willing to adopt older children on grounds of goodwill. Indeed children wishing to escape impossible family situations should be allowed a fair degree of initiative in finding and negotiating with possible future families.

Obviously the risk of rackets would be very high unless the exact terms of such provisions were framed very carefully, but the possibility of rackets is less frightening to anyone who thinks about it for long than the dangers of the present situation, which are evident and unrelieved by any signs of improvement. In barely a century this country has changed from a relatively loose society in which Huckleberry Finns were not uncommon, to a society of tense, airless nuclear families in which unhealthy and neurotic tendencies, once spawned in a family, tend to repeat themselves at a magnifying and accelerating rate. We may soon gain the distinction of being the only nation on earth to need not just medicare but "psychi-care." We have invested far too heavily in the unproved "equity" called the nuclear family; that stock is about to crash and we ought to begin finding escape options. In colonial days many New England colonies passed laws imposing fines or extra taxes on parents who kept their children under their own roofs after age 15 or 16, on the sensible notion that a person of that age ought to be out and doing on his own, whether going to Yale or apprenticing in a foundry. Even without the benefit of Freud, the colonial fathers had a good sense of what was wrong with a closely bound and centripetal family structure—it concentrates craziness like compound interest, and so they hit it with monetary penalties, a proper Protestant response, intolerant at once of both mystery and excuses. But this was the last gasp of a medieval and fundamentally Catholic idea that children, God help them, while they may be the children of *these* particular parents biologically, spiritually are the children of God, and more appositely are the children of the entire community, for which the entire community takes responsibility. The unguessed secret of the middle ages was not that monasteries relieved parents of unwanted children; more frequently, they relieved children of unwanted parents!

## Questions

1. What is the author's thesis? (Quote the thesis sentence.) Apart from his own experience, what evidence or other means does he offer to persuade you to accept his thesis?
2. What part does the *tone* of his article play in persuading you to agree with him, or in alienating you? Does his tone strike you, perhaps, as vigorous or belligerent, as ironic or bitter, as reasonable or hysterical?
3. The author admits (page 45, in the paragraph beginning "The reader may ask") that he is "a very cold-hearted man." Do you remember your initial reaction to that sentence? What was it? Overall, does the author strengthen or jeopardize his argument by this admission? Explain.
4. If you did not find the article persuasive, did you find it interesting? Can you explain why?

## Jonathan Swift

# A Modest Proposal

### For Preventing the Children of Poor People in Ireland from Being a Burden to Their Parents or Country, and for Making Them Beneficial to the Public

It is a melancholy object to those who walk through this great town or travel in the country, when they see the streets, the roads, and cabin doors, crowded with beggars of the female sex, followed by three, four, or six children, all in rags and importuning every passenger for an alms. These mothers, instead of being able to work for their honest livelihood, are forced to employ all their time in strolling to beg sustenance for their helpless infants: who as they grow up either turn thieves for want of work, or leave their dear native country to fight for the pretender in Spain, or sell themselves to the Barbadoes.

I think it is agreed by all parties that this prodigious number of children in the arms, or on the backs, or at the heels of their mothers, and frequently of their fathers, is in the present deplorable state of the kingdom a very great additional grievance; and, therefore, whoever could find out a fair, cheap, and easy method of making these children sound, useful members of the commonwealth, would deserve so well of the public as to have his statue set up for a preserver of the nation.

But my intention is very far from being confined to provide only for the children of professed beggars; it is of a much greater extent,

---

Jonathan Swift (1667–1745) was born in Ireland of an English family. He was ordained in the Church of Ireland in 1694, and in 1714 he became dean of St. Patrick's Cathedral, Dublin. He wrote abundantly on political and religious topics, often motivated (in his own words) by "savage indignation." It is ironic that *Gulliver's Travels,* the masterpiece by this master of irony, is most widely thought of as a book for children.

From the middle of the sixteenth century the English regulated the Irish economy so that it would enrich England. Heavy taxes and other repressive legislation impoverished Ireland, and in 1728, the year before Swift wrote "A Modest Proposal," Ireland was further weakened by a severe famine. Swift, deeply moved by the injustice, the stupidity, and the suffering that he found in Ireland, adopts the disguise or persona of an economist and offers an ironic suggestion on how Irish families may improve their conditions.

and shall take in the whole number of infants at a certain age who are born of parents in effect as little able to support them as those who demand our charity in the streets.

As to my own part, having turned my thoughts for many years upon this important subject, and maturely weighed the several schemes of our projectors, I have always found them grossly mistaken in their computation. It is true, a child just dropped from its dam may be supported by her milk for a solar year, with little other nourishment; at most not above the value of 2s.,[1] which the mother may certainly get, or the value in scraps, by her lawful occupation of begging; and it is exactly at one year old that I propose to provide for them in such a manner as instead of being a charge upon their parents or the parish, or wanting food and raiment for the rest of their lives, they shall on the contrary contribute to the feeding, and partly to the clothing, of many thousands.

There is likewise another great advantage in my scheme, that it will prevent those voluntary abortions, and that horrid practice of women murdering their bastard children, alas! too frequent among us! sacrificing the poor innocent babes I doubt more to avoid the expense than the shame, which would move tears and pity in the most savage and inhuman breast.

The number of souls in this kingdom being usually reckoned one million and a half, of these I calculate there may be about 200,000 couple whose wives are breeders; from which number I subtract 30,000 couple who are able to maintain their own children (although I apprehend there cannot be so many, under the present distress of the kingdom); but this being granted, there will remain 170,000 breeders. I again subtract 50,000 for those women who miscarry, or whose children die by accident or disease within the year. There only remain 120,000 children of poor parents annually born. The question therefore is, how this number shall be reared and provided for? which, as I have already said, under the present situation of affairs, is utterly impossible by all the methods hitherto proposed. For we can neither employ them in handicraft or agriculture; we neither build houses (I mean in the country) nor cultivate land; they can very seldom pick up a livelihood by stealing, till they arrive at six years old, except where they are of towardly parts; although I confess they learn the rudiments much earlier; during which time they can, how-

[1]2s.=two shillings. Later in the essay, "l" stands for pounds and "d" for pence. (Editor's note)

ever, be properly looked upon only as probationers; as I have been informed by a principal gentleman in the county of Cavan, who protested to me that he never knew above one or two instances under the age of six, even in a part of the kingdom so renowned for the quickest proficiency in that art.

I am assured by our merchants, that a boy or a girl before twelve years old is no saleable commodity; and even when they come to this age they will not yield above 3l. or 3l. 2s. 6d. at most on the exchange; which cannot turn to account either to the parents or kingdom, the charge of nutriment and rags having been at least four times that value.

I shall now therefore humbly propose my own thoughts, which I hope will not be liable to the least objection.

I have been assured by a very knowing American of my acquaintance in London, that a young healthy child well nursed is at a year old a most delicious, nourishing, and wholesome food, whether stewed, roasted, baked, or broiled; and I make no doubt that it will equally serve in a fricassee or a ragout.

I do therefore humbly offer it to public consideration that of the 120,000 children already computed, 20,000 may be reserved for breed, whereof only one-fourth part to be males; which is more than we allow to sheep, black cattle, or swine; and my reason is, that these children are seldom the fruits of marriage, a circumstance not much regarded by our savages; therefore one male will be sufficient to serve four females. That the remaining 100,000 may, at a year old, be offered in sale to the persons of quality and fortune through the kingdom; always advising the mother to let them suck plentifully in the last month, so as to render them plump and fat for a good table. A child will make two dishes at an entertainment for friends; and when the family dines alone, the fore or hind quarter will make a reasonable dish, and seasoned with a little pepper or salt will be very good boiled on the fourth day, especially in winter.

I have reckoned upon a medium that a child just born will weigh 12 pounds, and in a solar year, if tolerably nursed, will increase to 28 pounds.

I grant this food will be somewhat dear, and therefore very proper for landlords, who, as they have already devoured most of the parents, seem to have the best title to the children.

Infant's flesh will be in season throughout the year, but more plentiful in March, and a little before and after: for we are told by a grave author, an eminent French physician, that fish being a prolific diet, there are more children born in Roman Catholic countries about nine months after Lent than at any other season; therefore, reckoning a year after Lent, the markets will be more glutted than usual, because the number of popish infants is at least three to one in this kingdom: and therefore it will have one other collateral advantage, by lessening the number of papists among us.

I have already computed the charge of nursing a beggar's child (in which list I reckon all cottagers, laborers, and four-fifths of the farmers) to be about 2s. per annum, rags included; and I believe no gentleman would repine to give 10s. for the carcass of a good fat child, which, as I have said, will make four dishes of excellent nutritive meat, when he has only some particular friend or his own family to dine with him. Thus the squire will learn to be a good landlord, and grow popular among the tenants; the mother will have 8s. net profit, and be fit for work till she produces another child.

Those who are more thrifty (as I must confess the times require) may flay the carcass; the skin of which artificially dressed will make admirable gloves for ladies, and summer boots for fine gentlemen.

As to our city of Dublin, shambles may be appointed for this purpose in the most convenient parts of it, and butchers we may be assured will not be wanting: although I rather recommend buying the children alive, and dressing them hot from the knife as we do roasting pigs.

A very worthy person, a true lover of his country, and whose virtues I highly esteem, was lately pleased in discoursing on this matter to offer a refinement upon my scheme. He said that many gentlemen of this kingdom, having of late destroyed their deer, he conceived that the want of venison might be well supplied by the bodies of young lads and maidens, not exceeding fourteen years of age nor under twelve; so great a number of both sexes in every country being now ready to starve for want of work and service; and these to be disposed of by their parents, if alive, or otherwise by their nearest relations. But with due deference to so excellent a friend and so deserving a patriot, I cannot be altogether in his sentiments; for as to the males, my American acquaintance assured me from frequent experience that their flesh was generally tough and lean, like that of our schoolboys by continual exercise, and their taste disagreeable; and to fatten them would not answer the charge. Then as to the females, it would, I think, with humble submission be a loss to the public, because they soon would become breeders themselves: and besides, it is not improbable that some scrupulous people might be apt to censure such a practice (although indeed very unjustly), as a little bordering upon cruelty; which, I confess, has always been with me the strongest objection against any project, how well soever intended.

But in order to justify my friend, he confessed that this expedient was put into his head by the famous Psalmanazar, a native of the island Formosa, who came from thence to London about twenty years ago: and in conversation told my friend, that in his country when any young person happened to be put to death, the executioner sold the carcass to persons of quality as a prime dainty; and that in his time the body of a plump girl of fifteen, who was crucified for an attempt to poison the emperor, was sold to his imperial majesty's prime minister of state, and other great mandarins of the court, in joints from the gibbet, at 400 crowns. Neither indeed can I deny, that if the same use were made of several plump young girls in this town, who without one single groat to their fortunes cannot stir abroad without a chair, and appear at the playhouse and assemblies in foreign fineries which they never will pay for, the kingdom would not be the worse.

Some persons of a desponding spirit are in great concern about that vast number of poor people, who are aged, diseased, or maimed, and I have been desired to employ my thoughts what course may be taken to ease the nation of so grievous an encumbrance. But I am not in the least pain upon that matter, because it is very well known that they are every day dying and rotting by cold and famine, and filth and vermin, as fast as can be reasonably expected. And as to the young laborers, they are now in as hopeful a condition: they cannot get work, and consequently pine away for want of nourishment, to a degree that if at any time they are accidentally hired to common labor, they have not strength to perform it; and thus the country and themselves are happily delivered from the evils to come.

I have too long digressed, and therefore shall return to my subject. I think the advantages by the proposal which I have made are obvious and many, as well as of the highest importance.

For first, as I have already observed, it would greatly lessen the number of papists, with whom we are yearly overrun, being the principal breeders of the nation as well as our most dangerous enemies; and who stay at home on purpose to deliver the kingdom to the Pretender, hoping to take their advantage by the absence of so many good Protestants, who have chosen rather to leave their country than stay at home and pay tithes against their conscience to an Episcopal curate.

Secondly, The poor tenants will have something valuable of their own, which by law may be made liable to distress and help to pay their landlord's rent, their corn and cattle being already seized, and money a thing unknown.

Thirdly, Whereas the maintenance of 100,000 children from two years old and upward, cannot be computed at less than 10s. a-piece per annum, the nation's stock will be thereby increased £50,000 per annum, beside the profit of a new dish introduced to the tables of all gentlemen of fortune in the kingdom who have any refinement in taste. And the money will circulate among ourselves, the goods being entirely of our own growth and manufacture.

Fourthly, The constant breeders beside the gain of 8s. sterling per annum by the sale of their children, will be rid of the charge of maintaining them after the first year.

Fifthly, This food would likewise bring great custom to taverns, where the vintners will certainly be so prudent as to procure the best receipts for dressing it to perfection, and consequently have their houses frequented by all the fine gentlemen, who justly value themselves upon their knowledge in good eating; and a skilful cook who understands how to oblige his guests, will contrive to make it as expensive as they please.

Sixthly, This would be a great inducement to marriage, which all wise nations have either encouraged by rewards or enforced by laws and penalties. It would increase the care and tenderness of mothers toward their children, when they were sure of a settlement for life to the poor babes, provided in some sort by the public, to their annual profit instead of expense. We should see an honest emulation among the married women, which of them would bring the fattest child to the market. Men would become as fond of their wives during the time of their pregnancy as they are now of their mares in foal, their cows in calf, their sows when they are ready to farrow; nor offer to beat or kick them (as is too frequent a practice) for fear of a miscarriage.

Many other advantages might be enumerated. For instance, the addition of some thousand carcasses in our exportation of barreled beef, the propagation of swine's flesh, and improvement in the art of making good bacon, so much wanted among us by the great destruction of pigs, too frequent at our table; which are no way comparable in taste or magnificence to a well-grown, fat, yearling child, which roasted whole will make a considerable figure at a lord mayor's feast or any other public entertainment. But this and many others I omit, being studious of brevity.

Supposing that 1,000 families in this city would be constant customers for infants' flesh, besides others who might have it at merry-meetings, particularly at weddings and christenings, I compute that Dublin would take off annually about 20,000 carcasses; and the rest of the kingdom (where probably they will be sold somewhat cheaper) the remaining 80,000.

I can think of no one objection that will possibly be raised against this proposal, unless it should be urged that the number of people will be thereby much lessened in the kingdom. This I freely own, and it was indeed one principal design in offering it to the world. I desire the reader will observe, that I calculate my remedy for this one individual kingdom of Ireland and for no other that ever was, is, or I think ever can be upon earth. Therefore let no man talk to me of other expedients: of taxing our absentees at 5s. a pound: of using neither clothes nor household furniture except what is of our own growth and manufacture: of utterly rejecting the materials and instruments that promote foreign luxury: of curing the expensiveness of pride, vanity, idleness, and gaming in our women: of introducing a vein of parsimony, prudence, and temperance: of learning to love our country, in the want of which we differ even from Laplanders and the inhabitants of Topinamboo: of quitting our animosities and factions, nor acting any longer like the Jews, who were murdering one another at the very moment their city was taken: of being a little cautious not to sell our country and conscience for nothing: of teaching landlords to have at least one degree of mercy toward their tenants: lastly, of putting a spirit of honesty, industry, and skill into our shopkeepers; who, if a resolution could now be taken to buy only our native goods, would immediately unite to cheat and exact upon us in the price, the measure, and the goodness, nor could ever yet be brought to make one fair proposal of just dealing, though often and earnestly invited to it.

Therefore I repeat, let no man talk to me of these and the like expedients, till he has at least some glimpse of hope that there will be ever some hearty and sincere attempt to put them in practice.

But as to myself, having been wearied out for many years with offering vain, idle, visionary thoughts, and at length utterly despairing of success, I fortunately fell upon this proposal; which, as it is wholly new, so it has something solid and real, of no expense and little trouble, full in our own power, and whereby we can incur no danger in disobliging England. For this kind of commodity will not bear exportation, the flesh being of too tender a consistence to admit a long continuance in salt, although perhaps I could name a country which would be glad to eat up our whole nation without it.

After all, I am not so violently bent upon my own opinion as to reject any offer proposed by wise men, which shall be found equally innocent, cheap, easy, and effectual. But before something of that kind shall be advanced in contradiction to my scheme, and offering a better, I desire the author or authors will be pleased maturely to consider two points. First, as things now stand, how they will be able to find food and raiment for 100,000 useless mouths and backs. And secondly, there being a round million of creatures in human figure throughout this kingdom, whose subsistence put into a common stock would leave them in debt 2,000,000*l.* sterling, adding those who are beggars by profession to the bulk of farmers, cottagers, and laborers, with the wives and children who are beggars in effect; I desire those politicians who dislike my overture, and may perhaps be so bold as to attempt an answer, that they will first ask the parents of these mortals, whether they would not at this day think it a great happiness to have been sold for food at a year old in the manner I prescribe, and thereby have avoided such a perpetual scene of misfortunes as they have since gone through by the oppression of landlords, the impossibility of paying rent without money or trade, the want of common sustenance, with neither house nor clothes to cover them from the inclemencies of the weather, and the most inevitable prospect of entailing the like or greater miseries upon their breed for ever.

I profess, in the sincerity of my heart, that I have not the least personal interest in endeavoring to promote this necessary work, having no other motive than the public good of my country, by advancing our trade, providing for infants, relieving the poor, and giving some pleasure to the rich. I have no children by which I can propose to get a single penny; the youngest being nine years old, and my wife past child-bearing.

## Questions

1. In the fourth paragraph Swift speaks of "projectors." Check the *Oxford English Dictionary* to see the implications of this word in the eighteenth century. Keeping these implications in mind, characterize the pamph-

leteer (not Swift but his persona, an invented "projector") who offers his "modest proposal." What sort of man does he think he is? What sort of man do we regard him as? Support your assertions with evidence.

2. In the first paragraph the speaker says that the sight of mothers begging is "melancholy." In this paragraph what assumption does the speaker make about women that in part gives rise to this melancholy? Now that you are familiar with the entire essay, explain Swift's strategy in his first paragraph.
3. Explain the function of the "other expedients" (listed in the paragraph on page 55 beginning "I can think of no one objection").
4. How might you argue that although this satire is primarily ferocious, it also contains some playful touches? What specific passages might support your argument?
5. In the speaker's view, what underlies good family relationships?

**Peter Singer**

# Animal Liberation

## I

We are familiar with Black Liberation, Gay Liberation, and a variety of other movements. With Women's Liberation some thought we had come to the end of the road. Discrimination on the basis of sex, it has been said, is the last form of discrimination that is universally accepted and practiced without pretense, even in those liberal circles which have long prided themselves on their freedom from racial discrimination. But one should always be wary of talking of "the last remaining form of discrimination." If we have learned anything from the liberation movements, we should have learned how difficult it is to be aware of the ways in which we discriminate until they are forcefully pointed out to us. A liberation movement demands an expansion of our moral horizons, so that practices that

Peter Singer teaches philosophy at Monash University in Melbourne, Australia. This essay originally appeared as a review of *Animals, Men and Morals,* edited by Stanley and Roslind Godlovitch and John Harris.

were previously regarded as natural and inevitable are now seen as intolerable.

*Animals, Men and Morals* is a manifesto for an Animal Liberation movement. The contributors to the book may not all see the issue this way. They are a varied group. Philosophers, ranging from professors to graduate students, make up the largest contingent. There are five of them, including the three editors, and there is also an extract from the unjustly neglected German philosopher with an English name, Leonard Nelson, who died in 1927. There are essays by two novelist/critics, Brigid Brophy and Maureen Duffy, and another by Muriel the Lady Dowding, widow of Dowding of Battle of Britain fame and the founder of "Beauty Without Cruelty," a movement that campaigns against the use of animals for furs and cosmetics. The other pieces are by a psychologist, a botanist, a sociologist, and Ruth Harrison, who is probably best described as a professional campaigner for animal welfare.

Whether or not these people, as individuals, would all agree that they are launching a liberation movement for animals, the book as a whole amounts to no less. It is a demand for a complete change in our attitudes to nonhumans. It is a demand that we cease to regard the exploitation of other species as natural and inevitable, and that, instead, we see it as a continuing moral outrage. Patrick Corbett, Professor of Philosophy at Sussex University, captures the spirit of the book in his closing words:

> . . . We require now to extend the great principles of liberty, equality and fraternity over the lives of animals. Let animal slavery join human slavery in the graveyard of the past.

The reader is likely to be skeptical. "Animal Liberation" sounds more like a parody of liberation movements than a serious objective. The reader may think: We support the claims of blacks and women for equality because blacks and women really are equal to whites and males—equal in intelligence and in abilities, capacity for leadership, rationality, and so on. Humans and nonhumans obviously are not equal in these respects. Since justice demands only that we treat equals equally, unequal treatment of humans and nonhumans cannot be an injustice.

This is a tempting reply, but a dangerous one. It commits the non-racist and non-sexist to a dogmatic belief that blacks and women really are just as intelligent, able, etc., as whites and males—and no more. Quite possibly this happens to be the case. Certainly attempts to prove that racial or sexual differences in these respects have a genetic origin have not been conclusive. But do we really want to stake our demand for equality on the assumption that there are no genetic differences of this kind between the different races or sexes? Surely the appropriate response to those who claim to have found evidence for such genetic differences is not to stick to the belief that there are no differences, whatever the evidence to the contrary; rather one should be clear that the claim to equality does not depend on IQ. Moral equality is distinct from factual equality. Otherwise it would be nonsense to talk of the equality of human beings, since humans, as individuals, obviously differ in intelligence and almost any ability one cares to name. If possessing greater intelligence does not entitle one human to exploit another, why should it entitle humans to exploit nonhumans?

Jeremy Bentham expressed the essential basis of equality in his famous formula: "Each to count for one and none for more than one." In other words, the interests of every being that has interests are to be taken into account and treated equally with the like interests of any other being. Other moral philosophers, before and after Bentham, have made the same point in different ways. Our concern for others must not depend on whether they possess certain characteristics, though just what that concern involves may, of course, vary according to such characteristics.

Bentham, incidentally, was well aware that the logic of the demand for racial equality did not stop at the equality of humans. He wrote:

> The day *may* come when the rest of the animal creation may acquire those rights which never could have been withholden from them but by the hand of tyranny. The French have already discovered that the blackness of the skin is no reason why a human being should be abandoned without redress to the caprice of a tormentor. It may one day come to be recognized that the number of the legs, the villosity of the skin, or the termination of the *os sacrum,* are reasons equally insufficient for abandoning a sensitive being to the same fate. What else is it that should trace the insuperable line? Is it the faculty of reason, or perhaps the faculty of discourse? But a full-grown horse or dog is beyond comparison a more rational, as well as a more conversable animal, than an infant of a day, or a week, or even a month, old. But suppose they were otherwise, what would it avail? The question is not, Can they *reason?* nor Can they *talk?* but, Can they *suffer?*[1]

[1] *The Principles of Morals and Legislation,* ch. XVII, sec. 1, footnote to paragraph 4.

Surely Bentham was right. If a being suffers, there can be no moral justification for refusing to take that suffering into consideration, and, indeed, to count it equally with the like suffering (if rough comparisons can be made) of any other being.

So the only question is: Do animals other than man suffer? Most people agree unhesitatingly that animals like cats and dogs can and do suffer, and this seems also to be assumed by those laws that prohibit wanton cruelty to such animals. Personally, I have no doubt at all about this and find it hard to take seriously the doubts that a few people apparently do have. The editors and contributors of *Animals, Men and Morals* seem to feel the same way, for although the question is raised more than once, doubts are quickly dismissed each time. Nevertheless, because this is such a fundamental point, it is worth asking what grounds we have for attributing suffering to other animals.

It is best to begin by asking what grounds any individual human has for supposing that other humans feel pain. Since pain is a state of consciousness, a "mental event," it can never be directly observed. No observations, whether behavioral signs such as writhing or screaming or physiological or neurological recordings, are observations of pain itself. Pain is something one feels, and one can only infer that others are feeling it from various external indications. The fact that only philosophers are ever skeptical about whether other humans feel pain shows that we regard such inference as justifiable in the case of humans.

Is there any reason why the same inference should be unjustifiable for other animals? Nearly all the external signs which lead us to infer pain in other humans can be seen in other species, especially "higher" animals such as mammals and birds. Behavioral signs—writhing, yelping, or other forms of calling, attempts to avoid the source of pain, and many others—are present. We know, too, that these animals are biologically similar in the relevant respects, having nervous systems like ours which can be observed to function as ours do.

So the grounds for inferring that these animals can feel pain are nearly as good as the grounds for inferring other humans do. Only nearly, for there is one behavioral sign that humans have but nonhumans, with the exception of one or two specially raised chimpanzees, do not have. This, of course, is a developed language. As the quotation from Bentham indicates, this has long been regarded as an important distinction between man and other animals. Other animals may communicate with each other, but not in the way we do. Following Chomsky, many people now mark this distinction by saying that only humans communicate in a form that is governed by rules of syntax. (For the purposes of this argument, linguists allow those chimpanzees who have learned a syntactic sign language to rank as honorary humans.) Nevertheless, as Bentham pointed out, this distinction is not relevant to the question of how animals ought to be treated, unless it can be linked to the issue of whether animals suffer.

This link may be attempted in two ways. First, there is a hazy line of philosophical thought, stemming perhaps from some doctrines associated with Wittgenstein, which maintains that we cannot meaningfully attribute states of consciousness to beings without language. I have not seen this argument made explicit in print, though I have come across it in conversation. This position seems to me very implausible, and I doubt that it would be held at all if it were not thought to be a consequence of a broader view of the significance of language. It may be that the use of a public, rule-governed language is a precondition of conceptual thought. It may even be, although personally I doubt it, that we cannot meaningfully speak of a creature having an intention unless that creature can use a language. But states like pain, surely, are more primitive than either of these, and seem to have nothing to do with language.

Indeed, as Jane Goodall points out in her study of chimpanzees, when it comes to the expression of feelings and emotions, humans tend to fall back on non-linguistic modes of communication which are often found among apes, such as a cheering pat on the back, an exuberant embrace, a clasp of hands, and so on.[2] Michael Peters makes a similar point in his contribution to *Animals, Men and Morals* when he notes that the basic signals we use to convey pain, fear, sexual arousal, and so on are not specific to our species. So there seems to be no reason at all to believe that a creature without language cannot suffer.

The second, and more easily appreciated way of linking language and the existence of pain is to say that the best evidence that we can have that another creature is in pain is when he tells us that he is. This is a distinct line of argument, for it is not being denied that a non-language-user conceivably could suffer, but only that we could know that he is suffering. Still, this line of argument seems to me to fail, and for reasons similar to those just given. "I am in pain" is not

[2]Jane van Lawick-Goodall, *In the Shadow of Man* (Houghton Mifflin, 1971), p. 225.

the best possible evidence that the speaker is in pain (he might be lying) and it is certainly not the only possible evidence. Behavioral signs and knowledge of the animal's biological similarity to ourselves together provide adequate evidence that animals do suffer. After all, we would not accept linguistic evidence if it contradicted the rest of the evidence. If a man was severely burned, and behaved as if he were in pain, writhing, groaning, being very careful not to let his burned skin touch anything, and so on, but later said he had not been in pain at all, we would be more likely to conclude that he was lying or suffering from amnesia than that he had not been in pain.

Even if there were stronger grounds for refusing to attribute pain to those who do not have a language, the consequences of this refusal might lead us to examine these grounds unusually critically. Human infants, as well as some adults, are unable to use language. Are we to deny that a year-old infant can suffer? If not, how can language be crucial? Of course, most parents can understand the responses of even very young infants better than they understand the responses of other animals, and sometimes infant responses can be understood in the light of later development.

This, however, is just a fact about the relative knowledge we have of our own species and other species, and most of this knowledge is simply derived from closer contact. Those who have studied the behavior of other animals soon learn to understand their responses at least as well as we understand those of an infant. (I am not referring to Jane Goodall's and other well-known studies of apes. Consider, for example, the degree of understanding achieved by Tinbergen from watching herring gulls.)[3] Just as we can understand infant human behavior in the light of adult human behavior, so we can understand the behavior of other species in the light of our own behavior (and sometimes we can understand our own behavior better in the light of the behavior of other species).

The grounds we have for believing that other mammals and birds suffer are, then, closely analogous to the grounds we have for believing that other humans suffer. It remains to consider how far down the evolutionary scale this analogy holds. Obviously it becomes poorer when we get further away from man. To be more precise would require a detailed examination of all that we know about other forms of life. With fish, reptiles, and other vertebrates the analogy still seems strong, with molluscs like oysters it is much

[3]N. Tinbergen, *The Herring Gull's World* (Basic Books, 1961).

weaker. Insects are more difficult, and it may be that in our present state of knowledge we must be agnostic about whether they are capable of suffering.

If there is no moral justification for ignoring suffering when it occurs, and it does occur in other species, what are we to say of our attitudes toward these other species? Richard Ryder, one of the contributors to *Animals, Men and Morals,* uses the term "speciesism" to describe the belief that we are entitled to treat members of other species in a way in which it would be wrong to treat members of our own species. The term is not euphonious, but it neatly makes the analogy with racism. The non-racist would do well to bear the analogy in mind when he is inclined to defend human behavior toward nonhumans. "Shouldn't we worry about improving the lot of our own species before we concern ourselves with other species?" he may ask. If we substitute "race" for "species" we shall see that the question is better not asked. "Is a vegetarian diet nutritionally adequate?" resembles the slave-owner's claim that he and the whole economy of the South would be ruined without slave labor. There is even a parallel with skeptical doubts about whether animals suffer, for some defenders of slavery professed to doubt whether blacks really suffer in the way whites do.

I do not want to give the impression, however, that the case for Animal Liberation is based on the analogy with racism and no more. On the contrary, *Animals, Men and Morals* describes the various ways in which humans exploit nonhumans, and several contributors consider the defenses that have been offered, including the defense of meat-eating mentioned in the last paragraph. Sometimes the rebuttals are scornfully dismissive, rather than carefully designed to convince the detached critic. This may be a fault, but it is a fault that is inevitable, given the kind of book this is. The issue is not one on which one can remain detached. As the editors state in their Introduction:

> Once the full force of moral assessment has been made explicit there can be no rational excuse left for killing animals, be they killed for food, science, or sheer personal indulgence. We have not assembled this book to provide the reader with yet another manual on how to make brutalities less brutal. Compromise, in the traditional sense of the term, is simple unthinking weakness when one considers the actual reasons for our crude relationships with the other animals.

The point is that on this issue there are few critics who are genuinely detached. People who eat pieces of slaughtered nonhumans every day find it hard to believe that they are doing wrong; and they also find it hard to imagine what else they could eat. So for those who do not place nonhumans beyond the pale of morality, there comes a stage when further argument seems pointless, a stage at which one can only accuse one's opponent of hypocrisy and reach for the sort of sociological account of our practices and the way we defend them that is attempted by David Wood in his contribution to this book. On the other hand, to those unconvinced by the arguments, and unable to accept that they are merely rationalizing their dietary preferences and their fear of being thought peculiar, such sociological explanations can only seem insultingly arrogant.

## II

The logic of speciesism is most apparent in the practice of experimenting on nonhumans in order to benefit humans. This is because the issue is rarely obscured by allegations that nonhumans are so different from humans that we cannot know anything about whether they suffer. The defender of vivisection cannot use this argument because he needs to stress the similarities between man and other animals in order to justify the usefulness to the former of experiments on the latter. The researcher who makes rats choose between starvation and electric shocks to see if they develop ulcers (they do) does so because he knows that the rat has a nervous system very similar to man's, and presumably feels an electric shock in a similar way.

Richard Ryder's restrained account of experiments on animals made me angrier with my fellow men than anything else in this book. Ryder, a clinical psychologist by profession, himself experimented on animals before he came to hold the view he puts forward in his essay. Experimenting on animals is now a large industry, both academic and commercial. In 1969, more than 5 million experiments were performed in Britain, the vast majority without anesthetic (though how many of these involved pain is not known). There are no accurate U.S. figures, since there is no federal law on the subject, and in many cases no state law either. Estimates vary from 20 million to 200 million. Ryder suggests that 80 million may be the best guess. We tend to think that this is all for vital medical research, but of course it is not. Huge numbers of animals are used in university departments from Forestry to Psychology, and even more are used for commercial purposes, to test whether cosmetics can cause skin damage, or shampoos eye damage, or to test food additives or laxatives or sleeping pills or anything else.

A standard test for foodstuffs is the "LD50." The object of this test is to find the dosage level at which 50 percent of the test animals will die. This means that nearly all of them will become very sick before finally succumbing or surviving. When the substance is a harmless one, it may be necessary to force huge doses down the animals, until in some cases sheer volume or concentration causes death.

Ryder gives a selection of experiments, taken from recent scientific journals. I will quote two, not for the sake of indulging in gory details, but in order to give an idea of what normal researchers think they may legitimately do to other species. The point is not that the individual researchers are cruel men, but that they are behaving in a way that is allowed by our speciesist attitudes. As Ryder points out, even if only 1 percent of the experiments involve severe pain, that is 50,000 experiments in Britain each year, or nearly 150 every day (and about fifteen times as many in the United States, if Ryder's guess is right). Here then are two experiments:

> O. S. Ray and R. J. Barrett of Pittsburg gave electric shocks to the feet of 1,042 mice. They then caused convulsions by giving more intense shocks through cup-shaped electrodes applied to the animals' eyes or through pressure spring clips attached to their ears. Unfortunately some of the mice who "successfully completed Day One training were found sick or dead prior to testing on Day Two." [Journal of Comparative and Physiological Psychology, 1969, vol. 67, pp. 110–116]

> At the National Institute for Medical Research, Mill Hill, London, W. Feldberg and S. L. Sherwood injected chemicals into the brains of cats —"with a number of widely different substances, recurrent patterns of reaction were obtained. Retching, vomiting, defaecation, increased salivation and greatly accelerated respiration leading to panting were common features." . . .
>
> The injection into the brain of a large dose of Tubocuraine caused the cat to jump "from the table to the floor and then straight into its cage, where it started calling more and more noisily whilst moving about restlessly and jerkily . . . finally the cat fell with legs and neck flexed, jerking in rapid clonic movements, the condition being that of a major [epileptic] convulsion . . . within a few seconds the cat got up, ran for a few yards at high speed and fell in another fit. The whole process was repeated several times within the next ten minutes, during which the cat lost faeces and foamed at the mouth."
>
> This animal finally died thirty-five minutes after the brain injection. [*Journal of Physiology,* 1954, vol. 123, pp. 148–167]

There is nothing secret about these experiments. One has only to open any recent volume of a learned journal, such as the *Journal of Comparative and Physiological Psychology,* to find full descriptions of experiments of this sort, together with the results obtained—results that are frequently trivial and obvious. The experiments are often supported by public funds.

It is a significant indication of the level of acceptability of these practices that, although these experiments are taking place at this moment on university campuses throughout the country, there has, so far as I know, not been the slightest protest from the student movement. Students have been rightly concerned that their universities should not discriminate on grounds of race or sex, and that they should not serve the purposes of the military or big business. Speciesism continues undisturbed, and many students participate in it. There may be a few qualms at first, but since everyone regards it as normal, and it may even be a required part of a course, the student soon becomes hardened and, dismissing his earlier feelings as "mere sentiment," comes to regard animals as statistics rather than sentient beings with interests that warrant consideration.

Argument about vivisection has often missed the point because it has been put in absolutist terms: Would the abolitionist be prepared to let thousands die if they could be saved by experimenting on a single animal? The way to reply to this purely hypothetical question is to pose another: Would the experimenter be prepared to experiment on a human orphan under six months old, if it were the only way to save many lives? (I say "orphan" to avoid the complication of parental feelings, although in doing so I am being overfair to the experimenter, since the nonhuman subjects of experiments are not orphans.) A negative answer to this question indicates that the experimenter's readiness to use nonhumans is simple discrimination, for adult apes, cats, mice, and other mammals are more conscious of what is happening to them, more self-directing, and, so far as we can tell, just as sensitive to pain as a human infant. There is no characteristic that human infants possess that adult mammals do not have to the same or a higher degree.

(It might be possible to hold that what makes it wrong to experiment on a human infant is that the infant will in time develop into more than the nonhuman, but one would then, to be consistent, have to oppose abortion, and perhaps contraception, too, for the fetus and the egg and sperm have the same potential as the infant. Moreover, one would still have no reason for experimenting on a nonhuman rather than a human with brain damage severe enough to make it impossible for him to rise above infant level.)

The experimenter, then, shows a bias for his own species whenever he carries out an experiment on a nonhuman for a purpose that he would not think justified him in using a human being at an equal or lower level of sentience, awareness, ability to be self-directing, etc. No one familiar with the kind of results yielded by these experiments can have the slightest doubt that if this bias were eliminated the number of experiments performed would be zero or very close to it.

## III

If it is vivisection that shows the logic of speciesism most clearly, it is the use of other species for food that is at the heart of our attitudes toward them. Most of *Animals, Men and Morals* is an attack on meat-eating—an attack which is based solely on concern for nonhumans, without reference to arguments derived from considerations of ecology, macrobiotics, health, or religion.

The idea that nonhumans are utilities, means to our ends, pervades our thought. Even conservationists who are concerned about the slaughter of wild fowl but not about the vastly greater slaughter of chickens for our tables are thinking in this way—they are worried about what we would lose if there were less wildlife. Stanley Godlovitch, pursuing the Marxist idea that our thinking is formed by the activities we undertake in satisfying our needs, suggests that man's first classification of his environment was into Edibles and Inedibles. Most animals came into the first category, and there they have remained.

Man may always have killed other species for food, but he has never exploited them so ruthlessly as he does today. Farming has succumbed to business methods, the objective being to get the highest possible ratio of output (meat, eggs, milk) to input (fodder, labor costs, etc.). Ruth Harrison's essay "On Factory Farming" gives an account of some aspects of modern methods, and of the unsuccessful British campaign for effective controls, a campaign which was sparked off by her *Animal Machines* (Stuart: London, 1964).

Her article is in no way a substitute for her earlier book. This is a pity since, as she says, "Farm produce is still associated with mental pictures of animals browsing in the fields . . . of hens having a last forage before going to roost. . . . " Yet neither in her article nor elsewhere in *Animals, Men and Morals* is this false image replaced by a clear idea of the nature and extent of factory farming. We learn of this only indirectly, when we hear of the code of reform proposed by an advisory committee set up by the British government.

Among the proposals, which the government refused to implement on the grounds that they were too idealistic, were: *"Any animal should at least have room to turn around freely."*

Factory farm animals need liberation in the most literal sense. Veal calves are kept in stalls five feet by two feet. They are usually slaughtered when about four months old, and have been too big to turn in their stalls for at least a month. Intensive beef herds, kept in stalls only proportionately larger for much longer periods, account for a growing percentage of beef production. Sows are often similarly confined when pregnant, which, because of artificial methods of increasing fertility, can be most of the time. Animals confined in this way do not waste food by exercising, nor do they develop unpalatable muscle.

*"A dry bedded area should be provided for all stock."* Intensively kept animals usually have to stand and sleep on slatted floors without straw, because this makes cleaning easier.

*"Palatable roughage must be readily available to all calves after one week of age."* In order to produce the pale veal housewives are said to prefer, calves are fed on an all-liquid diet until slaughter, even though they are long past the age at which they would normally eat grass. They develop a craving for roughage, evidenced by attempts to gnaw wood from their stalls. (For the same reason, their diet is deficient in iron.)

*"Battery cages for poultry should be large enough for a bird to be able to stretch one wing at a time."* Under current British practice, a cage for four or five laying hens has a floor area of twenty inches by eighteen inches, scarcely larger than a double page of the *New York Review of Books.* In this space, on a sloping wire floor (sloping so the eggs roll down, wire so the dung drops through) the birds live for a year or eighteen months while artificial lighting and temperature conditions combine with drugs in their food to squeeze the maximum number of eggs out of them. Table birds are also sometimes kept in cages. More often they are reared in sheds, no less crowded. Under these conditions all the birds' natural activities are frustrated, and they develop "vices" such as pecking each other to death. To prevent this, beaks are often cut off, and the sheds kept dark.

How many of those who support factory farming by buying its produce know anything about the way it is produced? How many have heard something about it, but are reluctant to check up for fear that it will make them uncomfortable? To non-speciesists, the typical consumer's mixture of ignorance, reluctance to find out the truth, and vague belief that nothing really bad could be allowed seems analogous to the attitudes of "decent Germans" to the death camps.

There are, of course, some defenders of factory farming. Their arguments are considered, though again rather sketchily, by John Harris. Among the most common: "Since they have never known anything else, they don't suffer." This argument will not be put by anyone who knows anything about animal behavior, since he will know that not all behavior has to be learned. Chickens attempt to stretch wings, walk around, scratch, and even dustbathe or build a nest, even though they have never lived under conditions that allowed these activities. Calves can suffer from maternal deprivation no matter at what age they were taken from their mothers. "We need these intensive methods to provide protein for a growing population." As ecologists and famine relief organizations know, we can produce for more protein per acre if we grow the right vegetable crop, soy beans for instance, than if we use the land to grow crops to be converted into protein by animals who use nearly 90 percent of the protein themselves, even when unable to exercise.

There will be many readers of this book who will agree that factory farming involves an unjustifiable degree of exploitation of sentient creatures, and yet will want to say that there is nothing wrong with rearing animals for food, provided it is done "humanely." These people are saying, in effect, that although we should not cause animals to suffer, there is nothing wrong with killing them.

There are two possible replies to this view. One is to attempt to show that this combination of attitudes is absurd. Roslind Godlovitch takes this course in her essay, which is an examination of some common attitudes to animals. She argues that from the combination of "animal suffering is to be avoided" and "there is nothing wrong with killing animals" it follows that all animal life ought to be exterminated (since all sentient creatures will suffer to some degree at some point in their lives). Euthanasia is a contentious issue only because we place some value on living. If we did not, the least amount of suffering would justify it. Accordingly, if we deny that we have a duty to exterminate all animal life, we must concede that we are placing some value on animal life.

This argument seems to me valid, although one could still reply that the value of animal life is to be derived from the pleasures that life can have for them, so that, provided their lives have a balance of pleasure over pain, we are justified in rearing them. But this would imply that we ought to produce animals and let them live as pleasantly as possible, without suffering.

At this point, one can make the second of the two possible replies to the view that rearing and killing animals for food is all right so long as it is done humanely. This second reply is that so long as we think that a nonhuman may be killed simply so that a human can satisfy his taste for meat, we are still thinking of nonhumans as means rather than as ends in themselves. The factory farm is nothing more than the application of technology to this concept. Even traditional methods involve castration, the separation of mothers and their young, the breaking up of herds, branding or ear-punching, and of course transportation to the abattoirs and the final moments of terror when the animal smells blood and senses danger. If we were to try rearing animals so that they lived and died without suffering, we should find that to do so on anything like the scale of today's meat industry would be a sheer impossibility. Meat would become the prerogative of the rich.

I have been able to discuss only some of the contributions to this book, saying nothing about, for instance, the essays on killing for furs and for sport. Nor have I considered all the detailed questions that need to be asked once we start thinking about other species in the radically different way presented by this book. What, for instance, are we to do about genuine conflicts of interest like rats biting slum children? I am not sure of the answer, but the essential point is just that we *do* see this as a conflict of interests, that we recognize that rats have interests too. Then we may begin to think about other ways of resolving the conflict—perhaps by leaving out rat baits that sterilize the rats instead of killing them.

I have not discussed such problems because they are side issues compared with the exploitation of other species for food and for experimental purposes. On these central matters, I hope that I have said enough to show that this book, despite its flaws, is a challenge to every human to recognize his attitudes to nonhumans as a form of prejudice no less objectionable than racism or sexism. It is a challenge that demands not just a change of attitudes, but a change in our way of life, for it requires us to become vegetarians.

Can a purely moral demand of this kind succeed? The odds are certainly against it. The book holds out no inducements. It does not tell us that we will become healthier, or enjoy life more, if we cease exploiting animals. Animal Liberation will require greater altruism on the part of mankind than any other liberation movement, since animals are incapable of demanding it for themselves, or of protesting against their exploitation by votes, demonstrations, or bombs. Is man capable of such genuine altruism? Who knows? If this book does have a significant effect, however, it will be a vindication of all those who have believed that man has within himself the potential for more than cruelty and selfishness.

## Questions

1. Reread Singer's first seven paragraphs carefully, observing how he leads us to see that "animal liberation" is not a joke. It will help you to understand his strategy if for each of his paragraphs you write one sentence, either summarizing the paragraph or commenting on what it accomplishes in his argument.
2. What grounds does Singer find for attributing suffering to nonhumans? List the arguments he offers to dismiss the relevance of a developed language. Why does he find it necessary to offer these arguments?
3. Does Singer attribute the capacity to feel pain to all species? Explain.
4. How does Singer define speciesism? To what extent does he use the analogy of speciesism to racism?
5. What is vivisection? Why, according to Singer, *must* defenders of vivisection also defend speciesism? Why do many of us who would not be willing to defend speciesism tolerate or even participate in experiments on animals?
6. What use of animals does Singer analyze beginning on page 67? Why does he reserve this discussion for the last part of his essay? Why does he offer more detailed and more concrete examples in this section than in the second part, beginning on page 64?

## Jamaica Kincaid

# Girl

Wash the white clothes on Monday and put them on the stone heap; wash the color clothes on Tuesday and put them on the clothesline to dry; don't walk barehead in the hot sun; cook pumpkin fritters in very hot sweet oil; soak your little cloths right after you take them off; when buying cotton to make yourself a nice blouse, be sure that it doesn't have gum in it, because that way it won't hold up well after a wash; soak salt fish overnight before you cook it; is it true that you sing benna in Sunday school?; always eat your food in such a way that it won't turn someone else's stomach; on Sundays try to walk like a lady and not like the slut you are so bent on becoming; don't sing benna in Sunday school; you musn't speak to wharf-rat boys, not even to give directions; don't eat fruits on the street—flies will follow you; *but I don't sing benna on Sundays at all and never in Sunday school*; this is how to sew on a button; this is how to make a buttonhole for the button you have just sewed on; this is how to hem a dress when you see the hem coming down and so to prevent yourself from looking like the slut I know you are so bent on becoming; this is how you iron your father's khaki shirt so that it doesn't have a crease; this is how you iron your father's khaki pants so that they don't have a crease; this is how you grow okra—far from the house, because okra tree harbors red ants; when you are growing dasheen, make sure it gets plenty of water or else it makes your throat itch when you are eating it; this is how you sweep a corner; this is how you sweep a whole house; this is how you sweep a yard; this is how you smile to someone you don't like too much; this is how you smile to someone you don't like at all; this is how you smile to someone you like completely; this is how you set a table for tea; this is how you set a table for dinner; this is how you set a table for dinner with an important guest; this is how you set a table for lunch; this is how you set a table for breakfast; this is how to behave in the

Jamaica Kincaid was born in St. Johns, Antigua, in 1949, and was educated there at the Princess Margaret School. She writes for *The New Yorker.* Ms. Kincaid informs us that "benna," mentioned early in this piece, refers to "songs of the sort your parents didn't want you to sing, at first calypso and later rock and roll."

presence of men who don't know you very well, and this way they won't recognize immediately the slut I have warned you against becoming; be sure to wash every day, even if it is with your own spit; don't squat down to play marbles—you are not a boy, you know; don't pick people's flowers—you might catch something; don't throw stones at blackbirds, because it might not be a blackbird at all; this is how to make a bread pudding; this is how to make doukona; this is how to make pepper pot; this is how to make a good medicine for a cold; this is how to make a good medicine to throw away a child before it even becomes a child; this is how to catch a fish; this is how to throw back a fish you don't like, and that way something bad won't fall on you; this is how to bully a man; this is how a man bullies you; this is how to love a man, and if this doesn't work there are other ways, and if they don't work don't feel too bad about giving up; this is how to spit up in the air if you feel like it, and this is how to move quick so that it doesn't fall on you; this is how to make ends meet; always squeeze bread to make sure it's fresh; *but what if the baker won't let me feel the bread?*; you mean to say that after all you are really going to be the kind of woman who the baker won't let near the bread?

## Questions

1. We would classify "Girl" as a short story, a work of fiction. Ordinarily, short stories are said to have a *plot,* revealed in a series of *scenes* between *characters;* the scenes in turn reveal to us some particular qualities of the characters, and the circumstances in which they find themselves. The plot contains some *conflict* that by the end of the story comes to a *resolution.* Overall, a short story has some meaning that can be at least roughly stated as its *theme.*
   Examining "Girl" with these terms in mind, would you agree that it is a short story? If so, explain what elements of a short story you find in it, and where you find them. How does "Girl" differ from some more conventional stories you have read? If you find "Girl" effective, explain why you do to someone who does not.
2. Contrast Syfers (pages 40–42) and Kincaid on the freedom and restrictions of the traditional female role.

## Theodore Roethke

# My Papa's Waltz

The whiskey on your breath
Could make a small boy dizzy;
But I hung on like death:
Such waltzing was not easy.

We romped until the pans
Slid from the kitchen shelf;
My mother's countenance
Could not unfrown itself.

The hand that held my wrist
Was battered on one knuckle;
At every step you missed
My right ear scraped a buckle.

You beat time on my head
With a palm caked hard by dirt,
Then waltzed me off to bed
Still clinging to your shirt.

## Questions

1. Who is the speaker?
2. Summarize the scene presented. Which details suggest what has happened before the waltz began? Do any details suggest that there have been similar scenes before?
3. How does the speaker feel about his father?
4. Describe the rhythm of the poem. Is it appropriate to a waltz?

---

Theodore Roethke (1908–1963), author of eight volumes of poetry, was born in Saginaw, Michigan. Roethke's father ran a greenhouse, but the son earned his living by teaching English literature, chiefly at the University of Washington, in Seattle.

## Gregory Corso

# Marriage

*for Mr. and Mrs. Mike Goldberg*

Should I get married? Should I be good?
Astound the girl next door
with my velvet suit and faustus hood?
Don't take her to movies but to cemeteries
tell all about werewolf bathtubs and forked
clarinets
then desire her and kiss her and all the preliminaries
and she going just so far and I understanding why
not getting angry saying You must feel! It's beautiful to
feel!
Instead take her in my arms
lean against an old crooked tombstone
and woo her the entire night the constellations in the
sky—

When she introduces me to her parents
back straightened, hair finally combed, strangled by a tie,
should I sit knees together on their 3rd-degree sofa
and not ask Where's the bathroom?
How else to feel other than I am,
a young man who often thinks Flash Gordon soap—
O how terrible it must be for a young man
seated before a family and the family thinking
We never saw him before! He wants our Mary
Lou!
After tea and homemade cookies they ask What do you
do?

---

Gregory Corso was born in 1930 in New York City, of Italian immigrant parents. When his mother returned to Italy, Corso lived with various foster parents, then returned to his father, ran away, and was found and sent to a boys' home. At the age of seventeen he was sent to prison, where he remained for three years. During these years he began to read and to think and to write. In 1950 he met the poet Allen Ginsberg, "the first gentle person and dear friend to me."

Should I tell them? Would they like me then?
Say All right get married, we're losing a daughter
but we're gaining a son—
And should I then ask Where's the bathroom?

O God, and the wedding! All her family and her friends
and only a handful of mine all scroungy and bearded
just waiting to get at the drinks and food—
And the priest! he looking at me as if I masturbated
asking me Do you take this woman
for your lawful wedded wife?
And I, trembling what to say, say Pie Glue!
I kiss the bride all those corny men slapping me on the back:
She's all yours, boy! Ha-ha-ha!
And in their eyes you could see
some obscene honeymoon going on—
Then all that absurd rice and clanky cans and shoes
Niagara Falls! Hordes of us! Husbands! Wives! Flowers!
All streaming into cozy hotels
All going to do the same thing tonight
The indifferent clerk he knowing what was going to happen
The lobby zombies they knowing what
The whistling elevator man he knowing
The winking bellboy knowing
Everybody knows! I'd be almost inclined not to do anything!
Stay up all night! Stare that hotel clerk in the eye!
Screaming: I deny honeymoon! I deny honeymoon!
running rampant into those almost climactic suites
yelling Radio belly! Cat shovel!
O I'd live in Niagara forever! in a dark cave beneath the Falls
I'd sit there the Mad Honeymooner
devising ways to break marriages, a scourge of bigamy
a saint of divorce—

But I should get married I should be good
How nice it'd be to come home to her

and sit by the fireplace and she in the kitchen
apronned young and lovely wanting my baby
and so happy about me she burns the roast beef
and comes crying to me and I get up from my big papa chair
saying Christmas teeth! Radiant brains! Apple deaf!
God what a husband I'd make! Yes, I should get married!
So much to do! like sneaking into Mr. Jones' house late at night
and cover his golf clubs with 1920 Norwegian books
Like hanging a picture of Rimbaud on the lawnmower
Like pasting Tannu Tuva postage stamps
all over the picket fence
Like when Mrs. Kindhead comes to collect
for the Community Chest
grab her and tell her There are unfavorable omens in the sky!
And when the mayor comes to get my vote tell him
When are you going to stop people killing whales!
And when the milkman comes leave him a note in the bottle
Penguin dust, bring me penguin dust, I want penguin dust—

Yet if I should get married and it's Connecticut and snow
and she gives birth to a child and I am sleepless, worn,
up for nights, head bowed against a quiet window,
the past behind me,
finding myself in the most common of situations
a trembling man
knowledged with responsibility not twig-smear
nor Roman coin soup—
O what would that be like!
Surely I'd give it for a nipple a rubber Tacitus
For a rattle a bag of broken Bach records
Tack Della Francesca all over its crib
Sew the Greek alphabet on its bib
And build for its playpen a roofless Parthenon—

No, I doubt I'd be that kind of father
not rural not snow no quiet window
but hot smelly tight New York City
seven flights up, roaches and rats in the walls
a fat Reichian wife screeching over potatoes Get a job!
And five nose-running brats in love with Batman
And the neighbors all toothless and dry haired
like those hag masses of the 18th century
all wanting to come in and watch TV
The landlord wants his rent
Grocery store Blue Cross Gas & Electric Knights of Columbus
Impossible to lie back and dream Telephone snow,
ghost parking—
No! I should not get married I should never get married!

But—imagine if I were married to a beautiful
sophisticated woman
tall and pale wearing an elegant black dress
and long black gloves
holding a cigarette holder in one hand
and a highball in the other
and we lived high up in a penthouse with a huge window
from which we could see all of New York
and even farther on clearer days
No, can't imagine myself married to that pleasant prison dream—

O but what about love? I forget love
not that I am incapable of love
it's just that I see love as odd as wearing shoes—
I never wanted to marry a girl who was like my mother
And Ingrid Bergman was always impossible
And there's maybe a girl now but she's already married
And I don't like men and—
but there's got to be somebody!
Because what if I'm 60 years old and not married,
all alone in a furnished room with pee stains on my underwear

and everybody else is married! All the universe married
but me!

Ah, yet well I know that were a woman possible
as I am possible
then marriage would be possible—
Like SHE in her lonely alien gaud waiting her Egyptian
lover
so I wait—bereft of 2,000 years and the bath of life.

## Questions

1. The speaker in "Marriage" humorously exaggerates fears most young people have of getting married. Summarize the speaker's fears in a sentence or two.
2. In the first stanza what roles does the suitor imagine himself playing? Are there similarities between taking a girl to the movies and taking her to cemeteries (line 4), or is he spouting nonsense?
3. In the second stanza what lines express the speaker's feelings of worthlessness? What does he imagine the parents' values are? How do their values contribute to his anxiety?
4. Put into your own words what Corso is saying in stanzas 3 and 4 about conventional attitudes toward sex and marriage. Characterize the speaker's response to them in each stanza.
5. Stanzas 5 and 6 present two fantasies of parenthood. Summarize each. How do they contrast?
6. Describe the tone of the poem in the last three stanzas. What changes do you see?
7. Does "Marriage" answer the two questions asked in the first line? How?

# 2
# FOOD, CLOTHING, SHELTER

*Mr. and Mrs. A. B., on Their Farm, near Kersey, Colorado*
**Arthur Rothstein, 1939**

Farm Security Administration Photo, Library of Congress

*American Gothic*
**Grant Wood, 1930**

Friends of American Art Collection, The Art Institute of Chicago

*Louis XIV*
**William Makepeace Thackeray, 1840**

*The King* *Louis* *King Louis*

*AN HISTORICAL STUDY*

*A Graveyard and Steel Mill in Bethlehem, Pennsylvania*
**Walker Evans, 1935**

Photograph. Collection, The Museum of Modern Art, New York. Gift of the Farm Security Administration.

# Short Views

The discovery of a new dish does more for human happiness than the discovery of a new star.

**Anthelme Brillat-Savarin**

The great secret of vegetarianism is never to eat vegetables.

**George Bernard Shaw**

What is patriotism but the love of the good things we ate in our childhood?

**Lin Yutang**

Man ist was man isst (German saying: We are what we eat)

**Anonymous**

Coffee drunk out of wine glasses is really miserable stuff, as is meat cut at the table with a pair of scissors.

**G. C. Lichtenberg**

It is hard to provide and cook so simple and clean a diet as will not offend the imagination; but this, I think, is to be fed when we feed the body; they should both sit down at the same table. Yet perhaps this may be done. The fruits eaten temperately need not make us ashamed of our appetites, nor interrupt the worthiest pursuits. But put an extra condiment into your dish, and it will poison you. It is not worth the while to live by rich cookery. Most men would feel shame if caught preparing with their own hands precisely such a dinner, whether of animal or vegetable food, as is every day prepared for them by others. Yet till this is otherwise we are not civilized, and, if gentlemen and ladies, are not true men and women. This certainly suggests what change is to be made. It may be vain to ask why the imagination will not be reconciled to flesh and fat. I am satisfied that it is not. Is it not a reproach that man is a carnivorous animal? True, he can and does live, in a great measure, by preying on other animals; but this is a miserable way—as any one who will go to snaring rabbits, or slaughtering lambs, may learn—and he will be regarded as a benefactor of his race who shall teach man to confine himself to a more innocent and wholesome diet.

Whatever my own practice may be, I have no doubt that it is a part of the destiny of the human race, in its gradual improvement, to leave off eating animals, as surely as the savage tribes have left off eating each other when they came in contact with the more civilized.

**Henry David Thoreau**

This seems to be an era of gratuitous inventions and negative improvements. Consider the beer can. It was beautiful—as beautiful as the clothespin, as inevitable as the wine bottle, as dignified and reassuring as the fire hydrant. A tranquil cyclinder of delightfully resonant metal, it could be opened in an instant, requiring only the application of a handy gadget freely dispensed by every grocer. Who can forget the small, symmetrical thrill of those two triangular punctures, the dainty *pffff,* the little crest of suds that foamed eagerly in the exultation of release? Now we are given, instead, a top beetling with an ugly, shmoo-shaped "tab," which, after fiercely resisting the tugging, bleeding fingers of the thirsty man, threatens his lips with a dangerous and hideous hole. However, we have discovered a way to thwart Progress, usually so unthwartable. *Turn the beer can upside down and open the bottom.* The bottom is still the way the top used to be. True, this operation gives the beer an unsettling jolt, and the sight of a consistently inverted beer can might make people edgy, not to say queasy. But the latter difficulty could be eliminated if manufacturers would design cans that looked the same whichever end was up, like playing cards. What we need is Progress with an escape hatch.

**John Updike**

A man is in general better pleased when he has a good dinner upon his table than when his wife talks Greek.

**Samuel Johnson**

Better is a dinner of herbs where love is, than a stalled ox and hatred therewith.

**Proverbs 15:17**

I can't help thinking that the decline in table manners has something to do with fast food. There are no rules of etiquette for eating a Big Mac and a side of fries. The whole idea of fast food is to get eating out of the way as quickly as possible so you can get to something else. It's difficult, too, to have respect for a fast food cheeseburger. And if you don't have respect for what you're eating how can you have any respect for yourself or the people you're eating with?

**Diane White**

The fashion wears out more apparel than the man.

**William Shakespeare, *Much Ado About Nothing***

The more I think of it, the more it appears to me that dress is the foundation of society.

**Thomas Carlyle**

What would a man be—what would *any* man be—without his clothes? As soon as one stops and thinks over that proposition, one realizes that without his clothes a man would be nothing at all; that the clothes do not merely make the man, the clothes *are* the man; that without them he is a cipher, a vacancy, a nobody, a nothing.

Titles—another . . . artificiality—are a part of his clothing. They and the dry-goods conceal the wearer's inferiority and make him seem great and a wonder, when at bottom there is nothing remarkable about him. They can move a nation to fall on its knees and sincerely worship an Emperor who, without the clothes and the title, would drop to the rank of the cobbler and be swallowed up and lost sight of in the massed multitude of the inconsequentials. . . .

A policeman in plain clothes is one man; in his uniform he is ten. Clothes and title are the most potent thing, the most formidable influence, in the earth. They move the human race to willing and spontaneous respect for the judge, the general, the admiral, the bishop, the ambassador, the frivolous earl, the idiot duke, the sultan, the king, the emperor. No great title is efficient without clothes to support it.

. . . Is the human race a joke? Was it devised and patched together in a dull time when there was nothing important to do? Has it no respect for itself? . . . I think my respect of it is drooping, sinking—and my respect for myself along with it. . . . There is but one restorative—*clothes!* respect-reviving, spirit-uplifting clothes! heaven's kindliest gift to man, his only protection against finding himself out: they deceive him, they confer dignity upon him; without them he has none. How charitable are clothes, how beneficent, how puissant, how inestimably precious! Mine are able to expand a human cipher into a globe-shadowing portent; they can command the respect of the whole world—including my own, which is fading. I will put them on.

**Mark Twain**

Put on the costume of the country you visit, but keep the clothes you will need to go home in.

**Denis Diderot**

No one finds difficulty in assenting to the commonplace that the greater part of the expenditure incurred by all classes for apparel is incurred for the sake of respectable appearance rather than for the protection of the person. And probably at no other point is the sense of shabbiness so keenly felt as it is if we fall short of the standard set by social usage in this matter of dress. It is true of dress in even a higher degree than of most other items of consumption, that people will undergo a very considerable degree of privation in the comforts or the necessaries of life in order to afford what is considered a decent amount of wasteful consumption; so that it is by no means an uncommon occurrence, in an inclement climate, for people to go ill clad in order to appear well dressed. And the commercial value of the goods used for clothing in any modern community is made up to a much larger extent of the fashionableness, the reputability of the goods than of the mechanical service which they render in clothing the person of the wearer. The need of dress is eminently a "higher" or spiritual need.

**Thorstein Veblen**

Long before I am near enough to talk to you on the street, in a meeting, or at a party, you announce your sex, age and class to me through what you are wearing—and very possibly give me important information (or misinformation) as to your occupation, origin, personality, opinions, tastes, sexual desires and current mood. . . . By the time we meet and converse we have already spoken to each other in an older and more universal tongue.

**Alison Lurie**

Skin, if it is attractive, can be part of the design.
**Rudi Gernreich**

Architecture is to be regarded by us with the most serious thought. We may live without her, and worship without her, but we cannot remember without her. How cold is all history, how lifeless all imagery, compared to that which the living nation writes, and the uncorrupted marble bears!—how many pages of doubtful record might we not often spare, for a few stones left one upon another! The ambition of the old Babel builders was well directed for this world: there are but two strong conquerors of the forgetfulness of men. Poetry and Architecture; and the latter in some sort includes the former, and is mightier in its reality: it is well to have, not only what men have thought and felt, but what their hands have handled, and their strength wrought, and their eyes beheld, all the days of their life.
**John Ruskin**

We shall live to see the day, I trust, when no man shall build his house for posterity. . . . He might just as reasonably order a durable suit of clothes . . . so that his great-grandchildren should cut precisely the same figure in the world. . . . I doubt whether even one public edifice . . . should be built of such permanent materials. . . . Better that they should crumble to ruin, once in twenty years or thereabouts, as a hint to the people to reform the institutions which they symbolize.
**Nathaniel Hawthorne, *The House of the Seven Gables***

If I had to say which was telling the truth about society, a speech by a Minister of Housing or the actual buildings put up in his time, I should believe the buildings.
**Kenneth Clark**

A house is a machine for living.
**Le Corbusier**

I like a man who likes to see a fine barn as well as a good tragedy.
**Ralph Waldo Emerson**

Peter Farb and George Armelagos

# The Patterns of Eating

Among the important societal rules that represent one component of cuisine are table manners. As a socially instilled form of conduct, they reveal the attitudes typical of a society. Changes in table manners through time, as they have been documented for western Europe, likewise reflect fundamental changes in human relationships. Medieval courtiers saw their table manners as distinguishing them from crude peasants; but by modern standards, the manners were not exactly refined. Feudal lords used their unwashed hands to scoop food from a common bowl and they passed around a single goblet from which all drank. A finger or two would be extended while eating, so as to be kept free of grease and thus available for the next course, or for dipping into spices and condiments—possibly accounting for today's "polite" custom of extending the finger while holding a spoon or small fork. Soups and sauces were commonly drunk by lifting the bowl to the mouth; several diners frequently ate from the same bread trencher. Even lords and nobles would toss gnawed bones back into the common dish, wolf down their food, spit onto the table (preferred conduct called for spitting under it), and blew their noses into the tablecloth.

By about the beginning of the sixteenth century, table manners began to move in the direction of today's standards. The importance attached to them is indicated by the phenomenal success of a treatise, *On Civility in Children,* by the philosopher Erasmus, which appeared in 1530; reprinted more than thirty times in the next six years, it also appeared in numerous translations. Erasmus' idea of good table manners was far from modern, but it did represent an advance. He believed, for example, that an upper class diner was distinguished by putting only three fingers of one hand into the bowl, instead of the entire hand in the manner of the lower class. Wait a few moments after being seated before you dip into it, he advises. Do not poke

---

Peter Farb (1929–1980) was a naturalist, linguist, anthropologist, and spokesman for conservation. George Armelagos is a professor of anthropology at the University of Massachusetts, Amherst.

around in your dish, but take the first piece you touch. Do not put chewed food from the mouth back on your plate; instead, throw it under the table or behind your chair.

By the time of Erasmus, the changing table manners reveal a fundamental shift in society. People no longer ate from the same dish or drank from the same goblet, but were divided from one another by a new wall of constraint. Once the spontaneous, direct, and informal manners of the Middle Ages had been repressed, people began to feel shame. Defecation and urination were now regarded as private activities; handkerchiefs came into use for blowing the nose; nightclothes were now worn, and bedrooms were set apart as private areas. Before the sixteenth century, even nobles ate in their vast kitchens; only then did a special room designated for eating come into use away from the bloody sides of meat, the animals about to be slaughtered, and the bustling servants. These new inhibitions became the essence of "civilized" behavior, distinguishing adults from children, the upper classes from the lower, and Europeans from the "savages" then being discovered around the world. Restraint in eating habits became more marked in the centuries that followed. By about 1800, napkins were in common use, and before long they were placed on the thighs rather than wrapped around the neck; coffee and tea were no longer slurped out of the saucer; bread was genteelly broken into small pieces with the fingers rather than cut into large chunks with a knife.

Numerous paintings that depict meals—with subjects such as the Last Supper, the wedding at Cana, or Herod's feast—show what dining tables looked like before the seventeenth century. Forks were not depicted until about 1600 (when Jacopo Bassano painted one in a Last Supper), and very few spoons were shown. At least one knife is always depicted—an especially large one when it is the only one available for all the guests—but small individual knives were often at each place. Tin disks or oval pieces of wood had already replaced the bread trenchers. This change in eating utensils typified the new table manners in Europe. (In many other parts of the world, no utensils at all were used. In the Near East, for example, it was traditional to bring food to the mouth with the fingers of the right hand, the left being unacceptable because it was reserved for wiping the buttocks.) Utensils were employed in part because of a change in the attitude toward meat. During the Middle Ages, whole sides of meat, or even an entire dead animal, had been brought to the table and then carved in view of the diners. Beginning in the seventeenth century, at first in France but later elsewhere, the practice began to go out of fashion. One reason was that the family was ceasing to be a production unit that did its own slaughtering; as that function was transferred to specialists outside the home, the family became essentially a consumption unit. In addition, the size of the family was decreasing, and consequently whole animals, or even large parts of them, were uneconomical. The cuisines of Europe reflected these social and economic changes. The animal origin of meat dishes was concealed by the arts of preparation. Meat itself became distasteful to look upon, and carving was moved out of sight to the kitchen. Comparable changes had already taken place in Chinese cuisine, with meat being cut up beforehand, unobserved by the diners. England was an exception to the change in Europe, and in its former colonies—the United States, Canada, Australia, and South Africa—the custom has persisted of bringing a joint of meat to the table to be carved.

Once carving was no longer considered a necessary skill among the well-bred, changes inevitably took place in the use of the knife, unquestionably the earliest utensil used for manipulating food. (In fact, the earliest English cookbooks were not so much guides to recipes as guides to carving meat.) The attitude of diners toward the knife, going back to the Middle Ages and the Renaissance, had always been ambivalent. The knife served as a utensil, but it offered a potential threat because it was also a weapon. Thus taboos were increasingly placed upon its use: It was to be held by the point with the blunt handle presented; it was not to be placed anywhere near the face; and most important, the uses to which it was put were sharply restricted. It was not to be used for cutting soft foods such as boiled eggs or fish, or round ones such as potatoes, or to be lifted from the table for courses that did not need it. In short, good table manners in Europe gradually removed the threatening aspect of the knife from social occasions. A similar change had taken place much earlier in China when the warrior was supplanted by the scholar as a cultural model. The knife was banished completely from the table in favor of chopsticks, which is why the Chinese came to regard Europeans as barbarians at their table who "eat with swords."

The fork in particular enabled Europeans to separate themselves from the eating process, even avoiding manual contact with their food. When the fork first appeared in Europe, toward the end of the Middle Ages, it was used solely as an instrument for lifting chunks from the common bowl. Beginning in the sixteenth century, the fork was increasingly used by members of the upper classes—first in Italy, then in France, and finally in Germany and England. By then, social relations in western Europe had so changed that a utensil was needed to spare diners from the "uncivilized" and distasteful necessity of picking up food and putting it into the mouth with the fingers. The addition of the fork to the table was once said to be for reasons of hygiene, but this cannot be true. By the sixteen century people were no longer eating from a common bowl but from their own plates, and since they also washed their hands before meals, their fingers were now every bit as hygienic as a fork would have been. Nor can the reason for the adoption of the fork be connected with the wish not to soil the long ruff that was worn on the sleeve at the time, since the fork was also adopted in various countries where ruffs were not then in fashion.

Along with the appearance of the fork, all table utensils began to change and proliferate from the sixteenth century onward. Soup was no longer eaten directly from the dish, but each diner used an individual spoon for that purpose. When a diner wanted a second helping from the serving dish, a ladle or a fresh spoon was used. More and more special utensils were developed for each kind of food: soup spoons, oyster forks, salad forks, two-tined fondue forks, blunt butter knives, special utensils for various desserts and kinds of fruit, each one differently shaped, of a different size, with differently numbered prongs and with blunt or serrated edges. The present European pattern eventually emerged, in which each person is provided with a table setting of as many as a dozen utensils at a full-course meal. With that, the separation of the human body from the taking of food became virtually complete. Good table manners dictated that even the cobs of maize were to be held by prongs inserted in each end, and the bones of lamb chops covered by ruffled paper pantalettes. Only under special conditions—as when Western people consciously imitate an earlier stage in culture at a picnic, fish fry, cookout, or campfire—do they still tear food apart with their fingers and their teeth, in a nostalgic reenactment of eating behaviors long vanished.

Today's neighborhood barbecue recreates a world of sharing and hospitality that becomes rarer each year. We regard as a curiosity the behavior of hunters in exotic regions. But every year millions of North Americans take to the woods and lakes to kill a wide variety of animals—with a difference, of course: What hunters do for survival we do for sport (and also for proof of masculinity, for male bonding, and for various psychological rewards). Like hunters, too, we stuff ourselves almost whenever food is available. Nibbling on a roasted ear of maize gives us, in addition to nutrients, the satisfaction of participating in culturally simpler ways. A festive meal, however, is still thought of in Victorian terms, with the dominant male officiating over the roast, the dominant female apportioning vegetables, the extended family gathered around the table, with everything in its proper place—a revered picture, as indeed it was so painted by Norman Rockwell, yet one that becomes less accurate with each year that passes.

## Questions

1. Reverse the first sentence (begin with "Table manners" and end with "cuisine"). Which order is more usual? Why did the authors choose the order they did?
2. If your library has a copy of *On Civility in Children,* cull three other examples of Erasmus's recommendations.
3. Find the first edition (or at least an early edition) of Emily Post. What rules of etiquette strike you as being quaint?
4. How do Farb and Armelagos account for feelings of shame associated with urination and defecation? Does their reasoning strike you as plausible?
5. Study a reproduction of a painting before the seventeenth century that depicts a meal (for instance, da Vinci's *The Last Supper*). Then describe and analyze the food, the table utensils, and the postures and manners of the diners.
6. Describe and analyze a contemporary meal: a church or fraternal picnic, a family holiday meal, a dormitory breakfast. What social attitudes or values does it embody and reveal?
7. "Parents are often irritated by their childrens' table manners; equally often children are revulsed by the eating habits of their parents or other adults." Write a brief essay (approximately 500 words) using this sentence as your thesis.

## Ruth Gay

# Fear of Food

Supermarket shelves, the great barometer of what America eats, all seem to be colored brown now. Instant cereals, white flours, refined sugars appear solemnly packaged in their tan sacks to persuade us that there has been hardly any intervention between the manure that nourished them and the recycled paper that wraps them. What is this flight into the natural, the coarse, all about? Dr. Reuben, who told us all we ever wanted to know about sex, now tells us what we need to know about our health—or, more properly, about our digestion. And here, too, we learn that we have been too refined, our food too delicate, our palates too exquisite. With him, we are back to seeing man as a machine, and the machine, it seems, requires a certain amount of grit to keep functioning. This theory, based on a study by a pair of English investigators, is obviously an idea whose time has come. It was first presented in the popular press in the winter of 1974 in England. By the spring of 1975 it was getting a lot of attention in the German newspapers and feature stories in the women's magazines. By last summer, it was in full bloom in the United States.

These days, then, when Americans talk about food, they are not talking about something good to eat. They are talking about their health, or the stress of modern life, or about the world's surviving. A great fear has overwhelmed us in the last decade, as we have begun to contemplate not only the atom, but also ineradicable pollution, indestructible poison gases, harmful chemicals irretrievably soaked into the food chain. Less than two decades ago, when we feared the war and nuclear destruction epitomized in *Dr. Strangelove,* people sat in living rooms in the capitals of the world drawing concentric circles around their homes, calculating the distance of a weekend retreat from flash damage. The same anxiety at the irreversible process of pollution has now come to center on the domestic explosive that we ingest: our daily bread.

---

Ruth Gay has published a book, *Jews in America,* as well as many essays.

---

Although there does seem to be a reasonable connection between our perception of the poisoned food chain and our worry about what we eat, our newest crisis actually revives a very old pattern in Western life, a pattern in which food and medicine, food and magic have been inextricably mixed. It is an ancient tradition that potions for magic and potions for healing come out of the same caldron. Who does not have in his family some form of a story much cherished in mine? Our version took place at the turn of the century in the Ukraine when my great-aunt, then a child, lay ill of smallpox. Her case was so severe that she was expected to die and had been removed to a little hut away from the main house. At this point an old peasant woman came by and peeped in the window. Seeing the plight of the child, she hurried away and returned with a bowl of sour milk, which she fed her spoonful by spoonful. From that moment on, the child began to mend, and, as they say in old German fairy tales, if she hasn't died, she is still alive to this day.

There is much that is suggestive in this story. The old peasant woman, for example: is she not the prototype of the witch, the dangerous guardian of dangerous secrets, controlling health and sickness at her whim? And the sour milk is itself a dish most susceptible to magic, easily curdled by malign influences or evil presences. Yet sour milk was also a staple in the Ukraine, being one of the commonest ways of preserving milk—halfway between a drink and cheese—in a time before refrigeration. Whether the story is asserting the magical power of sour milk as a potion brewed by the knowing old woman or pointing out its inherent goodness as a primal food remains ambiguous, and properly so. The best stories, after all, always leave an echo of uncertainty in the air.

It is hard to remember that the science of nutrition is barely half a century old, so that many of our attitudes were formed, and are still propagated, by people who grew up with the helpless analogies or pragmatic conclusions available to medicine around the turn of the century. The English had learned something about scurvy and citrus fruit, about "fever" and quinine. Digitalis seemed to help certain heart conditions. But why or how these simple medicines worked no one understood.

The combination of our helplessness and our need for certainty, however, led us for decades to rely on principles whose origin we would now blush to acknowledge. I recently heard someone say that she had discovered why she had a certain kind of rash. A friend had pointed out to her the resemblance between her spots and tomato seeds. Her remedy, therefore, was to avoid eating tomatoes. Did she know that she was reasoning by the old medieval doctrine of Signatures?

According to this fascinating science, as expounded by Paracelsus in the sixteenth century, fruits and vegetables carry certain signs that reveal their properties for good or evil. "Behold the *Satyrion* root," he wrote; "is it not formed like the male privy parts? No one can deny this. Accordingly magic discovered it and revealed that it can restore a man's virility and passion. And then we have the thistle; do not its leaves prickle like needles? Thanks to this sign, the art of magic discovered that there is no better herb against internal prickling." Jerusalem artichokes that grew as stumpy, deformed-looking roots were thought, as late as the nineteenth century, to induce leprosy, because, as Paracelsus would say, were they not like the misshapen fingers of the late stages of leprosy? Similarly, the beloved port wine tonic so gravely prescribed by physicians to improve the blood of pale Victorian young ladies had no more relation to blood than artichokes had to leprosy. But the principle of analogy is persuasive and not easily shakable.

In the fields of food and drink we are still most vulnerable to the claims of superstition. The pseudo-scientific reasoning that introduces so many food fads comes dressed in the impressive language of medicine, and instantly quenches every spark of skepticism still feebly alive within us by satisfying our conscious need for "scientific" proof while feeding our simple credulity. Although we learned long ago to abandon magical thinking in connection with weather, crops, the care of animals, and other natural phenomena, it still has us in its grip when we think of diet. Our latest thinking about food, based on fear, is proportionately retrograde—willing to accept, indeed seeking out, the consolations of magic, the mute practice of peasants, and the quaint devices of folklore. Books on the saving properties of "honegar" (a mixture of honey and vinegar), of blackstrap molasses, of sprouting mung beans, succeed one another in unending succession. The *Foxfire* book of homely know-how has gone into a third volume in response to popular interest, just as the earlier *Whole Earth Catalogue* was the guide for all seekers of the true way. The dividing line between recipes for natural foods and other natural remedies, for illness, for making a garden, for building a house, has grown steadily fainter. The Department of Agriculture pamphlets that were once sought after for the best scientific solutions to problems in domestic economy are being supplanted in popularity by books reviving traditional methods of cultivation and cures, the more ancient and more bizarre the better. "Chicken shit," I heard one cosmopolite in New Hampshire say, "isn't that what you're supposed to put on cuts?"

With our sophisticated imaginations we endow all these stratagems with the patina of ancient wisdom, of lost truths, and we flee from the modern world, condemning packaged white bread with a passion we reserve for few other evils. We hardly notice, in this flight from reason, the disappearance of smallpox, or that we no longer expect a "cholera season," or that the eight million people who live in the squalor called New York are drinking safe water.

The unexamined residue of literal magic—the heritage of the Signature, or vaguer memories of aphrodisiacs—is augmented by the history of manners and social usage that has created a mystical hierarchy of foods, each with its own special and instantly identifiable attributes. It was in recognition of the power of this symbolism that the West German government recently barred a cigarette company from continuing a false advertisement. What was striking about it was that, although wordless, the meaning of the ad was unmistakable: in the foreground lay a package of cigarettes, in the background a loaf of crusty bread, an earthenware milk jug, and a picturesque cluster of wheat stalks, all bathed in a golden light. In any part of the Western world, the message was instantly decipherable: whatever is natural, elemental, is therefore wholesome. What could be purer and more innocent in our imaginations than bread and milk? With bread such a universal symbol, it is no wonder that so much feeling is again centering on it.

Much of the history of Europe could be written using the fine wheaten loaf as a barometer. For a long time, sumptuary laws forbade it to all but members of noble households. Like the Cadillac to the slum dweller today, it came to stand for all kinds of things that had nothing to do with its function. The peasant's black bread may have been ultimately more nutritious, but to him it was the sign of poverty and servitude, as white bread was the sign of wealth and freedom. The oldest prejudice of mankind has probably been in favor of wheat to the denigration of all other grains. While bread was not the first food of man, it has been a staple since Neolithic times, and has been the main, and sometimes the only, food for all but the tiny percentage of the privileged. What is visible from the earliest times is that all grains are not equal, and even in Egyptian wall paintings the priests are offering the gods beautiful cone-shaped loaves made of wheat flour, while the fellahin are eating millet.

We can endorse the prejudices of our ancestors, of course, by agreeing that fine wheaten bread is obviously "better" than bread made of rye or oats or millet or spelt or chestnuts. But the objective merits of wheat bread—its lightness, delicate flavor, rich texture—are all less significant to the imagination than its having been for so long an unattainable luxury. In England even the symbolic status of the brown-bread bakers was inferior to that of white-bread bakers. The arms granted to them in 1722, a quarter of a century after the white-bread bakers, are similar in most details, but are instantly perceptible as lesser by the lack of supporting festoons and a motto. During the nineteenth century, the brown-bread bakers began to find allies in various groups that had discovered the evils of white bread. "A Physician" in 1846 pointed out that the nourishing "ingredients are removed by the miller in his efforts to please the public so that fine flour, instead of being better than meal is the least nourishing. . . . It seems desirable that the poor be brought to inquire whether they do not purchase at too dear a rate the privilege of indulging in the use of it." All this was written under the old, relatively primitive conditions when grain was still stone-ground.

When the new roller mills were introduced in the 1870s, making the production of white flour cheaper and less nutritious than ever, one of the big brown-bread baking companies in London attempted to defend its product by inviting a "distinguished gathering of physicians, medical officers and representatives of the press" to view a newly installed set of steam ovens. At the luncheon that followed, the vice-chairman of the firm laid at the door of white bread "the sickly, stunted and ricketty children which infest the courts and alleys of all large towns where the poor congregate." Indeed, the chemicals used to produce the much-longed-for "nice white loaf," he concluded, produced in actuality nothing more than "whited sepulchers."

But neither the revelations of the brown-bread bakers nor the reasoning of the Bread Reform League had any effect. "Why," one of its members asked in 1888, "in our craze for white bread, should we raise so many feeble, nervous, undersized children upon an impoverished flour, because it looks white and light . . . ? White bread alone will not sustain life. Dogs fed on white bread died at the end of forty days, whilst those fed on wheat bread alone throve and flourished." Quite deaf to these pleas, the English working-class poor knew what they wanted and, as soon as they could, bought their white, wheaten loaf—although by the time they could afford it, they were getting the proverbial stone for bread. The fine white loaf, and the tea with canned, skimmed milk that became the basis of the working-class English diet, was nutritionally so valueless that, as George Orwell once said, it did no more than cheat hunger three times a day. Ironically enough, by the nineteenth century, when wheat was produced in sufficient quantity to supply the demand of all those who wanted it, bread consumption had begun to fall everywhere.

The powerful associations with rank that have survived underground will not be denied, and continue to endow ordinary items of food and drink with attributes more significant than their chemical composition. Montaigne's explanation is as succinct as it is enduring. "For to decree that none but princes shall eat turbot," he wrote, "and be allowed to wear velvet or gold lace, and forbid these things to the people, what is it but to bring them into a greater esteem, and increase the desire of everyone to enjoy them?" Under such circumstances, what is one century of availability against the yearnings of millenia? Even today, when white bread is commonplace, only bread or rolls of white wheat flour will be served at a festive meal. Solzhenitsyn—who writes, after all, about men in extreme circumstances—describes vividly in the *Gulag Archipelago* how the idea of white bread could be used to torment a prisoner at crucial moments: "the starvation technique," he wrote, "like interrogation at night was an integral element in the entire system of coercion. Chulpenyev was kept for a month on three and a half ounces of bread, after which—when he had just been brought from the pit—the interrogator Sokol placed in front of him a pot of thick borscht, and half a loaf of white bread sliced diagonally. [What does it matter one might ask, how it was sliced? But Chulpenyev even today would insist that it was really sliced very attractively.]"

In our search now for whole wheat bread and coarse pumpernickel, we have turned one of the oldest ideals of Europe upside down. One historian of diet Günther Wiegelmann, has pointed out that when new technolgy and changes in fashion make traditional ingredients scarce, they are suddenly revived as delicacies by the middle classes. Honey, for example, for centuries man's only sweetener, came back as a delicacy in the nineteenth century after sugar had long since driven it out. Buckwheat groats, bean soups, and now dark bread are restored out of the same impulses that brought back Morris dancing in England and societies for the preservation of local costume in Germany. Perhaps we should read some of the labels on the brown paper sacks. One of the biggest distributors of whole wheat flour notes (in small print, to be sure) that it has added malted barley. Someone there knows that customers will accept the newly desired brown loaf more readily if it is made tastier by the addition of malt. Despite our new aims, we are still buying the package rather than the contents, as we have for so long been in the habit of doing.

In America, unlike Europe, bread has been less than central to our diet, which makes the passionate search for the home-baked loaf all the more remarkable. It is one phenomenon that cannot be laid at the door of the wave of nostalgia that seems to be overtaking every other area of life. Requiring both time and real effort, baking appears as an active attempt to build up something original. Bread bakers are not looking for shortcuts and scorn the easy-no-knead breads. The whole point of the exercise is to go back as far in the breadmaking chain as possible. Some serious bakers even buy their wheat in the grain and grind it at home. Sourdough starters and homemade yeasts are commonplace. In an epoch that has been devoted to the development of convenience foods, this change must be seen as an attempt to regain control of what is eaten by manufacturing it at home.

In other areas as well, the primitive is reasserting itself. No one will be surprised to learn that seventy million Americans are overweight, and most of them at one time or another are on a diet. Some are impelled by vanity, but many are dieting for their lives, fearing fats, salt, sugar, carbohydrates, all those villains that bring on heart attacks and untimely death. Here mythology again offers sweet reassurances: in the Bulgarian peasants who live forever on yogurt, in the remote Mongol tribe that reaches a shapely and vigorous old age on a diet of cornmeal and cheese. In short, the ancient urban yearning for a largely imaginary pastoral, an idea already old when put into verse by Vergil, has reasserted itself in the headlong flights from refinement to soups, stews, and breads—the coarser, the better.

There was a time when it was rather a compliment to one's guests to serve them Beef Wellington. By now it is regarded as little better than putting a gun to their heads. Cheese had better be dry, chalky, and preferably of goats' milk. A creamy brie only shows a total lack of sensitivity. At dessert, the dense chocolate nut torte is no more than a memory, replaced everywhere by chaste and artistic arrangements of small fruits. One item, however, survives. As the German cigarette advertiser knew so well, at the heart of it all, white or brown, must be a crusty loaf of bread.

I worry now about a certain seepage. A recent visit to a drugstore revealed several companies pushing oatmeal soap. And Clairol, which until now brought us sparkling blondes enjoying champagne parties, has taken up a new ideal, printed in sepia ink. We are now confronted with a milkmaid churning butter in a well-mannered pastoral landscape. According to the Victorian Gothic script, she is there to call attention to a "BUTTERMILK shampoo with ten 100 percent chemically organic ingredients." I copied it all down in my notebook, and decided to go home and study it as yet another tributary to the rising brown tide.

Our new all-inclusive fear has led to a new all-purpose remedy. Whatever is natural, or colored brown, is good for you. At least, it is presumed harmless. Just as the fear has spilled over from food to cosmetics to the universe, the remedies, too, follow hard behind, echoing antiphonally the new danger, with new counsel for evasive action.

With our lives at stake, we find ourselves caught between two conflicting ideas. On the one hand, we still cherish the debonair worldling ordering his oysters (without regard to sewage), his filet mignon (without regard to the world grain supply), his grapes (without regard to César Chavez). His alter ego is the social hero: self-abnegating, placing public policy above private pleasure, and rigorously rational. Without sorrow or regret, he eliminates—as decreed by the FDA, the surgeon general, or the Third World—tobacco, cyclamates, red dye no. 2, butter, cream, and marbled beef.

Yet running through all this reasoned, politic behavior is a strange element of the irrational, in which we seek to ward off evil by talismans. As fresh dangers threaten us with every new edition of the newspaper, we renounce our butter, cream, and marbled beef as sacrifices to the gods, hoping to propitiate them with our good intentions. In our anxiety we have converted our lives into a daily morality play, assigning every morsel, every act its part in the grand drama. As time goes on, our worldly self, he who stood for a way of life based on a knowledge of pleasure, a love of ornamentation, an acceptance of self-indulgence, appears less and less frequently. When he does, he is an embarrassment, about as welcome as the stone guest at Don Giovanni's last supper party. None of us, it would seem, wants to be caught at the table.

# Questions

1. Characterize the tone of the first paragraph. Is the author sufficiently serious about her topic? Too serious? Or what?
2. In a sentence or two summarize Gay's thesis. In which paragraph do you find the thesis most clearly stated?
3. Ruth Gay tells a family story of a sick great-aunt in the Ukraine, whom a peasant woman supposedly saved by administering a bowl of sour milk. If your family has a cherished story about the virtue of some food, recount it in 250–500 words. Do not explicitly say whether or not you believe it, but indirectly let the reader know where you stand. (Note that Gay implies her position when she says, "The best stories . . . always leave an echo of uncertainty in the air.")
4. On page 98 Gay mentions "the pseudo-scientific reasoning that introduces so many food fads." Analyze a magazine or television advertisement for a food, indicating whether you find the reasoning scientific or pseudo-scientific.
5. Gay suggests that certain foods are associated with certain ranks. In 500 words write an essay on the association some food has with rank. Possible foods: hot dogs, pizza, quiche, gelatin salad, filet mignon, calves' brains, collard greens, roast chicken, pheasant, venison.
6. Gay suggests that we buy the package, rather than the contents. Analyze the packaging of a food—for instance, a box of Wheaties or a bag of ginger snaps.
7. In an essay of 500 words set forth your own preferences for certain kinds of bread and examine the reasons by which you support these preferences.

## Michael J. Arlen

# Ode to Thanksgiving

It is time, at last, to speak the truth about Thanksgiving, and the truth is this. Thanksgiving is really not such a terrific holiday. Consider the traditional symbols of the event: Dried cornhusks hanging on the door! Terrible wine! Cranberry jelly in little bowls of extremely doubtful provenance which everyone is required to handle with the greatest of care! Consider the participants, the merrymakers: men and women (also children) who have survived passably well throughout the years, mainly as a result of living at considerable distances from their dear parents and beloved siblings, who on this feast of feasts must apparently forgather (as if beckoned by an aberrant Fairy Godmother), usually by circuitous routes, through heavy traffic, at a common meeting place, where the very moods, distempers, and obtrusive personal habits that have kept them all happily apart since adulthood are then and there encouraged to slowly ferment beneath the cornhusks, and gradually rise with the aid of the terrible wine, and finally burst forth out of control under the stimulus of the cranberry jelly! No, it is a mockery of a holiday. For instance: *Thank you, O Lord, for what we are about to receive.* This is surely not a gala concept. There are no presents, unless one counts Aunt Bertha's sweet rolls a present, which no one does. There is precious little in the way of costumery: miniature plastic turkeys and those witless Pilgrim hats. There is no sex. Indeed, Thanksgiving is the one day of the year (a fact known to everybody) when all thoughts of sex completely vanish, evaporating from apartments, houses, condominiums, and mobile homes like steam from a bathroom mirror.

Consider also the nowhereness of the time of year: the last week or so in November. It is obviously not yet winter: winter, with its death-dealing blizzards and its girls in tiny skirts pirouetting on the ice. On the other hand, it is certainly not much use to anyone as fall;

---

Michael Arlen was born in London in 1930. He came to the United States in 1940, and in time became a reporter and then an essayist. He regularly writes on television for *The New Yorker.*

no golden leaves or Oktoberfests, and so forth. Instead, it is a no-man's-land between the seasons. In the cold and sobersides northern half of the country, it is a vaguely unsettling interregnum of long, mournful walks beneath leafless trees: the long, mournful walks following the midday repast with the dread inevitability of pie following turkey, and the leafless trees looming or standing about like eyesores, and the ground either as hard as iron or slightly mushy, and the light snow always beginning to fall when one is halfway to the old green gate—flecks of cold, watery stuff plopping between neck and collar, for the reason that, it being not yet winter, one has forgotten or not chosen to bring along a muffler. It is a corollary to the long, mournful Thanksgiving walk that the absence of this muffler is quickly noticed and that four weeks or so later, at Christmastime, instead of the Sony Betamax one had secretly hoped the children might have chipped in to purchase, one receives another muffler: by then the thirty-third. Thirty-three mufflers! Some walk! Of course, things are more fun in the warm and loony southern part of the country. No snow there of any kind. No need of mufflers. Also, no long, mournful walks, because in the warm and loony southern part of the country everybody drives. So everybody drives over to Uncle Jasper's house to watch the Cougars play the Gators, a not entirely unimportant conflict which will determine whether the Gators get a Bowl bid or must take another post-season exhibition tour of North Korea. But no sooner do the Cougars kick off (an astonishing end-over-end squiggly thing that floats lazily above the arena before plummeting down toward K. C. McCoy and catching him on the helmet) than Auntie Em starts hustling turkey. Soon Cousin May is slamming around the bowls and platters, and Cousin Bernice is oohing and ahing about "all the fixin's," and Uncle Bob is making low, insincere sounds of appreciation: "Yummy, yummy, Auntie Em, I'll have me some more of these delicious yams!" Delicious yams? Uncle Bob's eyes roll wildly in his head. Billy Joe Quaglino throws his long bomb in the middle of Grandpa Morris saying grace, Grandpa Morris speaking so low nobody can hear him, which is just as well, since he is reciting what he can remember of his last union contract. And then, just as J. B. (Speedy) Snood begins his ninety-two-yard punt return, Antie Em starts dealing everyone second helpings of her famous stuffing, as if she were pushing a controlled substance, which it well might be, since there are no easily recognizable ingredients visible to the naked eye.

Consider for a moment the Thanksgiving meal itself. It has become a sort of refuge for endangered species of starch: cauliflower, turnips, pumpkin, mince (whatever "mince" is), those blessed yams. Bowls of luridly colored yams, with no taste at all, lying torpid under a lava flow of marshmallow! And then the sacred turkey. One might as well try to construct a holiday repast around a fish—say, a nice piece of boiled haddock. After all, turkey tastes very similar to haddock: same consistency, same quite remarkable absence of flavor. But then, if the Thanksgiving *pièce de résistance* were a nice piece of boiled haddock instead of turkey, there wouldn't be all that fun for Dad when Mom hands him the sterling-silver, bone-handled carving set (a wedding present from her parents and not sharpened since) and then everyone sits around pretending not to watch while he saws and tears away at the bird as if he were trying to burrow his way into or out of some grotesque, fowllike prison.

What of the good side to Thanksgiving, you ask. There is always a good side to everything. Not to Thanksgiving. There is only a bad side and then a worse side. For instance, Grandmother's best linen tablecloth is a bad side: the fact that it is produced each year, in the manner of a red flag being produced before a bull, and then is always spilled upon by whichever child is doing poorest at school that term and so is in need of greatest reassurance. Thus: "Oh, my God, *Veronica,* you just spilled grape juice [or plum wine or tar] on Grandmother's best linen tablecloth!" But now comes worse. For at this point Cousin Bill, the one who lost all Cousin Edwina's money on the car dealership three years ago and has apparently been drinking steadily since Halloween, bizarrely chooses to say: "Seems to me those old glasses are always falling over." To which Auntie Meg is heard to add: "Somehow I don't remember receivin' any of those old glasses." To which Uncle Fred replies: "That's because you and George decided to go on vacation to Hawaii the summer Grandpa Sam was dying." Now Grandmother is sobbing, though not so uncontrollably that she can refrain from murmuring: "I think that volcano painting I threw away by mistake got sent me from Hawaii, heaven knows why." But the gods are merciful, even the Pilgrim-hatted god of cornhusks and soggy stuffing, and there is an end to everything, even to Thanksgiving. Indeed, there is a grandeur to the feelings of finality and doom which usually settle on a house after the Thanksgiving celebration is over, for with the completion of Thanksgiving Day the year itself has been properly terminated: shot through the cranium with a high-velocity candied yam. At this calendrical nadir, all energy on the planet has gone, all fun has fled, all the terrible wine has been drunk.

But then, overnight, life once again begins to stir, emerging, even by the next morning, in the form of Japanese window displays and Taiwanese Christmas lighting, from the primeval ooze of the nation's department stores. Thus, a new year dawns, bringing with it immediate and cheering possibilities of extended consumer debt, office-party flirtations, good—or, at least mediocre—wine and visions of Supersaver excursion fares to Montego Bay. It is worth noting, perhaps, that this true new year always starts with the same mute, powerful mythic ceremony: the surreptitious tossing out, in the early morning, of all those horrid aluminim-foil packages of yams and cauliflower and stuffing and red, gummy cranberry substance which have been squeezed into the refrigerator as if a reenactment of the siege of Paris were shortly expected. Soon afterward, the phoenix of Christmas can be observed as it slowly rises, beating its drumsticks, once again goggle-eyed with hope and unrealistic expectations.

## Questions

1. Judging from the first paragraph alone, do you think Arlen is entirely serious? Support your view with evidence.
2. Let's assume that at least some of Arlen's sentences strike you as interesting. Analyze a few sentences, accounting for their effect.

W. S. Merwin

# Make This Simple Test

Blindfold yourself with some suitable object. If time permits remain still for a moment. You may feel one or more of your senses begin to swim back toward you in the darkness, singly and without their names. Meanwhile have someone else arrange the products to be used in a row in front of you. It is preferable to have them in identical containers, though that is not necessary. Where possible, perform the test by having the other person feed you a portion—a spoonful—of each of the products in turn, without comment.

Guess what each one is, and have the other person write down what you say.

Then remove the blindfold. While arranging the products the other person should have detached part of the label or container from each and placed it in front of the product it belongs to, like a title. This bit of legend must not contain the product's trade name nor its generic name, nor any suggestion of the product's taste or desirability. Or price. It should be limited to that part of the label or container which enumerates the actual components of the product in question.

Thus, for instance:

"Contains dextrinized flours, cocoa processed with alkali, nonfat dry milk solids, yeast nutrients, vegetable proteins, agar, hydrogenated vegetable oil, dried egg yolk, GUAR, sodium cyclamate, soya lecithin, imitation lemon oil, acetyl tartaric esters of mono- and diglycerides as emulsifiers, polysorbate 60, 1/10 of 1% of sodium benzoate to retard spoilage."

Or:

"Contains anhydrated potatoes, powdered whey, vegetable gum, emulsifier (glycerol monostearate), invert syrup, shortening with freshness preserver, lactose, sorbic acid to retard mold growth,

W. S. Merwin, born in New York City in 1927, spent his early years in New Jersey and Pennsylvania. At Princeton University he became interested in poetry, and he is now best known as a poet and translator of Latin, Spanish, and French poetry. He has also written some highly imaginative prose.

caramel color, natural and artificial flavors, sodium acid pyrophosphate, sodium bisulfite."

Or:

"Contains beef extract, wheat and soya derivatives, food starch-modified, dry sweet whey, calcium carageenan, vegetable oil, sodium phosphates to preserve freshness, BHA, BHT, prophylene glycol, pectin, niacinamide, artificial flavor, U.S. certified color."

There should be not less than three separate products.

Taste again, without the blindfold. Guess again and have the other person record the answers. Replace the blindfold. Have the other person change the order of the products and again feed you a spoonful of each.

Guess again what you are eating or drinking in each case (if you can make the distinction.) But this time do not stop there. Guess why you are eating or drinking it. Guess what it may do for you. Guess what it was meant to do for you. By whom. When. Where. Why. Guess where in the course of evolution you took the first step toward it. Guess which of your organs recognize it. Guess whether it is welcomed to their temples. Guess how it figures in their prayers. Guess how completely you become what you eat. Guess how soon. Guess at the taste of locusts and wild honey. Guess at the taste of water. Guess what the rivers see as they die. Guess why the babies are burning. Guess why there is silence in heaven. Guess why you were ever born.

## Questions

1. What does Merwin's title echo? How does this echo prepare you for his essay?
2. Suppose Merwin began: "Blindfold yourself with a handkerchief, and then pause for a minute or two." Is there any difference between his first two sentences and this revision? Explain.
3. Do you intend to make this simple test? Why, or why not?

Paul Goldberger

# Quick! Before It Crumbles!

## An Architecture Critic Looks at Cookie Architecture

*Sugar Wafer (Nabisco)*

There is no attempt to imitate the ancient forms of traditional, individually baked cookies here—this is a modern cookie through and through. Its simple rectangular form, clean and pure, just reeks of mass production and modern technological methods. The two wafers, held together by the sugar-cream filling, appear to float, and the Nabisco trademark, stamped repeatedly across the top, confirms that this is a machine-age object. Clearly the Sugar Wafer is the Mies van der Rohe of cookies.

*Fig Newton (Nabisco)*

This, too, is a sandwich but different in every way from the Sugar Wafer. Here the imagery is more traditional, more sensual even; a rounded form of cookie dough arcs over the fig concoction inside, and

---

Paul Goldberger is the architecture critic for *The New York Times;* He has also contributed articles to various magazines, and is the author of *The City Observed,* a book about the architecture of Manhattan.

---

the whole is soft and pliable. Like all good pieces of design, it has an appropriate form for its use, since the insides of Fig Newtons can ooze and would not be held in place by a more rigid form. The thing could have had a somewhat different shape, but the rounded top is a comfortable, familiar image, and it's easy to hold. Not a revolutionary object but an intelligent one.

*Milano (Pepperidge Farms)*

This long, chocolate-filled cookie summons up contradictory associations. Its rounded ends suggest both the traditional image of stodgy ladyfingers and the curves of Art Deco, while the subtle yet forceful "V" embossed onto the surface creates an abstract image of force and movement. The "V" is the kind of ornament that wishes to appear modern without really being modern, which would have meant banning ornament altogether. That romantic symbolism of the modern was an Art Deco characteristic, of course; come to think of it the Milano is rather Art Deco in spirit.

*Mallomar (Nabisco)*

This marshmallow, chocolate and cracker combination is the ultimate sensual cookie—indeed, its resemblance to the female breast has been cited so often as to sound rather trite. But the cookie's imagery need not be read so literally—the voluptuousness of the form, which with its nipped waist rather resembles the New Orleans Superdome, is enough. Like all good pieces of design, the form of the cookie is primarily derived from functional needs, but with just enough distinction to make it instantly identifiable. The result is a cultural icon —the cookie equivalent, surely, of the Coke bottle.

*Lorna Doone (Nabisco)*

Like the Las Vegas casino that is overwhelmed by its sign, image is all in the Lorna Doone. It is a plain, simple cookie (of shortbread, in fact), but a cookie like all other cookies—except for its sign. The Lorna Doone logo, a four-pointed star with the cookie's name and a pair of fleur-de-lis-like decorations, covers the entire surface of the cookie in low relief. Cleverly, the designers of this cookie have placed the logo so that the points of the star align with the corners of the square, forcing one to pivot the cookie forty-five degrees, so that its shape appears instead to be a diamond. It is a superb example of the ordinary made extraordinary.

*Oatmeal Peanut Sandwich (Sunshine)*

If the Sugar Wafer is the Mies van der Rohe of cookies, this is the Robert Venturi—not pretentiously modern but, rather, eager to prove its ordinariness, its lack of real design, and in so zealous a way that it ends up looking far dowdier than a *really* ordinary cookie like your basic gingersnap. The Oatmeal Peanut Sandwich is frumpy, like a plump matron in a flower-print dress, or an old piece of linoleum. But it is frumpy in an intentional way and not by accident—one senses that the designers of this cookie knew the Venturi principle that the average user of architecture (read eater of cookies) is far more comfortable with plain, ordinary forms that do not require him to adjust radically any of his perceptions.

## Questions

1. How seriously do you take these descriptions? Do they have any point, or are they sheer fooling around?
2. Explain to someone who does not understand them—the references, in context, to Mies van der Rohe, Art Deco, the New Orleans Superdome, and Robert Venturi. If you had to do some research, explain what sources you used and how you located the sources. What difficulties, if any, did you encounter?
3. Explicate Goldberger's final sentence on "Mallomar": "The result is a cultural icon—the cookie equivalent, surely, of the Coke bottle."
4. Write a similar description of some cookie not discussed by Goldberger. Or write a description, along these lines, of a McDonald's hamburger, a BLT, and a hero sandwich. Other possibilities: a pizza, a bagel, and a taco.

Henry David Thoreau

# As for Clothing

As for Clothing, to come at once to the practical part of the question, perhaps we are led oftener by the love of novelty and a regard for the opinions of men, in procuring it, than by a true utility. Let him who has work to do recollect that the object of clothing is, first, to retain the vital heat, and secondly, in this state of society, to cover nakedness, and he may judge how much of any necessary or important work may be accomplished without adding to his wardrobe. Kings and queens who wear a suit but once, though made by some tailor or dressmaker to their majesties, cannot know the comfort of wearing a suit that fits. They are no better than wooden horses to hang the clean clothes on. Every day our garments become more assimilated to ourselves, receiving the impress of the wearer's character, until we hesitate to lay them aside, without such delay and medical appliances and some such solemnity even as our bodies. No man ever stood the lower in my estimation for having a patch in his clothes; yet I am sure that there is greater anxiety, commonly, to have fashionable, or at least clean and unpatched clothes, than to have a sound conscience. But even if the rent is not mended, perhaps the worst vice betrayed is improvidence. I sometimes try my acquaintances by such tests as this,—Who could wear a patch, or two extra seams only, over the knee? Most behave as if they believed that their prospects for life would be ruined if they should do it. It would be easier for them to hobble to town with a broken leg than with a broken pantaloon. Often if an accident happens to a gentleman's legs, they can be mended; but if a similar accident happens to the legs of his pantaloons, there is no help for it; for he considers, not what is truly respectable, but what is respected. We know but few men, a great many coats and breeches.

Henry David Thoreau (1817–1862) was born in Concord, Massachusetts, where he spent most of his life ("I have travelled a good deal in Concord"). He taught and lectured, but chiefly he observed, thought, and wrote. From July 5, 1845, to September 6, 1847, he lived near Concord in a cabin at Walden Pond, an experience recorded in *Walden* (1854).

"As for Clothing" (editors' title) comes from *Walden,* Chapter 1.

Dress a scarecrow in your last shift, you standing shiftless by, who would not soonest salute the scarecrow? Passing a cornfield the other day, close by a hat and coat on a stake, I recognized the owner of the farm. He was only a little more weather-beaten than when I saw him last. I have heard of a dog that barked at every stranger who approached his master's premises with clothes on, but was easily quieted by a naked thief. It is an interesting question how far men would retain their relative rank if they were divested of their clothes. Could you, in such a case, tell surely of any company of civilized men which belonged to the most respected class? When Madam Pfeiffer, in her adventurous travels round the world, from east to west, had got so near home as Asiatic Russia, she says that she felt the necessity of wearing other than a travelling dress, when she went to meet the authorities, for she "was now in a civilized country, where . . . people are judged of by their clothes." Even in our democratic New England towns the accidental possession of wealth, and its manifestation in dress and equipage alone, obtain for the possessor almost universal respect. But they who yield such respect, numerous as they are, are so far heathen, and need to have a missionary sent to them. Beside, clothes introduced sewing, a kind of work which you may call endless; a woman's dress, at least, is never done.

A man who has at length found something to do will not need to get a new suit to do it in; for him the old will do, that has lain dusty in the garret for an indeterminate period. Old shoes will serve a hero longer than they have served his valet,—if a hero even has a valet,—bare feet are older than shoes, and he can make them do. Only they who go to soirées and legislative halls must have new coats, coats to change as often as the man changes in them. But if my jacket and trousers, my hat and shoes, are fit to worship God in, they will do; will they not? Who ever saw his old clothes,—his old coat, actually worn out, resolved into its primitive elements, so that it was not a deed of charity to bestow it on some poor boy, by him perchance to be bestowed on some poorer still, or shall we say richer, who could do with less? I say, beware of all enterprises that require new clothes, and not rather a new wearer of clothes. If there is not a new man, how can the new clothes be made to fit? If you have any enterprise before you, try it in your old clothes. All men want, not something to *do with,* but something to *do,* or rather something to *be.* Perhaps we should never procure a new suit, however ragged or dirty the old, until we have so conducted, so enterprised or sailed in some way, that we feel like new men in the old, and that to retain it would be like keeping new wine in old bottles. Our moulting season, like that of the fowls, must be a crisis in our lives. The loon retires to solitary ponds to spend it. Thus also the snake casts its slough, and the caterpillar its wormy coat, by an internal industry and expansion; for clothes are but our outmost cuticle and mortal coil. Otherwise we shall be found sailing under false colors, and be inevitably cashiered at last by our own opinion, as well as that of mankind.

We don garment after garment, as if we grew like exogenous plants by addition without. Our outside and often thin and fanciful clothes are our epidermis, or false skin, which partakes not of our life, and may be stripped off here and there without fatal injury; our thicker garments, constantly worn, are our cellular integument, or cortex; but our shirts are our liber,[1] or true bark, which cannot be removed without girdling and so destroying the man. I believe that all races at some seasons wear something equivalent to the shirt. It is desirable that a man be clad so simply that he can lay his hands on himself in the dark, and that he live in all respects so compactly and preparedly, that, if an enemy take the town, he can, like the old philosopher, walk out the gate empty-handed without anxiety. While one thick garment is, for most purposes, as good as three thin ones, and cheap clothing can be obtained at prices really to suit customers; while a thick coat can be bought for five dollars, which will last as many years, thick pantaloons for two dollars, cowhide boots for a dollar and a half a pair, a summer hat for a quarter of a dollar, and a winter cap for sixty-two and a half cents, or a better be made at home at a nominal cost, where is he so poor that, clad in such a suit, *of his own earning,* there will not be found wise men to do him reverence?

When I ask for a garment of a particular form, my tailoress tells me gravely, "They do not make them so now," not emphasizing the "They" at all, as if she quoted an authority as impersonal as the Fates, and I find it difficult to get made what I want, simply because she cannot believe that I mean what I say, that I am so rash. When I hear this oracular sentence, I am for a moment absorbed in thought, emphasizing to myself each word separately that I may come at the meaning of it, that I may find out by what degree of consanguinity *They* are related to *me,* and what authority they may have in an affair which affects me so nearly; and finally, I am inclined to answer her with equal mystery, and without any more emphasis of the

[1]Inner bark of a tree. (Editors' note)

"they"—"It is true, they did not make them so recently, but they do now." Of what use this measuring of me if she does not measure my character, but only the breadth of my shoulders, as it were a peg to hang the coat on? We worship not the Graces, nor the Parcæ, but Fashion. She spins and weaves and cuts with full authority. The head monkey at Paris puts on a traveller's cap, and all the monkeys in America do the same. I sometimes despair of getting anything quite simple and honest done in this world by the help of men. They would have to be passed through a powerful press first, to squeeze their old notions out of them, so that they would not soon get upon their legs again; and then there would be some one in the company with a maggot in his head, hatched from an egg deposited there nobody knows when, for not even fire kills these things, and you would have lost your labor. Nevertheless, we will not forget that some Egyptian wheat was handed down to us by a mummy.

On the whole, I think that it cannot be maintained that dressing has in this or any country risen to the dignity of an art. At present men make shift to wear what they can get. Like shipwrecked sailors, they put on what they can find on the beach, and at a little distance, whether of space or time, laugh at each other's masquerade. Every generation laughs at the old fashions, but follows religiously the new. We are amused at beholding the costume of Henry VIII., or Queen Elizabeth, as much as if it was that of the King and Queen of the Cannibal Islands. All costume off a man is pitiful or grotesque. It is only the serious eye peering from and the sincere life passed within it which restrain laughter and consecrate the costume of any people. Let Harlequin be taken with a fit of the colic and his trappings will have to serve that mood too. When the soldier is hit by a cannon ball rags are as becoming as purple.

The childish and savage taste of men and women for new patterns keeps how many shaking and squinting through kaleidoscopes that they may discover the particular figure which this generation requires today. The manufacturers have learned that this taste is merely whimsical. Of two patterns which differ only by a few threads more or less of a particular color, the one will be sold readily, the other lie on the shelf, though it frequently happens that after the lapse of a season the latter becomes the most fashionable. Comparatively, tattooing is not the hideous custom which it is called. It is not barbarous merely because the printing is skin-deep and unalterable.

I cannot believe that our factory system is the best mode by which men may get clothing. The condition of the operatives is becoming every day more like that of the English; and it cannot be wondered at, since, as far as I have heard or observed, the principal object is, not that mankind may be well and honestly clad, but, unquestionably, that the corporations may be enriched. In the long run men hit only what they aim at. Therefore, though they should fail immediately, they had better aim at something high.

## Questions

1. What, according to Thoreau, are the legitimate functions of clothing? What other functions does he reject, or fail to consider?
2. In the last paragraph, Thoreau criticizes the factory system. Is the criticism mild or severe? Explain. Point out some of the earlier passages in which he touches on the relation of clothes to a faulty economic system.
3. Many of Thoreau's sentences mean both what they say literally and something more; often, like proverbs, they express abstract or general truths in concrete, homely language. How might these sentences be interpreted?
   a. We know but few men, a great many coats and breeches.
   b. Dress a scarecrow in your last shift, you standing shiftless by, who would not soonest salute the scarecrow?
   c. If you have any enterprise before you, try it in your old clothes.
   d. Every generation laughs at the old fashions, but follows religiously the new.
   e. When the soldier is hit by a cannon ball rags are as becoming as purple.

## Anne Hollander

# Clothes Make the Man—Uneasy

The last decade has made a large number of men more uneasy about what to wear than they might have believed possible. The idea that one might agonize over whether to grow sideburns (sideburns!) or wear trousers of a radically different shape had never occurred to a whole generation. Before the mid-'60s whether to wear a tie was about the most dramatic sartorial problem: everything else was a subtle matter of surface variation. Women have been so accustomed to dealing with extreme fashion for so long that they automatically brace themselves for whatever is coming next, including their own willingness to resist or conform and all the probable masculine responses. Men in modern times have only lately felt any pressure to pay that kind of attention. All the delicate shades of significance expressed by the small range of possible alternatives used to be absorbing enough: Double- or single-breasted cut? Sports jacket and slacks or a suit? Shoes with plain or wing tip? The choices men had had to make never looked very momentous to a feminine eye accustomed to a huge range of personally acceptable possibilities, but they always had an absolute and enormous meaning in the world of men, an identifying stamp usually incomprehensible to female judgment. A hat with a tiny bit of nearly invisible feather was separated as by an ocean from a hat with none, and white-on-white shirts, almost imperceptibly complex in weave, were totally shunned by those men who favored white oxford-cloth shirts. Women might remain mystified by the ferocity with which men felt and supported these tiny differences, and perhaps, they might pity such narrow sartorial vision attaching so much importance to half an inch of padding in the shoulders or an inch of trouser cuff.

But men knew how lucky they were. It was never very hard to dress the part of oneself. Even imaginative wives and mothers could eventually be trained to reject all seductive but incorrect choices with

Anne Hollander was born in Cleveland in 1930, and was educated at Barnard College. She has published essays on the history of fashion and a book on the clothed figure in art.

respect to tie fabric and collar shape that might connote the wrong flavor of spiritual outlook, the wrong level of education or the wrong sort of male bonding. It was a well ordered world, the double standard flourished without hindrance, and no man who stuck to the rules ever needed to suspect that he might look ridiculous.

Into this stable system the width-of-tie question erupted in the early '60s. Suddenly, and for the first time in centuries, the rate of change in masculine fashion accelerated with disconcerting violence, throwing a new light on all the steady old arrangements. Women looked on with secret satisfaction, as it became obvious that during the next few years men might think they could resist the changes, but they would find it impossible to ignore them. In fact to the discomfiture of many, the very look of having ignored the changes suddenly became a distinct and highly conspicuous way of dressing, and everyone ran for cover. Paying no attention whatever to nipped-in waistlines, vivid turtlenecks, long hair with sideburns and bell-bottom trousers could not guarantee any comfy anonymity, but rather stamped one as a convinced follower of the old order—thus adding three or four dangerous new meanings to all the formerly reliable signals. A look in the mirror suddenly revealed man to himself wearing his obvious chains and shackles, hopelessly unliberated.

Now that fashion is loose upon the whole male sex, many men are having to discard an old look for a new, if only to maintain the desired distance from the avant-garde, as women have always known how to do. Just after the first few spurts of creative masculine dress in the mid-'60s, like the Beatle haircut and the wide ties, daring young women began to appear in the miniskirt, and men were temporarily safe from scrutiny as those thousands of thighs came into view. The other truly momentous fashion phenomenon to arise at the same moment, the counterculture costume, established itself absolutely but almost unnoticeably among both sexes while all eyes were glued to those rising hems. In fact miniskirts were the last spectacular and successful sexist thunderbolt to be hurled by modern women, before the liberation movement began to conspire with the nature movement to prevent semi-nudity from being erotic (hot pants, rightly short lived, were too much like science fiction). Men who might have longed in adolescence for the sight of unconfined breasts were perhaps slightly disconcerted when breasts at last appeared, bouncing and swaying on the public streets in the late '60s, since they were often quite repellently presented to the accompaniment of costumes and facial expressions somehow calculated to quell the merest stirring of a lustful thought. But that was only at the beginning, of course. Since then the visible nipple has become delightfully effective under proper management.

Following bare legs, free breasts and the perverse affectation of poverty, dress suddenly became a hilarious parlor game, and men were playing too. Chains, zippers, nailheads and shiny leather were available in any sort of combination. Extremely limp, tired and stained old clothes could also be tastefully festooned on anybody who preferred those. Universal ethnic and gypsy effects, featuring extraordinary fringes and jewelry worn in unusual places, vied with general romantic and menace effects, featuring dark glasses, sinister hats and occasional black capes. In addition all the parts were interchangeable. Both sexes participated, but then finally many people got tired and felt foolish and gave it up. Men, however, had had a taste of what it could be like, and all the extreme possibilities still echoed long after the extreme practices had subsided, even in the consciousness of those who had observed and never tried to join.

During the whole trend men floundered, and still do, longing for the familiar feel of solid ground. Hoping to appease the unleashed tide with one decisive gesture, many men bought a turtleneck dress shirt and wore it uncomfortably but hopefully with a medallion on a chain, only to discover within three months that it would not do. Many a conservative minded but imaginative fellow, eager to avoid new possibilities for feeling foolish and to look at least attuned to the modern world, had expensive tailoring done in a bold and becoming new shape, hoping to stay exactly like that for the rest of his life, or at least for a few more years. He then discovered himself still handsome but hopelessly dated in a season or two. Mustaches sprouted and hastily vanished again, sideburns were cultivated and sometimes proved to grow in upsettingly silver gray. Hair, once carefully prevented from exhibiting wayward traits, was given its head. Men balding on top could daringly relish luxuriant growth about the sides, and the Allen Ginsberg phenomenon frequently occurred: a man once clean-shaven and well furred on top would compensate for a thinning poll by growing a lengthy fringe around its edges and often adding an enormous beard. The result was a sort of curious air of premature wisdom, evoking mental images of the young Walt Whitman spiced with swami. Other, more demanding solutions to the problem of thinning hair among those wishing to join the thick thatch with sideburns group required an elaborate styling of the remaining sparse growth, complete with teasing and spray and a consequent new dependence, quite equal to anything women submit to, upon the hairdressing skill of the professional, the family or the self.

Early in the game, of course, long hair for men had been just another badge. Most men had felt quite safe from any temptation to resemble those youthful and troublesome citizens who were always getting into the newspapers and the jails. Some young people, eager to maintain a low profile, had also found the hairy and ragged look an excellent disguise for masking a serious interest in studying the violin or any similar sort of heterodox concern. During all this time no one ever bothered girls about the length of *their* hair, or found any opportunity to throw them out of school for wearing crew cuts for instance. Even if half-inch fuzz had been the revolutionary mode for girls, they would have undoubtedly been exempt from official hassling, except possibly by their mothers. But, as it happened, the gradually evolved migrant worker, bowery bum costume worn by the armies of the young required long hair for both sexes. The very similarity of coiffure helped, paradoxically, to emphasize the difference of sex. After a while the potent influence of this important sub-fashion that was at first so easy to ridicule came steadily to bear on the general public's clothes-consciousness. The hairy heads and worn blue denim legs all got easier to take, and indeed they looked rather attractive on many of them. People became quite accustomed to having their children look as if they belonged to a foreign tribe, possibly hostile; after all under the hair it was still Tom and Kathy.

In general, men of all ages turn out not to want to give up the habit of fixing on a suitable self-image and then carefully tending it, instead of taking up all the new options. It seems too much of a strain to dress for all that complex multiple role-playing, like women. The creative use of male plumage for sexual display, after all, has had a very thin time for centuries: the whole habit became the special prerogative of certain clearly defined groups, ever since the overriding purpose of male dress had been established as that of precise identification. No stepping over the boundaries was thinkable—ruffled evening shirts were for them, not me; and the fear of the wrong associations was the strongest male emotion about clothes, not the smallest part being fear of association with the wrong sex.

The difference between men's and women's clothes used to be an easy matter from every point of view, all the more so when the same tailors made both. When long ago all elegant people wore brightly colored satin, lace and curls, nobody had any trouble sorting out the sexes or worrying whether certain small elements were sexually appropriate. So universal was the skirted female shape and the bifurcated male one that a woman in men's clothes was completely disguised (see the history of English drama), and long hair or gaudy trimmings were never the issue. It was the 19th century, which produced the look of the different sexes coming from different planets, that lasted such a very long time. It also gave men official exemption from fashion risk, and official sanction to laugh at women for perpetually incurring it.

Women apparently love the risk of course, and ignore the laughter. Men secretly hate it and dread the very possibility of a smile. Most of them find it impossible to leap backward across the traditional centuries into a comfortable renaissance zest for these dangers, since life is hard enough now anyway. Moreover along with fashion came the pitiless exposure of masculine narcissism and vanity, so long submerged and undiscussed. Men had lost the habit of having their concern with personal appearance show as blatantly as women's —the great dandies provided no continuing tradition, except perhaps among urban blacks. Men formerly free from doubt wore their new finery with colossal self-consciousness, staring covertly at everyone else to find out what the score really was about all this stuff. Soon enough the identifying compartments regrouped themselves to include the new material. High heels and platform soles, once worn by the Sun King and other cultivated gentlemen of the past, have been appropriated only by those willing to change not only their heights but their way of walking. They have been ruled out, along with the waist-length shirt opening that exposes trinkets nestling against the chest hair, by men who nevertheless find themselves willing to wear long hair and fur coats and carry handbags. Skirts, I need not add, never caught on.

What of women during the rest of this revolutionary decade? The furor over the miniskirt now seems quaint, like all furors about fashion, and the usual modifications have occurred in everybody's eyesight to make them seem quite ordinary. Trousers have a longer and more interesting history. Women only very recently learned that pants are sexy when fitted tightly over the female pelvis. When trousers were first worn by women, they were supposed to be another disturbing attractive masculine affectation, perfectly exemplified by Marlene Dietrich doing her white tie and tails number in *Morocco.* They were also supposed to be suitable for very slim, rangy outdoor types low on sex appeal. Jokes used to fly about huge female behinds looking dreadful in pants, and those who habitually wore them had to speak loudly about their comfort and practicality. Gradually, however, it became obvious that pants looked sensational, not in the least masculine, and the tighter the better. Long trousers, along with lots of hair, breasts and bareness, became sexy in their own right. Everybody promptly forgot all about how comfortable and practical they were supposed to be, since who cared when they obviously simply looked marvelous. They are in fact a great bore on slushy pavements and very hot in summer but nobody minds. Nevertheless the extremely ancient prejudice against women in trousers lingered for a very long time. Many schools forbade pants for girls even though they might wear their hair as they liked, and the same restaurants that required the male necktie prohibited the female trouser. Even in quite recent times pants still seemed to connote either excessively crude informality or slightly perverted, raunchy sex. The last decade has seen the end of all this, since those sleek housewives in TV ads who used to wear shirtdresses all wear pants now, and dignified elderly ladies at all economic levels wear them too, with crystal earrings and nice, neat handbags. After all these anxious and newsworthy borrowings, all the classes and the sexes remain as distinguishable as ever.

## Questions

1. How would you describe the tone of this essay? Point to three or four sentences that seem to you to be especially clear illustrations of the dominant tone.
2. This essay was originally published in 1974. Write a postscript of about 250 words, bringing the essay up to date.

Robert Sommer

# Hard Architecture

Prison fixtures are being installed in the restrooms of city parks. According to the manufacturers' statements, they are supposed to be vandal-proof. One advertisement shows a man attacking a toilet with a sledgehammer. According to Sacramento, California, Recreation Director Solon Wisham, Jr., "There is no exposed plumbing in the new buildings. The external fixtures are made of cast aluminum covered with hard epoxy. The buildings themselves are made of concrete blocks rather than wood or brick."[1] This same trend toward hard buildings is evident in public facilities across the country. Picnic tables are being cast of concrete rather than built of wood and are embedded several feet into the ground. It isn't possible to move these tables to a shady place or combine two tables to accommodate a large group, but that is an inconvenience for the users rather than the park officials. The older wood and metal tables remaining from a happier era are chained to blocks of concrete or steel posts.

The original inspiration for the park restroom, the prison cell, illustrates the hard facts of hard architecture. Human beings are enclosed in steel cages with the bare minimum of furnishings or amenities. In some cells there may be no furniture whatever except for the furthest advance in the field of vandal-proof plumbing, the hole in the concrete floor, otherwise known as a Chinese toilet. Because nothing is provided that the inmate might destroy, he may have to sleep on a bare concrete floor without mattress or blanket. I am not talking about the Middle Ages or some backward part of the nation. I have a clear image of an isolation cell circa 1973 with a man in a steel cage for 23 hours a day with nothing to do but pace the floor and curse the guard watching him through the slit in a steel door. The architecture of the isolation cell is based on a variant of Murphy's

---

Robert Sommer teaches psychology and environmental studies at the University of California at Davis. Our selection comes from *Tight Spaces*, a study of the "New Brutalism" manifested in windowless concrete buildings and in uncomfortable parks and airports.

---

[1]Jeff Raimundo, "Park Facilities Are Still Vulnerable," Sacramento *Bee*, February 8, 1973, p. B1.

Law—if something can be destroyed, it will be destroyed.[2] In mental hospitals of the early 1950s, the line was, "If you give the patients anything nice, they won't take care of it." For public housing tenants it went "If you provide good architecture they won't appreciate it." There is the same denigrating we/they dichotomy in all these assessments of people's response to their surroundings. We know what's best for them and they don't. Even if we provide what they say they'd like, they won't take care of it and will probably destroy it. Ergo, it is best for everyone, especially the taxpayers who foot the bill, to design things that cannot be destroyed.

The result is that architecture is designed to be strong and resistant to human imprint. To the inhabitants it seems impervious, impersonal, and inorganic. Lady Allen, who pioneered the adventure playground in Great Britain, was appalled at American play yards which she described as "an administrator's heaven and a child's hell . . . asphalt barracks yards behind wire mesh screen barriers" built primarily for ease and economy of maintenance.[3] There is a whole industry built around supplying steel cages for prisons, wire mesh fences for city parks, and graffiti-resistant paint for public buildings. On a larger scale, the hardening of the landscape is evident in the ever-growing freeway system, the residential and second-home subdivisions pushing aside orchards and forests, the straightening and cementing of river beds, the walled and guarded cities of suburbia, and the TV cameras in banks and apartment buildings.

Another characteristic of hard architecture is a lack of permeability between inside and out. Often this means an absence of windows, a style referred to in Berkeley as post-revolutionary architecture. At first glance the Bank of America on Berkeley's Telegraph Avenue seems to have windows but these are really reflecting metal surfaces. The new postal center in Oakland, with its tiny slit windows, looks as if it were intended for urban guerilla warfare. Older buildings that still have plate glass use steel shutters and gates that can be drawn across the exterior in a matter of minutes. Some corporations are moving their data-processing machinery underground where they are less vulnerable to attack. The fact that employees must work underground forty hours a week is a minor cost borne by the employees rather than the architect.

[2]Murphy's Law No. 1: If something can go wrong, it will. Law No. 2: The toast always falls butter side down.
[3]Lady Allen of Hurtwood, *Planning for Play* (Cambridge: M.I.T. Press, 1968).

Hard architecture means wall surfaces that resist human imprint. Dark colors and rough cement were satisfactory prior to the advent of the aerosol can. The counter response of the hard-line designers has taken two forms. The first is the legal effort to remove aerosol cans from the hands of potential graffitists. Ordinances have been proposed to make it illegal to carry open aerosol cans on city streets. A New York State Senator has proposed a bill to make it illegal for people under eighteen to purchase cans of spray paint. The other approach is to develop vandal-resistant surfaces and stronger kinds of paint remover. In a six-month period New York City purchased 7,000 gallons of a yellow jelly called DWR (dirty word remover) from a Moorestown, N.J., manufacturer of industrial chemicals. The remover comes in two strengths and the heavier duty version is optimistically called Enzitall.[4] Planners of President Nixon's inauguration sprayed the trees alongside the motorcade route with a material that prevented birds from roosting there. They didn't want the president being embarrassed by an occasional bird-dropping. The two-year interval during which the birds would be unable to roost on these trees is a minor inconvenience again borne by the users.

Most of these efforts to harden the environment have had the avowed purpose of increasing security. Frequently this reason is a coverup for a desire to maintain order, discipline, or control. Although these motives are related to security, there are important differences between security and control that must be recognized and heeded if a democratic society is to continue. . . .

## *Ideological Supports for Hard Buildings*

Any effort to soften hard buildings and improve the lot of the public housing tenant, the prisoner, or the park user will encounter the popular prejudice against "frills" in public facilities. As they say about army buildings, "It doesn't have to be cheap, it just has to look cheap." The taxpayer doesn't want to believe that people living in public housing are better off than he is. Almost every prison official advocates individual cells for prisoners. The logic behind single cells is compelling; it includes the physical protection of weaker inmates, reduces homosexual relationships, enables better control of inmates in single cells, as well as increased privacy and personal dignity. However, whenever prison officials argue for single cells, they are

[4]"Help Arrives," Cincinnati *Enquirer,* April 23, 1972.

accused of coddling convicts. The apocryphal question from the state legislature is how single rooms can be justified for people who have broken the law when army recruits are compelled to live in open barracks. Is it reasonable to provide more amenities for lawbreakers than for draftees?

There are several good answers to this question. First we can turn to Florence Nightingale's dictum that the first requisite of a hospital is that it do the patients no harm. The minimum criterion of a prison should be that an inmate emerges no worse than when he entered. At present this is not the case and prisons are accurately described as breeding grounds for criminal behavior. When someone is hurt and angry, there is no reason to believe that putting him in a degrading and dehumanizing environment will improve his outlook or behavior. Indeed there is every reason to suppose that this will worsen whatever antisocial attitudes presently exist.

The logic of subjecting the poor, the criminal, and the deviant to degrading conditions is also based on a puritanical attitude toward comfort. A belief in the redemptive value of hard work and frugality pervades much of our thinking about people who are public charges. The first American prison was developed in Pennsylvania in response to demands for the humane treatment of criminals by the Quaker sect, a group characterized both by its humane impulses and a disdain for anything beyond the minimum in personal comfort. Following Quaker precepts, lawbreakers were confined in solitary cells with ample time to consider their transgressions and become penitent. The cells were quite large and the inmate remained in his cell most of the day apart from a one-hour exercise period. Later, when large-scale workshops proved more efficient than individual craft work performed in a single cell, the solitary system of the Pennsylvania prison was replaced by the silent system of the Auburn Prison, in which inmates also lived in single cells but came together to work and eat but had to remain silent. The idea that an ascetic life would help to rehabilitate prisoners was used against any effort to humanize the institutions.

Even today, efforts to improve the drab conditions of army life, to permit recruits to personalize their sleeping quarters or choose their own hair styles, are regarded by many senior officers as responsible for breakdowns in order and discipline. Not too long ago architects who planned college classrooms and dormitories were advised against making the furnishings too pleasant or comfortable lest the students become distracted or fall asleep. Guidebooks for undergraduate students still warn against too many amenities in the student's room. Here is a sampling of advice on dormitory furnishing: "Choose a straight backed chair rather than a very comfortable one. . . ." "All of the votes are in favor of a simple, rugged, straight-backed chair with no cushion. You study best when you are not too comfortable or relaxed. . . ." "For obvious reasons, avoid studying on a couch, easy chair, or in bed. . . ." "A bed is no place to study. Neither is a sofa, nor a foam rubber lounge chair. When you are too relaxed and comfortable physically, your concentration also relaxes. A straight-backed wooden chair is best for most students; it allows them to work at maximum concentration for longer periods." Before analyzing the attitudes behind these recommendations, let me state emphatically that there is no evidence that people work better when they are uncomfortable. Let the reader examine his or her own circumstances while reading this book. Are you sitting bolt upright in a straight-backed chair or lying on a couch with your head against a cushion? My own observations of the way students read suggest that when a couch or easy chair is available, it will be chosen almost every time over the rugged, virtuous, and uncomfortable straight-backed chair.

Another ideological prop behind hard architecture is neo-behaviorism. Providing decent housing for public charges would be "rewarding" poverty or criminal behavior. The argument goes beyond the accusation of simply coddling convicts to the idea that improved conditions will actually "reinforce" criminal tendencies. Neo-behaviorism maintains that people won't be deterred from crime if the consequences are not sufficiently dire. This requires some form of punishment—if not actual torture then at least confinement without amenity. The critical question is whether confinement and removal from society constitute sufficient punishment or whether the transgressor must be punished still further during confinement. There is no evidence to indicate that such punishment exerts any positive influences on an inmate's character. Instead it increases his alienation from and his bitterness toward society. There is not much basis for believing that dehumanizing public housing will help to reduce welfare rolls, juvenile delinquency, or anything else society considers bad. Poor housing lowers the self-image of the tenant and helps to convince him how little society cares about his plight. This is not a terribly important consideration to a philosophy that is unabashedly beyond freedom and dignity. Hard, hard, hard, ain't it hard? Yes it is. But does it work? No, it doesn't. City officials across the country will testify that there is no such thing as a vandal-proof restroom or picnic bench. If restrooms are built out of concrete they will be dynamited and have concrete poured down the toilet holes. Vandals, thousands of helmeted Huns riding out of the East, have managed to dig out concrete blocks and haul away picnic tables weighing hundred of pounds. Bolt cutters and wire snippers can sever any chain-link fence manufactured today. In the People's Park disturbance of 1972, the metal poles for the fence were used to break up the macadam of the parking lot. Local police were very cooperative in carting away the broken macadam pieces lest they in turn be used to break the windows of local stores. The harder the architecture, the greater its potential as a weapon if it is used against the authorities. Prison inmates have learned how to make deadly knives from steel bedsprings. Hard architecture also costs more to adapt or remove. Pennsylvania's Eastern Penitentiary, built in 1829, was closed down in 1966, but has yet to be removed from the site because of the high razing expense. The extra costs of hard architecture are manifold; first in the initial purchase price because it costs twice as much as ordinary items, second in its potential for abuse once it is destroyed as well as the greater cost in repairing or removing a heavy and rigid item designed to be installed permanently, and finally the human costs resulting from being in cold, ugly, and impersonal buildings.

Challenge people to destroy something and they will find a way to do it. Many people prefer to ignore the great amount of technological ingenuity released in wartime. Although only sketchy accounts of the automated battlefield have been made public, it is evident that the Vietnam War has produced the most sophisticated gadgetry in the history of warfare. If city agencies use remote sensors and infrared photography to detect the presence of people in parks after closing time, it is likely that such methods will have the same success in New York parks that they had in Vietnam. Authorities who go the route of vandalproof facilities are deluding themselves. They are short-range thinkers who cost everyone money in the long run. Adversity puts human ingenuity to the test and the prison inmate naked in his strip cell is tested most severely. By law the California authorities are required to provide even strip-cell inmates with their own Bibles. The result is that the Bible has become a weapon in a manner unintended by the most ardent missionary. Inmates stuff the pages into the ventilator shaft and use the covers to stop up the Chinese toilet. Think of what the inmate could do if he had a table and chair to work with! An advisory committee on dental hygiene ran into problems when it suggested to the California Department of Corrections that inmates should be allowed to use dental floss. Prison officials pointed out that dental floss "when coated with an abrasive substance, could be as effective as metal blades in cutting through iron bars."[5]

The major defects of hard architecture are that it is costly, dehumanizing, and it isn't effective. Besides that, it doesn't look very nice. The prototype of hard architecture is the strip cell in the maximum security prison containing nothing but reinforced concrete poured over a steel cage without any amenities. If we can develop ways of humanizing the prison cell, perhaps we can also do so for schools, parks, and other public facilities.

The rationale of the hard prison is that the inmate will destroy anything that is provided for him. It is easy to prove the correctness of this view by giving a wooden chair to an inmate in a strip cell. It is likely that he will bang the chair against the wall until the legs have come loose and he has several clubs in his possession. Give him a mattress and sooner or later the authorities will have a fire or smoke problem on their hands. Just what does this prove? One can also supply numerous examples of maximum security cells that are equally secure and full of amenities including rugs, tables, desks, television sets, and stereo systems. In prison disturbances, where inmates are rampaging against virtually every part of the prison building, televisions sets purchased with inmate welfare funds remain undisturbed. Nor do inmates destroy the paintings made by their fellow prisoners.

The arguments against providing amenities for inmates do not discuss the costs of denying a human existence to the lawbreakers. I have never heard anyone maintain that the inmate's mental or physical health is improved by a bare, unheated cell with no exercise yard or outside stimulation. This experience does not teach him a greater respect for the law or the society that maintains him under such dehumanizing conditions. However, guards legitimately object to providing chairs for inmates who are going to break them apart and fashion clubs from the pieces. The typical solution has been to harden prison furnishings with indestructible materials and attach them to the walls. But human ingenuity can always find a way to destroy things that are physically or spiritually oppressive.

[5]Sacramento *Bee*, May 8, 1973, p. B2.

Another assumption behind hard architecture is that security through steel, concrete, and electronic surveillance is cheaper and more effective than security through public access. Stated another way, security can be gained through technological control of the environment. This is perhaps valid when one is working *with* people rather than against them. To design a highway to minimize ambiguity, error, and accidents increases everyone's sense of security. I feel more comfortable riding my bike on a well-planned bicycle path than on a street or highway that was designed with automobiles in mind. However, we have not been discussing situations in which everyone gains from good design, but rather those in which hard architecture is used by one group to exclude or oppress another.

The emulation of the prison as a security environment is the more ironic because the prison is a failing institution from everyone's standpoint. It provides no security for inmates, guards, wardens, and visitors. It does provide a short-run protection to outside society by segregating offenders for brief periods, but this must be weighed against the corrosive effects of incarceration in an oppressive and unnatural environment.

### *Soft Architecture*

If experience has shown that hard architecture isn't working from the standpoint of economics, aesthetics, or human dignity, what then is the answer? The solution, I believe, is to reverse course and make buildings more rather than less responsive to their users. Instead of hardening things to resist human imprint, let us design buildings, parks, and cities to welcome and reflect the presence of human beings —let us abandon the fruitless and costly search for ever more secure cell furnishings. There is another alternative to the completely empty cell. This would involve materials such as foam and inflatables as well as other types of plastics. Provided one selects materials that are fire proof, the security implications of an inexpensive air mattress or styrofoam chair are virtually zero, or at least they are considerably less than with ordinary prison furnishings. There is no justification for inmates in maximum security cells sleeping on hard concrete floors when the wholesale cost of an air mattress is twenty cents. At least an inmate should be offered a choice between the bare concrete floor and an air mattress which he can destroy if he chooses. If he elects to destroy the air mattress, the security implications to the guard as well as the cost to the taxpayers are minimal. However, if he does not destroy it, an equally inexpensive foam chair might be tried next. In this way a valid transaction between the inmate and the authorities regarding cell furnishings could be established.

Soft architecture can change the relationship between keeper and inmate. New Jersey State Penitentiary in Leesburg was deliberately built by the architects to include breakable materials; a necessary adjunct to a humane environment. Glass abounds and each cell has natural light with an exterior window in addition to the glazed walls separating cells from courtyards. Locally some people refer to this medium security facility as "the glass house." All windows face the interior courtyards and exterior security is provided by the back wall of the residential units, a deep overhang of the roof to prevent climbing, and a cyclone fence surrounding the entire site. However the interior of the prison contains a great amount of breakable material requiring inmates and guards to reach a mutually satisfactory accommodation, because any burst of anger would result in shattered glass.[6] It would indeed be difficult to run a repressive prison in "the glass house." On the other hand, it requires tremendous tact, patience, and sensitivity to run such a prison. Let the reader answer whether he or she would prefer to work (or be confined) in Leesburg or in a traditional institution.

Several years ago, the dormitories on my campus had strict rules against students hanging pictures or posters on the walls. There were constant inspections by university officials who removed illegal posters and fined the offenders. The basis for these regulations was that the tacks or tape used to mount these posters would scratch the walls. The prohibition against decorating dormitory rooms continued for years even though it was a constant irritant as well as being costly and ineffective. Besides the inspections there was the annual repainting bill, which mounted steadily over the years. Eventually the administration decided that it would be cheaper and happier for everyone to let students hang anything they wanted on their walls. The housing office now provides paint at the beginning of the year so that students can erase anything done by the previous occupants and have the colors they want. Students living on the same floor can decide jointly how the corridors and stairwells are to be painted. New dormitories now contain soft wall materials such as cork or burlap on

[6]Suzanne Stephens, "Pushing Prisons Aside," *The Architectural Forum* (March 1973), pp. 28–51.

wood so that students can hang pictures, mobiles, or macramé without marring the surface. They are built to be largely maintained by the users. This has proven cheaper and more satisfying than the previous arrangement of bare walls accompanied by constant inspections, fines, and reprimands, as well as periodic repainting by the maintenance staff. It costs $15 per room to allow students to do the painting themselves, compared to $75 charged by the physical plant office. In 1970, the repaint rate was 10 percent—that is, only one out of ten rooms was repainted by the subsequent occupant.[7]

On any college campus there is always a shortage of study space, particularly around exam time. There is also a great deal of unused space in the evenings, in the form of academic offices, laboratories, and even cafeterias, but it is difficult to get these opened for student use. I don't know of a single campus where faculty offices are available in the evenings as study space—the territorial feelings of the faculty toward their offices are too strong. However on a number of campuses there have been successful campaigns to open up the cafeterias in the evenings. These campaigns have been successful only sporadically and probably less than one-third of university cafeterias are routinely opened for evening studiers, another third are opened during examination periods, and the remainder are locked and available only during specified meal hours. The arguments against opening up cafeterias are custodial and security-oriented—the students will disturb the table arrangements and will steal the utensils and perhaps even the chairs and tables themselves. At a large university in Los Angeles where the silverware is automatically returned to the locked kitchen after meals, the explanation for closing the cafeteria in the evenings is that the students would steal the salt and pepper shakers. Like the belief that mental patients will flush magazines down the toilets, prisoners will destroy decent furnishings if they have them, or park users will chop up wooden benches, a few instances can always be cited, but the trade-offs in social utility and aesthetics are rarely considered. The best counterargument for opening up college cafeterias for evening studiers is that the system works on scores of campuses across the nation. The loss of twenty salt and pepper shakers and perhaps an extra $10 per evening in janitorial services to open up two cafeterias for around-the-clock use might provide the campus with an additional 15,000 feet of prime study

[7]Robbie Hart, "Room Painting in the Residence Halls." Unpublished report, University of California, Davis Housing Office, 1970.

space already equipped with tables and chairs. If need be, the student government or some dormitory organization can provide proctors or monitors in the late evening hours.

In all such illustrations—magazines for mental patients, amenities for prisoners, and study space for college students—the security and custodial opposition is largely specious, but this is obvious only to someone knowledgeable about the situation elsewhere. The argument that mental patients will immediately tear up magazines and flush them down the toilet has at least minimal logic *unless* one has worked on a psychiatric ward where magazines and newspapers are freely available. The arguments against amenity for prisoners seem equally ridiculous if one has seen maximum security cells equipped with carpets, stereos, green plants, and tropical fish. To the criticism that inmates will hide knives and drugs in flower pots and stereos, one can cite the fact that inmates presently secrete weapons and contraband even in the barest cells and sometimes as suppositories. It is also true that the majority of stabbings and other serious injuries have occurred at the most security-conscious institutions. The explanation always returns to the "type of inmate" and never to the type of place. The mental patients who had free access to newspapers and magazines and didn't flush them down the toilets were presumably a "better class of patients." Similarly, students at University *A* who have access to cafeterias for evening study and leave the salt and pepper shakers undisturbed are a "better class of students." This "class logic" treats people apart from their surroundings, as if there is some intrinsic self independent of the environment. This is a false model of any natural process, including person/environment transactions. There is no behavior apart from environment even *in utero.* People adapt themselves to their surroundings in diverse and complex ways. When those surroundings are cold and oppressive, people who can will avoid them. Unfortunately many people, for economic, social, or statutory reasons, cannot avoid places that oppress them. The result may be somatic disorders, anxiety, and irritation, but the probable outcome will be numbness to one's surroundings, with psychological withdrawal substituting for physical avoidance. . . .

The dream of a society in which people who share common goals will trust and respect one another is being suffocated in a torrent of concrete, steel, and sophisticated security equipment. I would feel less strongly if windowless buildings, barbed-wire fences, and electronic surveillance equipment were infrequent aberrations of paranoid homeowners and public officials, but they are not. Housing projects, schools, playgrounds, courtrooms, and commercial buildings reveal the hardening process at an advanced stage. If there is truth to Churchill's dictum that the buildings we shape will eventually shape us, then the inevitable result of hard buildings will be withdrawn, callous, and indifferent people. A security emphasis is being poured into concrete that will harden our children's children fifty years from now. . . .

### *Personalization*

There is no single best arrangement of office furniture and no way for a designer, building manager, or psychologist to intuit someone's space needs without meeting the person, seeing the sort of job he or she has to do, and how he or she does it. Every faculty office on my campus comes equipped with a standard complement of furniture—a desk, filing cabinet, table, two or three bookcases, coat rack, and so on. Because all these people have the same job title (professor) and the size and shape of all office pieces are identical, one could conceive of standardized office arrangements. However a walk down the hallways reveals a great diversity of arrangements. One man has placed his bookcase between his desk and the door for maximum privacy. Another has joined together his desk and table to yield a large work area and writing surface as well as considerable distance from any visitor, and a third has placed all furniture against the walls to remove any barriers between himself and the students. Numerous attempts at personalization are evident. Out of their own pocket, faculty purchased rugs, drapes, wall-hangings, and pictures of every description, as well as artifacts and symbols of their respective professions. The same diversity of arrangements is evident in the student dormitories, which also come equipped with a standardized complement of similar furniture. Sometimes I think I have seen every conceivable arrangement of two desks, two beds, two chairs, and two dressers, but invariably I am surprised to find a novel pattern.

Instead of guessing "user needs" one should aim at providing access to a pool or selection of furnishings and allow people to arrange their office areas as they see fit. During the occupation of the administration building during Berkeley's Free Speech Movement crisis in 1964, it was reported that the students had broken into and ransacked the office of President Emeritus Robert Gordon Sproul. When the police had removed the demonstrators, they found Sproul's office in disarray with papers strewn about the floor. The situation was resolved when Sproul's secretary reported that her employer often worked on the floor and left papers strewn about.

The idea that people should be able to control and personalize their work spaces is well within the technical capability of the building industry. It does call for a reversal of the tendency to centralize services and decision-making regarding the physical environment. In the short run it may be cheaper to omit the light switches in an office building, but this makes it difficult to show slides and it is also terribly wasteful of electric power. The same point applies to heating, air conditioning, and humidity controls. There is something tragic about an employee who is officially reprimanded for placing cardboard over her air conditioning vent or a poster on the wall to brighten an otherwise drab office. There is no contradiction between central design and local control provided one develops an overall design scheme that makes allowance for local inputs. One can design a soft building in which each occupant controls his own temperature —hotels and motels do this routinely—or one can design a hard building in which the custodian controls everyone's temperature. In the work on classroom seating . . . it was found that janitors arranged chairs in accordance with their educational philosophies. They also followed their own standards of temperature, humidity, and illumination. The custodian in my building has a clear conception of where my desk and chair belong. Every morning I move my chair over to the side of the room and every evening he returns it to my desk. He arranges the room according to his scheme and I to mine. Fortunately the rules allow me to move my chair. I visited a conference room in one government agency and found taped to the wall under the President's picture a diagram specifying how every item of furniture in the room was to be arranged.

Pleas for personalizing offices and work spaces are academic and even precious until one sees the drab and impersonal conditions under which many people work. At the offices of a large insurance company I found hundreds of clerk's desks in straight rows in a large open room with phones ringing, people scurrying about, and no one having any control over the thermal, acoustical, or visual environment. A federal agency building is liable to be a maze of offices of identical size, shape, and decor. All the furniture, including desks and bookcases, is government-issue grey and on every wall there is a framed photograph of the President and the agency director. A few executives are able to place maps on the walls for visual relief, but that is all. The quest for stimulating and attractive work places, the right to personalize one's own spaces and control temperature and illumination and noise are not academic issues to people who must spend eight hours a day in these settings. I don't feel it is necessary to "prove" that people in colorful offices will type more accurately, stay healthier, or buy more government bonds than people in drab offices. People should have the right to attractive and humane working conditions. Somehow the onus of the argument for a decent environment always falls upon the person who wants to improve things; the custodians and the rest of the grey wall crowd never have to defend drab and unresponsive buildings. This is a curious double standard. If an employee hangs up a poster by his desk, he is imposing his values and artistic tastes on the other employees, but if the management paints all the walls in the building grey or institutional green, that is part of the natural order. We eventually tune them out and thereby become alienated from the very buildings in which we spend our daylight hours.

Ugly and drab furnishings cannot be justified economically. For a corporation or government agency, colored items would cost only slightly more than grey ones and on a large order the difference would disappear entirely. There is some poetic justice that many of the drab furnishings of state office buildings are manufactured by the state prison system. In private corporations, which buy their furniture in the free market where a wide variety of styles and colors is available, standardization is less a result of economics or efficiency than of insensitivity and deliberate unconcern. There is also more than a hint of authoritarianism in the idea that each employee must accept the specific furniture arrangement provided by the company. In a large corporation or agency it would be feasible to give each employee a choice of desk, chair, file cabinet, table, and waste basket from a central furniture pool, not only at the time of employment, but every six months if the person felt like changing things around. This may sound utopian but it isn't. It doesn't take all that long to move furniture. The main objective is not so much to keep the furniture moving as it is to sensitize people to the connection between themselves and their surroundings and counteract the pervasive numbness and apathy. The idea of so many millions of people singlemindedly going to dingy little work stations in large skyscrapers, completely turned off to other people and places, is profoundly disturbing. This kind of numbness to one's surroundings can become a life style.

## Questions

1. List the chief characteristics of hard architecture. If any buildings on your campus or in its neighborhood embody some of the characteristics, specify the buildings in your list.
2. Among the common assumptions that Sommer challenges are these: public facilities should not have frills (page 128); a prisoner should not have the luxury of living in a single room (page 129); students study best when not too comfortable (page 129); decent public housing rewards poverty or criminal behavior (page 130). If you held any of these views, has Sommer persuaded you to drop them? If so, how? If not, why has he failed? Next, list three or four other assumptions that Sommer himself makes about human behavior and evaluate them.
3. On page 138 Sommer says that "janitors arranged chairs [in a classroom] in accordance with their educational philosophies." What do you think the arrangement was? What philosophy is implied in this arrangement?
4. Amplify Sommer's last sentence, showing how "numbness to one's surroundings can become a life style." (Many people find the words "life style" faddish and imprecise. Can you think of a better expression?)

Jane Jacobs

# A Good Neighborhood

Anthropologist Elena Padilla, author of *Up from Puerto Rico,* describing Puerto Rican life in a poor and squalid district of New York, tells how much people know about each other—who is to be trusted and who not, who is defiant of the law and who upholds it, who is competent and well informed and who is inept and ignorant—and how these things are known from the public life of the sidewalk and its associated enterprises. These are matters of public char-

Jane Jacobs was born in Scranton, Pennsylvania, in 1916. From 1952 until 1962 she served as an associate editor of *Architectural Forum.* In addition to *The Death and Life of Great American Cities,* from which "A Good Neighborhood" (editors' title) comes, she has written *The Economy of Cities.*

acter. But she also tells how select are those permitted to drop into the kitchen for a cup of coffee, how strong are the ties, and how limited the number of a person's genuine confidants, those who share in a person's private life and private affairs. She tells how it is not considered dignified for everyone to know one's affairs. Nor is it considered dignified to snoop on others beyond the face presented in public. It does violence to a person's privacy and rights. In this, the people she describes are essentially the same as the people of the mixed, Americanized city street on which I live, and essentially the same as the people who live in high-income apartments or fine town houses, too.

A good city street neighborhood achieves a marvel of balance between its people's determination to have essential privacy and their simultaneous wishes for differing degrees of contact, enjoyment or help from the people around. This balance is largely made up of small, sensitively managed details, practiced and accepted so casually that they are normally taken for granted.

Perhaps I can best explain this subtle but all-important balance in terms of the stores where people leave keys for their friends, a common custom in New York. In our family, for example, when a friend wants to use our place while we are away for a weekend or everyone happens to be out during the day, or a visitor for whom we do not wish to wait up is spending the night, we tell such a friend that he can pick up the key at the delicatessen across the street. Joe Cornacchia, who keeps the delicatessen, usually has a dozen or so keys at a time for handing out like this. He has a special drawer for them.

Now why do I, and many others, select Joe as a logical custodian for keys? Because we trust him, first, to be a responsible custodian, but equally important because we know that he combines a feeling of good will with a feeling of no personal responsibility about our private affairs. Joe considers it no concern of his whom we choose to permit in our places and why.

Around on the other side of our block, people leave their keys at a Spanish grocery. On the other side of Joe's block, people leave them at the candy store. Down a block they leave them at the coffee shop, and a few hundred feet around the corner from that, in a barber shop. Around one corner from two fashionable blocks of town houses and apartments in the Upper East Side, people leave their keys in a butcher shop and a bookshop; around another corner they leave them in a cleaner's and a drug store. In unfashionable East Harlem keys are left with at least one florist, in bakeries, in luncheonettes, in Spanish and Italian groceries.

The point, wherever they are left, is not the kind of ostensible service that the enterprise offers, but the kind of proprietor it has.

A service like this cannot be formalized. Identifications . . . questions . . . insurance against mishaps. The all-essential line between public service and privacy would be transgressed by institutionalization. Nobody in his right mind would leave his key in such a place. The service must be given as a favor by someone with an unshakable understanding of the difference between a person's key and a person's private life, or it cannot be given at all.

Or consider the line drawn by Mr. Jaffe at the candy store around our corner—a line so well understood by his customers and by other storekeepers too that they can spend their whole lives in its presence and never think about it consciously. One ordinary morning last winter, Mr. Jaffe, whose formal business name is Bernie, and his wife, whose formal business name is Ann, supervised the small children crossing at the corner on the way to P.S. 41, as Bernie always does because he sees the need; lent an umbrella to one customer and a dollar to another; took custody of two keys; took in some packages for people in the next building who were away; lectured two youngsters who asked for cigarettes; gave street directions; took custody of a watch to give the repair man across the street when he opened later; gave out information on the range of rents in the neighborhood to an apartment seeker; listened to a tale of domestic difficulty and offered reassurance; told some rowdies they could not come in unless they behaved and then defined (and got) good behavior; provided an incidental forum for half a dozen conversations among customers who dropped in for oddments; set aside certain newly arrived papers and magazines for regular customers who would depend on getting them; advised a mother who came for a birthday present not to get the ship-model kit because another child going to the same birthday party was giving that; and got a back copy (this was for me) of the previous day's newspaper out of the deliverer's surplus returns when he came by.

After considering this multiplicity of extra-merchandising services I asked Bernie, "Do you ever introduce your customers to each other?"

He looked startled at the idea, even dismayed. "No," he said thoughtfully. "That would just not be advisable. Sometimes, if I know two customers who are in at the same time have an interest in common, I bring up the subject in conversation and let them carry it on from there if they want to. But oh no, I wouldn't introduce them."

When I told this to an acquaintance in a suburb, she promptly assumed that Mr. Jaffe felt that to make an introduction would be to step above his social class. Not at all. In our neighborhood, storekeepers like the Jaffes enjoy an excellent social status, that of businessmen. In income they are apt to be the peers of the general run of customers and in independence they are the superiors. Their advice, as men or women of common sense and experience, is sought and respected. They are well known as individuals, rather than unknown as class symbols. No; this is that almost unconsciously enforced, well-balanced line showing, the line between the city public world and the world of privacy.

This line can be maintained, without awkwardness to anyone, because of the great plenty of opportunities for public contact in the enterprises along the sidewalks, or on the sidewalks themselves as people move to and fro or deliberately loiter when they feel like it, and also because of the presence of many public hosts, so to speak, proprietors of meeting places like Bernie's where one is free either to hang around or dash in and out, no strings attached.

Under this system, it is possible in a city street neighborhood to know all kinds of people without unwelcome entanglements, without boredom, necessity for excuses, explanations, fears of giving offense, embarrassments respecting impositions or commitments, and all such paraphernalia of obligations which can accompany less limited relationships. It is possible to be on excellent sidewalk terms with people who are very different from oneself, and even, as time passes, on familiar public terms with them. Such relationships can, and do, endure for many years, for decades; they could never have formed without that line, much less endured. They form precisely because they are by-the-way to people's normal public sorties.

## Questions

1. In the first two paragraphs Jacobs defines "a good city street neighborhood." Are her standards applicable to suburban or rural neighborhoods? If not, how might they be adapted?
2. What other qualities define a good neighborhood for you? What makes for a bad neighborhood?

3. Jacobs doesn't speak here of how good neighborhoods, or bad, come into existence. What forces, in your opinion, create good or bad neighborhoods? Can the evolution of neighborhoods be predicted, or controlled?
4. If you reread the first paragraph, you will notice that the first sentence is unusually long and that the second is unusually short; the third is fairly long and the fourth fairly short. What is the effect of these two shorter sentences, beyond mere variety? Elsewhere in the essay, too, Jacobs's prose includes some very long sentences, but they probably did not confuse you. Why?

E. B. White

# The Door

Everything (he kept saying) is something it isn't. And everybody is always somewhere else. Maybe it was the city, being in the city, that made him feel how queer everything was and that it was something else. Maybe (he kept thinking) it was the names of the things. The names were tex and frequently koid. Or they were flex and oid or they were duroid (sani) or flexsan (duro), but everything was glass (but not quite glass) and the thing that you touched (the surface, washable, crease-resistant) was rubber, only it wasn't quite rubber and you didn't quite touch it but almost. The wall, which was glass but thrutex, turned out on being approached not to be a wall, it was something else, it was an opening or doorway—and the doorway (through which he saw himself approaching) turned out to be something else, it was a wall. And what he had eaten not having agreed with him.

He was in a washable house, but he wasn't sure. Now about those rats, he kept saying to himself. He meant the rats that the

E[lwyn] B[rooks] White was born in 1899. In 1926 he joined *The New Yorker,* and he published essays and stories regularly in it until 1938, when he became a columnist for *Harper's.* He returned to *The New Yorker* in 1945. Now retired in Maine, he continues to write.

Professor had driven crazy by forcing them to deal with problems which were beyond the scope of rats, the insoluble problems. He meant the rats that had been trained to jump at the square card with the circle in the middle, and the card (because it was something it wasn't) would give way and let the rat into a place where the food was, but then one day it would be a trick played on the rat, and the card would be changed, and the rat would jump but the card wouldn't give way, and it was an impossible situation (for a rat) and the rat would go insane and into its eyes would come the unspeakably bright imploring look of the frustrated, and after the convulsions were over and the frantic racing around, then the passive stage would set in and the willingness to let anything be done to it, even if it was something else.

He didn't know which door (or wall) or opening in the house to jump at, to get through, because one was an opening that wasn't a door (it was a void, or koid) and the other was a wall that wasn't opening, it was a sanitary cupboard of the same color. He caught a glimpse of his eyes staring into his eyes, in the thrutex, and in them was the expression he had seen in the picture of the rats—weary after convulsions and the frantic racing around, when they were willing and did not mind having anything done to them. More and more (he kept saying) I am confronted by a problem which is incapable of solution (for this time even if he chose the right door, there would be no food behind it) and that is what madness is, and things seeming different from what they are. He heard, in the house where he was, in the city to which he had gone (as toward a door which might, or might not, give way), a noise—not a loud noise but more of a low prefabricated humming. It came from a place in the base of the wall (or stat) where the flue carrying the filterable air was, and not far from the Minipiano, which was made of the same material nailbrushes are made of, and which was under the stairs. "This, too, has been tested," she said, pointing, but not at it, "and found viable." It wasn't a loud noise, he kept thinking, sorry that he had seen his eyes, even though it was through his own eyes that he had seen them.

First will come the convulsions (he said), then the exhaustion, then the willingness to let anything be done. "And you better believe it *will* be."

All his life he had been confronted by situations which were incapable of being solved, and there was a deliberateness behind all this, behind this changing of the card (or door), because they would always wait till you had learned to jump at the certain card (or door) —the one with the circle—and then they would change it on you. There have been so many doors changed on me, he said, in the last twenty years, but it is now becoming clear that it is an impossible situation, and the question is whether to jump again, even though they ruffle you in the rump with a blast of air—to make you jump. He wished he wasn't standing by the Minipiano. First they would teach you the prayers and the Psalms, and that would be the right door (the one with the circle) and the long sweet words with the holy sound, and that would be the one to jump at to get where the food was. Then one day you jumped and it didn't give way, so that all you got was the bump on the nose, and the first bewilderment, the first young bewilderment.

I don't know whether to tell her about the door they substituted or not, he said, the one with the equation on it and the picture of the amoeba reproducing itself by division. Or the one with the photostatic copy of the check for thirty-two dollars and fifty cents. But the jumping was so long ago, although the bump is . . . how those old wounds hurt! Being crazy this way wouldn't be so bad if only, if only. If only when you put your foot forward to take a step, the ground wouldn't come up to meet your foot the way it does. And the same way in the street (only I may never get back to the street unless I jump at the right door), the curb coming up to meet your foot, anticipating ever so delicately the weight of the body, which is somewhere else. "We could take your name," she said, "and send it to you." And it wouldn't be so bad if only you could read a sentence all the way through without jumping (your eye) to something else on the same page; and then (he kept thinking) there was that man out in Jersey, the one who started to chop his trees down, one by one, the man who began talking about how he would take his house to pieces, brick by brick, because he faced a problem incapable of solution, probably, so he began to hack at the trees in the yard, began to pluck with trembling fingers at the bricks in the house. Even if a house is not washable, it is worth taking down. It is not till later that the exhaustion sets in.

But it is inevitable that they will keep changing the doors on you, he said, because that is what they are for; and the thing is to get used to it and not let it unsettle the mind. But that would mean not jumping, and you can't. Nobody can not jump. There will be no not-jumping. Among rats, perhaps, but among people never. Everybody has to keep jumping at a door (the one with the circle on it) because that is the way everybody is, especially some people. You wouldn't want me, standing here, to tell you, would you, about my friend the poet (deceased) who said, "My heart has followed all my days something I cannot name"? (It had the circle on it.) And like many poets, although few so beloved, he is gone. It killed him, the jumping. First, of course, there were the preliminary bouts, the convulsions, and the calm and the willingness.

I remember the door with the picture of the girl on it (only it was spring), her arms outstretched in loveliness, her dress (it was the one with the circle on it) uncaught, beginning the slow, clear, blinding cascade—and I guess we would all like to try that door again, for it seemed like the way and for a while it was the way, the door would open and you would go through winged and exalted (like any rat) and the food would be there, the way the Professor had it arranged, everything O.K., and you had chosen the right door for the world was young. The time they changed that door on me, my nose bled for a hundred hours—how do you like that, Madam? Or would you prefer to show me further through this so strange house, or you could take my name and send it to me, for although my heart has followed all my days something I cannot name, I am tired of the jumping and I do not know which way to go, Madam, and I am not even sure that I am not tried beyond the endurance of man (rat, if you will) and have taken leave of sanity. What are you following these days, old friend, after your recovery from the last bump? What is the name, or is it something you cannot name? The rats have a name for it by this time, perhaps, but I don't know what they call it. I call it plexikoid and it comes in sheets, something like insulating board, unattainable and ugli-proof.

And there was the man out in Jersey, because I keep thinking about his terrible necessity and the passion and trouble he had gone to all those years in the indescribable abundance of a householder's detail, building the estate and the planting of the trees and in spring the lawn-dressing and in fall the bulbs for the spring burgeoning, and the watering of the grass on the long light evenings in summer and the gravel for the driveway (all had to be thought out, planned) and the decorative borders, probably, the perennials and the bug spray, and the building of the house from plans of the architect, first the sills, then the studs, then the full corn in the ear, the floors laid on the floor timbers, smoothed, and then the carpets upon the smooth floors and the curtains and the rods therefor. And then, almost without warning, he would be jumping at the same old door and it wouldn't give: they had changed it on him, making life no longer supportable under the elms in the elm shade, under the maples in the maple shade.

"Here you have the maximum of openness in a small room."

It was impossible to say (maybe it was the city) what made him feel the way he did, and I am not the only one either, he kept thinking —ask any doctor if I am. The doctors, they know how many there are, they even know where the trouble is only they don't like to tell you about the prefrontal lobe because that means making a hole in your skull and removing the work of centuries. It took so long coming, this lobe, so many, many years. (Is it something you read in the paper, perhaps?) And now, the strain being so great, the door having been changed by the Professor once too often . . . but it only means a whiff of ether, a few deft strokes, and the higher animal becomes a little easier in his mind and more like the lower one. From now on, you see, that's the way it will be, the ones with the small prefrontal lobes will win because the other ones are hurt too much by this incessant bumping. They can stand just so much, eh, Doctor? (And what is that, pray, that you have in your hand?) Still, you never can tell, eh, Madam?

He crossed (carefully) the room, the thick carpet under him softly, and went toward the door carefully, which was glass and he could see himself in it, and which, at his approach, opened to allow him to pass through; and beyond he half expected to find one of the old doors that he had known, perhaps the one with the circle, the one with the girl her arms outstretched in loveliness and beauty before him. But he saw instead a moving stairway, and descended in light (he kept thinking) to the street below and to the other people. As he stepped off, the ground came up slightly, to meet his foot.

## Questions

1. What information does the first paragraph give us about the story's setting and about the main character? What is the effect of all the parenthetical interruptions? How can White's use of a fragmentary sentence at the end of the paragraph be defended?
2. In the second paragraph, the man recalls an account of a psychologist's experiment. What was the experiment's purpose? Why does the man recall it?

3. Beginning with the fifth paragraph (page 145, "All his life"), the man reflects on the last twenty years of his life and on the "doors" that were constantly changed on him. What do the doors and their constant changing symbolize? He gives four examples. What are they, and what does each represent? Do the examples suggest that the man's problem is unique, or that it is shared by many of us?
4. What do the "man out in Jersey" and the "poet (deceased)" and the man have in common? How are they dissimilar?
5. In the next-to-last paragraph, the doctor offers the man a solution of a kind. What is it? What does White think of this solution?
6. Does the story have a happy ending? Explain.

## William Carlos Williams

# The Poor

It's the anarchy of poverty
delights me, the old
yellow wooden house indented
among the new brick tenements

Or a cast iron balcony
with panels showing oak branches
in full leaf. It fits
the dress of the children

reflecting every stage and
custom of necessity—
Chimneys, roofs, fences of
wood and metal in an unfenced

William Carlos Williams (1883–1963) was a pediatrician with a wide practice among the industrial population in and around Rutherford, New Jersey. He was also a prolific writer. His works include short stories, novels, essays, plays, poems, and an autobiography.

age and enclosing next to
nothing at all: the old man
in a sweater and soft black
hat who sweeps the sidewalk—

his own ten feet of it—
in a wind that fitfully
turning his corner has
overwhelmed the entire city

## Questions

1. In the context of the poem, how would you define "anarchy"?
2. Poverty does not usually inspire delight. How does the poem support the opening statement?

# 3
# TEACHING AND LEARNING

*Instruction at Home, Transylvania, Louisiana*
**Russell Lee, 1939**

Farm Security Administration Photo, Library of Congress

*The Lesson—Planning a Career*
**Ron James, 1963**

*St. Jerome Studying in His Cell*
**Georges de la Tour, c. 1640**

Bulloz

Washoe Makes the Sign for "Drink"
**T. J. Kaminski**

Courtesy R. A. and B. T. Gardner

# Short Views

Knowledge is power.

**Francis Bacon**

Hard students are commonly troubled with gouts, catarrahs, rheums, cachexia, bradypepsia, bad eyes, stone, and collick, crudities, oppilations, vertigo, winds, consumptions, and all such diseases as come by over-much sitting: they are most part lean, dry, ill-colored . . . and all through immoderate pains and extraordinary studies.

**Robert Burton**

In my opinion, the only justification for high schools is as therapeutic halfway houses for the deranged. Normal adolescents can find themselves and grow further only by coping with the jobs, sex, and chances of the real world—it is useless to feed them curricular imitations. I would simply abolish the high schools, substituting apprenticeships and other alternatives and protecting the young from gross exploitation by putting the school money directly in their pockets. The very few who have authentic scholarly interests will gravitate to their own libraries, teachers, and academies, as they always did in the past, when they could afford it. In organic communities, adolescents cluster together in their own youth houses, for their fun and games and loud music, without bothering sober folk. I see no reason whatsoever for adults to set up or direct such nests or to be there at all unless invited.

**Paul Goodman**

I can judge one of the main effects of personal grading by the attitudes of students who land in my remedial course in college. They hate and fear writing more than anything else they have had to do in school. If they see a blank sheet of paper on which they are expected to write something, they look as though they want to scream. Apparently they have never written anything that anyone thought was good. At least, no one ever *told* them that anything in their writing was good. All their teachers looked for were mistakes, and there are so many kinds of mistakes in writing that their students despair of ever learning to avoid them.

The attitude toward writing that these students have developed is well illustrated by a story told by the Russian writer Chekhov about a kitten that was given to his uncle. The uncle wanted to make the kitten a champion killer of mice, so while it was still very young, he showed it a live mouse in a cage. Since the kitten's hunting instinct had not yet developed, it examined the mouse curiously but without any hostility. The uncle wanted to teach it that such fraternizing with the enemy was wrong, so he slapped the kitten, scolded it, and sent it away in disgrace. The next day the same mouse was shown to the kitten again. This time the kitten regarded it rather fearfully but without any aggressive intent. Again the uncle slapped it, scolded it, and sent it away. This treatment went on day after day. After some time, as soon as the kitten saw or smelled that mouse, it screamed and tried to climb up the walls. At that point the uncle lost patience and gave the kitten away, saying that it was stupid and would never learn. Of course the kitten had learned perfectly, and had learned exactly what it had been taught, but unfortunately not what the uncle intended to teach. "I can sympathize with that kitten," says Chekhov, "because that same uncle tried to teach me Latin."

**Paul B. Diederich**

A woman came to Rabbi Israel, the great maggid or teacher in Koznitz, and told him, with many tears, that she had been married a dozen years and still had not borne a son. "What are you willing to do about it?" he asked her. She did not know what to say. "My mother," so the maggid told her, "was aging and still had no child. Then she heard that the holy Baal Shem was stopping over in Apt in the course of a journey. She hurried to his inn and begged him to pray she might bear a son. 'What are you willing to do about it?' he asked. 'My husband is a poor book-binder,' she replied, 'but I do have one fine thing that I shall give to the rabbi.' She went home as fast as she could and fetched her good cape, her 'Katinka,' which was carefully stowed away in a chest. But when she returned to the inn with it, she heard that the Baal Shem had already left for Mezbizh. She immediately set out after him and since she had no money to ride, she walked from town to town with her 'Katinka' until she came to Mezbizh. The Baal Shem took the cape and hung it on the wall. 'It is well,' he said. My mother walked all the way back, from town to town, until she reached Apt. A year later, I was born."

"I, too," cried the woman, "will bring you a cape of mine so that I may get a son."

"That won't work," said the maggid. "You heard the story. My mother had no story to go by."

**Hasidic Tale**

You go to a great school not for knowledge so much as for arts and habits; for the habit of attention, for the art of expression, for the art of assuming at a moment's notice a new intellectual posture, for the art of entering quickly into another person's thought, for the habit of submitting to censure and refutation, for the art of indicating assent or dissent in graduated terms, for the habit of regarding minute points of accuracy, for the habit of working out what is possible in a given time, for taste, for discrimination, for mental courage and mental soberness. Above all, you go to a great school for self-knowledge.

**William Cory**

How people keep correcting us when we are young! There's always some bad habit or other they tell us we ought to get over. Yet most bad habits are tools to help us through life.

**Johann Wolfgang von Goethe**

Supposing anyone were to suggest that the best results for the individual and society could be derived through compulsory feeding. Would not the most ignorant rebel against such a stupid procedure? And yet the stomach has far greater adaptability to almost any situation than the brain. With all that, we find it quite natural to have compulsory mental feeding.

Indeed, we actually consider ourselves superior to other nations, because we have evolved a compulsory brain tube through which, for a certain number of hours every day, and for so many years, we can force into the child's mind a large quantity of mental nutrition.

. . . The great harm done by our system of education is not so much that it teaches nothing worth knowing, that it helps to perpetuate privileged classes, that it assists them in the criminal procedure of robbing and exploiting the masses; the harm of the system lies in its boastful proclamation that it stands for true education, thereby enslaving the masses a great deal more than could an absolute ruler.

**Emma Goldman**

The education of women should always be relative to that of men. To please, to be useful to us, to make us love and esteem them, to educate us when young, to take care of us when grown up; to advise, to console us, to render our lives easy and agreeable. These are the duties of women at all times, and what they should be taught in their infancy.

**Jean Jacques Rousseau, *Emile***

If Johnny can't learn because he is hungry, that's the fault of poverty. But if Johnny can't pay attention because he is sleepy, that's the fault of parents.

What does it matter if we have a new book or an old book, if we open neither?

**Jesse Jackson**

*Education.* An education in things is not. We all are involved in the condemnation of words, an age of words. We are shut up in schools and college recitation rooms for ten or fifteen years, and come out at last with a bellyfull of words and do not know a thing. We cannot use our hands, or our legs, or our eyes, or our arms. We do not know an edible root in the woods. We cannot tell our course by the stars, nor the hour of the day by the sun. It is well if we can swim and skate. We are afraid of a horse, of a cow, of a dog, of a cat, of a spider. Far better was the Roman rule to teach a boy nothing that he could not learn standing. Now here are my wise young neighbors who, instead of getting, like the woodmen, into a railroad-car, where they have not even the activity of holding the reins, have got into a boat which they have built with their own hands, with sails which they have contrived to serve as a tent by night, and gone up the Merrimack to live by their wits on the fish of the stream and the berries of the wood. My worthy neighbor Dr. Bartlett expressed a true parental instinct when he desired to send his boy with them to learn something. The farm, the farm, is the right school. The reason of my deep respect for the farmer is that he is a realist, and not a dictionary. The farm is a piece of the world, the school-house is not. The farm, by training the physical, rectifies and invigorates the metaphysical and moral nature.

**Ralph Waldo Emerson**

Universities are, of course, hostile to geniuses.

**Ralph Waldo Emerson**

The man who can make hard things easy is the educator.

**Ralph Waldo Emerson**

It is perhaps idle to wonder what, from my present point of view, would have been an ideal education. If I could provide such a curriculum for my own children they, in their turn, might find it all a bore. But the fantasy of what I would have liked to learn as a child may be revealing, since I feel unequipped by education for problems that lie outside the cloistered, literary domain in which I am competent and at home. Looking back, then, I would have arranged for myself to be taught survival techniques for both natural and urban wildernesses. I would want to have been instructed in self-hypnosis, in *aikido* (the esoteric and purely self-defensive style of judo), in elementary medicine, in sexual hygiene, in vegetable gardening, in astronomy, navigation, and sailing; in cookery and clothesmaking, in metalwork and carpentry, in drawing and painting, in printing and typography, in botany and biology, in optics and acoustics, in semantics and psychology, in mysticism and yoga, in electronics and mathematical fantasy, in drama and dancing, in singing and in playing an instrument by ear; in wandering, in advanced daydreaming, in prestidigitation, in techniques of escape from bondage, in disguise, in conversation with birds and beasts, in ventriloquism, in French and German conversation, in planetary history, in morphology, and in classical Chinese. Actually, the main thing left out of my education was a proper love for my own body, because one feared to cherish anything so obviously mortal and prone to sickness.

**Alan Watts**

If then a practical end must be assigned to a University course, I say it is that of training good members of society. Its art is the art of social life, and its end is fitness for the world. It neither confines its views to particular professions on the one hand, nor creates heroes or inspires genius on the other. Works indeed of genius fall under no art; heroic minds come under no rule; a University is not a birthplace of poets or of immortal authors, of founders of schools, leaders of colonies, or conquerors of nations.

It does not promise a generation of Aristotles or Newtons, of Napoleons or Washingtons, of Raphaels or Shakespeares, though such miracles of nature it has before now contained within its precincts. Nor is it content on the other hand with forming the critic or the experimentalist, the economist or the engineer, though such too it includes within its scope. But a University training is the great ordinary means to a great but ordinary end; it aims at raising the intellectual tone of society, at cultivating the public mind, at purifying the national taste, at supplying true principles to popular enthusiasm and fixed aims to popular aspiration, at giving enlargement and sobriety to the ideas of the age, at facilitating the exercise of political power, and refining the intercourse of private life. It is the education which gives a man a clear conscious view of his own opinions and judgments, a truth in developing them, an eloquence in expressing them, and a force in urging them. It teaches him to see things as they are, to go right to the point, to disentangle a skein of thought, to detect what is sophistical, and to discard what is irrelevant. It prepares him to fill any post with credit, and to master any subject with facility. It shows him how to accommodate himself to others, how to throw himself into their state of mind, how to bring before them his own, how to influence them, how to come to an understanding with them, how to bear with them.

**John Henry Newman**

Education! Which of the various me's do you propose to educate, and which do you propose to suppress?

**D. H. Lawrence**

Think about the kind of world you want to live and work in. What do you need to know to build the world? Demand that your teachers teach you that.

**Prince Kropotkin**

The entire object of true education is to make people not merely *do* the right things, but *enjoy* the right things.

**John Ruskin**

## Plato

# The Myth of the Cave

And now, I said, let me show in a figure how far our nature is enlightened or unenlightened:—Behold! human beings living in an underground den, which has a mouth open toward the light and reaching all along the den; here they have been from their childhood, and have their legs and necks chained so that they cannot

---

Plato (427–347 B.C.), born in Athens, the son of an aristocratic family, wrote thirty dialogues in which Socrates is the chief speaker. Socrates, about twenty-five years older than Plato, was a philosopher who called himself a gadfly to Athenians. For his efforts at stinging them into thought the Athenians executed him in 399 B.C. "The Myth of the Cave" is the beginning of Book VII of Plato's dialogue entitled *The Republic.* Socrates is talking with Glaucon.

For Plato, true knowledge is philosophic insight or awareness of the Good, not mere opinion or the knack of getting along in this world by remembering how things have usually worked in the past. To illustrate his idea that awareness of the Good is different from the ability to recognize the things of this shabby world, Plato (through his spokesman Socrates) resorts to an allegory: men imprisoned in a cave see on a wall in front of them the shadows or images of objects that are really behind them, and they hear echoes, not real voices. (The shadows are caused by the light from a fire behind the objects, and the echoes by the cave's acoustical properties.) The prisoners, unable to perceive the real objects and the real voices, mistakenly think that the shadows and the echoes are real, and some of them grow highly adept at dealing with this illusory world. Were Plato writing today, he might have made the cave a movie theater: we see on the screen in front of us images caused by an object (film, passing in front of light) that is behind us. Moreover, the film itself is an illusory image, for it bears only the traces of a yet more real world—the world that was photographed—outside of the movie theater. And when we leave the theater to go into the real world, our eyes have become so accustomed to the illusory world that we at first blink with discomfort—just as Plato's freed prisoners do when they move out of the cave—at the real world of bright day, and we long for the familiar darkness. So too, Plato suggests, dwellers in ignorance may prefer the familiar shadows of their unenlightened world ("the world of becoming") to the bright world of the eternal Good ("the world of being") that education reveals.

We have just used the word "education." You will notice that the first sentence in the translation (by Benjamin Jowett) says that the myth will show "how far our nature is enlightened or unenlightened." In the original Greek the words here translated "enlightened" and "unenlightened" are *paideia* and *apaideusia.* No translation can fully catch the exact meanings of these elusive words. Depending on the context, *paideia* may be translated as "enlightenment," "education," "civilization," "culture," "knowledge of the good."

---

move, and can only see before them, being prevented by the chains from turning round their heads. Above and behind them a fire is blazing at a distance, and between the fire and the prisoners there is a raised way; and you will see, if you look, a low wall built along the way, like the screen which marionette players have in front of them, over which they show the puppets.

I see.

And do you see, I said, men passing along the wall carrying all sorts of vessels, and statues and figures of animals made of wood and stone and various materials, which appear over the wall? Some of them are talking, others silent.

You have shown me a strange image, and they are strange prisoners.

Like ourselves, I replied; and they see only their own shadows, or the shadows of one another, which the fire throws on the opposite wall of the cave?

True, he said; how could they see anything but the shadows if they were never allowed to move their heads?

And of the objects which are being carried in like manner they would only see the shadows?

Yes, he said.

And if they were able to converse with one another, would they not suppose that they were naming what was actually before them?

Very true.

And suppose further that the prison had an echo which came from the other side, would they not be sure to fancy when one of the passers-by spoke that the voice which they heard came from the passing shadow?

No question, he replied.

To them, I said, the truth would be literally nothing but the shadows of the images.

That is certain.

And now look again, and see what will naturally follow if the prisoners are released and disabused of their error. At first, when any of them is liberated and compelled suddenly to stand up and turn his neck round and walk and look toward the light, he will suffer sharp pains; the glare will distress him, and he will be unable to see the realities of which in his former state he had seen the shadows; and then conceive some one saying to him, that what he saw before was an illusion, but that now, when he is approaching nearer to being and his eye is turned toward more real existence, he has a clearer vision

—what will be his reply? And you may further imagine that his instructor is pointing to the objects as they pass and requiring him to name them—will he not be perplexed? Will he not fancy that the shadows which he formerly saw are truer than the objects which are now shown to him?

Far truer.

And if he is compelled to look straight at the light, will he not have a pain in his eyes which will make him turn away to take refuge in the objects of vision which he can see, and which he will conceive to be in reality clearer than the things which are now being shown to him?

True, he said.

And suppose once more, that he is reluctantly dragged up a steep and rugged ascent, and held fast until he is forced into the presence of the sun himself, is he not likely to be pained and irritated? When he approaches the light his eyes will be dazzled, and he will not be able to see anything at all of what are now called realities.

Not all in a moment, he said.

He will require to grow accustomed to the sight of the upper world. And first he will see the shadows best, next the reflections of men and other objects in the water, and then the objects themselves; then he will gaze upon the light of the moon and the stars and the spangled heaven; and he will see the sky and the stars by night better than the sun or the light of the sun by day?

Certainly.

Last of all he will be able to see the sun, and not mere reflections of him in the water, but he will see him in his own proper place, and not in another; and he will contemplate him as he is.

Certainly.

He will then proceed to argue that this is he who gives the season and the years, and is the guardian of all that is in the visible world, and in a certain way the cause of all things which he and his fellows have been accustomed to behold?

Clearly, he said, he would first see the sun and then reason about him.

And when he remembered his old habitation, and the wisdom of the den and his fellow-prisoners, do you not suppose that he would felicitate himself on the change, and pity them?

Certainly, he would.

And if they were in the habit of conferring honors among themselves on those who were quickest to observe the passing shadows and to remark which of them went before, and which followed after, and which were together; and who were therefore best able to draw conclusions as to the future, do you think that he would care for such honors and glories, or envy the possessors of them? Would he not say with Homer,

> Better to be the poor servant of a poor master,

and to endure anything, rather than think as they do and live after their manner?

Yes, he said, I think that he would rather suffer anything than entertain these false notions and live in this miserable manner.

Imagine once more, I said, such an one coming suddenly out of the sun to be replaced in his old situation; would he not be certain to have his eyes full of darkness?

To be sure, he said.

And if there were a contest, and he had to compete in measuring the shadows with the prisoners who had never moved out of the den, while his sight was still weak, and before his eyes had become steady (and the time which would be needed to acquire this new habit of sight might be very considerable), would he not be ridiculous? Men would say of him that up he went and down he came without his eyes; and that it was better not even to think of ascending; and if any one tried to loose another and lead him up to the light, let them only catch the offender, and they would put him to death.

No question, he said.

This entire allegory, I said, you may now append, dear Glaucon, to the previous argument; the prison-house is the world of sight, the light of the fire is the sun, and you will not misapprehend me if you interpret the journey upwards to be the ascent of the soul into the intellectual world according to my poor belief, which, at your desire, I have expressed—whether rightly or wrongly God knows. But, whether true or false, my opinion is that in the world of knowledge the idea of good appears last of all, and is seen only with an effort; and, when seen, is also inferred to be the universal author of all things beautiful and right, parent of light and of the lord of light in this visible world, and the immediate source of reason and truth in the intellectual; and that this is the power upon which he who would act rationally either in public or private life must have his eye fixed.

I agree, he said, as far as I am able to understand you.

Moreover, I said, you must not wonder that those who attain to this beatific vision are unwilling to descend to human affairs; for their souls are ever hastening into the upper world where they desire to dwell; which desire of theirs is very natural, if our allegory may be trusted.

Yes, very natural.

And is there anything surprising in one who passes from divine contemplations to the evil state of man, misbehaving himself in a ridiculous manner; if, while his eyes are blinking and before he has become accustomed to the surrounding darkness, he is compelled to fight in courts of law, or in other places, about the images or the shadows of images of justice, and is endeavoring to meet the conceptions of those who have never yet seen absolute justice?

Anything but surprising, he replied.

Any one who has common sense will remember that the bewilderments of the eyes are of two kinds, and arise from two causes, either from coming out of the light or from going into the light, which is true of the mind's eye, quite as much as of the bodily eye; and he who remembers this when he sees any one whose vision is perplexed and weak, will not be too ready to laugh; he will first ask whether that soul of man has come out of the brighter life, and is unable to see because unaccustomed to the dark, or having turned from darkness to the day is dazzled by excess of light. And he will count the one happy in his condition and state of being, and he will pity the other; or, if he have a mind to laugh at the soul which comes from below into the light, there will be more reason in this than in the laugh which greets him who returns from above out of the light into the den.

That, he said, is a very just distinction.

But then, if I am right, certain professors of education must be wrong when they say that they can put a knowledge into the soul which was not there before, like sight into blind eyes.

They undoubtedly say this, he replied.

Whereas, our argument shows that the power and capacity of learning exists in the soul already; and that just as the eye was unable to turn from darkness to light without the whole body, so too the instrument of knowledge can only by the movement of the whole soul be turned from the world of becoming into that of being, and learn by degrees to endure the sight of being, and of the brightest and best of being, or in other words, of the good.

Very true.

And must there not be some art which will effect conversion in the easiest and quickest manner; not implanting the faculty of sight, for that exists already, but has been turned in the wrong direction, and is looking away from the truth?

Yes, he said, such an art may be presumed.

And whereas the other so-called virtues of the soul seem to be akin to bodily qualities, for even when they are not originally innate they can be implanted later by habit and exercise, the virtue of wisdom more than anything else contains a divine element which always remains, and by this conversion is rendered useful and profitable; or, on the other hand, hurtful and useless. Did you never observe the narrow intelligence flashing from the keen eye of a clever rogue—how eager he is, how clearly his paltry soul sees the way to his end; he is the reverse of blind, but his keen eyesight is forced into the service of evil, and he is mischievous in proportion to his cleverness?

Very true, he said.

But what if there had been a circumcision of such natures in the days of their youth; and they had been severed from those sensual pleasures, such as eating and drinking, which, like leaden weights, were attached to them at their birth, and which drag them down and turn the vision of their souls upon the things that are below—if, I say, they had been released from these impediments and turned in the opposite direction, the very same faculty in them would have seen the truth as keenly as they see what their eyes are turned to now.

Very likely.

Yes, I said; and there is another thing which is likely, or rather a necessary inference from what has preceded, that neither the uneducated and uninformed of the truth, nor yet those who never make an end of their education, will be able ministers of State; not the former, because they have no single aim of duty which is the rule of all their actions, private as well as public; nor the latter, because they will not act at all except upon compulsion, fancying that they are already dwelling apart in the islands of the blest.

Very true, he replied.

Then, I said, the business of us who are the founders of the State will be to compel the best minds to attain that knowledge which we have already shown to be the greatest of all—they must continue to ascend until they arrive at the good; but when they have ascended and seen enough we must not allow them to do as they do now.

What do you mean?

I mean that they remain in the upper world: but this must not be allowed; they must be made to descend again among the prisoners in the den, and partake of their labors and honors, whether they are worth having or not.

But is not this unjust? he said; ought we to give them a worse life, when they might have a better?

You have again forgotten, my friend, I said, the intention of the legislator, who did not aim at making any one class in the State happy above the rest; the happiness was to be in the whole State, and he held the citizens together by persuasion and necessity, making them benefactors of the State, and therefore benefactors of one another; to this end he created them, not to please themselves, but to be his instruments in binding up the State.

True, he said, I had forgotten.

Observe, Glaucon, that there will be no injustice in compelling our philosophers to have a care and providence of others; we shall explain to them that in other States, men of their class are not obliged to share in the toils of politics: and this is reasonable, for they grow up at their own sweet will, and the government would rather not have them. Being self-taught, they cannot be expected to show any gratitude for a culture which they have never received. But we have brought you into the world to be rulers of the hive, kings of yourselves and of the other citizens, and have educated you far better and more perfectly than they have been educated, and you are better able to share in the double duty. Wherefore each of you, when his turn comes, must go down to the general underground abode, and get the habit of seeing in the dark. When you have acquired the habit, you will see ten thousand times better than the inhabitants of the den, and you will know what the several images are, and what they represent, because you have seen the beautiful and just and good in their truth. And thus our State which is also yours will be a reality, and not a dream only, and will be administered in a spirit unlike that of other States, in which men fight with one another about shadows only and are distracted in the struggle for power, which in their eyes is a great good. Whereas the truth is that the State in which the rulers are most reluctant to govern is always the best and most quietly governed, and the State in which they are most eager, the worst.

Quite true, he replied.

And will our pupils, when they hear this, refuse to take their turn at the toils of State, when they are allowed to spend the greater part of their time with one another in the heavenly light?

Impossible, he answered; for they are just men, and the commands which we impose upon them are just; there can be no doubt that every one of them will take office as a stern necessity, and not after the fashion of our present rulers of State.

Yes, my friend, I said; and there lies the point. You must contrive for your future rulers another and a better life than that of a ruler, and then you may have a well-ordered State; for only in the State which offers this, will they rule who are truly rich, not in silver and gold, but in virtue and wisdom, which are the true blessings of life. Whereas if they go to the administration of public affairs, poor and hungering after their own private advantage, thinking that hence they are to snatch the chief good, order there can never be; for they will be fighting about office, and the civil and domestic broils which thus arise will be the ruin of the rulers themselves and of the whole State.

Most true, he replied.

And the only life which looks down upon the life of political ambition is that of true philosophy. Do you know of any other?

Indeed, I do not, he said.

And those who govern ought not to be lovers of the task? For, if they are, there will be rival lovers, and they will fight.

No question.

Who then are those whom we shall compel to be guardians? Surely they will be the men who are wisest about affairs of State, and by whom the State is best administered, and who at the same time have other honors and another and a better life than that of politics?

They are the men, and I will choose them, he replied.

And now shall we consider in what way such guardians will be produced, and how they are to be brought from darkness to light— as some are said to have ascended from the world below to the gods?

By all means, he replied.

The process, I said, is not the turning over of an oyster-shell,[1] but the turning round of a soul passing from a day which is little better than night to the true day of being, that is, the ascent from below which we affirm to be true philosophy?

Quite so.

[1]In allusion to a game in which two parties fled or pursued according as an oyster-shell which was thrown into the air fell with the dark or light side uppermost.

## Questions

1. Plato is not merely reporting one of Socrates' conversations; he is teaching. What advantages does a dialogue have over a narrative or an essay as a way of teaching philosophy? How is the form of a dialogue especially suited to solving a problem?
2. If you don't know the etymology of the word "conversion," look it up in a dictionary. How is the etymology appropriate to Plato's idea about education.
3. On page 164 describing the prisoner as "reluctantly dragged" upward and "forced" to look at the sun, Socrates asks: "Is he not likely to be pained and irritated?" Can you recall experiencing pain and irritation while learning something you later were glad to have learned? Can you recall learning something new *without* experiencing pain and irritation?
4. "The State in which the rulers are most reluctant to govern is always the best and most quietly governed, and the State in which they are most eager, the worst" (page 168). What does Socrates mean? Using examples from contemporary politics, defend this proposition, or argue against it.
5. Can you account for the power of this myth or fable? In our introductory comment (page 162) we tried to clarify the message by saying that a movie theater might serve as well as a cave, but in fact if the story were recast using a movie theater, would the emotional power be the same? Why or why not?
6. The metaphors of education as conversion and ascent are linked by the metaphor of light. Consider such expressions as "I see" (meaning "I understand") and "Let me give an illustration" (from the Latin *in* = in, and *lustrare* = to make bright). What other expressions about light are used metaphorically to describe intellectual comprehension?

## Ernesto Galarza

# Growing into Manhood

Up to the time a boy was between five and six years old, Jalcocotán was for the most part an easy place in which to live. The neighbors and *compadres* and *comadres* who scolded you for your bad manners or sent you on errands did not interfere much if you were respectful and stayed out of the way. With my two cousins and other boys of my own age I always had something to watch or to do.

The near side of the pond was shallow and fringed with reeds and tall clumps of grass that blossomed with plumes of cream-colored fluff. Around them the pond was always muddy and cool. In your bare feet you sank up to the ankles and by wriggling your toes you could raise oozy, iridescent bubbles. Trampling and squishing the mud, we made plopping hollow sounds and pretended we had gas on our stomachs. Pulling your foot out of the soft gumbo while your friends listened closely made noise remarkably like the mules in the corrals when they dropped manure.

Although we never collected polliwogs or frogs or lizards we chased them along the mud flat until they hopped into deep water or slithered away in the grass. Water snakes were everywhere, which we imagined were poisonous *víboras* or copperheads, like those the *jalcocotecanos* found in the forest. We spiced our play with a legend about an alligator that had crawled all the way up from Miramar and lay in wait for us somewhere in a deep pool of the arroyo—a monster no less real because he lived only in our imagination.

When the older boys of the village came to the pond on Sunday afternoons we watched them swim and dive. From a high branch of the big *nogal* they dropped a swing made of bush vines we called *liana,* braided like the women of the pueblo did their hair. The boy who was to dive next waited up in the *nogal.* Another handed him the end of the *liana.* The diver kicked off and let go as high as he could swing, his naked brown body twisting through the air like a

Ernesto Galarza, a teacher, writer, and lecturer, lives in San Jose, California. "Growing into Manhood" (editors' title) is from Part One of *Barrio Boy,* a book that began, Galarza says, "as anecdotes I told my family about Jalcocotán, the mountain village in western Mexico where I was born."

split string bean. On our side of the swimming hole the smaller boys stripped and paddled while the divers yelled instructions on strokes and kicks.

Once in a great while the older boys would also allow us to join them in the bullfights they organized in one corner of the pasture. The bulls, the matadores, and the picadores were the ten- to twelve-year-olds, and the master of the fight was the oldest of the gang. We were permitted to take part only as fans or *aficionados,* to provide the yelling, the catcalls and the cheers. The master of the *corrida* directed us to sit on the ground on the upper slope of the bullring, which was entirely imaginary.

From behind a tree a trumpeter stepped to the edge of the ring. Blowing on a make-believe bugle he sounded a call and the bull rushed in—a boy with a plain sarape over his shoulders, holding with both hands in front of his chest the bleached skull of a steer complete with horns. Between the horns a large, thick cactus leaf from which the thorns had been removed, was tied. It was at the cactus pad that the matadores and picadores aimed their wooden swords and bamboo spears.

If the fight went according to the rules, the master declared the bull dead after a few rushes, by counting the stabs into the cactus, and the dead bull was replaced by a live one. Sometimes a sword or a spear missed the cactus pad and poked the bull in the stomach or some more sensitive spot. If the bull suspected that the miss was on purpose and dropped his skull to charge the torero with his fists, there was a free-for-all. We *aficionados* fell on one another with grunts and kicks, wrestling on the ground to increase the bedlam. If the commotion got out of the hands of the master of the *corrida,* there was always an adult watching from the village across the arroyo, who would walk over to the ring to scatter the rioters and send them home.

The girls of the village, needless to say, did not take part in the swimming parties or in the action of the bullfights. Neither did we, the boys who were under seven years of age.

This by no means put us in the same class. Up to his third year, a boy could still be led by the hand or undressed by an older sister. He was a *chilpayate,* a toddler who could play on the street naked without anybody noticing it. Little by little the *chilpayates* became men of sorts. They noticed that only girls had their earlobes pierced, wearing bits of string until their parents could afford genuine rings. They had to sit for hours to have their hair braided. At five years of age girls began to learn to carry water up from the arroyo in *ollas,* holding them on top of their heads with both hands, something that no man in Jalco would think of doing. They played silly games like La Ronda, hopping around and around, we thought, like *zopilotes.* Boys did girls' chores only if, and everybody knew that it was only if, there were no girls in the family—like shaking and sunning the bed mats or sprinkling the street in front of your cottage.

Between five and six, the fact that girls belonged to a lower class became even more obvious. Boys went into the forest to gather firewood. If their father's *milpa* or banana patch was not too far away they would be sent off before noon with a hot lunch in the haversack. They picked coffee beans on the lower branches of the bushes. They were taught to halter the burros and water them at the arroyo. They cut and bundled weeds in the *milpa* to feed the hens and the stock.

When a Jalco boy was passing six years of age and had become used to such jobs, he spent more and more of his day with the men and less time with the women. He was given more important tasks, which had a great deal to do with his becoming a man: "para que se vaya haciendo hombre." At six, a boy stood about as tall as a machete, but he would not be able to use one for several years. By the time he was fourteen he would be a man, complete with a machete of his own, working the *milpa* or the coffee patch or the banana stand by the side of his father, and able to do it by himself, if necessary.

Somewhere between seven and fourteen the village noticed other signs of his coming manhood. The surest of these was his watching the girls when they went to the arroyo to scrub clothes and bathe. We under-sixers could do this anyway without anyone paying attention or chasing us off. Sitting high on a boulder just above the pond I could see them, with a white skirt pulled up and pinned over one shoulder, slapping the clothes on the rocks, dipping them in the water and wringing them. When the washing was over they slipped off the skirt and slid into a pool, dunking themselves, chattering and laughing above the noise of the current. That was how I found out, without my folks making any particular fuss, that there were at least two important differences between boys and girls besides the braids and the perforated ears.

That was not, however, real girl watching. Around twelve years, boys stood away, behind a tree or a bush. If someone noticed, they pretended that they were going into the forest or to the *milpa* to work.

After you picked out a girl you began watching her in the village, coming closer step by step until everybody knew it. In this way the girl was staked out and every other young man in the pueblo was on notice. Any other watcher would have to fight for it sooner or later. All this took time; if you began watching when you were around twelve by the time you were sixteen you could propose, asking your parents to ask hers for permission to get married.

All this happened only if the parents of the girl liked you. If they didn't, her father would let you know. Jalco was a small, tight town and you could easily be caught shadowing the girl or even speaking to her. She would most likely get a beating, and you might be chased away by her father or brothers.

But you were not ready to take the risks of going steady in Jalco until you had proved yourself a man at work. At six years of age or thereabouts you stopped being a playmate and became an apprentice. Jacinto and his father were a good example of this.

Chinto, as we called him, became an apprentice *campesino* when he was only a little older than I. I saw them pass in front of our cottage in the early dawn, Chinto following his *jefe* to their cornpatch down the mountain. The man walked ahead, his cotton pants cinched tightly to his waist, one side of the fly crossed over the other and tucked into the waistband. The legs of the *calzones* were wound snug to the ankles, like puttees. At this time of the day the grass along the path to the *milpa* would be heavy with dew; the puttees soaked up less moisture than the bell-bottoms of the pants legs when they were loose. The soles and leather thongs of the huaraches the father wore were the soiled brown color of his ankles and toes. The hat was the usual ice cream cone of straw set on a wide brim curving down over the eyes and upward above the neck. He carried a machete in a sheath with the rawhide loop over one shoulder, and over the other the lunch bag.

Jacinto walked behind, dressed exactly like his father, except that he did not carry a machete. Several paces behind, he trotted to keep up with the steady gait of the man, learning the first lesson of his life as a *campesino:* that he would spend the rest of his life walking, walking, walking. "Ay va Jacinto con su papá," someone said in the gloom of our kitchen. It was the end of another boy and the beginning of another man.

They came back at nightfall in the same way, the man leading the boy. Both had rolled their pants legs above the knees, their white cotton shirts open in front, their hats tilted back. The man carried his huaraches over his shoulder. When the trail had roughened and calloused the feet of the boy, he would do the same.

The daily rounds that Jacinto and his father made were either to the cornpatch, the *platanar* where they cultivated banana trees or to the few rows of peppers and *jitomate* they tended. We knew the day that Jacinto went to pick coffee berries with his father, because they both carried wicker baskets, the man a large one, Jacinto a small one. When they left the village for several days to herd cattle for a *patrón,* father and son carried rawhide slings, the father a long sling, the boy a short one. Rounding up heifers and calves, the father taught the boy to whirl the sling and let one end go, timing it so the pebble would strike the target. Jacinto showed us how, when he was practicing in the pasture.

Jacinto and the other seven-year-olds who were growing into manhood lost no time in making it clear to the rest of us that we were nothing but stay-at-homes. As we felt more important than girls, so Jacinto and his fellow apprentices felt more important than us. It took courage to walk toward the *milpa* through the forest where you could step on a rattler any moment, if you didn't see it coiled in the path or hear its tail buzzing. It took stamina to weed the corn hills and the banana trees under the broiling sun. Only a boy with manstuff in him could walk down the mountain and up the next ridge to spend the night tending heaps of burning wood to make charcoal that the burros carried to Tepic and San Blas. At night from Jalco we could see the orange bonfires high up on the mountain to the east. We saw Jacinto come back with his father from such work—jaunty *carboneros* with rolled-up pants legs, hats tilted back, face and legs and arms smeared with charcoal, dust, and sweat.

It was in the cultivated patches in the forest that boys grew into men. With machetes they cleared the steep slopes and the hollows, setting fire to the brush and the stumps. In the ashes they planted corn, beans, peppers, *jitomate,* and bananas. Under the shade of a tall tree they grew coffee bushes. The forest provided the rest of Jalcocotán's living—timber, charcoal, wild fruit, herbs, bears, deer, and hides from alligators and cougars.

Out of the forest a man took out only what he and his family could use. Not all the *campesinos* in Jalcocotán, or in all the pueblos on the mountain together took out so much that the *monte* and the arroyo could not replenish themselves. In the conversation of the townspeople there were ancient sayings—*dichos*—that showed how long the people and the forest had lived together: "Agua que no has de beber, déjala correr"—at the arroyo drink your fill, let the rest run down the hill. "El que a buen árbol se arrima buena sombra le da"—the shade beneath a goodly tree is good for you and good for me.

Other than the stone walls of their corrals, the *jalcocotecanos* did not build fences to separate one man's property from another's. When the soil wore out in a *milpa* and another one was cleared, there were no old fences to take down or new ones to put up.

The world of work into which Jacinto and the other seven-year-olds were apprenticed was within sight and sound of the pueblo. It was work under blazing suns, in rainstorms, in pitch-black nights. It was work that you were always walking to or walking from, work without wages and work without end. It was work that gave you a bone-tired feeling at the end of the day, so you learned to swing a machete, to tighten a cinch, and to walk without lost motion. Between seven and twelve you learned all this, each lesson driven home when your *jefe* said with a scowl: "Así no, hombre; así." And he showed you how.

But he knew that there was another world of work beyond Jalco. Over in Miramar, Los Cocos, Puga and such places there were haciendas where peasants from the pueblos could work for money. Some *jalcocotecanos* did this kind of hiring out. They cut sugarcane, herded cattle, butchered steers, tended the crops, gathered coconuts for the soap works, and cleared land *a puro machetazo*—with your bare hands and a machete.

Boys who went with their fathers to the haciendas soon learned the differences between making a living on the mountain and working for the *patrones.* One was that on the mountain you took home corn, bananas, peppers, coffee, and anything else you had raised, but never money. From the hacienda, when your contract ended, you never took anything to eat or wear except what you paid for at the *tienda de raya,* the company store. A peon could make as much as ten pesos a month at hard labor working from dawn to dusk, seven days a week, four weeks every month. It came to about two or three centavos per hour, plus your meals and a place to spread you straw sleeping mat.

The most important difference, however, was the *capataz,* the riding boss who watched the laborers all day long, just as the *guardia* watched them throughout the night. The business of the *capataz* was to keep the *peonanda,* as the crews of field hands were called, hustling at the assigned tasks. He carried a machete slung from his saddle, a whip, and often a pistol: the equipment of a top sergeant of the hacienda. The captain was the *Administrador,* who in turn took his orders from the *patrón* who probably lived in Tepic or Guadalajara or perhaps even in La Capital, as everyone called Mexico City.

The men who had worked on haciendas knew of these matters. We heard snatches of firsthand reports from them but mostly we learned from Don Catarino, José, Don Cleofas, and the muleteers who passed through Jalco. Whoever had been there came back cursing it. The riding boss was the Devil on horseback; in the company store every centavo you earned was taken back by a clerk who kept numbers in a book that proved you always owed him something. If a peon left the hacienda before his contract was over and his debts were paid, he became a fugitive. He either returned to his pueblo, his *compadres* and his *milpa* in some far-off place in the mountains, or he scratched for a living, lost in the forest. Old men in the village talked of the time they had worked on a hacienda as if they had served a sentence in prison or on a chain gang. They remembered capataces who had whipped them or cursed them fifty years before, and they still murmured a phrase: "Algún día me la pagan." There were a hundred blood debts of this kind in Jalcocotán, Doña Esther said, thousands of them in all the villages of the Sierra Madre, and millions in all the pueblos of Mexico.

"Algún día me la pagan."

"Tía, what does that mean?" I asked her more than once. She always sent me to my mother with the question. Her answer was: "It means that somebody owes him something."

"But what does somebody owe him?"

The anger and the foreboding in "algún día me la pagan" was in my mother's voice: "Something that hurts." She did not explain, just as she would not tell me why Catalino the bandit hated the *rurales* and shot so many of them.

Guessing at what people meant, I came to *feel* certain words rather than to *know* them. They were words which came from the lips of the *jalcocotecanos* with an accent of suspicion, of fear, and of hatred. These words were *los rurales,* the *jefe politico,* the *señor gobernador, las autoridades, el gobierno.* When a stranger rode into Jalco, people stopped talking. Every detail about him and his horse was observed for a clue as to whether he was one of the *autoridades.*

It was the same with all outsiders. They always came asking questions, which the *jalcocotecanos* answered politely but roundabout. For me the world began to divide itself into two kinds of people—the men on horseback and the men who walked.

## Questions

1. Summarize the contents of the first seven paragraphs. How has Galarza organized his materials in these paragraphs? What other ways of organizing them can you imagine? What is the function of the eighth paragraph?
2. In this chapter from *Barrio Boy* Galarza reflects on several distinct areas in the education and indoctrination of the child into the world of the adult. What are they? Could you outline, with comparable distinctness, parts of your own education and indoctrination? If not, why not?

E. B. White

# Education

I have an increasing admiration for the teacher in the country school where we have a third-grade scholar in attendance. She not only undertakes to instruct her charges in all the subjects of the first three grades, but she manages to function quietly and effectively as a guardian of their health, their clothes, their habits, their mothers, and their snowball engagements. She has been doing this sort of Augean task for twenty years, and is both kind and wise. She cooks for the children on the stove that heats the room, and she can cool their passions or warm their soup with equal competence. She conceives their costumes, cleans up their messes, and shares their confidences. My boy already regards his teacher as his great friend, and I think tells her a great deal more than he tells us.

The shift from city school to country school was something we worried about quietly all last summer. I have always rather favored public school over private school, if only because in public school you meet a greater variety of children. This bias of mine, I suspect,

For a biographical note on White, see page 144.

is partly an attempt to justify my own past (I never knew anything but public schools) and partly an involuntary defense against getting kicked in the shins by a young ceramist on his way to the kiln. My wife was unacquainted with public schools, never having been exposed (in her early life) to anything more public than the washroom of Miss Winsor's. Regardless of our backgrounds, we both knew that change in schools was something that concerned not us but the scholar himself. We hoped it would work out all right. In New York our son went to a medium-priced private institution with semi-progressive ideas of education, and modern plumbing. He learned fast, kept well, and we were satisfied. It was an electric, colorful, regimented existence with moments of pleasurable pause and giddy incident. The day the Christmas angel fainted and had to be carried out by one of the Wise Men was educational in the highest sense of the term. Our scholar gave imitations of it around the house for weeks afterward, and I doubt if it ever goes completely out of his mind.

His days were rich in formal experience. Wearing overalls and an old sweater (the accepted uniform of the private seminary), he sallied forth at morn accompanied by a nurse or a parent and walked (or was pulled) two blocks to a corner where the school bus made a flag stop. This flashy vehicle was as punctual as death: seeing us waiting at the cold curb, it would sweep to a halt, open its mouth, suck the boy in, and spring away with an angry growl. It was a good deal like a train picking up a bag of mail. At school the scholar was worked on for six or seven hours by half a dozen teachers and a nurse, and was revived on orange juice in mid-morning. In a cinder court he played games supervised by an athletic instructor, and in a cafeteria he ate lunch worked out by a dietitian. He soon learned to read with gratifying facility and discernment and to make Indian weapons of a semi-deadly nature. Whenever one of his classmates fell low of a fever the news was put on the wires and there were breathless phone calls to physicians, discussing periods of incubation and allied magic.

In the country all one can say is that the situation is different, and somehow more casual. Dressed in corduroys, sweatshirt, and short rubber boots, and carrying a tin dinner-pail pail, our scholar departs at crack of dawn for the village school, two and a half miles down the road, next to the cemetery. When the road is open and the car will start, he makes the journey by motor, courtesy of his old man. When the snow is deep or the motor is dead or both, he makes it on the hoof. In the afternoons he walks or hitches all or part of the way home in fair weather, gets transported in foul. The schoolhouse is a two-room frame building, bungalow type, shingles stained a burnt brown with weather-resistant stain. It has a chemical toilet in the basement and two teachers above stairs. One takes the first three grades, the other the fourth, fifth, and sixth. They have little or no time for individual instruction, and no time at all for the esoteric. They teach what they know themselves, just as fast and as hard as they can manage. The pupils sit still at their desks in class, and do their milling around outdoors during recess.

There is no supervised play. They play cops and robbers (only they call it "Jail") and throw things at one another—snowballs in winter, rose hips in fall. It seems to satisfy them. They also construct darts, pinwheels, and "pick-up sticks" (jackstraws), and the school itself does a brisk trade in penny candy, which is for sale right in the classroom and which contains "surprises." The most highly prized surprise is a fake cigarette, made of cardboard, fiendishly lifelike.

The memory of how apprehensive we were at the beginning is still strong. The boy was nervous about the change too. The tension, on that first fair morning in September when we drove him to school, almost blew the windows out of the sedan. And when later we picked him up on the road, wandering along with his little blue lunch-pail, and got his laconic report "All right" in answer to our inquiry about how the day had gone, our relief was vast. Now, after almost a year of it, the only difference we can discover in the two school experiences is that in the country he sleeps better at night—and *that* probably is more the air than the education. When grilled on the subject of school-in-country vs. school-in-city, he replied that the chief difference is that the day seems to go so much quicker in the country. "Just like lightning," he reported.

# Questions

1. Which school, public or private, does White prefer? Since White doesn't state his preference outright, from what evidence were you able to infer it?
2. In the first half of the second paragraph White admits to a bias in favor of public schools, and he speculates, half-seriously, about the origins of his bias. If his intention here is not simply to amuse us, what is it?
3. What is White's strongest argument in favor of the school he prefers? Where in the essay do you find it?

## Pauline Kael

# High School and Other Forms of Madness

Many of us grow to hate documentaries in school, because the use of movies to teach us something seems a cheat—a pill disguised as candy—and documentaries always seem to be about something we're not interested in. But Wiseman's documentaries show what is left out of both fictional movies and standard documentaries that simplify for a purpose, and his films deal with the primary institutions of our lives: *Titicut Follies* (Bridgewater, an institution in which we lock away the criminally insane), *High School* (a high school in a large Eastern city), and *Law and Order* (the Kansas City police force). Television has been accustoming us to a horrible false kind of "involvement"; sometimes it seems that the only thing the news shows can think of is to get close to emotion. They shove a camera and a microphone in front of people in moments of stress and disaster and grief, and ram their equipment into any pores and cavities they can reach. Wiseman made comparable mistakes in *Titicut Follies,* but he learned better fast.

*High School* is so familiar and so extraordinarily evocative that a feeling of empathy with the students floods over us. How did we live through it? How did we keep any spirit? When you see a kid trying to make a phone call and being interrupted with "Do you have a pass to use the phone?" it all floods back—the low ceilings and pale-green walls of the basement where the lockers were, the constant defensiveness, that sense of always being in danger of breaking some pointless, petty rule. When since that time has one ever needed a pass to make a phone call? This movie takes one back to where, one discovers, time has stood still. Here is the girl humiliated for having worn a short dress to the Senior Prom, being told it was "offensive" to the whole class. Here it is all over again—the insistence that you be "respectful," and the teachers' incredible instinct for "disrespect,"

Pauline Kael, born in 1919 in Petaluma, California, grew up in San Francisco and attended the University of California at Berkeley. She regularly writes film criticism for *The New Yorker.*

their antennae always extended for that little bit of reservation or irony in your tone, the tiny spark that you desperately need to preserve your *self*-respect. One can barely hear it in the way a boy says "Yes, sir" to the dean, but the dean, ever on the alert, snaps, "Don't give me that 'Yes, sir' business! . . . There's no sincereness behind it." Here, all over again, is the dullness of high-school education:

> *Teacher:* What on the horizon or what existed that forced labor to turn to collective bargaining? What was there a lack of?
> *Girl:* Communications?
> *Teacher:* Security, yes, communications, lack of security, concern for the job. The important thing is this, let's get to the beginning. First of all, there was the lack of security; second of all, there was a lack of communication. . . .

The same old pseudo-knowledge is used to support what the schools think is moral. The visiting gynecologist in a sex-education class lectures the boys:

> The more a fellow gets into bed with more different girls, the more insecure he is, and this shows up actually later in all the divorce statistics in America. . . . You can graph right on a graph, the more girls fellows got into bed with or vice-versa the higher the divorce rate, the greater the sexual inadequacy. . . .

And there's the beautiful military doubletalk when it's a question of a teacher's incompetence or unfairness. A boy protests a disciplinary action against him by a teacher, and after he has explained his innocence, the dean talks him into accepting the punishment "to establish that you can be a man and that you can take orders." The teachers are masters here; they're in a superior position for the only time in their lives, probably, and most of the petty tyrannies—like laying on the homework—aren't fully conscious. They justify each other's actions as a matter of course, and put the students in the wrong in the same indifferent way. They put a student down with "It's nice to be individualistic, but there are certain places to be individualistic," yet they never tell you where. How can one stand up against such bland authoritarianism? The teachers, crushing and processing, are the most insidious kind of enemy, the enemy with corrupt values who means well. The counsellor advising on college plans who says "You can have all your dream schools, but at the bottom you ought to have some college of last resort where you could be sure that you would go, if none of your dreams came through" certainly means to be realistic and helpful. But one can imagine what it must feel like to be a kid trudging off to the bottom college of last resort. There's a jolly good Joe of a teacher staging a fashion show who tells the girls, "Your legs are all too heavy. . . . Don't wear it too short; it looks miserable." And she's not wrong. But, given the beauty norms set up in this society, what are they to do? Cut off their legs? Emigrate? They're defeated from the legs up. Mediocrity and defeat sit in the offices and classrooms, and in those oppressive monitored halls.

We went through it all in order to graduate and be rid of passes forever, and once it was over we put it out of our minds, and here are the students still serving time until graduation, still sitting in class staring out the windows or watching the crawling hands of those ugly school clocks. So much of this education is part of an obsolete system of authority that broke down long ago, yet the teachers and administrators are still out there, persevering, "building character." *High School* seems an obvious kind of film to make, but as far as I know no one before has gone into an ordinary, middle-class, "good" (most of the students go to college) high school with a camera and looked around to see what it's like. The students are even more apathetic than we were. Probably the conflicts over the restrictions come earlier now—in junior high—and by high school the kids either are trying to cool it and get through to college or are just beaten down and sitting it out. We may have had a few teachers who really got us interested in something—it was one of the disappointments of the movie *Up the Down Staircase* that, treating this theme, it failed to be convincing—and, remembering our good luck, we could always say that even if a school was rotten, there were bound to be a few great teachers in it. This movie shows competent teachers and teachers who are trying their best but not one teacher who really makes contact in the way that means a difference in your life. The students are as apathetic toward the young English teacher playing and analyzing a Simon & Garfunkel record as toward the English teacher reciting "Casey at the Bat," and, even granted that as poetry there might not be much to choose between them—and perhaps Casey has the edge—still, one might think the students would, just as a *courtesy,* respond to the young teacher's attempt, the way one always gave the ingénue in the stock company a special round of applause. But it's very likely that high schools no longer *are* saved by live teachers, if hostility and cynicism and apathy set in right after children learn their basic skills. The students here sit on their hands even when a teacher tries. That's the only visible difference between this school and mine. I think we would have responded appreciatively to obvious effort, even if we thought the teacher was a jerk; these kids are beyond that. So the teachers are trapped, too. The teachers come off much worse than the police do in *Law and Order. High School* is a revelation because now that we see school from the outside, the teachers seem to give themselves away every time they open their mouths—and to be unaware of it.

At the end, the principal—a fine-looking woman—holds up a letter from a former student, on stationery marked "U.S.S. Okinawa," and reads it to the faculty:

> I have only a few hours before I go. Today I will take a plane trip from this ship. I pray that I'll make it back but it's all in God's hands now. You see, I am going with three other men. We are going to be dropped behind the D.M.Z. (the Demilitarized Zone). The reason for telling you this is that all my insurance money will be given for that scholarship I once started but never finished, if I don't make it back. I am only insured for $10,000. Maybe it could help someone. I have been trying to become a Big Brother in Vietnam, but it is very hard to do. I have to write back and forth to San Diego, California, and that takes time. I only hope that I am good enough to become one. God only knows. My personal family usually doesn't understand me. . . . They say: "Don't you value life? Are you crazy?" My answer is: "Yes. But I value all the lives of South Vietnam and the free world so that they and all of us can live in peace." Am I wrong? If I do my best and believe in what I do, believe that what I do is right—that is all I can do. . . . Please don't say anything to Mrs. C. She would only worry over me. I am not worth it. I am only a body doing a job. In closing I thank everyone for what they all have done for me.

And the principal comments, "Now, when you get a letter like this, to me it means that we are very successful at [this] high school. I think you will agree with me."

It's a great scene—a consummation of the educational process we've been watching: They are successful at turning out bodies to do a job. Yet it's also painfully clear that the school must have given this soldier more kindness and affection than he'd ever had before. There must be other students who respond to the genuine benevolence behind the cant and who are grateful to those who labor to turn them into men. For those students, this schooling in conformity is successful.

Wiseman extends our understanding of our common life the way novelists used to—a way largely abandoned by the modern novel and left to the journalists but not often picked up by them. What he's doing is so simple and so basic that it's like a rediscovery of what we knew, or should know. We often want more information about the people and their predicaments than he gives, but this is perhaps less a criticism of Wiseman's method than it is a testimonial to his success in making us care about his subjects. With fictional movies using so little of our shared experience, and the big TV news "specials" increasingly using that idiot "McLuhanite" fragmentation technique that scrambles all experience— as if the deliberate purpose were to make us indifferent to the life around us—it's a good sign when a movie sends us out wanting to know more and feeling that there is more to know. Wiseman is probably the most sophisticated intelligence to enter the documentary field in recent years.

## Questions

1. In her second paragraph Kael assumes that her readers share with her the view, based on experience, that high school is dull, dispiriting, and even humiliating. Is the assumption warranted?
2. At the end of the second paragraph Kael quotes a bit of dialogue. Pinpoint examples of dullness in the dialogue.
3. The language of the fourth paragraph (beginning "And there's the beautiful military doubletalk") suggests that high school is a battleground between teachers and students. Are the hostilities Kael cites familiar? If not, do you find them nevertheless convincing? With what weapons is each side armed?
4. In her first paragraph Kael writes: "Many of us grow to hate documentaries in school." Did you? If so, why? What reasons might you offer to argue that the documentary films you saw in school were educational or anti-educational?

Neil Postman

# Order in the Classroom

William O'Connor, who is unknown to me in a personal way, was once a member of the Boston School Committee, in which capacity he made the following remark: "We have no inferior education in our schools. What we have been getting is an inferior type of student."

The remark is easy to ridicule, and I have had some fun with it in the past. But there are a couple of senses in which it is perfectly sound.

In the first place, a classroom is a technique for the achievement of certain kinds of learning. It is a workable technique provided that both the teacher and the student have the skill and, particularly, the attitudes that are fundamental to it. Among these, from the student's point of view, are tolerance for delayed gratification, a certain measure of respect for and fear of authority, and a willingness to accommodate one's individual desires to the interests of group cohesion and purpose. These attitudes cannot be taught easily in school because they are a necessary component of the teaching situation itself. The problem is not unlike trying to find out how to spell a word by looking it up in the dictionary. If you do not know how a word is spelled, it is hard to look it up. In the same way, little can be taught in school unless these attitudes are present. And if they are not, to teach them is difficult.

Obviously, such attitudes must be learned during the years before a child starts school; that is, in the home. This is the real meaning of the phrase "preschool education." If a child is not made ready at home for the classroom experience, he or she usually cannot benefit from any normal school program. Just as important, the school is defenseless against such a child, who, typically, is a source of disorder in a situation that requires order. I raise this issue because education reform is impossible without order in the classroom. Without the

Neil Postman, born in New York City in 1931, has taught in elementary and secondary schools and is now a professor of communication arts and sciences at New York University.

attitudes that lead to order, the classroom is an entirely impotent technique. Therefore, one possible translation of Mr. O'Connor's remark is, "We have a useful technique for educating youth but too many of them have not been provided at home with the attitudes necessary for the technique to work."

In still another way Mr. O'Connor's remark makes plain sense. The electronic media, with their emphasis on visual imagery, immediacy, non-linearity, and fragmentation, do not give support to the attitudes that are fundamental to the classroom; that is, Mr. O'Conner's remark can be translated as, "We would not have an inferior education if it were the nineteenth century. Our problem is that we have been getting students who are products of the twentieth century." But there is nothing nonsensical about this, either. The nineteenth century had much to recommend it, and we certainly may be permitted to allow it to exert an influence on the twentieth. The classroom is a nineteenth-century invention, and we ought to prize what it has to offer. It is one of the few social organizations left to us in which sequence, social order, hierarchy, continuity, and deferred pleasure are important.

The problem of disorder in the classroom is created largely by two factors: a dissolving family structure, out of which come youngsters who are "unfit" for the presuppositions of a classroom; and a radically altered information environment, which undermines the foundation of school. The question, then, is, What should be done about the increasing tendency toward disorder in the classroom?

Liberal reformers, such as Kenneth Keniston, have answers, of a sort. Keniston argues that economic reforms should be made so that the integrity and authority of the family can be restored. He believes that poverty is the main cause of family dissolution, and that by improving the economic situation of families, we may kindle a sense of order and aspiration in the lives of children. Some of the reforms he suggests in his book *All Our Children* seem practical, although they are long-range and offer no immediate response to the problem of present disorder. Some Utopians, such as Ivan Illich, have offered other solutions; for example, dissolving the schools altogether, or so completely restructuring the school environment that its traditional assumptions are rendered irrelevant. To paraphrase Karl Kraus's epigram about psychoanalysis, these proposals are the Utopian disease of which they consider themselves the cure.

One of the best answers comes from Dr. Howard Hurwitz, who is neither a liberal reformer nor a Utopian. It is a good solution, I believe, because it tries to respond to the needs not only of children who are unprepared for school because of parental failure but of children of all backgrounds who are being made strangers to the assumptions of school by the biases of the electronic media.

During the eleven years Dr. Hurwitz was principal at Long Island City High School, the average number of suspensions each year was three, while in many New York City high schools the average runs close to one hundred. Also, during his tenure, not one instance of an assault on a teacher was reported, and daily student attendance averaged better than 90 percent, which in the context of the New York City school scene represents a riot of devotion.

Although I consider some of Dr. Hurwitz's curriculum ideas uninspired and even wrong-headed, he understands a few things of overriding importance that many educators of more expansive imagination do not. The first is that educators must devote at least as much attention to the immediate consequences of disorder as to its abstract causes. Whatever the causes of disorder and alienation, the consequences are severe and, if not curbed, result in making the school impotent. At the risk of becoming a symbol of reaction, Hurwitz ran "a tight ship." He holds to the belief, for example, that a child's right to an education is terminated at the point where the child interferes with the right of other children to have one.

Dr. Hurwitz also understands that disorder expands proportionately to the tolerance for it, and that children of all kinds of home backgrounds can learn, in varying degrees, to function in situations where disorder is not tolerated at all. He does not believe that it is inevitably or only the children of the poor who are disorderly. In spite of what the "revisionist" education historians may say, poor people still regard school as an avenue of social and economic advancement for their children, and do not object in the least to its being an orderly and structured experience.

All this adds up to the common sense view that the school ought not to accommodate itself to disorder, or to the biases of other communication systems. The children of the poor are likely to continue to be with us. Some parents will fail to assume competent responsibility for the preschool education of their children. The media will increase the intensity of their fragmenting influence. Educators must live with these facts. But Dr. Hurwitz believes that as a technique for learning, the classroom can work if students are oriented toward its assumptions, not the other way around. William O'Connor, wherever he is, would probably agree. And so do I. The school is not an extension of the street, the movie theater, a rock concert, or a playground. And it is certainly not an extension of the psychiatric clinic. It is a special environment that requires the enforcement of certain traditional rules of controlled group interaction. The school may be the only remaining public situation in which such rules have any meaning, and it would be a grave mistake to change those rules because some children find them hard or cannot function within them. Children who cannot ought to be removed from the environment in the interests of those who can.

Wholesale suspensions, however, are a symptom of disorder, not a cure for it. And what makes Hurwitz's school noteworthy is the small number of suspensions that have been necessary. This is not the result of his having "good" students or "bad" students. It is the result of his having created an unambiguous, rigorous, and serious attitude—a nineteenth-century attitude, if you will—toward what constitutes acceptable school behavior. In other words, Dr. Hurwitz's school turns out to be a place where children of all backgrounds—fit and unfit—can function, or can learn to function, and where the biases of our information environment are emphatically opposed.

At this point I should like to leave the particulars of Dr. Hurwitz's solution and, retaining their spirit, indicate some particulars of my own.

Let us start, for instance, with the idea of a dress code. A dress code signifies that school is a special place in which special kinds of behavior are required. The way one dresses is an indication of an attitude toward a situation. And the way one is *expected* to dress indicates what that attitude ought to be. You would not wear dungarees and a T-shirt that says "Feel Me" when attending a church wedding. That would be considered an outrage against the tone and meaning of the situation. The school has every right and reason, I believe, to expect the same sort of consideration.

Those who are inclined to think this is a superficial point are probably forgetting that symbols not only reflect our feelings but to some extent create them. One's kneeling in church, for example, reflects a sense of reverence but also engenders reverence. If we want school to *feel* like a special place, we can find no better way to begin than by requiring students to dress in a manner befitting the seriousness of the enterprise and the institution. I should include teachers in this requirement. I know of one high school in which the principal has put forward a dress code of sorts for teachers. (He has not, apparently, had the courage to propose one for the students.) For males the requirement is merely a jacket and tie. One of his teachers bitterly complained to me that such a regulation infringed upon his civil rights. And yet, this teacher will accept without complaint the same regulation when it is enforced by an elegant restaurant. His complaint and his acquiescence tell a great deal about how he values schools and how he values restaurants.

I do not have in mind, for students, uniforms of the type sometimes worn in parochial schools. I am referring here to some reasonable standard of dress which would mark school as a place of dignity and seriousness. And I might add that I do not believe for one moment the argument that poor people would be unable to clothe their children properly if such a code were in force. Furthermore, I do not believe that poor people have advanced that argument. It is an argument that middle-class education critics have made on behalf of the poor.

Another argument advanced in behalf of the poor and oppressed is the students' right to their own language. I have never heard this argument come from parents whose children are not competent to use Standard English. It is an argument, once again, put forward by "liberal" education critics whose children *are* competent in Standard English but who in some curious way wish to express their solidarity with and charity for those who are less capable. It is a case of pure condescension, and I do not think teachers should be taken in by it. Like the mode of dress, the mode of language in school ought to be relatively formal and exemplary, and therefore markedly different from the custom in less rigorous places. It is particularly important that teachers should avoid trying to win their students' affection by adopting the language of youth. Such teachers frequently win only the contempt of their students, who sense that the language of teachers and the language of students ought to be different; that is to say, the world of adults is different from the world of children.

In this connection, it is worth saying that the modern conception of childhood is a product of the sixteenth century, as Philippe Aries has documented in his *The Centuries of Childhood.* Prior to that century, children as young as six and seven were treated in all important respects as if they were adults. Their language, their dress, their legal status, their responsibilities, their labor, were much the same as those of adults. The concept of childhood as an identifiable stage in human growth began to develop in the sixteenth century and has continued into our own times. However, with the emergence of electronic media of communication, a reversal of this trend seems to be taking place. In a culture in which the distribution of information is almost wholly undifferentiated, age categories begin to disappear. Television, in itself, may bring an end to childhood. In truth, there is no such thing as "children's programming," at least not for children over the age of eight or nine. Everyone sees and hears the same things. We have already reached a point where crimes of youth are indistinguishable from those of adults, and we may soon reach a point where the punishments will be the same.

I raise this point because the school is one of our few remaining institutions based on firm distinctions between childhood and adulthood, and on the assumption that adults have something of value to teach the young. That is why teachers must avoid emulating in dress and speech the style of the young. It is also why the school ought to be a place for what we might call "manners education": the adults in school ought to be concerned with teaching youth a standard of civilized interaction.

Again those who are inclined to regard this as superficial may be underestimating the power of media such as television and radio to teach how one is to conduct oneself in public. In a general sense, the media "unprepare" the young for behavior in groups. A young man who goes through the day with a radio affixed to his ear is learning to be indifferent to any shared sound. A young woman who can turn off a television program that does not suit her needs at the moment is learning impatience with any stimulus that is not responsive to her interests.

But school is not a radio station or a television program. It is a social situation requiring the subordination of one's own impulses and interests to those of the group. In a word, manners. As a rule, elementary school teachers will exert considerable effort in teaching manners. I believe they refer to this effort as "socializing the child." But it is astonishing how precipitously this effort is diminished at higher levels. It is certainly neglected in the high schools, and where it is not, there is usually an excessive concern for "bad habits," such as smoking, drinking, and in some nineteenth-century schools, swearing. But, as William James noted, our virtues are as habitual as our vices. Where is the attention given to the "Good morning" habit, to the "I beg your pardon" habit, to the "Please forgive the interruption" habit?

The most civilized high school class I have ever seen was one in which students and teacher said "Good morning" to each other and in which the students stood up when they had something to say. The teacher, moreover, thanked each student for any contribution made to the class, did not sit with his feet on the desk, and did not interrupt a student unless he had asked permission to do so. The students, in turn, did not interrupt each other, or chew gum, or read comic books when they were bored. To avoid being a burden to others when one is bored is the essence of civilized behavior.

Of this teacher, I might also say that he made no attempt to entertain his students or model his classroom along the lines of a TV program. He was concerned not only to teach his students manners but to teach them how to attend in a classroom, which is partly a matter of manners but also necessary to their intellectual development. One of the more serious difficulties teachers now face in the classroom results from the fact that their students suffer media-shortened attention spans and have become accustomed, also through intense media exposure, to novelty, variety, and entertainment. Some teachers have made desperate attempts to keep their students "tuned in" by fashioning their classes along the lines of *Sesame Street* or the *Tonight* show. They tell jokes. They change the pace. They show films, play records, and avoid *anything* that would take more than eight minutes. Although their motivation is understandable, this is what their students least need. However difficult it may be, the teacher must try to achieve student attention and even enthusiasm through the attraction of ideas, not razzmatazz. Those who think I am speaking here in favor of "dull" classes may themselves, through media exposure, have lost an understanding of the potential for excitement contained in an idea. The media (one prays) are not so powerful that they can obliterate in the young, particularly in the adolescent, what William James referred to as a "theoretic instinct," a need to know reasons, causes, abstract conceptions. Such an "instinct" can be seen in its earliest stages in what he calls the "sporadic metaphysical inquiries of children as to who made God, and why they have five fingers. . . ."

I trust that the reader is not misled by what I have been saying. As I see it, nothing in any of the above leads to the conclusion that I favor a classromm that is authoritarian or coldhearted, or dominated by a teacher insensitive to students and how they learn. I merely want to affirm the importance of the classroom as a special place, aloof from the biases of the media; a place in which the uses of the intellect are given prominence in a setting of elevated language, civilized manners, and respect for social symbols.

## Questions

1. In the third paragraph what does Postman mean by "tolerance for delayed gratification"? By the way, two paragraphs later Postman uses an expression that is approximately synonymous with "delayed gratification." What is this expression?
2. Postman in part blames "the electronic media," because (he says in the paragraph beginning "In still another way," page 187) they emphasize "fragmentation." Does he give any examples in his essay? Do you think that you know what he means? And do you think he is right?
3. Who is Postman's audience? High school students? Parents and teachers? Professors of education? And who is Postman—that is, putting aside the biographical note on page 186, what sort of person does the author of the essay reveal himself to be? A frustrated high school teacher? A professor of education? An intelligent layperson? Does he seem to know what he is talking about?
4. On page 188 we are told, with approval, that a principal named Dr. Howard Hurwitz "ran 'a tight ship.' " First, make sure that you know what the term means, and then write an essay of 500 words evaluating the degree of success of some instructor or administrator who ran a tight ship in your school. Your essay will, of course, have to give us a sense of what the instructor or administrator did, as well as your evaluation of the results of his or her teaching or administrating.
5. If you disagree with Postman on the value of a dress code, set forth your disagreement in a persuasive essay of 500 words.
6. Write an editorial—as an alumnus or alumna—for your high school newspaper, summarizing Postman in a paragraph, and then comparing your school with Postman's idea of a good school, and, finally, evaluating your school and Postman's essay. You may, for example, conclude that, thank heavens, your school was nothing like Postman's ideal school.

John Holt

# The Right to Control One's Learning

Young people should have the right to control and direct their own learning, that is, to decide what they want to learn, and when, where, how, how much, how fast, and with what help they want to learn it. To be still more specific, I want them to have the right to decide if, when, how much, and by whom they want to be *taught* and the right to decide whether they want to learn in a school and if so which one and for how much of the time.

No human right, except the right to life itself, is more fundamental than this. A person's freedom of learning is part of his freedom of thought, even more basic than his freedom of speech. If we take from someone his right to decide what he will be curious about, we destroy his freedom of thought. We say, in effect, you must think not about what interests and concerns *you,* but about what interests and concerns *us.*

We might call this the right of curiosity, the right to ask whatever questions are most important to us. As adults, we assume that we have the right to decide what does or does not interest us, what we will look into and what we will leave alone. We take this right for granted, cannot imagine that it might be taken away from us. Indeed, as far as I know, it has never been written into any body of law. Even the writers of our Constitution did not mention it. They thought it was enough to guarantee citizens the freedom of speech and the freedom to spread their ideas as widely as they wished and could. It did not occur to them that even the most tyrannical government would try to control people's minds, what they thought and knew. That idea was to come later, under the benevolent guise of compulsory universal education.

This right of each of us to control our own learning is now in danger. When we put into our laws the highly authoritarian notion

John Holt, born in New York City in 1923, has taught in schools and colleges. He is the author of numerous books and is widely known as an educational consultant.

that someone should and could decide what all young people were to learn and beyond that, could do whatever might seem necessary (which now includes dosing them with drugs) to compel them to learn it, we took a long step down a very steep and dangerous path. The requirement that a child go to school, for about six hours a day, 180 days a year, for about ten years, whether or not he learns anything there, whether or not he already knows it or could learn it faster or better somewhere else, is such a gross violation of civil liberties that few adults would stand for it. But the child who resists is treated as a criminal. With this requirement we created an industry, an army of people whose whole work was to tell young people what they had to learn and to try to make them learn it. Some of these people, wanting to exercise even more power over others, to be even more "helpful," or simply because the industry is not growing fast enough to hold all the people who want to get into it, are now beginning to say, "If it is good for children for us to decide what they shall learn and to make them learn it, why wouldn't it be good for everyone? If compulsory education is a good thing, how can there be too much of it? Why should we allow anyone, of any age, to decide that he has had enough of it? Why should we allow older people, any more than young, not to know what we know when their ignorance may have bad consequences for all of us? Why should we not *make* them know what they *ought* to know?"

They are beginning to talk, as one man did on a nationwide TV show, about "womb-to-tomb" schooling. If hours of homework every night are good for the young, why wouldn't they be good for us all—they would keep us away from the TV set and other frivolous pursuits. Some group of experts, somewhere, would be glad to decide what we all ought to know and then every so often check up on us to make sure we knew it—with, of course, appropriate penalties if we did not.

I am very serious in saying that I think this is coming unless we prepare against it and take steps to prevent it. The right I ask for the young is a right that I want to preserve for the rest of us, the right *to decide what goes into our minds.* This is much more than the right to decide whether or when or how much to go to school or what school you want to go to. That right is important, but it is only part of a much larger and more fundamental right, which I might call the right to Learn, as opposed to being Educated, *i.e.,* made to learn what someone else thinks would be good for you. It is not just compulsory schooling but compulsory Education that I oppose and want to do away with.

That children might have the control of their own learning, including the right to decide if, when, how much, and where they wanted to go to school, frightens and angers many people. They ask me, "Are you saying that if the parents wanted the child to go to school, and the child didn't want to go, that he wouldn't have to go? Are you saying that if the parents wanted the child to go to one school, and the child wanted to go to another, that the child would have the right to decide?" Yes, that is what I say. Some people ask, "If school wasn't compulsory, wouldn't many parents take their children out of school to exploit their labor in one way or another?" Such questions are often both snobbish and hypocritical. The questioner assumes and implies (though rarely says) that these bad parents are people poorer and less schooled than he. Also, though he appears to be defending the right of children to go to school, what he really is defending is the right of the state to compel them to go whether they want to or not. What he wants, in short, is that children should be in school, not that they should have any choice about going.

But saying that children should have the right to choose to go or not to go to school does not mean that the ideas and wishes of the parents would have no weight. Unless he is estranged from his parents and rebelling against them, a child cares very much about what they think and want. Most of the time, he doesn't want to anger or worry or disappoint them. Right now, in families where the parents feel that they have some choice about their children's schooling, there is much bargaining about schools. Such parents, when their children are little, often ask them whether they want to go to nursery school or kindergarten. Or they may take them to school for a while to try it out. Or, if they have a choice of schools, they may take them to several to see which they think they will like the best. Later, they care whether the child likes his school. If he does not, they try to do something about it, get him out of it, find a school he will like.

I know some parents who for years had a running bargain with their children, "If on a given day you just can't stand the thought of school, you don't feel well, you are afraid of something that may happen, you have something of your own that you very much want to do—well, you can stay home." Needless to say, the schools, with their supporting experts, fight it with all their might—Don't Give in to Your Child, Make Him Go to School, He's Got to Learn. Some parents, when their own plans make it possible for them to take an interesting trip, take their children with them. They don't ask the school's permission, they just go. If the child doesn't want to make the trip and would rather stay in school, they work out a way for him to do that. Some parents, when their child is frightened, unhappy, and suffering in school, as many children are, just take him out. Hal Bennett, in his excellent book *No More Public School,* talks about ways to do this.

A friend of mine told me that when her boy was in third grade, he had a bad teacher, bullying, contemptuous, sarcastic, cruel. Many of the class switched to another section, but this eight-year-old, being tough, defiant, and stubborn, hung on. One day—his parents did not learn this until about two years later—having had enough of the teacher's meanness, he just got up from his desk and without saying a word, walked out of the room and went home. But for all his toughness and resiliency of spirit, the experience was hard on him. He grew more timid and quarrelsome, less outgoing and confident. He lost his ordinary good humor. Even his handwriting began to go to pieces—was much worse in the spring of the school year than in the previous fall. One spring day he sat at breakfast, eating his cereal. After a while he stopped eating and sat silently thinking about the day ahead. His eyes filled up with tears, and two big ones slowly rolled down his cheeks. His mother, who ordinarily stays out of the school life of her children, saw this and knew what it was about. "Listen," she said to him, "we don't have to go on with this. If you've had enough of that teacher, if she's making school so bad for you that you don't want to go any more, I'll be perfectly happy just to pull you right out. We can manage it. Just say the word." He was horrified and indignant. "No!" he said, "I couldn't do that." "Okay," she said, "whatever you want is fine. Just let me know." And so they left it. He had decided that he was going to tough it out, and he did. But I am sure knowing that he had the support of his mother and the chance to give it up if it got too much for him gave him the strength he needed to go on.

To say that children should have the right to control and direct their own learning, to go to school or not as they chose, does not mean that the law would forbid the parents to express an opinion or wish or strong desire on the matter. It only means that if their natural authority is not strong enough the parents can't call in the cops to make the child do what they are not able to persuade him to do. And the law may say that there is a limit to the amount of pressure or coercion the parents can apply to the child to deny him a choice that he has a legal right to make.

When I urge that children should control their learning there is one argument that people bring up so often that I feel I must anticipate and meet it here. It says that schools are a place where children can for a while be protected against the bad influences of the world outside, particularly from its greed, dishonesty, and commercialism. It says that in school children may have a glimpse of a higher way of life, of people acting from other and better motives than greed and fear. People say, "We know that society is bad enough as it is and that children will be exposed to it and corrupted by it soon enough. But if we let children go out into the larger world as soon as they wanted, they would be tempted and corrupted just that much sooner."

They seem to believe that schools are better, more honorable places than the world outside—what a friend of mine at Harvard once called "museums of virtue." Or that people in school, both children and adults, act from higher and better motives than people outside. In this they are mistaken. There are, of course, some good schools. But on the whole, far from being the opposite of, or an antidote to, the world outside, with all its envy, fear, greed, and obsessive competitiveness, the schools are very much like it. If anything, they are worse, a terrible, abstract, simplified caricature of it. In the world outside the school, some work, at least, is done honestly and well, for its own sake, not just to get ahead of others; people are not everywhere and always being set in competition against each other; people are not (or not yet) in every minute of their lives subject to the arbitrary, irrevocable orders and judgment of others. But in most schools, a student is every minute doing what others tell him, subject to their judgment, in situations in which he can only win at the expense of other students.

This is a harsh judgment. Let me say again, as I have before, that schools are worse than most of the people in them and that many of these people do many harmful things they would rather not do, and a great many other harmful things that they do not even see as harmful. The whole of school is much worse than the sum of its parts. There are very few people in the U.S. today (or perhaps anywhere, any time) in *any* occupation, who could be trusted with the kind of power that schools give most teachers over their students. Schools seem to me among the most anti-democratic, most authoritarian, most destructive, and most dangerous institutions of modern society.

No other institution does more harm or more lasting harm to more people or destroys so much of their curiosity, independence, trust, dignity, and sense of identity and worth. Even quite kindly schools are inhibited and corrupted by the knowledge of children and teachers alike that they are *performing* for the judgment and approval of others—the children for the teachers; the teachers for the parents, supervisors, school board, or the state. No one is ever free from feeling that he is being judged all the time, or soon may be. Even after the best class experiences teachers must ask themselves, "Were we right to do that? Can we prove we were right? Will it get us in trouble?"

What corrupts the school, and makes it so much worse than most of the people in it, or than they would like it to be, is its power–just as their powerlessness corrupts the students. The school is corrupted by the endless anxious demand of the parents to know how their child is doing—meaning is he ahead of the other kids—and their demand that he be kept ahead. Schools do not protect children from the badness of the world outside. They are at least as bad as the world outside, and the harm they do to the children in their power creates much of the badness of the world outside. The sickness of the modern world is in many ways a school-induced sickness. It is in school that most people learn to expect and accept that some expert can always place them in some sort of rank or hierarchy. It is in school that we meet, become used to, and learn to believe in the totally controlled society. We do not learn much science, but we learn to worship "scientists" and to believe that anything we might conceivably need or want can only come, and someday will come, from them. The school is the closest we have yet been able to come to Huxley's *Brave New World,* with its alphas and betas, deltas and epsilons—and now it even has its soma. Everyone, including children, should have the right to say "No!" to it.[1]

[1]Aldous Huxley's *Brave New World* (1932) depicts a totalitarian society that scientifically controls the populace. Babies are created in laboratories and are conditioned; adults are given *soma* pills to prevent depression. John Holt plays on the Greek letters for A, B, D, and E, suggesting that the grading system of our schools turns into a doping system. (Editor's note)

# Questions

1. Holt's opening sentence pretty much dismisses the idea of compulsory education. What arguments can be offered on behalf of compulsory education? How can you defend the requirement that children be schooled—even if the children and their parents don't wish them to go to school?
2. In his fourth paragraph, Holt refers to "an industry, an army of people." To whom does he refer? What is the effect of describing them as an "industry" and an "army"?
3. Read the paragraph beginning "When I urge" (page 198), and the next paragraph, and then write an essay of 500 words, evaluating your high school in the light of Holt's comment that most schools encourage morally destructive competition.
4. If you have read Postman's essay (page 186), write an essay of 500–750 words comparing and evaluating the two essays as examples of persuasive writing. Note: your topic is not "Which of the Two Essays I Subscribe To"; rather, it is an analysis and an evaluation of the essays *as persuasion.*
5. If you have read Anonymous, "Confessions of an Erstwhile Child" (page 43), what ideas do you find there that are similar to Holt's? In a paragraph or two, point out the similarities, citing specific passages in each essay.

## Maya Angelou

# Graduation

The children in Stamps trembled visibly with anticipation. Some adults were excited too, but to be certain the whole young population had come down with graduation epidemic. Large classes were graduating from both the grammar school and the high school. Even those who were years removed from their own day of glorious release were anxious to help with preparations as a kind of dry run. The junior students who were moving into the vacating classes' chairs were tradition-bound to show their talents for leadership and management. They strutted through the school and around the campus exerting pressure on the lower grades. Their authority was so new that occasionally if they pressed a little too hard it had to be overlooked. After all, next term was coming, and it never hurt a sixth grader to have a play sister in the eighth grade, or a tenth-year student to be able to call a twelfth grader Bubba. So all was endured in a spirit of shared understanding. But the graduating classes themselves were the nobility. Like travelers with exotic destinations on their minds, the graduates were remarkably forgetful. They came to school without their books, or tablets or even pencils. Volunteers fell over themselves to secure replacements for the missing equipment. When accepted, the willing workers might or might not be thanked, and it was of no importance to the pregraduation rites. Even teachers were respectful of the now quiet and aging seniors, and tended to speak to them, if not as equals, as beings only slightly lower than themselves. After tests were returned and grades given, the student body, which acted like an extended family, knew who did well, who excelled, and what piteous ones had failed.

Unlike the white high school, Lafayette County Training School distinguished itself by having neither lawn, nor hedges, nor tennis court, nor climbing ivy. Its two buildings (main classrooms, the grade school and home economics) were set on a dirt hill with no fence to

---

Maya Angelou was born in St. Louis in 1928. She has written two books of poetry and three autobiographic books.

"Graduation" (editors' title) is from her first autobiography, *I Know Why the Caged Bird Sings,* chapter 23.

---

limit either its boundaries or those of bordering farms. There was a large expanse to the left of the school which was used alternately as a baseball diamond or a basketball court. Rusty hoops on the swaying poles represented the permanent recreational equipment, although bats and balls could be borrowed from the P.E. teacher if the borrower was qualified and if the diamond wasn't occupied.

Over this rocky area relieved by a few shady tall persimmon trees the graduating class walked. The girls often held hands and no longer bothered to speak to the lower students. There was a sadness about them, as if this old world was not their home and they were bound for higher ground. The boys, on the other hand, had become more friendly, more outgoing. A decided change from the closed attitude they projected while studying for finals. Now they seemed not ready to give up the old school, the familiar paths and classrooms. Only a small percentage would be continuing on to college—one of the South's A & M (agricultural and mechanical) schools, which trained Negro youths to be carpenters, farmers, handymen, masons, maids, cooks and baby nurses. Their future rode heavily on their shoulders, and blinded them to the collective joy that had pervaded the lives of the boys and girls in the grammar school graduating class.

Parents who could afford it had ordered new shoes and ready-made clothes for themselves from Sears and Roebuck or Montgomery Ward. They also engaged the best seamstresses to make the floating graduating dresses and to cut down secondhand pants which would be pressed to a military slickness for the important event.

Oh, it was important, all right. Whitefolks would attend the ceremony, and two or three would speak of God and home, and the Southern way of life, and Mrs. Parsons, the principal's wife, would play the graduation march while the lower-grade graduates paraded down the aisles and took their seats below the platform. The high school seniors would wait in empty classrooms to make their dramatic entrance.

In the Store I was the person of the moment. The birthday girl. The center. Bailey had graduated the year before, although to do so he had had to forfeit all pleasures to make up for his time lost in Baton Rouge.

My class was wearing butter-yellow piqué dresses, and Momma launched out on mine. She smocked the yoke into tiny crisscrossing puckers, then shirred the rest of the bodice. Her dark fingers ducked in and out of the lemony cloth as she embroidered raised daisies around the hem. Before she considered herself finished she had added a crocheted cuff on the puff sleeves, and a pointy crocheted collar.

I was going to be lovely. A walking model of all the various styles of fine hand sewing and it didn't worry me that I was only twelve years old and merely graduating from the eighth grade. Besides, many teachers in Arkansas Negro schools had only that diploma and were licensed to impart wisdom.

The days had become longer and more noticeable. The faded beige of former times had been replaced with strong and sure colors. I began to see my classmates' clothes, their skin tones, and the dust that waved off pussy willows. Clouds that lazed across the sky were objects of great concern to me. Their shiftier shapes might have held a message that in my new happiness and with a little bit of time I'd soon decipher. During that period I looked at the arch of heaven so religiously my neck kept a steady ache. I had taken to smiling more often, and my jaws hurt from the unaccustomed activity. Between the two physical sore spots, I suppose I could have been uncomfortable, but that was not the case. As a member of the winning team (the graduating class of 1940) I had outdistanced unpleasant sensations by miles. I was headed for the freedom of open fields.

Youth and social approval allied themselves with me and we trammeled memories of slights and insults. The wind of our swift passage remodeled my features. Lost tears were pounded to mud and then to dust. Years of withdrawal were brushed aside and left behind, as hanging ropes of parasitic moss.

My work alone had awarded me a top place and I was going to be one of the first called in the graduating ceremonies. On the classroom blackboard, as well as on the bulletin board in the auditorium, there were blue stars and white stars and red stars. No absences, no tardinesses, and my academic work was among the best of the year. I could say the preamble to the Constitution even faster than Bailey. We timed ourselves often: "WethepeopleoftheUnitedStatesinordertoformamoreperfectunion . . ." I had memorized the Presidents of the United States from Washington to Roosevelt in chronological as well as alphabetical order.

My hair pleased me too. Gradually the black mass had lengthened and thickened, so that it kept at last to its braided pattern, and I didn't have to yank my scalp off when I tried to comb it.

Louise and I had rehearsed the exercises until we tired out ourselves. Henry Reed was class valedictorian. He was a small, very black boy with hooded eyes, a long, broad nose and an oddly shaped head. I had admired him for years because each term he and I vied for the best grades in our class. Most often he bested me, but instead of being disappointed I was pleased that we shared top places between us. Like many Southern Black children, he lived with his grandmother, who was as strict as Momma and as kind as she knew how to be. He was courteous, respectful and soft-spoken to elders, but on the playground he chose to play the roughest games. I admired him. Anyone, I reckoned, sufficiently afraid or sufficiently dull could be polite. But to be able to operate at a top level with both adults and children was admirable.

His valedictory speech was entitled "To Be or Not to Be." The rigid tenth-grade teacher had helped him to write it. He'd been working on the dramatic stresses for months.

The weeks until graduation were filled with heady activities. A group of small children were to be presented in a play about buttercups and daisies and bunny rabbits. They could be heard throughout the building practicing their hops and their little songs that sounded like silver bells. The older girls (non-graduates, of course) were assigned the task of making refreshments for the night's festivities. A tangy scent of ginger, cinnamon, nutmeg and chocolate wafted around the home economics building as the budding cooks made samples for themselves and their teachers.

In every corner of the workshop, axes and saws split fresh timber as the woodshop boys made sets and stage scenery. Only the graduates were left out of the general bustle. We were free to sit in the library at the back of the building or look in quite detachedly, naturally, on the measures being taken for our event.

Even the minister preached on graduation the Sunday before. His subject was, "Let your light so shine that men will see your good works and praise your Father, Who is in Heaven." Although the sermon was purported to be addressed to us, he used the occasion to speak to backsliders, gamblers, and general ne'er-do-wells. But since he had called our names at the beginning of the service we were mollified.

Among Negroes the tradition was to give presents to children going only from one grade to another. How much more important this was when the person was graduating at the top of the class. Uncle Willie and Momma had sent away for a Mickey Mouse watch like Bailey's. Louise gave me four embroidered handkerchiefs. (I gave her three crocheted doilies.) Mrs. Sneed, the minister's wife, made me an underskirt to wear for graduation, and nearly every customer gave me a nickel or maybe even a dime with the instruction "Keep on moving to higher ground," or some such encouragement.

Amazingly the great day finally dawned and I was out of bed before I knew it. I threw open the back door to see it more clearly, but Momma said, "Sister, come away from that door and put your robe on."

I hoped the memory of that morning would never leave me. Sunlight was itself still young, and the day had none of the insistence maturity would bring it in a few hours. In my robe and barefoot in the backyard, under cover of going to see about my new beans, I gave myself up to the gentle warmth and thanked God that no matter what evil I had done in my life He had allowed me to live to see this day. Somewhere in my fatalism I had expected to die, accidentally, and never have the chance to walk up the stairs in the auditorium and gracefully receive my hard-earned diploma. Out of God's merciful bosom I had won reprieve.

Bailey came out in his robe and gave me a box wrapped in Christmas paper. He said he had saved his money for months to pay for it. It felt like a box of chocolates, but I knew Bailey wouldn't save money to buy candy when we had all we could want under our noses.

He was as proud of the gift as I. It was a soft-leather-bound copy of a collection of poems by Edgar Allan Poe, or, as Bailey and I called him, "Eap." I turned to "Annabel Lee" and we walked up and down the garden rows, the cool dirt between our toes, reciting the beautifully sad lines.

Momma made a Sunday breakfast although it was only Friday. After we finished the blessing, I opened my eyes to find the watch on my plate. It was a dream of a day. Everything went smoothly and to my credit. I didn't have to be reminded or scolded for anything. Near evening I was too jittery to attend to chores, so Bailey volunteered to do all before his bath.

Days before, we had made a sign for the Store and as we turned out the lights Momma hung the cardboard over the doorknob. It read clearly: CLOSED. GRADUATION.

My dress fitted perfectly and everyone said that I looked like a sunbeam in it. On the hill, going toward the school, Bailey walked behind with Uncle Willie, who muttered, "Go on, Ju." He wanted him to walk ahead with us because it embarrassed him to have to walk so slowly. Bailey said he'd let the ladies walk together, and the men would bring up the rear. We all laughed, nicely.

Little children dashed by out of the dark like fireflies. Their crepe-paper dresses and butterfly wings were not made for running and we heard more than one rip, dryly, and the regretful "uh uh" that followed.

The school blazed without gaiety. The windows seemed cold and unfriendly from the lower hill. A sense of ill-fated timing crept over me, and if Momma hadn't reached for my hand I would have drifted back to Bailey and Uncle Willie, and possibly beyond. She made a few slow jokes about my feet getting cold, and tugged me along to the now-strange building.

Around the front steps, assurance came back. There were my fellow "greats," the graduating class. Hair brushed back, legs oiled, new dresses and pressed pleats, fresh pocket handkerchiefs and little handbags, all homesewn. Oh, we were up to snuff, all right. I joined my comrades and didn't even see my family go in to find seats in the crowded auditorium.

The school band struck up a march and all classes filed in as had been rehearsed. We stood in front of our seats, as assigned, and on a signal from the choir director, we sat. No sooner had this been accomplished than the band started to play the national anthem. We rose again and sang the song, after which we recited the pledge of allegiance. We remained standing for a brief minute before the choir director and the principal signaled to us, rather desperately I thought, to take our seats. The command was so unusual that our carefully rehearsed and smooth-running machine was thrown off. For a full minute we fumbled for our chairs and bumped into each other awkwardly. Habits change or solidify under pressure, so in our state of nervous tension we had been ready to follow our usual assembly pattern: the American National Anthem, then the pledge of allegiance, then the song every Black person I knew called the Negro National Anthem. All done in the same key, with the same passion and most often standing on the same foot.

Finding my seat at last, I was overcome with a presentiment of worse things to come. Something unrehearsed, unplanned, was going to happen, and we were going to be made to look bad. I distinctly remember being explicit in the choice of pronoun. It was "we," the graduating class, the unit, that concerned me then.

The principal welcomed "parents and friends" and asked the Baptist minister to lead us in prayer. His invocation was brief and punchy, and for a second I thought we were getting back on the high road to right action. When the principal came back to the dais, however, his voice had changed. Sounds always affected me profoundly and the principal's voice was one of my favorites. During assembly it melted and lowed weakly into the audience. It had not been in my plan to listen to him, but my curiosity was piqued and I straightened up to give him my attention.

He was talking about Booker T. Washington, our "late great leader," who said we can be as close as the fingers on the hand, etc. . . . Then he said a few vague things about friendship and the friendship of kindly people to those less fortunate than themselves. With that his voice nearly faded, thin, away. Like a river diminishing to a stream and then to a trickle. But he cleared his throat and said, "Our speaker tonight, who is also our friend, came from Texarkana to deliver the commencement address, but due to the irregularity of the train schedule, he's going to, as they say, 'speak and run.' " He said that we understood and wanted the man to know that we were most grateful for the time he was able to give us and then something about how we were willing always to adjust to another's program, and without more ado—"I give you Mr. Edward Donleavy."

Not one but two white men came through the door offstage. The shorter one walked to the speaker's platform, and the tall one moved over to the center seat and sat down. But that was our principal's seat, and already occupied. The dislodged gentleman bounced around for a long breath or two before the Baptist minister gave him his chair, then with more dignity than the situation deserved, the minister walked off the stage.

Donleavy looked at the audience once (on reflection, I'm sure that he wanted only to reassure himself that we were really there), adjusted his glasses and began to read from a sheaf of papers.

He was glad "to be here and to see the work going on just as it was in the other schools."

At the first "Amen" from the audience I willed the offender to immediate death by choking on the word. But Amens and Yes, sir's began to fall around the room like rain through a ragged umbrella.

He told us of the wonderful changes we children in Stamps had in store. The Central School (naturally, the white school was Central) had already been granted improvements that would be in use in the fall. A well-known artist was coming from Little Rock to teach art to them. They were going to have the newest microscopes and chemistry equipment for their laboratory. Mr. Donleavy didn't leave us long in the dark over who made these improvements available to Central High. Nor were we to be ignored in the general betterment scheme he had in mind.

He said that he had pointed out to people at a very high level that one of the first-line football tacklers at Arkansas Agricultural and Mechanical College had graduated from good old Lafayette County Training School. Here fewer Amen's were heard. Those few that did break through lay dully in the air with the heaviness of habit.

He went on to praise us. He went on to say how he had bragged that "one of the best basketball players at Fisk sank his first ball right here at Lafayette County Training School."

The white kids were going to have a chance to become Galileos and Madame Curies and Edisons and Gauguins, and our boys (the girls weren't even in on it) would try to be Jesse Owenses and Joe Louises.

Owens and the Brown Bomber were great heroes in our world, but what school official in the white-goddom of Little Rock had the right to decide that those two men must be our only heroes? Who decided that for Henry Reed to become a scientist he had to work like George Washington Carver, as a bootblack, to buy a lousy microscope? Bailey was obviously always going to be too small to be an athlete, so which concrete angel glued to what country seat had decided that if my brother wanted to become a lawyer he had to first pay penance for his skin by picking cotton and hoeing corn and studying correspondence books at night for twenty years?

The man's dead words fell like bricks around the auditorium and too many settled in my belly. Constrained by hard-learned manners I couldn't look behind me, but to my left and right the proud graduating class of 1940 had dropped their heads. Every girl in my row had found something new to do with her handkerchief. Some folded the tiny squares into love knots, some into triangles, but most were wadding them, then pressing them flat on their yellow laps.

On the dais, the ancient tragedy was being replayed. Professor Parsons sat, a sculptor's reject, rigid. His large, heavy body seemed devoid of will or willingness, and his eyes said he was no longer with us. The other teachers examined the flag (which was draped stage right) or their notes, or the windows which opened on our now-famous playing diamond.

Graduation, the hush-hush magic time of frills and gifts and congratulations and diplomas, was finished for me before my name was called. The accomplishment was nothing. The meticulous maps, drawn in three colors of ink, learning and spelling decasyllabic words, memorizing the whole of *The Rape of Lucrece*—it was nothing. Donleavy had exposed us.

We were maids and farmers, handymen and washerwomen, and anything higher that we aspired to was farcical and presumptuous. Then I wished that Gabriel Prosser and Nat Turner had killed all whitefolks in their beds and that Abraham Lincoln had been assassinated before the signing of the Emancipation Proclamation, and that Harriet Tubman had been killed by that blow on her head and Christopher Columbus had drowned in the *Santa Maria.*

It was awful to be Negro and have no control over my life. It was brutal to be young and already trained to sit quietly and listen to charges brought against my color with no chance of defense. We should all be dead. I thought I should like to see us all dead, one on top of the other. A pyramid of flesh with the whitefolks on the bottom, as the broad base, then the Indians with their silly tomahawks and teepees and wigwams and treaties, the Negroes with their mops and recipes and cotton sacks and spirituals sticking out of their mouths. The Dutch children should all stumble in their wooden shoes and break their necks. The French should choke to death on the Louisiana Purchase (1803) while silkworms ate all the Chinese with their stupid pigtails. As a species, we were an abomination. All of us.

Donleavy was running for election, and assured our parents that if he won we could count on having the only colored paved playing field in that part of Arkansas. Also—he never looked up to acknowledge the grunts of acceptance—also, we were bound to get some new equipment for the home economics building and the workshop.

He finished, and since there was no need to give any more than the most perfunctory thank-you's, he nodded to the men on the stage, and the tall white man who was never introduced joined him at the door. They left with the attitude that now they were off to something really important. (The graduation ceremonies at Lafayette County Training School had been a mere preliminary.)

The ugliness they left was palpable. An uninvited guest who wouldn't leave. The choir was summoned and sang a modern arrangement of "Onward, Christian Soldiers," with new words pertaining to graduates seeking their place in the world. But it didn't work. Elouise, the daughter of the Baptist minister, recited "Invictus," and I could have cried at the impertinence of "I am the master of my fate, I am the captain of my soul."

My name had lost its ring of familiarity and I had to be nudged to go and receive my diploma. All my preparations had fled. I neither marched up to the stage like a conquering Amazon, nor did I look in the audience for Bailey's nod of approval. Marguerite Johnson, I heard the name again, my honors were read, there were noises in the audience of appreciation, and I took my place on the stage as rehearsed.

I thought about colors I hated: ecru, puce, lavender, beige and black.

There was shuffling and rustling around me, then Henry Reed was giving his valedictory address, "To Be or Not to Be." Hadn't he heard the whitefolks? We couldn't *be,* so the question was a waste of time. Henry's voice came out clear and strong. I feared to look at him. Hadn't he got the message? There was no "nobler in the mind" for Negroes because the world didn't think we had minds, and they let us know it. "Outrageous fortune"? Now, that was a joke. When the ceremony was over I had to tell Henry Reed some things. That is, if I still cared. Not "rub," Henry, "erase." "Ah, there's the erase." Us.

Henry had been a good student in elocution. His voice rose on tides of promise and fell on waves of warnings. The English teacher had helped him to create a sermon winging through Hamlet's soliloquy. To be a man, a doer, a builder, a leader, or to be a tool, an unfunny joke, a crusher of funky toadstools. I marveled that Henry could go through with the speech as if we had a choice.

I had been listening and silently rebutting each sentence with my eyes closed; then there was a hush, which in an audience warns that something unplanned is happening. I looked up and saw Henry Reed, the conservative, the proper, the A student, turn his back to the audience and turn to us (the proud graduating class of 1940) and sing, nearly speaking,

> Lift ev'ry voice and sing
> Till earth and heaven ring
> Ring with the harmonies of Liberty . . .

It was the poem written by James Weldon Johnson. It was the music composed by J. Rosamond Johnson. It was the Negro National Anthem. Out of habit we were singing it.

Our mothers and fathers stood in the dark hall and joined the hymn of encouragement. A kindergarten teacher led the small children onto the stage and the buttercups and daisies and bunny rabbits marked time and tried to follow:

Stony the road we trod
Bitter the chastening rod
Felt in the days when hope, unborn, had died.
Yet with a steady beat
Have not our weary feet
Come to the place for which our fathers sighed?

Every child I knew had learned that song with his ABC's and along with "Jesus Loves Me This I Know." But I personally had never heard it before. Never heard the words, despite the thousands of times I had sung them. Never thought they had anything to do with me.

On the other hand, the words of Patrick Henry had made such an impression on me that I had been able to stretch myself tall and trembling and say, "I know not what course others may take, but as for me, give me liberty or give me death."

And now I heard, really for the first time:

We have come over a way that with tears has been watered,
We have come, treading our path through the blood of the
slaughtered.

While echoes of the song shivered in the air, Henry Reed bowed his head, said "Thank you," and returned to his place in the line. The tears that slipped down many faces were not wiped away in shame.

We were on top again. As always, again. We survived. The depths had been icy and dark, but now a bright sun spoke to our souls. I was no longer simply a member of the proud graduating class of 1940; I was a proud member of the wonderful, beautiful Negro race.

Oh, Black known and unknown poets, how often have your auctioned pains sustained us? Who will compute the lonely nights made less lonely by your songs, or by the empty pots made less tragic by your tales?

If we were a people much given to revealing secrets, we might raise monuments and sacrifice to the memories of our poets, but slavery cured us of that weakness. It may be enough, however, to have it said that we survive in exact relationship to the dedication of our poets (include preachers, musicians and blues singers).

## Questions

1. In the first paragraph notice such overstatements as "glorious release," "the graduating classes themselves were the nobility," and "exotic destinations." Find further examples in the next few pages. What is the function of this diction?
2. Characterize the writer as you perceive her at the end of the first section (page 206). Support your characterization with references to specific passages. Next, characterize her in the paragraph beginning "It was awful to be Negro" (page 209). Next, characterize her on the basis of the entire essay. Finally, in a sentence, try to describe the change, telling the main attitudes or moods that she goes through.
3. How would you define "poets" as Angelou uses the word in the last sentence?

Paul Goodman

# A Proposal to Abolish Grading

Let half a dozen of the prestigious Universities—Chicago, Stanford, the Ivy League—abolish grading, and use testing only and entirely for pedagogic purposes as teachers see fit.

Anyone who knows the frantic temper of the present schools will understand the transvaluation of values that would be effected by this modest innovation. For most of the students, the competitive grade has come to be the essence. The naïve teacher points to the beauty of the subject and the ingenuity of the research; the shrewd student asks if he is responsible for that on the final exam.

---

Paul Goodman (1911–1972) received his bachelor's degree from City College in New York and his Ph.D. from the University of Chicago. He taught in several colleges and universities, and he wrote prolifically on literature, politics, and education. Goodman's view that students were victims of a corrupt society made him especially popular on campuses, even in the 1960s when students tended to distrust anyone over thirty. "A Proposal to Abolish Grading" (editors' title) is an extract from *Compulsory Miseducation and the Community of Scholars* (1966).

Let me at once dispose of an objection whose unanimity is quite fascinating. I think that the great majority of professors agree that grading hinders teaching and creates a bad spirit, going as far as cheating and plagiarizing. I have before me the collection of essays, *Examining in Harvard College,* and this is the consensus. It is uniformly asserted, however, that the grading is inevitable; for how else will the graduate schools, the foundations the corporations *know* whom to accept, reward, hire? How will the talent scouts know whom to tap?

By testing the applicants, of course, according to the specific task-requirements of the inducting institution, just as applicants for the Civil Service or for licenses in medicine, law, and architecture are tested. Why should Harvard professors do the testing *for* corporations and graduate-schools?

The objection is ludicrous. Dean Whitla, of the Harvard Office of Tests, points out that the scholastic-aptitude and achievement tests used for *admission* to Harvard are a super-excellent index for all-around Harvard performance, better than high-school grades or particular Harvard course-grades. Presumably, these college-entrance tests are tailored for what Harvard and similar institutions want. By the same logic, would not an employer do far better to apply his own job-aptitude test rather than to rely on the vagaries of Harvard section-men. Indeed, I doubt that many employers bother to look at such grades; they are more likely to be interested merely in the fact of a Harvard diploma, whatever that connotes to them. The grades have most of their weight with the graduate schools—here, as elsewhere, the system runs mainly for its own sake.

It is really necessary to remind our academics of the ancient history of Examination. In the medieval university, the whole point of the gruelling trial of the candidate was whether or not to accept him as a peer. His disputation and lecture for the Master's was just that, a master-piece to enter the guild. It was not to make comparative evaluations. It was not to weed out and select for an extra-mural licensor or employer. It was certainly not to pit one young fellow against another in an ugly competition. My philosophic impression is that the medievals thought they knew what a good job of work was and that we are competitive because we do not know. But the more status is achieved by largely irrelevant competitive evaluation, the less will we ever know.

(Of course, our American examinations never did have this purely guild orientation, just as our faculties have rarely had absolute autonomy; the examining was to satisfy Overseers, Elders, distant

Regents—and they as paternal superiors have always doted on giving grades, rather than accepting peers. But I submit that this set-up itself makes it impossible for the student to *become* a master, to *have* grown up, and to commence on his own. He will always be making A or B for some overseer. And in the present atmosphere, he will always be climbing on his friend's neck.)

Perhaps the chief objectors to abolishing grading would be the students and their parents. The parents should be simply disregarded; their anxiety has done enough damage already. For the students, it seems to me that a primary duty of the university is to deprive them of their props, their dependence on extrinsic valuation and motivation, and to force them to confront the difficult enterprise itself and finally lose themselves in it.

A miserable effect of grading is to nullify the various uses of testing. Testing, for both student and teacher, is a means of structuring, and also of finding out what is blank or wrong and what has been assimilated and can be taken for granted. Review—including high-pressure review—is a means of bringing together the fragments, so that there are flashes of synoptic insight.

There are several good reasons for testing, and kinds of test. But if the aim is to discover weakness, what is the point of down-grading and punishing it, and thereby inviting the student to conceal his weakness, by faking and bulling, if not cheating? The natural conclusion of synthesis is the insight itself, not a grade for having had it. For the important purpose of placement, if one can establish in the student the belief that one is testing *not* to grade and make invidious comparisons but for his own advantage, the student should normally seek his own level, where he is challenged and yet capable, rather than trying to get by. If the student dares to accept himself as he is, a teacher's grade is a crude instrument compared with a student's self-awareness. But it is rare in our universities that students are encouraged to notice objectively their vast confusion. Unlike Socrates, our teachers rely on power-drives rather than shame and ingenuous idealism.

Many students are lazy, so teachers try to goad or threaten them by grading. In the long run this must do more harm than good. Laziness is a character-defense. It may be a way of avoiding learning, in order to protect the conceit that one is already perfect (deeper, the despair that one *never* can). It may be a way of avoiding just the risk of failing and being down-graded. Sometimes it is a way of politely saying, "I won't." But since it is the authoritarian grown-up demands that have created such attitudes in the first place, why repeat the trauma? There comes a time when we must treat people as adult, laziness and all. It is one thing courageously to fire a do-nothing out of your class; it is quite another thing to evaluate him with a lordly F.

Most important of all, it is often obvious that balking in doing the work, especially among bright young people who get to great universities, means exactly what it says: The work does not suit me, not this subject, or not at this time, or not in this school, or not in school altogether. The student might not be bookish; he might be school-tired; perhaps his development ought now to take another direction. Yet unfortunately, if such a student is intelligent and is not sure of himself, he *can* be bullied into passing, and this obscures everything. My hunch is that I am describing a common situation. What a grim waste of young life and teacherly effort! Such a student will retain nothing of what he has "passed" in. Sometimes he must get mononucleosis to tell his story and be believed.

And ironically, the converse is also probably commonly true. A student flunks and is mechanically weeded out, who is really ready and eager to learn in a scholastic setting, but he has not quite caught on. A good teacher can recognize the situation, but the computer wreaks its will.

## Questions

1. In his opening paragraph Goodman limits his suggestion about grading and testing to "half a dozen of the prestigious Universities." Does he offer any reason for this limitation? Can you?
2. In the third paragraph Goodman says that "the great majority of professors agree that grading hinders teaching." What evidence does he offer to support this claim? What arguments might be made that grading assists teaching? Should Goodman have made them?
3. As a student, have grades helped you to learn, or have grades hindered you? Explain.

## Paul Robinson

# TV Can't Educate

On July 20 [1978] NBC aired a documentary on life in Marin County, a bedroom community just across the Golden Gate Bridge from San Francisco. The program was called "I Want It All Now" and its single theme was the predominance of narcissism in Marin. The program's host, Edwin Newman, introduced viewers, in his studied casual manner, to a variety of "consciousness raising" groups ensconced in Marin and insinuated that this new narcissistic manner was leading to a breakdown not only of the family (a divorce rate of 75 percent was mentioned three times) but also of traditional civic virtue. The following day the *San Francisco Chronicle* carried a long, front-page article on the outraged reaction of Marin's respectable citizenry to what is considered a grossly distorted portrait of itself. Several residents argued, persuasively, that Marin was in fact a highly political suburb—that it had been a hot spot of the anti-Vietnam war movement, and that only last year it had responded dramatically to the water crisis in California, cutting back on water use much more than was required by law. Television journalism appeared to be up to its old tricks: producers saw what they wanted to see, and they were not about to pass up the chance to show a woman being massaged by two nude men and chirping about how delightful it was to "receive" without having to "give."

I was reminded, however improbably, of an experience in Berlin, where I had spent the previous six months teaching. The Germans are all exercised over a recent movie about Adolf Hitler *(Hitler: Eine Karriere)*, which is based on a biography by the journalist Joachim Fest. The charge leveled against the film is that it glorifies Hitler (though it uses nothing but documentary footage; there are no actors), and it has been linked with a supposed resurgence of Nazism in Germany, particularly among the young. I saw only parts of the film and therefore can't speak to the justice of the charge. What I wish to report on—and what the Marin program brought to mind—is a lecture I attended by a young German historian from the Free

Paul Robinson was born in San Diego in 1940. He teaches history at Stanford University, specializing in modern European intellectual history.

University of Berlin, in which he took issue with the film because it had failed to treat Hitler's relations with the German industrialists, who were crucial in supporting the Nazi Party before it came to power and apparently benefited from its success.

The critics of the Newman program and my young scholar friend in Berlin were guilty of the same error. They both bought the assumption that television and movies can be a source of knowledge, that one can "learn" from them. By knowledge and learning I obviously don't mean an assortment of facts. Rather I have in mind the analytic process that locates pieces of information within a larger context of argument and meaning. Movies and TV are structurally unsuited to that process.

There is no great mystery here. It's a simple matter of time. Learning requires one kind of time, visual media are bound to another. In learning one must be able to freeze the absorption of fact or proposition at any moment in order to make mental comparisons, to test the fact or proposition against known facts and propositions, to measure it against the formal rules of logic and evidence—in short, to carry on a mental debate. Television is a matter of seconds, minutes and hours, it moves inexorably forward, and thus even with the best will in the world (a utopian assumption), it can never teach. In the last analysis there is only one way to learn: by reading. That's how you'll find out about Hitler's relations with the German industrialists, if you can find out about them at all. Such a complex, many-layered phenomenon simply cannot be reduced to a scene (which would presumably meet my scholar-friend's objection) in which Hitler has dinner with Baron Krupp. Similarly, you will not find out about life in Marin County from an hour-long TV program or, for that matter, from a 24-hour-long one. What are the control populations? What statistical methods are being used? Is there more consciousness raising going on in Marin than in Cambridge? What is the correlation between narcissism and income level, educational background, employment, religious affiliation, marital status, sexual inclination and so forth? If these questions have answers, they are to be found in the books and articles of sociologists, not on TV.

I am prepared, indeed eager, to follow my argument to its logical conclusion: the worst thing on TV is educational TV (and not just on educational stations). By comparison the gratuitous violence of most commercial shows is a mere peccadillo. Educational TV corrupts the very notion of education and renders its victims uneducable. I hear grown-ups launching conversations with, "Mike Wallace says that . . ." as if Mike Wallace actually knew something. Viewers hold forth authoritatively about South Africa, or DNA, or black holes, or whatever because they have watched a segment about them on "60 Minutes" or some such program. Complete ignorance really would be preferable, because ignorance at least preserves a mental space that might someday be filled with real knowledge, or some approximation of it.

There is a new form of slumming popular among intellectuals: watching "bad" (i.e. commercial) TV and even writing books about it (as Dan Wakefield has about the afternoon soap opera "All My Children"). I would like to think that the motive behind this development is revulsion against the intellectual pretensions of "good" TV. But, as often happens with academics, the reaction has been dressed up in phony theoretical garb. "All My Children," we're supposed to believe, is the great American novel, heir to the tradition of Dickens and Trollope. Of course it's nothing of the sort. But it *is* very good entertainment. And that is precisely what TV is prepared to do: to entertain, to divert, above all to amuse. It is superbly amusing, ironically, for the same reason that it can't educate: it is tied to the clock, which has enormous comic potential. It is not accidental that one speaks of a comedian's "timing." Jack Benny would not be funny in print. He must wait just the right length of time after the robber threatens, "Your money or your life," before responding. (Imagine the situation in a novel: "The robber said, 'Your money or your life.' Jack took ten seconds trying to make up his mind.") Nor can you do a double-take in print, only on the screen. The brilliant manipulation of time made "The Honeymooners" so funny: Art Carney squandered it while Jackie Gleason, whose clock ran at double-time, burned. Audrey Meadows stood immobile, producing a magnificently sustained and silent obbligato to Gleason's frantic buffo patter.

Television, then, is superbly fit to amuse. And amusement is not to be despised. At the very least it provides an escape from the world and from ourselves. It is pleasurable (by definition, one might say), and it gives us a sense of union with humanity, if only in its foibles. Herbert Marcuse might even contend that it keeps alive the image of an unrepressed existence. Television can provide all this. But it can't educate.

Movies are faced with the same dilemma. The desire to educate accounts, I believe, for the increasingly deliberate pace of movies. It is as if the director were trying to provide room within his time-bound narrative for the kind of reflection associated with analysis. This was brought home to me recently when, during the same week, I saw the movie *Julia* in the theater and *Jezebel* on TV. The latter, made in 1938, portrays the tragedy of a strong-willed southern girl who refuses to conform to the rules of antebellum New Orleans society. The most striking difference between the two movies is their pace. *Jezebel* moves along swiftly (there is probably more dialogue in the first 15 minutes than in all of *Julia*), treats its theme with appropriate superficiality and entertains effortlessly. *Julia,* on the other hand, is lugubrious and obviously beyond its depth. It succeeds only with the character of Julia herself, who, like Jezebel, is powerful, beautiful, virtuous and unburdened by intellectual or psychological complexity. By way of contrast, the narrative figure, Lilli, tries vainly to deal with issues that movies can't manage: the difficulty of writing, a relationship with an older man who is at once lover, mentor, and patient-to-be, the tension between literary success and political commitment. All of these are wonderfully captured in Lillian Hellman's memoir, but not even two fine actors like Jane Fonda and Jason Robards can bring such uncinematic matters to life on the screen. The "issue" of the memoir—despite all those meaningful silences—inevitably eluded the movie.

Let us, then, not ask more of movies and TV than they can deliver. In fact, let us discourage them from trying to "educate" us.

## Questions

1. The first paragraph speaks of the "new narcissistic manner." What is narcissism? How is the etymology of the word (like "narcotic," it derives ultimately from the Greek *narkē,* "numbness") relevant to the meaning of narcissism?
2. In the paragraph beginning "There is no great mystery here" (page 217), Robinson argues that one can't learn from television because television doesn't allow the viewer time "to make mental comparisons, to test the fact or proposition against known facts and propositions, . . . in short, to carry on a mental debate." If this is true, does it follow that the lecture method of teaching is also inherently ineffective? Is Robinson defining teaching and learning (see especially his third paragraph) too narrowly?

Toni Cade Bambara

# The Lesson

Back in the days when everyone was old and stupid or young and foolish and me and Sugar were the only ones just right, this lady moved on our block with nappy hair and proper speech and no makeup. And quite naturally we laughed at her, laughed the way we did at the junk man who went about his business like he was some big-time president and his sorry-ass horse his secretary. And we kinda hated her too, hated the way we did the winos who cluttered up our parks and pissed on our handball walls and stank up our hallways and stairs so you couldn't halfway play hide-and-seek without a goddamn gas mask. Miss Moore was her name. The only woman on the block with no first name. And she was black as hell, cept for her feet, which were fish-white and spooky. And she was always planning these boring-ass things for us to do, us being my cousin, mostly, who lived on the block cause we all moved North the same time and to the same apartment then spread out gradual to breathe. And our parents would yank our heads into some kinda shape and crisp up our clothes so we'd be presentable for travel with Miss Moore, who always looked like she was going to church, though she never did. Which is just one of things the grownups talked about when they talked behind her back like a dog. But when she came calling with some sachet she'd sewed up or some gingerbread she'd made or some book, why then they'd all be too embarrassed to turn her down and we'd get handed over all spruced up. She'd been to college and said it was only right that she should take responsibility for the young ones' education, and she not even related by marriage or blood. So they'd go for it. Specially Aunt Gretchen. She was the main gofer in the family. You got some ole dumb shit foolishness you want somebody to go for, you send for Aunt Gretchen. She been

---

Toni Cade Bambara, born in New York City in 1939, received her B.A. from Queens College in 1959 and her M.A. from City College in 1964. Both schools are part of the City University of New York. She has studied mime and dance, has taught at Livingston College of Rutgers University, and has worked for the New York State Department of Welfare.

screwed into the go-along for so long, it's a blood-deep natural thing with her. Which is how she got saddled with me and Sugar and Junior in the first place while our mothers were in a la-de-da apartment up the block having a good ole time.

So this one day Miss Moore rounds us all up at the mailbox and it's puredee hot and she's knockin herself out about arithmetic. And school suppose to let up in summer I heard, but she don't never let up. And the starch in my pinafore scratching the shit outta me and I'm really hating this nappy-head bitch and her goddamn college degree. I'd much rather go to the pool or to the show where it's cool. So me and Sugar leaning on the mailbox being surly, which is a Miss Moore word. And Flyboy checking out what everybody brought for lunch. And Fat Butt already wasting his peanut-butter-and-jelly sandwich like the pig he is. And Junebug punchin on Q.T.'s arm for potato chips. And Rosie Giraffe shifting from one hip to the other waiting for somebody to step on her foot or ask her if she from Georgia so she can kick ass, preferably Mercedes'. And Miss Moore asking us do we know what money is, like we a bunch of retards. I mean real money, she say, like it's only poker chips or monopoly papers we lay on the grocer. So right away I'm tired of this and say so. And would much rather snatch Sugar and go to the Sunset and terrorize the West Indian kids and take their hair ribbons and their money too. And Miss Moore files that remark away for next week's lesson on brotherhood, I can tell. And finally I say we oughta get to the subway cause it's cooler and besides we might meet some cute boys. Sugar done swiped her mama's lipstick, so we ready.

So we heading down the street and she's boring us silly about what things cost and what our parents make and how much goes for rent and how money ain't divided up right in this country. And then she gets to the part about we all poor and live in the slums, which I don't feature. And I'm ready to speak on that, but she steps out in the street and hails two cabs just like that. Then she hustles half the crew in with her and hands me a five-dollar bill and tells me to calculate 10 percent tip for the driver. And we're off. Me and Sugar and Junebug and Flyboy hanging out the window and hollering to everybody, putting lipstick on each other cause Flyboy a faggot anyway, and making farts with our sweaty armpits. But I'm mostly trying to figure how to spend this money. But they all fascinated with the meter ticking and Junebug starts laying bets as to how much it'll read when Flyboy can't hold his breath no more. Then Sugar lay bets as to how much it'll be when we get there. So I'm stuck. Don't nobody want to go for my plan, which is to jump out at the next light and run off to the first bar-b-que we can find. Then the driver tells us to get the hell out cause we there already. And the meter reads eight-five cents. And I'm stalling to figure out the tip and Sugar say give him a dime. And I decide he don't need it bad as I do, so later for him. But then he tries to take off with Junebug foot still in the door so we talk about his mama something ferocious. Then we check out that we on Fifth Avenue and everybody dressed up in stockings. One lady in a fur coat, hot as it is. White folks crazy.

"This is the place," Miss Moore say, presenting it to us in the voice she uses at the museum. "Let's look in the windows before we go in."

"Can we steal?" Sugar asks very serious like she's getting the ground rules squared away before she plays. "I beg your pardon," say Miss Moore, and we fall out. So she leads us around the windows of the toy store and me and Sugar screamin, "This is mine, that's mine, I gotta have that, that was made for me, I was born for that," till Big Butt drowns us out.

"Hey, I'm goin to buy that there."

"That there? You don't even know what it is, stupid."

"I do so," he say punchin on Rosie Giraffe. "It's a microscope."

"Whatcha gonna do with a microscope, fool?"

"Look at things."

"Like what, Ronald?" ask Miss Moore. And Big Butt ain't got the first notion. So here go Miss Moore gabbing about the thousands of bacteria in a drop of water and the somethinorother in a speck of blood and the million and one living things in the air around us is invisible to the naked eye. And what she say that for? Junebug go to town on that "naked" and we rolling. Then Miss Moore ask what it cost. So we all jam into the window smudgin it up and the price tag say $300. So then she ask how long'd take for Big Butt and Junebug to save up their allowances. "Too long," I say. "Yeh," adds Sugar, "outgrown it by that time." And Miss Moore say no, you never outgrow learning instruments. "Why, even medical students and interns and," blah, blah, blah. And we ready to choke Big Butt for bringing it up in the first damn place.

"This here costs four hundred eighty dollars," say Rosie Giraffe. So we pile up all over her to see what she pointin out. My eyes tell me it's a chunk of glass cracked with something heavy, and different-color inks dripped into the splits, then the whole thing put into a oven or something. But for $480 it don't make sense.

"That's a paperweight made of semi-precious stones fused together under tremendous pressure," she explains slowly, with her hands doing the mining and all the factory work.

"So what's a paperweight?" asks Rosie Giraffe.

"To weigh paper with, dumbbell," say Flyboy, the wise man from the East.

"Not exactly," say Miss Moore, which is what she say when you warm or way off too. "It's to weigh paper down so it won't scatter and make your desk untidy." So right away me and Sugar curtsy to each other and then to Mercedes who is more the tidy type.

"We don't keep paper on top of the desk in my class," say Junebug, figuring Miss Moore crazy or lyin one.

"At home, then," she say. "Don't you have a calendar and a pencil case and a blotter and a letter-opener on your desk at home where you do your homework?" And she know damn well what our homes look like cause she nosys around in them every chance she gets.

"I don't even have a desk," say Junebug. "Do we?"

"No. And I don't get no homework neither," says Big Butt.

"And I don't even have a home," say Flyboy like he do at school to keep the white folks off his back and sorry for him. Send this poor kid to camp posters, is his specialty.

"I do," says Mercedes. "I have a box of stationery on my desk and a picture of my cat. My godmother bought the stationery and the desk. There's a big rose on each sheet and the envelopes smell like roses."

"Who wants to know about your smelly-ass stationery," say Rosie Giraffe fore I can get my two cents in.

"It's important to have a work area all your own so that . . ."

"Will you look at this sailboat, please," say Flyboy, cuttin her off and pointin to the thing like it was his. So once again we tumble all over each other to gaze at this magnificent thing in the toy store which is just big enough to maybe sail two kittens across the pond if you strap them to the posts tight. We all start reciting the price tag like we in assembly. "Handcrafted sailboat of fiberglass at one thousand one hundred ninety-five dollars."

"Unbelievable," I hear myself say and am really stunned. I read it again for myself just in case the group recitation put me in a trance. Same thing. For some reason this pisses me off. We look at Miss Moore and she lookin at us, waiting for I dunno what.

"Who'd pay all that when you can buy a sailboat set for a

quarter at Pop's, a tube of glue for a dime, and a ball of string for eight cents? It must have a motor and a whole lot else besides," I say. "My sailboat cost me about fifty cents."

"But will it take water?" say Mercedes with her smart ass.

"Took mine to Alley Pond Park once," say Flyboy. "String broke. Lost it. Pity."

"Sailed mine in Central Park and it keeled over and sank. Had to ask my father for another dollar."

"And you got the strap," laugh Big Butt. "The jerk didn't even have a string on it. My old man wailed on his behind."

"Little Q.T. was staring hard at the sailboat and you could see he wanted it bad. But he too little and somebody'd just take it from him. So what the hell. "This boat for kids, Miss Moore?"

"Parents silly to buy something like that just to get all broke up," say Rosie Giraffe.

"That much money it should last forever," I figure.

"My father'd buy it for me if I wanted it."

"Your father, my ass," say Rosie Giraffe getting a chance to finally push Mercedes.

"Must be rich people shop here," say Q.T.

"You are a very bright boy," say Flyboy. "What was your first clue?" And he rap him on the head with the back of his knuckles, since Q.T. the only one he could get away with. Though Q.T. liable to come up behind you years later and get his licks in when you half expect it.

"What I want to know is," I says to Miss Moore though I never talk to her, I wouldn't give the bitch that satisfaction, "is how much a real boat costs? I figure a thousand'd get you a yacht any day."

"Why don't you check that out," she says, "and report back to the group?" Which really pains my ass. If you gonna mess up a perfectly good swim day least you could do is have some answers. "Let's go in," she say like she got something up her sleeve. Only she don't lead the way. So me and Sugar turn the corner to where the entrance is, but when we get there I kinda hang back. Not that I'm scared, what's there to be afraid of, just a toy store. But I feel funny, shame. But what I got to be shamed about? Got as much right to go in as anybody. But somehow I can't seem to get hold of the door, so I step away for Sugar to lead. But she hangs back too. And I look at her and she looks at me and this is ridiculous. I mean, damn, I have never ever been shy about doing nothing or going nowhere. But then Mercedes steps up and then Rosie Giraffe and Big Butt crowd in behind and shove, and next thing we all stuffed into the doorway with only Mercedes squeezing past us, smoothing out her jumper and walking right down the aisle. Then the rest of us tumble in like a glued-together jigsaw done all wrong. And people lookin at us. And it's like the time me and Sugar crashed into the Catholic church on a dare. But once we got in there and everything so hushed and holy and the candles and the bowin and the handkerchiefs on all the drooping heads, I just couldn't go through with the plan. Which was for me to run up to the altar and do a tap dance while Sugar played the nose flute and messed around in the holy water. And Sugar kept givin me the elbow. Then later teased me so bad I tied her up in the shower and turned it on and locked her in. And she'd be there till this day if Aunt Gretchen hadn't finally figured I was lyin about the boarder takin a shower.

Same thing in the store. We all walkin on tiptoe and hardly touchin the games and puzzles and things. And I watched Miss Moore who is steady watchin us like she waiting for a sign. Like Mama Drewery watches the sky and sniffs the air and takes note of just how much slant is in the bird formation. Then me and Sugar bump smack into each other, so busy gazing at the toys, 'specially the sailboat. But we don't laugh and go into our fat-lady bump-stomach routine. We just stare at that price tag. Then Sugar run a finger over the whole boat. And I'm jealous and want to hit her. Maybe not her, but I sure want to punch somebody in the mouth.

"Watcha bring us here for, Miss Moore?"

"You sound angry, Sylvia. Are you mad about something?" Givin me one of them grins like she tellin a grown-up joke that never turns out to be funny. And she's lookin very closely at me like maybe she plannin to do my portrait from memory. I'm mad, but I won't give her that satisfaction. So I slouch around the store bein very bored and say, "Let's go."

Me and Sugar at the back of the train watchin the tracks whizzin by large then small then gettin gobbled up in the dark. I'm thinkin about this tricky toy I saw in the store. A clown that somersaults on a bar then does chin-ups just cause you yank lightly at his leg. Cost $35. I could see me askin my mother for a $35 birthday clown. "You wanna who that costs what?" she'd say, cocking her head to the side to get a better view of the hole in my head. Thirty-five dollars and the whole household could go visit Grandaddy Nelson in the country. Thirty-five dollars would pay for the rent and the piano bill too. Who are these people that spend that much for performing clowns and $1000 for toy sailboats? What kinda work they do and how they live and how come we ain't in on it? Where we are is who we are, Miss Moore always pointin out. But it don't necessarily have to be that way, she always adds then waits for somebody to say that poor people have to wake up and demand their share of the pie and don't none of us know what kind of pie she talkin about in the first damn place. But she ain't so smart cause I still got her four dollars from the taxi and she sure ain't gettin it. Messin up my day with this shit. Sugar nudges me in my pocket and winks.

Miss Moore lines us up in front of the mailbox where we started from, seem like years ago, and I got a headache for thinkin so hard. And we lean all over each other so we can hold up under the draggy-ass lecture she always finishes us off with at the end before we thank her for borin us to tears. But she just looks at us like she readin tea leaves. Finally she say, "Well, what did you think of F.A.O. Schwartz?"

Rosie Giraffe mumbles, "White folks crazy."

"I'd like to go there again when I get my birthday money," says Mercedes, and we shove her out the pack so she has to lean on the mailbox by herself.

"I'd like a shower. Tiring day," say Flyboy.

Then Sugar surprises me by sayin, "You know, Miss Moore, I don't think all of us here put together eat in a year what that sailboat costs." And Miss Moore lights up like somebody goosed her. "And?" she say, urging Sugar on. Only I'm standin on her foot so she don't continue.

"Imagine for a minute what kind of society it is in which some people can spend on a toy what it would cost to feed a family of six or seven. What do you think?"

"I think," say Sugar pushing me off her feet like she never done before, cause I whip her ass in a minute, "that this is not much of a democracy if you ask me. Equal chance to pursue happiness means an equal crack at the dough, don't it?" Miss Moore is besides herself and I am disgusted with Sugar's treachery. So I stand on her foot one more time to see if she'll shove me. She shuts up, and Miss Moore looks at me, sorrowfully I'm thinkin. And somethin weird is goin on. I can feel it in my chest.

"Anybody else learn anything today?" lookin dead at me. I walk away and Sugar has to run to catch up and don't even seem to notice when I shrug her arm off my shoulder.

"Well, we got four dollars anyway," she says.

"Uh hunh."

"We could go to Hascombs and get half a chocolate layer and then to the Sunset and still have plenty money for potato chips and ice cream sodas."

"Uh hunh."

"Race you to Hascombs," she say.

We start down the block and she gets ahead which is O.K. by me cause I'm goin to the West End and then over to the Drive to think this day through. She can run if she want to and even run faster. But ain't nobody gonna beat me at nuthin.

## Questions

1. What is the point of Miss Moore's lesson? Why does Sylvia resist it?
2. Describe the relationship between Sugar and Sylvia. What is Sugar's function in the story?
3. What does the last line of the story suggest?

## Wu-tsu Fa-yen

# Zen and the Art of Burglary

If people ask me what Zen is like, I will say that it is like learning the art of burglary. The son of a burglar saw his father growing older and thought, "If he is unable to carry on his profession, who will be the breadwinner of the family, except myself? I must learn the trade." He intimated the idea to his father, who approved of it.

One night the father took the son to a big house, broke through the fence, entered the house, and, opening one of the large chests, told the son to go in and pick out the clothing. As soon as the son got into it, the father dropped the lid and securely applied the lock. The father now came out to the courtyard and loudly knocked at the door, waking up the whole family; then he quietly slipped away by the hole in the fence. The residents got excited and lighted candles, but they found that the burglar had already gone.

The son, who remained all the time securely confined in the chest, thought of his cruel father. He was greatly mortified, then a fine idea flashed upon him. He made a noise like the gnawing of a rat. The family told the maid to take a candle and examine the chest. When the lid was unlocked, out came the prisoner, who blew out the light, pushed away the maid, and fled. The people ran after him. Noticing a well by the road, he picked up a large stone and threw it into the water. The pursuers all gathered around the well trying to find the burglar drowning himself in the dark hole.

---

Wu-tsu Fa-yen (1025–1104) was a Chinese Zen Buddhist priest. More exactly, he was a Ch'an priest; *Zen* is Japanese for the Chinese *Ch'an.*

The practitioner of Zen (to use the more common name) seeks *satori,* "enlightenment" or "awakening." The awakening is from a world of blind strivings (including those of reason and of morality). The awakened being, free from a sense of the self in opposition to all other things, perceives the unity of all things. Wu-tsu belonged to the branch of Zen that uses "shock therapy, the purpose of which is to jolt the student out of his analytical and conceptual way of thinking and lead him back to his natural and spontaneous faculty" (Kenneth Ch'en, *Buddhism in China* [1964, rptd. 1972], p. 359).

The title of this story, from *The Sayings of Goso Hōyen,* is the editors'.

---

In the meantime he went safely back to his father's house. He blamed his father deeply for his narrow escape. Said the father, "Be not offended, my son. Just tell me how you got out of it." When the son told him all about his adventures, the father remarked, "There you are, you have learned the art."

## Questions

1. What assumptions about knowledge did the father make? Can you think of any of your own experiences that substantiate this assumption?
2. Is there anything you have studied or are studying to which Zen pedagogical methods would be applicable? If so, explain by setting forth a sample lesson.

Marianne Moore

# The Student

"In America," began
the lecturer, "everyone must have a
degree. The French do not think that
all can have it, they don't say everyone
 must go to college." We
do incline to feel
 that although it may be unnecessary

to know fifteen languages,
one degree is not too much. With us, a
school—like the singing tree of which
the leaves were mouths singing in concert—is
 both a tree of knowledge
and of liberty,—
 seen in the unanimity of college

---

Marianne Moore (1887–1972) was educated at Bryn Mawr and at Carlisle Commercial College. From 1911 to 1915 she taught stenography at the government Indian school in Carlisle, Pennsylvania. Later she served as a secretary, as an assistant in the New York Public Library, and as the editor of the *Dial,* a literary journal. During her long career as a poet she received numerous awards, including the Cross of the Legion of Honor, in France.

Miss Moore provides the following note to "The Student":

"In America." Les Idéals de l'éducation française; lecture, December 3, 1931, by M. Auguste Desclos, Director-adjoint, Office National des Universités et Écoles Françaises de Paris.

The singing tree. Each leaf was a mouth, and every leaf joined in concert. *Arabian Nights.*

*Lux et veritas* (Yale); *Christo et ecclesiae* (Harvard); *sapiet felici,*——

"Science is never finished." Professor Einstein to an American student; *New York Times.*

Jack Bookworm, in Goldsmith's *The Double Transformation.*

A variety of hero: Emerson in *The American Scholar;* "there can be no scholar without the heroic mind;" "let him hold by himself; . . . patient of neglect, patient of reproach."

The wolf. Edmund Burke, November, 1781, in reply to Fox: "there is excellent wool on the back of a wolf and therefore he must be sheared. . . . But will he comply?"

"Gives his opinion." Henry McBride in the *New York Sun,* December 12, 1931: "Dr. Valentiner . . . has the typical reserve of the student. He does not enjoy the active battle of opinion that invariably rages when a decision is announced that can be weighed in great sums of money. He gives his opinion firmly and rests upon that."

mottoes, *lux et veritas,*
*Christo et ecclesiae, sapiet*
*felici.* It may be that we
have not knowledge, just opinions, that we
    are undergraduates,
not students; we know
    we have been told with smiles, by expatriates

of whom we had asked "When will
your experiment be finished?" "Science
is never finished." Secluded
from domestic strife, Jack Bookworm led a
    college life, says Goldsmith;
and here also as
    in France or Oxford, study is beset with

dangers,—with bookworms, mildews,
and complaisancies. But someone in New
England has known enough to say
the student is patience personified,
    is a variety
of hero, "patient
    of neglect and of reproach,"—who can "hold by

himself." You can't beat hens to
make them lay. Wolf's wool is the best of wool,
but it cannot be sheared because
the wolf will not comply. With knowledge as
    with the wolf's surliness,
the student studies
    voluntarily refusing to be less

than individual. He
"gives his opinion and then rests on it;"
he renders service when there is
no reward, and is too reclusive for
    some things to seem to touch
him, not because he
    has no feeling but because he has so much.

## Questions

1. What is the tone of the lecturer's remarks in lines 1–5? Of the reply in lines 5–9?
2. Explain: "a / school . . . / is / both a tree of knowledge / and of liberty." How do the college mottoes support this notion of what a school is? (Moore gives the Latin version—*lux et veritas,* "light and truth,"—of Yale's Hebrew motto, and she gives a Latin expression—*Christo et ecclesiae,* "for Christ and church,"— that used to appear on the Harvard seal. But *sapiet felici* makes no sense. Moore must have garbled some expression such as *sapiens est felix,* or "the wise man is happy.")
3. What difference is there between "knowledge" and "opinions" (line 18)? What differences between "undergraduates" and "students" (lines 19, 20) are implied?
4. What dangers to the student appear in lines 29–30? What dangers are named or implied from line 35 to the end of the poem? How do the "dangers" contrast? What dangers justify the description of the student as "a variety of hero" (lines 33–34)?

# 4

# WORK AND PLAY

*Lettuce Cutters, Salinas Valley*
**Dorothea Lange, 1935**

Farm Security Administration Photo, Library of Congress

*E. B. White*
**Jill Krementz**

*High School Football*
**Edward Hausner, 1967**

Courtesy NYT Pictures

*Children*
**Helen Levitt, 1940**

# Short Views

Work and play are words used to describe the same thing under differing conditions.

**Mark Twain**

The Battle of Waterloo was won on the playing fields of Eton.

**Attributed to the Duke of Wellington**

The competitive spirit goes by many names. Most simply and directly, it is called "the work ethic." As the name implies, the work ethic holds that labor is good in itself; that a man or woman at work not only makes a contribution to his fellow man, but becomes a better person by virtue of the act of working. That work ethic is ingrained in the American character. That is why most of us consider it immoral to be lazy or slothful—even if a person is well off enough not to have to work or deliberately avoids work by going on welfare.

**Richard Milhous Nixon**

In the laws of political economy, the alienation of the worker from his product is expressed as follows: the more the worker produces, the less he has to consume; the more value he creates, the more valueless, the more unworthy he becomes; the better formed is his product, the more deformed becomes the worker; the more civilized his product, the more brutalized becomes the worker; the mightier the work, the more powerless the worker; the more ingenious the work, the duller becomes the worker and the more he becomes nature's bondsman.

Political economy conceals the alienation inherent in labor by avoiding any mention of the evil effects of work on those who work. Thus, whereas labor produces miracles for the rich, for the worker it produces destitution. Labor produces palaces, but for the worker, hovels. It produces beauty, but it cripples the worker. It replaces labor by machines, but how does it treat the worker? By throwing some workers back into a barbarous kind of work, and by turning the rest into machines. It produces intelligence, but for the worker, stupidity and cretinism.

**Karl Marx**

My young men shall never work. Men who work cannot dream, and wisdom comes in dreams.

**Smohalla, of the Nez Perce**

Everyone who is prosperous or successful must have dreamed of something. It is not because he is a good worker that he is prosperous, but because he dreamed.

**Lost Star, of the Maricopa**

The possible quantity of play depends on the possible quantity of pay.

**John Ruskin**

It can't be just a job. It's not worth playing just for money. It's a way of life. When we were kids there was the release in playing, the sweetness in being able to move and control your body. This is what play is. Beating somebody is secondary. When I was a kid, to really *move* was my delight. I felt released because I could move around anybody. I was free.

**Eric Nesterenko, Professional Hockey Player**

Winning is not the most important thing; it's everything.

**Vince Lombardi**

Serious sport has nothing to do with fair play. It is bound up with hatred, jealousy, boastfulness, disregard of all rules and sadistic pleasure in witnessing violence: in other words, it is war minus the shooting.

**George Orwell**

The maturity of man—that means, to have reacquired the seriousness that one had as a child at play.

**Friedrich Nietzsche**

The boys throw stones at the frogs in sport, but the frogs die not in sport but in earnest.

**Bion**

## Bertrand Russell

# Work

Whether work should be placed among the causes of happiness or among the causes of unhappiness may perhaps be regarded as a doubtful question. There is certainly much work which is exceedingly irksome, and an excess of work is always very painful. I think, however, that, provided work is not excessive in amount, even the dullest work is to most people less painful than idleness. There are in work all grades, from mere relief of tedium up to the profoundest delights, according to the nature of the work and the abilities of the worker. Most of the work that most people have to do is not in itself interesting, but even such work has certain great advantages. To begin with, it fills a good many hours of the day without the need of deciding what one shall do. Most people, when they are left free to fill their own time according to their own choice, are at a loss to think of anything sufficiently pleasant to be worth doing. And whatever they decide on, they are troubled by the feeling that something else would have been pleasanter. To be able to fill leisure intelligently is the last product of civilization, and at present very few people have reached this level. Moreover the exercise of choice is in itself tiresome. Except to people with unusual initiative it is positively agreeable to be told what to do at each hour of the day, provided the orders are not too unpleasant. Most of the idle rich suffer unspeakable boredom as the price of their freedom from drudgery. At times, they may find relief by hunting big game in Africa, or by flying round the world, but the number of such sensa-

Bertrand Russell (1872–1970) was educated at Trinity College, Cambridge. He published his first book, *The Study of German Social Democracy,* in 1896; subsequent books on mathematics and on philosophy quickly established his international reputation. His pacifist opposition to World War I cost him his appointment at Trinity College, and won him a prison sentence of six months. While serving this sentence he wrote his *Introduction to Mathematical Philosophy.* In 1940 an appointment to teach at the College of the City of New York was withdrawn because of Russell's unorthodox moral views. But he was not always treated shabbily; he won numerous awards, including (in 1950) a Nobel Prize. After World War II he devoted most of his energy to warning the world about the dangers of nuclear war.

In reading the first sentence of the essay that we reprint, you should know that the essay comes from a book called *The Conquest of Happiness.*

tions is limited, especially after youth is past. Accordingly the more intelligent rich men work nearly as hard as if they were poor, while rich women for the most part keep themselves busy with innumerable trifles of whose earth-shaking importance they are firmly persuaded.

Work therefore is desirable, first and foremost, as a preventive of boredom, for the boredom that a man feels when he is doing necessary though uninteresting work is as nothing in comparison with the boredom that he feels when he has nothing to do with his days. With this advantage of work another is associated, namely that it makes holidays much more delicious when they come. Provided a man does not have to work so hard as to impair his vigor, he is likely to find far more zest in his free time than an idle man could possibly find.

The second advantage of most paid work and of some unpaid work is that it gives chances of success and opportunities for ambition. In most work success is measured by income, and while our capitalistic society continues, this is inevitable. It is only where the best work is concerned that this measure ceases to be the natural one to apply. The desire that men feel to increase their income is quite as much a desire for success as for the extra comforts that a higher income can procure. However dull work may be, it becomes bearable if it is a means of building up a reputation, whether in the world at large or only in one's own circle. Continuity of purpose is one of the most essential ingredients of happiness in the long run, and for most men this comes chiefly through their work. In this respect those women whose lives are occupied with housework are much less fortunate than men, or than women who work outside the home. The domesticated wife does not receive wages, has no means of bettering herself, is taken for granted by her husband (who sees practically nothing of what she does), and is valued by him not for her housework but for quite other qualities. Of course this does not apply to those women who are sufficiently well-to-do to make beautiful houses and beautiful gardens and become the envy of their neighbors; but such women are comparatively few, and for the great majority housework cannot bring as much satisfaction as work of other kinds brings to men and to professional women.

The satisfaction of killing time and of affording some outlet, however modest, for ambition, belongs to most work, and is sufficient to make even a man whose work is dull happier on the average than a man who has no work at all. But when work is interesting, it is capable of giving satisfaction of a far higher order than mere relief from tedium. The kinds of work in which there is some interest may be arranged in a hierarchy. I shall begin with those which are only mildly interesting and end with those that are worthy to absorb the whole energies of a great man.

Two chief elements make work interesting; first, the exercise of skill, and second, construction.

Every man who has acquired some unusual skill enjoys exercising it until it has become a matter of course, or until he can no longer improve himself. This motive to activity begins in early childhood: a boy who can stand on his head becomes reluctant to stand on his feet. A great deal of work gives the same pleasure that is to be derived from games of skill. The work of a lawyer or a politician must contain in a more delectable form a great deal of the same pleasure that is to be derived from playing bridge. Here of course there is not only the exercise of skill but the outwitting of a skilled opponent. Even where this competitive element is absent, however, the performance of difficult feats is agreeable. A man who can do stunts in an aëroplane finds the pleasure so great that for the sake of it he is willing to risk his life. I imagine that an able surgeon, in spite of the painful circumstances in which his work is done, derives satisfaction from the exquisite precision of his operations. The same kind of pleasure, though in a less intense form, is to be derived from a great deal of work of a humbler kind. All skilled work can be pleasurable, provided the skill required is either variable or capable of indefinite improvement. If these conditions are absent, it will cease to be interesting when a man has acquired his maximum skill. A man who runs three-mile races will cease to find pleasure in this occupation when he passes the age at which he can beat his own previous record. Fortunately there is a very considerable amount of work in which new circumstances call for new skill and a man can go on improving, at any rate until he has reached middle age. In some kinds of skilled work, such as politics, for example, it seems that men are at their best between sixty and seventy, the reason being that in such occupations a wide experience of other men is essential. For this reason successful politicians are apt to be happier at the age of seventy than any other men of equal age. Their only competitors in this respect are the men who are the heads of big businesses.

There is, however, another element possessed by the best work, which is even more important as a source of happiness than is the exercise of skill. This is the element of constructiveness. In some work, though by no means in most, something is built up which remains as a monument when the work is completed. We may distinguish construction from destruction by the following criterion. In construction the initial state of affairs is comparatively haphazard, while the final state of affairs embodies a purpose: in destruction the reverse is the case; the initial state of affairs embodies a purpose, while the final state of affairs is haphazard, that is to say, all that is intended by the destroyer is to produce a state of affairs which does not embody a certain purpose. This criterion applies in the most literal and obvious case, namely the construction and destruction of buildings. In constructing a building a previously made plan is carried out, whereas in destroying it no one decides exactly how the materials are to lie when the demolition is complete. Destruction is of course necessary very often as a preliminary to subsequent construction; in that case it is part of a whole which is constructive. But not infrequently a man will engage in activities of which the purpose is destructive without regard to any construction that may come after. Frequently he will conceal this from himself by the belief that he is only sweeping away in order to build afresh, but it is generally possible to unmask this pretense, when it is a pretense, by asking him what the subsequent construction is to be. On this subject it will be found that he will speak vaguely and without enthusiasm, whereas on the preliminary destruction he has spoken precisely and with zest. This applies to not a few revolutionaries and militarists and other apostles of violence. They are actuated, usually without their own knowledge, by hatred: the destruction of what they hate is their real purpose, and they are comparatively indifferent to the question what is to come after it. Now I cannot deny that in the work of destruction as in the work of construction there may be joy. It is a fiercer joy, perhaps at moments more intense, but it is less profoundly satisfying, since the result is one in which little satisfaction is to be found. You kill your enemy, and when he is dead your occupation is gone, and the satisfaction that you derive from victory quickly fades. The work of construction, on the other hand, when completed is delightful to contemplate, and moreover is never so fully completed that there is nothing further to do about it. The most satisfactory purposes are those that lead on indefinitely from one success to another without ever coming to a dead end; and in this respect it will be found that construction is a greater source of happiness than destruction. Perhaps it would be more correct to say that those who find satisfaction in construction find in it greater satisfaction than the lovers of destruction can find in destruction, for if once you have become filled with hate you will not easily derive from construction the pleasure which another man would derive from it.

At the same time few things are so likely to cure the habit of hatred as the opportunity to do constructive work of an important kind.

The satisfaction to be derived from success in a great constructive enterprise is one of the most massive that life has to offer, although unfortunately in its highest forms it is open only to men of exceptional ability. Nothing can rob a man of the happiness of successful achievement in an important piece of work, unless it be the proof that after all his work was bad. There are many forms of such satisfaction. The man who by a scheme of irrigation has caused the wilderness to blossom like the rose enjoys it in one of its most tangible forms. The creation of an organization may be a work of supreme importance. So is the work of those few statesmen who have devoted their lives to producing order out of chaos, of whom Lenin is the supreme type in our day. The most obvious examples are artists and men of science. Shakespeare says of his verse: "So long as men can breathe, or eyes can see, so long lives this." And it cannot be doubted that the thought consoled him for misfortune. In his sonnets he maintains that the thought of his friend reconciled him to life, but I cannot help suspecting that the sonnets he wrote to his friend were even more effective for this purpose than the friend himself. Great artists and great men of science do work which is in itself delightful; while they are doing it, it secures them the respect of those whose respect is worth having, which gives them the most fundamental kind of power, namely power over men's thoughts and feelings. They have also the most solid reasons for thinking well of themselves. This combination of fortunate circumstances ought, one would think, to be enough to make any man happy. Nevertheless it is not so. Michael Angelo, for example, was a profoundly unhappy man, and maintained (not, I am sure, with truth) that he would not have troubled to produce works of art if he had not had to pay the debts of his impecunious relations. The power to produce great art is very often, though by no means always, associated with a temperamental unhappiness, so great that but for the joy which the artist derives from his work, he would be driven to suicide. We cannot, therefore, maintain that even the greatest work must make a man happy; we can only maintain that it must make him less unhappy. Men of science, however, are far less often temperamentally unhappy than artists are, and in the main the men who do great work in science are happy men, whose happiness is derived primarily from their work.

One of the causes of unhappiness among intellectuals in the present day is that so many of them, especially those whose skill is literary, find no opportunity for the independent exercise of their talents, but have to hire themselves out to rich corporations directed by Philistines, who insist upon their producing what they themselves regard as pernicious nonsense. If you were to inquire among journalists in either England or America whether they believed in the policy of the newspaper for which they worked, you would find, I believe, that only a small minority do so; the rest, for the sake of a livelihood, prostitute their skill to purposes which they believe to be harmful. Such work cannot bring any real satisfaction, and in the course of reconciling himself to the doing of it, a man has to make himself so cynical that he can no longer derive whole-hearted satisfaction from anything whatever. I cannot condemn men who undertake work of this sort, since starvation is too serious an alternative, but I think that where it is possible to do work that is satisfactory to a man's constructive impulses without entirely starving, he will be well advised from the point of view of his own happiness if he chooses it in preference to work much more highly paid but not seeming to him worth doing on its own account. Without self-respect genuine happiness is scarcely possible. And the man who is ashamed of his work can hardly achieve self-respect.

The satisfaction of constructive work, though it may, as things are, be the privilege of a minority, can nevertheless be the privilege of a quite large minority. Any man who is his own master in his work can feel it; so can any man whose work appears to him useful and requires considerable skill. The production of satisfactory children is a difficult constructive work capable of affording profound satisfaction. Any woman who has achieved this can feel that as a result of her labor the world contains something of value which it would not otherwise contain.

Human beings differ profoundly in regard to the tendency to regard their lives as a whole. To some men it is natural to do so, and essential to happiness to be able to do so with some satisfaction. To others life is a series of detached incidents without directed movement and without unity. I think the former sort are more likely to achieve happiness than the latter, since they will gradually build up those circumstances from which they can derive contentment and self-respect, whereas the others will be blown about by the winds of circumstance now this way, now that, without ever arriving at any haven. The habit of viewing life as a whole is an essential part both of wisdom and of true morality, and is one of the things which ought to be encouraged in education. Consistent purpose is not enough to make life happy, but it is an almost indispensable condition of a happy life. And consistent purpose embodies itself mainly in work.

## Questions

1. Russell is generally admired for his exceptionally clear prose. List some of the devices that make for clarity in this essay.
2. Russell is thought of as a left-winger. Aside from the casual reference to Lenin on page 244, is there anything in "Work" to which Barry Goldwater, Ronald Reagan, or William Buckley might object? Of which statements might they especially approve?
3. Russell says (page 241): "The desire that men feel to increase their income is quite as much a desire for success as for the extra comforts that a higher income can procure." In its context, what does "success" mean? In your experience, do Russell's words ring true? Why, or why not?

W. H. Auden

# Work, Labor, and Play

So far as I know, Miss Hannah Arendt was the first person to define the essential difference between work and labor. To be happy, a man must feel, firstly, free and, secondly, important. He

W[ystan] H[ugh] Auden (1907–1973) was born and educated in England. In 1939 he came to the United States and he became an American citizen. In 1972, however, he returned to England to live. Although Auden established his reputation chiefly with his poetry, he also wrote plays, libretti, and essays, all of high quality.

One of Auden's most unusual books is *A Certain World: A Commonplace Book.* It is an anthology of some of his favorite passages from other people's books, along with brief reflections on his reading. The passage we print here begins with a reference to Hannah Arendt's *The Human Condition.*

cannot be really happy if he is compelled by society to do what he does not enjoy doing, or if what he enjoys doing is ignored by society as of no value or importance. In a society where slavery in the strict sense has been abolished, the sign that what a man does is of social value is that he is paid money to do it, but a laborer today can rightly be called a wage slave. A man is a laborer if the job society offers him is of no interest to himself but he is compelled to take it by the necessity of earning a living and supporting his family.

The antithesis to labor is play. When we play a game, we enjoy what we are doing, otherwise we should not play it, but it is a purely private activity; society could not care less whether we play it or not.

Between labor and play stands work. A man is a worker if he is personally interested in the job which society pays him to do; what from the point of view of society is necessary labor is from his own point of view voluntary play. Whether a job is to be classified as labor or work depends, not on the job itself, but on the tastes of the individual who undertakes it. The difference does not, for example, coincide with the difference between a manual and a mental job; a gardener or a cobbler may be a worker, a bank clerk a laborer. Which a man is can be seen from his attitude toward leisure. To a worker, leisure means simply the hours he needs to relax and rest in order to work efficiently. He is therefore more likely to take too little leisure than too much; workers die of coronaries and forget their wives' birthdays. To the laborer, on the other hand, leisure means freedom from compulsion, so that it is natural for him to imagine that the fewer hours he has to spend laboring, and the more hours he is free to play, the better.

What percentage of the population in a modern technological society are, like myself, in the fortunate position of being workers? At a guess I would say sixteen per cent, and I do not think that figure is likely to get bigger in the future.

Technology and the division of labor have done two things: by eliminating in many fields the need for special strength or skill, they have made a very large number of paid occupations which formerly were enjoyable work into boring labor, and by increasing productivity they have reduced the number of necessary laboring hours. It is already possible to imagine a society in which the majority of the population, that is to say, its laborers, will have almost as much leisure as in earlier times was enjoyed by the aristocracy. When one recalls how aristocracies in the past actually behaved, the prospect is not cheerful. Indeed, the problem of dealing with boredom may be even more difficult for such a future mass society than it was for aristocracies. The latter, for example, ritualized their time; there was a season to shoot grouse, a season to spend in town, etc. The masses are more likely to replace an unchanging ritual by fashion which it will be in the economic interest of certain people to change as often as possible. Again, the masses cannot go in for hunting, for very soon there would be no animals left to hunt. For other aristocratic amusements like gambling, dueling, and warfare, it may be only too easy to find equivalents in dangerous driving, drug-taking, and senseless acts of violence. Workers seldom commit acts of violence, because they can put their aggression into their work, be it physical like the work of a smith, or mental like the work of a scientist or an artist. The role of aggression in mental work is aptly expressed by the phrase "getting one's teeth into a problem."

## Questions

1. Some readers have had trouble following Auden in his first three paragraphs, although by the end of the third paragraph the difficulties have disappeared. Can you summarize the first paragraph in a sentence? If you think that the development of the idea in these first three paragraphs could be clearer, insert the necessary phrases or sentences, or with arrows indicate the places to which sentences should be moved.
2. If you have read the entries from John R. Coleman's *Blue-Collar Journal* (pages 257–261), decide whether, by Auden's definitions and Coleman's implied purposes (see the editors' footnote, page 257), Coleman was working, laboring, or playing.

Arturo Vivante

# The Orchard

They all have this prejudice against fruit trees," he keeps saying. Though no one wishes to remind him, there is some reason for it. Thirty-five years ago, when he was forty-three and a novice to agriculture—philosophy until that time had been his only field—soon after moving to the Tuscan estate his father bought him, with extraordinary energy he set himself to looking for spring water, of which the house was till then deprived, found it ("It was there," he said,) ordered two hundred peach trees from a nursery in Pistoia, and had them planted down on a fertile plain below the spring. Peaches, he claimed, would fetch far more than wine, wheat, or olive oil—the produce that the farmers in this, the Chianti region, prized. In the nearby town, he argued, much of the fruit had to be brought in from far away, so that there surely was a market here for perishable fruit like peaches, plums, apricots, and cherries—but expecially for peaches. Peach trees grew fast. "In three years, they begin to bear," he said, and started counting, though when not on the subject of fruit trees he was fond of quoting the Latin dictum that he who begins to count begins to err. The figures he came to! Two hundred trees by twenty kilos by two lire. Eight thousand lire from just two hundred trees. Walking the fields, looking at the ground, hands clasped behind his back, he had his sons excited. Only the farmers remained skeptical. They understood vines, olive trees, and wheat. Anything else they rather distrusted. Their attitude didn't daunt him. It only made him bolder.

In the moist soil of the plain, the trees grew well, and in the fall he ordered more—three hundred this time. "Five hundred trees by twenty kilos by two lire," he now said. In the spring of their second year, the little trees had their first blossoms—the most delicate pink, a few to each plant. One or two became peaches—tiny slips of substances with a silvery, soft fuzz ending in a cowlick. At first the faintest green, they swelled, they reddened, they were ripe. And at

---

Arturo Vivante was born in Rome in 1923 and practiced medicine there from 1950 to 1958. He now lives in Wellfleet, Massachusetts, and devotes all of his time to writing.

the same time the price of wine was falling. It cost less than a lira a bottle—hardly a dime. He joked about it. "Please, *please* have another glass and help us drink it." Wheat, too, was low, and so was olive oil. Only the taxes rose.

But in the plain the five hundred trees, growing up and florid, promised harvests that would once and for all solve what he called the "disastrous financial situation." In the house, one heard a lot about it. "The water is level with our throats," he'd say, creating a feeling that made everyone uneasy and drew long sighs from his wife. "But oh, dear me, what can we do?" she'd say, stretching her arms down in a helpless gesture. Any big new purchase was put off till the peach trees would start producing. And in the meantime, to save on electricity, he bought weak light bulbs. The house grew dim. Never mind, his eyes were on the trees.

Every day, over his shoulders the threadbare charcoal-gray mantle he had worn since his young days when he had climbed Mont Blanc, the Matterhorn, the Giant's Tooth, Monte Rosa, and a hundred lesser peaks both of the Alps and of the Apennines, he would go down to the plain to look at his peach trees.

The next March, there weren't just one or two blossoms to each tree but myriads. Each flower a peach. Well, perhaps not quite. Say three to one—three blossoms to one peach. Say even four to one. He counted the blossoms on a branch, and then the branches; he divided by four to be on the safe side; again he divided, to get the weight in kilos; then he started multiplying. It was like coasting on a bicycle down a mountain road and having the horizon at one's feet. He looked at the plain, only a portion of which had trees. "If all goes well," he said, "we'll plant some more."

All *did* go well. When the wind blew away the petals of the blossoms, there remained the greenish-white, tiny, rounded mass. A little bead of fluff it seemed at first, but if you squeezed it you felt it was pulpy even then, and if you squashed it there was a green smear left on your thumb. That downy light green was alive, and it clung hard by its minuscule stem. It was not about to drop or to come off at the least touch. And it seemed as though there was no blossom that did not turn into a fruit. The peaches were so thick that here and there the trees had to be thinned. When the peaches ripened, he hired some help—mainly girls from nearby farms—to pick them. Into the barn came the full baskets and the crates, filling it with fragrance.

"They are as beautiful as flowers," he said, watching the fruit being put in rows and layers inside the boxes.

From town, the buyers came with their wallets bulging, and the trucks left with heavy loads. There were so many peaches they tempted thieves. After some had been stolen, a barbed-wire fence was set up around the orchard, and a big white shepherd dog put there to guard it. Signs claiming the peaches were from his farm appeared on the pushcarts in the squares. He beamed. He saw the world peach-colored. So he ordered more trees—a thousand this time—and since the water of the spring wasn't sufficient to irrigate them all, some workmen who specialized in building wells dug a trench, spectacularly deep and long. Enough water was found to irrigate three or four thousand trees. To him agriculture was irrigation and fruit trees. Even as a child he had had a passion for water and watercourses. Once, he ran away from home and was found with a bundle on his back, walking along a stream, trying to trace it to its source. And now nothing was nicer than in a summer drought seeing water gushing out and making mud of the dry, the brittle earth—nothing more beautiful than fruit or than girls picking the fruit.

The blooming that took place the following spring! The bees seemed driven crazy. They buzzed from one blossom to the other, gathering pollen, bringing it around. Again the blossoms blew away petal after petal, leaving the tiny, almond-shaped, thin, fuzzy peaches that by and by swelled and captured color from the sun, except where the leaves cast their sharp, sleek shadows on them, and, swelling more and more, became so heavy some of the branches had to be sustained. Again the girls came, and the buyers. Again the trucks left laden. Again the farm's name appeared on the pushcarts. And before winter two thousand more peach trees were planted.

That made thirty-five hundred on the plain, and there were other fruit trees near the house—apricot, cherry, plum, persimmon, apple, fig, and pear. The peach trees were of several varieties, from the early kind, which ripened in June, to some that got ripe in November. Foreign-sounding names like Hale, Crawford, and Late Elberta became household words. In the next season, he said, there would be at least fifteen hundred trees producing. Winter came. Now the peach trees stood, bare of their foliage, in long, stern rows down in the plain, asleep and silent except when the wind blew strong, and then it whistled through them and they seemed to stir. They stood naked, yet so far from dead: each tiny twig intact, waiting and ready—heedful almost. Then in March a softening of the air, and very quickly, as if they could wait no longer, the first buds, the blossoms, and their petals falling to disclose the velvet of the newborn peach.

Still March. Mist and gentle showers, and the sun shining out of speckled clouds; then clouds fringed with silver, followed by skies completely overcast. For days there was no sun, no stars, but under the dim days and the black nights the peach trees were safe, as though under a cover. Then, late one evening, the two flag-shaped, rusty weathervanes over the house were heard distincly turning on the roof—a grating, creaking sound. Slowly they turned, taking what seemed a long time about it, opposing as they did a fair amount of resistance to the wind and indicating a marked change in its direction. It was the north wind. Quickly it cleared the sky. Over the house now, the stars were shining in all their wintry brightness. One couldn't help but admire them. But to the not so different blossoms on the plain this change of wind, this polished starlit sky was baneful, and all the members of the household knew it. In the morning, when they woke up, the sun was shining, the fields down in the valleys were hoary and stiff with frost. A workman who had got up at dawn reported that in the plain the frost had "burned" all of the peaches.

"All of them?"

"Hardly any left, you'll see. Why, it was like crunching through snow down there this morning," he said, and swore, impressed—no, almost awed by what nature could work when it put its mind to it. A robust frost, no doubt.

In the next few days, its full effect became apparent. The tiny, beadlike peaches, as you could readily see if you cut into them with your thumbnail, were black inside, had lost their firmness, had a shrivelled feel, and they came off at the slightest touch, without a sound, as if they were bits of matter that had got there by chance. On tree after tree, one looked in vain for a whole peach, for one that wasn't black and wizened.

The leaves came out of the buds, deep green and thick, so thick sometimes that you parted them to see if by chance they weren't hiding a peach. But you would never find one.

"Still, the trees are growing," he said, unperturbed. "Without fruit they may develop more, and next spring we'll try and protect them."

In the late fall, he bought an extraordinary number of cane mats, put up tall poles along the rows of peach trees, strung wires from pole to pole, and in March, just before blossomtime, hoisted the mats up. At the same time he had piles of kindling, brambles, and moist straw placed here and there ready to be burned if a cold night should come. A cold night came—frosty, sparkling with stars. The fires were lit. The smoke rose, hiding the stars. And the mats hung like magic carpets over the three thousand five hundred trees. But in the morning, when the sun rose in the blue sky, the little peaches had fared no better than the previous year.

Another summer without fruit. Though fruitless, the trees still had to be pruned, the ground around them hoed and irrigated. It was discouraging, however; the workmen clipped and dug without believing in their work.

The following March, the mats went up again. They could be seen from the main road—a tented army. Some passersby wondered what they were. And those who knew laughed or made remarks like "The good money he wasted on that place!"

"Two good seasons and two bad ones," he said "We have an even chance."

In March, there was no frost. No frost in April. The peaches, tens of thousands of them, were fair-sized. "They are out of danger now," everyone confidently said. Then, on May 2nd, the frost. The spectacle this time was worse than it had ever been. The peaches withered, and grew as black as mushrooms rotting, then fell from their branches. The workmen shook their heads. "That plain is lethal," his wife said, but—he took it in his stride, like the philosopher he was, and continued hoping.

It was clear, though, that those first two good years had been exceptional, for the following spring, too, there came a deadly frost. The land—valuable, fertile land—could not be kept unproductive. The older peach trees were cut down; the younger ones were left in the hope that there might be a crop. There wasn't. Not for two more years was there a good season. By then, however, the Second World War had broken out, and he, being Jewish and alert to what might happen, had taken the family out of Italy to England, leaving the estate in the care of a bailiff. For the duration of the war, the peach trees were forgotten. For so long they had been the subject of so much conversation, and now suddently they didn't matter anymore.

After the war, in 1946, when the family returned, of the three thousand five hundred peach trees only two trees were left. They stood by the barn, old and barren, many of their branches without leaves. Why they had been spared nobody knew. Perhaps because they weren't in anybody's way, perhaps to stretch a clothesline to—there was a font nearby where women did the washing. Or perhaps just as a souvenir.

But if the trees were gone, his passion for them wasn't. He read an American pamphlet on peach trees, which one of his sons had sent for and given to him. It was one of those booklets that the American goverment prints and sends out free upon request as a public service —a plainly written, informative thing. The choice of location for an orchard, it said, was crucial; since warm air tends to rise and cold air fall, in hilly country where there's danger of frost peach trees ought never to be planted at the foot of hills or on a plain, no matter how fertile and rich in water that low ground might be. Scarcity of water, it stressed, was far less dangerous than frost, since very little could be done to save the peaches on a frosty night, while in a drought the trees could be irrigated wherever they might be. These remarks were so pertinent that they seemed a comment on what had happened, and read as though they had been written for him. "Not one of those agricultural experts I consulted ever told me," he said.

He began again, went right ahead and planted a batch of peach trees high on the slope of a hill above the plain. People cautioned him. Irritated, he said, "Everyone is against fruit trees," and he complained about this "hostile attitude" as though it were absurd. If someone mentioned the word "frost" to him, he patiently explained that since warm air rises and cold air falls, up on the hill where the new orchard was, frost wasn't a danger anymore. And he repeated his old arguments in favor of peach trees—about the good market for perishable fruit in the hill town, about the low price of wine and wheat. People looked at him. They knew better than to contradict him. They knew that if they did he would come looking for them wherever they were—in their bedrooms, even—and bring up the subject almost as though they were heathens who had to be converted. One knew his step approaching, knew what was on his mind, knew what he would say, and either one didn't answer or was reduced to saying, "Oh, well, maybe you are right."

He certainly planted the trees with conviction; they were a sort of cause. It was as if some future need, hardly surmised or suspected, were directing the course of his actions. And there was no dissuading him. He went straight on putting all his savings into the new orchard, selling his shares, keeping workmen on it. They brought water to the new plants in a barrel on an oxcart. And he himself, though frail and aging, was often seen going up to the orchard in the heat, his arms stretched by two full pails. Finally, as the trees grew in size and number, he piped the water up to them. To increase its volume, he even repaired an ancient, leaking cistern into which rainwater drained from the roofs of the house.

"Sink money into that hole!" one of his sons said, without considering that his father led a very frugal life indeed and that the money he spent on the orchard was his only outlay of any size.

"What about men who have mistresses, go to Paris, bet on horses, drive expensive cars, drink the best cognacs, or, hypochondriacs, fill the house with drugs?" another of his sons retorted.

"There are those, too."

"He—he smokes Alfas, goes into town by bus, buys a book or takes in a movie once in a while. Why shouldn't he spend money on fruit trees if he wants to?"

"It's all right to say that. But when you see those deep new trenches he has dug—more than three feet deep, you know—"

"After all, the land is his, isn't it?"

*Was* it his land? Just before the war, in 1938, when the Fascists threatened to confiscate Jewish property, he transferred it to his sons, who, because his wife wasn't Jewish, were exempt from expropriation. In name, at least, the land was theirs. Morally, though, it was still his, for the transfer had been no more than a temporary expedient made necessary by an evil government for an evil reason. Those circumstances were now conveniently forgotten, and when a piece of land was up for sale, as his signature was not required, no one asked for his approval. He became more and more removed from the running of the estate. He cared only for his orchard and his books, went from one to the other, over his shoulders still wearing the cape, as threadbare as an ancient flag, darned many times over.

And now the peach trees on the hill were in their third year, the year in which they were supposed to start producing. He waited confidently. No cane mats or piles of straw and kindling up here. No need. The warm air rises from the plain, the cold air sinks. The stars can shine unutterably bright, the north wind blow, the frost fall. It won't affect them. Not up here, unless, of course, it is one of those exceptionally cold years that come once, and maybe not even once, in a decade, and we all hope it won't be one of those.

A frost came that made the plain and all the low ground white. But the hilltops were green, and so was the slope on which the peach trees stood, all clothed in pink. The cold persisted; sometimes the fringe of white—the frost coating with a silver edge the blades of grass—rose almost to the level of the orchard, skirting it like a tide. Each day, a workman, now become a real expert in fruit trees, disclosed the tiny peaches in their blossoms, and assayed them. They were still whole, still firm, still whitish-green and pulpy, their skin still fuzzy. "So far it hasn't touched them," he reported.

"If they'd been down in the plain . . ."

"Down there, there wouldn't have been one left; you can be sure of that."

The peaches ripened. The girls came to pick them. Girls picking fruit—the way he watched them, the way he spoke about them, sometimes it seemed he wanted nothing more in return for all his labors. Oh, the peaches weren't as large as they had been down in the fertile plain, but perhaps they had more taste. Nor were there truckfuls of them, but every day a station wagon left, loaded.

Each summer, there's a crop. Though he has high hopes and keeps planting peaches, cherries, figs, the orchard hasn't solved the estate's heavy financial situation—but it has solved *his.* At at time when, to pay the taxes, the land has to be sold bit after bit and two of his sons have left to go and live elsewhere—one in Milan, the other in America—he, without having to ask anything from anybody, earns from his orchard enough money for his books, the bus fare into town, the cup of coffee, the movie, the Alfas that he smokes, the little gifts he buys once in a while, and new fruit trees. The orchard fills his needs. Year after year, he watches the trees blossom in the spring, the girls gathering the peaches in the summer.

## Questions

1. Read the first paragraph a few times, perhaps even aloud. Now characterize the voice of the narrator. Does he seem condescending, friendly, sarcastic, or what? Next, try to locate—by rereading the passage—the words, phrases, or constructions that especially give this voice its character.
2. The second sentence from the end is: "The orchard fills his needs." What are his needs? How does the orchard fill them?
3. In a paragraph characterize the farmer who is the subject of Vivante's essay. You may want to quote a few phrases, but the paragraph should chiefly be a description of the man in your own voice.

## John R. Coleman

# Blue-Collar Journal

*Monday, March 26*

Cold rain after the warmth of Sunday. Spring has pulled back to wait for a while. Few people seemed to want to eat, even Oyster House food. Not many customers, not much excitement, not much work.

This was a half day for me. Because I'd be getting my own dinner on the hot plate back in my room, I slipped over to the Faneuil Hall markets about 2:00 to get a piece of meat and some vegetables. My uniform worked wonders this time. At the three counters where I stopped, I got warm greetings and questions about how business was at the Oyster House. Had I been in my Haverford clothes, I'd have received the polite "May-I-help-you" treatment that I get at the Wayne Farmers' Market near home every Saturday morning at 7:00. But today the butcher and the vegetable men gave me the "Here's-one-of-us" treatment. It felt good.

I didn't pay any less for what I bought. But I did get told at one counter, "No, you don't want that one," and had a better squash placed in my hand. That's almost the same as paying less.

*Tuesday, March 27*

One of the waitresses I find hard to take asked me at one point today, "Are you the boy who cuts the lemons?"

"I'm the man who does," I replied.

---

John Royston Coleman, born in Ontario in 1921, did his undergraduate work at the University of Toronto. He came to the United States for graduate work in economics at the University of Chicago, and in 1946 he became a U.S. citizen. He has taught economics (his specialty is labor relations) at Massachusetts Institute of Technology and at Carnegie Institute of Technology, and he has served as a labor arbitrator. In 1967 he became president of Haverford College.

In 1973, during a sabbatical leave of absence from his job at Haverford, instead of engaging in academic research on labor, Coleman held blue-collar jobs. He worked on sewers in Georgia, in kitchens in Boston, and on a garbage truck in Maryland. He wrote entries in a journal every night, and later he expanded the entries for publication. A few selections on his work in kitchens and on a garbage truck follow.

"Well, there are none cut." There wasn't a hint that she heard my point.

Dana, who has cooked here for twelve years or so, heard that exchange.

"It's no use, Jack," he said when she was gone. "If she doesn't know now, she never will." There was a trace of a smile on his face, but it was a sad look all the same.

In that moment, I learned the full thrust of those billboard ads of a few years ago that said, "BOY. Drop out of school and that's what they'll call you the rest of your life." I had read those ads before with a certain feeling of pride; education matters, they said, and that gave a lift to my field. Today I saw them saying something else. They were untrue in part; it turns out that you'll get called "boy" if you do work that others don't respect even if you have a Ph.D. It isn't education that counts, but the job in which you land. And the ads spoke too of a sad resignation about the world. They assumed that some people just won't learn respect for others, so you should adapt yourself to them. Don't try to change them. Get the right job and they won't call *you* boy any more. They'll save it for the next man.

It isn't just people like this one waitress who learn slowly, if at all. Haverford College has prided itself on being a caring, considerate community in the Quaker tradition for many long years. Yet when I came there I soon learned that the cleaning women in the dormitories were called "wombats" by all the students. No one seemed to know where the name came from or what connection, if any, it had with the dictionary definition. *The American College Dictionary* says a wombat is "any of three species of burrowing marsupials of Australia . . . somewhat resembling ground hogs." The name was just one of Haverford's unexamined ways of doing things.

It didn't take much persuasion to get the name dropped. Today there are few students who remember it at all. But I imagine the cleaning women remember it well.

Certainly I won't forget being called a boy today.

*Wednesday, March 28*

A day off once again.

I went into a restaurant downtown, the first time since I started work as a sandwich man. My curiosity won out. I ordered a club sandwich just to see how well it held together. It was noon, and I knew the man or woman in the kitchen must be having a rough time at that hour, but I ordered it just the same.

The sandwich looked fine, and its ingredients were fresh. I sent my compliments to the sandwich man, but I think the waitress thought I was nuts.

The place where I really wanted to eat was the Oyster House. I wanted to sit down at one of the tables and have someone—one of the many waitresses I like—bring me the menu. I wanted to order that stuffed fillet of sole, after some oysters at the bar. And I wanted the salad on the side, complete with cherry tomato and cucumber slice, and blue cheese dressing on top. I know some of the inside secrets of the place. I know, for example, that yesterday a customer got a thumbtack in his corn chowder (he was very nice about it). But I know too that the sanitation is generally good and that the people who work here care. I just wanted to see the whole meal come together as a production, fashioned by people whom I knew.

I'll eat there someday as a customer. And nothing that happens will escape my eye.

*Sunday, April 1*

It was hard, steady work all day long.

The rhythm of each day and even of each week is familiar enough that it should be getting boring by now. It doesn't seem that way yet. There is enough variety in the flow of orders and of people too that I seldom feel I have been through all this before. Cleaning up the aluminum trays, where my supplies are kept, at the end of each day is dull; I'd happily skip that if I could. But even in that there is a small element of suspense: the question each time is how far I can get with closing up for the night before the last waitress comes in with an order that requires getting the supplies out again.

I wonder how many loaves of bread and heads of lettuce I'd go through if I stuck at this job until retirement age.

*Friday, April 6*

We made the first stop. I had thought to bring gloves along with the work clothes in my gear, and I had them with me now. I was the only one who pulled gloves on. Each of us took a very large green or orange plastic barrel out of the back of the truck. Each barrel had a hole near the top to hold it by.

Steve took me into the first yard with him. "This is the way it's done," he said as he dumped the contents from three containers at the back door into his tub. Then in a flash he jumped into the barrel and trampled down what was there. "This way we can get more houses in one trip," he said as he jumped. In another flash he was out of the barrel, the load was on his back, and he was off for the house next door.

That was the training course.

He told me which houses to "pull." With three of us on the crew and only two sides to the street, Steve had some maneuvers to work out as to who pulled where. For the most part, he left Kenny on one side and me on the other, while he crossed back and forth to get the trash a few doors ahead of where we were. He also moved the truck.

I don't know just what I expected to find in the first householder's can on my route, but I know I took the lid off gingerly. It was full of garbage. Right on, I thought.

I couldn't quite bring myself to jump in and out of the barrel the way Steve had done. Instead, I pushed down hard with my gloved hand to make room for the next set of cans. With two houses pulled, the barrel was full. I lifted it up to my shoulder with a grunt (that seemed easier than swinging it around and onto my back) and headed for the truck. All kids—and many grown men—have an urge to throw at least one load of garbage into the waiting jaws of a sanitation truck and to pull the lever that sets the compacting unit to work. I threw my first load in with a feeling of fulfillment.

One thing about being a trashman is that, after your first load, you pretty well know the job. The only progress from then on comes in learning your route, developing your muscles, and picking up speed. I could never have imagined how heavy some of those barrels could be. Most times I got three households' worth of trash into one load, since that was the best way to save time on the route. But sometimes the resulting weight was more than I could lift even to my waist, let alone shoulder high. I had to drag some of those loads down the driveway or across the lawn to the truck. The noise of the barrel being dragged on the road gave me away, of course. Steve smiled patiently at that, and Kenny pretended not to see. It sobered me too to note that, while they never once dragged a load, they both cursed the weight on their backs a couple of times. I knew then that there's no such thing as getting used to what we had to heave.

This work was a far cry from what I had watched the Haverford Township sanitation men do back home. They work hard and fast, and they probably pull a longer route than we do. But their work consists of lifting the householders' cartons or cans from the curb to the truck. They miss the extra miles of walking through yards, the hoisting of loads to the shoulder or back, and the extra physical contact with the trash as it goes from the cans into the barrel. The driver there stays in the truck; perhaps he is someone who has done his share of years on the dirty end of the truck. Here he pulls trash with his crew. Still, I now feel an affinity with the Haverford Township men that I hadn't quite felt before.

Steve was in charge at all times. He directed us where to go, kept tabs on us, and kept the truck moving ahead so that we never had far to walk once we got out loads from the backyards to the street. This has been his route for well over a year and he knows every house on the route well. (We are the only crew working this part of town. The other trucks from Liberty Refuse go to other towns in this county, and the part of Dryden lying across the county line is serviced by some other firm.) He had scared me with that talk early in the morning about keeping up with him. A look at his muscles and the way he moved told me I was in for a test. But, as the day went by, I saw I didn't have to be afraid of him. I was not as fast as he or Kenny, but he never once got on my back. He set an example instead.

Two mysteries about the job were cleared up for me on this first day. One was where we could have lunch. The answer to that one was that we didn't have any. We worked straight through until the route was done. Then we drove back to the yard, punched the clock, and went home to eat as we chose. I was glad my breakfast was big.

The other mystery was about taking care of bodily functions at work. Dryden is strictly residential. There are no gas stations on our route and no cafés. There are woods at the end of a few streets but they're spaced far apart. There didn't seem to be householders who were about to invite us into their homes. But happily we carried our own facilities with us. Next time I see a trashman jump into the open space where the garbage goes at the back of the truck and seem to stare at the curved metal wall in front of him, I'll know he's not looking for flaws. He's taking a leak.

It was after 3:30 when we pulled back into the yard. I knew I had done a day's work. Nothing I saw in the cans today took away from the joy of a big meal tonight, nor did I leave any scraps on my plate. I wasn't going to make extra work for the trashman tomorrow.

## Questions

1. Reread the first entry (page 257). Speaking in general, when you go shopping, which would you rather have, a polite "May-I-help-you?" or questions about how business is where you work? Why?

2. What, exactly, was the waitress implying (page 257) when she addressed Coleman as "boy"? Analyze some similar uses of "girl."
3. What "small element of suspense" (page 259) have you found yourself introducing into a dull job? (A dull job can include listening to a lecturer.)
4. Did any of Coleman's ideas surprise you, coming from a college president? How would you describe Coleman's style? Does it conflict with ideas you have about what a college president is or ought to be like?
5. In the Foreword to *Blue-Collar Journal* Coleman writes: "This book is dedicated to my parents. But it could have been dedicated to Walter Mitty. He too would have understood." If you have read "The Secret Life of Walter Mitty" (pages 432–437), explain Coleman's dedication.

## Malcolm X

# The Shoeshine Boy

When I got home, Ella said there had been a telephone call from somebody named Shorty. He had left a message that over at the Roseland State Ballroom, the shoeshine boy was quitting that night, and Shorty had told him to hold the job for me.

"Malcolm, you haven't had any experience shining shoes," Ella said. Her expression and tone of voice told me she wasn't happy about my taking that job. I didn't particularly care, because I was already speechless thinking about being somewhere close to the greatest bands in the world. I didn't even wait to eat any dinner.

---

Malcolm X, born Malcolm Little in Nebraska in 1925, was the son of a Baptist minister. He completed the eighth grade, but then he got into trouble and was sent to a reformatory. After his release he became a thief, dope peddler, and pimp. In 1944 he was sent to jail, where he spent six and a half years. During his years in jail he became a convert to the Black Muslim faith. Paroled in 1950, he served as a minister and founded Muslim temples throughout the United States. In 1964, however, he broke with Elijah Muhammad, leader of the Black Muslims and a powerful advocate of separation of whites and blacks. Malcolm X formed a new group, the Organization of Afro-American Unity, but a year later he was assassinated in New York. His *Autobiography,* written with Alex Haley, was published in 1964. Haley (b. 1921) is also the author of *Roots,* a study tracing a black family back through seven generations.

"The Shoeshine Boy" (editors' title) is from *The Autobiography of Malcolm X,* chapter 3.

The ballroom was all lighted when I got there. A man at the front door was letting in members of Benny Goodman's band. I told him I wanted to see the shoeshine boy, Freddie.

"You're going to be the new one?" he asked. I said I thought I was, and he laughed, "Well, maybe you'll hit the numbers and get a Cadillac, too." He told me that I'd find Freddie upstairs in the men's room on the second floor.

But downstairs before I went up, I stepped over and snatched a glimpse inside the ballroom. I just couldn't believe the size of that waxed floor! At the far end, under the soft, rose-colored lights, was the bandstand with the Benny Goodman musicians moving around, laughing and talking, arranging their horns and stands.

A wiry, brown-skinned, conked fellow upstairs in the men's room greeted me. "You Shorty's homeboy?" I said I was, and he said he was Freddie. "Good old boy," he said. "He called me, he just heard I hit the big number, and he figured right I'd be quitting." I told Freddie what the man at the front door had said about a Cadillac. He laughed and said, "Burns them white cats up when you get yourself something. Yeah, I told them I was going to get me one—just to bug them."

Freddie then said for me to pay close attention, that he was going to be busy and for me to watch but not get in the way, and he'd try to get me ready to take over at the next dance, a couple of nights later.

As Freddie busied himself setting up the shoeshine stand, he told me, "Get here early . . . your shoeshine rags and brushes by this footstand . . . your polish bottles, paste wax, suede brushes over here . . . everything in place, you get rushed, you never need to waste motion. . . ."

While you shined shoes, I learned, you also kept watch on customers inside, leaving the urinals. You darted over and offered a small white hand towel. "A lot of cats who ain't planning to wash their hands, sometimes you can run up with a towel and shame them. Your towels are really your best hustle in here. Cost you a penny apiece to launder—you always get at least a nickel tip."

The shoeshine customers, and any from the inside rest room who took a towel, you whiskbroomed a couple of licks. "A nickel or a dime tip, just give 'em that," Freddie said. "But for two bits, Uncle Tom a little—white cats especially like that. I've had them to come back two, three times a dance."

From down below, the sound of the music had begun floating

up. I guess I stood transfixed. "You never seen a big dance?" asked Freddie. "Run on awhile, and watch."

There were a few couples already dancing under the rose-covered lights. But even more exciting to me was the crowd thronging in. The most glamorous-looking white women I'd ever seen—young ones, old ones, white cats buying tickets at the window, sticking big wads of green bills back into their pockets, checking the women's coats, and taking their arms and squiring them inside.

Freddie had some early customers when I got back upstairs. Between the shoeshine stand and thrusting towels to me just as they approached the wash basin, Freddie seemed to be doing four things at once. "Here, you can take over the whiskbroom," he said, "just two or three licks—but let 'em feel it."

When things slowed a little, he said, "You ain't seen nothing tonight. You wait until you see a spooks' dance! Man, our own people carry *on!*" Whenever he had a moment, he kept schooling me. "Shoelaces, this drawer here. You just starting out, I'm going to make these to you as a present. Buy them for a nickel a pair, tell cats they need laces if they do, and charge two bits."

Every Benny Goodman record I'd ever heard in my life, it seemed, was filtering faintly into where we were. During another customer lull, Freddie let me slip back outside again to listen. Peggy Lee was at the mike singing. Beautiful! She had just joined the band and she was from North Dakota and had been singing with a group in Chicago when Mrs. Benny Goodman discovered her, we had heard some customers say. She finished the song and the crowd burst into applause. She was a big hit.

"It knocked me out, too, when I first broke in here," Freddie said, grinning, when I went back in there. "But, look, you ever shined any shoes?" He laughed when I said I hadn't, excepting my own. "Well, let's get to work. I never had neither. " Freddie got on the stand and went to work on his own shoes. Brush, liquid polish, brush, paste wax, shine rag, lacquer sole dressing . . . step by step, Freddie showed me what to do.

"But you got to get a whole lot faster. You can't waste time!" Freddie showed me how fast on my own shoes. Then, because business was tapering off, he had time to give me a demonstration of how to make the shine rag pop like a firecracker. "Dig the action?" he asked. He did it in slow motion. I got down and tried it on his shoes. I had the principle of it. "Just got to do it faster," Freddie said. "It's a jive noise, that's all. Cats tip better, they figure you're knocking yourself out!"

## Questions

1. In this selection Malcolm X is more concerned with Benny Goodman than with learning about shining shoes. Freddie is concerned with teaching Malcolm the trade. What are *we* concerned with in this selection?
2. How would you characterize Freddie's attitude toward his job? Compare it with Maggie Holmes's attitude (pages 285–291) toward her job.
3. In the last paragraph Freddie demonstrates a "jive noise." Using evidence from this selection, the library, mother wit, or what you will, define "jive."
4. On what date did Malcolm begin his apprenticeship as a shoeshine boy? How did you arrive at that date?

**Studs Terkel**

# Three Workers

### I. Terry Mason, Airline Stewardess

*She has been an airline stewardess for six years. She is twenty-six-years old, recently married. "The majority of airline stewardesses are from small towns. I myself am from Nebraska. It's supposed to be one of the nicest professions for a woman—if she can't be a model or in the movies. All the great benefits: flying around the world, meeting all those people. It is a nice status symbol.*

*"I have five older sisters and they were all married before they were twenty. The minute they got out of high school, they would end up getting married. That was the thing everybody did, was get married. When I told my parents I was going to the airlines, they got excited. They were so happy that one of the girls could go out and see the world and spend some time being*

Studs Terkel was born Louis Terkel in New York City in 1912. He was brought up in Chicago, and was graduated from the University of Chicago. Terkel has been an actor, playwright, columnist, and disc jockey, but he is best known as the man who makes books out of tape recordings of people he gets to talk. These oral histories are *Division Street: America* (1966), *Hard Times* (1970), and *Working* (1974).

"Three Workers" (editors' title) is from the last of these books.

*single. I didn't get married until I was almost twenty-five. My mother especially thought it would be great that I could have the ambition, the nerve to go to the big city on my own and try to accomplish being a stewardess."*

When people ask you what you're doing and you say stewardess, you're really proud, you think it's great. It's like a stepping stone. The first two months I started flying I had already been to London, Paris, and Rome. And me from Broken Bow, Nebraska. But after you start working, it's not as glamorous as you thought it was going to be.

They like girls that have a nice personality and that are pleasant to look at. If a woman has a problem with blemishes, they take her off. Until the appearance counselor thinks she's ready to go back on. One day this girl showed up, she had a very slight black eye. They took her off. Little things like that.

We had to go to stew school for five weeks. We'd go through a whole week of make-up and poise. I didn't like this. They make you feel like you've never been out in public. They showed you how to smoke a cigarette, when to smoke a cigarette, how to look at a man's eyes. Our teacher, she had this idea we had to be sexy. One day in class she was showing us how to accept a light for a cigarette from a man and never blow it out. When he lights it, just look in his eyes. It was really funny, all the girls laughed.

It's never proper for a woman to light her own cigarette. You hold it up and of course you're out with a guy who knows the right way to light the cigarette. You look into their eyes as they're lighting your cigarette and you're cupping his hand, but holding it just very light, so that he can feel your touch and your warmth. (Laughs.) You do not blow the match out. It used to be really great for a woman to blow the match out when she looked in his eyes, but she said now the man blows the match out.

The idea is not to be too obvious about it. They don't want you to look too forward. That's the whole thing, being a lady but still giving out that womanly appeal, like the body movement and the lips and the eyes. The guy's supposed to look in your eyes. You could be a real mean woman. You're a lady and doing all these evil things with your eyes.

She did try to promote people smoking. She said smoking can be part of your conversation. If you don't know what to say, you can always pull out a cigarette. She says it makes you more comfortable. I started smoking when I was on the airlines.

Our airline picks the girl-next-door type. At one time they wouldn't let us wear false eyelashes and false fingernails. Now it's required that you wear false eyelashes, and if you do not have the right length nails, you wear false nails. Everything is supposed to be becoming to the passenger.

That's the whole thing: meeting all these great men that either have great business backgrounds or good looking or different. You do meet a lot of movie stars and a lot of political people, but you don't get to really visit with them that much. You never really get to go out with these men. Stewardesses are impressed only by name people. But a normal millionaire that you don't know you're not impressed about. The only thing that really thrills a stewardess is a passenger like Kennedy or movie stars or somebody political. Celebrities.

I think our average age is twenty-six. But our supervisors tell us what kind of make-up to wear, what kind of lipstick to wear, if our hair is not the right style for us, if we're not smiling enough. They even tell us how to act when you're on a pass. Like last night I met my husband. I was in plain clothes. I wanted to kiss him. But I'm not supposed to kiss anybody at the terminal. You're not supposed to walk off with a passenger, hand in hand. After you get out of the terminal, that's all yours.

The majority of passengers do make passes. The ones that do make passes are married and are business people. When I tell them I'm married, they say, "I'm married and you're married and you're away from home and so am I and nobody's gonna find out." The majority of those who make passes at you, you wouldn't accept a date if they were friends of yours at home.

After I was a stewardess for a year, and I was single, I came down to the near North Side of Chicago, which is the swinging place for singles. Stewardess, that was a dirty name. In a big city, it's an easy woman. I didn't like this at all. All these books—*Coffee, Tea and Me.*

I lived in an apartment complex where the majority there were stewardesses.[1] The other women were secretaries and teachers. They would go to our parties and they would end up being among the worst. They never had stories about these secretaries and nurses, but they sure had good ones about stewardesses.

[1]"In New York, stewardesses live five or six girls to one apartment. They think they can get by because they're in and out so much. But there's gonna be a few nights they're all gonna be home at once and a couple of 'em will have to sleep on the floor."

I meet a lot of other wives or single women. The first minute they start talking to me, they're really cold. They think the majority of stewardesses are snobs or they may be jealous. These women think we have a great time, that we are playgirls, that we have the advantage to go out with every type of man we want. So when they first meet us, they really turn off on us.

When you first start flying, the majority of girls do live in apartment complexes by the airport. The men they meet are airport employees: ramp rats, cleaning airplanes and things like that, mechanics, and young pilots, not married, ones just coming in fresh.

After a year we get tired of that, so we move into the city to get involved with men that are usually young executives, like at Xerox or something. Young businessmen in the early thirties and late twenties, they really think stewardesses are the gals to go out with if they want to get so far. They wear their hats and their suits and in the winter their black gloves. The women are getting older, they're getting twenty-four, twenty-five. They get involved with bartenders too. Stewardesses and bartenders are a pair. (Laughs.)

One time I went down into the area of swinging bars with two other girls. We just didn't want anybody to know that we were stewardesses, so we had this story made up that we were going to a women's college in Colorado. That went over. We had people that were talking to us, being nice to us, being polite. Down there, they wouldn't even be polite. They'd buy you drinks but then they'd steal your stool if you got up to go to the restroom. But when they knew you weren't stewardesses, just young ladies that were going to a women's college, they were really nice to us.

They say you can spot a stewardess by the way she wears her makeup. At that time we all had short hair and everybody had it cut in stew school exactly alike. If there's two blondes that have their hair cut very short, wearing the same shade of makeup, and they get into uniform, people say, "Oh, you look like sisters." Wonder why? (Laughs.)

The majority of us were against it because they wouldn't let you say how *you'd* like your hair cut, they wouldn't let you have your own personality, *your* makeup, *your* clothes. They'd tell you what length skirts to wear. At one time they told us we couldn't wear anything one inch above the knees. And no pants at that time. It's different now.

Wigs used to be forbidden. Now it's the style. Now it's permissible for nice women to wear wigs, eyelashes, and false fingernails.

Before it was the harder looking women that wore them. Women showing up in pants, it wasn't ladylike. Hot pants are in now. Most airlines change style every year.

*She describes stewardess schools in the past as being like college dorms: it was forbidden to go out during the week; signing in and out on Friday and Saturday nights. "They've cut down stewardess school quite a bit. Cut down on how-to-serve-meal classes and paperwork. A lot of girls get on aircraft these days and don't know where a magazine is, where the tray tables are for passengers. . . . Every day we used to have an examination. If you missed over two questions, that was a failure. They'd ask us ten questions. If you failed two tests out of the whole five weeks, you would have to leave. Now they don't have any exams at all. Usually we get a raise every year. We haven't been getting that lately."*

We have long duty hours. We can be on duty for thirteen hours. But we're not supposed to fly over eight hours. This is in a twenty-four-hour period. During the eight hours, you could be flying from Chicago to Flint, to Moline, short runs. You stop twenty minutes. So you get to New York finally, after five stops, let's say. You have an hour on your own. But you have to be on the plane thirty minutes before departure time. How many restaurants can serve you food in thirty minutes? So you've gone thirteen hours, off and on duty, having half-hours and no time to eat. This is the normal thing. If we have only thirty minutes and we don't have time to eat, it's our hard luck.

Pilots have the same thing too. They end up grabbing a sandwich and eating in the cockpit. When I first started flying we were not supposed to eat at all on the aircraft, even though there was an extra meal left over. Now we can eat in the buffet. We have to stand there with all those dirty dishes and eat our meals—if there's one left over. We cannot eat in the public eye. We cannot bring it out if there's an extra seat. You can smoke in the cockpit, in the restrooms, but not in the public's eye.

*"We have a union. It's a division of the pilots union. It helps us out on duty time and working privileges. It makes sure that if we're in Cleveland and stuck because of weather and thirteen hours have gone by, we can go to bed. Before we had a union the stew office would call and say, 'You're working another seven.' I worked one time thirty-six hours straight."*

The other day I had fifty-five minutes to serve 101 coach passengers, a cocktail and full-meal service. You do it fast and terrible. You're very rude. You don't mean to be rude, you just don't have time to answer questions. You smile and you just ignore it. You get three drink orders in a hurry. There's been many times when you miss the glass, pouring, and you pour it in the man's lap. You just don't say I'm sorry. You give him a cloth and you keep going. That's the bad part of the job.

Sometimes I get tired of working first class. These people think they're great, paying for more, and want more. Also I get tired of coach passengers asking for something that he thinks he's a first-class passenger. We get this attitude of difference from our airlines. They're just dividing the class of people. If we're on a first-class pass, the women are to wear a dress or a nice pants suit that has a matching jacket, and the men are to dress with suit jacket and tie and white shirt. And yet so many types of first-class passengers: some have grubby clothes, jeans and moccasins and everything. They can afford to dress the way they feel. . . .

If I want to fly first class, I pay the five dollars difference. I like the idea of getting free drinks, free champagne, free wine. In a coach, you don't. A coach passenger might say, "Could I have a pillow?" So you give him a pillow. Then he'll say, "Could you bring me a glass of water?" A step behind him there's the water fountain. In first class, if the guy says, "I want a glass of water," even if the water fountain is right by his arm, you'd bring it for him. We give him all this extra because he's first class. Which isn't fair. . . .

When you're in a coach, you feel like there's just heads and heads and heads of people. That's all you can see. In first class, being less people, you're more relaxed, you have more time. When you get on a 727, we have one coatroom. Our airline tells us you hang up first-class coats only. When a coach passenger says, "Could you hang up my coat?" most of the time I'll hang it up. Why should I hang up first class and not coach?

One girl is for first class only and there's two girls for coach. The senior girl will be first class. That first-class girl gets used to working first class. If she happens to walk through the coach, if someone asks her for something, she'll make the other girls do it. The first stew always stays at the door and welcomes everybody aboard and says good-by to everybody when they leave. That's why a lot of girls don't like to be first class.

There's an old story on the airline. The stewardess asks if he'd like something to drink, him and his wife. He says, "I'd like a martini." The stewardess asks the wife, "Would you like a drink?" She doesn't say anything, and the husband says, "I'm sorry, she's not used to talking to the help." (Laughs.) When I started flying, that was the first story I heard.

I've never had the nerve to speak up to anybody that's pinched me or said something dirty. Because I've always been afraid of these onion letters. These are bad letters. If you get a certain amount of bad letters, you're fired. When you get a bad letter you have to go in and talk to the supervisor. Other girls now, there are many of 'em that are coming around and telling them what they feel. The passenger reacts: She's telling me off! He doesn't believe it. Sometimes the passenger needs it.

One guy got his steak and he said, "This is too medium, I want mine rarer." The girl said, "I'm sorry, I don't cook the food, it's precooked." He picked up the meal and threw it on the floor. She says, "If you don't pick the meal up right now, I'll make sure the crew members come back here and make you pick it up." (With awe) She's talking right back at him and loud, right in front of everybody. He really didn't think she would yell at him. Man, he picked up the meal. . . . The younger girls don't take that guff any more, like we used to. When the passenger is giving you a bad time, you talk back to him.

It's always: the passenger is right. When a passenger says something mean, we're supposed to smile and say, "I understand." We're supposed to *really* smile because stewardesses' supervisors have been getting reports that the girls have been back-talking passengers. Even when they pinch us or say dirty things, we're supposed to smile at them. That's one thing they taught us at stew school. Like he's rubbing your body somewhere, you're supposed to just put his hand down and not say anything and smile at him. That's the main thing, smile.

When I first went to class, they told me I had a crooked smile. She showed me how to smile. She said, "Kinda press a little smile on" —which I did. "Oh, that's great," she said, "that's a *good* smile." But I couldn't do it. I didn't feel like I was doing it on my own. Even if we're sad, we're supposed to have a smile on our face.

I came in after a flight one day, my grandfather had died. Usually they call you up or meet you at the flight and say, "We have some bad news for you." I pick up this piece of paper in my mailbox and it says, "Mother called in. Your grandfather died today." It was written like, say, two cups of sugar. Was I mad! They wouldn't give me time off for the funeral. You can only have time off for your parents or somebody you have lived with. I had never lived with my grandparents. I went anyway.

A lot of our girls are teachers, nurses, everything. They do this part-time, 'cause you have enough time off for another kind of job. I personally work for conventions. I work electronic and auto shows. Companies hire me to stay in their booth and talk about products. I have this speech to tell. At others, all I do is pass out matches or candy. Nowadays every booth has a young girl in it.

People just love to drink on airplanes. They feel adventurous. So you're serving drinks and meals and there's very few times that you can sit down. If she does sit down, she's forgotten how to sit down and talk to passengers. I used to play bridge with passengers. But that doesn't happen any more. We're not supposed to be sitting down, or have a magazine or read a newspaper. If it's a flight from Boston to Los Angeles, you're supposed to have a half an hour talking to passengers. But the only time we can sit down is when we go to the cockpit. You're not supposed to spend any more than five minutes up there for a cigarette.

We could be sitting down on our jump seat and if you had a supervisor on board, she would write you up—for not mixing with the crowd. We're supposed to be told when she walks on board. Many times you don't know. They do have personnel that ride the flights that don't give their names—checking, and they don't tell you about it. Sometimes a girl gets caught smoking in the cabin. Say it's a long flight, maybe a night flight. You're playing cards with a passenger and you say, "Would it bother you if I smoke?" And he says no. She would write you up and get you fired for smoking in the airplane.

They have a limit on how far you can mix. They want you to be sociable, but if he offers you a cigarette, not to take it. When you're outside, they encourage you to take cigarettes.

You give your time to everybody, you share it, not too much with one passenger. Everybody else may be snoring away and there's three guys, maybe military, and they're awake 'cause they're going home and excited. So you're playing cards with 'em. If you have a supervisor on, that would be a no-no. They call a lot of things no-no's.

They call us professional people but they talk to us as very young, childishly. They check us all the time on appearance. They check our weight every month. Even though you've been flying twenty years, they check you and say that's a no-no. If you're not spreading yourself around passengers enough, that's a no-no. Not hanging up first-class passenger's coats, that's a no-no, even though there's no room in the coatroom. You're supposed to somehow make room. If you're a pound over, they can take you off flight until you get under.

Accidents? I've never yet been so scared that I didn't want to get in the airplane. But there've been times at take-offs, there's been something funny. Here I am thinking, What if I die today? I've got too much to do. I can't die today. I use it as a joke.

I've had emergencies where I've had to evacuate the aircraft. I was coming back from Las Vegas and being a lively stewardess I stayed up all night, gambled. We had a load full of passengers. The captain tells me we're going to have an emergency landing in Chicago because we lost a pin out of the nose gear. When we land, the nose gear is gonna collapse. He wants me to prepare the whole cabin for the landing, but not for two more hours. And not to tell the other stewardesses, because they were new girls and would get all excited. So I had to keep this in me for two more hours, wondering, Am I gonna die today? And this is Easter Sunday. And I was serving the passengers drinks and food and this guy got mad at me because his omelet was too cold. And I was gonna say, "You just wait, buddy, you're not gonna worry about that omelet." But I was nice about it, because I didn't want to have trouble with a passenger, especially when I have to prepare him for an emergency.

I told the passengers over the intercom: "The captain says it's just a precaution, there's nothing to worry about." I'm just gonna explain how to get out of the airplane fast, how to be in a braced position. They can't wear glasses or high heels, purses, things out of aisles, under the seats. And make sure everybody's pretty quiet. We had a blind woman on with a dog. We had to get people to help her off and all this stuff.

They were fantastic. Nobody screamed, cried, or hollered. When we got on the ground, everything was fine. The captain landed perfect. But there was a little jolt, and the passengers started screaming and hollering. They held it all back and all of a sudden we got on the ground, blah.

I was great. (Laughs.) That's what was funny. I thought, I have a husband now. I don't know how he would take it, my dying on an airplane. So I thought, I can't die. When I got on the intercom, I was so calm. Also we're supposed to keep a smile on our face. Even during an emergency, you're supposed to walk through the cabin and make everybody feel comfortable with a smile. When you're on the jump seat everybody's looking at you. You're supposed to sit there, holding your ankles, in a position to get out of that airplane fast with a big fat smile on your face.

Doctors tell stewardesses two bad things about them. They're gonna get wrinkles all over their face because they smile with their mouth and their eyes. And also with the pressurization on the airplane, we're not supposed to get up while we're climbing because it causes varicose veins in our legs. So they say being a stewardess ruins your looks.

A lot of stewardesses wanted to be models. The Tanya girl used to be a stewardess on our airline. A stewardess is what they could get and a model is what they couldn't get. They weren't the type of person, they weren't that beautiful, they weren't that thin. So their second choice would be stewardess.

*What did you want to be?* I wanted to get out of Broken Bow, Nebraska. (Laughs.)

POSTSCRIPT: *"Everytime I go home, they all meet me at the airplane. Not one of my sisters has been on an airplane. All their children think that Terry is just fantastic, because their mom and dad—my sisters and their husbands—feel so stupid, 'Look at us. I wish I could have done that.' I know they feel bad, that they never had the chance. But they're happy I can come home and tell them about things. I send them things from Europe. They get to tell all their friends that their sister's a stewardess. They get real excited about that. The first thing they come out and say, 'One of my sisters is a stewardess.'*

*"My father got a promotion with his company and they wrote in their business news that he had a family of seven, six girls and a boy, and one girl is a stewardess in Chicago. And went on to say what I did, and didn't say a word about anything else."*[2]

## II. Roberta Victor, Hooker

*She had been a prostitute, starting at the age of fifteen. During the first five or six years, she worked as a high-priced call girl in Manhattan. Later she was a streetwalker. . . .*

[2]Questions on this selection appear on page 291.

You never used your own name in hustling. I used a different name practically every week. If you got busted, it was more difficult for them to find out who you really were. The role one plays when hustling has nothing to do with who you are. It's only fitting and proper you take another name.

There were certain names that were in great demand. Every second hustler had the name Kim or Tracy or Stacy and a couple others that were in vogue. These were all young women from seventeen to twenty-five, and we picked these very non-ethnic-oriented WASP names, rich names.

A hustler is any woman in American society. I was the kind of hustler who received money for favors granted rather than the type of hustler who signs a lifetime contract for her trick. Or the kind of hustler who carefully reads women's magazines and learns what it is proper to give for each date, depending on how much money her date or trick spends on her.

The favors I granted were not always sexual. When I was a call girl, men were not paying for sex. They were paying for something else. They were either paying to act out a fantasy or they were paying for companionship or they were paying to be seen with a well-dressed young woman. Or they were paying for somebody to listen to them. They were paying for a *lot* of things. Some men were paying for sex that *they* felt was deviant. They were paying so that nobody would accuse them them of being perverted or dirty or nasty. A large proportion of these guys asked things that were not at all deviant. Many of them wanted oral sex. They felt they couldn't ask their wives or girl friends because they'd be repulsed. Many of them wanted somebody to talk dirty to them. Every good call girl in New York used to share her book and we all knew the same tricks.

We know a guy who used to lie in a coffin in the middle of his bedroom and he would see the girl only once. He got his kicks when the door would be open, the lights would be out, and there would be candles in the living room, and all you could see was his coffin on wheels. As you walked into the living room, he'd suddenly sit up. Of course, you screamed. He got his kicks when you screamed. Or the guy who set a table like the Last Supper and sat in a robe and sandals and wanted you to play Mary Magdalene. (Laughs.)

I was about fifteen, going on sixteen. I was sitting in a coffee shop in the Village, and a friend of mine came by. She said; "I've got a cab waiting. Hurry up. You can make fifty dollars in twenty minutes." Looking back, I wonder why I was so willing to run out of the coffee shop, get in a cab, and turn a trick. It wasn't traumatic because my training had been in how to be a hustler anyway.

I learned it from the society around me, just as a woman. We're taught how to hustle, how to attract, hold a man, and give sexual favors in return. The language that you hear all the time, "Don't sell yourself cheap." "Hold out for the highest bidder." "Is it proper to kiss a man good night on the first date?" The implication is it may not be proper on the first date, but if he takes you out to dinner on the second date, it's proper. If he brings you a bottle of perfume on the third date, you should let him touch you above the waist. And go on from here. It's a market place transaction.

Somehow I managed to absorb that when I was quite young. So it wasn't even a moment of truth when this woman came into the coffee shop and said; "Come on." I was back in twenty-five minutes and I felt no guilt.

*She was a virgin until she was fourteen. A jazz musician, with whom she had fallen in love, avoided her. "So I went out to have sex with somebody to present him with an accomplished fact. I found it nonpleasurable. I did a lot of sleeping around before I ever took money."*

*A precocious child, she was already attending a high school of demanding academic standards. "I was very lonely. I didn't experience myself as being attractive. I had always felt I was too big, too fat, too awkward, didn't look like a Pepsi-Cola ad, was not anywhere near the American Dream. Guys were mostly scared of me. I was athletic, I was bright, and I didn't know how to keep my mouth shut. I didn't know how to play the games right.*

*"I understood very clearly they were not attracted to me for what I was, but as a sexual object. I was attractive. The year before I started hustling there were a lot of guys that wanted to go to bed with me. They didn't want to get involved emotionally, but they did want to ball. For a while I was willing to accept that. It was feeling intimacy, feeling close, feeling warm.*

*"The time spent in bed wasn't unpleasant. It just wasn't terribly pleasant. It was a way of feeling somebody cared about me, at least for a moment. And it mattered that I was there, that I was important. I discovered that in bed it was possible. It was one skill that I had and I was proud of my reputation as an amateur.*

*"I viewed all girls as being threats. That's what we were all taught. You can't be friends with another woman, she might take your man. If you tell her anything about how you really feel, she'll use it against you. You smile at other girls and you spend time with them when there's nothing better to do, but you'd leave any girl sitting anywhere if you had an opportunity*

*to go somewhere with a man. Because the most important thing in life is the way men feel about you."*

How could you forget your first trick? (Laughs.) We took a cab to midtown Manhattan, we went to a penthouse. The guy up there was quite well known. What he really wanted to do was watch two women make love, and then he wanted to have sex with me. It was barely sex. He was almost finished by the time we started. He barely touched me and we were finished.

Of course, we faked it, the woman and me. The ethic was: You don't participate in a sexual act with another woman if a trick is watching. You always fake it. You're putting something over on him and he's paying for something he didn't really get. That's the only way you can keep any sense of self-respect.

The call girl ethic is very strong. You were the lowest of the low if you allowed yourself to feel anything with a trick. The bed puts you on their level. The way you maintain your integrity is by acting all the way through. It's not too far removed from what most American women do—which is to put on a big smile and act.

It was a tremendous kick. Here I was doing absolutely nothing, *feeling* nothing, and in twenty minutes I was going to walk out with fifty dollars in my pocket. That just made me feel absolutely marvelous. I came downtown. I can't believe this! I'm not changed, I'm the same as I was twenty minutes ago, except that now I have fifty dollars in my pocket. It really was tremendous status. How many people coud make fifty dollars for twenty minutes' work? Folks work for eighty dollars take-home pay. I worked twenty minutes for fifty dollars clear, no taxes, nothing! I was still in school, I was smoking grass, I was shooting heroin, I wasn't hooked yet, and I had money. It was terrific.

After that, I made it my business to let my friend know that I was available for more of these situations. (Laughs.) She had good connections. Very shortly I linked up with a couple of others who had a good call book.

Books of phone numbers are passed around from call girl to call girl. They're numbers of folks who are quite respectable and with whom there is little risk. They're not liable to pull a knife on you, they're not going to cheat you out of money. Businessmen and society figures. There's three or four groups. The wealthy executive, who makes periodic trips into the city and is known to several girls. There's the social figure, whose name appears quite regularly in the society pages and who's a regular one-a-week John. Or there's the quiet, independently wealthy type. Nobody knows how they got their money. I know one of them made his money off munitions in World War II. Then there's the entertainer. There's another crowd that runs around the night spots, the 21 Club. . . .

These were the people whose names you saw in the paper almost every day. But I knew what they were really like. Any John who was obnoxious or aggressive was just crossed out of your book. You passed the word around that this person was not somebody other people should call.

We used to share numbers—standard procedure. The book I had I got from a guy who got it from a very good call girl. We kept a copy of that book in a safe deposit box. The standard procedure was that somebody new gave half of what they got the first time for each number. You'd tell them: "Call so-and-so, that's a fifty-dollar trick." They would give you twenty-five dollars. Then the number was theirs. My first book, I paid half of each trick to the person who gave it to me. After that, it was my book.

The book had the name and phone number coded, the price, what the person wants, and the contact name. For four years I didn't turn a trick for less than fifty dollars. They were all fifty to one hundred dollars and up for twenty minutes, an hour. The understanding is: it doesn't get conducted as a business transaction. The myth is that it's a social occasion.

You're expected to be well dressed, well made up, appear glad to see the man. I would get a book from somebody and I would call and say, "I'm a friend of so-and-so's, and she thought it would be nice if we got together." The next move was his. Invariably he'd say, "Why don't we do that? Tonight or tomorrow night. Why don't you come over for a drink?" I would get very carefully dressed and made up. . . .

There's a given way of dressing in that league—that's to dress well but not ostentatiously. You have to pass doormen, cabdrivers. You have to look as if you belong in those buildings on Park Avenue or Central Park West. You're expected not to look cheap, not to look hard. Youth is the premium. I was quite young, but I looked older, so I had to work very hard at looking my age. Most men want girls who are eighteen. They really want girls who are younger, but they're afraid of trouble.

Preparations are very elaborate. It has to do with beauty parlors and shopping for clothes and taking long baths and spending money on preserving the kind of front that gives you a respectable address and telephone and being seen at the right clubs and drinking at the right bars. And being able to read the newspapers faithfully, so that not only can you talk about current events, you can talk about the society columns as well.

It's a social ritual. Being able to talk about what is happening and learn from this great master, and be properly respectful and know the names that he mentions. They always drop names of their friends, their contacts, and their clients. You should recognize these. Playing a role. . . .

At the beginning I was very excited. But in order to continue I had to turn myself off. I had to disassociate who I was from what I was doing.

It's a process of numbing yourself. I couldn't associate with people who were not in the life—either the drug life or the hustling life. I found I couldn't turn myself back on when I finished working. When I turned myself off, I was numb—emotionally, sexually numb.

At first I felt like I was putting one over on all the other poor slobs that would go to work at eight-thirty in the morning and come home at five. I was coming home at four in the morning and I could sleep all day. I really thought a lot of people would change places with me because of the romantic image: being able to spend two hours out, riding cabs, and coming home with a hundred dollars. I could spend my mornings doing my nails, going to the beauty parlor, taking long baths, going shopping. . . .

It was usually two tricks a night. That was easily a hundred, a hundred and a quarter. I always had money in my pocket. I didn't know what the inside of a subway smelled like. Nobody traveled any other way except by cab. I ate in all the best restaurants and I drank in all the best clubs. A lot of people wanted you to go out to dinner with them. All you had to do was be an ornament.

Almost all the call girls I knew were involved in drugs. The fast life, the night hours. At after-hours clubs, if you're not a big drinker, you usually find somebody who has cocaine, 'cause that's the big drug in those places. You wake up at noon, there's not very much to do till nine or ten that night. Everybody else is at work, so you shoot heroin. After a while the work became a means of supplying drugs, rather than drugs being something we took when we were bored.

The work becomes boring because you're not part of the life. You're the part that's always hidden. The doormen smirk when you come in, 'cause they know what's going on. The cabdriver, when you give him a certain address—he knows exactly where you're going when you're riding up Park Avenue at ten o'clock at night, for Christ sake. You leave there and go back—to what? Really, to what? To an emptiness. You've got all this money in your pocket and nobody you care about.

When I was a call girl I looked down on streetwalkers. I couldn't understand why anybody would put themselves in that position. It seemed to me to be hard work and very dangerous. What I was doing was basically riskless. You never had to worry about disease. These were folks who you know took care of themselves and saw the doctor regularly. Their apartments were always immaculate and the liquor was always good. They were always polite. You didn't have to ask them for money first. It was always implicit: when you were ready to leave, there would be an envelope under the lamp or there'd be something in your pocketbook. It never had to be discussed.

I had to work an awful lot harder for the same money when I was a streetwalker. I remember having knives pulled on me, broken bottles held over my head, being raped, having my money stolen back from me, having to jump out of a second-story window, having a gun pointed at me.

As a call girl, I had lunch at the same places society women had lunch. There was no way of telling me apart from anybody else in the upper tax bracket. I made my own hours, no more than three or so hours of work an evening. I didn't have to accept calls. All I had to do was play a role.

As a streetwalker, I didn't have to act. I let myself show the contempt I felt for the tricks. They weren't paying enough to make it worth performing for them. As a call girl, I pretended I enjoyed it sexually. You have to act as if you had an orgasm. As a streetwalker, I didn't. I used to lie there with my hands behind my head and do mathematics equations in my head or memorize the keyboard typewriter.

It was strictly a transaction. No conversation, no acting, no myth around it, no romanticism. It was purely a business transaction. You always asked for your money in front. If you could get away without undressing totally, you did that.

It's not too different than the distinction between an executive secretary and somebody in the typing pool. As an executive secretary you really identify with your boss. When you're part of the typing pool, you're a body, you're hired labor, a set of hands on the typewriter. You have nothing to do with whoever is passing the work down to you. You do it as quickly as you can.

*What led you to the streets?*

My drug habit. It got a lot larger. I started looking bad. All my money was going for drugs. I didn't have any money to spend on keeping myself up and going to beauty parlors and having a decent address and telephone.

If you can't keep yourself up, you can't call on your old tricks. You drop out of circulation. As a call girl, you have to maintain a whole image. The trick wants to know he can call you at a certain number and you have to have a stable address. You must look presentable, not like death on a soda cracker.

I looked terrible. When I hit the streets, I tried to stick to at least twenty dollars and folks would laugh. I needed a hundred dollars a night to maintain a drug habit and keep a room somewhere. It meant turning seven or eight tricks a night. I was out on the street from nine o'clock at night till four in the morning. I was taking subways and eating in hamburger stands.

For the first time I ran the risk of being busted. I was never arrested as a call girl. Every once in a while a cop would get hold of somebody's book. They would call one of the girls and say, "I'm a friend of so-and-so's." They would try to trap them. I never took calls from people I didn't know. But on the streets, how do you know who you're gonna pick up?

As a call girl, some of my tricks were upper echelon cops, not patrolmen. Priests, financiers, garment industry folks, bigtimers. On the street, they ranged from *junior* executive types, blue-collar workers, upwardly striving postal workers, college kids, suburban white collars who were in the city for the big night, restaurant workers. . . .

You walk a cerain area, usually five or six blocks. It has a couple of restaurants, a couple of bars. There's the step in-between: hanging out in a given bar, where people come to you. I did that briefly.

You'd walk very slowly, you'd stop and look in the window. Somebody would come up to you. There was a ritual here too. The law says in order to arrest a woman for prostitution, she has to mention money and she has to tell you what she'll do for the money. We would keep within the letter of the law, even though the cops never did.

Somebody would come up and say, "It's a nice night, isn't it?" "Yes." They'd say, "Are you busy?" I'd say, "Not particularly." "Would you like to come with me and have a drink?" You start walking and they say, "I have fifteen dollars or twelve dollars and I'm very lonely." Something to preserve the myth. Then they want you to spell out exactly what you're willing to do for the money.

I never approached anybody on the street. That was the ultimate risk. Even if he weren't a cop, he could be some kind of supersquare, who would call a cop. I was trapped by cops several times.

The first one didn't even trap me as a trick. It was three in the morning. I was in Chinatown. I ran into a trick I knew. We made contact in a restaurant. He went home and I followed him a few minutes later. I knew the address. I remember passing a banana truck. It didn't dawn on me that it was strange for somebody to be selling bananas at three in the morning. I spent about twenty minutes with my friend. He paid me. I put the money in my shoe. I opened the door and got thrown back against the wall. The banana salesman was a vice squad cop. He'd stood on the garbage can to peer in the window. I got three years for that one.

I was under age. I was four months short of twenty-one. They sent me to what was then called Girls' Term Court. They wouldn't allow me a lawyer because I wasn't an adult, so it wasn't really a criminal charge. The judge said I was rehabilitable. Instead of giving me thirty days, he gave me three years in the reformatory. It was very friendly of him. I was out on parole a couple of times before I'd get caught and sent back.

I once really got trapped. It was about midnight and a guy came down the street. He said he was a postal worker who just got off the shift. He told me how much money he had and what he wanted. I took him to my room. The cop isn't supposed to undress. If you can describe the color of his shorts, it's an invalid arrest. Not only did he show me the color of his shorts, he went to bed with me. Then he pulled a badge and a gun and busted me.

He lied to me. He told me he was a narc and didn't want to bust me for hustling. If I would tell him who was dealing in the neighborhood, he'd cut me loose. I lied to him, but he won. He got me to walk out of the building past all my friends and when we got to the car, he threw me in. (Laughs.) It was great fun. I did time for that—close to four years.

*What's the status of the streetwalker in prison?*

It's fine. Everybody there has been hustling. It's status in reverse. Anybody who comes in saying things like they could never hustle is looked down on as being somewhat crazy.

*She speaks of a profound love she had for a woman who she's met in prison; of her nursing her lover after the woman had become blind.*

*"I was out of the country for a couple of years. I worked a house in Mexico. It had heavy velour curtains—a Mexican version of a French whorehouse. There was a reception area, where the men would come and we'd parade in front of them.*

*"The Mexicans wanted American girls. The Americans wanted Mexican girls. So I didn't get any American tricks. I had to give a certain amount to the house for each trick I turned and anything I negotiated over that amount was mine. It was far less than anything I had taken in the States.*

*"I was in great demand even though I wasn't a blonde. A girl friend of mine worked there two nights. She was Norwegian and very blonde. Every trick who came in wanted her. Her head couldn't handle it all. She quit after two nights. So I was the only American.*

*"That was really hard work. The Mexicans would play* macho. *American tricks will come as quickly as they can. Mexicans will hold back and make me work for my money. I swear to God they were doing multiplication tables in their heads to keep from having an orgasm. I would use every trick I knew to get them to finish. It was crazy!*

*I was teaching school at the same time. I used* Alice in Wonderland *as the text in my English class. During the day I tutored English for fifth- and sixth-grade kids. In the evening, I worked in the call house.*

*"The junk down there was quite cheap and quite good. My habit was quite large. I loved dope more than anything else around. After a while I couldn't differentiate between working and not working. All men were tricks, all relationships were acting. I was completely turned off."*

*She quit shooting dope the moment she was slugged, brutally beaten by a dealer who wanted her. This was her revelatory experience. "It was the final indignity. I'd had tricks pulling broken bottles on me, I'd been in razor fights, but nobody had ever* hit me." *It was a threat to her status. "I was strong. I could handle myself. A tough broad. This was threatened, so . . ."*

I can't talk for women who were involved with pimps. That was where I always drew the line. I always thought pimps were lower than pregnant cockroaches. I didn't want anything to do with them. I was involved from time to time with some men. They were either selling dope or stealing, but they were not depending on my income. Nor were they telling me to get my ass out on the street. I never supported a man.

As a call girl I got satisfaction, an unbelievable joy—perhaps perverted—in knowing what these reputable folks were really like. Being able to open a newspaper every morning, read about this pillar of society, and know what a pig he really was. The tremendous kick in knowing that I didn't feel anything, that I was acting and they weren't. It's sick, but no sicker than what every woman is taught, all right?

I was in *control* with every one of those relationships. You're vulnerable if you allow yourself to be involved sexually. I wasn't. They were. I called it. Being able to manipulate somebody sexually, I could determine when I wanted that particular transaction to end. 'Cause I could make the guy come. I could play all kinds of games. See? It was a tremendous sense of power.

What I did was no different from what ninety-nine percent of American women are taught to do. I took the money from under the lamp instead of in Arpege. What would I do with 150 bottles of Arpege a week?

You become your job. I became what I did. I became a hustler. I became cold, I became hard, I became turned off, I became numb. Even when I wasn't hustling, I was a hustler. I don't think it's terribly different from somebody who works on the assembly line forty hours a week and comes home cut off, numb, dehumanized. People aren't built to switch on and off like water faucets.

What was really horrifying about jail is that it really isn't horrifying. You adjust very easily. The same thing with hustling. It became my life. It was too much of an effort to try to make contact with another human being, to force myself to care, to feel.

I didn't care about me. It didn't matter whether I got up or didn't get up. I got high as soon as I awoke. The first thing I'd reach for, with my eyes half-closed, was my dope. I didn't like my work. It was messy. That was the biggest feeling about it. Here's all these guys slobbering over you all night long. I'm lying there, doing math or conjugations or Spanish poetry in my head. (Laughs.) And they're slobbering. God! God! What enabled me to do it was being high—high and numb.

The overt hustling society is the microcosm of the rest of the society. The power relationships are the same and the games are the same. Only this one I was in control of. The greater one I wasn't. In the outside society, if I tried to be me, I wasn't in control of anything. As a bright, assertive woman, I had no power. As a cold, manipulative hustler, I had a lot. I knew I was playing a role. Most women are taught to become what they act. All I did was act out the reality of American womanhood.[3]

## III. Maggie Holmes, Domestic

What bugs me now, since I'm on welfare, is people saying they give you the money for nothin'. When I think back what we had to come through, up from the South, comin' here. The hard work we had to do. It really gets me, when I hear people . . . It do somethin' to me. I think violence.

I think what we had to work for. I used to work for $1.50 a week. This is five days a week, sometimes six. If you live in the servant quarter, your time is never off, because if they decide to have a party at night, you gotta come out. My grandmother, I remember when she used to work, we'd get milk and a pound of butter. I mean this was pay. I'm thinkin' about what my poor parents worked for, gettin' nothing. What do the white think about when they think? Do they ever think about what *they* would do?

*She had worked as a domestic, hotel chambermaid, and as "kitchen help in cafés" for the past twenty-five years, up North and down South. She lives with her four children.*

When it come to housework, I can't do it now. I can't stand it, cause it do somethin' to my mind. They want you to clean the house, want you to wash, even the windows, want you to iron. You not supposed to wash no dishes. You ain't supposed to make no beds up. Lots of 'em try to sneak it in on you, think you don't know that. So the doorbell rings and I didn't answer to. The bell's ringin' and I'm still doin' my work. She ask me why I don't answer the bell. I say; "Do I come here to be a butler?" And I don't see myself to be no doormaid. I came to do some work and I'm gonna do my work. When you end up, you's nursemaid, you's cook. They puts all this on you. If you want a job to cleanin', you ask for just cleanin'. She wants you to do in one day what she hasn't did all year.

Now this bug me: the first thing she gonna do is pull out this damn rubber thing—just fittin' for your knees. Knee pads—like you're workin' in the fields, like people pickin' cotton. No mop or

[3]Questions on this selection appear on page 292.

nothin'. That's why you find so many black women here got rheumatism in their legs, knees. When you gets on that cold floor, I don't care how warm the house is, you can feel the cold on the floor, the water and stuff. I never see nobody on their knees until I come North. In the South, they had mops. Most times, if they had real heavy work, they always had a man to come in. Washin' windows, that's a man's job. They don't think nothin' about askin' you to do that here. They don't have no feeling that that's what bothers you. I think to myself; My God, if I had somebody come and do my floors, clean up for me, I'd appreciate it. They don't say nothin' about it. Act like you haven't even done anything. They has no feelin's.

I worked for one old hen on Lake Shore Drive. You remember that big snow they had there?[4] Remember when you couldn't get there? When I gets to work she says: "Call the office." She complained to the lady where I got the job, said I was late to work. So I called. So I said, in the phone (Shouts), *"What do you want with me?* I got home four black, beautiful kids. Before I go to anybody's job in the morning I see that my kids are at school. I gonna see that they have warm clothes on and they fed." I'm lookin' right at the woman I'm workin' for. (Laughs.) When I get through the phone I tell this employer: "That goes for you too. The only thing I live for is my kids. There's nothin', you and nobody else." The expression on her face: What is this? (Laughs.) She thought I was gonna be like (mimics "Aunt Jemima"): "Yes ma'am, I'll try to get here a little early." But it wasn't like that. (Laughs.)

When I come in the door that day she told me pull my shoes off. I said, "For what? I can wipe my feet at the door here, but I'm not gettin' out of my shoes, it's cold." She look at me like she said: Oh my God, what I got here? (Laughs.) I'm knowin' I ain't gonna make no eight hours here. I can't take it.

She had everything in there snow white. And that means work, believe me. In the dining room she had a blue set, she had sky-blue chairs. They had a bedroom with pink and blue. I look and say, "I know what this means." It means sho' 'nough—knees. I said, "I'm gonna try and make it today, *if* I can make it." Usually when they're so bad, you have to leave.

I ask her where the mop is. She say she don't have no mop. I said, "Don't tell me you mop the floor on your knees. I know you don't."

[4]It was the week of Chicago's Big Snow-In, beginning January 25, 1967. Traffic was hopelessly snarled. Scores of thousands couldn't get to work.

They usually hid these mops in the clothes closet. I go out behind all these clothes and get the mop out. (Laughs.) They don't get on their knees, but they don't think nothin' about askin' a black woman. She says, "All you—you girls. . . . " She stop. I say, "All you *niggers,* is that what you want to say?" She give me this stupid look. I say, "I'm glad you tellin' me that there's more like me." (Laughs.) I told her, "You better give me my money and let me go, 'cause I'm gettin' angry." So I made her give me my carfare and what I had worked that day.

Most when you find decent work is when you find one that work themselves. They know what it's like to get up in the morning and go to work. In the suburbs they ain't got nothin' to do. They has nothin' else to think about. Their mind's just about blowed.

It's just like they're talkin' about mental health. Poor people's mental health is different than the rich white. Mine could come from a job or not havin' enough money for my kids. Mine is from me being poor. That don't mean you're sick. His sickness is from money, graftin' where he want more. I don't have *any.* You live like that day to day, penny to penny.

I worked for a woman, her husband's a judge. I cleaned the whole house. When it was time for me to go home, she decided she wants some ironing. She goes in the basement, she turn on the air conditioner. She said, "I think you can go down in the basement and finish your day out. It's air conditioned." I said, "I don't care what you got down there, I'm not ironing. You look at that slip, it says cleanin'. Don't say no ironin'. She wanted me to wash the walls in the bathroom. I said, "If you look at that telephone book they got all kinds of ads there under house cleanin'." She said the same thing as the other one, "All you girls—" I said same thing I said to the other one; "You mean niggers." (Laughs.)

*They ever call you by your last name?*

Oh God, they wouldn't do that. (Laughs.)

*Do you call her by her last name?*

Most time I don't call her, period. I don't say anything to her. I don't talk nasty to nobody, but when I go to work I don't talk to people. Most time they don't like what you're gonna say. So I keeps quiet.

*Most of her jobs were "way out in the suburbs. You get a bus and you ride till you get a subway. After you gets to Howard,[5] you gets the El. If you get to the end of the line and there's no bus, they pick you up. I don't like to work in the city, 'cause they don't pay you nothin'. And these old buildings are so nasty. It takes so much time to clean 'em. They are not kept up so good, like suburbs. Most of the new homes out there, it's easier to clean."*

*A commonly observed phenomenon: during the early evening hour, trains, crowded, predominantly by young white men carrying attaché cases, pass trains headed in the opposite direction, crowded, predominantly by middle-aged black women carrying brown paper bags. Neither group, it appears, glances at the other.*

*"We spend most of the time ridin'. You get caught goin' out from the suburbs at nighttime, man, you're really sittin' there for hours. There's nothin' movin'. You got a certain hour to meet trains. You get a transfer, you have to get that train. It's a shuffle to get in and out of the job. If you miss that train at five o'clock, what time you gonna get out that end? Sometime you don't get home till eight o'clock. . . ."*

You don't feel like washin' your own window when you come from out there, scrubbin'. If you work in one of them houses eight hours, you gotta come home do the same thing over . . . you don't feel like . . . (sighs softly) . . . tired. You gotta come home, take care of your kids, you gotta cook, you gotta wash. Most of the time, you gotta wash for the kids for somethin' to wear to school. You gotta clean up, 'cause you didn't have time in the morning. You gotta wash and iron and whatever you do, nights. You be so tired, until you don't feel like even doin' nothin'.

You get up at six, you fix breakfast for the kids, you get them ready to go on to school. Leave home about eight. Most of the time I make biscuits for my kids, cornbread you gotta make. I don't mean the canned kind. This I don't call cookin', when you go in that refrigerator and get some beans and drop 'em in a pot. And TV dinners, they go stick 'em in the stove and she say she cooked. This is not cookin'.

And *she's* tired. Tired from doin' what? You got a washing dryer, you got an electric sweeper, anything at fingertips. All she gotta do is unfroze 'em, dump 'em in the pot, and she's tired! I go to the store, I get my vegetables, greens, I wash 'em. I gotta pick 'em first. I don't eat none of that stuff, like in the cans. She don't do that, and she says she's tired.

[5]The boundary line separating Chicago from the North Shore suburb, Evanston.

When you work for them, when you get in that house in the morning, boy, they got one arm in their coat and a scarf on their head. And when you open that door, she shoots by you, she's gone. Know what I mean? They want you to come there and keep the kids and let them get out. What she think about how am I gonna do? Like I gets tired of my kids too. I'd like to go out too. It bugs you to think that they don't have no feelin's about that.

Most of the time I work for them and they be out. I don't like to work for 'em when they be in the house so much. They don't have no work to do. All they do is get on the telephone and talk about one another. Make you sick. I'll go and close the door. They're all the same, everybody's house is the same. You think they rehearse it . . .

When I work, only thing I be worryin' about is my kids. I just don't like to leave 'em too long. When they get out of school, you wonder if they out on the street. The only thing I worry is if they had a place to play in easy. I always call two, three times. When she don't like you to call, I'm in a hurry to get out of there. (Laughs.) My mind is gettin' home, what are you gonna find to cook before the stores close.

This Nixon was sayin' he don't see nothin' wrong with people doin' scrubbin'. For generations that's all we done. He should know we wants to be doctors and teachers and lawyers like him. I don't want my kids to come up and do domestic work. It's degrading. You can't see no tomorrow there. We done this for generation and generation—cooks and butlers all your life. They want their kids to be lawyers, doctors, and things. You don't want 'em in no cafés workin'. . . .

When they say about the neighborhood we live in is dirty, why do they ask me to come and clean their house? We, the people in the slums, the same nasty women they have come to their house in the suburbs every day. If these women are so filthy, why you want them to clean for you? They don't go and clean for us. We go and clean for them.

I worked one day where this white person did some housework. I'm lookin' at the difference how she with me and her. She had a guilt feeling towards that lady. They feel they shouldn't ask them to do this type of work, but they don't mind askin' me.

They want you to get in a uniform. You take me and my mother, she work in what she wear. She tells you, "If that place so dirty where I can't wear my dress, I won't do the job." You can't go to work dressed like they do, 'cause they think you're not working—like you should get dirty, at least. They don't say what kind of uniform, just say uniform. This is in case anybody come in, the black be workin'. They don't want you walkin' around dressed up, lookin' like them. They asks you sometimes, "Don't you have somethin' else to put on?" I say, "No, 'cause I'm not gettin' on my knees."

They move with caution now, believe me. They want to know, "What should I call you?" I say, "Don't call me a Negro, I'm black." So they say, "Okay, I don't want to make you angry with me." (Laughs.) The old-timers, a lot of 'em was real religious. "Lord'll make a way." I say, "I'm makin' my own way." I'm not anti-Bible or anti-God, but I just let 'em know I don't think thataway.

The younger women, they don't pay you too much attention. Most of 'em work. The older women, they behind you, wiping. I don't like nobody checkin' behind me. When you go to work, they want to show you how to clean. That really gets me, somebody showin' me how to clean. I been doin' it all my life. They come and get the rag and show you how to do it. (Laughs.) I stand there, look at 'em. Lotta times I ask her, "You finished?" I say, "If there's anything you gotta go and do, I wish you'd go." I don't need nobody to show me how to clean.

I had them put money down and pretend they can't find it and have me look for it. I worked for one, she had dropped ten dollars on the floor, and I was sweepin' and I'm glad I seen it, because if I had put that sweeper on it, she coulda said I got it. I had to push the couch back and the ten dollars was there. Oh, I had 'em, when you go to dust, they put something . . . to test you.

I worked at a hotel. A hotel's the same thing. You makin' beds, scrubbin' toilets, and things. You gotta put in linens and towels. You still cleanin'. When people come in the room—that's what bugs me—they give you that look: You just a maid. It do somethin' to me. It really gets into me.

Some of the guests are nice. The only thing you try to do is to hurry up and get this bed made and get outa here, 'cause they'll get you to do somethin' else. If they take that room, they want everything they paid for. (Laughs.) They get so many towels, they can't use 'em all. But you gotta put up all those towels. They want that pillow, they want that blanket. You gotta be trottin' back and forth and gettin' all those things.

In the meantime, when they have the hotel full, we put in extra beds—the little foldin' things. They say they didn't order the bed. They stand and look at you like you crazy. Now you gotta take this bed back all the way from the twelfth floor to the second. The guy at the desk, he got the wrong room. He don't say, "I made a mistake." You take the blame.

And you get some guys . . . you can't work with afightin' 'em. He'll call down and say he wants some towels. When you knock, he says, "Come in." He's standing there without a stitch of clothes on, buck naked. You're not goin' in there. You only throw those towels and go back. Most of the time you wait till he got out of there.

When somethin's missin', it's always the maid took it. If we find one of those type people, we tell the house lady, "You have to go in there and clean it yourself." If I crack that door, and nobody's in, I wouldn't go in there. If a girl had been in there, they would call and tell you, "Did you see something?" They won't say you got it. It's the same thing. You say no. They say, "It *musta* been in there."

Last summer I worked at a place and she missed a purse. I didn't work on that floor that day. She called the office, "Did you see that lady's purse?" I said, "No, I haven't been in the room." He asked me again, Did I . . . ? I had to stay till twelve o'clock. She found it. It was under some papers. I quit, 'cause they end up sayin' you stole somethin'.

You know what I wanted to do all my life? I wanted to play piano. And I'd want to write songs and things, that's what I really wanted to do. If I could just get myself enough to buy a piano. . . . And I'd like to write about my life, if I could sit long enough: How I growed up in the South and my grandparents and my father—I'd like to do that. I would like to dig up more of black history, too. I would love to for my kids.

Lotta times I'm tellin' 'em about things, they'll be sayin', "Mom, that's olden days." (Laughs.) They don't understand, because it's so far from what's happening now. Mighty few young black women are doin' domestic work. And I'm glad. That's why I want my kids to go to school. This one lady told me, "All you people are gettin' like that." I said, "I'm glad." There's no more gettin' on their knees.

## Questions

*Terry Mason, Airline Stewardess*

1. How satisfied is Terry Mason with her job? What are the sources of her satisfactions? her dissatisfactions? Try to sketch her values, and to characterize her.

2. Using Mason's remarks as evidence, evaluate the training program for stewardesses (now called flight attendants). Is it intelligent? Is it immoral? Do you think that after stew school the airlines deal fairly with the stewardesses?
3. Has this selection changed your idea of the job of a stewardess? If so, in what ways?

*Roberta Victor, Hooker*

1. In the second paragraph (page 275) Victor lists some desirable ("very non-ethnic-oriented WASP") names: Kim, Tracy, Stacy. Why are such names considered desirable?
2. In the first paragraph Victor says: "The role one plays when hustling has nothing to do with who you are." Judging from the interview as a whole, is she deceiving herself? In her third paragraph she says that all women in America are hustlers, and she returns to this notion, especially in the final paragraph. Again, is she deceiving herself, or has she put her finger on a truth, or at least a partial truth? Terkel tells us (page 276) that she was a bright child. During the interview does Victor say anything that strikes you as especially perceptive? Does her language occasionally show unusual vitality? Are there touches of wit?

*Maggie Holmes, Domestic*

1. How do you account for the difference in treatment (page 286) of domestic help in the North and the South?
2. What evidence is there that Holmes is witty? resourceful? insightful?
3. How would you describe Holmes's attitude toward suburban housewives? Does it make sense?

Virginia Woolf

# Professions for Women

When your secretary invited me to come here, she told me that your Society is concerned with the employment of women and she suggested that I might tell you something about my own professional experiences. It is true I am a woman; it is true I am employed, but what professional experiences have I had? It is difficult to say. My profession is literature; and in that profession there are fewer experiences for women than in any other, with the exception of the stage—fewer, I mean, that are peculiar to women. For the road was cut many years ago—by Fanny Burney, by Aphra Behn, by Harriet Martineau, by Jane Austen, by George Eliot—many famous women, and many more unknown and forgotten, have been before me, making the path smooth, and regulating my steps. Thus, when I came to write, there were very few material obstacles in my way. Writing was a reputable and harmless occupation. The family peace was not broken by the scratching of a pen. No demand was made upon the family purse. For ten and sixpence one can buy paper enough to write all the plays of Shakespeare—if one has a mind that way. Pianos and models, Paris, Vienna and Berlin, masters and mistresses, are not needed by a writer. The cheapness of writing paper is, of course, the reason why women have succeeded as writers before they have succeeded in the other professions.

But to tell you my story—it is a simple one. You have only got to figure to yourselves a girl in a bedroom with a pen in her hand. She had only to move that pen from left to right—from ten o'clock to one. Then it occurred to her to do what is simple and cheap enough after all—to slip a few of those pages into an envelope, fix a penny stamp in the corner, and drop the envelope into the red box at the corner. It was thus that I became a journalist; and my effort was

Virginia Woolf (1882–1941) was born in London into an upper-middle-class literary family. In 1912 she married a writer, and with him she founded the Hogarth Press, whose important publications included not only books by T. S. Eliot but her own novels.

This essay was originally a talk delivered in 1931 to The Women's Service League.

rewarded on the first day of the following month—a very glorious day it was for me—by a letter from an editor containing a check for one pound ten shillings and sixpence. But to show you how little I deserve to be called a professional woman, how little I know of the struggles and difficulties of such lives, I have to admit that instead of spending that sum upon bread and butter, rent, shoes and stockings, or butcher's bills, I went out and bought a cat—a beautiful cat, a Persian cat, which very soon involved me in bitter disputes with my neighbors.

What could be easier than to write articles and to buy Persian cats with the profits? But wait a moment. Articles have to be about something. Mine, I seem to remember, was about a novel by a famous man. And while I was writing this review, I discovered that if I were going to review books I should need to do battle with a certain phantom. And the phantom was a woman, and when I came to know her better I called her after the heroine of a famous poem, The Angel in the House. It was she who used to come between me and my paper when I was writing reviews. It was she who bothered me and wasted my time and so tormented me that at last I killed her. You who come of a younger and happier generation may not have heard of her—you may not know what I mean by the Angel in the House. I will describe her as shortly as I can. She was intensely sympathetic. She was immensely charming. She was utterly unselfish. She excelled in the difficult arts of family life. She sacrificed herself daily. If there was chicken, she took the leg; if there was a draught she sat in it—in short she was so constituted that she never had a mind or a wish of her own, but preferred to sympathize always with the minds and wishes of others. Above all—I need not say it—she was pure. Her purity was supposed to be her chief beauty—her blushes, her great grace. In those days—the last of Queen Victoria—every house had its Angel. And when I came to write I encountered her with the very first words. The shadow of her wings fell on my page; I heard the rustling of her skirts in the room. Directly, that is to say, I took my pen in hand to review that novel by a famous man, she slipped behind me and whispered: "My dear, you are a young woman. You are writing about a book that has been written by a man. Be sympathetic; be tender; flatter; deceive; use all the arts and wiles of our sex. Never let anybody guess that you have a mind of your own. Above all, be pure." And she made as if to guide my pen. I now record the one act for which I take some credit to myself, though the credit rightly belongs to some excellent ancestors of mine who left me a certain sum of money—shall we say five hundred pounds a year?—so that it was not necessary for me to depend solely on charm for my living. I turned upon her and caught her by the throat. I did my best to kill her. My excuse, if I were to be had up in a court of law, would be that I acted in self-defense. Had I not killed her she would have killed me. She would have plucked the heart out of my writing. For, as I found, directly I put pen to paper, you cannot review even a novel without having a mind of your own, without expressing what you think to be the truth about human relations, morality, sex. And all these questions, according to the Angel in the House, cannot be dealt with freely and openly by women; they must charm, they must conciliate, they must—to put it bluntly—tell lies if they are to succeed. Thus, whenever I felt the shadow of her wing or the radiance of her halo upon my page, I took up the inkpot and flung it at her. She died hard. Her fictitious nature was of great assistance to her. It is far harder to kill a phantom than a reality. She was always creeping back when I thought I had despatched her. Though I flatter myself that I killed her in the end, the struggle was severe; it took much time that had better have been spent upon learning Greek grammar; or in roaming the world in search of adventures. But it was a real experience; it was an experience that was bound to befall all women writers at that time. Killing the Angel in the House was part of the occupation of a woman writer.

But to continue my story. The Angel was dead; what then remained? You may say that what remained was a simple and common object—a young woman in a bedroom with an inkpot. In other words, now that she had rid herself of falsehood, that young woman had only to be herself. Ah, but what is "herself"? I mean, what is a woman? I assure you, I do not know. I do not believe that you know. I do not believe that anybody can know until she has expressed herself in all the arts and professions open to human skill. That indeed is one of the reasons why I have come here—out of respect for you, who are in process of showing us by your experiments what a woman is, who are in process of providing us, by your failures and successes, with that extremely important piece of information.

But to continue the story of my professional experiences. I made one pound ten and six by my first review; and I bought a Persian cat with the proceeds. Then I grew ambitious. A Persian cat is all very well, I said; but a Persian cat is not enough. I must have a motor car. And it was thus that I became a novelist—for it is a very strange thing that people will give you a motor car if you will tell them a story.

It is a still stranger thing that there is nothing so delightful in the world as telling stories. It is far pleasanter than writing reviews of famous novels. And yet, if I am to obey your secretary and tell you my professional experiences as a novelist, I must tell you about a very strange experience that befell me as a novelist. And to understand it you must try first to imagine a novelist's state of mind. I hope I am not giving away professional secrets if I say that a novelist's chief desire is to be as unconscious as possible. He has to induce in himself a state of perpetual lethargy. He wants life to proceed with the utmost quiet and regularity. He wants to see the same faces, to read the same books, to do the same things day after day, month after month, while he is writing, so that nothing may break the illusion in which he is living—so that nothing may disturb or disquiet the mysterious nosings about, feelings round, darts, dashes and sudden discoveries of that very shy and illusive spirit, the imagination. I suspect that this state is the same both for men and women. Be that as it may, I want you to imagine me writing a novel in a state of trance. I want you to figure to yourselves a girl sitting with a pen in her hand, which for minutes, and indeed for hours, she never dips into the inkpot. The image that comes to my mind when I think of this girl is the image of a fisherman lying sunk in dreams on the verge of a deep lake with a rod held out over the water. She was letting her imagination sweep unchecked round every rock and cranny of the world that lies submerged in the depths of our unconscious being. Now came the experience, the experience that I believe to be far commoner with women writers than with men. The line raced through the girl's fingers. Her imagination had rushed away. It had sought the pools, the depths, the dark places where the largest fish slumber. And then there was a smash. There was an explosion. There was foam and confusion. The imagination had dashed itself against something hard. The girl was roused from her dream. She was indeed in a state of the most acute and difficult distress. To speak without figure she had thought of something, something about the body, about the passions which it was unfitting for her as a woman to say. Men, her reason told her, would be shocked. The consciousness of what men will say of a woman who speaks the truth about her passions had roused her from her artist's state of unconsciousness. She could write no more. The trance was over. Her imagination could work no longer. This I believe to be a very common experience with women writers—they are impeded by the extreme conventionality of the other sex. For though men sensibly allow themselves great freedom in these respects, I doubt that they realize or can control the extreme severity with which they condemn such freedom in women.

These then were two very genuine experiences of my own. These were two of the adventures of my professional life. The first —killing the Angel in the House—I think I solved. She died. But the second, telling the truth about my own experiences as a body, I do not think I solved. I doubt that any woman has solved it yet. The obstacles against her are still immensely powerful—and yet they are very difficult to define. Outwardly, what is simpler than to write books? Outwardly, what obstacles are there for a woman rather than for a man? Inwardly, I think, the case is very different; she has still many ghosts to fight, many prejudices to overcome. Indeed it will be a long time still, I think, before a woman can sit down to write a book without finding a phantom to be slain, a rock to be dashed against. And if this is so in literature, the freest of all professions for women, how is it in the new professions which you are now for the first time entering?

Those are the questions that I should like, had I time, to ask you. And indeed, if I have laid stress upon these professional experiences of mine, it is because I believe that they are, though in different forms, yours also. Even when the path is nominally open—when there is nothing to prevent a woman from being a doctor, a lawyer, a civil servant—there are many phantoms and obstacles, as I believe, looming in her way. To discuss and define them is I think of great value and importance; for thus only can the labor be shared, the difficulties be solved. But besides this, it is necessary also to discuss the ends and the aims for which we are fighting, for which we are doing battle with these formidable obstacles. Those aims cannot be taken for granted; they must be perpetually questioned and examined. The whole position, as I see it—here in this hall surrounded by women practising for the first time in history I know not how many different professions—is one of extraordinary interest and importance. You have won rooms of your own in the house hitherto exclusively owned by men. You are able, though not without great labor and effort, to pay the rent. You are earning your five hundred pounds a year. But this freedom is only a beginning; the room is your own, but it is still bare. It has to be furnished; it has to be decorated; it has to be shared. How are you going to furnish it, how are you going to decorate it? With whom are you going to share it, and upon what terms? These, I think, are questions of the utmost importance and interest. For the first time in history you are able to ask them; for the first time you are able to decide for yourselves what the answers should be. Willingly would I stay and discuss those questions and answers—but not tonight. My time is up; and I must cease.

# Questions

1. How would you characterize Woolf's tone, especially her attitude toward her subject and herself, in the first paragraph?
2. What do you think Woolf means when she says (page 295): "It is far harder to kill a phantom than a reality"?
3. Woolf conjectures (page 297) that she has not solved the problem of "telling the truth about my own experiences as a body." Is there any reason to believe that today a woman has more difficulty than a man in telling the truth about the experiences of the body?
4. In her final paragraph Woolf suggests that phantoms as well as obstacles impede women from becoming doctors and lawyers. What might some of these phantoms be?
5. This essay is highly metaphoric. Speaking roughly (or, rather, as precisely as possible), what is the meaning of the metaphor of "rooms" in the final paragraph? What does Woolf mean when she says: "The room is your own, but it is still bare. . . . With whom are you going to share it, and upon what terms?"
6. Evaluate the last two sentences. Are they too abrupt and mechanical? Or do they provide a fitting conclusion to the speech?

Sir Thomas More

# Work and Play in Utopia

## Their Occupations

Agriculture is the one occupation at which everyone works, men and women alike, with no exceptions. They are trained in it from childhood, partly in the schools where they learn theory, and partly through field trips to nearby farms, which make something like a game of practical instruction. On these trips they not only watch the work being done, but frequently pitch in and get a workout by doing the jobs themselves.

Besides farm work (which, as I said, everybody performs), each person is taught a particular trade of his own, such as wool-working, linen-making, masonry, metal-work, or carpentry. There is no other craft that is practiced by any considerable number of them. Throughout the island people wear, and down through the centuries they have always worn, the same style of clothing, except for the distinction between the sexes, and between married and unmarried persons. Their clothing is attractive, does not hamper bodily movement, and serves for warm as well as cold weather; what is more, each household can make its own.

Every person (and this includes women as well as men) learns a second trade, besides agriculture. As the weaker sex, women practice the lighter crafts, such as working in wool or linen; the heavier crafts are assigned to the men. As a rule, the son is trained to his father's craft, for which most feel a natural inclination. But if anyone

---

Sir Thomas More (1478–1535) was an extremely able English administrator and diplomat who rose to high rank in the government of King Henry VIII, but when he opposed the King's break with Roman Catholicism (Henry demanded that his subjects recognize him as Supreme Head of the Church), More was beheaded. Four hundred years later, in 1935, he was canonized.

More wrote *Utopia* in Latin (the international language of the Renaissance) in 1516. The word is Greek for "no place," but the Greek-sounding names for officials in this imaginary land—a syphogrant is elected by a group of thirty households, and a tranibor governs a group of ten syphogrants—have no meaning. Though the book is fictional, setting forth a playful vision of an ideal society, there is no story; it is not a novel but a sort of essay.

"Work and Play" (editors' title) is about a tenth of the book.

is attracted to another occupation, he is transferred by adoption into a family practicing the trade he prefers. When anyone makes such a change, both his father and the authorities make sure that he is assigned to a grave and responsible householder. After a man has learned one trade, if he wants to learn another, he gets the same permission. When he has learned both, he pursues whichever he likes better, unless the city needs one more than the other.

The chief and almost the only business of the syphogrants is to manage matters so that no one sits around in idleness, and assure that everyone works hard at his trade. But no one has to exhaust himself with endless toil from early morning to late at night, as if he were a beast of burden. Such wretchedness, really worse than slavery, is the common lot of workmen in all countries, except Utopia. Of the day's twenty-four hours, the Utopians devote only six to work. They work three hours before noon, when they go to dinner. After dinner they rest for a couple of hours, then go to work for another three hours. Then they have supper, and at eight o'clock (counting the first hour after noon as one), they go to bed and sleep eight hours.

The other hours of the day, when they are not working, eating, or sleeping, are left to each man's individual discretion, provided he does not waste them in roistering or sloth, but uses them busily in some occupation that pleases him. Generally these periods are devoted to intellectual activity. For they have an established custom of giving public lectures before daybreak; attendance at these lectures is required only of those who have been specially chosen to devote themselves to learning, but a great many other people, both men and women, choose voluntarily to attend. Depending on their interests, some go to one lecture, some to another. But if anyone would rather devote his spare time to his trade, as many do who don't care for the intellectual life, this is not discouraged; in fact, such persons are commended as especially useful to the commonwealth.

After supper, they devote an hour to recreation, in their gardens when the weather is fine, or during winter weather in the common halls where they have their meals. There they either play music or amuse themselves with conversation. They know nothing about gambling with dice, or other such foolish and ruinous games. They do play two games not unlike our own chess. One is a battle of numbers, in which one number captures another. The other is a game in which the vices fight a battle against the virtues. The game is set up to show how the vices oppose one another, yet readily combine against the virtues; then, what vices oppose what virtues, how they try to assault them openly or undermine them in secret; how the virtues can break the strength of the vices or turn their purposes to good; and finally, by what means one side or the other gains the victory.

But in all this, you may get a wrong impression, if we don't go back and consider one point more carefully. Because they allot only six hours to work, you might think the necessities of life would be in scant supply. This is far from the case. Their working hours are ample to provide not only enough but more than enough of the necessities and even the conveniences of life. You will easily appreciate this if you consider how large a part of the population in other countries exists without doing any work at all. In the first place, hardly any of the women, who are a full half of the population, work; or, if they do, then as a rule their husbands lie snoring in the bed. Then there is a great lazy gang of priests and so-called religious men. Add to them all the rich, especially the landlords, who are commonly called gentlemen and nobility. Include with them their retainers, that mob of swaggering bullies. Finally, reckon in with these the sturdy and lusty beggars, who go about feigning some disease as an excuse for their idleness. You will certainly find that the things which satisfy our needs are produced by far fewer hands than you had supposed.

And now consider how few of those who do work are doing really essential things. For where money is the standard of everything, many superfluous trades are bound to be carried on simply to satisfy luxury and licentiousness. Suppose the multitude of those who now work were limited to a few trades, and set to producing more and more of those conveniences and commodities that nature really requires. They would be bound to produce so much that the prices would drop, and the workmen would be unable to gain a living. But suppose again that all the workers in useless trades were put to useful ones, and that all the idlers (who now guzzle twice as much as the workingmen who make what they consume) were assigned to productive tasks—well, you can easily see how little time each man would have to spend working, in order to produce all the goods that human needs and conveniences require—yes, and human pleasure too, as long as it's true and natural pleasure.

The experience of Utopia makes this perfectly apparent. In each city and its surrounding countryside barely five hundred of those men and women whose age and strength make them fit for work are exempted from it. Among these are the syphogrants, who by law are free not to work; yet they don't take advantage of the privilege, preferring to set a good example to their fellow-citizens. Some others are permanently exempted from work so that they may devote themselves to study, but only on the recommendation of the priests and through a secret vote of the syphogrants. If any of these scholars disappoints their hopes, he becomes a workman again. On the other hand, it happens from time to time that a craftsman devotes his leisure so earnestly to study, and makes such progress as a result, that he is relieved of manual labor, and promoted to the class of learned men. From this class of scholars are chosen ambassadors, priests, tranibors, and the prince himself, who used to be called Barzanes, but in their modern tongue is known as Ademus. Since all the rest of the population is neither idle nor occupied in useless trades, it is easy to see why they produce so much in so short a working day.

Apart from all this, in several of the necessary crafts their way of life requires less total labor than does that of people elsewhere. In other countries, building and repairing houses requires the constant work of many men, because what a father has built, his thriftless heir lets fall into ruin; and then his successor has to repair, at great expense, what could easily have been maintained at a very small charge. Further, even when a man has built a splendid house at large cost, someone else may think he has finer taste, let the first house fall to ruin, and then build another one somewhere else for just as much money. But among the Utopians, where everything has been established, and the commonwealth is carefully regulated, building a brand-new home on a new site is a rare event. They are not only quick to repair damage, but foresighted in preventing it. The result is that their buildings last for a very long time with minimum repairs; and the carpenters and masons sometimes have so little to do, that they are set to hewing timber and cutting stone in case some future need for it should arise.

Consider, too, how little labor their clothing requires. Their work clothes are loose garments made of leather which last as long as seven years. When they go out in public, they cover these rough working-clothes with a cloak. Throughout the entire island, everyone wears the same colored cloak, which is the color of natural wool. As a result, they not only need less wool than people in other countries, but what they do need is less expensive. They use linen cloth most, because it requires least labor. They like linen cloth to be white and wool cloth to be clean; but they put no price on fineness of texture. Elsewhere a man is not satisfied with four or five woolen cloaks of different colors and as many silk shirts, or if he's a show-off, even ten of each are not enough. But a Utopian is content with a single cloak, and generally wears it for two seasons. There is no reason at all why he should want any others, for if he had them, he would not be better protected against the cold, nor would he appear in any way better dressed.

When there is an abundance of everything, as a result of everyone working at useful trades, and nobody consuming to excess, then great numbers of the people often go out to work on the roads, if any of them need repairing. And when there is no need even for this sort of public work, then the officials very often proclaim a short work day, since they never force their citizens to perform useless labor. The chief aim of their constitution and government is that, whenever public needs permit, all citizens should be free, so far as possible, to withdraw their time and energy from the service of the body, and devote themselves to the freedom and culture of the mind. For that, they think, is the real happiness of life. . . .

## Their Moral Philosophy

They conclude, after carefully considering and weighing the matter, that all our actions and the virtues exercised within them look toward pleasure and happiness as their ultimate end.

By pleasure they understand every state or movement of body or mind in which man naturally finds delight. They are right in considering man's appetites natural. By simply following his senses and his right reason a man may discover what is pleasant by nature —it is a delight which does not injure others, which does not preclude a greater pleasure, and which is not followed by pain. But a pleasure which is against nature, and which men call "delightful" only by the emptiest of fictions (as if one could change the real nature of things just by changing their names), does not really make for happiness; in fact they say, it destroys happiness. And the reason is that men whose minds are filled with false ideas of pleasure have no room left for true and genuine delight. As a matter of fact, there are a great many things which have no sweetness in them, but are mainly or entirely bitter—yet which through the perverse enticements of evil lusts are considered very great pleasures, and even the supreme goals of life.

Among those who pursue this false pleasure the Utopians include those whom I mentioned before, the men who think themselves finer fellows because they wear finer clothes. These people are twice mistaken: first in thinking their clothes better than anyone else's, and then in thinking themselves better because of their clothes. As far as a coat's usefulness goes, what does it matter if it was woven of thin thread or thick? Yet they act as if they were set apart by nature herself, rather than their own fantasies; they strut about, and put on airs. Because they have a fancy suit, they think themselves entitled to honors they would never have expected if they were poorly dressed, and they get very angry if someone passes them by without showing special respect.

It is the same kind of absurdity to be pleased by empty, ceremonial honors. What true and natural pleasure can you get from someone's bent knee or bared head? Will the creaks in your own knees be eased thereby, or the madness in your head? The phantom of false pleasure is illustrated by other men who run mad with delight over their own blue blood, plume themselves on their nobility, and applaud themselves for all their rich ancestors (the only ancestors worth having nowadays), and all their ancient family estates. Even if they don't have the shred of an estate themselves, or if they've squandered every penny of their inheritance, they don't consider themselves a bit less noble.

In the same class the Utopians put those people I described before, who are mad for jewelry and gems, and think themselves divinely happy if they find a good specimen, especially of the sort which happens to be fashionable in their country at the time—for stones vary in value from one market to another. The collector will not make an offer for the stone till it's taken out of its setting, and even then he will not buy unless the dealer guarantees and gives security that it is a true and genuine stone. What he fears is that his eyes will be deceived by a counterfeit. But if you consider the matter, why should a counterfeit give any less pleasure when your eyes cannot distinguish it from a real gem? Both should be of equal value to you, as they would be, in fact, to a blind man.

Speaking of false pleasure, what about those who pile up money, not because they want to do anything with the heap, but so they can sit and look at it? Is that true pleasure they experience, or aren't they simply cheated by a show of pleasure? Or what of those with the opposite vice, the men who hide away money they will never use and perhaps never even see again? In their anxiety to hold onto their money, they actually lose it. For what else happens when you deprive yourself, and perhaps other people too, of a chance to use money, by burying it in the ground? And yet when the miser has hidden his treasure, he exults over it as if his mind were now free to rejoice. Suppose someone stole it, and the miser died ten years later, knowing nothing of the theft. During all those ten years, what did it matter whether the money was stolen or not? In either case, it was equally useless to the owner.

To these false and foolish pleasures they add gambling, which they have heard about, though they've never tried it, as well as hunting and hawking. What pleasure can there be, they wonder, in throwing dice on a table? If there were any pleasure in the action, wouldn't doing it over and over again quickly make one tired of it? What pleasure can there be in listening to the barking and yelping of dogs—isn't that rather a disgusting noise? Is there any more real pleasure when a dog chases a rabbit than there is when a dog chases a dog? If what you like is fast running, there's plenty of that in both cases; they're just about the same. But if what you really want is slaughter, if you want to see a living creature torn apart under your eyes, then the whole thing is wrong. You ought to feel nothing but pity when you see the hare fleeing from the hound, the weak creature tormented by the stronger, the fearful and timid beast brutalized by the savage one, the harmless hare killed by the cruel dog. The Utopians, who regard this whole activity of hunting as unworthy of free men, have assigned it, accordingly, to their butchers, who as I said before, are all slaves. In their eyes, hunting is the lowest thing even butchers can do. In the slaughterhouse, their work is more useful and honest—besides which, they kill animals only from necessity; but in hunting they seek merely their own pleasure from the killing and mutilating of some poor little creature. Taking such relish in the sight of death, even if it's only beasts, reveals, in the opinion of the Utopians, a cruel disposition. Or if he isn't cruel to start with, the hunter quickly becomes so through the constant practice of such brutal pleasures.

Most men consider these activities, and countless others like them, to be pleasures; but the Utopians say flatly they have nothing at all to do with real pleasure since there's nothing naturally pleasant about them. They often please the senses, and in this they are like pleasure, but that does not alter their basic nature. The enjoyment doesn't arise from the experience itself, but only from the perverse mind of the individual, as a result of which he mistakes the bitter for the sweet, just as pregnant women, whose taste has been turned awry, sometimes think pitch and tallow taste sweeter than honey. A man's taste may be similarly depraved, by disease or by custom, but that does not change the nature of pleasure, or of anything else.

# Questions

1. What does More assume are the only functions of clothing? Do you agree with More, or do you find other important reasons why people wear the clothes that they wear?
2. The "work ethic" assumes that labor is good in itself—that there is some sort of virtue in work. Further, many people assume that work, at least certain kinds of work done under certain conditions, affords happiness to the worker. What does More's attitude seem to be on these two related points?
3. What is More's opinion of hunting? What arguments in support of hunting are commonly offered? In your opinion, does More successfully counter those arguments?
4. In approximately 500 words set forth More's assumptions about the sources of happiness.
5. More says that each Utopian is free to do what he wishes with leisure hours, "provided he does not waste them in roistering or sloth." (By the way, since the Utopians work six hours a day, if they sleep eight hours they have ten hours of free time.) In 500 words develop an argument for or against this proviso concerning the pursuit of happiness. (You may want to recall that our own government to some degree regulates our pleasure, for instance by outlawing bullfights.)
6. Note the passage in which More describes a game enjoyed by Utopians. Imitating More's style, write a paragraph describing a video game as a Utopian, or anti-Utopian, recreation.

Lin Yutang

# Art as Play and Personality

Art is both creation and recreation. Of the two ideas, I think art as recreation or as sheer play of the human spirit is more important. Much as I appreciate all forms of immortal creative work, whether in painting, architecture or literature, I think the spirit of true art can become more general and permeate society only when a lot of people are enjoying art as a pastime, without any hope of achieving immortality. As it is more important that all college students should play tennis or football with indifferent skill than that a college should produce a few champion athletes or football players for the national contests, so it is also more important that all children and all grown-ups should be able to create something of their own as their pastime than that the nation should produce a Rodin. I would rather have all school children taught to model clay and all bank presidents and economic experts able to make their own Christmas cards, however ridiculous the attempt may be, than to have only a few artists who work at art as a profession. That is to say, I am for amateurism in all fields. I like amateur philosophers, amateur poets, amateur photographers, amateur magicians, amateur architects who build their own houses, amateur musicians, amateur botanists and amateur aviators. I get as much pleasure out of listening to a friend playing a sonatina of an evening in an indifferent manner as out of listening to a first-class professional concert. And everyone enjoys an amateur parlor magician, who is one of his friends, more than he enjoys a professional magician on the stage, and every parent enjoys the amateur dramatics of his own children much more heartily than he enjoys a Shakespearean play. We know that it is spontaneous, and in spontaneity alone lies the true spirit of art. That is why I regard

Lin Yutang (1895–1976) was educated in China and then in the United States. Lin (the Chinese put the family-name first) returned to teach in China in 1923, but after 1928 he spent most of his time in the United States. He translated and wrote many books: *The Importance of Living* (1937), from which we reprint a selection, is a good introduction to his work. "Art as Play and Personality" is the editors' title.

it as so important that in China painting is essentially the pastime of a scholar and not of a professional artist. It is only when the spirit of play is kept that art can escape being commercialized.

Now it is characteristic of play that one plays without reason and there must be no reason for it. Play is its own good reason. This view is borne out by the history of evolution. Beauty is something that cannot be accounted for by the struggle for existence, and there are forms of beauty that are destructive even to the animal, like the over-developed horns of a deer. Darwin saw that he could never account for the beauties of plant and animal life by natural selection, and he had to introduce the great secondary principle of sexual selection. We fail to understand art and the essence of art if we do not recognize it as merely an overflow of physical and mental energy, free and unhampered and existing for its own sake. This is the much decried formula of "art for art's sake." I regard this not as a question upon which the politicians have the right to say anything, but merely as an incontrovertible fact regarding the psychological origin of all artistic creation. Hitler has denounced many forms of modern art as immoral, but I consider that those painters who paint portraits of Hitler, to be shown at the new Art Museum in order to please the powerful ruler, are the most immoral of all. That is not art, but prostitution. If commercial art often injures the spirit of artistic creation, political art is sure to kill it. For freedom is the very soul of art. Modern dictators are attempting the impossible when they try to produce a political art. They don't seem to realize that you cannot produce art by the force of the bayonet any more than you can buy real love from a prostitute.

In order to understand the essence of art at all, we have to go back to the physical basis of art as an overflow of energy. This is known as an artistic or creative impulse. The use of the very word "inspiration" shows that the artist himself hardly knows where the impulse comes from. It is merely a matter of inner urge, like the scientist's impulse for the discovery of truth, or the explorer's impulse for discovering a new island. There is no accounting for it. We are beginning to see today, with the help of biological knowledge, that the whole organization of our mental life is regulated by the increase or decrease and distribution of hormones in the blood, acting on the various organs and the nervous system controlling these organs. Even anger or fear is merely a matter of the supply of adrenalin. Genius itself, it seems to me, is but an oversupply of glandular secretions. An obscure Chinese novelist, without the modern knowledge of hormones, made a correct guess about the origin of all activity as due to "worms" in our body. Adultery is a matter of worms gnawing our intestines and impelling the man to satisfy his desire. Ambition and aggressiveness and love of fame or power are also due to certain other worms giving the person no rest until he has achieved the object of his ambition. The writing of a book, say a novel, is again due to a species of worms which impel and urge the author to create for no reason whatsoever. Between hormones and worms, I prefer to believe in the latter. The term is more vivid.

Given an over-supply or even a normal supply of worms, a man is bound to create something or other, because he cannot help himself. When a child has an over-supply of energy, his normal walking is transformed into hopping or skipping. When a man has an over-supply of energy, his walking becomes transformed into prancing or dancing. So, then, dancing is nothing but inefficient walking, inefficient in the sense that there is a waste of energy from an utilitarian, not an aesthetic, point of view. Instead of going straight to a point, which is the quickest road, a dancer waltzes and goes in a circle. No one really tries to be patriotic when he is dancing, and to command a man to dance according to the capitalist or fascist or proletarian ideology is to destroy the spirit of play and glorious inefficiency in dancing. If a Communist is trying to attain a political objective, or trying to be a loyal comrade, he should just walk, and not dance. The Communists seem to know the sacredness of labor, and not the sacredness of play. As if man in civilization didn't work too much already, in comparison with every other species and variety of the animal kingdom, so that even the little leisure he has, the little time for play and art, must too be invaded by the claims of that monster, the State!

## Questions

1. In his first paragraph Lin implies that it is important that all students should engage in athletics. How can such a claim be defended?
2. In his first paragraph Lin says he would like to see "all bank presidents and economic experts able to make their own Christmas cards." What is his point?
3. In a paragraph or two, indicate what sort of a person the author strikes you as. Your paragraph(s) should include a few brief quotations to support your characterization of Lin.
4. If "dancing is nothing but inefficient walking," what are diving, playing soccer, swimming, hang-gliding, playing Pac-Man, and singing? What is watching television? Write one sentence "defining" each activity.

**Jeff Greenfield**

# The Black and White Truth About Basketball

## A Skin-deep Theory of Style

The dominance of black athletes over professional basketball is beyond dispute. Two thirds of the players are black, and the number would be greater were it not for the continuing practice of picking white bench warmers for the sake of balance. The Most Valuable Player award of the National Basketball Association has gone to blacks for sixteen of the last twenty years, and in the newer American Basketball Association, blacks have won it all but once in the league's eight years. In the 1974–75 season, four of the top five All-Stars and seven of the top ten were black. The N.B.A. was the first pro sports league of any stature to hire a black coach (Bill Russell of the Celtics) and the first black general manager (Wayne Embry of the Bucks). What discrimination remains—lack of opportunity for lucrative benefits such as speaking engagements and product endorsements—has more to do with society than with basketball.

This dominance reflects a natural inheritance; basketball is a pastime of the urban poor. The current generation of black athletes are heirs to a tradition half a century old: in a neighborhood without the money for bats, gloves, hockey sticks, tennis rackets, or shoulder pads, basketball is accessible. "Once it was the game of the Irish and Italian Catholics in Rockaway and the Jews on Fordham Road in the Bronx," writes David Wolf in his brilliant book, *Foul!* "It was recreation, status, and a way out." But now the ethnic names are changed; instead of Red Holzmans, Red Auerbachs, and McGuire brothers, there are Earl Monroes and Connie Hawkins and Nate Archibalds. And professional basketball is a sport with a national television contract and million-dollar salaries.

But the mark on basketball of today's players can be measured by more than money or visibility. It is a question of style. For there

---

Jeff Greenfield has written speeches for Robert F. Kennedy and for former New York mayor John V. Lindsay. He has published books and essays on sports and on other popular entertainments.

is a clear difference between "black" and "white" styles of play that is as clear as the difference between 155th Street at Eighth Avenue and Crystal City, Missouri. Most simply (remembering we are talking about culture, not chromosomes), "black" basketball is the use of superb athletic skill to adapt to the limits of space imposed by the game. "White" ball is the pulverization of that space by sheer intensity.

It takes a conscious effort to realize how constricted the space is on a basketball court. Place a regulation court (ninety-four by fifty feet) on a football field, and it will reach from the back of the end zone to the twenty-one-yard line; its width will cover less than a third of the field. On a baseball diamond, a basketball court will reach from home plate to just beyond first base. Compared to its principal indoor rival, ice hockey, basketball covers about one fourth the playing area. And during the normal flow of the game, most of the action takes place on about the third of the court nearest the basket. It is in this dollhouse space that ten men, each of them half a foot taller than the average man, come together to battle each other.

There is, thus, no room; basketball is a struggle for the edge: the half step with which to cut around the defender for a lay-up, the half second of freedom with which to release a jump shot, the instant a head turns allowing a pass to a teammate breaking for the basket. It is an arena for the subtlest of skills: the head fake, the shoulder fake, the shift of body weight to the right and the sudden cut to the left. Deception is crucial to success; and to young men who have learned early and painfully that life is a battle for survival, basketball is one of the few games in which the weapon of deception is a legitimate rule and not the source of trouble.

If there is, then, the need to compete in a crowd, to battle for the edge, then the surest strategy is to develop the *unexpected;* to develop a shot that is simply and fundamentally different from the usual methods of putting the ball in the basket. Drive to the hoop, but go under it and come up the other side; hold the ball at waist level and shoot from there instead of bringing the ball up to eye level; leap into the air and fall away from the basket instead of toward it. All these tactics take maximum advantage of the crowding on a court; they also stamp uniqueness on young men who may feel it nowhere else.

"For many young men in the slums," David Wolf writes, "the school yard is the only place they can feel true pride in what they do, where they can move free of inhibitions and where they can, by being spectacular, rise for the moment against the drabness and anonymity of their lives. Thus, when a player develops extraordinary 'school yard' moves and shots . . . [they] become his measure as a man."

So the moves that begin as tactics for scoring soon become calling cards. You don't just lay the ball in for an uncontested basket; you take the ball in both hands, leap as high as you can, and slam the ball through the hoop. When you jump in the air, fake a shot, bring the ball back to your body, and throw up a shot, all without coming back down, you have proven your worth in uncontestable fashion.

This liquid grace is an integral part of "black" ball, almost exclusively the province of the playground player. Some white stars like Richie Guerin, Bob Cousy, and Billy Cunningham have it: the body control, the moves to the basket, the free-ranging mobility. They also have the surface ease that is integral to the "black" style; an incorporation of the ethic of mean streets—to "make it" is not just to have wealth, but to have it without strain. Whatever the muscles and organs are doing, the face of the "black" star almost never shows it. Bob McAdoo of the Buffalo Braves can drive to the basket with two men on him, pull up, turn around, and hit a basket without the least flicker of emotion. The Knicks' Walt Frazier, flamboyant in dress, cars, and companions, displays nothing but a quickly raised fist after scoring a particularly important basket. (Interestingly, the black coaches in the N.B.A. exhibit far less emotion on the bench than their white counterparts; Washington's K. C. Jones and Seattle's Bill Russell are statuelike compared with Tommy Heinsohn, Jack Ramsay, or Dick Motta.)

If there is a single trait that characterizes "black" ball it is leaping agility. Bob Cousy, ex-Celtic great and former pro coach, says that "when coaches get together, one is sure to say, 'I've got the one black kid in the country who can't jump.' When coaches see a white boy who can jump or who moves with extraordinary quickness, they say, 'He should have been born black, he's that good.' "

Don Nelson of the Celtics recalls that in 1970, Dave Cowens, then a relatively unknown Florida State graduate, prepared for his rookie season by playing in the Rucker League, an outdoor Harlem competition that pits pros against playground stars and college kids. So ferocious was Cowens' leaping power, Nelson says, that "when the summer was over, everyone wanted to know who the white son of a bitch was who could jump so high." That's another way to overcome a crowd around the basket—just go over it.

Speed, mobility, quickness, acceleration, "the moves"—all of these are catchphrases that surround the "black" playground style of play. So does the most racially tinged of attributes, "rhythm." Yet rhythm is what the black stars themselves talk about; feeling the flow of the game, finding the tempo of the dribble, the step, the shot. It is an instinctive quality, one that has led to difficulty between systematic coaches and free-form players. "Cats from the street have their own rhythm when they play," said college dropout Bill Spivey, onetime New York high-school star. "It's not a matter of somebody setting you up and you shooting. You *feel* the shot. When a coach holds you back, you lose the feel and it isn't fun anymore.

Connie Hawkins, the legendary Brooklyn playground star, said of Laker coach Bill Sharman's methodical style of teaching, "He's systematic to the point where it begins to be a little too much. It's such an action-reaction type of game that when you have to do everything the same way, I think you lose something."

There is another kind of basketball that has grown up in America. It is not played on asphalt playgrounds with a crowd of kids competing for the court; it is played on macadam driveways by one boy with a ball and a backboard nailed over the garage; it is played in Midwestern gyms and on Southern dirt courts. It is a mechanical, precise development of skills (when Don Nelson was an Iowa farm boy, his incentive to make his shots was that an errant rebound would land in the middle of chicken droppings), without frills, without flow, but with effectiveness. It is "white" basketball: jagged, sweaty, stumbling, intense. A "black" player overcomes an obstacle with finesse and body control; a "white" player reacts by outrunning or outpowering the obstacle.

By this definition, the Boston Celtics and the Chicago Bulls are classically "white" teams. The Celtics almost never use a player with dazzling moves; that would probably make Red Auerbach swallow his cigar. Instead, the Celtics wear you down with execution, with constant running, with the same play run again and again. The rebound triggers the fast break, with everyone racing downcourt; the ball goes to John Havlicek, who pulls up and takes the jump shot, or who fakes the shot and passes off to the man following, the "trailer," who has the momentum to go inside for a relatively easy shot.

The Bulls wear you down with punishing intensity, hustling, and defensive tactics which are either aggressive or illegal, depending on what side you're on. The Bulls—particularly Jerry Sloan and Norm Van Lier (one white, one black for the quota-minded)—seem to reject the concept of an out-of-bounds line. They are as likely to be found under the press table or wrapped around the ushers as on the court.

Perhaps the most classically "white" position is that of the quick forward, one without great moves to the basket, without highly developed shots, without the height and mobility for rebounding effectiveness. What does he do? He runs. He runs from the opening jump to the last horn. He runs up and down the court, from base line to base line, back and forth under the basket, looking for the opening, for the pass, for the chance to take a quick step and the high-percentage shot. To watch Boston's Don Nelson, a player without speed or moves, is to wonder what this thirty-five-year-old is doing in the N.B.A.—until you see him swing free and throw up a shot that, without demanding any apparent skill, somehow goes in the basket more frequently than the shots of any of his teammates. And to watch his teammate John Havlicek, also thirty-five, is to see "white" ball at its best.

Havlicek stands in dramatic contrast to Julius Erving of the New York Nets. Erving has the capacity to make legends come true; leaping from the foul line and slam-dunking the ball on his way down; going up for a lay-up, pulling the ball to his body and throwing under and up the other side of the rim, defying gravity and probability with moves and jumps. Havlicek looks like the living embodiment of his small-town Ohio background. He brings the ball downcourt, weaving left, then right, looking for the path. He swings the ball to a teammate, cuts behind a pick, takes the pass and releases the shot in a flicker of time. It looks plain, unvarnished. But there are not half a dozen players in the league who can see such possibilities for a free shot, then get that shot off as quickly and efficiently as Havlicek.

To Jim McMillian of Buffalo, a black with "white" attributes, himself a quick forward, "it's a matter of environment. Julius Erving grew up in a different environment from Havlicek—John came from a very small town in Ohio. There everything was done the easy way, the shortest distance between two points. It's nothing fancy, very few times will he go one-on-one; he hits the lay-up, hits the jump shot, makes the free throw, and after the game you look and you say, 'How did he hurt us that much?' "

"White" ball, then, is the basketball of patience and method. "Black" ball is the basketball of electric self-expression. One player has all the time in the world to perfect his skills, the other a need to prove himself. These are slippery categories, because a poor boy who is black can play "white" and a white boy of middle-class parents can play "black." K. C. Jones and Pete Maravich are athletes who seem to defy these categories. And what makes basketball the most intriguing of sports is how these styles do not necessarily clash; how the punishing intensity of "white" players and the dazzling moves of the "blacks" can fit together, a fusion of cultures that seems more and more difficult in the world beyond the out-of-bounds line.

## Questions

1. In a sentence or two summarize Greenfield's theory about how the "black" style of basketball began.
2. In a few sentences summarize the "black" style as Greenfield describes it. Next summarize the "white" style. If you are familiar with professional basketball, take two teams and test Greenfield's views against the players. Do most of the blacks play "black" basketball, and do most of the whites play "white"? Which whites play "black" basketball; which blacks play "white"?
3. What does Greenfield mean when he says (page 313) that the word "rhythm" is "the most racially tinged of attributes"?
4. Outline the organization of Greenfield's essay. (One way to do this is to write a topic sentence for each paragraph and then see if the succession of sentences makes a pattern.)
5. Are there differences in the styles of blacks and whites in some other sport with which you are familiar? If so, try to characterize them. If not, is there something in the sport that allows for only one style?

## Black Elk

# War Games

When it was summer again we were camping on the Rosebud, and I did not feel so much afraid, because the Wasichus seemed farther away and there was peace there in the valley and there was plenty of meat. But all the boys from five or six years up were playing war. The little boys would gather together from the different bands of the tribe and fight each other with mud balls that they threw with willow sticks. And the big boys played the game called Throwing-Them-Off-Their-Horses, which is a battle all but the killing; and sometimes they got hurt. The horsebacks from the different bands would line up and charge upon each other, yelling; and when the ponies came together on the run, they would rear and flounder and scream in a big dust, and the riders would seize each other, wrestling until one side had lost all its men, for those who fell upon the ground were counted dead.

When I was older, I, too, often played this game. We were always naked when we played it, just as warriors are when they go into battle if it is not too cold, because they are swifter without clothes. Once I fell off on my back right in the middle of a bed of prickly pears, and it took my mother a long while to pick all the stickers out of me. I was still too little to play war that summer, but I can remember watching the other boys, and I thought that when we all grew up and were big together, maybe we could kill all the Wasichus or drive them far away from our country. . . .

There was a war game that we little boys played after a big hunt. We went out a little way from the village and built some grass tepees, playing we were enemies and this was our village. We had an adviser, and when it got dark he would order us to go and steal some dried meat from the big people. He would hold a stick up to us and we had to bite off a piece of it. If we bit a big piece we had to get a big piece of meat, and if we bit a little piece, we did not have to get so much. Then we started for the big people's village, crawling on our bellies,

For a biographical note on Black Elk, see page 35. "War Games" (editors' title) is from *Black Elk Speaks.*

and when we got back without getting caught, we would have a big feast and a dance and make kill talks, telling of our brave deeds like warriors. Once, I remember, I had no brave deed to tell. I crawled up to a leaning tree beside a tepee and there was meat hanging on the limbs. I wanted a tongue I saw up there in the moonlight, so I climbed up. But just as I was about to reach it, the man in the tepee yelled "Ye-a-a!" He was saying this to his dog, who was stealing some meat too, but I thought the man had seen me, and I was so scared I fell out of the tree and ran away crying.

Then we used to have what we called a chapped breast dance. Our adviser would look us over to see whose breast was burned most from not having it covered with the robe we wore; and the boy chosen would lead the dance while we all sang like this:

I have a chapped breast.
My breast is red.
My breast is yellow.

And we practiced endurance too. Our adviser would put dry sunflower seeds on our wrists. These were lit at the top, and we had to let them burn clear down to the skin. They hurt and made sores, but if we knocked them off or cried Owh!, we would be called women.

## Questions

1. Notice the subjective passages in Black Elk's descriptions of the games he played as a child. What do they reveal about Black Elk as a child and as an adult? How appropriate are these revelations to his topic?
2. The Duke of Wellington is reported to have said that the Battle of Waterloo was won on the playing fields of Eton. Try to describe a game that is a small version of an adult activity that teaches adult habits, good or bad. As an experiment, write the description as objectively as you can. Then rewrite it, allowing your description to reveal your attitudes, then and now, to the game, to other children, and to the adult world.

## John Updike

# The Playground

UP from the hardball diamond, on a plateau bounded on three sides by cornfields, a pavilion contained some tables and a shed for equipment. I spent my summer weekdays there from the age I was so small that the dust stirred by the feet of roof-ball players got into my eyes. Roof ball was the favorite game. It was played with a red rubber ball smaller than a basketball. The object was to hit it back up on the roof of the pavilion, the whole line of children in succession. Those who failed dropped out. When there was just one person left, a new game began with the cry "*Noo*-oo *gay*-ame," and we lined up in the order in which we had gone out, so that the lines began with the strongest and tallest and ended with the weakest and youngest. But there was never any doubt that everybody could play; it was perfect democracy. Often the line contained as many as thirty pairs of legs, arranged chronologically. By the time we moved away, I had become a regular front-runner; I knew how to flick the ball to give it spin, how to leap up and send the ball skimming the length of the roof edge, how to plump it with my knuckles when there was a high bounce. Somehow the game never palled; the sight of the ball bouncing along the tarpaper of the foreshortened roof was always important. Many days I was at the playground from nine o'clock, when they ran up the American flag, until four, when they called the equipment in, and played nothing else.

If you hit the ball too hard, and it went over the peak of the roof, you were out, and you had to retrieve the ball, going down a steep bank into a field where the poorhouse men had stopped planting corn because it all got mashed down. If the person ahead of you hit the ball into the air without touching the roof, or missed it entirely, you had the option of "saving," by hitting the ball onto the roof before it struck the ground; this created complex opportunities for strategy and gallantry. I would always try to save the Nightingale, for instance, and there was a girl who came from Louisiana with a French

---

John Updike was born in Shillington, Pennsylvania, in 1932. He has published stories, novels, and essays. In 1963 *The Centaur*, a novel, won the National Book Award.

---

name whom everybody wanted to save. At twelve, she seemed already mature, and I can remember standing with a pack of other boys under the swings looking up at the undersides of her long tense dark-skinned legs as she kicked into the air to give herself more height. The tendons on the underside of her smooth knees jumping, her sneakered feet pointing like a ballerina's shoes.

The walls of the pavilion shed were scribbled all over with dirty drawings and words and detailed slanders on the prettier girls. After hours, when the supervisors were gone, if you were tall enough you could grab hold of a crossbeam and get on top of the shed, where there was an intimate wedge of space under the slanting roof; here no adult ever bothered to scrub away the pencilings, and the wood fairly breathed of the forbidden. The very silence of the pavilion, after the day-long click of checkers and *pokabok* of ping-pong, was like a love-choked hush.

Reality seemed slightly more intense at the playground. There was a dust, a daring. It was a children's world; nowhere else did we gather in such numbers with so few adults over us. The playground occupied a platform of earth; we were exposed, it seems now, to the sun and sky.

# Questions

1. Although variety in sentence structure is not necessarily a primary goal in writing (as clarity is), it is often desirable. Study Updike's first three sentences. Then, writing from your own experience, imitate the structure and length of these sentences as closely as you can.
2. Compare Black Elk's description of childhood games (page 316) with Updike's on any two or three matters of content or style that you find interesting.
3. Describe a childhood game you either enjoyed intensely or detested. Try to account for the pleasure, or lack of pleasure, it gave you.

Laurence Wylie

# Having a Good Time in Peyrane, 1950

The only organized activity for adolescents that has a measure of success is dancing. There are two important dances in Peyrane every year. One is organized by the Volunteer Firemen, the other by the Comité des Fêtes appointed by the mayor for the Michaelmas celebration. The Volunteer Firemen are not adolescents, but most of them are young bachelors who still enjoy dancing. At a dance they meet girls among whom they may find a sexual partner or even a wife. The firemen work hard to put on their dance and it is usually a success.

To manage the Michaelmas celebration, however, a new committee must be appointed every year. The mayor would prefer to see the same group function over a period of years, but he can never appoint a committee which will last. Anyone who shows initiative is accused by the others of trying to boss them, so by the time the celebration is over the Committee resigns, and the mayor must persuade a different group of people to take charge of the next year's celebration.

Arranging for the dances entails responsibility and hard work. First there must be a decision on the orchestra that will be asked to play. The Firemen usually try to hire a "big name" orchestra from Cavaillon; for the Michaelmas dance any orchestra will do since people will attend a free dance whether the orchestra is good or not. Once the date and the orchestra have been chosen the Committee must worry about publicity. An item is sent in to the Marseille newspapers so that it may be printed in the Vaucluse edition. Arrangements are made with a job printer in Apt for handbills and posters. When they are ready, the Committee delegates two or three

---

Laurence Wylie, born in Indianapolis in 1909, taught French civilization at Haverford and later at Harvard until his recent retirement. In 1950 he went with his wife and two sons to live for a year in a rural French village composed chiefly of artisans and shopkeepers who catered to the farmers in the surrounding countryside.

"Having a Good Time in Peyranne" (editors' title) is from Wylie's *Village in the Vaucluse,* which describes this French community.

members with cars or motorcycles to go around the countryside posting them on walls and in cafés. Bus companies serving the region must be told to send special buses through the surrounding communities the night of the dance to bring people who have no other means of transportation. An effort is made to make the *Salle des Fêtes* look less dreary and feel less damp. The orchestra platform is decorated with evergreen boughs and a few flowers. The fire chief drives the fire truck down to Sansom Favre's sawmill for sacks of sawdust to burn in the drum stove.

The dances are scheduled to begin at nine o'clock, but they never begin that early. Even the orchestra arrives after nine. The people coming by bus arrive earlier than the people of Peyrane because the bus driver has a schedule to keep, though the schedule is neither hard nor fast.

As the young people arrive at the *Salle des Fêtes,* the boys drift toward one corner and the girls toward another. Within each group they talk and joke and pretend to be unaware of the existence of the group on the other side of the hall. In fact, there is much eyeing between the two. Now and then, two or three boys, obviously discussing one of the girls, may even turn around and stare at her. She makes a desperate effort to ignore the attention she is receiving.

As the orchestra starts to play these two groups remain aloof, but the dancing begins because the young people are not the only ones in the hall. Some families in Peyrane—not many families, but a few of them—are always eager to participate in any form of amusement. They go to all the movies, traveling circuses, political meetings; they turn up immediately after any accident. So the Favres and the Bellets and Pougets always come to the dances. As the orchestra starts to play Henri Favre dances with his thirteen-year-old daughter Jacqueline, and seven-year-old Colette waltzes around the floor with her three-year-old brother Dédou. The older Bellet girls are dancing together. Léon Favre's little boys are not dancing but playing tag around the floor and teasing their cousins who are pretending to dance. The mothers of these children sit together at the side of the hall, talking and paying little attention to the rest of the family.

Soon a few young married couples join the dance: the schoolteacher and her husband, the baker's son and his wife, young Aubenas and his wife, who were married a few months ago and have come up from Apt. They are joined in a few minutes by some of the girls who have been standing in the girls' corner. Tired of waiting for the boys to make up their minds, these girls start dancing together. Some of them know that no boy will ever ask them to dance; others believe they can attract a partner better by dancing in front of him with another girl than by standing in a corner.

After one or two dances the boys prepare to act. The eyeing becomes more intense. Suddenly a boy breaks away from the security of his corner and walks across the hall. He stands before a girl and mutters something. She seems not to reply—often she does not even look at the boy—but they begin to dance. They do not look at each other; they do not smile. If they are poor dancers, they walk, rather than dance, round and round the hall. If they are good dancers, they execute intricate steps. Some of them even jitterbug. Both the good dancers and the poor dancers cling to each other but seem to dance only with their legs. The upper part of their body is rigid; their faces retain a blank expression. It is surprising how gracefully active their legs and feet can be when the rest of the body seems not to coöperate.

When the music stops the boy and girl, without a word or a glance, separate and go to their own groups. Once they have reached the security of their corner, they relax and smile and talk. Even engaged couples separate; only the married couples remain together and chat in a relaxed way between dances. However, when the music begins again there is the same wooden expression on the faces of the married couples as on the faces of the unmarried dancers.

From this one would not think that dancing is the favorite amusement for the young people in Peyrane, and yet their constant problem is to find means to attend every dance in the region. They never miss one if they can help it. Of course, there are only the two dances in Peyrane, but a dance can be found in some neighboring community every Saturday night. The boy who has a motorcycle is lucky; he can go to all the dances. If he has an adolescent sister, she is lucky, too, for she can ride on the back of his motorcycle. Every Saturday night Roger and Lucienne Prayal roar out of Peyrane on Roger's motorcycle. At about the same time the barber from Bonnieux comes into town on his motorcycle. He has come for his fiancée, Henri Favre's oldest daughter, to take her to a dance.

Some people criticize the Favres for letting their daughter go out unchaperoned with a man to whom she is not married, even though they are engaged. But it is admitted that times have changed and young people cannot be expected to conform to the pattern which older people had to accept in their youth. Restrictions were relaxed during the war, but still it is considered in better taste for a group of girls to go to a dance with the father or the older brother of one of them. Some fathers enjoy the task of escorting a group of girls to a dance, although they complain of having to stay up too late. After they tire of watching the dance, they go to a café and play cards until their wards can be persuaded to go home.

During the course of the evening the young people drift off to the café, too. The dance floor is almost deserted at times. A few of the older unmarried men "on the make" have located willing partners and have left. Most of the young people walk in groups to the café to relax as they never do at the dance. In the café they sit around tables laughing, joking, drinking. The drinking is moderate. Boys may become a bit stimulated, girls very rarely.

A group of young men on a spree is often the exception to this rule of moderation. They have little interest in dancing; they have little interest in girls beyond making remarks about them that are almost objectionable. If a boy has drunk more than he should and seems about to cross the line of decency, his comrades will keep him in check. They are interested in having a good time and have no desire to get into trouble.

Finally at two or three o'clock the orchestra stops playing, stows its instruments in a car and drives away. Buses go off with dancers returning to Bonnieux, Apt, and Cavaillon. Fathers and older brothers collect the girls for whose safe return they are responsible. The *Salle des Fêtes* is closed. The owner of the café finally succeeds in persuading people to leave. Soon the town is quiet except for the young men on a spree. For them the night is beginning. When they are evicted from the café, they pile into a car which roars out of town and heads for Apt or Cavaillon.

Although the two dances are the only organized activity for the adolescents, the adolescents themselves do not complain. Only the adults keep saying, "Somebody ought to organize something for the young people." When I talked to Philippe Aubenas and Robert Paul and Louise Imbert, they said they had plenty to do. Philippe said, "And besides we'd rather do what we want to do when we want to do it. Suppose we had a club and it was decided to have a party on such-and-such a date. Maybe when that day came we wouldn't feel like going to the party."

The amusement the young people are most enthusiastic about, after dancing, is taking a *promenade.* A *promenade* is so vague and formless that it can be defined only as "an occasion on which people go somewhere for recreational purposes only." It may be a short walk through the village, a picnic in the woods, or a long anticipated trip to the top of Mont Ventoux. It may be made by a family group to celebrate a first communion, by a group of girls to see the annual parade at Apt, or by a boy and girl in love. Even a single person walking in what seems to be an aimless manner may be said to be taking a *promenade.*

As I used to make my rounds through the village at different times during the day to see what was going on, the purpose of my walk seemed recreational to all those I met on the street. They would invariably greet me with "Well, out for a *promenade*?" It was difficult not to reply that it was my business to walk around and see what was going on. Their greeting did not imply reproach; if anything, it implied envy. The people of Peyrane think it is good to be able to take a walk any time of the day—especially when the sun is shining and the mistral is not blowing.

The dances, the *promenades,* and the usual forms of adult recreational activity are supposed to offer adolescent girls adequate opportunities to have a good time. A well-behaved girl will not seek others, and most of the girls seem content. Their work takes most of their time. They can go to the movie on Tuesday evening. They go to a dance on Saturday night. They go on a *promenade* on Sunday afternoons and holidays. They may go to the market in Apt on Saturday morning and remain in the city to spend the night with a friend. During the day and in the evening when they have spare time they may drop in at a friend's house for a cup of coffee. As they get older they can expect suitors to call in the evening.

Boys are expected to seek wilder forms of amusement. Three years ago there was a group of older boys called the "Bombonne peyranaise," perhaps best translated as the "Peyrane Jug," because the group seemed capable of holding an extraordinary quantity of wine. Louis Pascal had decided he wanted to become the village cobbler and had left his father's farm to set up his shop in one of the run-down houses of the village. After a year or so he gave up cobbling and went back to the farm, but during the year that he halfheartedly exercised his craft, his house was the center of activity for most of the young men of the village. Every evening and every holiday they congregated there and played cards and drank until late at night. Occasionally they went on a spree that lasted two or three days.

A spree usually began when the gang decided to go somewhere for a good meal. They would take the Borel car to Apt or to the Fontaine de Vaucluse for a dinner which would last two or three hours. The rounds of pastis before dinner, the bottles of wine consumed during the meal, the brandy or rum drunk after coffee kept them in good spirits until eleven o'clock when they would decide to go to a dance somewhere in the region. Even at the dance the group retained its unity. They would stand around and watch the dancers for a while, laughing and making remarks about the girls. As the effects of dinner wore off they would go to the café for a drink. There they played a pinball game or a few rounds of belote[1] so wildly that the café keeper would threaten to kick them out. They kept distinct from the groups of dancers who now and then came from the dance. When the dance ended and the café closed, there was nothing more to do in the village, but with a car they could carry on elsewhere. In Apt and Cavaillon most of the cafés were closed, too, but there were always the brothels, now called "hotels" since brothels have been abolished, and these institutions remain open all night. The boys were not primarily interested in the prostitutes; they wanted a place where they could sit and drink and joke and play cards as long as they wanted. They enjoyed the girls who hovered around them because they could joke with them and dance if they felt like it. But on most of these occasions females were definitely of secondary importance.

By the time the sun came up the group was bored with the brothel and with sitting around drinking. Back in the car, they dashed up to Peyrane to get their guns and dogs, and in an hour they were off in the woods hunting hare or thrushes. The hunting lasted until they got tired and hungry and went back home to eat and drink. But then they were ready to start out again—this time perhaps for a fête in a neighboring town where they could "check up on things" and enter the boules tournament. Either success or failure in the tournament called for a few rounds of drinks, and eventually it would be time for dinner—a good dinner, since they had not eaten well for twenty-four hours. When someone suggested that there was a new restaurant in Gordes which was supposed to be good, they would set off and the night would begin again.

The "Bombonne peyranaise" took the idea of having a good time more seriously than most of the young people of Peyrane. They represented the extreme to which young people may go. Sometimes adults were inclined to feel that Pascal, Borel, Vidal, and others were going too far, but on the whole they approved. They respected them more than they did Roger Prayal who never did anything wild. The proof that their confidence was well placed lies in the fact that Pascal,

[1]A card game. (Editors' note)

Borel, and Vidal are now, three years later, serious, hard-working young men.

## Questions

1. Reread the paragraph beginning "As the young people arrive" (page 321), and the next four paragraphs describing behavior at the dance. In what ways does the behavior seem familiar to you, and in what ways utterly foreign? Are the resemblances essential, and the differences superficial, or vice versa?
2. Wylie is a social anthropologist. In the preface to his account of life in a French village in 1950, Wylie says that he attempted "to depict living personalities in the framework of a systematic description of their culture." How would you characterize his attitude toward the people he is studying? (Clinical, affectionate, patronizing, or what?) Is his attitude "scientific"? What can you infer about the attitude of the villagers toward him? Write a paragraph or two embodying your answers and supporting them with appropriate references to the text.
3. Wylie says that in Peyrane the two activities most preferred by young people were dancing and taking a promenade. What are the first and second preferences in your home community? Do they fulfill the functions of the dance and the promenade in Peyrane?

Theodore Roethke

# Child on Top of a Greenhouse

The wind billowing out the seat of my britches,
My feet crackling splinters of glass and dried putty,
The half-grown chrysanthemums staring up like accusers,
Up through the streaked glass, flashing with sunlight,
A few white clouds all rushing eastward,
A line of elms plunging and tossing like horses,
And everyone, everyone pointing up and shouting!

## Questions

1. What must have happened just before the scene described in the poem? What details serve as clues?
2. How does the child feel about being on top of the greenhouse? How do you know?
3. The poem is an incomplete or fragmentary sentence. By changing the present participles (from "billowing" in the first line to "shouting" in the last line) to verbs, convert the fragment to a sentence. Read the "revised" poem through, then explain what has been lost.

For a biographical note on Roethke, see page 74.

# 5
# MESSAGES

*Behind the Bar, Birney, Montana*
**Post Wolcott, 1941**

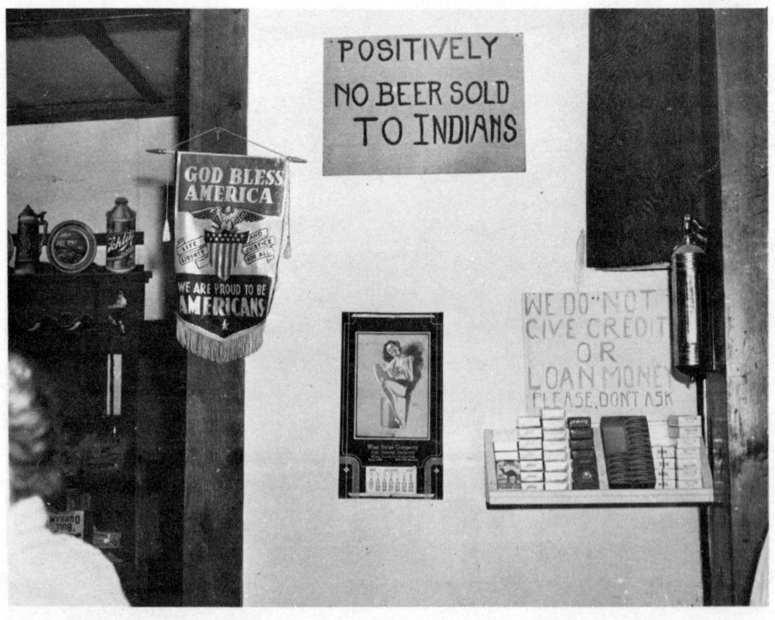


Farm Security Administration Photo, Library of Congress

*The Argument*
**Leonard Freed, 1965**

Magnum Photos

*I Want YOU*
**James Montgomery Flagg, 1917**

Franklin D. Roosevelt Library

*The Computer Operator*
**Arthur Tress, 1976**

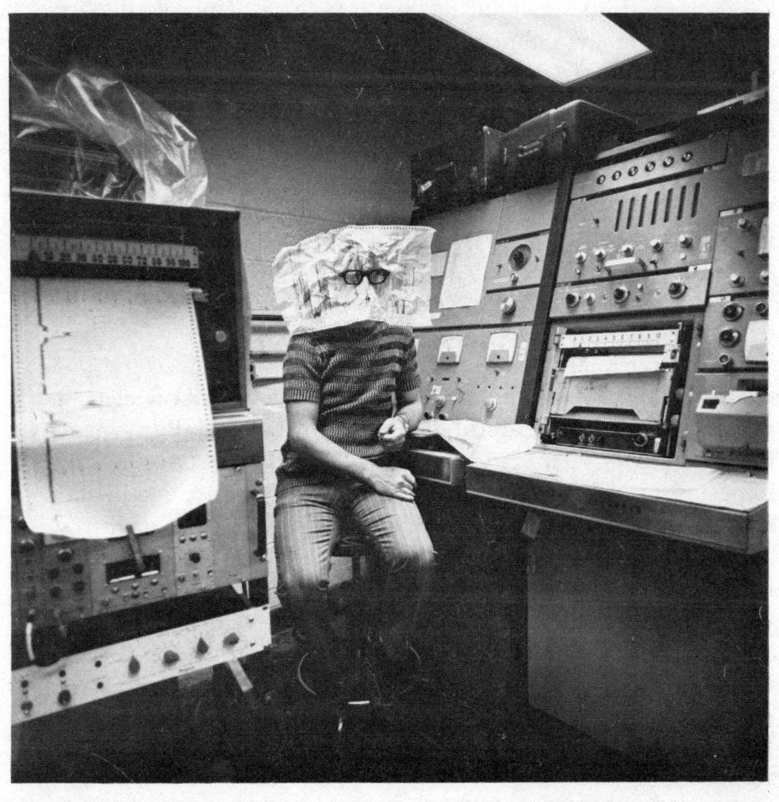

# Short Views

We must be as clear as our natural reticence allows us to be.
**Marianne Moore**

To talk much about oneself may also be a means of concealing oneself.
**Friedrich Nietzsche**

Politeness ruins conversations.
**Ralph Waldo Emerson**

While I am thinking about metaphor, a flock of purple finches arrives on the lawn. Since I haven't seen these birds for some years, I am only fairly sure of their being in fact purple finches, so I get down Peterson's *Field Guide* and read his description: "Male: About size of House Sparrow, rosy-red, brightest on head and rump." That checks quite well, but his next remark—"a sparrow dipped in raspberry juice,"—is decisive: it fits. I look out the window again, and now I know that I am seeing purple finches.
**Howard Nemerov**

We will understand the world, and preserve ourselves and our values in it, only insofar as we have a language that is alert and responsive to it, and careful of it. I mean that literally. When we give our plows such brand names as "Sod Blaster," we are imposing on their use conceptual limits which raise the likelihood that they will be used destructively. When we speak of man's "war against nature," or of a "peace offensive," we are accepting the limitations of a metaphor that suggests, and even proposes, violent solutions. When students ask for the right of "participatory input" at the meetings of a faculty organization, they are thinking of democratic process, but they are *speaking* of a convocation of robots, and are thus devaluing the very traditions that they invoke.
**Wendell Berry**

Because it deals with struggle, sports writing is required to be vigorous, and because it scorns formality it must be slangy and colloquial. But slang is particularly unfitted for frequent repetition and sports writing is, above any other type of contemporary writing, repetitious, laden with clichés. The wretched sports writer, with slight material and often (one suspects) even slighter interest, is compelled to assume concern he does not feel and to conceal his yawns under forced shouts of simulated excitement. A tyrannical convention of his dreary craft prevents him from repeating his verbs; yet there are only a certain number of synonyms for win and lose. He has done what he can with *win, top, upset, pace, defeat, trounce, decision* (verb), *crush, sock, blitz, spank, clobber, whip, wallop, down, spill,* and the like, but the demand far exceeds the capacity of the language. No one, apparently, using only the normal resources of the richest language known, can make sports interesting.

The strained variation is interspersed with the strained periphrasis. An injured thumb is *the dislocated digit* and the backfield is *a bevy of backs.* Alliteration is freely employed. Not since *Widsith* has its artful aid been so assiduously sought.

**Bergen and Cornelia Evans**

A man is known by the books he reads, by the company he keeps, by the praise he gives, by his dress, by his tastes, by his distastes, by the stories he tells, by his gait, by the motion of his eye, by the look of his house, of his chamber; for nothing on earth is solitary, but everything hath affinities infinite. . . .

**Ralph Waldo Emerson**

Gifts from parents to children always carry the most meaningful messages. The way parents think about presents goes one step beyond the objects themselves—the ties, dolls, sleds, record players, kerchiefs, bicycles and model airplanes that wait by the Christmas tree. The gifts are, if effect, one way of telling boys and girls, "We love you even though you have been a bad boy all month" or, "We love having a daughter" or, "We treat all our children alike" or, "It is all right for girls to have some toys made for boys" or, "This alarm clock will help you get started in the morning all by yourself." Throughout all the centuries since the invention of a Santa Claus figure who represented a special recognition of children's behavior, good and bad, presents have given parents a way of telling children about their love and hopes and expectations for them.

**Margaret Mead**

A good painter is to paint two main things, namely, man and the working of man's mind. The first is easy, the second difficult, for it is to be represented through the gestures and movements of the limbs.

**Leonardo da Vinci**

If you saw a bullet hit a bird, and he told you he wasn't shot, you might weep at his courtesy, but you would certainly doubt his word.

**Emily Dickinson**

Abraham Lincoln

# Address at the Dedication of the Gettysburg National Cemetery

Four score and seven years ago our fathers brought forth on this continent, a new nation, conceived in Liberty, and dedicated to the proposition that all men are created equal.

Now we are engaged in a great civil war; testing whether that nation, or any nation so conceived and so dedicated, can long endure. We are met on a great battlefield of that war. We have come to dedicate a portion of that field as a final resting-place for those who here gave their lives that that nation might live. It is altogether fitting and proper that we should do this.

But, in a larger sense, we cannot dedicate—we cannot consecrate—we cannot hallow—this ground. The brave men, living and dead, who struggled here have consecrated it, far above our poor power to add or detract. The world will little note, nor long remember, what we say here, but it can never forget what they did here. It is for us the living, rather, to be dedicated here to the unfinished work which they who fought here have thus far so nobly advanced. It is rather for us to be here dedicated to the great task remaining before us—that from these honored dead we take increased devotion to that cause for which they gave the last full measure of devotion; that we here highly resolve that these dead shall not have died in vain; that this nation, under God, shall have a new birth of freedom; and that government of the people, by the people, for the people, shall not perish from the earth.

Abraham Lincoln (1809–1865), sixteenth president of the United States, is not usually thought of as a writer, but his published speeches and writings comprise about 1,078,000 words, the equivalent of about 4,000 pages of double-spaced typing. They were all composed without the assistance of a speech writer.

Gilbert Highet

# The Gettysburg Address

Fourscore and seven years ago. . . .

These five words stand at the entrance to the best-known monument of American prose, one of the finest utterances in the entire language, and surely one of the greatest speeches in all history. Greatness is like granite: it is molded in fire, and it lasts for many centuries.

Fourscore and seven years ago. . . . It is strange to think that President Lincoln was looking back to the 4th of July 1776, and that he and his speech are now further removed from us than he himself was from George Washington and the Declaration of Independence. Fourscore and seven years before the Gettysburg Address, a small group of patriots signed the Declaration. Fourscore and seven years after the Gettysburg Address, it was the year 1950, and that date is already receding rapidly into our troubled, adventurous, and valiant past.

Inadequately prepared and at first scarcely realized in its full importance, the dedication of the graveyard at Gettysburg was one of the supreme moments of American history. The battle itself had been a turning point of the war. On the 4th of July 1863, General Meade repelled Lee's invasion of Pennsylvania. Although he did not follow up his victory, he had broken one of the most formidable aggressive enterprises of the Confederate armies. Losses were heavy on both sides. Thousands of dead were left on the field, and thousands of wounded died in the hot days following the battle. At first, their burial was more or less haphazard; but thoughtful men gradually came to feel that an adequate burying place and memorial were required. These were established by an interstate commission that autumn, and the finest speaker in the North was invited to dedicate

---

Gilbert Highet (1906–1978) was born in Glasgow, Scotland, and was educated at Glasgow University and at Oxford University. In 1937 he came to the United States, and in 1951 he was naturalized. Until his retirement in 1972 he taught Latin, Greek, and comparative literature at Columbia University. In addition to writing scholarly studies of classical authors he has written several general and more popular books.

them. This was the scholar and statesman Edward Everett of Harvard. He made a good speech—which is still extant: not at all academic, it is full of close strategic analysis and deep historical understanding.

Lincoln was not invited to speak, at first. Although people knew him as an effective debater, they were not sure whether he was capable of making a serious speech on such a solemn occasion. But one of the impressive things about Lincoln's career is that he constantly strove to *grow.* He was anxious to appear on that occasion and to say something worthy of it. (Also, it has been suggested, he was anxious to remove the impression that he did not know how to behave properly—an impression which had been strengthened by a shocking story about his clowning on the battlefield of Antietam the previous year.) Therefore when he was invited he took considerable care with his speech. He drafted rather more than half of it in the White House before leaving, finished it in the hotel at Gettysburg the night before the ceremony (not in the train, as sometimes reported), and wrote a fair copy next morning.

There are many accounts of the day itself, 19 November 1863. There are many descriptions of Lincoln, all showing the same curious blend of grandeur and awkwardness, or lack of dignity, or—it would be best to call it humility. In the procession he rode horseback: a tall lean man in a high plug hat, straddling a short horse, with his feet too near the ground. He arrived before the chief speaker, and had to wait patiently for half an hour or more. His own speech came right at the end of a long and exhausting ceremony, lasted less than three minutes, and made little impression on the audience. In part this was because they were tired, in part because (as eyewitnesses said) he ended almost before they knew he had begun, and in part because he did not speak the Address, but read it, very slowly, in a thin high voice, with a marked Kentucky accent, pronouncing "to" as "toe" and dropping his final R's.

Some people of course were alert enough to be impressed. Everett congratulated him at once. But most of the newspapers paid little attention to the speech, and some sneered at it. The *Patriot and Union* of Harrisburg wrote, "We pass over the silly remarks of the President; for the credit of the nation we are willing . . . that they shall no more be repeated or thought of"; and the London *Times* said, "The ceremony was rendered ludicrous by some of the sallies of that poor President Lincoln," calling his remarks "dull and commonplace." The first commendation of the Address came in a single sentence of the Chicago *Tribune,* and the first discriminating and detailed praise of it appeared in the Springfield *Republican,* the Providence *Journal,* and the Philadelphia *Bulletin.* However, three weeks after the ceremony and then again the following spring, the editor of *Harper's Weekly* published a sincere and thorough eulogy of the Address, and soon it was attaining recognition as a masterpiece.

At the time, Lincoln could not care much about the reception of his words. He was exhausted and ill. In the train back to Washington, he lay down with a wet towel on his head. He had caught smallpox. At that moment he was incubating it, and he was stricken down soon after he re-entered the White House. Fortunately it was a mild attack, and it evoked one of his best jokes: he told his visitors, "At last I have something I can give to everybody."

He had more than that to give to everybody. He was a unique person, far greater than most people realize until they read his life with care. The wisdom of his policy, the sources of his statesmanship —these were things too complex to be discussed in a brief essay. But we can say something about the Gettysburg Address as a work of art.[1]

A work of art. Yes: for Lincoln was a literary artist, trained both by others and by himself. The textbooks he used as a boy were full of difficult exercises and skillful devices in formal rhetoric, stressing the qualities he practiced in his own speaking: antithesis, parallelism, and verbal harmony. Then he read and reread many admirable models of thought and expression: the King James Bible, the essays of Bacon, the best plays of Shakespeare. His favorities were *Hamlet, Lear, Macbeth, Richard III,* and *Henry VIII,* which he had read dozens of times. He loved reading aloud, too, and spent hours reading poetry to his friends. (He told his partner Herndon that he preferred getting the sense of any document by reading it aloud.) Therefore his serious speeches are important parts of the long and noble classical tradition of oratory which begins in Greece, runs through Rome to the modern world, and is still capable (if we do not neglect it) of producing masterpieces.

The first proof of this is that the Gettysburg Address is full of quotations—or rather of adaptations—which give it strength. It is

[1]For further reference, see W. E. Barton, *Lincoln at Gettysburg* (Bobbs-Merrill, 1930); R. P. Basier, "Abraham Lincoln's Rhetoric," *American Literature* 11 (1939–40), 167–182; and L. E. Robinson, *Abraham Lincoln as a Man of Letters* (Chicago, 1918).

partly religious, partly (in the highest sense) political: therefore it is interwoven with memories of the Bible and memories of American history. The first and the last words are Biblical cadences. Normally Lincoln did not say "fourscore" when he meant eighty; but on this solemn occasion he recalled the important dates in the Bible—such as the age of Abraham when his first son was born to him, and he was "fourscore and six years old." Similarly he did not say there was a chance that democracy might die out: he recalled the somber phrasing in the Book of Job—where Bildad speaks of the destruction of one who shall vanish without a trace, and says that "his branch shall be cut off; his remembrance shall perish from the earth." Then again, the famous description of our State as "government of the people, by the people, for the people" was adumbrated by Daniel Webster in 1830 (he spoke of "the people's government, made for the people, made by the people, and answerable to the people") and then elaborated in 1854 by the abolitionist Theodore Parker (as "government of all the people, by all the people, for all the people"). There is good reason to think that Lincoln took the important phrase "under God" (which he interpolated at the last moment) from Weems, the biographer of Washington; and we know that it had been used at least once by Washington himself.

Analyzing the Address further, we find that it is based on a highly imaginative theme, or group of themes. The subject is—how can we put it so as not to disfigure it?—the subject is the kinship of life and death, that mysterious linkage which we see sometimes as the physical succession of birth and death in our world, sometimes as the contrast, which is perhaps a unity, between death and immortality. The first sentence is concerned with birth:

> Our *fathers brought forth* a *new* nation, *conceived* in liberty.

The final phrase but one expresses the hope that

> this nation, under God, shall have a *new birth* of freedom.

And the last phrase of all speaks of continuing life as the triumph over death. Again and again throughout the speech, this mystical contrast and kinship reappear: "those who *gave their lives* that that nation might *live,*" "the brave men *living* and *dead,*" and so in the central assertion that the dead have already consecrated their own burial place, while "it is for us, the *living,* rather to be dedicated . . .

to the great task remaining." The Gettysburg Address is a prose poem; it belongs to the same world as the great elegies, and the adagios of Beethoven.

Its structure, however, is that of a skillfully contrived speech. The oratorical pattern is perfectly clear. Lincoln describes the occasion, dedicates the ground, and then draws a larger conclusion by calling on his hearers to dedicate themselves to the preservation of the Union. But within that, we can trace his constant use of at least two important rhetorical devices.

The first of these is *antithesis:* opposition, contrast. The speech is full of it. Listen:

> The world will little *note*<br>
> nor long *remember* what *we say* here<br>
> but it can never *forget* what *they did* here.

And so in nearly every sentence: "brave men, *living* and *dead*"; "to *add* or *detract.*" There is the antithesis of the Founding Fathers and men of Lincoln's own time:

> Our *fathers brought forth* a new nation . . .<br>
> now *we* are testing whether that nation . . . can *long endure.*

And there is the more terrible antithesis of those who have already died and those who still live to do their duty. Now, antithesis is the figure of contrast and conflict. Lincoln was speaking in the midst of a great civil war.

The other important pattern is different. It is technically called *tricolon*—the division of an idea into three harmonious parts, usually of increasing power. The most famous phrase of the Address is a tricolon:

> government of the people<br>
> by the people<br>
> for the people.

The most solemn sentence is a tricolon:

> we cannot dedicate<br>
> we cannot consecrate<br>
> we cannot hallow this ground.

And above all, the last sentence (which has sometimes been criticized as too complex) is essentially two parallel phrases, with a tricolon growing out of the second and then producing another tricolon: a trunk, three branches, and a cluster of flowers. Lincoln says that it is for his hearers to be dedicated to the great task remaining before them. Then he goes on,

> that from these honored dead

—apparently he means "in such a way that from these honored dead"—

> we take increased devotion to that cause.

Next, he restates this more briefly:

> that we here highly resolve. . . .

And now the actual resolution follows, in three parts of growing intensity:

> that these dead shall not have died in vain
> that this nation, under God, shall have a new birth
> of freedom

and that (one more tricolon)

> government of the people
> by the people
> for the people
> shall not perish from the earth.

Now, the tricolon is the figure which, through division, emphasizes basic harmony and unity. Lincoln used antithesis because he was speaking to a people at war. He used the tricolon because he was hoping, planning, praying for peace.

No one thinks that when he was drafting the Gettysburg Address, Lincoln deliberately looked up these quotations and consciously chose these particular patterns of thought. No, he chose the theme. From its development and from the emotional tone of the entire occasion, all the rest followed, or grew—by that marvelous process of choice and rejection which is essential to artistic creation. It does not spoil such a work of art to analyze it as closely as we have done; it is altogether fitting and proper that we should do this: for it helps us to penetrate more deeply into the rich meaning of the Gettysburg Address, and it allows us the very rare privilege of watching the workings of a great man's mind.

## Questions

1. At the start of his essay, after quoting the opening words of Lincoln's speech, Highet uses a metaphor and a simile: he says that the words "stand at the entrance to the best-known monument," and that "greatness is like granite: it is molded in fire, and it lasts for many centuries." Are these figures of speech effective? Why or why not? How are the two figures related to each other?
2. Analyze the structure of Highet's essay.
3. This essay was a talk given on the radio, presumably to a large general public. Find passages in the essay that suggest oral delivery to an unspecialized audience. How would you describe Highet's tone?
4. It has been suggested that "government of the people, by the people" is redundant; a government *of* the people, it is argued, must be the same as a government *by* the people. Did Lincoln repeat himself merely to get a triad: "of the people, by the people, for the people"? If so, is this a fault? Or can it be argued that "government of the people" really means "government over the people"? If so, what does the entire expression mean?

## Oliver Jensen

# The Gettysburg Address in Eisenhowese

I haven't checked these figures but 87 years ago, I think it was, a number of individuals organized a governmental set-up here in this country. I believe it covered certain Eastern areas, with this

Oliver Jensen, born in 1914, has been an editor or founder of several magazines, including *American Heritage* and *Horizon.*

idea they were following up based on a sort of national independence arrangement and the program that every individual is just as good as every other individual. Well, now, of course, we are dealing with this big difference of opinion, civil disturbance you might say, although I don't like to appear to take sides or name any individuals, and the point is naturally to check up, by actual experience in the field, to see whether any governmental set-up with a basis like the one I was mentioning has any validity and find out whether that dedication by those early individuals will pay off in lasting values and things of that kind.

Well, here we are, at the scene where one of these disturbances between different sides got going. We want to pay our tribute to those loved ones, those departed individuals who made the supreme sacrifice here on the basis of their opinions about how this thing ought to be handled. And I would say this. It is absolutely in order to do this.

But if you look at the over-all picture of this, we can't pay any tribute—we can't sanctify this area, you might say—we can't hallow according to whatever individual creeds or faiths or sort of religious outlooks are involved like I said about this particular area. It was those individuals themselves, including the enlisted men, very brave individuals, who have given this religious character to the area. The way I see it, the rest of the world will not remember any statements issued here but it will never forget how these men put their shoulders to the wheel and carried this idea down the fairway.

Now frankly, our job, the living individuals' job here, is to pick up the burden and sink the putt they made these big efforts here for. It is our job to get on with the assignment— and from these deceased fine individuals to take extra inspiration, you could call it, for the same theories about the set-up for which they made such a big contribution. We have to make up our minds right here and now, as I see it, that they didn't put out all that blood, perspiration and—well —that they didn't just make a dry run here, and that all of us here, under God, that is, the God of our choice, shall beef up this idea about freedom and liberty and those kind of arrangements, and that government of all individuals, by all individuals and for the individuals, shall not pass out of the world-picture.

## Questions

1. Describe the features of presidential prose that Jensen is parodying. Indicate a few passages that exemplify these features. (On parody, see page 646.)
2. Read Orwell's "Politics and the English Language" (page 346), marking passages that are particularly well supported by this parody. What reasons can you give for the influence of politics on prose style?

**George Orwell**

# Politics and the English Language

Most people who bother with the matter at all would admit that the English language is in a bad way, but it is generally assumed that we cannot by conscious action do anything about it. Our civilization is decadent and our language—so the argument runs—must inevitably share in the general collapse. It follows that any struggle against the abuse of language is a sentimental archaism, like preferring candles to electric light or hansom cabs to aeroplanes. Underneath this lies the half-conscious belief that language is a natural growth and not an instrument which we shape for our own purposes.

Now, it is clear that the decline of a language must ultimately have political and economic causes: it is not due simply to the bad influence of this or that individual writer. But an effect can become a cause, reinforcing the original cause and producing the same effect

---

George Orwell (1903–1950) was the pen name adopted by Eric Blair, an Englishman born in India. Orwell was educated at Eton, in England, but in 1921 he went back to the East and served for five years as a police officer in Burma. He then returned to Europe, doing odd jobs while writing novels and stories. In 1936 he fought in the Spanish Civil War on the side of the Republicans, an experience reported in *Homage to Catalonia* (1938). His last years were spent writing in England.

in an intensified form, and so on indefinitely. A man may take to drink because he feels himself to be a failure, and then fail all the more completely because he drinks. It is rather the same thing that is happening to the English language. It becomes ugly and inaccurate because our thoughts are foolish, but the slovenliness of our language makes it easier for us to have foolish thoughts. The point is that the process is reversible. Modern English, especially written English, is full of bad habits which spread by imitation and which can be avoided if one is willing to take the necessary trouble. If one gets rid of these habits one can think more clearly, and to think clearly is a necessary first step towards political regeneration: so that the fight against bad English is not frivolous and is not the exclusive concern of professional writers. I will come back to this presently, and I hope that by that time the meaning of what I have said here will have become clearer. Meanwhile, here are five specimens of the English language as it is now habitually written.

These five passages have not been picked out because they are especially bad—I could have quoted far worse if I had chosen—but because they illustrate various of the mental vices from which we now suffer. They are a little below the average, but are fairly representative samples. I number them so that I can refer back to them when necessary:

1. I am not, indeed, sure whether it is not true to say that the Milton who once seemed not unlike a seventeenth-century Shelley had not become, out of an experience ever more bitter in each year, more alien [*sic*] to the founder of that Jesuit sect which nothing could induce him to tolerate.

   Professor Harold Laski (Essay in *Freedom of Expression*)

2. Above all, we cannot play ducks and drakes with a native battery of idioms which prescribes such egregious collocations of vocables as the Basic *put up with* for *tolerate* or *put at a loss* for *bewilder.*

   Professor Lancelot Hogben *(Interglossa)*

3. On the one side we have the free personality: by definition it is not neurotic, for it has neither conflict nor dream. Its desires, such as they are, are transparent, for they are just what institutional approval keeps in the forefront of consciousness; another institutional pattern would alter their number and intensity; there is little in

them that is natural, irreducible, or culturally dangerous. But *on the other side,* the social bond itself is nothing but the mutual reflection of these self-secure integrities. Recall the definition of love. Is not this the very picture of a small academic? Where is there a place in this hall of mirrors for either personality or fraternity?

Essay on Psychology in *Politics* (New York)

4. All the "best people" from the gentlemen's clubs, and all the frantic fascist captains, united in common hatred of Socialism and bestial horror of the rising tide of the mass revolutionary movement, have turned to acts of provocation, to foul incendiarism, to medieval legends of poisoned wells, to legalize their own destruction of proletarian organizations, and rouse the agitated petty-bourgeoisie to chauvinistic fervor on behalf of the fight against the revolutionary way out of the crisis.

Communist Pamphlet

5. If a new spirit *is* to be infused into this old country, there is one thorny and contentious reform which must be tackled, and that is the humanization and galvanization of the B.B.C. Timidity here will bespeak canker and atrophy of the soul. The heart of Britain may be sound and of strong beat, for instance, but the British lion's roar at present is like that of Bottom in Shakespeare's *Midsummer Night's Dream*—as gentle as any sucking dove. A virile new Britain cannot continue indefinitely to be traduced in the eyes or rather ears, of the world by the effete languors of Langham Place, brazenly masquerading as "standard English." When the voice of Britain is heard at nine o'clock, better far and infinitely less ludicrous to hear aitches honestly dropped than the present priggish, inflated, inhibited, school-ma'amish arch braying of blameless bashful mewing maidens!

Letter in *Tribune*

Each of these passages has faults of its own, but, quite apart from avoidable ugliness, two qualities are common to all of them. The first is staleness of imagery; the other is lack of precision. The writer either has a meaning and cannot express it, or he inadvertently says something else, or he is almost indifferent as to whether his words mean anything or not. This mixture of vagueness and sheer incompetence is the most marked characteristic of modern English prose, and especially of any kind of political writing. As soon as certain topics are raised, the concrete melts into the abstract and no one seems able to think of turns of speech that are not hackneyed: prose consists less and less of *words* chosen for the sake of their meaning, and more and more of *phrases* tacked together like the sections of a prefabricated hen-house. I list below, with notes and examples, various of the tricks by means of which the work of prose-construction is habitually dodged:

### *Dying Metaphors*

A newly invented metaphor assists thought by evoking a visual image, while on the other hand a metaphor which is technically "dead" (e.g. *iron resolution*) has in effect reverted to being an ordinary word and can generally be used without loss of vividness. But in between these two classes there is a huge dump of worn-out metaphors which have lost all evocative power and are merely used because they save people the trouble of inventing phrases for themselves. Examples are: *Ring the changes on, take up the cudgels for, toe the line, ride roughshod over, stand shoulder to shoulder with, play into the hands of, no axe to grind, grist to the mill, fishing in troubled waters, on the order of the day, Achilles' heel, swan song, hotbed.* Many of these are used without knowledge of their meaning (what is a "rift," for instance?), and incompatible metaphors are frequently mixed, a sure sign that the writer is not interested in what he is saying. Some metaphors now current have been twisted out of their original meaning without those who use them even being aware of the fact. For example, *toe the line* is sometimes written *tow the line.* Another example is *the hammer and the anvil,* now always used with the implication that the anvil gets the worst of it. In real life it is always the anvil that breaks the hammer, never the other way about: a writer who stopped to think what he was saying would be aware of this, and would avoid perverting the original phrase.

### *Operators or Verbal False Limbs*

These save the trouble of picking out appropriate verbs and nouns, and at the same time pad each sentence with extra syllables which give it an appearance of symmetry. Characteristic phrases are *render inoperative, militate against, make contact with, be subjected to, give rise to, give grounds for, have the effect of, play a leading part (role) in, make itself felt, take effect, exhibit a tendency to, serve the purpose of, etc., etc.* The keynote is the elimination of simple verbs. Instead of being a single word, such as *break, stop, spoil, mend, kill,* a verb becomes *a phrase,* made up of a noun or adjective tacked on to some general-purpose verb such as *prove, serve, form, play, render.* In addition, the passive voice is wherever possible used in preference to the active, and noun constructions are used instead of gerunds (*by examination of* instead of *by examining*). The range of verbs is further cut down by means of the *-ize* and *de-* formations, and the banal statements are given an appearance of profundity by means of the *not un-* formation. Simple conjunctions and prepositions are replaced by such phrases as *with respect to, having regard to, the fact that, by dint of, in view of, in the interests of, on the hypothesis that;* and the ends of sentences are saved from anticlimax by such resounding common-places as *greatly to be desired, cannot be left out of account, a development to be expected in the near future, deserving of serious consideration, brought to a satisfactory conclusion,* and so on and so forth.

### *Pretentious Diction*

Words like *phenomenon, element, individual* (as noun), *objective, categorical, effective, virtual, basic, primary, promote, constitute, exhibit, exploit, utilize, eliminate, liquidate,* are used to dress up simple statements and give an air of scientific impartiality to biased judgments. Adjectives like *epoch-making, epic, historic, unforgettable, triumphant, age-old, inevitable, inexorable, veritable,* are used to dignify the sordid processes of international politics, while writing that aims at glorifying war usually takes on an archaic color, its characteristic words being: *realm, throne, chariot, mailed fist, trident, sword, shield, buckler, banner, jackboot, clarion.* Foreign words and expressions such as *cul de sac, ancien régime, deus ex machina, mutatis mutandis, status quo, gleichschaltung, weltanschauung,* are used to give an air of culture and elegance. Except for the useful abbreviations *i.e., e.g.,* and *etc.,* there is no real need for any of the hundreds of foreign phrases now current in English. Bad writers, and especially scientific, political and sociological writers, are nearly always haunted by the notion that Latin or Greek words are grander than Saxon ones, and unnecessary words like *expedite, ameliorate, predict, extraneous, deracinated, clandestine, subaqueous* and hundreds of others constantly gain ground from their Anglo-Saxon opposite numbers.[1] The jargon peculiar to Marxist writing (*hyena, hangman, cannibal, petty bourgeois, these gentry, lacquey, flunkey, mad dog, White Guard,* etc.) consists largely of words and phrases translated from Russian, German or French; but the normal way of coining a new word is to use a Latin or Greek root with the appropriate affix and, where necessary, the *-ize* formation. It is often easier to make up words of this kind (*deregionalize, impermissible, extramarital, non-fragmentary* and so forth) than to think up the English words that will cover one's meaning. The result, in general, is an increase in slovenliness and vagueness.

## *Meaningless Words*

In certain kinds of writing, particularly in art criticism and literary criticism, it is normal to come across long passages which are almost completely lacking in meaning.[2] Words like *romantic, plastic, values, human, dead, sentimental, natural, vitality,* as used in art criticism, are strictly meaningless, in the sense that they not only do not point to any discoverable object, but are hardly ever expected to do so by the reader. When one critic writes, "The outstanding feature of Mr. X's work is its living quality," while another writes, "The immediately striking thing about Mr. X's work is its peculiar deadness," the reader accepts this as a simple difference of opinion. If words like *black* and *white* were involved, instead of the jargon words *dead* and *living,* he would see at once that language was being used in an improper way. Many political words are similarly abused. The word *Fascism* has now no meaning except in so far as it signifies "something not desirable." The words *democracy, socialism, freedom, patriotic, realistic, justice,* have each of them several different meanings which cannot be reconciled with one another. In the case of a word like *democracy,* not only is there no agreed definition, but the attempt to make one is resisted

[1] An interesting illustration of this is the way in which the English flower names which were in use till very recently are being ousted by Greek ones, *snapdragon* becoming *antirrhinum, forget-me-not* becoming *myosotis,* etc. It is hard to see any practical reason for this change of fashion: it is probably due to an instinctive turning-away from the more homely word and a vague feeling that the Greek word is scientific.

[2] Example: "Comfort's catholicity of perception and image, strangely Whitmanesque in range, almost the exact opposite in aesthetic compulsion, continues to evoke that trembling atmospheric accumulative hinting at a cruel, an inexorably serene timelessness. . . . Wrey Gardiner scores by aiming at simple bull's-eyes with precision. Only they are not so simple, and through this contented sadness runs more than the surface bitter-sweet of resignation." (*Poetry Quarterly.*)

from all sides. It is almost universally felt that when we call a country democratic we are praising it: consequently the defenders of every kind of régime claim that it is a democracy, and fear that they might have to stop using the word if it were tied down to any one meaning. Words of this kind are often used in a consciously dishonest way. That is, the person who uses them has his own private definition, but allows his hearer to think he means something quite different. Statements like *Marshal Pétain was a true patriot, The Soviet Press is the freest in the world, The Catholic Church is opposed to persecution,* are almost always made with intent to deceive. Other words used in variable meanings, in most cases more or less dishonestly, are: *class, totalitarian, science, progressive, reactionary, bourgeois, equality.*

Now that I have made this catalogue of swindles and perversions, let me give another example of the kind of writing that they lead to. This time it must of its nature be an imaginary one. I am going to translate a passage of good English into modern English of the worst sort. Here is a well-known verse from *Ecclesiastes:*

> I returned and saw under the sun, that the race is not to the swift, nor the battle to the strong, neither yet bread to the wise, nor yet riches to men of understanding, nor yet favour to men of skill; but time and chance happeneth to them all.

Here it is in modern English:

> Objective consideration of contemporary phenomena compels the conclusion that success or failure in competitive activities exhibits no tendency to be commensurate with innate capacity, but that a considerable element of the unpredictable must invariably be taken into account.

This is a parody, but not a very gross one. Exhibit (3), above, for instance, contains several patches of the same kind of English. It will be seen that I have not made a full translation. The beginning and ending of the sentence follow the original meaning fairly closely, but in the middle the concrete illustrations—race, battle, bread—dissolve into the vague phrase "success or failure in competitive activities." This had to be so, because no modern writer of the kind I am discussing—no one capable of using phrases like "objective consideration of contemporary phenomena"—would ever tabulate his thoughts in that precise and detailed way. The whole tendency of modern prose is away from concreteness. Now analyze these two sentences a little more closely. The first contains forty-nine words but only sixty syllables, and all its words are those of everyday life. The second contains thirty-eight words of ninety syllables: eighteen of its words are from Latin roots, and one from Greek. The first sentence contains six vivid images, and only one phrase ("time and chance") that could be called vague. The second contains not a single fresh, arresting phrase, and in spite of its ninety syllables it gives only a shortened version of the meaning contained in the first. Yet without a doubt it is the second kind of sentence that is gaining ground in modern English. I do not want to exaggerate. This kind of writing is not yet universal, and outcrops of simplicity will occur here and there in the worst-written page. Still, if you or I were told to write a few lines on the uncertainty of human fortunes, we should probably come much nearer to my imaginary sentence than to the one from *Ecclesiastes.*

As I have tried to show, modern writing at its worst does not consist in picking out words for the sake of their meaning and inventing images in order to make the meaning clearer. It consists in gumming together long strips of words which have already been set in order by someone else, and making the results presentable by sheer humbug. The attraction of this way of writing is that it is easy. It is easier—even quicker, once you have the habit—to say *In my opinion it is not an unjustifiable assumption that* than to say *I think.* If you use ready-made phrases, you not only don't have to hunt about for words; you also don't have to bother with the rhythms of your sentences, since these phrases are generally so arranged as to be more or less euphonious. When you are composing in a hurry—when you are dictating to a stenographer, for instance, or making a public speech—it is natural to fall into a pretentious, Latinized style. Tags like *a consideration which we should do well to bear in mind* or *a conclusion to which all of us would readily assent* will save many a sentence from coming down with a bump. By using stale metaphors, similes and idioms, you save much mental effort, at the cost of leaving your meaning vague, not only for your reader but for yourself. This is the significance of mixed metaphors. The sole aim of a metaphor is to call up a visual image. When these images clash—as in *The Fascist octopus has sung its swan song, the jackboot is thrown into the melting pot*—it can be taken as certain that the writer is not seeing a mental image of the objects he is naming; in other words he is not really thinking. Look again at the examples I gave at the beginning of this essay. Professor Laski (1) uses five negatives in fifty-three words. One of these is superfluous, making nonsense of the whole passage, and in addition there is the slip *alien* for *akin,* making further nonsense, and several avoidable pieces of clumsiness which increase the general vagueness. Professor Hogben (2) plays ducks and drakes with a battery which is able to write prescriptions, and while, disapproving of the everyday phrase *put up with,* is unwilling to look *egregious* up in the dictionary and see what it means; (3), if one takes an uncharitable attitude towards it, is simply meaningless: probably one could work out its intended meaning by reading the whole of the article in which it occurs. In (4), the writer knows more or less what he wants to say, but an accumulation of stale phrases chokes him like tea leaves blocking a sink. In (5), words and meaning have almost parted company. People who write in this manner usually have a general emotional meaning—they dislike one thing and want to express solidarity with another—but they are not interested in the detail of what they are saying. A scrupulous writer, in every sentence that he writes, will ask himself at least four questions, thus: What am I trying to say? What words will express it? What image or idiom will make it clearer? Is this image fresh enough to have an effect? And he will probably ask himself two more: Could I put it more shortly? Have I said anything that is avoidably ugly? But you are not obliged to go to all this trouble. You can shirk it by simply throwing your mind open and letting the ready-made phrases come crowding in. They will construct your sentences for you—even think your thoughts for you, to a certain extent—and at need they will perform the important service of partially concealing your meaning even from yourself. It is at this point that the special connection between politics and the debasement of language becomes clear.

In our time it is broadly true that political writing is bad writing. Where it is not true, it will generally be found that the writer is some kind of rebel, expressing his private opinions and not a "party line." Orthodoxy, of whatever color, seems to demand a lifeless, imitative style. The political dialects to be found in pamphlets, leading articles, manifestos, White Papers and the speeches of undersecretaries do, of course, vary from party to party, but they are all alike in that one almost never finds in them a fresh, vivid, home-made turn of speech. When one watches some tired hack on the platform mechanically repeating the familiar phrases—*bestial atrocities, iron heel, bloodstained tyranny, free peoples of the world, stand shoulder to shoulder*—one often has a curious feeling that one is not watching a live human being but some kind of dummy: a feeling which suddenly becomes stronger at moments when the light catches the speaker's spectacles and turns them into blank discs which seem to have no eyes behind them. And this is not altogether fanciful. A speaker who uses that kind of phraseology has gone some distance towards turning himself into a machine. The appropriate noises are coming out of his larynx, but his brain is not involved as it would be if he were choosing his words for himself. If the speech he is making is one that he is accustomed to make over and over again, he may be almost unconscious of what he is saying, as one is when one utters the responses in church. And this reduced state of consciousness, if not indispensable, is at any rate favorable to political conformity.

In our time, political speech and writing are largely the defense of the indefensible. Things like the continuance of British rule in India, the Russian purges and deportations, the dropping of the atom bombs on Japan, can indeed be defended, but only by arguments which are too brutal for most people to face, and which do not square with the professed aims of political parties. Thus political language has to consist largely of euphemism, question-begging and sheer cloudy vagueness. Defenseless villages are bombarded from the air, the inhabitants driven out into the countryside, the cattle machine-gunned, the huts set on fire with incendiary bullets: this is called *pacification.* Millions of peasants are robbed of their farms and sent trudging along the roads with no more than they can carry: this is called *transfer of population* or *rectification of frontiers.* People are imprisoned for years without trial, or shot in the back of the neck or sent to die of scurvy in Arctic lumber camps: this is called *elimination of unreliable elements.* Such phraseology is needed if one wants to name things without calling up mental pictures of them. Consider for instance some comfortable English professor defending Russian totalitarianism. He cannot say outright, "I believe in killing off your opponents when you can get good results by doing so." Probably, therefore, he will say something like this:

> While freely conceding that the Soviet regime exhibits certain features which the humanitarian may be inclined to deplore, we must, I think, agree that a certain curtailment of the right to political opposition is an unavoidable concomitant of transitional periods, and that the rigors which the Russian people have been called upon to undergo have been amply justified in the sphere of concrete achievement.

The inflated style is itself a kind of euphemism. A mass of Latin words falls upon the facts like soft snow, blurring the outlines and covering up all the details. The great enemy of clear language is insincerity. When there is a gap between one's real and one's declared aims, one turns as it were instinctively to long words and exhausted idioms, like a cuttlefish squirting out ink. In our age there is no such thing as "keeping out of politics." All issues are political issues, and politics itself is a mass of lies, evasions, folly, hatred and schizophrenia. When the general atmosphere is bad, language must suffer. I should expect to find—this is a guess which I have not sufficient knowledge to verify—that the German, Russian and Italian languages have all deteriorated in the last ten to fifteen years, as a result of dictatorship.

But if thought corrupts language, language can also corrupt thought. A bad usage can spread by tradition and imitation, even among people who should and do know better. The debased language that I have been discussing is in some ways very convenient. Phrases like *a not unjustifiable assumption, leaves much to be desired, would serve no good purpose, a consideration which we should do well to bear in mind,* are a continuous temptation, a packet of aspirins always at one's elbow. Look back through this essay, and for certain you will find that I have again and again committed the very faults I am protesting against. By this morning's post I have received a pamphlet dealing with conditions in Germany. The author tells me that he "felt impelled" to write it. I open it at random, and here is almost the first sentence that I see: "[The Allies] have an opportunity not only of achieving a radical transformation of Germany's social and political structure in such a way as to avoid a nationalistic reaction in Germany itself, but at the same time of laying the foundations of a cooperative and unified Europe." You see, he "feels impelled" to write—feels, presumably, that he has something new to say—and yet his words, like cavalry horses answering the bugle, group themselves automatically into the familiar dreary pattern. This invasion of one's mind by ready-made phrases (*lay the foundations, achieve a radical transformation*) can only be prevented if one is constantly on guard against them, and every such phrase anaesthetizes a portion of one's brain.

I said earlier that the decadence of our language is probably curable. Those who deny this would argue, if they produced an argument at all, that language merely reflects existing social conditions, and that we cannot influence its development by any direct tinkering with words and constructions. So far as the general tone or spirit of a language goes, this may be true, but it is not true in detail. Silly words and expressions have often disappeared, not through any evolutionary process but owing to the conscious action of a minority. Two recent examples were *explore every avenue* and *leave no stone unturned,* which were killed by the jeers of a few journalists. There is a long list of flyblown metaphors which could similarly be got rid of if enough people would interest themselves in the job; and it should also be possible to laugh the *not un-* formation out of existence,[3] to reduce the amount of Latin and Greek in the average sentence, to drive out foreign phrases and strayed scientific words, and, in general, to make pretentiousness unfashionable. But all these are minor points. The defense of the English language implies more than this, and perhaps it is best to start by saying what it does *not* imply.

To begin with it has nothing to do with archaism, with the salvaging of obsolete words and turns of speech, or with the setting up of a "standard English" which must never be departed from. On the contrary, it is especially concerned with the scrapping of every word or idiom which has outworn its usefulness. It has nothing to do with correct grammar and syntax, which are of no importance so long as one makes one's meaning clear, or with the avoidance of Americanisms, or with having what is called a "good prose style." On the other hand it is not concerned with fake simplicity and the attempt to make written English colloquial. Nor does it even imply in every case preferring the Saxon word to the Latin one, though it does imply using the fewest and shortest words that will cover one's meaning. What is above all needed is to let the meaning choose the word, and not the other way about. In prose, the worst thing one can do with words is to surrender to them. When you think of a concrete object, you think wordlessly, and then, if you want to describe the thing you have been visualizing you probably hunt about till you find the exact words that seem to fit it. When you think of something abstract you are more inclined to use words from the start, and unless you make a conscious effort to prevent it, the existing dialect will come rushing in and do the job for you, at the expense of blurring or even changing your meaning. Probably it is better to put off using words as long as possible and get one's meaning as clear as one can through pictures or sensations. Afterwards one can choose—not simply *accept*—the phrases that will best cover the meaning, and then switch round and decide what impression one's words are likely to make on another person. This last effort of the mind cuts out all stale

[3]One can cure oneself of the *not un-* formation by memorizing this sentence: *A not unblack dog was chasing a not unsmall rabbit across a not ungreen field.*

or mixed images, all prefabricated phrases, needless repetitions, and humbug and vagueness generally. But one can often be in doubt about the effect of a word or a phrase, and one needs rules that one can rely on when instinct fails. I think the following rules will cover most cases:

(i) Never use a metaphor, simile or other figure of speech which you are used to seeing in print.
(ii) Never use a long word where a short one will do.
(iii) If it is possible to cut a word out, always cut it out.
(iv) Never use the passive where you can use the active.
(v) Never use a foreign phrase, a scientific word or a jargon word if you can think of an everyday English equivalent.
(vi) Break any of these rules sooner than say anything outright barbarous.

These rules sound elementary, and so they are, but they demand a deep change of attitude in anyone who has grown used to writing in the style now fashionable. One could keep all of them and still write bad English, but one could not write the kind of stuff that I quoted in those five specimens at the beginning of this article.

I have not here been considering the literary use of language, but merely language as an instrument for expressing and not for concealing or preventing thought. Stuart Chase and others have come near to claiming that all abstract words are meaningless, and have used this as a pretext for advocating a kind of political quietism. Since you don't know what Fascism is, how can you struggle against Fascism? One need not swallow such absurdities as this, but one ought to recognize that the present political chaos is connected with the decay of language, and that one can probably bring about some improvement by starting at the verbal end. If you simplify your English, you are freed from the worst follies of orthodoxy. You cannot speak any of the necessary dialects, and when you make a stupid remark its stupidity will be obvious, even to yourself. Political language—and with variations this is true of all political parties, from Conservatives to Anarchists—is designed to make lies sound truthful and murder respectable, and to give an appearance of solidity to pure wind. One cannot change this all in a moment, but one can at least change one's own habits, and from time to time one can even, if one jeers loudly enough, send some worn-out and useless phrase—some *jackboot, Achilles' heel, hotbed, melting pot, acid test, veritable inferno* or other lump of verbal refuse—into the dustbin where it belongs.

## Questions

1. Revise one or two of Orwell's examples of bad writing.
2. Examine Orwell's metaphors. Do they fulfill his requirements for good writing?
3. Look again at Orwell's grotesque revision (page 352) of a passage from the Bible. Write a similar version of another passage from the Bible.
4. Can you recall any occasion when you have used words, in writing or speaking, in a consciously dishonest way? If so, can you explain why, or go further and justify your behavior?
5. In the second paragraph Orwell says: "Written English is full of bad habits which spread by imitation." Are you aware of having acquired any bad writing habits by imitation? If so, imitation of what or whom?

Barbara Lawrence

# Four-Letter Words Can Hurt You

Why should any words be called obscene? Don't they all describe natural human functions? Am I trying to tell them, my students demand, that the "strong, earthy, gut-honest"—or, if they are fans of Norman Mailer, the "rich, liberating, existential"—language they use to describe sexual activity isn't preferable to "phony-sounding, middle-class words like 'intercourse' and 'copulate'?" "Cop You Late!" they say with fancy inflections and gagging grimaces. "Now, what is *that* supposed to mean?"

Well, what is it supposed to mean? And why indeed should one group of words describing human functions and human organs be acceptable in ordinary conversation and another, describing presumably the same organs and functions, be tabooed—so much so, in fact,

Barbara Lawrence was born in Hanover, New Hampshire, and she was educated at Connecticut College and at New York University. She teaches at the State University of New York, at Old Westbury.

that some of these words still cannot appear in print in many parts of the English-speaking world?

The argument that these taboos exist only because of "sexual hangups" (middle-class, middle-age, feminist), or even that they are a result of class oppression (the contempt of the Norman conquerors for the language of their Anglo-Saxon serfs), ignores a much more likely explanation, it seems to me, and that is the sources and functions of the words themselves.

The best known of the tabooed sexual verbs, for example, comes from the German *ficken,* meaning "to strike"; combined, according to Partridge's etymological dictionary *Origins,* with the Latin sexual verb *futuere;* associated in turn with the Latin *fustis,* "a staff or cudgel"; the Celtic *buc,* "a point, hence to pierce"; the Irish *bot,* "the male member"; the Latin *battuere,* "to beat"; the Gaelic *batair,* "a cudgeller"; the Early Irish *bualaim,* "I strike"; and so forth. It is one of what etymologists sometimes call "the sadistic group of words for the man's part in copulation."

The brutality of this word, then, and its equivalents ("screw," "bang," etc.), is not an illusion of the middle class or a crotchet of Women's Liberation. In their origins and imagery these words carry undeniably painful, if not sadistic, implications, the object of which is almost always female. Consider, for example, what a "screw" actually does to the wood it penetrates; what a painful, even mutilating, activity this kind of analogy suggests. "Screw" is particularly interesting in this context, since the noun, according to Partridge, comes from words meaning "groove," "nut," "ditch," "breeding sow," "scrofula" and "swelling," while the verb, besides its explicit imagery, has antecedent associations to "write on," "scratch," "scarify," and so forth—a revealing fusion of a mechanical or painful action with an obviously denigrated object.

Not all obscene words, of course, are as implicitly sadistic or denigrating to women as these, but all that I know seem to serve a similar purpose: to reduce the human organism (especially the female organism) and human functions (especially sexual and procreative) to their least organic, most mechanical dimension; to substitute a trivializing or deforming resemblance for the complex human reality of what is being described.

Tabooed male descriptives, when they are not openly denigrating to women, often serve to divorce a male organ or function from any significant interaction with the female. Take the word "testes," for example, suggesting "witnesses" (from the Latin *testis*) to the sexual and procreative strengths of the male organ; and the obscene counterpart of this word, which suggests little more than a mechanical shape. Or compare almost any of the "rich," "liberating" sexual verbs, so fashionable today among male writers, with that much-derided Latin word "copulate" ("to bind or join together") or even that Anglo-Saxon phrase (which seems to have had no trouble surviving the Norman Conquest) "make love."

How arrogantly self-involved the tabooed words seem in comparison to either of the other terms, and how contemptuous of the female partner. Understandably so, of course, if she is only a "skirt," a "broad," a "chick," a "pussycat" or a "piece." If she is, in other words, no more than her skirt, or what her skirt conceals; no more than a breeder, or the broadest part of her; no more than a piece of a human being or a "piece of tail."

The most severely tabooed of all the female descriptives, incidentally, are those like a "piece of tail," which suggest (either explicitly or through antecedents) that there is no significant difference between the female channel through which we are all conceived and born and the anal outlet common to both sexes—a distinction that pornographers have always enjoyed obscuring.

This effort to deny women their biological identity, their individuality, their humanness, is such an important aspect of obscene language that one can only marvel at how seldom, in an era preoccupied with definitions of obscenity, this fact is brought to our attention. One problem, of course, is that many of the people in the best position to do this (critics, teachers, writers) are so reluctant today to admit that they are angered or shocked by obscenity. Bored, maybe, unimpressed, aesthetically displeased, but—no matter how brutal or denigrating the material—never angered, never shocked.

And yet how eloquently angered, how piously shocked many of these same people become if denigrating language is used about any minority group other than women; if the obscenities are racial or ethnic, that is, rather than sexual. Words like "coon," "kike," "spic," "wop," after all, deform identity, deny individuality and humanness in almost exactly the same way that sexual vulgarisms and obscenities do.

No one that I know, least of all my students, would fail to question the values of a society whose literature and entertainment rested heavily on racial or ethnic pejoratives. Are the values of a society whose literature and entertainment rest as heavily as ours on sexual pejoratives any less questionable?

## Question

In addition to giving evidence to support her view, what persuasive devices (such as irony, analogy) does Lawrence use?

C. S. Lewis

# Xmas and Christmas

### A Lost Chapter from Herodotus

And Beyond this there lies in the ocean, turned towards the west and north, the island of Niatirb which Hecataeus indeed declares to be the same size and shape as Sicily, but it is larger, though in calling it triangular a man would not miss the mark. It is densely inhabited by men who wear clothes not very different from the other barbarians who occupy the north-western parts of Europe though they do not agree with them in language. These islanders, surpassing all the men of whom we know in patience and endurance, use the following customs.

In the middle of winter when fogs and rains most abound they have a great festival which they call Exmas, and for fifty days they prepare for it in the fashion I shall describe. First of all, every citizen is obliged to send to each of his friends and relations a square piece of hard paper stamped with a picture, which in their speech is called an Exmas-card. But the pictures represent birds sitting on branches, or trees with a dark green prickly leaf, or else men in such garments as the Niatirbians believe that their ancestors wore two hundred years ago riding in coaches such as their ancestors used, or houses with snow on their roofs. And the Niatirbians are unwilling to say what these pictures have to do with the festival, guarding (as I suppose) some sacred mystery. And because all men must send these

---

C[live] S[taples] Lewis (1898–1963) taught medieval and Renaissance literature at Oxford and later at Cambridge. He wrote about literature, and he wrote fiction (including children's books), poetry, and numerous essays and books on Christianity, from the point of view of a believer.

cards the market-place is filled with the crowd of those buying them, so that there is great labour and weariness.

But having bought as many as they suppose to be sufficient, they return to their houses and find there the like cards which others have sent to them. And when they find cards from any to whom they also have sent cards, they throw them away and give thanks to the gods that this labour at least is over for another year. But when they find cards from any to whom they have not sent, then they beat their breasts and wail and utter curses against the sender; and, having sufficiently lamented their misfortune, they put on their boots again and go out into the fog and rain and buy a card for him also. And let this account suffice about Exmas-cards.

They also send gifts to one another, suffering the same things about the gifts as about the cards, or even worse. For every citizen has to guess the value of the gift which every friend will send to him so that he may send one of equal value, whether he can afford it or not. And they buy as gifts for one another such things as no man ever bought for himself. For the sellers, understanding the custom, put forth all kinds of trumpery, and whatever, being useless and ridiculous, they have been unable to sell throughout the year they now sell as an Exmas gift. And though the Niatirbians profess themselves to lack sufficient necessary things, such as metal, leather, wood and paper, yet an incredible quantity of these things is wasted every year, being made into the gifts.

But during these fifty days the oldest, poorest and most miserable of the citizens put on false beards and red robes and walk about the market-place; being disguised (in my opinion) as *Cronos.* And the sellers of gifts no less than the purchasers become pale and weary, because of the crowds and the fog, so that any man who came into a Niatirbian city at this season would think some great public calamity had fallen on Niatirb. This fifty days of preparation is called in their barbarian speech the Exmas *Rush.*

But when the day of the festival comes, then most of the citizens, being exhausted with the *Rush,* lie in bed till noon. But in the evening they eat fives times as much supper as on other days and, crowning themselves with crowns of paper, they become intoxicated. And on the day after Exmas they are very grave, being internally disordered by the supper and the drinking and reckoning how much they have spent on gifts and on the wine. For wine is so dear among the Niatirbians that a man must swallow the worth of a talent before he is well intoxicated.

Such, then, are their customs about the Exmas. But the few

among the Niatirbians have also a festival, separate and to themselves, called Crissmas, which is on the same day as Exmas. And those who keep Crissmas, doing the opposite to the majority of the Niatirbians, rise early on that day with shining faces and go before sunrise to certain temples where they partake of a sacred feast. And in most of the temples they set out images of a fair woman with a new-born Child on her knees and certain animals and shepherds adoring the Child. (The reason of these images is given in a certain sacred story which I know but do not repeat.)

But I myself conversed with a priest in one of these temples and asked him why they kept Crissmas on the same day as Exmas; for it appeared to me inconvenient. But the priest replied, It is not lawful, O Stranger, for us to change the date of Crissmas, but would that Zeus would put it into the minds of the Niatirbians to keep Exmas at some other time or not to keep it at all. For Exmas and the *Rush* distract the minds even of the few from sacred things. And we indeed are glad that men should make merry at Crissmas; but in Exmas there is no merriment left. And when I asked him why they endured the *Rush,* he replied, It is, O Stranger, a *racket;* using (as I suppose) the words of some oracle and speaking unintelligibly to me (for a *racket* is an instrument which the barbarians use in a game called *tennis*).

But what Hecataeus says, that Exmas and Crissmas are the same, is not credible. For first, the pictures which are stamped on the Exmas-cards have nothing to do with the sacred story which the priests tell about Crissmas. And secondly, the most part of the Niatirbians, not believing the religion of the few, nevertheless send the gifts and cards and participate in the *Rush* and drink, wearing paper caps. But it is not likely that men, even being barbarians, should suffer so many and great things in honour of a god they do not believe in. And now, enough about Niatirb.

## Questions

1. An encyclopedia, or even a dictionary, will give you some information about Herodotus. Check your library for a copy of Herodotus's *History,* read a few pages in it, and then point to two or three places where Lewis has captured something of the flavor of Herodotus.
2. In this semicomic piece, Lewis is making a serious point. What is it?
3. Lewis, an Englishman (let's say a citizen of Great Britain) wrote about Niatirb. Write another lost chapter from Herodotus, describing a custom celebrated in Acirema (or your college, dormitory, or wherever).

4. In an essay of 500 words, compare Lewis's essay with Arlen's "Ode to Thanksgiving" (page 105). What is the main point of each? By what means does each essay make its point? (Explain both the similarities and differences.) Evaluate and compare the success of each essay as (a) persuasion and (b) entertainment.

## Edward T. Hall

# Proxemics in the Arab World

In spite of over two thousand years of contact, Westerners and Arabs still do not understand each other. Proxemic research reveals some insights into this difficulty. Americans in the Middle East are immediately struck by two conflicting sensations. In public they are compressed and overwhelmed by smells, crowding, and high noise levels; in Arab homes Americans are apt to rattle around, feeling exposed and often somewhat inadequate because of too much space! (The Arab houses and apartments of the middle and upper classes which Americans stationed abroad commonly occupy are much larger than the dwellings such Americans usually inhabit.) Both the high sensory stimulation which is experienced in public places and the basic insecurity which comes from being in a dwelling that is too large provide Americans with an introduction to the sensory world of the Arab.

---

Edward T. Hall was born in Missouri in 1914. He is a professor of anthropology at Northwestern University.

Hall is especially concerned with "proxemics," a word derived from the Latin *proximus,* "nearest." Proxemics is the study of people's responses to spatial relationships—for example, their ways of marking out their territory in public places, and their responses to what they consider to be crowding. In these pages from his book *The Hidden Dimension* (1966), Hall suggests that Arabs and Westerners must understand the proxemic customs of each other's culture; without such understanding, other communications between them are likely to be misunderstood.

*Behavior in Public*

Pushing and shoving in public places is characteristic of Middle Eastern culture. Yet it is not entirely what Americans think it is (being pushy and rude) but stems from a different set of assumptions concerning not only the relations between people but how one experiences the body as well. Paradoxically, Arabs consider northern Europeans and Americans pushy, too. This was very puzzling to me when I started investigating these two views. How could Americans who stand aside and avoid touching be considered pushy? I used to ask Arabs to explain this paradox. None of my subjects was able to tell me specifically what particulars of American behavior were responsible, yet they all agreed that the impression was widespread among Arabs. After repeated unsuccessful attempts to gain insight into the cognitive world of the Arab on this particular point, I filed it away as a question that only time would answer. When the answer came, it was because of a seemingly inconsequential annoyance.

While waiting for a friend in a Washington, D.C., hotel lobby and wanting to be both visible and alone, I had seated myself in a solitary chair outside the normal stream of traffic. In such a setting most Americans follow a rule, which is all the more binding because we seldom think about it, that can be stated as follows: as soon as a person stops or is seated in a public place, there balloons around him a small sphere of privacy which is considered inviolate. The size of the sphere varies with the degree of crowding, the age, sex, and the importance of the person, as well as the general surroundings. Anyone who enters this zone and stays there is intruding. In fact, a stranger who intrudes, even for a specific purpose, acknowledges the fact that he has intruded by beginning his request with "Pardon me, but can you tell me . . . ?"

To continue, as I waited in the deserted lobby, a stranger walked up to where I was sitting and stood close enough so that not only could I easily touch him but I could even hear him breathing. In addition, the dark mass of his body filled the peripheral field of vision on my left side. If the lobby had been crowded with people, I would have understood his behavior, but in an empty lobby his presence made me exceedingly uncomfortable. Feeling annoyed by this intrusion, I moved my body in such a way as to communicate annoyance. Strangely enough, instead of moving away, my actions seemed only to encourage him, because he moved even closer. In spite of the temptation to escape the annoyance, I put aside thoughts of abandoning my post, thinking, "To hell with it. Why should I move? I was here first and I'm not going to let this fellow drive me out even if he is a boor." Fortunately, a group of people soon arrived whom my tormentor immediately joined. Their mannerisms explained his behavior, for I knew from both speech and gestures that they were Arabs. I had not been able to make this crucial identification by looking at my subject when he was alone because he wasn't talking and he was wearing American clothes.

In describing the scene later to an Arab colleague, two contrasting patterns emerged. My concept and my feelings about my own circle of privacy in a "public" place immediately struck my Arab friend as strange and puzzling. He said, "After all, it's a public place, isn't it?" Pursuing this line of inquiry, I found that an Arab thought I had no rights whatsoever by virtue of occupying a given spot; neither my place nor my body was inviolate! For the Arab, there is no such thing as an intrusion in public. Public means public. With this insight, a great range of Arab behavior that had been puzzling, annoying, and sometimes even frightening began to make sense. I learned, for example, that if *A* is standing on a street corner and *B* wants his spot, *B* is within his rights if he does what he can to make *A* uncomfortable enough to move. In Beirut only the hardy sit in the last row in a movie theater, because there are usually standees who want seats and who push and shove and make such a nuisance that most people give up and leave. Seen in this light, the Arab who "intruded" on my space in the hotel lobby had apparently selected it for the very reason I had: it was a good place to watch two doors and the elevator. My show of annoyance, instead of driving him away, had only encouraged him. He thought he was about to get me to move.

Another silent source of friction between Americans and Arabs is in an area that Americans treat very informally—the manners and rights of the road. In general, in the United States we tend to defer to the vehicle that is bigger, more powerful, faster, and heavily laden. While a pedestrian walking along a road may feel annoyed he will not think it unusual to step aside for a fast-moving automobile. He knows that because he is moving he does not have the right to the space around him that he has when he is standing still (as I was in the hotel lobby). It appears that the reverse is true with the Arabs who apparently *take on rights to space as they move.* For someone else to move into a space an Arab is also moving into is a violation of his rights. It is infuriating to an Arab to have someone else cut in front of him on the highway. It is the American's cavalier treatment of moving space that makes the Arab call him aggressive and pushy.

*Concepts of Privacy*

The experience described above and many others suggested to me that Arabs might actually have a wholly contrasting set of assumptions concerning the body and the rights associated with it. Certainly the Arab tendency to shove and push each other in public and to feel and pinch women in public conveyances would not be tolerated by Westerners. It appeared to me that they must not have any concept of a private zone outside the body. This proved to be precisely the case.

In the Western world, the person is synonymous with an individual inside a skin. And in northern Europe generally, the skin and even the clothes may be inviolate. You need permission to touch either if you are a stranger. This rule applies in some parts of France, where the mere touching of another person during an argument used to be legally defined as assault. For the Arab the location of the person in relation to the body is quite different. The person exists somewhere down inside the body. The ego is not completely hidden, however, because it can be reached very easily with an insult. It is protected from touch but not from words. The dissociation of the body and the ego may explain why the public amputation of a thief's hand is tolerated as standard punishment in Saudi Arabia. It also sheds light on why an Arab employer living in a modern apartment can provide his servant with a room that is a boxlike cubicle approximately 5 by 10 by 4 feet in size that is not only hung from the ceiling to conserve floor space but has an opening so that the servant can be spied on.

As one might suspect, deep orientations toward the self such as the one just described are also reflected in the language. This was brought to my attention one afternoon when an Arab colleague who is the author of an Arab-English dictionary arrived in my office and threw himself into a chair in a state of obvious exhaustion. When I asked him what had been going on, he said: "I have spent the entire afternoon trying to find the Arab equivalent of the English word 'rape.' There is no such word in Arabic. All my sources, both written and spoken, can come up with no more than an approximation, such as 'He took her against her will.' There is nothing in Arabic approaching your meaning as it is expressed in that one word."

Differing concepts of the placement of the ego in relation to the body are not easily grasped. Once an idea like this is accepted, however, it is possible to understand many other facets of Arab life that would otherwise be difficult to explain. One of these is the high population density of Arab cities like Cairo, Beirut, and Damascus. According to the animal studies described in the earlier chapters, the Arabs should be living in a perpetual behavioral sink. While it is probable that Arabs are suffering from population pressures, it is also just as possible that continued pressure from the desert has resulted in a cultural adaptation to high density which takes the form described above. Tucking the ego down inside the body shell not only would permit higher population densities but would explain why it is that Arab communications are stepped up as much as they are when compared to northern European communication patterns. Not only is the sheer noise level much higher, but the piercing look of the eyes, the touch of the hands, and the mutual bathing in the warm moist breath during conversation represent stepped-up sensory inputs to a level which many Europeans find unbearably intense.

The Arab dream is for lots of space in the home, which unfortunately many Arabs cannot afford. Yet when he has space, it is very different from what one finds in most American homes. Arab spaces inside their upper middle-class homes are tremendous by our standards. They avoid partitions because Arabs *do not like to be alone.* The form of the home is such as to hold the family together inside a single protective shell, because Arabs are deeply involved with each other. Their personalities are intermingled and take nourishment from each other like the roots and soil. If one is not with people and actively involved in some way, one is deprived of life. An old Arab saying reflects this value: "Paradise without people should not be entered because it is Hell." Therefore, Arabs in the United States often feel socially and sensorially deprived and long to be back where there is human warmth and contact.

Since there is no physical privacy as we know it in the Arab family, not even a word for privacy, one could expect that the Arabs might use some other means to be alone. Their way to be alone is to stop talking. Like the English, an Arab who shuts himself off in this way is not indicating that anything is wrong or that he is withdrawing, only that he wants to be alone with his own thoughts or does not want to be intruded upon. One subject said that her father would come and go for days at a time without saying a word, and no one in the family thought anything of it. Yet for this very reason, an Arab exchange student visiting a Kansas farm failed to pick up the cue that his American hosts were mad at him when they gave him the "silent treatment." He only discovered something was wrong when they took him to town and tried forcibly to put him on a bus to Washington, D.C., the headquarters of the exchange program responsible for his presence in the U.S.

## *Arab Personal Distances*

Like everyone else in the world, Arabs are unable to formulate specific rules for their informal behavior patterns. In fact, they often deny that there are any rules, and they are made anxious by suggestions that such is the case. Therefore, in order to determine how the Arab sets distances, I investigated the use of each sense separately. Gradually, definite and distinctive behavioral patterns began to emerge.

Olfaction occupies a prominent place in the Arab life. Not only is it one of the distance-setting mechanisms, but it is a vital part of a complex system of behavior. Arabs consistently breathe on people when they talk. However, this habit is more than a matter of different manners. To the Arab good smells are pleasing and a way of being involved with each other. To smell one's friend is not only nice but desirable, for to deny him your breath is to act ashamed. Americans, on the other hand, trained as they are not to breathe in people's faces, automatically communicate shame in trying to be polite. Who would expect that when our highest diplomats are putting on their best manners they are also communicating shame? Yet this is what occurs constantly, because diplomacy is not only "eyeball to eyeball" but breath to breath.

By stressing olfaction, Arabs do not try to eliminate all the body's odors, only to enhance them and use them in building human relationships. Nor are they self-conscious about telling others when they don't like the way they smell. A man leaving his house in the morning may be told by his uncle, "Habib, your stomach is sour and your breath doesn't smell too good. Better not talk too close to people today." Smell is even considered in the choice of a mate. When couples are being matched for marriage, the man's go-between will sometimes ask to smell the girl, who may be turned down if she doesn't "smell nice." Arabs recognize that smell and disposition may be linked.

In a word, the olfactory boundary performs two roles in Arab life. It enfolds those who want to relate and separates those who don't. The Arab finds it essential to stay inside the olfactory zone as a means of keeping tab on changes in emotion. What is more, he may feel crowded as soon as he smells something unpleasant. While not much is known about "olfactory crowding," this may prove to be as significant as any other variable in the crowding complex because it is tied directly to the body chemistry and hence to the state of health and emotions. It is not surprising, therefore, that the olfactory boundary constitutes for the Arabs an informal distance-setting mechanism in contrast to the visual mechanisms of the Westerner.

### *Facing and Not Facing*

One of my earliest discoveries in the field of intercultural communication was that the position of the bodies of people in conversation varies with the culture. Even so, it used to puzzle me that a special Arab friend seemed unable to walk and talk at the same time. After years in the United States, he could not bring himself to stroll along, facing forward while talking. Our progress would be arrested while he edged ahead, cutting slightly in front of me and turning sideways so we could see each other. Once in this position, he would stop. His behavior was explained when I learned that for the Arabs to view the other person peripherally is regarded as impolite, and to sit or stand back-to-back is considered very rude. You must be involved when interacting with Arabs who are friends.

One mistaken American notion is that Arabs conduct all conversations at close distances. This is not the case at all. On social occasions, they may sit on opposite sides of the room and talk across the room to each other. They are, however, apt to take offense when Americans use what are to them ambiguous distances, such as the four- to seven-foot social-consultative distance. They frequently complain that Americans are cold or aloof or "don't care." This was what an elderly Arab diplomat in an American hospital thought when the American nurses used "professional" distance. He had the feeling that he was being ignored, that they might not take good care of him. Another Arab subject remarked, referring to American behavior, "What's the matter? Do I smell bad? Or are they afraid of me?"

Arabs who interact with Americans report experiencing a certain flatness traceable in part to a very different use of the eyes in private and in public as well as between friends and strangers. Even though it is rude for a guest to walk around the Arab home eying things, Arabs look at each other in ways which seem hostile or challenging to the American. One Arab informant said that he was in constant hot water with Americans because of the way he looked at them without the slightest intention of offending. In fact, he had on several occasions barely avoided fights with American men who apparently thought their masculinity was being challenged because of the way he was looking at them. As noted earlier, Arabs look each other in the eye when talking with an intensity that makes most Americans highly uncomfortable.

### *Involvement*

As the reader must gather by now, Arabs are involved with each other on many different levels simultaneously. Privacy in a public place is foreign to them. Business transactions in the bazaar, for example, are not just between buyer and seller, but are participated in by everyone. Anyone who is standing around may join in. If a grownup sees a boy breaking a window, he must stop him even if he doesn't know him. Involvement and participation are expressed in other ways as well. If two men are fighting, the crowd must intervene. On the political level, *to fail to intervene* when trouble is brewing is to take sides, which is what our State Department always seems to be doing. Given the fact that few people in the world today are even remotely aware of the cultural mold that forms their thoughts, it is normal for Arabs to view *our* behavior as though it stemmed from *their* own hidden set of assumptions.

### *Feelings About Enclosed Spaces*

In the course of my interviews with Arabs the term "tomb" kept cropping up in conjunction with enclosed space. In a word, Arabs don't mind being crowded by people but hate to be hemmed in by walls. They show a much greater overt sensitivity to architectural crowding than we do. Enclosed space must meet at least three requirements that I know of if it is to satisfy the Arabs: there must be plenty of unobstructed space in which to move around (possibly as much as a thousand square feet); very high ceilings—so high in fact that they do not normally impinge on the visual field; and, in addition, there must be an unobstructed view. It was spaces such as these in which the Americans referred to earlier felt so uncomfortable. One sees the Arab's need for a view expressed in many ways, even negatively, for to cut off a neighbor's view is one of the most effective ways of spiting him. In Beirut one can see what is known locally as the "spite house." It is nothing more than a thick, four-story wall, built at the end of a long fight between neighbors, on a narrow strip of land, for the express purpose of denying a view of the Mediterranean to any house built on the land behind. According to one of my informants, there is also a house on a small plot of land between Beirut and Damascus which is completely surrounded by a neighbor's wall built high enough to cut off the view from all windows!

### *Boundaries*

Proxemic patterns tell us other things about Arab culture. For example, the whole concept of the boundary as an abstraction is almost impossible to pin down. In one sense, there are no boundaries. "Edges" of towns, yes, but permanent boundaries out in the country (hidden lines), no. In the course of my work with Arab subjects I had a difficult time translating our concept of a boundary into terms which could be equated with theirs. In order to clarify the distinction's between the two very different definitions, I thought it might be helpful to pinpoint acts which constituted trespass. To date, I have been unable to discover anything even remotely resembling our own legal concept of trespass.

Arab behavior in regard to their own real estate is apparently an extension of, and therefore consistent with, their approach to the body. My subjects simply failed to respond whenever trespass was mentioned. They didn't seem to understand what I meant by this term. This may be explained by the fact that they organize relationships with each other according to closed social systems rather than spatially. For thousands of years Moslems, Marinites, Druses, and Jews have lived in their own villages, each with strong kin affiliations. Their hierarchy of loyalties is: first to one's self, then to kinsman, townsman, or tribesman, co-religionist and/or countryman. Anyone not in these categories is a stranger. Strangers and enemies are very closely linked, if not synonymous, in Arab thought. Trespass in this context is a matter of who you are, rather than a piece of land or a space with a boundary that can be denied to anyone and everyone, friend and foe alike.

In summary, proxemic patterns differ. By examining them it is possible to reveal hidden cultural frames that determine the structure of a given people's perceptual world. Perceiving the world differently leads to differential definitions of what constitutes crowded living, different interpersonal relations, and a different approach to both local and international politics.

## Questions

1. According to Hall, why do Arabs think Americans are pushy? And, again according to Hall, why do Arabs not consider themselves pushy?
2. Explain what Hall means by "cognitive world" (page 366, in the paragraph beginning "Pushing and shoving"); by "ego" (page 369, in the paragraph beginning "Differing concepts"); by "behavioral sink" (in the same paragraph, page 369). Then explain, for the benefit of someone who did not understand the terms, how you know what Hall means by each.
3. On page 368 Hall points out that there is no Arabic equivalent of the English word "rape." Can you provide an example of a similar gap in English or in another language? Does a cultural difference account for the linguistic difference?
4. On page 366 Hall says of a rule that it "is all the more binding because we seldom think about it." Is this generally true of rules? What examples or counter-examples support your view?

## Flannery O'Connor

# Revelation

The doctor's waiting room, which was very small, was almost full when the Turpins entered and Mrs. Turpin, who was very large, made it look even smaller by her presence. She stood looming at the head of the magazine table set in the center of it, a living demonstration that the room was inadequate and ridiculous. Her little bright black eyes took in all the patients as she sized up the seating situation. There was one vacant chair and a place on the sofa occupied by a blond child in a dirty blue romper who should have been told to move over and make room for the lady. He was five or six, but Mrs. Turpin saw at once that no one was going to tell him to move over. He was slumped down in the seat, his arms idle at his sides and his eyes idle in his head; his nose ran unchecked.

Mrs. Turpin put a firm hand on Claud's shoulder and said in a voice that included everyone that wanted to listen, "Claud, you sit in that chair there," and gave him a push down into the vacant one. Claud was florid and bald and sturdy, somewhat shorter than Mrs. Turpin, but he sat down as if he were accustomed to doing what she told him to.

Mrs. Turpin remained standing. The only man in the room besides Claud was a lean stringy old fellow with a rusty hand spread out on each knee, whose eyes were closed as if he were asleep or dead or pretending to be so as not to get up and offer her his seat. Her gaze settled agreeably on a well-dressed grey-haired lady whose eyes met hers and whose expression said: if that child belonged to me, he would have some manners and move over—there's plenty of room there for you and him too.

Claud looked up with a sigh and made as if to rise.

"Sit down," Mrs. Turpin said. "You know you're not supposed to stand on that leg. He has an ulcer on his leg," she explained.

---

Flannery O'Connor (1925–1964) was born in Georgia and spent most of her short life there. *The Complete Stories of Flannery O'Connor* received the National Book Award for fiction in 1971. Another posthumous volume, *Mystery and Manners,* includes essays on literature and an account of her experiences raising peacocks in Georgia. The most recent posthumous volume is a fascinating collection of letters, *The Habit of Being.*

Claud lifted his foot onto the magazine table and rolled his trouser leg up to reveal a purple swelling on a plump marble-white calf.

"My!" the pleasant lady said. "How did you do that?"

"A cow kicked him," Mrs. Turpin said.

"Goodness!" said the lady.

Claud rolled his trouser leg down.

"Maybe the little boy would move over," the lady suggested, but the child did not stir.

"Somebody will be leaving in a minute," Mrs. Turpin said. She could not understand why a doctor—with as much money as they made charging five dollars a day just to stick their head in the hospital door and look at you—couldn't afford a decent-sized waiting room. This one was hardly bigger than a garage. The table was cluttered with limp-looking magazines and at one end of it there was a big green glass ash tray full of cigaret butts and cotton wads with little blood spots on them. If she had had anything to do with the running of the place, that would have been emptied every so often. There were no chairs against the wall at the head of the room. It had a rectangular-shaped panel in it that permitted a view of the office where the nurse came and went and the secretary listened to the radio. A plastic fern in a gold pot sat in the opening and trailed its fronds down almost to the floor. The radio was softly playing gospel music.

Just then the inner door opened and a nurse with the highest stack of yellow hair Mrs. Turpin had ever seen put her face in the crack and called for the next patient. The woman sitting beside Claud grasped the two arms of her chair and hoisted herself up; she pulled her dress free from her legs and lumbered through the door where the nurse had disappeared.

Mrs. Turpin eased into the vacant chair, which held her tight as a corset. "I wish I could reduce," she said, and rolled her eyes and gave a comic sigh.

"Oh, *you* aren't fat," the stylish lady said.

"Ooooo I am too," Mrs. Turpin said. "Claud he eats all he wants to and never weighs over one hundred and seventy-five pounds, but me I just look at something good to eat and I gain some weight," and her stomach and shoulders shook with laughter. "You can eat all you want to, can't you, Claud?" she asked turning to him.

Claud only grinned.

"Well, as long as you have such a good disposition," the stylish lady said, "I don't think it makes a bit of difference what size you are. You just can't beat a good disposition."

Next to her was a fat girl of eighteen or nineteen, scowling into a thick blue book which Mrs. Turpin saw was entitled *Human Development.* The girl raised her head and directed her scowl at Mrs. Turpin as if she did not like her looks. She appeared annoyed that anyone should speak while she tried to read. The poor girl's face was blue with acne and Mrs. Turpin thought how pitiful it was to have a face like that at that age. She gave the girl a friendly smile but the girl only scowled the harder. Mrs. Turpin herself was fat but she had always had good skin, and, though she was forty-seven years old, there was not a wrinkle in her face except around her eyes from laughing too much.

Next to the ugly girl was the child, still in exactly the same position, and next to him was a thin leathery old woman in a cotton print dress. She and Claud had three sacks of chicken feed in their pump house that was in the same print. She had seen from the first that the child belonged with the old woman. She could tell by the way they sat—kind of vacant and white-trashy, as if they would sit there until Doomsday if nobody called and told them to get up. And at right angles but next to the well-dressed pleasant lady was a lank-faced woman who was certainly the child's mother. She had on a yellow sweat shirt and wine-colored slacks, both gritty-looking, and the rims of her lips were stained with snuff. Her dirty yellow hair was tied behind with a piece of red paper ribbon. Worse than niggers any day, Mrs. Turpin thought.

The gospel hymn playing was, "When I looked up and He looked down," and Mrs. Turpin, who knew it, supplied the last line mentally, "And wona these days I know I'll we-eara crown."

Without appearing to, Mrs. Turpin always noticed people's feet. The well-dressed lady had on red and grey suede shoes to match her dress. Mrs. Turpin had on her good black patent leather pumps. The ugly girl had on Girl Scout shoes and heavy socks. The old woman had on tennis shoes and the white-trashy mother had on what appeared to be bedroom slippers, black straw with gold braid threaded through them—exactly what you would have expected her to have on.

Sometimes at night when she couldn't go to sleep, Mrs. Turpin would occupy herself with the question of who she would have chosen to be if she couldn't have been herself. If Jesus had said to her before he made her, "There's only two places available for you. You can either be a nigger or white-trash," what would she have said? "Please, Jesus, please," she would have said, "just let me wait until there's another place available," and he would have said, "No, you have to go right now and I have only those two places so make up your mind." She would have wiggled and squirmed and begged and pleaded but it would have been no use and finally she would have said, "All right, make me a nigger then—but that don't mean a trashy one." And he would have made her a neat clean respectable Negro woman, herself but black.

Next to the child's mother was a red-headed youngish woman, reading one of the magazines and working a piece of chewing gum, hell for leather, as Claud would say. Mrs. Turpin could not see the woman's feet. She was not white-trash, just common. Sometimes Mrs. Turpin occupied herself at night naming the classes of people. On the bottom of the heap were most colored people, not the kind she would have been if she had been one, but most of them; then next to them—not above, just away from—were the white-trash; then above them were the home-owners, and above them the home-and-land owners, to which she and Claud belonged. Above she and Claud were people with a lot of money and much bigger houses and much more land. But here the complexity of it would begin to bear in on her, for some of the people with a lot of money were common and ought to be below she and Claud and some of the people who had good blood had lost their money and had to rent and then there were colored people who owned their homes and land as well. There was a colored dentist in town who had two red Lincolns and a swimming pool and a farm with registered white-face cattle on it. Usually by the time she had fallen asleep all the classes of people were moiling and roiling around in her head, and she would dream they were all crammed in together in a box car, being ridden off to be put in a gas oven.

"That's a beautiful clock," she said and nodded to her right. It was a big wall clock, the face encased in a brass sunburst.

"Yes, it's very pretty," the stylish lady said agreeably. "And right on the dot too," she added, glancing at her watch.

The ugly girl beside her cast an eye upward at the clock, smirked, then looked directly at Mrs. Turpin and smirked again. Then she returned her eyes to her book. She was obviously the lady's daughter because, although they didn't look anything alike as to disposition, they both had the same shape of face and the same blue eyes. On the lady they sparkled pleasantly but in the girl's seared face they appeared alternately to smolder and to blaze.

What if Jesus had said, "All right, you can be white-trash or a nigger or ugly"!

Mrs. Turpin felt an awful pity for the girl, though she thought it was one thing to be ugly and another to act ugly.

The woman with the snuff-stained lips turned around in her chair and looked up at the clock. Then she turned back and appeared to look a little to the side of Mrs. Turpin. There was a cast in one of her eyes. "You want to know wher you can get one of themther clocks?" she asked in a loud voice.

"No, I already have a nice clock," Mrs. Turpin said. Once somebody like her got a leg in the conversation, she would be all over it.

"You can get you one with green stamps," the woman said. "That's most likely wher he got hisn. Save you up enough, you can get you most anythang. I got me some joo'ry."

Ought to have got you a wash rag and some soap, Mrs. Turpin thought.

"I get contour sheets with mine," the pleasant lady said.

The daughter slammed her book shut. She looked straight in front of her, directly through Mrs. Turpin and on through the yellow curtain and the plate glass window which made the wall behind her. The girl's eyes seemed lit all of a sudden with a peculiar light, an unnatural light like night road signs give. Mrs. Turpin turned her head to see if there was anything going on outside that she should see, but she could not see anything. Figures passing cast only a pale shadow through the curtain. There was no reason the girl should single her out for her ugly looks.

"Miss Finley," the nurse said, cracking the door. The gum-chewing woman got up and passed in front of her and Claud and went into the office. She had on red high-heeled shoes.

Directly across the table, the ugly girl's eyes were fixed on Mrs. Turpin as if she had some very special reason for disliking her.

"This is wonderful weather, isn't it?" the girl's mother said.

"It's good weather for cotton if you can get the niggers to pick it," Mrs. Turpin said, "but niggers don't want to pick cotton any more. You can't get the white folks to pick it and now you can't get the niggers—because they got to be right up there with the white folks."

"They gonna *try* anyways," the white-trash woman said, leaning forward.

"Do you have one of those cotton-picking machines?" the pleasant lady asked.

"No," Mrs. Turpin said, "they leave half the cotton in the field. We don't have much cotton anyway. If you want to make it farming now, you have to have a little of everything. We got a couple of acres of cotton and a few hogs and chickens and just enough white-face that Claud can look after them himself."

"One thang I don't want," the white-trash woman said, wiping her mouth with the back of her hand. "Hogs. Nasty stinking things, a-gruntin and a-rootin all over the place."

Mrs. Turpin gave her the merest edge of her attention. "Our hogs are not dirty and they don't stink," she said. "They're cleaner than some children I've seen. Their feet never touch the ground. We have a pig-parlor—that's where you raise them on concrete," she explained to the pleasant lady, "and Claud scoots them down with the hose every afternoon and washes off the floor." Cleaner by far than that child right there, she thought. Poor nasty little thing. He had not moved except to put the thumb of his dirty hand into his mouth.

The woman turned her face away from Mrs. Turpin. "I know I wouldn't scoot down no hog with no hose," she said to the wall.

You wouldn't have no hog to scoot down, Mrs. Turpin said to herself.

"A-gruntin and a-rootin and a-groanin," the woman muttered.

"We got a little of everything," Mrs. Turpin said to the pleasant lady. "It's no use in having more than you can handle yourself with help like it is. We found enough niggers to pick our cotton this year but Claud he has to go after them and take them home again in the evening. They can't walk that half a mile. No they can't. I tell you," she said and laughed merrily, "I sure am tired of buttering up niggers, but you got to love em if you want em to work for you. When they come in the morning, I run out and I say, 'Hi yawl this morning?' and when Claud drives them off to the field I just wave to beat the band and they just wave back." And she waved her hand rapidly to illustrate.

"Like you read out of the same book," the lady said, showing she understood perfectly.

"Child, yes," Mrs. Turpin said. "And when they come in from

the field, I run out with a bucket of icewater. That's the way it's going to be from now on," she said. "You may as well face it."

"One thang I know," the white-trash woman said. "Two thangs I ain't going to do: love no niggers or scoot down no hog with no hose." And she let out a bark of contempt.

The look that Mrs. Turpin and the pleasant lady exchanged indicated they both understood that you had to *have* certain things before you could *know* certain things. But every time Mrs. Turpin exchanged a look with the lady, she was aware that the ugly girl's peculiar eyes were still on her, and she had trouble bringing her attention back to the conversation.

"When you got something," she said, "you got to look after it." And when you ain't got a thing but breath and britches, she added to herself, you can afford to come to town every morning and just sit on the Court House coping and spit.

A grotesque revolving shadow passed across the curtain behind her and was thrown palely on the opposite wall. Then a bicycle clattered down against the outside of the building. The door opened and a colored boy glided in with a tray from the drug store. It had two large red and white paper cups on it with tops on them. He was a tall, very black boy in discolored white pants and a green nylon shirt. He was chewing gum slowly, as if to music. He set the tray down in the office opening next to the fern and stuck his head through to look for the secretary. She was not in there. He rested his arms on the ledge and waited, his narrow bottom stuck out, swaying slowly to the left and right. He raised a hand over his head and scratched the base of his skull.

"You see that button there, boy?" Mrs. Turpin said. "You can punch that and she'll come. She's probably in the back somewhere."

"Is thas right?" the boy said agreeably, as if he had never seen the button before. He leaned to the right and put his finger on it. "She sometime out," he said and twisted around to face his audience, his elbows behind him on the counter. The nurse appeared and he twisted back again. She handed him a dollar and he rooted in his pocket and made the change and counted it out to her. She gave him fifteen cents for a tip and he went out with the empty tray. The heavy door swung to slowly and closed at length with the sound of suction. For a moment no one spoke.

"They ought to send all them niggers back to Africa," the white-trash woman said. "That's wher they come from in the first place."

"Oh, I couldn't do without my good colored friends," the pleasant lady said.

"There's a heap of things worse than a nigger," Mrs. Turpin agreed. "It's all kinds of them just like it's all kinds of us."

"Yes, and it takes all kinds to make the world go round," the lady said in her musical voice.

As she said it, the raw-complexioned girl snapped her teeth together. Her lower lip turned downwards and inside out, revealing the pale pink inside her mouth. After a second it rolled back up. It was the ugliest face Mrs. Turpin had ever seen anyone make and for a moment she was certain that the girl had made it at her. She was looking at her as if she had known and disliked her all her life—all of Mrs. Turpin's life, it seemed too, not just all the girl's life. Why, girl, I don't even know you, Mrs. Turpin said silently.

She forced her attention back to the discussion. "It wouldn't be practical to send them back to Africa," she said. "They wouldn't want to go. They got it too good here."

"Wouldn't be what they wanted—if I had anythang to do with it," the woman said.

"It wouldn't be a way in the world you could get all the niggers back over there," Mrs. Turpin said. "They'd be hiding out and lying down and turning sick on you and wailing and hollering and raring and pitching. It wouldn't be a way in the world to get them over there."

"They got over here," the trashy woman said. "Get back like they got over."

"It wasn't so many of them then," Mrs. Turpin explained.

The woman looked at Mrs. Turpin as if here was an idiot indeed but Mrs. Turpin was not bothered by the look, considering where it came from.

"Nooo," she said, "they're going to stay here where they can go to New York and marry white folks and improve their color. That's what they all want to do, every one of them, improve their color."

"You know what comes of that, don't you?" Claud asked.

"No, Claud, what?" Mrs Turpin said.

Claud's eyes twinkled. "White-faced niggers," he said with never a smile.

Everybody in the office laughed except the white-trash and the ugly girl. The girl gripped the book in her lap with white fingers. The trashy woman looked around her from face to face as if she thought they were all idiots. The old woman in the feed sack dress continued to gaze expressionless across the floor at the high-top shoes of the man opposite her, the one who had been pretending to be asleep when the Turpins came in. He was laughing heartily, his hands still spread out on his knees. The child had fallen to the side and was lying now almost face down in the old woman's lap.

While they recovered from their laughter, the nasal chorus on the radio kept the room from silence.

You go to blank blank
And I'll go to mine
But we'll all blank along
To-geth-ther,
And all along the blank
We'll hep eachother out
Smile-ling in any kind of
Weath-ther!

Mrs. Turpin didn't catch every word but she caught enough to agree with the spirit of the song and it turned her thoughts sober. To help anybody out that needed it was her philosophy of life. She never spared herself when she found somebody in need, whether they were white or black, trash or decent. And of all she had to be thankful for, she was most thankful that this was so. If Jesus had said, "You can be high society and have all the money you want and be thin and svelte-like, but you can't be a good woman with it," she would have had to say, "Well don't make me that then. Make me a good woman and it don't matter what else, how fat or how ugly or how poor!" Her heart rose. He had not made her a nigger or white-trash or ugly! He had made her herself and given her a little of everything. Jesus, thank you! she said. Thank you thank you thank you! Whenever she counted her blessings she felt as buoyant as if she weighed one hundred and twenty-five pounds instead of one hundred and eighty.

"What's wrong with your little boy?" the pleasant lady asked the white-trashy woman.

"He has a ulcer," the woman said proudly. "He ain't give me a minute's peace since he was born. Him and her are just alike," she said, nodding at the old woman, who was running her leathery fingers through the child's pale hair. "Look like I can't get nothing down them two but Co' Cola and candy."

That's all you try to get down em, Mrs. Turpin said to herself. Too lazy to light the fire. There was nothing you could tell her about people like them that she didn't know already. And it was not just that they didn't have anything. Because if you gave them everything, in two weeks it would all be broken or filthy or they would have chopped it up for lightwood. She knew all this from her own experience. Help them you must, but help them you couldn't.

All at once the ugly girl turned her lips inside out again. Her eyes were fixed like two drills on Mrs. Turpin. This time there was no mistaking that there was something urgent behind them.

Girl, Mrs. Turpin exclaimed silently, I haven't done a thing to you! The girl might be confusing her with somebody else. There was no need to sit by and let herself be intimidated. "You must be in college," she said boldly, looking directly at the girl. "I see you reading a book there."

The girl continued to stare and pointedly did not answer.

Her mother blushed at this rudeness. "The lady asked you a question, Mary Grace," she said under her breath.

"I have ears," Mary Grace said.

The poor mother blushed again. "Mary Grace goes to Wellesley College," she explained. She twisted one of the buttons on her dress. "In Massachusetts," she added with a grimace. "And in the summer she just keeps right on studying. Just reads all the time, a real book worm. She's done real well at Wellesley; she's taking English and Math and History and Psychology and Social Studies," she rattled on, "and I think it's too much. I think she ought to get out and have fun."

The girl looked as if she would like to hurl them all through the plate glass window.

"Way up north," Mrs. Turpin murmured and thought, well, it hasn't done much for her manners.

"I'd almost rather to have him sick," the white-trash woman said, wrenching the attention back to herself. "He's so mean when he ain't. Look like some children just take natural to meanness. It's some gets bad when they get sick but he was the opposite. Took sick and turned good. He don't give me no trouble now. It's me waitin to see the doctor," she said.

If I was going to send anybody back to Africa, Mrs. Turpin thought, it would be your kind, woman. "Yes, indeed," she said aloud, but looking up at the ceiling, "it's a heap of things worse than a nigger." And dirtier than a hog, she added to herself.

"I think people with bad dispositions are more to be pitied than anyone on earth," the pleasant lady said in a voice that was decidedly thin.

"I thank the Lord he has blessed me with a good one," Mrs. Turpin said. "The day has never dawned that I couldn't find something to laugh at."

"Not since she married me anyways," Claud said with a comical straight face.

Everybody laughed except the girl and the white-trash.

Mrs. Turpin's stomach shook. "He's such a caution," she said, "that I can't help but laugh at him."

The girl made a loud ugly noise through her teeth.

Her mother's mouth grew thin and tight. "I think the worst thing in the world," she said, "is an ungrateful person. To have everything and not appreciate it. I know a girl," she said, "who has parents who would give her anything, a little brother who loves her dearly, who is getting a good education, who wears the best clothes, but who can never say a kind word to anyone, who never smiles, who just criticizes and complains all day long."

"Is she too old to paddle?" Claud asked.

The girl's face was almost purple.

"Yes," the lady said, "I'm afraid there's nothing to do but leave her to her folly. Some day she'll wake up and it'll be too late."

"It never hurt anyone to smile," Mrs. Turpin said. "It just makes you feel better all over."

"Of course," the lady said sadly, "but there are just some people you can't tell anything to. They can't take criticism."

"If it's one thing I am," Mrs. Turpin said with feeling, "it's grateful. When I think who all I could have been besides myself and what all I got, a little of everything, and a good disposition besides, I just feel like shouting, 'Thank you, Jesus, for making everything the way it is!' It could have been different!" For one thing, somebody else could have got Claud. At the thought of this, she was flooded with gratitude and a terrible pang of joy ran through her. "Oh thank you, Jesus, Jesus, thank you!" she cried aloud.

The book struck her directly over her left eye. It struck almost at the same instant that she realized the girl was about to hurl it. Before she could utter a sound, the raw face came crashing across the table toward her, howling. The girl's fingers sank like clamps into the soft flesh of her neck. She heard the mother cry out and Claud shout, "Whoa!" There was an instant when she was certain that she was about to be in an earthquake.

All at once her vision narrowed and she saw everything as if it were happening in a small room far away, or as if she were looking at it through the wrong end of a telescope. Claud's face crumpled and fell out of sight. The nurse ran in, then out, then in again. Then the gangling figure of the doctor rushed out of the inner door. Magazines flew this way and that as the table turned over. The girl fell with a thud and Mrs. Turpin's vision suddenly reversed itself and she saw everything large instead of small. The eyes of the white-trashy woman were staring hugely at the floor. There the girl, held down on one side by the nurse and on the other by her mother, was wrenching and turning in their grasp. The doctor was kneeling astride her, trying to hold her arm down. He managed after a second to sink a long needle into it.

Mrs. Turpin felt entirely hollow except for her heart which swung from side to side as if it were agitated in a great empty drum of flesh.

"Somebody that's not busy call for the ambulance," the doctor said in the off-hand voice young doctors adopt for terrible occasions.

Mrs. Turpin could not have moved a finger. The old man who had been sitting next to her skipped nimbly into the office and made the call, for the secretary still seemed to be gone.

"Claud!" Mrs. Turpin called.

He was not in his chair. She knew she must jump up and find him but she felt like some one trying to catch a train in a dream, when everything moves in slow motion and the faster you try to run the slower you go.

"Here I am," a suffocated voice, very unlike Claud's, said.

He was doubled up in the corner on the floor, pale as paper, holding his leg. She wanted to get up and go to him but she could not move. Instead, her gaze was drawn slowly downward to the churning face on the floor, which she could see over the doctor's shoulder.

The girl's eyes stopped rolling and focused on her. They seemed a much lighter blue than before, as if a door that had been tightly closed behind them was now open to admit light and air.

Mrs. Turpin's head cleared and her power of motion returned. She leaned forward until she was looking directly into the fierce brilliant eyes. There was no doubt in her mind that the girl did know her, knew her in some intense and personal way, beyond time and place and condition. "What you got to say to me?" she asked hoarsely and held her breath, waiting, as for a revelation.

The girl raised her head. Her gaze locked with Mrs. Turpin's. "Go back to hell where you came from, you old wart hog," she whispered. Her voice was low but clear. Her eyes burned for a moment as if she saw with pleasure that her message had struck its target.

Mrs. Turpin sank back in her chair.

After a moment the girl's eyes closed and she turned her head wearily to the side.

The doctor rose and handed the nurse the empty syringe. He leaned over and put both hands for a moment on the mother's shoulders, which were shaking. She was sitting on the floor, her lips pressed together, holding Mary Grace's hand in her lap. The girl's fingers were gripped like a baby's around her thumb. "Go on to the hospital," he said. "I'll call and make the arrangements."

"Now let's see that neck," he said in a jovial voice to Mrs. Turpin. He began to inspect her neck with his two fingers. Two little moon-shaped lines like pink fish bones were indented over her windpipe. There was the beginning of an angry red swelling above her eye. His fingers passed over this also.

"Let me be," she said thickly and shook him off. "See about Claud. She kicked him."

"I'll see about him in a minute," he said and felt her pulse. He was a thin grey-haired man, given to pleasantries. "Go home and have yourself a vacation the rest of the day," he said and patted her on the shoulder.

Quit your pattin me, Mrs. Turpin growled to herself.

"And put an ice pack over that eye," he said. Then he went and squatted down beside Claud and looked at his leg. After a moment he pulled him up and Claud limped after him into the office.

Until the ambulance came, the only sounds in the room were the tremulous moans of the girl's mother, who continued to sit on the floor. The white-trash woman did not take her eyes off the girl. Mrs. Turpin looked straight ahead at nothing. Presently the ambulance drew up, a long dark shadow, behind the curtain. The attendants came in and set the stretcher down beside the girl and lifted her expertly onto it and carried her out. The nurse helped the mother gather up her things. The shadow of the ambulance moved silently away and the nurse came back in the office.

"That ther girl is going to be a lunatic, ain't she?" the white-trash woman asked the nurse, but the nurse kept on to the back and never answered her.

"Yes, she's going to be a lunatic," the white-trash woman said to the rest of them.

"Po' critter," the old woman murmured. The child's face was still in her lap. His eyes looked idly out over her knees. He had not moved during the disturbance except to draw one leg up under him.

"I thank Gawd," the white-trash woman said fervently, "I ain't a lunatic."

Claud came limping out and the Turpins went home.

As their pick-up truck turned into their own dirt road and made the crest of the hill, Mrs. Turpin gripped the window ledge and looked out suspiciously. The land sloped gracefully down through a field dotted with lavender weeds and at the start of the rise their small yellow frame house, with its little flower beds spread out around it like a fancy apron, sat primly in its accustomed place between two giant hickory trees. She would not have been startled to see a burnt wound between two blackened chimneys.

Neither of them felt like eating so they put on their house clothes and lowered the shade in the bedroom and lay down, Claud with his leg on a pillow and herself with a damp washcloth over her eye. The instant she was flat on her back, the image of a razor-backed hog with warts on its face and horns coming out behind its ears snorted into her head. She moaned, a low quiet moan.

"I am not," she said tearfully, "a wart hog. From hell." But the denial had no force. The girl's eyes and her words, even the tone of her voice, low but clear, directed only to her, brooked no repudiation. She had been singled out for the message, though there was trash in the room to whom it might justly have been applied. The full force of this fact struck her only now. There was a woman there who was neglecting her own child but she had been overlooked. The message had been given to Ruby Turpin, a respectable, hard-working, church-going woman. The tears dried. Her eyes began to burn instead with wrath.

She rose on her elbow and the washcloth fell into her hand. Claud was lying on his back, snoring. She wanted to tell him what the girl had said. At the same time, she did not wish to put the image of herself as a wart hog from hell into his mind.

"Hey, Claud," she muttered and pushed his shoulder.

Claud opened one pale baby blue eye.

She looked into it warily. He did not think about anything. He just went his way.

"Wha, whasit?" he said and closed the eye again.

"Nothing," she said. "Does your leg pain you?"

"Hurts like hell," Claud said.

"It'll quit terreckly," she said and lay back down. In a moment Claud was snoring again. For the rest of the afternoon they lay there. Claud slept. She scowled at the ceiling. Occasionally she raised her fist and made a small stabbing motion over her chest as if she was defending her innocence to invisible guests who were like the comforters of Job, reasonable-seeming but wrong.

About five-thirty Claud stirred. "Got to go after those niggers," he sighed, not moving.

She was looking straight up as if there were unintelligible handwriting on the ceiling. The protuberance over her eye had turned a greenish-blue. "Listen here," she said.

"What?"

"Kiss me."

Claud leaned over and kissed her loudly on the mouth. He pinched her side and their hands interlocked. Her expression of ferocious concentration did not change. Claud got up, groaning and growling, and limped off. She continued to study the ceiling.

She did not get up until she heard the pick-up truck coming back with the Negroes. Then she rose and thrust her feet in her brown oxfords, which she did not bother to lace, and stumped out onto the back porch and got her red plastic bucket. She emptied a tray of ice cubes into it and filled it half full of water and went out into the back yard. Every afternoon after Claud brought the hands in, one of the boys helped him put out hay and the rest waited in the back of the truck until he was ready to take them home. The truck was parked in the shade under one of the hickory trees.

"Hi yawl this evening?" Mrs. Turpin asked grimly, appearing with the bucket and the dipper. There were three women and a boy in the truck.

"Us doin nicely," the oldest woman said. "Hi you doin?" and her gaze struck immediately on the dark lump on Mrs. Turpin's forehead. "You done fell down, ain't you?" she asked in a solicitous voice. The old woman was dark and almost toothless. She had on an old felt hat of Claud's set back on her head. The other two women were younger and lighter and they both had new bright green sun hats. One of them had hers on her head; the other had taken hers off and the boy was grinning beneath it.

Mrs. Turpin set the bucket down on the floor of the truck. "Yawl hep yourselves," she said. She looked around to make sure Claud had gone. "No. I didn't fall down," she said, folding her arms. "It was something worse than that."

"Ain't nothing bad happen to you!" the old woman said. She said it as if they all knew that Mrs. Turpin was protected in some special way by Divine Providence. "You just had you a little fall."

"We were in town at the doctor's office for where the cow kicked Mr. Turpin," Mrs. Turpin said in a flat tone that indicated they could leave off their foolishness. "And there was this girl there. A big fat girl with her face all broke out. I could look at that girl and tell she was peculiar but I couldn't tell how. And me and her mama were just talking and going along and all of a sudden WHAM! She throws this big book she was reading at me and . . ."

"Naw!" the old woman cried out.

"And then she jumps over the table and commences to choke me."

"Naw!" they all exclaimed, "naw!"

"Hi come she do that?" the old woman asked. "What ail her?"

Mrs. Turpin only glared in front of her.

"Somethin ail her," the old woman said.

"They carried her off in an ambulance," Mrs. Turpin continued, "but before she went she was rolling on the floor and they were trying to hold her down to give her a shot and she said something to me." She paused. "You know what she said to me?"

"What she say?" they asked.

"She said," Mrs. Turpin began, and stopped, her face very dark and heavy. The sun was getting whiter and whiter, blanching the sky overhead so that the leaves of the hickory tree were black in the face of it. She could not bring forth the words. "Something real ugly," she muttered.

"She sho shouldn't said nothin ugly to you," the old woman said. "You so sweet. You the sweetest lady I know."

"She pretty too," the one with the hat on said.

"And stout," the other one said. "I never knowed no sweeter white lady."

"That's the truth befo' Jesus," the old woman said. "Amen! You jes as sweet and pretty as you can be."

Mrs. Turpin knew just exactly how much Negro flattery was worth and it added to her rage. "She said," she began again and finished this time with a fierce rush of breath, "that I was an old wart hog from hell."

There was an astounded silence.

"Where she at?" the youngest woman cried in a piercing voice.

"Lemme see her. I'll kill her!"

"I'll kill her with you!" the other one cried.

"She b'long in the sylum," the old woman said emphatically. "You the sweetest white lady I know."

"She pretty too," the other two said. "Stout as she can be and sweet. Jesus satisfied with her!"

"Deed he is," the old woman declared.

Idiots! Mrs. Turpin growled to herself. You could never say anything intelligent to a nigger. You could talk at them but not with them. "Yawl ain't drunk your water," she said shortly. "Leave the bucket in the truck when you're finished with it. I got more to do than just stand around and pass the time of day," and she moved off and into the house.

She stood for a moment in the middle of the kitchen. The dark protuberance over her eye looked like a miniature tornado cloud which might any moment sweep across the horizon of her brow. Her lower lip protruded dangerously. She squared her massive shoulders. Then she marched into the front of the house and out the side door and started down the road to the pig parlor. She had the look of a woman going single-handed, weaponless, into battle.

The sun was a deep yellow now like a harvest moon and was rising westward very fast over the far tree line as if it meant to reach the hogs before she did. The road was rutted and she kicked several good-sized stones out of her path as she strode along. The pig parlor was on a little knoll at the end of a lane that ran off from the side of the barn. It was a square of concrete as large as a small room, with a board fence about four feet high around it. The concrete floor sloped slightly so that the hog wash could drain off into a trench where it was carried to the field for fertilizer. Claud was standing on the outside, on the edge of the concrete, hanging onto the top board, hosing down the floor inside. The hose was connected to the faucet of a water trough nearby.

Mrs. Turpin climbed up beside him and glowered down at the hogs inside. There were seven long-snouted bristly shoats in it—tan with liver-colored spots—and an old sow a few weeks off from farrowing. She was lying on her side grunting. The shoats were running about shaking themselves like idiot children, their little slit pig eyes searching the floor for anything left. She had read that pigs were the most intelligent animal. She doubted it. They were supposed to be smarter than dogs. There had even been a pig astronaut. He had performed his assignment perfectly but died of a heart attack afterwards because they left him in his electric suit, sitting upright throughout his examination when naturally a hog should be on all fours.

A-gruntin and a-rootin and a-groanin.

"Gimme that hose," she said, yanking it away from Claud. "Go on and carry them niggers home and then get off that leg."

"You look like you might have swallowed a mad dog," Claud observed, but he got down and limped off. He paid no attention to her humors.

Until he was out of earshot, Mrs. Turpin stood on the side of the pen, holding the hose and pointing the stream of water at the hind quarters of any shoat that looked as if it might try to lie down. When he had had time to get over the hill, she turned her head slightly and her wrathful eyes scanned the path. He was nowhere in sight. She turned back again and seemed to gather herself up. Her shoulders rose and she drew in her breath.

"What do you send me a message like that for?" she said in a low fierce voice, barely above a whisper but with the force of a shout in its concentrated fury. "How am I a hog and me both? How am I saved and from hell too?" Her free fist was knotted and with the other she gripped the hose, blindly pointing the stream of water in and out of the eye of the old sow whose outraged squeal she did not hear.

The pig parlor commanded a view of the back pasture where their twenty beef cows were gathered around the hay-bales Claud and the boy had put out. The freshly cut pasture sloped down to the highway. Across it was their cotton field and beyond that a dark green dusty wood which they owned as well. The sun was behind the wood, very red, looking over the paling of trees like a farmer inspecting his own hogs.

"Why me?" she rumbled. "It's no trash around here, black or white, that I haven't given to. And break my back to the bone every day working. And do for the church."

She appeared to be the right size woman to command the arena before her. "How am I a hog?" she demanded. "Exactly how am I like them?" and she jabbed the stream of water at the shoats. "There was plenty of trash there. It didn't have to be me.

"If you like trash better, go get yourself some trash then," she railed. "You could have made me trash. Or a nigger. If trash is what you wanted why didn't you make me trash?" She shook her fist with the hose in it and a watery snake appeared momentarily in the air. "I could quit working and take it easy and be filthy," she growled.

"Lounge about the sidewalks all day drinking root beer. Dip snuff and spit in every puddle and have it all over my face. I could be nasty.

"Or you could have made me a nigger. It's too late for me to be a nigger," she said with deep sarcasm, "but I could act like one. Lay down in the middle of the road and stop traffic. Roll on the ground."

In the deepening light everything was taking on a mysterious hue. The pasture was growing a peculiar glassy green and the streak of highway had turned lavender. She braced herself for a final assault and this time her voice rolled out over the pasture. "Go on," she yelled, "call me a hog! Call me a hog again. From hell. Call me a wart hog from hell. Put that bottom rail on top. There'll still be a top and bottom!"

A garbled echo returned to her.

A final surge of fury shook her and she roared, "Who do you think you are?"

The color of everything, field and crimson sky, burned for a moment with a transparent intensity. The question carried over the pasture and across the highway and the cotton field and returned to her clearly like an answer from beyond the wood.

She opened her mouth but no sound came out of it.

A tiny truck, Claud's, appeared on the highway, heading rapidly out of sight. Its gears scraped thinly. It looked like a child's toy. At any moment a bigger truck might smash into it and scatter Claud's and the niggers' brains all over the road.

Mrs. Turpin stood there, her gaze fixed on the highway, all her muscles rigid, until in five or six minutes the truck reappeared, returning. She waited until it had had time to turn into their own road. Then like a monumental statue coming to life, she bent her head slowly and gazed, as if through the very heart of mystery, down into the pig parlor at the hogs. They had settled all in one corner around the old sow who was grunting softly. A red glow suffused them. They appeared to pant with a secret life.

Until the sun slipped finally behind the tree line, Mrs. Turpin remained there with her gaze bent to them as if she were absorbing some abysmal life-giving knowledge. At last she lifted her head. There was only a purple streak in the sky, cutting through a field of crimson and leading, like an extension of the highway, into the descending dusk. She raised her hands from the side of the pen in a gesture hieratic and profound. A visionary light settled in her eyes. She saw the streak as a vast swinging bridge extending upward from the earth through a field of living fire. Upon it a vast horde of souls were rumbling toward heaven. There were whole companies of white-trash, clean for the first time in their lives, and bands of black niggers in white robes, and battalions of freaks and lunatics shouting and clapping and leaping like frogs. And bringing up the end of the procession was a tribe of people whom she recognized at once as those who, like herself and Claud, had always had a little of everything and the God-given wit to use it right. She leaned forward to observe them closer. They were marching behind the others with great dignity, accountable as they had always been for good order and common sense and respectable behavior. They alone were on key. Yet she could see by their shocked and altered faces that even their virtues were being burned away. She lowered her hands and gripped the rail of the hog pen, her eyes small but fixed unblinkingly on what lay ahead. In a moment the vision faded but she remained where she was, immobile.

At length she got down and turned off the faucet and made her slow way on the darkening path to the house. In the woods around her the invisible cricket choruses had struck up, but what she heard were the voices of the souls climbing upward into the starry field and shouting hallelujah.

## Questions

1. Drawing on the first four or five pages, characterize Mrs. Turpin. What do her actions and appearance tell us about her personality? Drawing on these same pages, point out passages that indicate how some other characters in the story send messages without using words.
2. On page 386 Mary Grace says: "Go back to hell where you came from, you old wart hog," and we are then told that the girl's "message had struck its target." Exactly what is the meaning of the message? Judging from the end of the story, what is the effect of the message?
3. Why is Mrs. Turpin willing to tell the blacks what her assailant said but not willing to tell Claud?

Stevie Smith

# Not Waving but Drowning

Nobody heard him, the dead man,
But still he lay moaning:
I was much further out than you thought
And not waving but drowning.

Poor chap, he always loved larking
And now he's dead
It must have been too cold for him his heart gave way,
They said

Oh, no no no, it was too cold always
(Still the dead one lay moaning)
I was much too far out all my life
And not waving but drowning.

## Questions

1. The first line, "Nobody heard him, the dead man," is, of course, literally true. Dead men do not speak. In what other ways is it true?
2. Who are "they" whose voices we hear in the second stanza? What does the punctuation—or lack of it—in line 7 tell us of their feelings for the dead man? What effect is produced by the brevity of line 6? of line 8?
3. In the last stanza, does the man reproach himself, or others, or simply bemoan his fate? What was the cause of his death?

Stevie Smith (1902–1971) was born Florence Margaret Smith in England. She published her first book, a novel, in 1936. She is best known, however, for her several volumes of poetry.

# 6
# NETWORKS

*Restaurant—US 1 Leaving Columbia, South Carolina*
**Robert Frank, 1955**

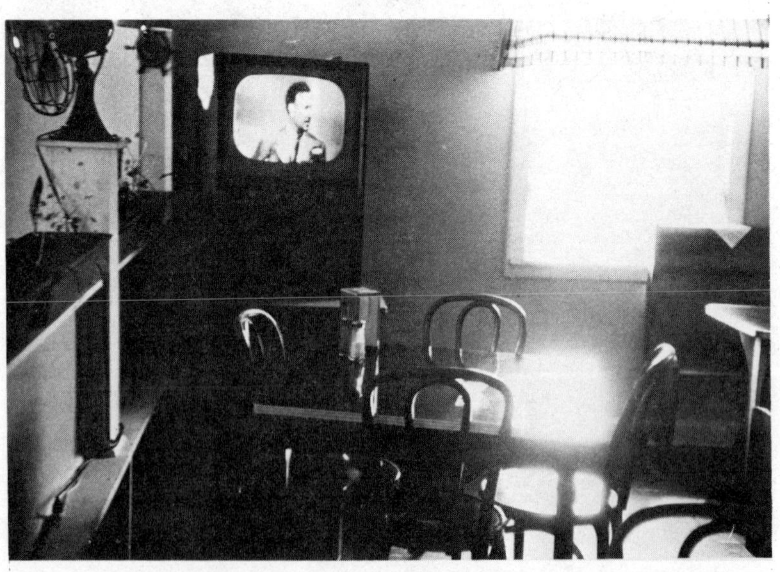

*Punch and Judy Show at Ilfracombe*
**Paul Martin, 1894**

The Victoria and Albert Museum, London

*Just what is it that makes today's homes so different, so appealing?*
**Richard Hamilton, 1956**

Courtesy of Kunsthalle Tubingen, Germany
Collection of Prof. Dr. Georg Zundel

*Sapolio*
**Anonymous, 1909**

Reprinted with permission from *LSA Magazine,* published by The College of Literature, Science and the Arts at The University of Michigan

# Short Views

Ballads, *bon mots,* anecdotes, give us better insight into the depths of past centuries than grave and voluminous chronicles. "A Straw," says Selden, "thrown up into the air will show how the wind sits, which cannot be learned by casting up a stone."

**Ralph Waldo Emerson**

For a while everybody was laughing at Marvel because we were going after the college crowd. But I've always felt comics were a very valid form of entertainment. There's no reason to look down on telling a good story in the comic book medium. It's just dialogue and illustrations, after all, like film, except that it's a little harder than film because our action is frozen. If Ernest Hemingway had written comic books, they would have been just as good as his novels.

**Stan Lee, of *Marvel Comics***

If there is one consistently dishonest element in every situation comedy, no matter how realistic, how bold, how relevant or controversial it may be, it is that no one in a situation comedy is isolated, alone, atomized. In a country where broken marriages are increasing almost geometrically, and where the trend of living alone is becoming an important national fact of life, the world of the situation comedy depicts strong bonds between friends, coworkers, and family. No one sits home at night watching television: the most pervasive habit in American life today usually goes unrecorded in even the most "realistic" comedies because it is not funny. Instead, the sturdiest barriers of isolation vanish under the power of the family bond. The students of Gabe Kotter in *Welcome Back, Kotter* pal around together—an Italian, a black, a Puerto Rican, a Jew, a white eastern European ethnic—in poverty-stricken Brooklyn where, in reality, racial polarization has been at a flash point for a decade or more. And they frequently arrive, alone or together, at the apartment of their teacher, an event which for many New York teachers in such a neighborhood would trigger an emergency call to the police.

**Jeff Greenfield**

Watching television is a habit.
**Martin Meyer**

The medium is the message.
**Marshall McLuhan**

I beheld the wretch—the miserable monster whom I had created.
**Mary Shelley, *Frankenstein***

We hear a great deal nowadays about "the importance of communication" and about "improved methods of communication"; but though certain supplementary methods of limited usefulness have recently been invented there are no *improved* methods, because the printed page remains the best and most flexible "means of communication" ever devised.

Even some colleges have joined what seems to be a conspiracy to ignore this fact. A year or two ago I visited a campus where they no longer had an English Department because it had become a Communications Department instead. And I remember saying to one of the professors whom I met on the campus that I thought it a sad day when a professor was seen—as at the moment he was—carrying under his arm, not books, but three film cans.

Just suppose that the radio, the phonograph, the film strip, and all the rest of it had been in existence since the Fifteenth Century but that books had just been invented. What a marvelous advance in communication that would be! And how many advantages the book would be seen to have over any previously known means, including ready availability and the possibility of wide choice. What comes over the air is chosen for you by somebody else and you must receive the communication at a particular moment, or not at all. A book, on the other hand, you can choose for yourself and you can read it at your own convenience. It is always available while a broadcast is gone, usually forever. And how much more economical in time a book is! Deduct from a half-hour broadcast the musical fanfare, the station announcement, the sponsor's commercial, etc., etc., and you can learn by five minutes with a book more than you can get in a half-hour broadcast. "Why," we would say, "this marvelous new invention, the book, just about makes radio obsolete."

But perhaps the greatest of all the advantages of the book as a means of communication is simply that by reading you learn to read, become more and more capable of receiving more and more completely more subtle and complicated communications. By listening to the radio or looking at film strips you become only more and more passive, less and less capable of giving your attention.

**Joseph Wood Krutch**

Richard A. Hawley

# Television and Adolescents

## A Teacher's View

Ever since its novelty wore off in the fifties, we have all known, really, that television in its commercial form wasn't up to much good. This isn't to say that millions of people don't still depend on it, but dependency is hardly a sign of virtue. Except for Marshall McLuhan's grab-bag theoretics, few claims have been advanced for the improving effects of television. In fact, recently there has been a flurry of publishing activity, most notably Marie Winn's *The Plug-in Drug,* about television as a cause of downright mental erosion. But what I think Marie Winn and others need is a concrete, closely observed, and intensely felt illustration of the larger thesis. That's what I offer here.

Television has a way of intruding into our lives, and last year it intruded into my life and into the life of the school where I work in a way that many of us there will never forget. We had all taken our seats for morning assembly. The usual announcements were read, after which the morning's senior speaker was introduced. Like many independent schools, ours requires each senior to address the student body in some manner before he graduates. Since public speaking is not a widely distributed gift these days, the senior speeches are infrequently a source of much interest or intentional amusement.

Richard A Hawley, dean of students at University School in Hunting Valley, Ohio, is writing a book on contemporary school life.

As the curtains parted, we could see that the speaker had opted for a skit. On the stage were a covered table and a number of cooking implements. Out stepped the speaker wearing an apron and chef's hat, which very quickly established that he was going to satirize one of my colleagues who has a national reputation as a gourmet chef. Since this colleague is also a man who can take a joke, the prospects for the skit seemed bright. But not for long.

At first, I think almost all of us pretended that we didn't hear, that we were making too much of certain, possibly accidental, double entendres. But then came the direct statements and a few blatant physical gestures. Then it was clear! This boy was standing before five hundred of us making fun of what he suggested at some length was the deviant sexual nature of one of his teachers. The response to this was at first stupefaction, then some outbursts of laughter (the groaning kind of laughter that says, "I don't believe you said that"), then a quieting, as the speech progressed, to periodic oohs (the kind that say, "You *did* say that, and you're in for it").

When he had finished, there was a nearly nauseating level of tension afloat. As the students filed off to class, I made my way backstage to find the speaker. It had by now dawned on him that he had done something wrong, even seriously wrong. We met in my office.

He expressed remorse at having offended a teacher whom he said he particularly liked. (Before the conference I had checked briefly with the teacher and found him badly flustered and deeply hurt.) The remorse was, I felt, genuine. But something was decidedly missing in the boy's explanation of how he came to think that such a presentation might, under any circumstances, have been appropriate. He hadn't, he admitted, really thought about it, and some of his friends thought the idea was funny, and, well, he didn't know. When it occurred to him that serious school action was in the offing, he protested that in no way had he intended the sexual references to be taken seriously—they were, you know, a joke.

I pointed out to him that the objects of such jokes have no way to respond: To ignore the insinuation might affirm its validity; on the other hand, to object vigorously would draw additional attention to the offense and sustain the embarrassment connected with it. I pointed out further that sometimes innocent parties *never* regain their stature after being offended in this manner, and that the injured party was, at the very least, in for a terrible day of school.

The boy became reflective and said, "Was it *that* bad? You can see worse on 'Saturday Night Live.' " I told him I doubted this, but if it were true, and were I in a position to judge, I would be in favor of expelling "Saturday Night Live" from the air. He left the office, and subsequently endured the appropriate consequences.

For my part, I resolved to turn on "Saturday Night Live," and when I did, I realized the student had spoken truly. The show's quick-succession, absurdist comedy spots depended for their appeal on establishing an almost dangerous sense of inappropriateness: exactly that sense created by our senior speaker. To me, for some years a lapsed viewer, it seemed that both the variety and specificity of sexual innuendo had developed considerably since, say, the once daring Smothers Brothers show of the sixties. What struck me more, however, was how many punch lines and visual gags depended on suddenly introducing the idea of injury or violent death.

I happened to tune in the night a funny caption was put over the documentary shot of Middle Eastern political partisans being dragged to death behind an automobile. Was this funny? I asked my students. They said it was "sick" and laughed. Does this kind of fun trivialize crisis? Trivialize cruelty? Inure us to both? Or is it, you know, a joke?

The right things were said, I think, to our students about the boy's speech. But I can't say the situation improved. Not more than a couple of weeks later, a speaker garbed in a woman's tennis dress took the podium and began to talk humorously about the transsexual tennis player Renee Richards. I can't think of a subject harder for an adolescent to discuss before an adolescent audience. Rarely noted for their confidence and breadth of vision in matters of human sexuality, adolescents are unlikely to be objective, sympathetic, or (let me tell you) funny about so disturbing a phenomenon as sex change. This particular boy, whose inflection is very flat and whose normal countenance is especially stony, managed to convey almost a sense of bitterness in making his string of insulting and, in his references to genitals and to menstruation, awfully tasteless cracks.

So there it was again: the inappropriateness, the tension. This time the injured party was remote from our particular world, so the hastily arranged conference with the boy turned on general considerations of taste and judgment. This time, however, the speaker was recalcitrant: We could disapprove of his speech and discipline him if we chose, but we ought to know that we could hear the same thing on television.

At that moment something clicked for me. Not only did my brief exposure to "Saturday Night Live" convince me that, yes, I would hear the same thing on television, but I was suddenly struck with the realization that he was using television as an arbiter of taste—that is, *as an arbiter of good taste.* I began to see in this premise a common ground upon which he and I could at least argue. Both of us were in agreement that what is broadcast over televsion ought to be acceptable; our point of disagreement was his feeling that broadcasting something over television *made* it acceptable. Alarming as such a feeling is to me, it is not hard to see how it has developed over the past few decades.

Until the middle sixties, with the exception of the very earthiest plays and novels, the values of home and school and the values of the popular culture were fairly continuous; if anything, radio, television, and motion pictures were more staid than real life. Of course, all this would change very quickly—not because change was requested or even consented to, but because it wasn't, perhaps couldn't be, resisted. And suddenly there it all was at once: the most embarrassing expletives as common speech; every imaginable kind of sexual coupling depicted in ever increasing candor; obsessively specific wounds, mutilations.

These formerly unacceptable kinds of stimulation made their way more easily into the relatively insulated world of print and film than they did into the more communal world of the television set. Television is typically viewed in homes, and what is communally seen and heard must be communally integrated, or there will be friction. Since American households—set-holds?—share this communal experience for an estimated two to seven hours per day, the potential for friction is considerable. This is why, on grounds of taste, criticism of television programming tends to be more bitter and more relentless than criticism of books and films.

Television foes and partisans alike continue to advise, with some reason, that those who object to certain programs ought not to watch them. But given the impossibility of monitoring the set at all hours, control over the amount and quality of viewing is difficult to maintain even in principled, surveillant households. Too, some viewers will insist on being their brother's keeper. Not everyone who is convinced that what is beaming over the national airwaves is inhumane, unscrupulous, or scurrilous is going to fight to the death for the networks' right to be so.

For many people, television is no longer on the polite side of real life. This is an obvious observation about a novel development, one whose consequences are only just dawning on us. A realist or an existentialist may argue that the unflappably suburban world of "Father Knows Best" revealed none of the complex, ambivalent, and often irrational forces at work in real families: But it is hard to argue that "Father Knows Best" in any way *contributed* to those dark forces. On the contrary, it is possible to argue—although one hesitates to carry it too far—that the theme of Father Knowing Best serves as a psychologically soothing backdrop to the prickly dynamics of real family life. And while today's most highly rated shows suggest that the prevailing seventies' theme is Nobody Knows Anything, there are still apparently enough viewers who like Father Knowing Best to support series like "The Waltons" and "Little House on the Prairie."

Sometimes the theme is compromised in a typical seventies' manner, of which "James at 16" provides a good example: The parents are cast very much in the Robert Young–Jane Wyatt mold, but their son James is, to borrow a phrase, kind of now. By far the most interesting thing he did was to lose his virginity on prime time. The fifteen-going-on-sixteen-year-old boys I work with, many of them at least as sophisticated as James, typically hold on to their virginity a bit longer, until the disposition of their sexual feelings is under surer control. The best clinical evidence maintains that the process of bringing newly emergent sexuality under control is *inherently* delicate and troublesome. James's television plunge planted the anxiety-provoking notion in the mind of the adolescent viewer that he was sexually lagging behind not only the precocious kid down the block, but the Average American Boy character of James. (One was allowed to be less anxious when Father Knew Best.)

Why shouldn't television make people anxious? say the producers of programs that make people anxious. After all, the *world* is anxious. (An awfully self-serving position: Programs that arouse anxiety are relevant; those that don't are enjoyable.) Before long, this line of argument begins to lay claim that programs which bring up irritating subjects in an irritating manner are performing a valuable social mission. Norman Lear, the producer of comedies such as "All in the Family" and "Maude," makes such a claim. According to the Lear formula, a controversial topic will be raised, tossed around for laughs, then either discarded or resolved. Resolution occurs when one of the characters tolerates or forgives the controversial person or practice, while some other character, usually a combination of lovable old coot and ass, does not.

As many critics have pointed out, this is only apparent resolution. Nothing much really happens to a racial or sexual conflict when it is laughed at (a device that is supposed to soften outright slurring and stereotyping), discarded, tolerated, or forgiven. The idea that "if we can joke about it this way, we have taken a humanitarian stride" is mistaken. There is plenty of evidence, particularly among the student population, that, for one thing, race relations are more strained today than they were a decade ago. No one would want to claim that racism among youth disappeared during the politically active sixties; however, a claim can be made that when a student was confronted then with having made a racial slur, he seemed to be aware of having violated a standard.

Who is to say that Archie Bunker hath no sting? More and more television comedians, in the manner of Don Rickles, seek *only* to sting. It is really an empirical question, not a matter of taste, whether or not it is harmless, much less healing, to denigrate everybody, including oneself. A hit song by Randy Newman insults small people: this is no parody of unkindness or bigotry, but the real thing. My students understand it perfectly and parrot it enthusiastically. Rebuked, they grimace in exasperation. Nothing in their youthful experience tells them that bigotry is a sign of cultural regression ("It isn't bigotry; it's, you know, a joke"). They prefer to see whatever wicked delights crop up in the media as a progressive casting off of prudish inhibitions. According to such a view, progress is whatever happens next.

Toleration of the intolerable is always worrying, but it is especially so when it takes place among the young, in whom we want to invest so much hope. Tolerating the intolerable is part of a dynamic, not a static, process; the intolerable, when it is nurtured, grows.

Which brings me back to the senior speeches. Two so thoroughly inappropriate presentations in a single year represented a high count for us, so we were not ready, at least I wasn't, for the third.

This time the talk was about a summer spent working on a ranch, and the format was that of a commentary with slides. No apparent harm in this, but there were a number of factors working against the speech's success. The first was that the speaker was renowned for being a card, a reputation the welcoming ovation insisted he live up to. Second, he had not adequately rehearsed the projection of the slides, so that they tended to appear out of order and askew, the effect of which was to provide a subtextual comedy of visual non sequiturs. Third, he chose to capitalize on the audience's nearly unrestrained hilarity by playing up certain questionable references.

The speaker made a fairly good, not too inappropriate crack about a slide which depicted a bull mounting a cow—"Sometimes the corrals get so crowded we have to stack the cattle on top of one another." But he chose to exploit his references to the gelding of bulls. There were, in all, four jokey and brutal evocations of this process which served to keep the image of bull genitalia before our minds for quite a few minutes. Since laughter had already been spent, the castration jokes were met with a kind of nervous applause. Bolstered by this, the speaker closed with a coda to the effect that he would be available after assembly to anybody who wanted tips on "cutting meat."

Since I happened to be in charge that day, I sent him home. It seemed to me, in light of the various reprisals and forewarnings connected with the previous speeches, that this particular performance, though perhaps less offensive in its specific references than the other two, ought to be the last straw. The speaker had clearly exceeded anything required by either schoolboy or cowboy saltiness. He had created an anything-goes atmosphere, and then he had let it go—for which he was applauded. "That was great!" said the boy next to me on the way out of the auditorium.

That morning and afterward scores of students, most, but not all, of them civil, hastened to let me know that they felt it was unfair to have sent the speaker home. Not one of them failed to remind me that I could see worse on television. Had I never seen "Saturday Night Live"? That afternoon an opinion poll went up requesting signatures from those who disapproved of the action I had taken and, in an opposing column, those who approved. Within the hour, hundreds expressed disapproval, only one approved.

For a day or two at school there was an animated atmosphere of martyrdom (the speaker's, not mine), but it dissipated rapidly, possibly because the right to make castration jokes from the stage was not, as a cause, very catalytic. The banished speaker, a very likable boy, returned, was received warmly, and apologized not at all cringingly.

In the calm that has followed, my colleagues and I have taken pains to stress to our students, especially at the commencement of the new school year, that whenever somebody addresses an assembly, it is a special occasion. Speakers are expected to observe definite standards when they speak or perform; audiences are expected to be courteous and restrained. Humor at someone else's expense is out, unless it is prearranged with the party lampooned, and even then it ought not to be inhumane. Excretory and copulatory humor is out; it's too easy. Preparation is important. Being persuasive is important. Being controversial is important. Being funny is a delight to all, though it is harder than it looks.

Perhaps these expectations are high. However, schools, especially parochial and independent schools, are gloriously unencumbered in setting such standards: Schools are often *chosen* for the standards they set, the difference they represent. One of the things schools have an opportunity to be different from is television, for although we are all wired into it and it feels public, like the law, it is actually private, like a door-to-door salesman. We don't have to buy the goods.

Since children who watch a fair amount of television will quite naturally assume they are being told and shown the truth, it seems to me crucial that they are exposed to models who view it selectively and critically, who judge it by criteria other than its potential to engage. My own experience has been that students are surprised, but not hostile, when television programming is harshly judged. I think they may even come to like the idea that they themselves, at their discriminating best, are in the process of becoming people television ought to measure up to.

## Questions

1. The three speeches that disturbed Hawley all had to do with sex, yet (aside from a few casual references, such as the one to the Smothers Brothers) his references to television are to violence, including verbal violence. Is Hawley muddling things?
2. On page 408 Hawley begins a paragraph by asking: "Why shouldn't television make people anxious?" and he goes on to repeat the word "anxious." What is the meaning of "anxious" in this context?
3. Judging from this essay, what sort of person is Hawley? In a paragraph, try to characterize him. (Don't attempt to summarize his argument; confine your remarks to his personality.)

## Marya Mannes

# Television Advertising

### The Splitting Image

A bride who looks scarcely fourteen whispers, "Oh, Mom, I'm so *happy!*" while a doting family adjust her gown and veil and a male voice croons softly, "A woman is a harder thing to be than a man. She has more feelings to feel." The mitigation of these excesses, it appears, is a feminine deodorant called Secret, which allows our bride to approach the altar with security as well as emotion.

Eddie Albert, a successful actor turned pitchman, bestows his attention on a lady with two suitcases, which prompt him to ask her whether she has been on a journey. "No," she says, or words to that effect, as she opens the suitcases. "My two boys bring back their soiled clothes every weekend from college for me to wash." And she goes into the familiar litany of grease, chocolate, mud, coffee, and fruit-juice stains, which presumably record the life of the average American male from two to fifty. Mr. Albert compliments her on this happy device to bring her boys home every week and hands her a box of Biz, because "Biz *is* better."

Two women with stony faces meet cart to cart in a supermarket as one takes a jar of peanut butter off a shelf. When the other asks her in a voice of nitric acid why she takes that brand, the first snaps, "Because I'm choosy for my family!" The two then break into delighted smiles as Number Two makes Number One taste Jif for "mothers who are choosy."

If you have not come across these dramatic interludes, it is because you are not home during the day and do not watch daytime television. It also means that your intestinal tract is spared from severe assaults, your credibility unstrained. Or, for that matter, you may look at commercials like these every day and manage either to ignore them or find nothing—given the fact of advertising—wrong with them. In that case, you are either so brainwashed or so innocent that you remain unaware of what this daily infusion may have done

Marya Mannes has published in many journals, from *TV Guide* to *The New Republic.*

and is doing to an entire people as the long-accepted adjunct of free enterprise and support of "free" television.

"Given the fact" and "long-accepted" are the key words here. Only socialists, communists, idealists (or the BBC) fail to realize that a mass television system cannot exist without the support of sponsors, that the massive cost of maintaining it as a free service cannot be met without the massive income from selling products. You have only to read of the unending struggle to provide financial support for public, noncommercial television for further evidence.

Besides, aren't commercials in the public interest? Don't they help you choose what to buy? Don't they provide needed breaks from programing? Aren't many of them brilliantly done, and some of them funny? And now, with the new sexual freedom, all those gorgeous chicks with their shining hair and gleaming smiles? And if you didn't have commercials taking up a good part of each hour, how on earth would you find enough program material to fill the endless space/time void.

Tick off the yesses and what have you left? You have, I venture to submit, these intangible but possibly high costs: the diminution of human worth, the infusion and hardening of social attitudes no longer valid or desirable, pervasive discontent, and psychic fragmentation.

Should anyone wonder why deception is not an included detriment, I suggest that our public is so conditioned to promotion as a way of life, whether in art or politics or products, that elements of exaggeration or distortion are taken for granted. Nobody really believes that a certain shampoo will get a certain swain, or that an unclogged sinus can make a man a swinger. People are merely prepared to hope it will.

But the diminution of human worth is much more subtle and just as pervasive. In the guise of what they consider comedy, the producers of television commercials have created a loathsome gallery of men and women patterned, presumably, on Mr. and Mrs. America. Women liberationists have a major target in the commercial image of woman flashed hourly and daily to the vast majority. There are, indeed, only four kinds of females in this relentless sales procession: the gorgeous teen-age swinger with bouncing locks; the young mother teaching her baby girl the right soap for skin care; the middle-aged housewife with a voice like a power saw; and the old lady with dentures and irregularity. All these women, to be sure, exist. But between the swinging sex object and the constipated granny there are millions of females never shown in commercials. These are—married or single—intelligent, sensitive women who bring charm to their homes, who work at jobs as well as lend grace to their marriage, who support themselves, who have talents or hobbies or commitments, or who are skilled at their professions.

To my knowledge, as a frequent if reluctant observer, I know of only one woman on a commercial who has a job; a comic plumber pushing Comet. Funny, heh? Think of a dame with a plunger.

With this one representative of our labor force, which is well over thirty million women, we are left with nothing but the full-time housewife in all her whining glory: obsessed with whiter wash, moister cakes, shinier floors, cleaner children, softer diapers, and greaseless fried chicken. In the rare instances when these ladies are not in the kitchen, at the washing machine, or waiting on hubby, they are buying beauty shops (fantasy, see?) to take home so that their hair will have more body. Or out at the supermarket being choosy.

If they were attractive in their obsessions, they might be bearable. But they are not. They are pushy, loud-mouthed, stupid, and —of all things now—bereft of sexuality. Presumably, the argument in the tenets of advertising is that once a woman marries she changes overnight from plaything to floor-waxer.

To be fair, men make an equivalent transition in commercials. The swinging male with the mod hair and the beautiful chick turns inevitably into the paunchy slob who chokes on his wife's cake. You will notice, however, that the voice urging the viewer to buy the product is nearly always male: gentle, wise, helpful, seductive. And the visible presence telling the housewife how to get shinier floors and whiter wash and lovelier hair is almost invariably a man: the Svengali in modern dress, the Trilby (if only she were!), his willing object.[1]

Woman, in short, is consumer first and human being fourth. A wife and mother who stays home all day buys a lot more than a woman who lives alone or who—married or single—has a job. The young girl hell-bent on marriage is the next most susceptible consumer. It is entirely understandable, then, that the potential buyers of detergents, foods, polishes, toothpastes, pills, and housewares are the housewives, and that the sex object spends more of *her* money on cosmetics, hair lotions, soaps, mouthwashes, and soft drinks.

Here we come, of course, to the youngest class of consumers, the

[1]In George Du Maurier's novel, *Trilby* (1894), Svengali mesmerizes Trilby and causes her to become a famous singer; when Svengali dies, Trilby loses her voice, dwindles, and soon dies. (Editors' note)

swinging teen-agers so beloved by advertisers keen on telling them (and us) that they've "got a lot to live, and Pepsi's got a lot to give." This affords a chance to show a squirming, leaping, jiggling group of beautiful kids having a very loud high on rock and—of all things—soda pop. One of commercial TV's most dubious achievements, in fact, is the reinforcement of the self-adulation characteristic of the young as a group.

As for the aging female citizen, the less shown of her the better. She is useful for ailments, but since she buys very little of anything, not having a husband or any children to feed or house to keep, nor —of course—sex appeal to burnish, society and commercials have little place for her. The same is true, to be sure, of older men, who are handy for Bosses with Bad Breath or Doctors with Remedies. Yet, on the whole, men hold up better than women at any age—in life or on television. Lines on their faces are marks of distinction, while on women they are signatures of decay.

There is no question, in any case, that television commercials (and many of the entertainment programs, notably the soap serials that are part of the selling package) reinforce, like an insistent drill, the assumption that a woman's only valid function is that of wife, mother, and servant of men: the inevitable sequel to her earlier function as sex object and swinger.

At a time when more and more women are at long last learning to reject these assumptions as archaic and demeaning, and to grow into individual human beings with a wide option of lives to live, the sellers of the nation are bent upon reinforcing the ancient pattern. They know only too well that by beaming their message to the Consumer Queen they can justify her existence as the housebound Mrs. America: dumber than dumb, whiter than white.

The conditioning starts very early: with the girl child who wants the skin Ivory soap has reputedly given her mother, with the nine-year-old who brings back a cake of Camay instead of the male deodorant her father wanted. (When she confesses that she bought it so she could be "feminine," her father hugs her, and, with the voice of a child-molester, whispers, "My little girl is growing up on me, huh.") And then, before long, comes the teen-aged bride who "has feelings to feel." It is the little boys who dream of wings, in an airplane commercial; who grow up (with fewer cavities) into the doers. Their little sisters turn into *Cosmopolitan* girls, who in turn become housewives furious that their neighbors' wash is cleaner than theirs.

There is good reason to suspect that this manic obsession with cleanliness, fostered, quite naturally, by the giant soap and detergent interests, may bear some responsibility for the cultivated sloppiness of so many of the young in their clothing as well as in their chosen hideouts. The compulsive housewife who spends more time washing and vacuuming and polishing her possessions than communicating to, or stimulating her children creates a kind of sterility that the young would instinctively reject. The impeccably tidy home, the impeccably tidy lawn are—in a very real sense—unnatural and confining. Yet the commercials confront us with broods of happy children, some of whom—believe it or not—notice the new fresh smell their clean, white sweatshirts exhale thanks to Mom's new "softener."

Some major advertisers, for that matter, can even cast a benign eye on the population explosion. In another Biz commercial, the genial Eddie Albert surveys with surprise a long row of dirty clothes heaped before him by a young matron. She answers his natural query by telling him gaily they are the products of her brood of eleven "with one more to come!" she adds as the twelfth turns up. "That's great!" says Mr. Albert, curdling the soul of Planned Parenthood and the future of this planet.

Who are, one cannot help but ask, the writers who manage to combine the sales of products with the selling-out of human dreams and dignity? Who people this cosmos of commercials with dolts and fools and shrews and narcissists? Who know so much about quirks and mannerisms and ailments and so little about life? So much about presumed wants and so little about crying needs?

Can women advertisers so demean their own sex? Or are there no women in positions of decision high enough to see that their real selves stand up? Do they not know, these extremely clever creators of commercials, what they could do for their audience even while they exploit and entertain them? How they could raise the levels of manners and attitudes while they sell their wares? Or do they really share the worm's-eye view of mass communication that sees, and addresses, only the lowest common denominator?

It can be argued that commercials are taken too seriously, that their function is merely to amuse, engage, and sell, and that they do this brilliantly. If that were all to this wheedling of millions, well and good. But it is not. There are two more fallouts from this chronic sales explosion that cannot be measured but that at least can be expected. One has to do with the continual celebration of youth at the expense of maturity. In commercials only the young have access to beauty, sex, and joy in life. What do older women feel, day after day, when love is the exclusive possession of a teen-age girl with a bobbing mantle of hair? What older man would not covet her in restless impotence?

The constant reminder of what is inaccessible must inevitably produce a subterranean but real discontent, just as the continual sight of things and places beyond reach has eaten deeply into the ghetto soul. If we are constantly presented with what we are not or cannot have, the dislocation deepens, contentment vanishes, and frustration reigns. Even for the substantially secure, there is always a better thing, a better way, to buy. That none of these things makes a better life may be consciously acknowledged, but still the desire lodges in the spirit, nagging and pulling.

This kind of fragmentation works in potent ways above and beyond the mere fact of program interruption, which is much of the time more of a blessing than a curse, especially in those rare instances when the commercial is deft and funny: the soft and subtle sell. Its overall curse, due to the large number of commercials in each hour, is that it reduces the attention span of a people already so conditioned to constant change and distraction that they cannot tolerate continuity in print or on the air.

Specifically, commercial interruption is most damaging during that 10 per cent of programing (a charitable estimate) most important to the mind and spirit of a people: news and public affairs, and drama. To many (and among these are network news producers), commercials have no place or business during the vital process of informing the public. There is something obscene about a newscaster pausing to introduce a deodorant or shampoo commercial between an airplane crash and a body count. It is more than an interruption; it tends to reduce news to a form of running entertainment, to smudge the edges of reality by treating death or disaster or diplomacy on the same level as household appliances or a new gasoline.

The answer to this would presumably be to lump the commercials before and after the news or public affairs broadcasts—an answer unpalatable, needless to say, to the sponsors who support them.

The same is doubly true of that most unprofitable sector of television, the original play. Essential to any creative composition, whether drama, music or dance, are mood and continuity, both inseparable from form and meaning. They are shattered by the periodic intrusion of commercials, which have become intolerable to the serious artists who have deserted commercial television in droves because the system allows them no real freedom or autonomy. The selling comes first, the creation must accommodate itself. It is the rare and admirable sponsor who restricts or fashions his commercials so as to provide a minimum of intrusion or damaging inappropriateness.

If all these assumptions and imponderables are true, as many suspect, what is the answer or alleviation?

One is in the course of difficult emergence: the establishment of a public television system sufficiently funded so that it can give a maximum number of people an alternate diet of pleasure, enlightenment, and stimulation free from commercial fragmentation. So far, for lack of funds to buy talent and equipment, this effort has been in terms of public attention a distinctly minor operation. Even if public television should greatly increase its scope and impact, it cannot in the nature of things and through long public conditioning equal the impact and reach the size of audience now tuned to commercial television.

Enormous amounts of time, money, and talent go into commercials. Technically they are often brilliant and innovative, the product not only of the new skills and devices but of imaginative minds. A few of them are both funny and endearing. Who, for instance, will forget the miserable young man with the appalling cold, or the kids taught to use—as an initiation into manhood—a fork instead of a spoon with a certain spaghetti? Among the enlightened sponsors, moreover, are some who manage to combine an image of their corporation and their products with accuracy and restraint.

What has to happen to mass medium advertisers as a whole, and especially on TV, is a totally new approach to their function not only as sellers but as social influencers. They have the same obligation as the broadcast medium itself: not only to entertain but to reflect, not only to reflect but to enlarge public consciousness and human stature.

This may be a tall order, but it is a vital one at a time when Americans have ceased to know who they are and where they are going, and when all the multiple forces acting upon them are daily diminishing their sense of their own value and purpose in life, when social upheaval and social fragmentation have destroyed old patterns, and when survival depends on new ones.

If we continue to see ourselves as the advertisers see us, we have no place to go. Nor, I might add, has commercial broadcasting itself.

## Questions

1. Spend an hour or two looking at daytime television and see if Mannes's observations about the advertisements are accurate.
2. Compare the image of women in daytime advertisements with the image of women in evening advertisements. Are there differences?
3. Mannes says (page 415) that advertisements assume that "a woman's only valid function is that of wife, mother, and servant of men." What do television advertisers assume about a man's "valid function"?
4. On page 415 Mannes suggests: "There is good reason to suspect that this manic obsession with cleanliness, fostered, quite naturally, by the giant soap and detergent interests, may bear some responsibility for the cultivated sloppiness of so many of the young in their clothing as well as in their chosen hideouts." Is there really good reason to suspect this connection? Does Mannes sometimes make doubtful assumptions? If so, point them out.
5. Examine some of Mannes's metaphors, such as "There are two more fallouts from this chronic sales explosion" (page 416), and evaluate them. Are they effective or strained?

X. J. Kennedy

# Who Killed King Kong?

The ordeal and spectacular death of King Kong, the giant ape, undoubtedly have been witnessed by more Americans than have ever seen a performance of *Hamlet, Iphigenia at Aulis,* or even *Tobacco Road.* Since RKO-Radio Pictures first released *King Kong,* a quarter-century has gone by; yet year after year, from prints that grow more rain-beaten, from sound tracks that grow more tinny, ticket-buyers by thousands still pursue Kong's luckless fight against the forces of technology, tabloid journalism, and the DAR. They see him chloroformed to sleep, see him whisked from his jungle isle to New York and placed on show, see him burst his chains to roam the city (lug-

X. J. Kennedy was born in 1929 in New Jersey. He has published several books of poetry (including a book for children) and several textbooks.

ging a frightened blonde), at last to plunge from the spire of the Empire State Building, machine-gunned by model airplanes.

Though Kong may die, one begins to think his legend unkillable. No clearer proof of his hold upon the popular imagination may be seen than what emerged one catastrophic week in March 1955, when New York WOR-TV programmed *Kong* for seven evenings in a row (a total of sixteen showings). Many a rival network vice-president must have scowled when surveys showed that *Kong*—the 1933 B-picture—had lured away fat segments of the viewing populace from such powerful competitors as Ed Sullivan, Groucho Marx and Bishop Sheen.

But even television has failed to run *King Kong* into oblivion. Coffee-in-the-lobby cinemas still show the old hunk of hokum, with the apology that in its use of composite shots and animated models the film remains technically interesting. And no other monster in movie history has won so devoted a popular audience. None of the plodding mummies, the stultified Draculas, the white-coated Lugosis with their shiny pinball-machine laboratories, none of the invisible stranglers, berserk robots, or menaces from Mars has ever enjoyed so many resurrections.

Why does the American public refuse to let King Kong rest in peace? It is true, I'll admit, that *Kong* outdid every monster movie before or since in sheer carnage. Producers Cooper and Schoedsack crammed into it dinosaurs, headhunters, riots, aerial battles, bullets, bombs, bloodletting. Heroine Fay Wray, whose function is mainly to scream, shuts her mouth for hardly one uninterrupted minute from first reel to last. It is also true that *Kong* is larded with good healthy sadism, for those whose joy it is to see the frantic girl dangled from cliffs and harried by pterodactyls. But it seems to me that the abiding appeal of the giant ape rests on other foundations.

Kong has, first of all, the attraction of being manlike. His simian nature gives him one huge advantage over giant ants and walking vegetables in that an audience may conceivably identify with him. Kong's appeal has the quality that established the Tarzan series as American myth—for what man doesn't secretly image himself a huge hairy howler aginst whom no other monster has a chance? If Tarzan recalls the ape in us, then Kong may well appeal to that great-granddaddy primordial brute from whose tribe we have all deteriorated.

Intentionally or not, the producers of *King Kong* encourage this identification by etching the character of Kong with keen sympathy.

For the ape is a figure in a tradition familiar to moviegoers: the tradition of the pitiable monster. We think of Lon Chaney in the role of Quasimodo, of Karloff in the original *Frankenstein.* As we watch the Frankenstein monster's fumbling and disastrous attempts to befriend a flower-picking child, our sympathies are enlisted with the monster in his impenetrable loneliness. And so with Kong. As he roars in his chains, while barkers sell tickets to boobs who gape at him, we perhaps feel something more deep than pathos. We begin to sense something of the problem that engaged Eugene O'Neill in *The Hairy Ape*: the dilemma of a displaced animal spirit forced to live in a jungle built by machines.

*King Kong,* it is true, had special relevance in 1933. Landscapes of the depression are glimpsed early in the film when an impresario, seeking some desperate pretty girl to play the lead in a jungle movie, visits souplines and a Woman's Home Mission. In Fay Wray—who's been caught snitching an apple from a fruitstand—his search is ended. When he gives her a big feed and a movie contract, the girl is magic-carpeted out of the world of the National Recovery Act. And when, in the film's climax, Kong smashes that very Third Avenue landscape in which Fay had wandered hungry, audiences of 1933 may well have felt a personal satisfaction.

What is curious is that audiences of 1960 remain hooked. For in the heart of urban man, one suspects, lurks the impulse to fling a bomb. Though machines speed him to the scene of his daily grind, though IBM comptometers ("freeing the human mind from drudgery") enable him to drudge more efficiently once he arrives, there comes a moment when he wishes to turn upon his machines and kick hell out of them. He wants to hurl his combination radio-alarmclock out the bedroom window and listen to its smash. What subway commuter wouldn't love—just for once—to see the downtown express smack head-on into the uptown local? Such a wish is gratified in that memorable scene in *Kong* that opens with a wide-angle shot: interior of a railway car on the Third Avenue El. Straphangers are nodding, the literate refold their newspapers. Unknown to them, Kong has torn away a section of trestle toward which the train now speeds. The motorman spies Kong up ahead, jams on the brakes. Passengers hurtle together like so many peas in a pail. In a window of the car appear Kong's bloodshot eyes. Women shriek. Kong picks up the railway car as if it were a rat, flips it to the street and ties knots in it, or something. To any commuter the scene must appear one of the most satisfactory pieces of celluloid ever exposed.

Yet however violent his acts, Kong remains a gentleman. Remarkable is his sense of chivalry. Whenever a fresh boa constrictor threatens Fay, Kong first sees that the lady is safely parked, then manfully thrashes her attacker. (And she, the ingrate, runs away every time his back is turned.) Atop the Empire State Building, ignoring his pursuers, Kong places Fay on a ledge as tenderly as if she were a dozen eggs. He fondles her, then turns to face the Army Air Force. And Kong is perhaps the most disinterested lover since Cyrano: His attentions to the lady are utterly without hope of reward. After all, between a five-foot blonde and a fifty-foot ape, love can hardly be more than an intellectual flirtation. In his simian way King Kong is the hopelessly yearning lover of Petrarchan convention. His forced exit from his jungle, in chains, results directly from his single-minded pursuit of Fay. He smashes a Broadway theater when the notion enters his dull brain that the flashbulbs of photographers somehow endanger the lady. His perilous shinnying up a skyscraper to pluck Fay from her boudoir is an act of the kindliest of hearts. He's impossible to discourage even though the love of his life can't lay eyes on him without shrieking murder.

The tragedy of King Kong then, is to be the beast who at the end of the fable fails to turn into the handsome prince. This is the conviction that the scriptwriters would leave with us in the film's closing line. As Kong's corpse lies blocking traffic in the street, the entrepreneur who brought Kong to New York turns to the assembled reporters and proclaims: "That's your story, boys—it was Beauty killed the Beast!" But greater forces than those of the screaming Lady have combined to lay Kong low, if you ask me. Kong lives for a time as one of those persecuted near-animal souls bewildered in the middle of an industrial order, whose simple desires are thwarted at every turn. He climbs the Empire State Building because in all New York it's the closest thing he can find to the clifftop of his jungle isle. He dies, a pitiful dolt, and the army brass and publicity-men cackle over him. His death is the only possible outcome to as neat a tragic dilemma as you can ask for. The machine-guns do him in, while the manicured human hero (a nice clean Dartmouth boy) carries away Kong's sweetheart to the altar. O, the misery of it all. There's far more truth about upper-middle-class American life in *King Kong* than in the last seven dozen novels of John P. Marquand.

A Negro friend from Atlanta tells me that in movie houses in colored neighborhoods throughout the South, *Kong* does a constant business. They show the thing in Atlanta at least every year, presumably to the same audiences. Perhaps this popularity may simply be due to the fact that Kong is one of the most watchable movies ever constructed, but I wonder whether Negro audiences may not find some archetypical appeal in this serio-comic tale of a huge black powerful free spirit whom all the hardworking white policemen are out to kill.

Every day in the week on a screen somewhere in the world, King Kong relives his agony. Again and again he expires on the Empire State Building, as audiences of the devout assist his sacrifice. We watch him die, and by extension kill the ape within our bones, but these little deaths of ours occur in prosaic surroundings. We do not die on a tower, New York before our feet, nor do we give our lives to smash a few flying machines. It is not for us to bring to a momentary standstill the civilization in which we move. King Kong does this for us. And so we kill him again and again, in much-spliced celluloid, while the ape in us expires from day to day, obscure, in desperation.

## Questions

1. What is your response to Kennedy's colloquial expressions, such as "lugging a frightened blonde," "hunk of hokum," "snitching an apple"? Are they used for a purpose?
2. In the third paragraph Kennedy calls *King Kong* "the old hunk of hokum." Does he consistently maintain the attitude implied here?
3. How persuasive do you find Kennedy's analysis? Is any of it useful in explaining the appeal of other films you have seen?
4. Kennedy refers to *King Kong* as a "monster movie." Can you think of other films you would place in that category? How would you define "horror movie" or "disaster film" or "science fiction film"? Are these, and "monster movie," distinct or overlapping categories?

Stanley Milgram

# Confessions of a News Addict

Let me begin with a confession. I am a news addict. Upon awakening I flip on the *Today* show to learn what events transpired during the night. On the commuter train which takes me to work, I scour *The New York Times,* and find myself absorbed in tales of earthquakes, diplomacy, and economics. I read the newspaper as religiously as my grandparents read their prayerbooks. The sacramental character of the news extends into the evening. The length of my workday is determined precisely by my need to get home in time for Walter Cronkite. My children understand that my communion with Cronkite is something serious and cannot be interrupted for light and transient causes.

But what is it, precisely, that is happening when I and millions of others scour our newspapers, stare at the tube, and pour over the news magazines that surround us? Does it make sense? What is news, and why does it occupy a place of special significance for so many people?

Let us proceed from a simple definition: news is information about events that are going on outside immediate experience. In this sense, news has always been a part of the human situation. In its earliest form, it took the shape of an account brought by a traveler, or a member of the group who wandered further than the rest and found water, game, or signs of a nearby enemy. The utility of such information is self-evident. News is a social mechanism that extends our own eyes and ears to embrace an ever wider domain of events. A knowledge of remote events allows us to prepare for them and take whatever steps are needed to deal with them. This is the classic function of news.

News is the consciousness of Society. It is the means whereby events in the body politic are brought into awareness. And it is curious that regimes which we call *repressive* tend to exhibit the same

Stanley Milgram, a professor of social psychology at the Graduate Center of the City University of New York, is the author of *Obedience to Authority.*

characteristic of repressed personalities; they are unable, or unwilling, to allow conflictive material into awareness. The disability stems from deep insecurities. The censoring of the repressed material does not eliminate it, but forces it to fester without anyone's rationally coming to grips with it.

Inevitably news comes to be controlled by the dominant political forces of a society. In a totalitarian regime the government attempts to create the image of a world, and of events, that reflects most favorably on those in power. The democratization of news, which goes hand in hand with the diffusion of political power among those governed, is a relatively recent development whose permanence cannot be assured. Democracies are far better able to cope with the reality of events than are totalitarian regimes. Such regimes promulgate a myth of their omnipotence, and are threatened even by events outside the control of the political process. Thus, typically, the Soviet press does not report air crashes, and even natural disasters such as earthquakes are suppressed, out of the notion—rooted in political insecurity—that the event in some manner reflects badly on the regime.

The question for any society is not whether there shall be news, but rather who shall have access to it. Every political system may be characterized by the proportion of information it has which is shared with the people and the proportion withheld. That is why the growth of secret news-gathering agencies, such as the C.I.A., is a troubling one for a democracy. It appears our government wants to keep some news to itself.

At a deeper historical level we can see that news in its present form is closely tied to the rise of the economy, and specifically to the exploitative and risk elements of capitalism. For the nineteenth-century merchant, news meant reports of his ship, of resources to exploit, and the means of minimizing the risk element inherent in entrepreneurship by gaining as much information as possible before his competitors. News services, such as Reuters, developed to serve business and investment interests, who discovered that getting the news quickly was the first step to financial gain.

In a civilization in which all activities tend toward commercial expression—for example, our own—news becomes a product to manufacture and dispense to the consumer. Thus a large-scale industry for the production and consumption of news has evolved. We ingest it with the same insatiable appetite that moves us to purchase the manifold products of our commercial civilization.

News under such circumstances tends toward decadent use. It no longer serves first the classic function of giving us information on which to act, or even to help us construct a mental model of the larger world. It serves mainly as entertainment. The tales of earthquakes, political assassinations, and bitterly fought elections are the heady stuff of which drama or melodrama is made. Happily, we are able to indulge our taste for thriller, romance, or murder mystery under the guise of a patently respectable pursuit. All enlightened people are supposed to know what is going on in the world. If what is going on also happens to be thrilling and exciting, so much the better.

Another feature of the decadent use of news is its increasing ritualization. The information becomes subservient to the form in which it is delivered. News is broadcast every evening, whether or not there is vital information to be conveyed. Indeed, the problem for the news networks is to generate sufficient news to fill a given time period. The time period becomes the fundamental fact, the framework into which events must be fitted. As in any ritual, the form persists even when a meaningful content is missing.

Those groups whose survival and well-being are most affected by remote events will be most persistently attuned to them. For example, Israelis, who view the survival of their state as a day-to-day contingency, are among the most news-oriented people in the world. During periods of crisis, portable radios blare in buses and in the market place. Jews, in general, have felt the need to develop antennae for remote events because of a communal insecurity. Any event, no matter how remote—even a farcical *putsch* in Munich led by a paper hanger—may grow into a formidable threat. Thus, constant monitoring of events is strongly reinforced.

Although I am a news addict, my addiction is strongest for news that in many respects seems most remote from my own life and experience. International news receives top priority, followed by national domestic news, and finally—and of least interest—local news. I feel more concerned reading about a student strike in Paris than a murder in my own neighborhood. I am especially uninterested in those news programs that provide a constant litany of fires and local crimes as their standard fare. Yet there is a paradox in this. Surely a criminal loose in my city is of greater personal consequence than an election outcome in Uruguay. Indeed, I sometimes ask what difference it makes to the actual conduct of my life to know about a fracas in Zaire, or a train wreck in Sweden. The total inconsequences of the news for my life is most strikingly brought home when we return from a vacation of several weeks where we have been without any news. I normally scan the accumulated pile of newspapers, but cannot help noticing how little difference it all made to me. And least consequential of all were those remote international events that so rivet my attention in the normal course of the week.

Why this interest in things far away, with a lesser interest in events close at home? Perhaps it is essentially a romantic impulse in the projection of meaning into remote countries, places, and people. Such a romantic impulse stems from a dissatisfaction with the mundane reality of everyday life. The events and places described in the news are remote, and thus we can more readily fix our imaginative sentiments to them. Moreover, an interest in news reinforces the "cosmopolitan" attitude which characterizes modern life, a desire to focus not only on the immediate community, but on the larger world. It is thus the opposite of the "provincialism" which characterized an earlier rural existence.

Living in the modern world, I cannot help but be shaped by it, suckered by the influence and impact of our great institutions. *The New York Times, CBS,* and *Newsweek* have made me into a news addict. In daily life I have come to accept the supposition that if *The New York Times* places a story on the front page, it deserves my attention. I feel obligated to know what is going on. But sometimes, in quieter moments, another voice asks: If the news went away, would the world be any worse for it?

# Questions

1. Why does Milgram describe himself as an "addict" and call his essay "confessions"? How seriously is he using the term? (Consider the connotations of "addict" compared with "reader," "consumer," and "fan.")
2. What reasons does Milgram give for being more interested in "things far away" than in "events close at home"? Do you find his reasons adequate? In answering this question reflect on the three or four items of news that have been of absorbing interest to you. What did those items have in common? Why did they interest you?

Lewis Thomas

# On Committees

The marks of selfness are laid out in our behavior irreversibly, unequivocally, whether we are assembled in groups or off on a stroll alone. Nobody can be aware of the unique immunologic labels of anyone else, outside a laboratory, nor can we smell with any reliability the pheromonal differences among ourselves. So, all we have to go by is how we walk, sound, write letters, turn our heads. We are infallible at this. Nobody is really quite like anyone else; there are reminders here and there, but no exact duplicates; we are four billion unique individuals.

Thus when committees gather, each member is necessarily an actor, uncontrollably acting out the part of himself, reading the lines that identify him, asserting his identity. This takes quite a lot of time and energy, and while it is going on there is little chance of anything else getting done. Many committees have been appointed in one year and gone on working well into the next decade, with nothing much happening beyond these extended, uninterruptible displays by each member of his special behavioral marks.

If it were not for such compulsive behavior by the individuals, committees would be a marvelous invention for getting collective thinking done. But there it is. We are designed, coded, it seems, to place the highest priority on being individuals, and we must do this first, at whatever cost, even if it means disability for the group.

This is surely the driving idea behind democracy, and it is astonishing that the system works at all, let alone well. The individual is the real human treasure, and only when he has been cultivated to full expression of his selfness can he become of full value to society. Like many attractive social ideas, it is authentic, ancient Chinese. Integrity is the most personal of qualities; groups and societies cannot possess it until single mortals have it in hand. It is hard work for civilization.

---

Lewis Thomas was born in 1913. A distinguished medical researcher and administrator, he is president of the Memorial Sloan-Kettering Cancer Center in New York. He is also a writer; his *The Lives of a Cell* (a collection of twenty-nine short essays) won a National Book Award in 1974.

---

But individuality can be carried too far, and you can see it happening almost all the time in committees. There are some very old words for critizing the display of too much individuality. When someone becomes too separate, too removed, out of communication, his behavior is called egregious. This was once a nice word, meaning "out of the herd," signifying distinction and accomplishment, but by the linguistic process of pejoration the word took on an antisocial significance. Overindividuals are called peculiar, strange, eccentric. The worst sort are idiots, from *idios,* originally meaning personal and private.

These days, with the increasing complexity of the organizations in which we live and the great numbers of us becoming more densely packed together, the work of committees can be a deadly serious business. This is especially so when there is need to forecast the future. By instinct, each of us knows that this is a responsibility not to be trusted to any single person; we have to do it together.

Because of the urgency of the problems ahead, various modifications of the old standard committee have been devised in recent years, in efforts to achieve better grades of collective thought. There are the think tanks, hybrids between committee and factory, little corporations for thinking. There are governmental commissions and panels, made up of people brought to Washington and told to sit down together and think out collective thoughts. Industries have organized their own encounter groups, in which executives stride around crowded rooms bumping and shouting at each other in hopes of prodding out new ideas. But the old trouble persists: people assembled for group thought are still, first of all, individuals in need of expressing selfness.

The latest invention for getting around this is the Delphi technique. This was an invention of the 1960s, worked out by some RAND Corporation people dissatisfied with the way committees laid plans for the future. The method has a simple, almost silly sound. Instead of having meetings, questionnaires are circulated to the members of a group, and each person writes his answers out and sends them back, in silence. Then the answers are circulated to all members and they are asked to reconsider and fill out the questionnaires again, after paying attention to the other views. And so forth. Three cycles are usually enough. By that time as much of a consensus has been reached as can be reached, and the final answers are said to be substantially more reliable, and often more interesting, than first time around. In some versions, new questions can be introduced by the participants at the same time that they are providing answers.

It is almost humiliating to be told that Delphi works, sometimes wonderfully well. One's first reaction is resentment at still another example of social manipulation, social-science trickery, behavior control.

But, then, confronted by the considerable evidence that the technique really does work—at least for future-forecasting in industry and government—one is bound to look for the possibly good things about it.

Maybe, after all, this is a way of preserving the individual and all his selfness, and at the same time linking minds together so that a group can do collective figuring. The best of both worlds, in short.

What Delphi is, is a really quiet, thoughtful conversation, in which everyone gets a chance to *listen.* The background noise of small talk, and the recurrent sonic booms of vanity, are eliminated at the outset, and there is time to think. There are no voices, and therefore no rising voices. It is, when you look at it this way, a great discovery. Before Delphi, real listening in a committee meeting has always been a near impossibility. Each member's function was to talk, and while other people were talking the individual member was busy figuring out what he ought to say next in order to shore up his own original position. Debating is what committees really do, not thinking. Take away the need for winning points, leading the discussion, protecting one's face, gaining applause, shouting down opposition, scaring opponents, all that kind of noisy activity, and a group of bright people can get down to quiet thought. It is a nice idea, and I'm glad it works.

It is interesting that Delphi is the name chosen, obviously to suggest the oracular prophetic function served. The original Delphi was Apollo's place, and Apollo was the god of prophecy, but more than that. He was also the source of some of the best Greek values: moderation, sanity, care, attention to the rules, deliberation. Etymologically, in fact, Apollo may have had his start as a committee. The word *apollo* (and perhaps the related word *apello*) originally meant a political gathering. The importance of public meetings for figuring out what to do next must have been perceived very early as fundamental to human society, therefore needing incorporation into myth and the creation of an administrative deity; hence Apollo, the Dorian god of prophecy.

The Pythian prophetess of Delphi was not really supposed to enunciate clear answers to questions about the future. On the contrary, her pronouncements often contained as much vagueness as the *I Ching,* and were similarly designed to provide options among which choice was possible. She symbolized something more like the committee's agenda. When she collapsed in ecstasy on the tripod, murmuring ambiguities, she became today's questionnaire. The working out of the details involved a meticulous exegesis of the oracle's statements, and this was the task of the *exegetai,* a committee of citizens, partly elected by the citizens of Athens and partly appointed by the Delphi oracle. The system seems to have worked well enough for a long time, constructing the statutory and legal basis for Greek religion.

Today's Delphi thus represents a refinement of an ancient social device, with a novel modification of committee procedure constraining groups of people to think more quietly, and to listen. The method seems new, as a formal procedure, but it is really very old, perhaps as old as human society itself. For in real life, this is the way we've always arrived at decisions, even though it has always been done in a disorganized way. We pass the word around; we ponder how the case is put by different people; we read the poetry; we mediate over the literature; we play the music; we change our minds; we reach an understanding. Society evolves this way, not by shouting each other down, but by the unique capacity of unique, individual human beings to comprehend each other.

## Questions

1. Locate the transition between the first and second paragraphs. Do you find it adequate? If so, explain to someone who does not understand it, the connection between the ideas in these two paragraphs. If not, try to explain where you get lost.
2. Why does Lewis find it "astonishing" that democracy "works at all, let alone well"?
3. The paragraph beginning "It is almost humiliating" (page 430) and the next two paragraphs are all extremely short. Were you ever taught, as some of us were, to avoid one- or two-sentence paragraphs? Would you recommend that Thomas take a writing course? Or how might you justify his paragraphs?
4. Drawing on this essay only, in a paragraph set forth your impression of Lewis Thomas. What sort of "voice" do you hear in the printed words?

5. Drawing on your own experience, evaluate Thomas's statement "Debating is what committees really do, not thinking."
6. Committees have a bad reputation. Ibsen said that he laughed whenever he heard the words "A committee has been appointed," and some nameless wag said that a camel is a horse designed by a committee. In an essay of 500 words explain exactly why some committee that you were on was notably successful or notably unsuccessful.

## James Thurber

# The Secret Life of Walter Mitty

"We're going through!" The Commander's voice was like thin ice breaking. He wore his full-dress uniform, with the heavily braided white cap pulled down rakishly over one cold gray eye. "We can't make it, sir. It's spoiling for a hurricane, if you ask me." "I'm not asking you, Lieutenant Berg," said the Commander. "Throw on the power lights! Rev her up to 8,500! We're going through!" The pounding of the cylinders increased; ta-pocketa-pocketa-pocketa-*pocketa-pocketa.* The Commander stared at the ice forming on the pilot window. He walked over and twisted a row of complicated dials. "Switch on No. 8 auxiliary!" he shouted. "Switch on No. 8 auxiliary!" repeated Lieutenant Berg. "Full strength in No. 3 turret!" shouted the Commander. "Full strength in No. 3 turret!" The crew, bending to their various tasks in the huge, hurtling eight-engined Navy hydroplane, looked at each other and grinned. "The Old Man'll get us through," they said to one another. "The Old Man ain't afraid of Hell!" . . .

"Not so fast! You're driving too fast!" said Mrs. Mitty. "What are you driving so fast for?"

"Hmm?" said Walter Mitty. He looked at his wife, in the seat beside him, with shocked astonishment. She seemed grossly unfamiliar, like a strange woman who had yelled at him in a crowd. "You

James Thurber (1894–1961) published most of his essays, stories, and cartoons in *The New Yorker.*

were up to fifty-five," she said. "You know I don't like to go more than forty. You were up to fifty-five." Walter Mitty drove on toward Waterbury in silence, the roaring of the SN202 through the worst storm in twenty years of Navy flying fading in the remote, intimate airways of his mind. "You're tensed up again," said Mrs. Mitty. "It's one of your days. I wish you'd let Dr. Renshaw look you over."

Walter Mitty stopped the car in front of the building where his wife went to have her hair done. "Remember to get those overshoes while I'm having my hair done," she said. "I don't need overshoes," said Mitty. She put her mirror back into her bag. "We've been all through that," she said, getting out of the car. "You're not a young man any longer." He raced the engine a little. "Why don't you wear your gloves? Have you lost your gloves?" Walter Mitty reached in a pocket and brought out the gloves. He put them on, but after she had turned and gone into the building and he had driven on to a red light, he took them off again. "Pick it up, brother," snapped a cop as the light changed, and Mitty hastily pulled on his gloves and lurched ahead. He drove around the streets aimlessly for a time, and then he drove past the hospital on his way to the parking lot.

. . . "It's the millionaire banker, Wellington McMillan," said the pretty nurse. "Yes?" said Walter Mitty, removing his gloves slowly. "Who has the case?" "Dr. Renshaw and Dr. Benbow, but there are two specialists here, Dr. Remington from New York and Dr. Pritchard-Mitford from London. He flew over." A door opened down a long, cool corridor and Dr. Renshaw came out. He looked distraught and haggard. "Hello, Mitty," he said. "We're having the devil's own time with McMillan, the millionaire banker and close personal friend of Roosevelt. Obstreosis of the ductal tract. Tertiary. Wish you'd take a look at him." "Glad to," said Mitty.

In the operating room there were whispered introductions: "Dr. Remington, Dr. Mitty. Dr. Pritchard-Mitford, Dr. Mitty." "I've read your book on streptothricosis," said Pritchard-Mitford, shaking hands. "A brilliant performance, sir." "Thank you," said Walter Mitty. "Didn't know you were in the States, Mitty," grumbled Remington. "Coals to Newcastle, bringing Mitford and me up here for a tertiary." "You are very kind," said Mitty. A huge, complicated machine, connected to the operating table, with many tubes and wires, began at this moment to go pocketa-pocketa-pocketa. "The new anaesthetizer is giving away!" shouted an interne. "There is no one in the East who knows how to fix it!" "Quiet, man!" said Mitty, in a low, cool voice. He sprang to the machine, which was now going pocketa-pocketa-queep-pocketa-queep. He began fingering delicately a row of glistening dials. "Give me a fountain pen!" he snapped. Someone handed him a fountain pen. He pulled a faulty piston out of the machine and inserted the pen in its place. "That will hold for ten minutes," he said. "Get on with the operation." A nurse hurried over and whispered to Renshaw, and Mitty saw the man turn pale. "Coreopsis has set in," said Renshaw nervously. "If you would take over, Mitty?" Mitty looked at him and at the craven figure of Benbow, who drank, and at the grave, uncertain faces of the two great specialists. "If you wish," he said. They slipped a white gown on him; he adjusted a mask and drew on thin gloves; nurses handed him shining . . .

"Back it up, Mac! Look out for that Buick!" Walter Mitty jammed on the brakes. "Wrong lane, Mac," said the parking-lot attendant, looking at Mitty closely. "Gee. Yeh," muttered Mitty. He began cautiously to back out of the lane marked "Exit Only." "Leave her sit there," said the attendant. "I'll put her away." Mitty got out of the car. "Hey, better leave the key." "Oh," said Mitty, handing the man the ignition key. The attendant vaulted into the car, backed it up with insolent skill, and put it where it belonged.

They're so damn cocky, thought Walter Mitty, walking along Main Street; they think they know everything. Once he had tried to take his chains off, outside New Milford, and he had got them wound around the axles. A man had had to come out in a wrecking car and unwind them, a young, grinning garage man. Since then Mrs. Mitty always made him drive to a garage to have the chains taken off. The next time, he thought, I'll wear my right arm in a sling; they won't grin at me then. I'll have my right arm in a sling and they'll see I couldn't possibly take the chains off myself. He kicked at the slush on the sidewalk. "Overshoes," he said to himself, and he began looking for a shoe store.

When he came out into the street again, with the overshoes in a box under his arm, Walter Mitty began to wonder what the other thing was his wife had told him to get. She had told him, twice before they set out from their house for Waterbury. In a way he hated these weekly trips to town—he was always getting something wrong. Kleenex, he thought, Squibb's, razor blades? No. Toothpaste, toothbrush, bicarbonate, carborundum, initiative and referendum? He gave it up. But she would remember it. "Where's the what's-its-name?" She would ask. "Don't tell me you forgot the what's-its-name." A newsboy went by shouting something about the Waterbury trial.

. . ."Perhaps this will refresh your memory." The District Attorney suddenly thrust a heavy automatic at the quiet figure on the witness stand. "Have you ever seen this before?" Walter Mitty took the gun and examined it expertly. "This is my Webley-Vickers 50.-80," he said calmly. An excited buzz ran around the courtroom. The judge rapped for order. "You are a crack shot with any sort of firearms, I believe?" said the District Attorney, insinuatingly. "Objection!" shouted Mitty's attorney. "We have shown that the defendant could not have fired the shot. We have shown that he wore his right arm in a sling on the night of the fourteenth of July." Walter Mitty raised his hand briefly and the bickering attorneys were stilled. "With any known make of gun," he said evenly, "I could have killed Gregory Fitzhurst at three hundred feet *with my left hand.*" Pandemonium broke loose in the courtroom. A woman's scream rose above the bedlam and suddenly a lovely, dark-haired girl was in Walter Mitty's arms. The District Attorney struck at her savagely. Without rising from his chair, Mitty let the man have it on the point of the chin. "You miserable cur!"

"Puppy biscuit," said Walter Mitty. He stopped walking and the buildings of Waterbury rose up out of the misty courtroom and surrounded him again. A woman who was passing laughed. "He said 'Puppy biscuit,' " she said to her companion. "That man said 'Puppy biscuit' to himself." Walter Mitty hurried on. He went into an A. & P., not the first one he came to but a smaller one farther up the street. "I want some biscuit for small, young dogs," he said to the clerk. "Any special brand, sir?" The greatest pistol shot in the world thought a moment. "It says 'Puppies Bark for It' on the box," said Walter Mitty.

His wife would be through at the hairdresser's in fifteen minutes, Mitty saw in looking at his watch, unless they had trouble drying it; sometimes they had trouble drying it. She didn't like to get to the hotel first; she would want him to be there waiting for her as usual. He found a big leather chair in the lobby, facing a window, and he put the overshoes and the puppy biscuit on the floor beside it. He picked up an old copy of *Liberty* and sank down into the chair. "Can Germany Conquer the World through the Air?" Walter Mitty looked at the pictures of bombing planes and of ruined streets.

. . ."The cannonading has got the wind up in young Raleigh, sir," said the sergeant. Captain Mitty looked up at him through tousled hair. "Get him to bed," he said wearily, "with the others. I'll fly alone." "But you can't, sir," said the sergeant anxiously. "It takes two men to handle that bomber and the Archies are pounding hell out of the air. Von Richtman's circus is between here and Saulier." "Somebody's got to get that ammunition dump," said Mitty. "I'm going over. Spot of brandy?" He poured a drink for the sergeant and one for himself. War thundered and whined around the dugout and battered at the door. There was a rending of wood and splinters flew through the room. "A bit of a near thing," said Captain Mitty carelessly. "The box barrage is closing in," said the sergeant. "We only live once, sergeant," said Mitty, with his faint, fleeting smile. "Or do we?" He poured another brandy and tossed it off. "I never see a man could hold his brandy like you, sir," said the sergeant. "Begging your pardon, sir." Captain Mitty stood up and strapped on his huge Webley-Vickers automatic. "It's forty kilometers through hell, sir," said the sergeant. Mitty finished one last brandy. "After all," he said softly, "what isn't?" The pounding of the cannon increased; there was the rat-tat-tatting of machine guns, and from somewhere came the menacing pocketa-pocketa-pocketa of the new flame-throwers. Walter Mitty walked to the door of the dugout humming "Après de Ma Blonde." He turned and waved to the sergeant. "Cheerio!" he said. . . .

Something struck his shoulder. "I've been looking all over this hotel for you," said Mrs. Mitty. "Why do you have to hide in this old chair? How did you expect me to find you?" "Things close in," said Walter Mitty vaguely. "What?" Mrs. Mitty said. "Did you get the what's-its-name? The puppy biscuit? What's in that box?" "Overshoes," said Mitty. "Couldn't you have put them on in the store?" "I was thinking," said Walter Mitty. "Does it ever occur to you that I am sometimes thinking?" She looked at him. "I'm going to take your temperature when I get you home," she said.

They went out through the revolving doors that made a faintly derisive whistling sound when you pushed them. It was two blocks to the parking lot. At the drugstore on the corner she said, "Wait here for me. I forgot something. I won't be a minute." She was more than a minute. Walter Mitty lighted a cigarette. It began to rain, rain with sleet in it. He stood up against the wall of the drugstore, smoking. . . . He put his shoulders back and his heels together. "To hell with the handkerchief," said Walter Mitty scornfully. He took one last drag on his cigarette and snapped it away. Then, with that faint, fleeting smile playing about his lips, he faced the firing squad; erect and motionless, proud and disdainful, Walter Mitty the Undefeated, inscrutable to the last.

## Questions

1. Why does Mitty have daydreams? From what sources has he derived the substance of his daydreams?
2. We may sympathize with Mitty, but we laugh at him, too. Why do we find this story primarily comic instead of pathetic? If it were intended to move us deeply, rather than to amuse us, what kinds of changes would have to be made in Mitty's daydreams? What other changes would have to be made in the characterization of Mitty and of his wife?
3. In the last sentence Mitty imagines himself facing a firing squad, "Mitty the Undefeated, inscrutable to the last." To what degree can it be argued that he is undefeated and inscrutable?

# 7

# RIVALS AND ENEMIES

*Sitting Bull and Buffalo Bill*
**William McFarlane Notman, 1885**

Notman Photographic Archives, McCord Museum

*John Pierpont Morgan*
**Edward Steichen, 1903**

Courtesy of The Trustees of The Pierpont Morgan Library

*A Situation Well in Hand*
**Anthony Bruculere**

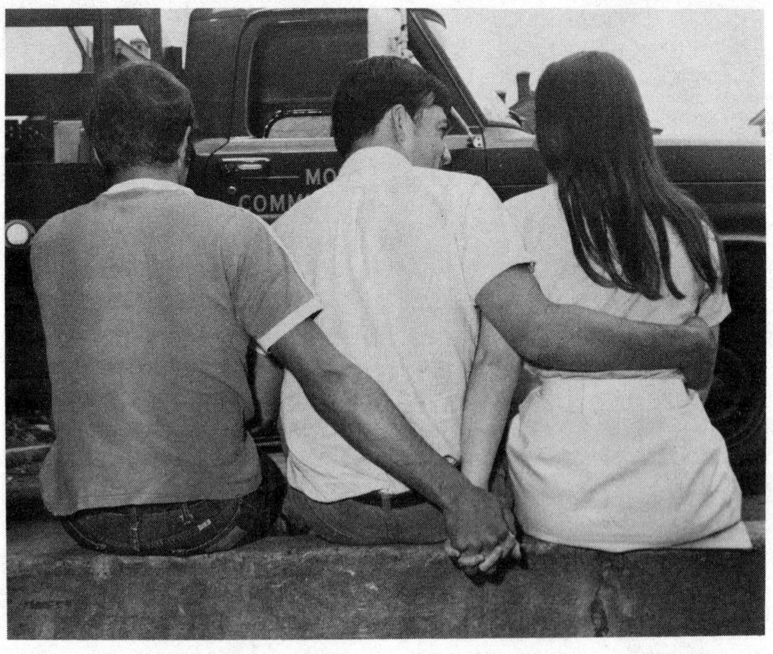

*The Soiling of Old Glory*
**Stanley J. Forman, 1976**

Courtesy of *The Boston Herald American*

## Short Views

Thou shalt not kill.

**Exodus 20:13**

Then said Jesus unto him, "Put up again thy sword into his place: for all they that take the sword shall perish with the sword."

**Matthew 26:52**

Then went the jury out, whose names were Mr. Blindman, Mr. No-good, Mr. Malice, Mr. Love-lust, Mr. Live-loose, Mr. Heady, Mr. High-mind, Mr. Enmity, Mr. Liar, Mr. Cruelty, Mr. Hate-light, Mr. Implacable, who every one gave in his private verdict against him among themselves, and afterwards unanimously concluded to bring him in guilty before the judge. And first among themselves, Mr. Blindman, the foreman, said, I see clearly that this man is a heretic. Then said Mr. No-good, Away with such a fellow from the earth! Ay, said Mr. Malice, for I hate the very look of him. Then said Mr. Love-lust, I could never endure him. Nor I, said Mr. Live-loose; for he would be always condemning my way. Hang him, hang him, said Mr. Heady. A sorry scrub, said Mr. High-mind. My heart riseth against him, said Mr. Enmity. He is a rogue, said Mr. Liar. Hanging is too good for him, said Mr. Cruelty. Let us despatch him out the way, said Mr. Hate-light. Then said Mr. Implacable, Might I have all the world given me, I could not be reconciled to him; therefore let us forthwith bring him in guilty of death.

**John Bunyan, *Pilgrim's Progress***

"I dislike him."—Why?—"I am not a match for him"—Did anyone ever answer so?

**Friedrich Nietzsche**

We mortals, men and women, devour many a disappointment between breakfast and dinner-time; keep back the tears and look a little pale about the lips, and in answer to inquiries say, "Oh, nothing!" Pride helps us; and pride is not a bad thing when it only urges us to hide our own hurts—not to hurt others.

**George Eliot, *Middlemarch***

America—Love It or Leave It.

**Anonymous**

To define force—it is that $x$ that turns anybody who is subjected to it into a *thing.* Exercised to the limit, it turns man into a thing in the most literal sense: it makes a corpse out of him. Somebody was here, and the next minute there is nobody here at all; this is a spectacle the *Iliad* never wearies of showing us:

> . . . the horses
> Rattled the empty chariots through the files of battle,
> Longing for their noble drivers. But they on the ground
> Lay, dearer to the vultures than to their wives.

The hero becomes a *thing* dragged behind a chariot in the dust:

> All around, his black hair
> Was spread; in the dust his whole head lay,
> That once-charming head; now Zeus had let his enemies
> Defile it on his native soil.

The bitterness of such a spectacle is offered us absolutely undiluted. No comforting fiction intervenes; no consoling prospect of immortality; and on the hero's head no washed-out halo of patriotism descends.

> His soul, fleeing his limbs, passed to Hades,
> Mourning its fate, forsaking its youth and its vigor.

Still more poignant—so painful is the contrast—is the sudden evocation, as quickly rubbed out, of another world: the faraway, precarious, touching world of peace, of the family, the world in which each man counts more than anything else to those about him.

> She ordered her bright-haired maids to the palace
> To place on the fire a large tripod, preparing
> A hot bath for Hector, returning from battle.
> Foolish woman! Already he lay, far from hot baths,
> Slain by grey-eyed Athena, who guided Achilles' arm.

Far from hot baths he was indeed, poor man. And not he alone. Nearly all the *Iliad* takes place far from hot baths. Nearly all of human life, then and now, takes place far from hot baths.

**Simone Weil**

War is hell.

**William Tecumseh Sherman**

Thomas Hobbes

# Of the Natural Condition of Mankind, as Concerning Their Felicity, and Misery

Nature has made men so equal in the faculties of body and mind as that though there be found one man sometimes manifestly stronger in body or of quicker mind than another, yet when all is reckoned together the difference between man and man is not so considerable as that one man can thereupon claim to himself any benefit to which another may not pretend as well as he. For as to the strength of body, the weakest has strength enough to kill the strongest, either by secret machination, or by confederacy with others that are in the same danger with himself.

And as to the faculties of the mind (setting aside the arts grounded upon words, and especially that skill of proceeding upon general and infallible rules called science, which very few have, and but in few things as being not a native faculty, born with us, nor attained—as prudence—while we look after somewhat else), I find yet a greater equality amongst men than that of strength. For prudence is but experience, which equal time equally bestows on all men in those things they equally apply themselves unto. That which may perhaps make such equality incredible is but a vain conceit of one's own wisdom, which almost all men think they have in a greater degree than the vulgar, that is, than all men but themselves and a few others, whom by fame, or for concurring with themselves, they approve. For such is the nature of men, that howsoever they may acknowledge many others to be more witty, or more eloquent, or

---

Thomas Hobbes (1588–1679) was Francis Bacon's student and for a while his secretary. In 1640, when Charles I was defeated by the Puritan army, Hobbes left England for Paris. In 1651 he published *Leviathan* there, but returned to England a few months later. In *Leviathan* Hobbes argues that men must "confer all their power and strength upon one man, or upon one assembly of men." The Leviathan is a state in which all people are united in one. The book so pleased Charles II that he pensioned Hobbes. We reprint chapter 13.

---

more learned, yet they will hardly believe there be many so wise as themselves, for they see their own wit at hand, and other men's at a distance. But this proves rather that men are in that point equal, than unequal. For there is not ordinarily a greater sign of the equal distribution of anything than that every man is contented with his share.

From this equality of ability arises equality of hope in the attaining of our ends. And therefore if any two men desire the same thing, which nevertheless they cannot both enjoy, they become enemies; and in the way to their end (which is principally their own conservation, and sometimes their delectation only), endeavor to destroy or subdue one another. And from hence it comes to pass that where an invader has no more to fear than another man's single power, if one plant, sow, build, or possess a convenient seat, others may probably be expected to come prepared with forces united to dispossess and deprive him, not only of the fruit of his labor, but also of his life, or liberty. And the invader again is in the like danger of another.

And from this diffidence of one another, there is no way for any man to secure himself so reasonable as anticipation; that is, by force, or wiles, to master the persons of all men he can, so long till he sees no other power great enough to endanger him, and this is no more than his own conservation requires, and is generally allowed. Also because there be some that taking pleasure in contemplating their own power in the acts of conquest, which they pursue farther than their security requires; if others, that otherwise would be glad to be at ease within modest bounds should not by invasion increase their power, they would not be able, long time, by standing only on their defense, to subsist. And by consequence, such augmentation of dominion over men, being necessary to man's conservation, it ought to be allowed him.

Again, men have no pleasure (but on the contrary a great deal of grief) in keeping company where there is no power able to overawe them all. For every man looks that his companion should value him at the same rate he sets upon himself, and upon all signs of contempt, or undervaluing, naturally endeavors, as far as he dares (which amongst them that have no common power to keep them in quiet is far enough to make them destroy each other), to extort a greater value from his contemners by homage, and from others by the example.

So that in the nature of man we find three principal causes of quarrel. First, competition; secondly, diffidence; thirdly, glory.

The first makes men invade for gain; the second for safety; and the third for reputation. The first use violence to make themselves masters of other men's persons, wives, children, and cattle; the second, to defend them; the third, for trifles, as a word, a smile, a different opinion, and any other sign of undervalue, either direct in their persons, or by reflection in their kindred, their friends, their nation, their profession, or their name.

Hereby it is manifest that during the time men live without a common power to keep them all in awe, they are in that condition which is called war; and such a war, as is of every man, against every man. For *war* consists not in battle only, or the act of fighting, but in a tract of time wherein the will to contend by battle is sufficiently known, and therefore the notion of *time* is to be considered in the nature of war, as it is in the nature of weather. For as the nature of foul weather lies not in a shower or two of rain but in an inclination thereto of many days together, the nature of war consists not in actual fighting, but in the known disposition thereto during all the time there is no assurance to the contrary. All other time is *peace.*

Whatsoever therefore is consequent to a time of war, where every man is enemy to every man, the same is consequent to the time wherein men live without other security than what their own strength and their own invention shall furnish them withal. In such condition there is no place for industry, because the fruit thereof is uncertain, and consequently no culture of the earth, no navigation, nor use of the commodities that may be imported by sea, no commodious building, no instruments of moving and removing such things as require much force, no knowledge of the face of the earth, no account of time, no arts, no letters, no society; and which is worst of all, continual fear, and danger of violent death; and the life of man, solitary, poor, nasty, brutish, and short.

It may seem strange to some man that has not well weighed these things that nature should thus dissociate and render men apt to invade and destroy one another, and he may therefore, not trusting to this inference made from the passions, desire perhaps to have the same confirmed by experience. Let him therefore consider with himself: when taking a journey he arms himself and seeks to go well accompanied; when going to sleep he locks his doors; when even in his house he locks his chests; and this when he knows there be laws and public officers armed to revenge all injuries that shall be done him; what opinion he has of his fellow subjects, when he rides armed; of his fellow citizens, when he locks his doors; and of his children and servants, when he locks his chests. Does he not there as much accuse mankind by his actions, as I do by my words? But neither of us accuse man's nature in it. The desires and other passions of men are in themselves no sin. No more are the actions that proceed from those passions, till they know a law that forbids them, which till laws be made they cannot know; nor can any law be made till they have agreed upon the person that shall make it.

It may peradventure be thought there was never such a time nor condition of war as this, and I believe it was never generally so over all the world, but there are many places where they live so now. For the savage people in many places of *America,* except the government of small families, the concord whereof depends on natural lust, have no government at all, and live at this day in that brutish manner as I said before. Howsoever, it may be perceived what manner of life there would be where there were no common power to fear by the manner of life which men that have formerly lived under a peaceful government use to degenerate into, in a civil war.

But though there had never been any time wherein particular men were in a condition of war one against another, yet in all times, kings, and persons of sovereign authority, because of their independence, are in continual jealousies, and in the state and posture of gladiators, having their weapons pointing, and their eyes fixed on one another; that is, their forts, garrisons, and guns upon the frontiers of their kingdoms, and continual spies upon their neighbors, which is a posture of war. But because they uphold thereby the industry of their subjects, there does not follow from it that misery which accompanies the liberty of particular men.

To this war of every man against every man, this also is consequent: that nothing can be unjust. The notions of right and wrong, justice and injustice, have there no place. Where there is no common power, there is no law; where no law, no injustice. Force and fraud are in war the two cardinal virtues. Justice and injustice are none of the faculties neither of the body nor mind. If they were, they might be in a man that were alone in the world, as well as his senses and passions. They are qualities that relate to men in society, not in solitude. It is consequent also to the same condition that there be no propriety, no dominion, no *mine* and *thine* distinct; but only that to be every man's that he can get, and for so long as he can keep it. And thus much for the ill condition which man by mere nature is actually placed in, though with a possibility to come out of it, consisting partly in the passions, partly in his reason.

The passions that incline men to peace are fear of death, desire of such things as are necessary to commodious living, and a hope by their industry to obtain them. And reason suggests convenient articles of peace upon which men may be drawn to agreement. These articles are they which otherwise are called the laws of nature. . . .

## Questions

1. Hobbes asserts that all men are roughly equal in power. What evidence of equality does he offer? Why does he establish the premise of equality at the beginning of his argument?
2. In his third paragraph Hobbes speaks of the "ends" we hope to attain. What are these ends? What do we most fear?
3. Restate in your own words Hobbes's definition of war. What is peace, and how is it achieved?
4. What does Hobbes seem to mean by felicity? Does he find the cause of man's misery in the nature of the world that man finds himself in or in some defect in human nature?
5. Do you find Hobbes's analysis of the causes of the "war of every man against every man" and the path to peace applicable to wars between modern nations? Explain.
6. Hobbes sees men as motivated in part by their passions and in part by their reason. Does he argue for the moral superiority of one over the other?
7. Hobbes has been criticized, both by those who respect his philosophy and by those who do not, for indulging in exaggeration, or overstatement. Point out some examples of overstatement in these pages and explain why these are overstatements. Then give and evaluate the argument or arguments for or against his use of overstatement.

## Mark Stevens

# Goya's *Third of May, 1808*

On May 2, 1808, the citizens of Madrid rose against the occupying forces of Napoleon, attacking his Egyptian Mameluke cavalry in the city's Puerta del Sol. The next night the French retaliated by slaughtering Spanish hostages. It was an ugly, brutish exchange. Six years later, Goya commemorated the event in two large canvases: *Second of May, 1808,* which shows the mob attacking the Mamelukes, and *Third of May 1808,* which portrays the execution of the hostages.

Both are extraordinary paintings. *Third of May,* however, has attained an importance beyond what is customary for great works of art. It is a painting of archetypal significance, a picture that seems to signal an essential change in the temper of Western civilization. Many observers have called it the first modern picture. They are right, not because Goya's formal approach was innovative, although it was, but because he was the first to portray, without false consolation, the horror near the heart of modern life.

I admire Goya's courage. Today it is not unusual to present an unsugared view of modern warfare or to bemoan the loss of heroism and religious solace; existential screams (and sighs) are commonplace. It was not so in Goya's day. A lesser painter, given the commission to commemorate the second and third of May, would have followed the traditional practice of the period. For example, he might have created a great historical panorama of nobility and heroism, in which the oppressed rise against their oppressors; the doomed would face death with the courage of martyrs. Goya, however, watched human beings, not fashion. He told the truth: what happened on the third of May was a butchering.

The iconography, the color and light, the composition—all contribute to the power of this picture. Its most impressive aspect, in my view, is that Goya was able to recall, even as he destroyed, those

Mark Stevens is an art critic for *Newsweek* and other journals, and is a novelist.

*The Third of May, 1808*
**Francisco Goya, 1814**

Alinari/Editorial Photocolor Archives

conventions that once provided solace; he transformed the conventions of hope into those of despair. This makes the horror all the greater, for we can see what we have lost, in addition to what we have. In the background, for example, the spire of the church is a dark, dim reminder, certainly not cause for hope. The cruelty of the execution, which takes place in a melodramatic light, reminds us of acts of martyrdom—but without the traditional promise of heavenly reward.

Of course, the outstretched arms of the central figure also recall the Crucifixion, and the man's hands bear stigmata. However, the traditional religious gesture of acceptance—the outstretched arms of Christ—has here been turned into an expression of outrage, terror and meaninglessness. What is the victim saying? There is nothing he can say, for his situation is one in which neither faith nor reason matter. His outflung arms are mirrored by those of the corpse in the foreground: such is the promise of resurrection. The corpse itself is perhaps the most truthful ever painted, for it exhibits the unbearable banality, the crumpled emptiness of death.

The men around the central victim display a variety of other reactions to their fate, none noble. One looks heavenward, but his expression is groveling. The praying man cannot raise his eyes. A third hides his face, as do the victims who await execution. Goya's use of light enhances their horror. The light contains no spiritual overtone, but rather emanates from a common lantern; an intense glow is cast on the small, grisly scene, but it cannot pierce the dark reaches. This light—glaring, without delicacy, lurid, almost artificial—seems peculiarly modern.

Goya anticipated certain other traits of modern violence that later artists would also explore. The ragged humanity of the victims is contrasted to the repetitive regularity of the line of executioners. Although the faces of most of the victims can be seen, the executioners remain faceless. There is even a certain mechanical gruesomeness to the execution, since the victims are led to the wall in assembly-line fashion, one batch after another.

In addition to his brilliant use of light and shade, which isolates the central figure, Goya used several other formal devices to make his point. He employed sweeping diagonal lines to scissor the picture into sharp, claustrophobic spaces. He foreshortened the corpse, so that the body seems to draw toward the viewer. (It almost looks as though the dead man is bidding the viewer welcome.) Otherwise, Goya has positioned the figures so that the viewer, curiously, is placed on the side of the executioners. You and I, observing, are implicated in mankind's folly.

Some critics have accused Goya of slapdash effects and sloppy handling. In this painting, however, the spots of gritty brushwork further suggest the horror of the situation, and any dissonance of line, light or color seems appropriate to the subject matter; too much artiness, or visual delectation, would have weakened the picture's power. The application of gummy, drying paint suggests, with horrible particularity, the clotting of blood.

Perhaps the chief terror of *Third of May,* however, is its shocking intimacy. Goya had a gift in that direction. His earlier portraits of the royal family, though rather unforgiving, were intimate in their insight, and his *Naked Maja* is one of the most erotic pictures ever painted. By 1814, however, Goya, through his experience of war and ill health, was forced into an intimate relation with death. He stripped away hope. He bared pain. He displayed, for all to see, the moment before death. What could be more intimate than the cold prick of a rifle against a white tunic?

## Questions

1. Wbat does it mean to say, in the second paragraph, that *The Third of May* "is a painting of archetypal significance"?
2. The writer begins the third paragraph with "I admire Goyas's courage." Does the essay as a whole seem too personal? If so, cite some bothersome passages. If not, cite some passages that, when one thinks about them, reflect personal opinions but do not obviously and obstrusively do so.
3. If Mark Stevens wrote an essay on the companion picture, *Second of May, 1808,* would you read it? Why, or why not?

Lewis Thomas

# The Iks

The small tribe of Iks, formerly nomadic hunters and gatherers in the mountain valleys of northern Uganda, have become celebrities, literary symbols for the ultimate fate of disheartened, heartless mankind at large. Two disastrously conclusive things happened to them: the government decided to have a national park, so they were compelled by law to give up hunting in the valleys and become farmers on poor hillside soil, and then they were visited for two years by an anthropologist who detested them and wrote a book about them.

The message of the book is that the Iks have transformed themselves into an irreversibly disagreeable collection of unattached, brutish creatures, totally selfish and loveless, in response to the dismantling of their traditional culture. Moreover, this is what the rest of us are like in our inner selves, and we will all turn into Iks when the structure of our society comes all unhinged.

The argument rests, of course, on certain assumptions about the core of human beings, and is necessarily speculative. You have to agree in advance that man is fundamentally a bad lot, out for himself alone, displaying such graces as affection and compassion only as learned habits. If you take this view, the story of the Iks can be used to confirm it. These people seem to be living together, clustered in small, dense villages, but they are really solitary, unrelated individuals with no evident use for each other. They talk, but only to make ill-tempered demands and cold refusals. They share nothing. They never sing. They turn the children out to forage as soon as they can walk, and desert the elders to starve whenever they can, and the foraging children snatch food from the mouths of the helpless elders. It is a mean society.

They breed without love or even casual regard. They defecate on each other's doorsteps. They watch their neighbors for signs of misfortune, and only then do they laugh. In the book they do a lot of

For a biographical note on Thomas, see page 428.

laughing, having so much bad luck. Several times they even laughed at the anthropologist, who found this especially repellent (one senses, between the lines, that the scholar is not himself the world's luckiest man). Worse, they took him into the family, snatched his food, defecated on his doorstep, and hooted dislike at him. They gave him two bad years.

It is a depressing book. If, as he suggests, there is only Ikness at the center of each of us, our sole hope for hanging onto the name of humanity will be in endlessly mending the structure of our society, and it is changing so quickly and completely that we may never find the threads in time. Meanwhile, left to ourselves alone, solitary, we will become the same joyless, zestless, untouching lone animals.

But this may be too narrow a view. For one thing, the Iks are extraordinary. They are absolutely astonishing, in fact. The anthropologist has never seen people like them anywhere, nor have I. You'd think, if they were simply examples of the common essence of mankind, they'd seem more recognizable. Instead, they are bizarre, anomalous. I have known my share of peculiar, difficult, nervous, grabby people, but I've never encountered any genuinely, consistently detestable human beings in all my life. The Iks sound more like abnormalities, maladies.

I cannot accept it. I do not believe that the Iks are representative of isolated, revealed man, unobscured by social habits. I believe their behavior is something extra, something laid on. This unremitting, compulsive repellence is a kind of complicated ritual. They must have learned to act this way; they copied it, somehow.

I have a theory, then. The Iks have gone crazy.

The solitary Ik, isolated in the ruins of an exploded culture, has built a new defense for himself. If you live in an unworkable society you can make up one of your own, and this is what the Iks have done. Each Ik has become a group, a one-man tribe on its own, a constituency.

Now everything falls into place. This is why they do seem, after all, vaguely familiar to all of us. We've seen them before. This is precisely the way groups of one size or another, ranging from committees to nations, behave. It is, of course, this aspect of humanity that has lagged behind the rest of evolution, and this is why the Ik seems so primitive. In his absolute selfishness, his incapacity to give anything away, no matter what, he is a successful committee. When he stands at the door of his hut, shouting insults at his neighbors in a loud harangue, he is a city addressing another city.

Cities have all the Ik characteristics. They defecate on doorsteps, in rivers and lakes, their own or anyone else's. They leave rubbish. They detest all neighboring cities, give nothing away. They even build institutions for deserting elders out of sight.

Nations are the most Iklike of all. No wonder the Iks seem familiar. For total greed, rapacity, heartlessness, and irresponsibility there is nothing to match a nation. Nations, by law, are solitary, self-centered, withdrawn into themselves. There is no such thing as affection between nations, and certainly no nation ever loved another. They bawl insults from their doorsteps, defecate into whole oceans, snatch all the food, survive by detestation, take joy in the bad luck of others, celebrate the death of others, live for the death of others.

That's it, and I shall stop worrying about the book. It does not signify that man is a sparse, inhuman thing at his center. He's all right. It only says what we've always known and never had enough time to worry about, that we haven't yet learned how to stay human when assembled in masses. The Ik, in his despair, is acting out this failure, and perhaps we should pay closer attention. Nations have themselves become too frightening to think about, but we might learn some things by watching these people.

## Questions

1. Find the grim joke in the first paragraph.
2. In the third and fourth paragraphs, what is the effect of repeating the structure of subject and verb: "They talk . . . ," "They share . . . ," "They never sing," "They turn . . . ," "They breed . . . ," and so on?
3. Pick out a few colloquial expressions, and a few notably informal sentences. Do you find them inappropriate to a discussion of a serious topic?
4. What is Thomas's attitude toward the anthropologist and his book? Cite some passages that convey his attitude, and explain how they convey it, or how they are meant to persuade us to share it.
5. From this essay, try to conjecture what Thomas's view of human nature is.
6. If you have read Hobbes's essay (pages 446–50), explain how well the Iks' behavior confirms Hobbes's analysis of human nature. Does Thomas's explanation of the Iks' behavior offer arguments to refute Hobbes? Does it suggest how such an argument might be constructed?

## Desmond Morris

# Altruistic Behavior

### How Do We Help Others at Our Own Expense?

Altruism is the performance of an unselfish act. As a pattern of behavior this act must have two properties: it must benefit someone else, and it must do so to the disadvantage of the benefactor. It is not merely a matter of being helpful, it is helpfulness at a cost to yourself.

This simple definition conceals a difficult biological problem. If I harm myself to help you, then I am increasing your chances of success relative to mine. In broad evolutionary terms, if I do this, your offspring (or potential offspring) will have better prospects than mine. Because I have been altruistic, your genetic line will stand a better chance of survival than mine. Over a period of time, my unselfish line will die out and your selfish line will survive. So altruism will not be a viable proposition in evolutionary terms.

Since human beings are animals whose ancestors have won the long struggle for survival during their evolutionary history, they cannot be genetically programmed to display true altruism. Evolution theory suggests that they must, like all other animals, be entirely selfish in their actions, even when they appear to be at their most self-sacrificing and philanthropic.

This is the biological, evolutionary argument and it is completely convincing as far as it goes, but it does not seem to explain many of mankind's "finer moments." If a man sees a burning house and inside it his small daughter, an old friend, a complete stranger, or even a screaming kitten, he may, without pausing to think, rush headlong into the building and be badly burned in a desperate attempt to save a life. How can actions of this sort be described as selfish? The fact is that they can, but it requires a special definition of the term "self."

When you think of your "self," you probably think of your living body, complete, as it is at this moment. But biologically it is more correct to think of yourself as merely a temporary housing, a disposable container, for your genes. Your genes—the genetic mate-

Desmond Morris, born in 1928, is the author of numerous books about animal (including human) behavior.

rial that you inherited from your parents and which you will pass on to your children—are in a sense immortal. Our bodies are merely the carriers which they use to transport themselves from one generation to the next. It is they, not we, who are the basic units of evolution. We are only their guardians, protecting them from destruction as best we can, for the brief span of our lives.

Religion pictures man as having an immortal soul which leaves his body at death and floats off to heaven (or hell, as the case may be), but the more useful image is to visualize a man's immortal soul as sperm-shaped and a woman's as egg-shaped, and to think of them as leaving the body during the breeding process rather than at death. Following this line of thought through, there is, of course, an after-life, but it is not in some mysterious "other world"; it is right here in the heaven (or hell) of the nursery and the playground, where our genes continue their immortal journey down the tunnel of time, re-housed now in the brand-new flesh-containers we call children.

So, genetically speaking, our children are us—or, rather, half of us, since our mate has a half share of the genes of each child. This makes our devoted and apparently selfless parental care nothing more than *genetic self-care.* The man who risks death to save his small daughter from a fire is in reality saving his own genes in their new body-package. And in saving his genes, his act becomes biologically selfish, rather than altruistic.

But supposing the man leaping into the fire is trying to save, not his daughter, but an old friend? How can this be selfish? The answer here lies in the ancient history of mankind. For more than a million years, man was a simple tribal being, living in small groups where everyone knew everyone else and everyone was closely genetically related to everyone else. Despite a certain amount of out-breeding, the chances were that every member of your own tribe was a relative of some kind, even if a rather remote one. A certain degree of altruism was therefore appropriate where all the other members of your tribe were concerned. You would be helping copies of your own genes, and although you might not respond so intensely to their calls for help as you would do with your own children, you would nevertheless give them a degree of help, again on a basis of genetic selfishness.

This is not, of course, a calculated process. It operates unconsciously and is based on an emotion we call "love." Our love for our children is what we say we are obeying when we act "selflessly" for them, and our love of our fellow-men is what we feel when we come to the aid of our friends. These are inborn tendencies and when we are faced with calls for help we feel ourselves obeying these deep-seated urges unquestioningly and unanalytically. It is only because we see ourselves as "persons" rather than as "gene machines" that we think of these acts of love as unselfish rather than selfish.

So far, so good, but what about the man who rushes headlong into the fire to save a complete stranger? The stranger is probably *not* genetically related to the man who helps him, so this act must surely be truly unselfish and altruistic? The answer is Yes, but only by accident. The accident is caused by the rapid growth of human populations in the last few thousand years. Previously, for millions of years, man was tribal and any inborn urge to help his fellow-men would have meant automatically that he was helping gene-sharing relatives, even if only remote ones. There was no need for this urge to be selective, because there were no strangers around to create problems. But with the urban explosion, man rapidly found himself in huge communities, surrounded by strangers, and with no time for his genetic constitution to alter to fit the startlingly new circumstances. So his altruism inevitably spread to include all his new fellow-citizens, even though many of them may have been genetically quite unrelated to him.

Politicians, exploiting this ancient urge, were easily able to spread the aid-system even further, to a national level called patriotism, so that men would go and die for their country as if it were their ancient tribe or their family.

The man who leaps into the fire to save a small kitten is a special case. To many people, animals are child-substitutes and receive the same care and love as real children. The kitten-saver is explicable as a man who is going to the aid of his symbolic child. This process of symbolizing, of seeing one thing as a metaphorical equivalent of another, is a powerful tendency of the human animal and it accounts for a great deal of the spread of helpfulness across the human environment.

In particular it explains the phenomenon of dying for a cause. This always gives the appearance of the ultimate in altruistic behavior, but a careful examination of the nature of each cause reveals that there is some basic symbolism at work. A nun who gives her life for Christ is already technically a "bride" of Christ and looks upon all people as the "children" of God. Her symbolism has brought the whole of humanity into her "family circle" and her altruism is for her symbolic family, which to her can become as real as other people's natural families.

In this manner it is possible to explain the biological bases for man's seemingly altruistic behavior. This is in no way intended to belittle such activities, but merely to point out that the more usual, alternative explanations are not necessary. For example, it is often stated that man is fundamentally wicked and that his kind acts are largely the result of the teachings of moralists, philosophers and priests; that if he is left to his own devices he will become increasingly savage, violent and cruel. The confidence trick involved here is that if we accept this viewpoint we will attribute all society's good qualities to the brilliant work of these great teachers. The biological truth appears to be rather different. Since selfishness is genetic rather than personal, we will have a natural tendency to help our blood-relatives and hence our whole tribe. Since our tribes have swollen into nations, our helpfulness becomes stretched further and further, aided and abetted by our tendency towards accepting symbolic substitutes for the real thing. Altogether this means that we are now, by nature, a remarkably helpful species. If there are break-downs in this helpfulness, they are probably due, not to our "savage nature" reasserting itself, but to the unbearable tensions under which people so often find themselves in the strained and over-crowded world of today.

It would be a mistake, nevertheless, to overstate man's angelic helpfulness. He is also intensely competitive. But under normal circumstances these rival tendencies balance each other out, and this balance accounts for a great deal of human intercourse, in the form of *transactional behavior.* This is behavior of the "I'll-scratch-your-back-if-you'll-scratch-mine" type. We do deals with one another. My actions help you, but they are not altruistic because they also help me at the same time. This co-operative behavior is perhaps the dominant feature of day-to-day social interaction. It is the basis of trade and commerce and it explains why such activities do not become more ruthless. If the competitive element were not tempered by the basic urge to help one another, business practices would rapidly become much more savage and brutal than they are, even today.

An important extension of this two-way cooperative behavior is embodied in the phrase: "one good turn now deserves another later." This is delayed, or nonspecific cooperation. I give help to you now, even though you cannot help me in return. I do this daily to many people I meet. One day I will need help and then, as part of a "long-term deal," they will return my help. I do not keep a check on what I am owed or by whom. Indeed, the person who finally helps me may not be one of the ones I have helped. But a whole network of social debts will have built up in a community and, as there is a great division of labor and skills in our species today, such a system will be beneficial to all the members of the society. This has been called "reciprocal altruism." But once again it is not true altruism because sooner or later, one way or another, I will be rewarded for my acts of helpfulness.

Anticipation of a delayed reward of this kind is often the hidden motive for a great deal of what is claimed to be purely altruistic behavior. Many countries hand out official awards to their citizens for "services to the community," but frequently these services have been deliberately undertaken in the anticipation that they are award-worthy. Comparatively few public honors ever come as a surprise. And many other "good works" are undertaken with later social (or heavenly) rewards in mind. This does not necessarily make the "works" any less good, of course; it merely explains the motives involved.

The following table sums up the relationship between competitiveness and helpfulness, and their intermediates:

| | | | |
|---|---|---|---|
| 1 Self-assertive behavior | Helps me | Harms you | Mild competitiveness to full criminality |
| 2 Self-indulgent behavior | Helps me | No effect on you | The private, non-social pleasures |
| 3 Co-operative behavior | Helps me | Helps you | Transaction, trade, barter and negotiation |
| 4 Courteous behavior | No effect on me | Helps you | Kindness and generosity |
| 5 "Altruistic" behavior | Harms me | Helps you | Loving devotion, philanthropy, self-sacrifice and patriotism |

## Questions

1. At the beginning of his second paragraph Morris says that the definition of altruism offered in his first paragraph "conceals a difficult biological problem." In your own words, explain the problem. At the end of this paragraph Morris summarizes his own explanation of the problem: "So altruism will not be a viable proposition in evolutionary terms." Look up "viable" in a good dictionary. Would a different adjective have made his explanation clearer? How else might the sentence be made clearer? Try rewriting the sentence.
2. How does Morris explain or define immortality? Is his definition consistent with (even though it may not be identical with) your own beliefs?
3. Morris explains patriotism as the exploitation by politicians of a genetic urge. Do you find this explanation adequate? How might Morris explain the behavior of politicians?
4. In the paragraph beginning "In this manner" (page 461), does Morris belittle good deeds and moral teachings? If you accept his explanation (and his dismissal of "alternative explanations"), is there any way to say that this act is good, that act evil? What function is left to "moralists, philosophers and priests"?
5. In the next-to-last paragraph Morris talks about the "anticipation of a delayed reward." How might he explain the bequests that wealthy philanthropists make to charitable causes in their last wills and testaments? Would he (in order to be consistent) have to take the view that they are all anticipating rewards in heaven? Or has his essay suggested more flexible explanations of charitable bequests?

# James Baldwin

# Stranger in the Village

From all available evidence no black man had ever set foot in this tiny Swiss village before I came. I was told before arriving that I would probably be a "sight" for the village; I took this to mean that people of my complexion were rarely seen in Switzerland, and also that city people are always something of a "sight" outside of the city. It did not occur to me—possibly because I am an American—that there could be people anywhere who had never seen a Negro.

It is a fact that cannot be explained on the basis of the inaccessibility of the village. The village is very high, but it is only four hours from Milan and three hours from Lausanne. It is true that it is virtually unknown. Few people making plans for a holiday would elect to come here. On the other hand, the villagers are able, presumably, to come and go as they please—which they do: to another town at the foot of the mountain, with a population of approximately five thousand, the nearest place to see a movie or go to the bank. In the village there is no movie house, no bank, no library, no theater; very few radios, one jeep, one station wagon; and at the moment, one typewriter, mine, an invention which the woman next door to me here had never seen. There are about six hundred people living here, all Catholic—I conclude this from the fact that the Catholic church is open all year round, whereas the Protestant chapel, set off on a hill a little removed from the village, is open only in the summertime when the tourists arrive. There are four or five hotels, all closed now, and four or five *bistros,* of which, however, only two do any business during the winter. These two do not do a great deal, for life in the village seems to end around nine or ten o'clock. There are a few stores, butcher, baker, *épicerie,* a hardware store, and a money-changer—who cannot change travelers' checks, but must send them down to the bank, an operation which takes two or three days. There

James Baldwin was born in Harlem in 1924 and was graduated from DeWitt Clinton High School. For a while he did odd jobs, but he also wrote, and in 1948 he received a fellowship that enabled him to go to Paris. There he wrote two novels (*Go Tell It on the Mountain* and *Giovanni's Room*) and some essays, published in *Notes of a Native Son.* He returned to the United States in 1955, where he has continued to publish fiction, plays, and essays.

is something called the *Ballet Haus,* closed in the winter and used for God knows what, certainly not ballet, during the summer. There seems to be only one schoolhouse in the village, and this for the quite young children; I suppose this to mean that their older brothers and sisters at some point descend from these mountains in order to complete their education—possibly, again, to the town just below. The landscape is absolutely forbidding, mountains towering on all four sides, ice and snow as far as the eye can reach. In this white wilderness, men and women and children move all day, carrying washing, wood, buckets of milk or water, sometimes skiing on Sunday afternoons. All week long boys and young men are to be seen shoveling snow off the rooftops, or dragging wood down from the forest in sleds.

The village's only real attraction, which explains the tourist season, is the hot spring water. A disquietingly high proportion of these tourists are cripples, or semi-cripples, who come year after year —from other parts of Switzerland, usually—to take the waters. This lends the village, at the height of the season, a rather terrifying air of sanctity, as though it were a lesser Lourdes. There is often something beautiful, there is always something awful, in the spectacle of a person who has lost one of his faculties, a faculty he never questioned until it was gone, and who struggles to recover it. Yet people remain people, on crutches or indeed on deathbeds; and wherever I passed, the first summer I was here, among the native villagers or among the lame, a wind passed with me—of astonishment, curiosity, amusement, and outrage. That first summer I stayed two weeks and never intended to return. But I did return in the winter, to work; the village offers, obviously, no distractions whatever and has the further advantage of being extremely cheap. Now it is winter again, a year later, and I am here again. Everyone in the village knows my name, though they scarcely ever use it, knows that I come from America—though this, apparently, they will never really believe: black men come from Africa—and everyone knows that I am the friend of the son of a woman who was born here, and that I am staying in their chalet. But I remain as much a stranger today as I was the first day I arrived, and the children shout *Neger! Neger!* as I walk along the streets.

It must be admitted that in the beginning I was far too shocked to have any real reaction. In so far as I reacted at all, I reacted by trying to be pleasant—it being a great part of the American Negro's education (long before he goes to school) that he must make people "like" him. This smile-and-the-world-smiles-with-you routine worked about as well in this situation as it had in the situation for which it was designed, which is to say that it did not work at all. No one, after all, can be liked whose human weight and complexity cannot be, or has not been, admitted. My smile was simply another unheard-of phenomenon which allowed them to see my teeth—they did not, really, see my smile and I began to think that, should I take to snarling, no one would notice any difference. All of the physical characteristics of the Negro which had caused me, in America, a very different and almost forgotten pain were nothing less than miraculous—or infernal—in the eyes of the village people. Some thought my hair was the color of tar, that it had the texture of wire, or the texture of cotton. It was jocularly suggested that I might let it all grow long and make myself a winter coat. If I sat in the sun for more than five minutes some daring creature was certain to come along and gingerly put his fingers on my hair, as though he were afraid of an electric shock, or put his hand on my hand, astonished that the color did not rub off. In all of this, in which it must be conceded there was the charm of genuine wonder and in which there were certainly no elements of intentional unkindness, there was yet no suggestion that I was human: I was simply a living wonder.

I knew that they did not mean to be unkind, and I know it now; it is necessary, nevertheless, for me to repeat this to myself each time that I walk out of the chalet. The children who shout *Neger!* have no way of knowing the echoes this sound raises in me. They are brimming with good humor and the more daring swell with pride when I stop to speak with them. Just the same, there are days when I cannot pause and smile, when I have no heart to play with them; when, indeed, I mutter sourly to myself, exactly as I muttered on the streets of a city these children have never seen, when I was no bigger than these children are now: *Your* mother *was a nigger.* Joyce is right about history being a nightmare—but it may be the nightmare from which no one *can* awaken. People are trapped in history and history is trapped in them.

There is a custom in the village—I am told it is repeated in many villages—of "buying" African natives for the purpose of converting them to Christianity. There stands in the church all year round a small box with a slot for money, decorated with a black figurine, and into this box the villagers drop their francs. During the *carnaval* which precedes Lent, two village children have their faces blackened —out of which bloodless darkness their blue eyes shine like ice—and fantastic horsehair wigs are placed on their blond heads; thus disguised, they solicit among the villagers for money for the missionaries in Africa. Between the box in the church and the blackened children, the village "bought" last year six or eight African natives. This was reported to me with pride by the wife of one of the bistro owners and I was careful to express astonishment and pleasure at the solicitude shown by the village for the souls of black folks. The bistro owner's wife beamed with a pleasure far more genuine than my own and seemed to feel that I might now breathe more easily concerning the souls of at least six of my kinsmen.

I tried not to think of these so lately baptized kinsmen, of the price paid for them, or the peculiar price they themselves would pay, and said nothing about my father, who having taken his own conversion too literally never, at bottom, forgave the white world (which he described as heathen) for having saddled him with a Christ in whom, to judge at least from their treatment of him, they themselves no longer believed. I thought of white men arriving for the first time in an African village, strangers there, as I am a stranger here, and tried to imagine the astounded populace touching their hair and marveling at the color of their skin. But there is a great difference between being the first white man to be seen by Africans and being the first black man to be seen by whites. The white man takes the astonishment as tribute, for he arrives to conquer and to convert the natives, whose inferiority in relation to himself is not even to be questioned; whereas I, without a thought of conquest, find myself among a people whose culture controls me, has even, in a sense, created me, people who have cost me more in anguish and rage than they will ever know, who yet do not even know of my existence. The astonishment with which I might have greeted them, should they have stumbled into my African village a few hundred years ago, might have rejoiced their hearts. But the astonishment with which they greet me today can only poison mine.

And this is so despite everything I may do to feel differently, despite my friendly conversations with the bistro owner's wife, despite their three-year-old son who has at last become my friend, despite the *saluts* and *bonsoirs* which I exchange with people as I walk, despite the fact that I know that no individual can be taken to task for what history is doing, or has done. I say that the culture of these people controls me—but they can scarcely be held responsible for European culture. America comes out of Europe, but these people have never seen America, nor have most of them seen more of Europe than the hamlet at the foot of their mountain. Yet they move with an authority which I shall never have; and they regard me, quite rightly, not only as a stranger in their village but as a suspect latecomer, bearing no credentials, to everything they have—however unconsciously—inherited.

For this village, even were it incomparably more remote and incredibly more primitive, is the West, the West onto which I have been so strangely grafted. These people cannot be, from the point of view of power, strangers anywhere in the world; they have made the modern world, in effect, even if they do not know it. The most illiterate among them is related, in a way that I am not, to Dante, Shakespeare, Michelangelo, Aeschylus, Da Vinci, Rembrandt, and Racine; the cathedral at Chartres says something to them which it cannot say to me, as indeed would New York's Empire State Building, should anyone here ever see it. Out of their hymns and dances come Beethoven and Bach. Go back a few centuries and they are in their full glory—but I am in Africa, watching the conquerors arrive.

The rage of the disesteemed is personally fruitless, but it is also absolutely inevitable; this rage, so generally discounted, so little understood even among the people whose daily bread it is, is one of the things that makes history. Rage can only with difficulty, and never entirely, be brought under the domination of the intelligence and is therefore not susceptible to any arguments whatever. This is a fact which ordinary representatives of the *Herrenvolk,*[1] having never felt this rage and being unable to imagine, quite fail to understand. Also, rage cannot be hidden, it can only be dissembled. This dissembling deludes the thoughtless, and strengthens rage and adds, to rage, contempt. There are, no doubt, as many ways of coping with the resulting complex of tensions as there are black men in the world, but no black man can hope ever to be entirely liberated from this internal warfare—rage, dissembling, and contempt having inevitably accompanied his first realization of the power of white men. What is crucial here is that, since white men represent in the black man's world so heavy a weight, white men have for black men a reality which is far from being reciprocal; and hence all black men have toward all white men an attitude which is designed, really, either to rob the white man of the jewel of his naiveté, or else to make it cost him dear.

The black man insists, by whatever means he finds at his disposal, that the white man cease to regard him as an exotic rarity and

[1]Master race. (Editors' note)

recognize him as a human being. This is a very charged and difficult moment, for there is a great deal of will power involved in the white man's naiveté. Most people are not naturally reflective any more than they are naturally malicious, and the white man prefers to keep the black man at a certain human remove because it is easier for him thus to preserve his simplicity and avoid being called to account for crimes committed by his forefathers, or his neighbors. He is inescapably aware, nevertheless, that he is in a better position in the world than black men are, nor can he quite put to death the suspicion that he is hated by black men therefore. He does not wish to be hated, neither does he wish to change places, and at this point in his uneasiness he can scarcely avoid having recourse to those legends which white men have created about black men, the most usual effect of which is that the white man finds himself enmeshed, so to speak, in his own language which describes hell, as well as the attributes which lead one to hell, as being as black as night.

Every legend, moreover, contains its residuum of truth, and the root function of language is to control the universe by describing it. It is of quite considerable significance that black men remain, in the imagination, and in overwhelming numbers in fact, beyond the disciplines of salvation; and this despite the fact that the West has been "buying" African natives for centuries. There is, I should hazard, an instantaneous necessity to be divorced from this so visibly unsaved stranger, in whose heart, moreover, one cannot guess what dreams of vengeance are being nourished; and, at the same time, there are few things on earth more attractive than the idea of the unspeakable liberty which is allowed the unredeemed. When, beneath the black mask, a human being begins to make himself felt one cannot escape a certain awful wonder as to what kind of human being it is. What one's imagination makes of other people is dictated, of course, by the laws of one's own personality and it is one of the ironies of black-white relations that, by means of what the white man imagines the black man to be, the black man is enabled to know who the white man is.

I have said, for example, that I am as much a stranger in this village today as I was the first summer I arrived, but this is not quite true. The villagers wonder less about the texture of my hair than they did then, and wonder rather more about me. And the fact that their wonder now exists on another level is reflected in their attitudes and in their eyes. There are the children who make those delightful, hilarious, sometimes astonishingly grave overtures of friendship in the unpredictable fashion of children; other children, having been taught that the devil is a black man, scream in genuine anguish as I approach. Some of the older women never pass without a friendly greeting, never pass, indeed, if it seems that they will be able to engage me in conversation; other women look down or look away or rather contemptuously smirk. Some of the men drink with me and suggest that I learn how to ski—partly, I gather, because they cannot imagine what I would look like on skis—and want to know if I am married, and ask questions about my métier. But some of the men have accused *le sale nègre*—behind my back—of stealing wood and there is already in the eyes of some of them that peculiar, intent, paranoiac malevolence which one sometimes surprises in the eyes of American white men when, out walking with their Sunday girl, they see a Negro male approach.

There is a dreadful abyss between the streets of this village and the streets of the city in which I was born, between the children who shout *Neger!* today and those who shouted *Nigger!* yesterday—the abyss is experience, the American experience. The syllable hurled behind me today expresses, above all, wonder: I am a stranger here. But I am not a stranger in America and the same syllable riding on the American air expresses the war my presence has occasioned in the American soul.

For this village brings home to me this fact: that there was a day, and not really a very distant day, when Americans were scarcely Americans at all but discontented Europeans, facing a great unconquered continent and strolling, say, into a marketplace and seeing black men for the first time. The shock this spectacle afforded is suggested, surely, by the promptness with which they decided that these black men were not really men but cattle. It is true that the necessity on the part of the settlers of the New World of reconciling their moral assumptions with the fact—and the necessity—of slavery enhanced immensely the charm of this idea, and it is also true that this idea expresses, with a truly American bluntness, the attitude which to varying extents all masters have had toward all slaves.

But between all former slaves and slave-owners and the drama which begins for Americans over three hundred years ago at Jamestown, there are at least two differences to be observed. The American Negro slave could not suppose, for one thing, as slaves in past epochs had supposed and often done, that he would ever be able to wrest the power from his master's hands. This was a supposition which the modern era, which was to bring about such vast changes in the aims and dimensions of power, put to death; it only begins, in unprecedented fashion, and with dreadful implications, to be resurrected today. But even had this supposition persisted with undiminished force, the American Negro slave could not have used it to lend his condition dignity, for the reason that this supposition rests on another: that the slave in exile yet remains related to his past, has some means—if only in memory—of revering and sustaining the forms of his former life, is able, in short, to maintain his identity.

This was not the case with the American Negro slave. He is unique among the black men of the world in that his past was taken from him, almost literally, at one blow. One wonders what on earth the first slave found to say to the first dark child he bore. I am told that there are Haitians able to trace their ancestry back to African kings, but any American Negro wishing to go back so far will find his journey through time abruptly arrested by the signature on the bill of sale which served as the entrance paper for his ancestor. At the time—to say nothing of the circumstances—of the enslavement of the captive black man who was to become the American Negro, there was not the remotest possibility that he would ever take power from his master's hands. There was no reason to suppose that his situation would ever change, nor was there, shortly, anything to indicate that his situation had ever been different. It was his necessity, in the words of E. Franklin Frazier, to find a "motive for living under American culture or die." The identity of the American Negro comes out of this extreme situation, and the evolution of this identity was a source of the most intolerable anxiety in the minds and the lives of his masters.

For the history of the American Negro is unique also in this: that the question of his humanity, and of his rights therefore as a human being, became a burning one for several generations of Americans, so burning a question that it ultimately became one of those used to divide the nation. It is out of this argument that the venom of the epithet *Nigger!* is derived. It is an argument which Europe has never had, and hence Europe quite sincerely fails to understand how or why the argument arose in the first place, why its effects are frequently disastrous and always so unpredictable, why it refuses until today to be entirely settled. Europe's black possessions remained—and do remain—in Europe's colonies, at which remove they represented no threat whatever to European identity. If they posed any problem at all for the European conscience, it was a problem which remained comfortingly abstract: in effect, the black man, as a *man,* did not exist for Europe. But in America, even as a slave, he was an inescapable part of the general social fabric and no American could escape having an attitude toward him. Americans attempt until today to make an abstraction of the Negro, but the very nature of these abstractions reveals the tremendous effects the presence of the Negro has had on the American character.

When one considers the history of the Negro in America it is of the greatest importance to recognize that the moral beliefs of a person, or a people, are never really as tenuous as life—which is not moral—very often causes them to appear; these create for them a frame of reference and a necessary hope, and the hope being, that when life has done its worst they will be enabled to rise above themselves and to triumph over life. Life would scarcely be bearable if this hope did not exist. Again, even when the worst has been said, to betray a belief is not by any means to have put oneself beyond its power; the betrayal of a belief is not the same thing as ceasing to believe. If this were not so there would be no moral standards in the world at all. Yet one must also recognize that morality is based on ideas and that all ideas are dangerous—dangerous because ideas can only lead to action and where the action leads no man can say. And dangerous in this respect: that confronted with the impossibility of remaining faithful to one's beliefs, and the equal impossibility of becoming free of them, one can be driven to the most inhuman excesses. The ideas on which American beliefs are based are not, though Americans often seem to think so, ideas which originated in America. They came out of Europe. And the establishment of democracy on the American continent was scarcely as radical a break with the past as was the necessity, which Americans faced, of broadening this concept to include black men.

This was, literally, a hard necessity. It was impossible, for one thing, for Americans to abandon their beliefs, not only because these beliefs alone seemed able to justify the sacrifices they had endured and the blood that they had spilled, but also because these beliefs afforded them their only bulwark against a moral chaos as absolute as the physical chaos of the continent it was their destiny to conquer. But in the situation in which Americans found themselves, these beliefs threatened an idea which, whether or not one likes to think so, is the very warp and woof of the heritage of the West, the idea of white supremacy.

Americans have made themselves notorious by the shrillness and the brutality with which they have insisted on this idea, but they did not invent it; and it has escaped the world's notice that those very excesses of which Americans have been guilty imply a certain, unprecedented uneasiness over the idea's life and power, if not, indeed, the idea's validity. The idea of white supremacy rests simply on the fact that white men are the creators of civilization (the present civilization, which is the only one that matters; all previous civilizations are simply "contributions" to our own) and are therefore civilization's guardians and defenders. Thus it was impossible for Americans to accept the black man as one of themselves, for to do so was to jeopardize their status as white men. But not so to accept him was to deny his human reality, his human weight and complexity, and the strain of denying the overwhelmingly undeniable forced Americans into rationalizations so fantastic that they approached the pathological.

At the root of the American Negro problem is the necessity of the American white man to find a way of living with the Negro in order to be able to live with himself. And the history of this problem can be reduced to the means used by Americans—lynch law and law, segregation and legal acceptance, terrorization and concession—either to come to terms with this necessity, or to find a way around it, or (most usually) to find a way of doing both these things at once. The resulting spectacle, at once foolish and dreadful, led someone to make the quite accurate observation that "the Negro-in-America is a form of insanity which overtakes white men."

In this long battle, a battle by no means finished, the unforeseeable effects of which will be felt by many future generations, the white man's motive was the protection of his identity; the black man was motivated by the need to establish an identity. And despite the terrorization which the Negro in America endured and endures sporadically until today, despite the cruel and totally inescapable ambivalence of his status in his country, the battle for his identity has long ago been won. He is not a visitor to the West, but a citizen there, an American; as American as the Americans who despise him, the Americans who fear him, the Americans who love him—the Americans who became less than themselves, or rose to be greater than themselves by virtue of the fact that the challenge he represented was inescapable. He is perhaps the only black man in the world whose relationship to white men is more terrible, more subtle, and more meaningful than the relationship of bitter possessed to uncertain possessors. His survival depended, and his development depends, on his ability to turn his peculiar status in the Western world to his own advantage and, it may be, to the very great advantage of that world. It remains for him to fashion out of his experience that which will give him sustenance, and a voice.

The cathedral at Chartres, I have said, says something to the people of this village which it cannot say to me; but it is important to understand that this cathedral says something to me which it cannot say to them. Perhaps they are struck by the power of the spires, the glory of the windows; but they have known God, after all, longer than I have known him, and in a different way, and I am terrified by the slippery bottomless well to be found in the crypt, down which heretics were hurled to death, and by the obscene, inescapable gargoyles jutting out of the stone and seeming to say that God and the devil can never be divorced. I doubt that the villagers think of the devil when they face a cathedral because they have never been identified with the devil. But I must accept the status which myth, if nothing else, gives me in the West before I can hope to change the myth.

Yet, if the American Negro has arrived at his identity by virtue of the absoluteness of his estrangement from his past, American white men still nourish the illusion that there is some means of recovering the European innocence, of returning to a state in which black men do not exist. This is one of the greatest errors Americans can make. The identity they fought so hard to protect has, by virtue of that battle, undergone a change: Americans are as unlike any other white people in the world as it is possible to be. I do not think, for example, that it is too much to suggest that the American vision of the world—which allows so little reality, generally speaking, for any of the darker forces in human life, which tends until today to paint moral issues in glaring black and white—owes a great deal to the battle waged by Americans to maintain between themselves and black men a human separation which could not be bridged. It is only now beginning to be borne in on us—very faintly, it must be admitted, very slowly, and very much against our will—that this vision of the world is dangerously inaccurate, and perfectly useless. For it protects our moral high-mindedness at the terrible expense of weakening our grasp of reality. People who shut their eyes to reality simply invite their own destruction, and anyone who insists on remaining in a state of innocence long after that innocence is dead turns himself into a monster.

The time has come to realize that the interracial drama acted out on the American continent has not only created a new black man, it has created a new white man, too. No road whatever will lead Americans back to the simplicity of this European village where white men still have the luxury of looking on me as a stranger. I am not, really, a stranger any longer for any American alive. One of the things that distinguishes Americans from other people is that no other people has ever been so deeply involved in the lives of black men, and vice versa. This fact faced, with all its implication, it can be seen that the history of the American Negro problem is not merely shameful, it is also something of an achievement. For even when the worst has been said, it must also be added that the perpetual challenge posed by this problem was always, somehow, perpetually met. It is precisely this black-white experience which may prove of indispensable value to us in the world we face today. This world is white no longer, and it will never be white again.

## Questions

1. Why does Baldwin establish at the beginning of the essay, and at some length, the village's isolation?
2. Explain in your own words the chief differences, according to Baldwin, between the experience of a white man arriving as a stranger in an African village and of a black man arriving as a stranger in a white village.
3. Baldwin's densely packed, highly allusive sentences often require close study. Try to paraphrase (rewrite in your own words) or to explain the meaning of these sentences:
   a. The rage of the disesteemed is personally fruitless, but it is also absolutely inevitable; this rage, so generally discounted, so little understood even among the people whose daily bread it is, is one of the things that makes history.
   b. For this village, even were it incomparably more remote and incredibly more primitive, is the West, the West onto which I have been so strangely grafted.
4. Why, according to Baldwin, have whites created legends about blacks? To what legends does Baldwin allude?
5. On page 472, Baldwin alludes to American beliefs threatened by the idea of white supremacy. What were those beliefs?
6. Baldwin wrote, "Stranger in the Village" in the early 1950s. Does his conclusion appear true today?

George Orwell

# Shooting an Elephant

In Moulmein, in Lower Burma, I was hated by large numbers of people—the only time in my life that I have been important enough for this to happen to me. I was sub-divisional police officer of the town, and in an aimless, petty kind of way anti-European feeling was very bitter. No one had the guts to raise a riot, but if a European woman went through the bazaars alone somebody would probably spit betel juice over her dress. As a police officer I was an obvious target and was baited whenever it seemed safe to do so. When a nimble Burman tripped me up on the football field and the referee (another Burman) looked the other way, the crowd yelled with hideous laughter. This happened more than once. In the end the sneering yellow faces of young men that met me everywhere, the insults hooted after me when I was at a safe distance, got badly on my nerves. The young Buddhist priests were the worst of all. There were several thousands of them in the town and none of them seemed to have anything to do except stand on street corners and jeer at Europeans.

All this was perplexing and upsetting. For at that time I had already made up my mind that imperialism was an evil thing and the sooner I chucked up my job and got out of it the better. Theoretically—and secretly, of course—I was all for the Burmese and all against their oppressors, the British. As for the job I was doing, I hated it more bitterly than I can perhaps make clear. In a job like that you see the dirty work of Empire at close quarters. The wretched prisoners huddling in the stinking cages of the lock-ups, the grey, cowed faces of the long-term convicts, the scarred buttocks of the men who had been flogged with bamboos—all these oppressed me with an intolerable sense of guilt. But I could get nothing into perspective. I was young and ill-educated and I had had to think out my problems in the utter silence that is imposed on every Englishman in the East. I did not even know that the British Empire is dying, still less did I know that it is a great deal better than the younger empires that are going to supplant it. All I knew was that I was stuck between my

For a biographical note on Orwell, see page 346.

hatred of the empire I served and my rage against the evil-spirited little beasts who tried to make my job impossible. With one part of my mind I thought of the British Raj as an unbreakable tyranny, as something clamped down, in *saecula saeculorum,*[1] upon the will of prostrate peoples; with another part I thought that the greatest joy in the world would be to drive a bayonet into a Buddhist priest's guts. Feelings like these are the normal by-products of imperialism; ask any Anglo-Indian official, if you can catch him off duty.

One day something happened which in a roundabout way was enlightening. It was a tiny incident in itself, but it gave me a better glimpse than I had had before of the real nature of imperialism—the real motives for which despotic governments act. Early one morning the sub-inspector at a police station the other end of town rang me up on the 'phone and said that an elephant was ravaging the bazaar. Would I please come and do something about it? I did not know what I could do, but I wanted to see what was happening and I got on to a pony and started out. I took my rifle, an old .44 Winchester and much too small to kill an elephant, but I thought the noise might be useful *in terrorem.*[2] Various Burmans stopped me on the way and told me about the elephant's doings. It was not, of course, a wild elephant, but a tame one which had gone "must." It had been chained up, as tame elephants always are when their attack of "must" is due, but on the previous night it had broken its chain and escaped. Its mahout, the only person who could manage it when it was in that state, had set out in pursuit, but had taken the wrong direction and was now twelve hours' journey away, and in the morning the elephant had suddenly reappeared in the town. The Burmese population had no weapons and were quite helpless against it. It had already destroyed somebody's bamboo hut, killed a cow and raided some fruit-stalls and devoured the stock; also it had met the municipal rubbish van and, when the driver jumped out and took to his heels, had turned the van over and inflicted violences upon it.

The Burmese sub-inspector and some Indian constables were waiting for me in the quarter where the elephant had been seen. It was a very poor quarter, a labyrinth of squalid bamboo huts, thatched with palmleaf, winding all over a steep hillside. I remember that it was a cloudy, stuffy morning at the beginning of the rains. We

[1]For world without end. (Editors' note)
[2]As a warning. (Editors' note)

began questioning the people as to where the elephant had gone and, as usual, failed to get any definite information. That is invariably the case in the East; a story always sounds clear enough at a distance, but the nearer you get to the scene of events the vaguer it becomes. Some of the people said that the elephant had gone in one direction, some said that he had gone in another, some professed not even to have heard of any elephant. I had almost made up my mind that the whole story was a pack of lies, when we heard yells a little distance away. There was a loud, scandalized cry of "Go away, child! Go away this instant!" and an old woman with a switch in her hand came round the corner of a hut, violently shooing away a crowd of naked children. Some more women followed, clicking their tongues and exclaiming; evidently there was something that the children ought not to have seen. I rounded the hut and saw a man's dead body sprawling in the mud. He was an Indian, a black Dravidian coolie, almost naked, and he could not have been dead many minutes. The people said that the elephant had come suddenly upon him round the corner of the hut, caught him with its trunk, put its foot on his back and ground him into the earth. This was the rainy season and the ground was soft, and his face had scored a trench a foot deep and a couple of yards long. He was lying on his belly with arms crucified and head sharply twisted to one side. His face was coated with mud, the eyes wide open, the teeth bared and grinning with an expression of unendurable agony. (Never tell me, by the way, that the dead look peaceful. Most of the corpses I have seen looked devilish.) The friction of the great beast's foot had stripped the skin from his back as neatly as one skins a rabbit. As soon as I saw the dead man I sent an orderly to a friend's house nearby to borrow an elephant rifle. I had already sent back the pony, not wanting it to go mad with fright and throw me if it smelt the elephant.

The orderly came back in a few minutes with a rifle and five cartridges, and meanwhile some Burmans had arrived and told us that the elephant was in the paddy fields below, only a few hundred yards away. As I started forward practically the whole population of the quarter flocked out of the houses and followed me. They had seen the rifle and were all shouting excitedly that I was going to shoot the elephant. They had not shown much interest in the elephant when he was merely ravaging their homes, but it was different now that he was going to be shot. It was a bit of fun to them, as it would be to an English crowd; besides they wanted the meat. It made me vaguely uneasy. I had no intention of shooting the elephant—I had merely sent for the rifle to defend myself if necessary—and it is always unnerving to have a crowd following you. I marched down the hill, looking and feeling a fool, with the rifle over my shoulder and an ever-growing army of people jostling at my heels. At the bottom, when you got away from the huts, there was a metalled road and beyond that a miry waste of paddy fields a thousand yards across, not yet ploughed but soggy from the first rains and dotted with coarse grass. The elephant was standing eight yards from the road, his left side towards us. He took not the slightest notice of the crowd's approach. He was tearing up bunches of grass, beating them against his knees to clean them and stuffing them into his mouth.

I had halted on the road. As soon as I saw the elephant I knew with perfect certainty that I ought not to shoot him. It is a serious matter to shoot a working elephant—it is comparable to destroying a huge and costly piece of machinery—and obviously one ought not to do it if it can possibly be avoided. And at that distance, peacefully eating, the elephant looked no more dangerous than a cow. I thought then and I think now that his attack of "must" was already passing off; in which case he would merely wander harmlessly about until the mahout came back and caught him. Moreover, I did not in the least want to shoot him. I decided that I would watch him for a little while to make sure that he did not turn savage again, and then go home.

But at that moment, I glanced round at the crowd that had followed me. It was an immense crowd, two thousand at the least and growing every minute. It blocked the road for a long distance on either side. I looked at the sea of yellow faces above the garish clothes — faces all happy and excited over this bit of fun, all certain that the elephant was going to be shot. They were watching me as they would watch a conjuror about to perform a trick. They did not like me, but with the magical rifle in my hands I was momentarily worth watching. And suddenly I realized that I should have to shoot the elephant after all. The people expected it of me and I had got to do it; I could feel their two thousand wills pressing me forward, irresistibly. And it was at this moment, as I stood there with the rifle in my hands, that I first grasped the hollowness, the futility of the white man's dominion in the East. Here was I, the white man with his gun, standing in front of the unarmed native crowd—seemingly the leading actor of the piece; but in reality I was only an absurd puppet pushed to and fro by the will of those yellow faces behind. I perceived in this moment that when the white man turns tyrant it is his own freedom that he destroys. He becomes a sort of hollow, posing dummy, the conventionalized figure of a sahib. For it is the condition of his rule that he shall spend his life in trying to impress the "natives," and so in every crisis he has got to do what the "natives" expect of him. He wears a mask, and his face grows to fit it. I had got to shoot the elephant. I had committed myself to doing it when I sent for the rifle. A sahib has got to act like a sahib; he has got to appear resolute, to know his own mind and do definite things. To come all that way, rifle in hand, with two thousand people marching at my heels, and then to trail feebly away, having done nothing—no, that was impossible. The crowd would laugh at me. And my whole life, every white man's life in the East, was one long struggle not to be laughed at.

But I did not want to shoot the elephant. I watched him beating his bunch of grass against his knees, with that preoccupied grandmotherly air that elephants have. It seemed to me that it would be murder to shoot him. At that age I was not squeamish about killing animals, but I had never shot an elephant and never wanted to. (Somehow it always seems worse to kill a *large* animal.) Besides, there was the beast's owner to be considered. Alive, the elephant was worth at least a hundred pounds; dead, he would only be worth the value of his tusks, five pounds, possibly. But I had got to act quickly. I turned to some experienced-looking Burmans who had been there when we arrived, and asked them how the elephant had been behaving. They all said the same thing: he took no notice of you if you left him alone, but he might charge if you went too close to him.

It was perfectly clear to me what I ought to do. I ought to walk up to within, say, twenty-five yards of the elephant and test his behavior. If he charged, I could shoot; if he took no notice of me, it would be safe to leave him until the mahout came back. But also I knew that I was going to do no such thing. I was a poor shot with a rifle and the ground was soft mud into which one would sink at every step. If the elephant charged and I missed him, I should have about as much chance as a toad under a steam-roller. But even then I was not thinking particularly of my own skin, only of the watchful yellow faces behind. For at that moment, with the crowd watching me, I was not afraid in the ordinary sense, as I would have been if I had been alone. A white man mustn't be frightened in front of "natives"; and so, in general, he isn't frightened. The sole thought in my mind was that if anything went wrong those two thousand Burmans would see me pursued, caught, trampled on and reduced to a grinning corpse like that Indian up the hill. And if that happened it was quite probable that some of them would laugh. That would never do. There was only one alternative. I shoved the cartridges into the magazine and lay down on the road to get a better aim.

The crowd grew very still, and a deep, low, happy sigh, as of people who see the theatre curtain go up at last, breathed from innumerable throats. They were going to have their bit of fun after all. The rifle was a beautiful German thing with cross-hair sights. I did not then know that in shooting an elephant one would shoot to cut an imaginary bar running from ear-hole to ear-hole. I ought, therefore, as the elephant was sideways on, to have aimed straight at his ear-hole; actually I aimed several inches in front of this, thinking the brain would be further forward.

When I pulled the trigger I did not hear the bang or feel the kick —one never does when a shot goes home—but I heard the devilish roar of glee that went up from the crowd. In that instant, in too short a time, one would have thought, even for the bullet to get there, a mysterious, terrible change had come over the elephant. He neither stirred nor fell, but every line of his body had altered. He looked suddenly stricken, shrunken, immensely old, as though the frightful impact of the bullet had paralysed him without knocking him down. At last, after what seemed a long time—it might have been five seconds, I dare say—he sagged flabbily to his knees. His mouth slobbered. An enormous senility seemed to have settled upon him. One could have imagined him thousands of years old. I fired again into the same spot. At the second shot he did not collapse but climbed with desperate slowness to his feet and stood weakly upright, with legs sagging and head drooping. I fired a third time. That was the shot that did for him. You could see the agony of it jolt his whole body and knock the last remnant of strength from his legs. But in falling he seemed for a moment to rise, for as his hind legs collapsed beneath him he seemed to tower upward like a huge rock toppling, his trunk reaching skywards like a tree. He trumpeted, for the first and only time. And then down he came, his belly towards me, with a crash that seemed to shake the ground even where I lay.

I got up. The Burmans were already racing past me across the mud. It was obvious that the elephant would never rise again, but he was not dead. He was breathing very rhythmically with long rattling gasps, his great mound of a side painfully rising and falling. His mouth was wide open. I could see far down into caverns of pale pink throat. I waited a long time for him to die, but his breathing did not weaken. Finally I fired my two remaining shots into the spot where I thought his heart must be. The thick blood welled out of him like red velvet, but still he did not die. His body did not even jerk when the shots hit him, the tortured breathing continued without a pause. He was dying, very slowly and in great agony, but in some world remote from me where not even a bullet could damage him further. I felt I had got to put an end to that dreadful noise. It seemed dreadful to see the great beast lying there, powerless to move and yet powerless to die, and not even to be able to finish him. I sent back for my small rifle and poured shot after shot into his heart and down his throat. They seemed to make no impression. The tortured gasps continued as steadily as the ticking of a clock.

In the end I could not stand it any longer and went away. I heard later that it took him half an hour to die. Burmans were bringing dahs and baskets even before I left, and I was told they had stripped his body almost to the bones by the afternoon.

Afterwards, of course, there were endless discussions about the shooting of the elephant. The owner was furious, but he was only an Indian and could do nothing. Besides, legally I had done the right thing, for a mad elephant has to be killed, like a mad dog, if its owner fails to control it. Among the Europeans opinion was divided. The older men said I was right, the younger men said it was a damn shame to shoot an elephant for killing a coolie, because the elephant was worth more than any damn Coringhee coolie. And afterwards I was very glad that the coolie had been killed; it put me legally in the right and it gave me sufficient pretext for shooting the elephant. I often wondered whether any of the others grasped that I had done it solely to avoid looking a fool.

## Questions

1. How does Orwell characterize himself at the time of the events he describes? What evidence in the essay suggests that he wrote it some years later?
2. Orwell says that the incident was "enlightening." What does he mean? Picking up this clue, state in a sentence or two the main point of the essay.
3. Compare Orwell's description of the dead coolie (page 478) with his description of the death of the elephant (pages 481–82). Why does Orwell devote more space to the death of the elephant?
4. How would you describe the tone of the last paragraph, particularly of the last two sentences? Do you find the paragraph an effective conclusion? Explain.

## Albert Camus

# The Guest

The schoolmaster was watching the two men climb toward him. One was on horseback, the other on foot. They had not yet tackled the abrupt rise leading to the schoolhouse built on the hillside. They were toiling onward, making slow progress in the snow, among the stones, on the vast expanse of the high, deserted plateau. From time to time the horse stumbled. Without hearing anything yet, he could see the breath issuing from the horse's nostrils. One of the men, at least, knew the region. They were following the trail although it had disappeared days ago under a layer of dirty white snow. The schoolmaster calculated that it would take them half an hour to get onto the hill. It was cold; he went back into the school to get a sweater.

He crossed the empty, frigid classroom. On the blackboard the four rivers of France, drawn with four different colored chalks, had been flowing toward their estuaries for the past three days. Snow had suddenly fallen in mid-October after eight months of drought without the transition of rain, and the twenty pupils, more or less, who lived in the villages scattered over the plateau had stopped coming. With fair weather they would return. Daru now heated only the single room that was his lodging, adjoining the classroom and giving also onto the plateau to the east. Like the class windows, his window looked to the south. On that side the school was a few kilometers from the point where the plateau began to slope toward the south. In clear weather could be seen the purple mass of the mountain range where the gap opened onto the desert.

Somewhat warmed, Daru returned to the window from which he had first seen the two men. They were no longer visible. Hence they must have tackled the rise. The sky was not so dark, for the snow had stopped falling during the night. The morning had opened with a dirty light which had scarcely become brighter as the ceiling

Albert Camus (1913–1960) was born in Algeria of French parents. During World War II he was active in the French Resistance, editing an underground newspaper. After the war he published fiction, philosophic essays, and plays. In 1957 he was awarded the Nobel Prize for literature. This story was translated by Justin O'Brien.

of clouds lifted. At two in the afternoon it seemed as if the day were merely beginning. But still this was better than those three days when the thick snow was falling amidst unbroken darkness with little gusts of wind that rattled the double door of the classroom. Then Daru had spent long hours in his room, leaving it only to go to the shed and feed the chickens or get some coal. Fortunately the delivery truck from Tadjid, the nearest village to the north, had brought his supplies two days before the blizzard. It would return in forty-eight hours.

Besides, he had enough to resist a siege, for the little room was cluttered with bags of wheat that the administration left as a stock to distribute to those of his pupils whose families had suffered from the drought. Actually they had all been victims because they were all poor. Every day Daru would distribute a ration to the children. They had missed it, he knew, during these bad days. Possibly one of the fathers or big brothers would come this afternoon and he could supply them with grain. It was just a matter of carrying them over to the next harvest. Now shiploads of wheat were arriving from France and the worst was over. But it would be hard to forget that poverty, that army of ragged ghosts wandering in the sunlight, the plateaus burned to a cinder month after month, the earth shriveled up little by little, literally scorched, every stone bursting into dust under one's foot. The sheep had died then by thousands and even a few men, here and there, sometimes without anyone's knowing.

In contrast with such poverty, he who lived almost like a monk in his remote schoolhouse, nonetheless satisfied with the little he had and with the rough life, had felt like a lord with his whitewashed walls, his narrow couch, his unpainted shelves, his well, and his weekly provision of water and food. And suddenly this snow, without warning, without the foretaste of rain. This is the way the region was, cruel to live in, even without men—who didn't help matters either. But Daru had been born here. Everywhere else, he felt exiled.

He stepped out onto the terrace in front of the schoolhouse. The two men were now halfway up the slope. He recognized the horseman as Balducci, the old gendarme he had known for a long time. Balducci was holding on the end of a rope an Arab who was walking behind him with hands bound and head lowered. The gendarme waved a greeting to which Daru did not reply, lost as he was in contemplation of the Arab dressed in a faded blue jellaba, his feet in sandals but covered with socks of heavy raw wool, his head surmounted by a narrow, short *chèche.* They were approaching. Balducci was holding back his horse in order not to hurt the Arab, and the group was advancing slowly.

Within earshot, Balducci shouted: "One hour to do the three kilometers from El Ameur!" Daru did not answer. Short and square in his thick sweater, he watched them climb. Not once had the Arab raised his head. "Hello," said Daru when they got up onto the terrace. "Come and warm up." Balducci painfully got down from his horse without letting go of the rope. From under his bristling mustache he smiled at the schoolmaster. His little dark eyes, deep-set under a tanned forehead, and his mouth surrounded with wrinkles made him look attentive and studious. Daru took the bridle, led the horse to the shed, and came back to the two men, who were now waiting for him in the school. He led them into his room. "I am going to heat up the classroom," he said. "We'll be more comfortable there." When he entered the room again Balducci was on the couch. He had undone the rope tying him to the Arab, who had squatted near the stove. His hands still bound, the chèche pushed back on his head, he was looking toward the window. At first Daru noticed only his huge lips, fat, smooth, almost Negroid; yet his nose was straight, his eyes were dark and full of fever. The chèche revealed an obstinate forehead and, under the weathered skin now rather discolored by the cold, the whole face had a restless and rebellious look that struck Daru when the Arab, turning his face toward him, looked him straight in the eyes. "Go into the other room," said the schoolmaster, "and I'll make you some mint tea." "Thanks," Balducci said. "What a chore! How I long for retirement." And addressing his prisoner in Arabic: "Come on, you." The Arab got up and, slowly, holding his bound wrists in front of him, went into the classroom.

With the tea, Daru brought a chair. But Balducci was already enthroned on the nearest pupil's desk and the Arab had squatted against the teacher's platform facing the stove, which stood between the desk and the window. When he held out the glass of tea to the prisoner, Daru hesitated at the sight of his bound hands. "He might perhaps be untied." "Sure," said Balducci. "That was for the trip." He started to get to his feet. But Daru, setting the glass on the floor, had knelt beside the Arab. Without saying anything, the Arab watched him with his feverish eyes. Once his hands were free, he rubbed his swollen wrists against each other, took the glass of tea, and sucked up the burning liquid in swift little sips.

"Good," said Daru. "And where are you headed?"

Balducci withdrew his mustache from the tea. "Here, son."

"Odd pupils! And you're spending the night?"

"No. I'm going back to El Ameur. And you will deliver this fellow to Tinguit. He is expected at police headquarters."

Balducci was looking at Daru with a friendly little smile.

"What's this story?" asked the schoolmaster. "Are you pulling my leg?"

"No, son. Those are the orders."

"The orders? I'm not . . . " Daru hesitated, not wanting to hurt the old Corsican. "I mean, that's not my job."

"What! What's the meaning of that? In wartime people do all kinds of jobs."

"Then I'll wait for the declaration of war!"

Balducci nodded.

"O.K. But the orders exist and they concern you too. Things are brewing, it appears. There is talk of a forthcoming revolt. We are mobilized, in a way."

Daru still had his obstinate look.

"Listen, son," Balducci said. "I like you and you must understand. There's only a dozen of us at El Ameur to patrol throughout the whole territory of a small department and I must get back in a hurry. I was told to hand this guy over to you and return without delay. He couldn't be kept there. His village was beginning to stir; they wanted to take him back. You must take him to Tinguit tomorrow before the day is over. Twenty kilometers shouldn't faze a husky fellow like you. After that, all will be over. You'll come back to your pupils and your comfortable life."

Behind the wall the horse could be heard snorting and pawing the earth. Daru was looking out the window. Decidedly, the weather was clearing and the light was increasing over the snowy plateau. When all the snow was melted, the sun would take over again and once more would burn the fields of stone. For days, still, the unchanging sky would shed its dry light on the solitary expanse where nothing had any connection with man.

"After all," he said, turning around toward Balducci, "what did he do?" And, before the gendarme had opened his mouth, he asked: "Does he speak French?"

"No, not a word. We had been looking for him for a month, but they were hiding him. He killed his cousin."

"Is he against us?"

"I don't think so. But you can never be sure."

"Why did he kill?"

"A family squabble, I think. One owed the other grain, it seems.

It's not at all clear. In short, he killed his cousin with a billhook. You know, like a sheep, *kreezk!*"

Balducci made the gesture of drawing a blade across his throat and the Arab, his attention attracted, watched him with a sort of anxiety. Daru felt a sudden wrath against the man, against all men with their rotten spite, their tireless hates, their blood lust.

But the kettle was singing on the stove. He served Balducci more tea, hesitated, then served the Arab again, who, a second time, drank avidly. His raised arms made the jellaba fall open and the schoolmaster saw his thin, muscular chest.

"Thanks, kid," Balducci said. "And now, I'm off."

He got up and went toward the Arab, taking a small rope from his pocket.

"What are you doing?" Daru asked dryly.

Balducci, disconcerted, showed him the rope.

"Don't bother."

The old gendarme hesitated. "It's up to you. Of course, you are armed?"

"I have my shotgun."

"Where?"

"In the trunk."

"You ought to have it near your bed."

"Why? I have nothing to fear."

"You're crazy, son. If there's an uprising, no one is safe, we're all in the same boat."

"I'll defend myself. I'll have time to see them coming."

Balducci began to laugh, then suddenly the mustache covered the white teeth. "You'll have time? O.K. That's just what I was saying. You have always been a little cracked. That's why I like you, my son was like that."

At the same time he took out his revolver and put it on the desk.

"Keep it; I don't need two weapons from here to El Ameur."

The revolver shone against the black paint of the table. When the gendarme turned toward him, the schoolmaster caught the smell of leather and horseflesh.

"Listen, Balducci," Daru said suddenly, "every bit of this disgusts me, and first of all your fellow here. But I won't hand him over. Fight, yes, if I have to. But not that."

The old gendarme stood in front of him and looked at him severely.

"You're being a fool," he said slowly. "I don't like it either. You don't get used to putting a rope on a man even after years of it, and you're even ashamed—yes, ashamed. But you can't let them have their way."

"I won't hand him over," Daru said again.

"It's an order, son, and I repeat it."

"That's right. Repeat to them what I've said to you: I won't hand him over."

Balducci made a visible effort to reflect. He looked at the Arab and at Daru. At last he decided.

"No, I won't tell them anything. If you want to drop us, go ahead; I'll not denounce you. I have an order to deliver the prisoner and I'm doing so. And now you'll just sign this paper for me."

"There's no need. I'll not deny that you left him with me."

"Don't be mean with me. I know you'll tell the truth. You're from hereabouts and you are a man. But you must sign, that's the rule."

Daru opened his drawer, took out a little square bottle of purple ink, the red wooden penholder with the "sergeant-major" pen he used for making models of penmanship, and signed. The gendarme carefully folded the paper and put it into his wallet. Then he moved toward the door.

"I'll see you off," Daru said.

"No," said Balducci. "There's no use being polite. You insulted me."

He looked at the Arab, motionless in the same spot, sniffed peevishly, and turned away toward the door. "Good-by, son," he said. The door shut behind him. Balducci appeared suddenly outside the window and then disappeared. His footsteps were muffled by the snow. The horse stirred on the other side of the wall and several chickens fluttered in fright. A moment later Balducci reappeared outside the window leading the horse by the bridle. He walked toward the little rise without turning around and disappeared from sight with the horse following him. A big stone could be heard bouncing down. Daru walked back toward the prisoner, who, without stirring, never took his eyes off him. "Wait," the schoolmaster said in Arabic and went toward the bedroom. As he was going through the door, he had a second thought, went to the desk, took the revolver, and stuck it in his pocket. Then, without looking back, he went into his room.

For some time he lay on his couch watching the sky gradually close over, listening to the silence. It was this silence that had seemed painful to him during the first days here, after the war. He had requested a post in the little town at the base of the foothills separating the upper plateaus from the desert. There, rocky walls, green and black to the north, pink and lavender to the south, marked the frontier of eternal summer. He had been named to a post farther north, on the plateau itself. In the beginning, the solitude and the silence had been hard for him on these wastelands peopled only by stones. Occasionally, furrows suggested cultivation, but they had been dug to uncover a certain kind of stone good for building. The only plowing here was to harvest rocks. Elsewhere a thin layer of soil accumulated in the hollows would be scraped out to enrich paltry village gardens. This is the way it was: bare rock covered three quarters of the region. Towns sprang up, flourished, then disappeared; men came by, loved one another or fought bitterly, then died. No one in this desert, neither he nor his guest, mattered. And yet, outside this desert neither of them, Daru knew, could have really lived.

When he got up, no noise came from the classroom. He was amazed at the unmixed joy he derived from the mere thought that the Arab might have fled and that he would be alone with no decision to make. But the prisoner was there. He had merely stretched out between the stove and the desk. With eyes open, he was staring at the ceiling. In that position, his thick lips were particularly noticeable, giving him a pouting look. "Come," said Daru. The Arab got up and followed him. In the bedroom, the schoolmaster pointed to a chair near the table under the window. The Arab sat down without taking his eyes off Daru.

"Are you hungry?"

"Yes," the prisoner said.

Daru set the table for two. He took flour and oil, shaped a cake in a frying-pan, and lighted the little stove that functioned on bottled gas. While the cake was cooking, he went out to the shed to get cheese, eggs, dates, and condensed milk. When the cake was done he set it on the window sill to cool, heated some condensed milk diluted with water, and beat up the eggs into an omelette. In one of his motions he knocked against the revolver stuck in his right pocket. He set the bowl down, went into the classroom, and put the revolver in his desk drawer. When he came back to the room, night was falling. He put on the light and served the Arab. "Eat," he said. The Arab took a piece of the cake, lifted it eagerly to his mouth, and stopped short.

"And you?" he asked.

"After you. I'll eat too."

The thick lips opened slightly. The Arab hesitated, then bit into the cake determinedly.

The meal over, the Arab looked at the schoolmaster. "Are you the judge?"

"No, I'm simply keeping you until tomorrow."

"Why do you eat with me?"

"I'm hungry."

The Arab fell silent. Daru got up and went out. He brought back a folding bed from the shed, set it up between the table and the stove, perpendicular to his own bed. From a large suitcase which, upright in a corner, served as a shelf for papers, he took two blankets and arranged them on the camp bed. Then he stopped, felt useless, and sat down on his bed. There was nothing more to do or to get ready. He had to look at this man. He looked at him, therefore, trying to imagine his face bursting with rage. He couldn't do so. He could see nothing but the dark yet shining eyes and the animal mouth.

"Why did you kill him?" he asked in a voice whose hostile tone surprised him.

The Arab looked away. "He ran away. I ran after him."

He raised his eyes to Daru again and they were full of a sort of woeful interrogation. "Now what will they do to me?"

"Are you afraid?"

He stiffened, turning his eyes away.

"Are you sorry?"

The Arab stared at him openmouthed. Obviously he did not understand. Daru's annoyance was growing. At the same time he felt awkward and self-conscious with his big body wedged between the two beds.

"Lie down there," he said impatiently. "That's your bed."

The Arab didn't move. He called to Daru:

"Tell me!"

The schoolmaster looked at him.

"Is the gendarme coming back tomorrow?"

"I don't know."

"Are you coming with us?"

"I don't know. Why?"

The prisoner got up and stretched out on top of the blankets, his feet toward the window. The light from the electric bulb shone straight into his eyes and he closed them at once.

"Why?" Daru repeated, standing beside the bed.

The Arab opened his eyes under the blinding light and looked at him, trying not to blink.

"Come with us," he said.

In the middle of the night, Daru was still not asleep. He had gone to bed after undressing completely; he generally slept naked. But when he suddenly realized that he had nothing on, he hesitated. He felt vulnerable and the temptation came to him to put his clothes back on. Then he shrugged his shoulders; after all, he wasn't a child and, if need be, he could break his adversary in two. From his bed he could observe him, lying on his back, still motionless with his eyes closed under the harsh light. When Daru turned out the light, the darkness seemed to coagulate all of a sudden. Little by little, the night came back to life in the window where the starless sky was stirring gently. The schoolmaster soon made out the body lying at his feet. The Arab still did not move, but his eyes seemed open. A faint wind was prowling around the schoolhouse. Perhaps it would drive away the clouds and the sun would reappear.

During the night the wind increased. The hens fluttered a little and then were silent. The Arab turned over on his side with his back to Daru, who thought he heard him moan. Then he listened for his guest's breathing, become heavier and more regular. He listened to that breath so close to him and mused without being able to go to sleep. In this room where he had been sleeping alone for a year, this presence bothered him. But it bothered him also by imposing on him a sort of brotherhood he knew well but refused to accept in the present circumstances. Men who share the same rooms, soldiers or prisoners, develop a strange alliance as if, having cast off their armor with their clothing, they fraternized every evening, over and above their differences, in the ancient community of dream and fatigue. But Daru shook himself; he didn't like such musings, and it was essential to sleep.

A little later, however, when the Arab stirred slightly, the schoolmaster was still not asleep. When the prisoner made a second move, he stiffened, on the alert. The Arab was lifting himself slowly on his arms with almost the motion of a sleepwalker. Seated upright in bed, he waited motionless without turning his head toward Daru, as if he were listening attentively. Daru did not stir; it had just occurred to him that the revolver was still in the drawer of his desk. It was better to act at once. Yet he continued to observe the prisoner, who, with the same slithery motion, put his feet on the ground, waited again, then began to stand up slowly. Daru was about to call out to him when the Arab began to walk, in a quite natural but extraordinary silent way. He was heading toward the door at the end of the room that opened into the shed. He lifted the latch with precaution and went out, pushing the door behind him but without shutting it. Daru had not stirred. "He is running away," he merely thought. "Good riddance!" Yet he listened attentively. The hens were not fluttering; the guest must be on the plateau. A faint sound of water reached him, and he didn't know what it was until the Arab again stood framed in the doorway, closed the door carefully, and came back to bed without a sound. Then Daru turned his back on him and fell asleep. Still later he seemed, from the depths of his sleep, to hear furtive steps around the schoolhouse. "I'm dreaming! I'm dreaming!" he repeated to himself. And he went on sleeping.

When he awoke, the sky was clear; the loose window let in a cold, pure air. The Arab was asleep, hunched up under the blankets now, his mouth open, utterly relaxed. But when Daru shook him, he started dreadfully, staring at Daru with wild eyes as if he had never seen him and such a frightened expression that the schoolmaster stepped back. "Don't be afraid. It's me. You must eat." The Arab nodded and said yes. Calm had returned to his face, but his expression was vacant and listless.

The coffee was ready. They drank it seated together on the folding bed as they munched their pieces of the cake. Then Daru led the Arab under the shed and showed him the faucet where he washed. He went back into the room, folded the blankets and the bed, made his own bed and put room in order. Then he went through the classroom and out onto the terrace. The sun was already rising in the blue sky; a soft, bright light was bathing the deserted plateau. On the ridge the snow was melting in spots. The stones were about to reappear. Crouched on the edge of the plateau, the schoolmaster looked at the deserted expanse. He thought of Balducci. He had hurt him, for he had sent him off in a way as if he didn't want to be associated with him. He could hear the gendarme's farewell and, without knowing why, he felt strangely empty and vulnerable. At that moment, from the other side of the schoolhouse, the prisoner coughed. Daru listened to him almost despite himself and then, furious, threw a pebble that whistled through the air before sinking into the snow. That man's stupid crime revolted him, but to hand him over was contrary to honor. Merely thinking of it made him smart with humiliation. And he cursed at one and the same time his own people who had sent him this Arab and the Arab too who had dared to kill and not managed to get away. Daru got up, walked in a circle on the terrace, waited motionless, and then went back into the schoolhouse.

The Arab, leaning over the cement floor of the shed, was washing his teeth with two fingers. Daru looked at him and said: "Come." He went back into the room ahead of the prisoner. He slipped a hunting-jacket on over his sweater and put on walking-shoes. Standing, he waited until the Arab had put on his chèche and sandals. They went into the classroom and the schoolmaster pointed to the exit, saying: "Go ahead." The fellow didn't budge. "I'm coming," said Daru. The Arab went out. Daru went back into the room and made a package of pieces of rusk, dates, and sugar. In the classroom, before going out, he hesitated a second in front of his desk, then crossed the threshold and locked the door. "That's the way," he said. He started toward the east, followed by the prisoner. But, a short distance from the schoolhouse, he thought he heard a slight sound behind them. He retraced his steps and examined the surroundings of the house; there was no one there. The Arab watched him without seeming to understand. "Come on," said Daru.

They walked for a hour and rested beside a sharp peak of limestone. The snow was melting faster and faster and the sun was drinking up the puddles at once, rapidly cleaning the plateau, which gradually dried and vibrated like the air itself. When they resumed walking, the ground rang under their feet. From time to time a bird rent the space in front of them with a joyful cry. Daru breathed in deeply the fresh morning light. He felt a sort of rapture before the vast familiar expanse, now almost entirely yellow under its dome of blue sky. They walked an hour or more, descending toward the south. They reached a level height made up of crumbly rocks. From there on, the plateau sloped down, eastward toward a low plain where there were a few spindly trees and, to the south, toward outcroppings of rock that gave the landscape a chaotic look.

Daru surveyed the two directions. There was nothing but the sky on the horizon. Not a man could be seen. He turned toward the Arab, who was looking at him blankly. Daru held out the package to him. "Take it," he said. "There are dates, bread, and sugar. You can hold out for two days. Here are a thousand francs too." The Arab took the package and the money but kept his full hands at chest level as if he didn't know what to do with what was being given him.

"Now look," the schoolmaster said as he pointed in the direction of the east, "there's the way to Tinguit. You have a two-hour walk. At Tinguit you'll find the administration and the police. They are expecting you." The Arab looked toward the east, still holding the package and the money against his chest. Daru took his elbow and turned him rather roughly toward the south. At the foot of the height on which they stood could be seen a faint path. "That's the trail across the plateau. In a day's walk from here you'll find pasturelands and the first nomads. They'll take you in and shelter you according to their law." The Arab had now turned toward Daru and a sort of panic was visible in his expression. "Listen," he said. Daru shook his head: "No, be quiet. Now I'm leaving you." He turned his back on him, took two long steps in the direction of the school, looked hesitantly at the motionless Arab, and started off again. For a few minutes he heard nothing but his own step resounding on the cold ground and did not turn his head. A moment later, however, he turned around. The Arab was still there on the edge of the hill, his arms hanging now, and he was looking at the schoolmaster. Daru felt something rise in his throat. But he swore with impatience, waved vaguely, and started off again. He had already gone some distance when he again stopped and looked. There was no longer anyone on the hill.

Daru hesitated. The sun was now rather high in the sky and was beginning to beat down on his head. The schoolmaster retraced his steps, at first somewhat uncertainly, then with decision. When he reached the little hill, he was bathed in sweat. He climbed it as fast as he could and stopped, out of breath, at the top. The rock-fields to the south stood out sharply against the blue sky, but on the plain to the east a steamy heat was already rising. And in that slight haze, Daru, with heavy heart, made out the Arab walking slowly on the road to prison.

A little later, standing before the window of the classroom, the schoolmaster was watching the clear light bathing the whole surface of the plateau, but he hardly saw it. Behind him on the blackboard, among the winding French rivers, sprawled the clumsily chalked-up words he had just read: "You handed over our brother. You will pay for this." Daru looked at the sky, the plateau, and, beyond, the invisible lands stretching all the way to the sea. In this vast landscape he had loved so much, he was alone.

## Questions

1. Explain the relationship between Daru and Balducci. With what conflict in loyalties does Balducci's order present Daru?
2. Faced with conflict, what is Daru's choice?
3. Characterize the Arab. Can you explain the choice he makes? What evidence in the story supports your explanation?
4. Briefly recapitulate the final events of the story. What light do they cast on Daru's choice?
5. How do the descriptions of the landscape and of the weather contribute to the story?
6. Do you find yourself sympathizing with one character more than another? Or with each character at different times in the story? Explain.

**Thomas Hardy**

---

# The Man He Killed

Had he and I but met
By some old ancient inn,
We should have sat us down to wet
Right many a nipperkin![1]

But ranged as infantry,
And staring face to face,
I shot at him as he at me,
And killed him in his place.

I shot him dead because—
Because he was my foe,
Just so: my foe of course he was;
That's clear enough; although

---

Thomas Hardy (1840–1928) worked as an assistant to an architect before he established himself as a novelist. After *Jude the Obscure* was badly received, however, he abandoned novel writing and produced only poetry.

---

[1]Half-pint cup. (Editors' note)

He thought he'd 'list, perhaps
Off-hand-like—just as I—
Was out of work—had sold his traps—[2]
No other reason why.

Yes; quaint and curious war is!
You shoot a fellow down
You'd treat if met where any bar is,
Or help to half-a-crown.

## Questions

1. What do we learn about the speaker's life before he enlisted in the infantry? How does his diction characterize him?
2. What is the effect of the series of monosyllables in lines 7 and 8?
3. Consider the punctuation of the third and fourth stanzas. Why are the heavy, frequent pauses appropriate? What question is the speaker trying to answer?
4. In the last stanza what attitudes toward war does the speaker express? What, from the evidence of this poem, would you infer Hardy's attitude toward war to be?

[2]Personal belongings. (Editors' note)

# 8

# LAW AND ORDER

*Flower Power*
**Bernie Boston, 1967**

*The Problem We All Live With*
**Norman Rockwell, 1963**

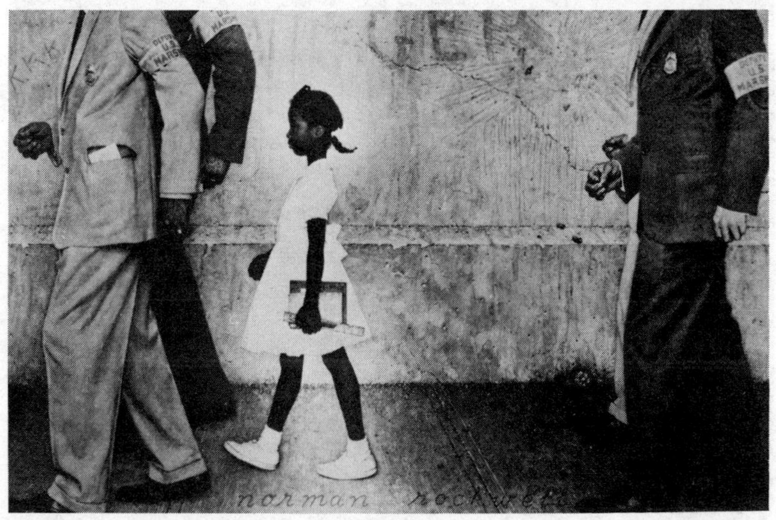

Courtesy Danenberg-Beilen Gallery Inc., New York

*The Death of Socrates*
**Jacques-Louis David, 1787**

The Metropolitan Museum of Art, Wolfe Fund, 1931

*United States Supreme Court*
**Fred Ward**

Black Star

# Short Views

Spare the rod and spoil the child.

**Anonymous**

The trouble for the thief is not how to steal the bugle, but where to blow it.

**African proverb**

And God spake all these words, saying, "I am the LORD thy God, which have brought thee out of the land of Egypt, out of the house of bondage.

"Thou shalt have no other gods before me.

"Thou shalt not make unto thee any graven image, or any likeness of any thing that is in heaven above, or that is in the earth beneath, or that is in the water under the earth: thou shalt not bow down thyself to them, nor serve them: for I the LORD thy God am a jealous God, visiting the iniquity of the fathers upon the children unto the third and fourth generation of them that hate me; and shewing mercy unto thousands of them that love me, and keep my commandments.

"Thou shalt not take the name of the LORD thy God in vain; for the LORD will not hold him guiltless that taketh his name in vain.

"Remember the sabbath day, to keep it holy. Six days shalt thou labour, and do all thy work: but the seventh day is the sabbath of the LORD thy God: in it thou shalt not do any work, thou, nor thy son, nor thy daughter, thy manservant, nor thy maidservant, nor thy cattle, nor thy stranger that is within thy gates: for in six days the LORD made heaven and earth, the sea, and all that in them is, and rested the seventh day: wherefore the LORD blessed the sabbath day, and hallowed it.

"Honour thy father and thy mother: that thy days may be long upon the land which the LORD thy God giveth thee.

"Thou shalt not kill.

"Thou shalt not commit adultery.

"Thou shalt not steal.

"Thou shalt not bear false witness against thy neighbour.

"Thou shalt not covet thy neighbour's house, thou shalt not covet thy neighbour's wife, nor his manservant, nor his maidservant, nor his ox, nor his ass, nor any thing that is thy neighbour's."

**Exodus 20:1–17**

*He Commits Theft with His Companions, Not Urged on by Poverty, but from a Certain Distaste of Well-doing.* Theft is punished by Thy law, O Lord, and by the law written in men's hearts, which iniquity itself cannot blot out. For what thief will suffer a thief? Even a rich thief will not suffer him who is driven to it by want. Yet had I a desire to commit robbery, and did so, compelled neither by hunger, nor poverty, but through a distaste for well-doing, and a lustiness of iniquity. For I pilfered that of which I had already sufficient, and much better. Nor did I desire to enjoy what I pilfered, but the theft and sin itself. There was a pear-tree close to our vineyard, heavily laden with fruit, which was tempting neither for its color nor its flavor. To shake and rob this some of us wanton young fellows went, late one night (having, according to our disgraceful habit, prolonged our games in the streets until then), and carried away great loads, not to eat ourselves, but to fling to the very swine, having only eaten some of them; and to do this pleased us all the more because it was not permitted. Behold my heart, O my God; behold my heart, which Thou hadst pity upon when in the bottomless pit. Behold, now, let my heart tell Thee what it was seeking there, that I should be gratuitously wanton, having no inducement to evil but the evil itself. It was foul, and I loved it. I loved to perish. I loved my own error—not that for which I erred; but the error itself. Base soul, falling from Thy firmament to utter destruction—not seeking aught through the shame but the shame itself!

**St. Augustine**

Whoever desires to found a state and give it laws, must start with assuming that all men are bad and ever ready to display their vicious nature, whenever they may find occasion for it.

**Niccolò Machiavelli**

Every prince must wish to be thought merciful and not cruel. But he must be careful not to misuse this mercifulness. Cesare Borgia was thought cruel, but his cruelty pacified the Romagna, united it, and reduced it to peace and loyalty. If this is carefully considered, it will be seen that Cesare was really much more merciful than the Florentines, who, to escape the name of cruelty, allowed Pistoia to be destroyed. A prince, therefore, should not mind being called cruel so long as he keeps his subjects united and faithful. With a few examples of cruelty he can be more merciful than those who, through too much tenderness, allow disturbances to arise, from which spring murder and plunder, for lawless acts injure the whole community, but the executions ordered by the prince injure only individuals. And of all princes, the new prince cannot escape a reputation for cruelty, because new states are always full of dangers. Virgil says, through the mouth of Dido: "My cruel fate and the newness of my realm force me to do such things, and to keep guard over all my lands."

Still, he must be cautious in believing and in acting, and he should not be easily frightened. He should proceed temperately, with prudence and humanity, so that overconfidence does not make him incautious, and suspicion does not make him intolerable.

**Niccolò Machiavelli**

It is questionable whether, when we break a murderer on the wheel, we aren't lapsing into precisely the mistake of the child who hits the chair he bumps into.

**G. C. Lichtenberg**

If a man were permitted to make all the ballads, he need not care who should make the laws of a nation.

**Andrew Fletcher**

Nature has given women so much power that the law has very wisely given them very little.

**Samuel Johnson**

I asked him whether, as a moralist, he did not think that the practice of the law, in some degree hurt the nice feeling of honesty. JOHNSON. "Why no, Sir, if you act properly. You are not to deceive your clients with false representations of your opinion: you are not to tell lies to a judge." BOSWELL. "But what do you think of supporting a cause which you know to be bad?" JOHNSON. "Sir, you do not know it to be good or bad till the Judge determines it. I have said that you are to state facts fairly; so that your thinking, or what you call knowing, a cause to be bad, must be from reasoning, must be from your supposing your arguments to be weak and inconclusive. But, Sir, that is not enough. An argument which does not convince yourself, may convince the Judge to whom you urge it; and if it does convince him, why, then, Sir, you are wrong, and he is right. It is his business to judge; and you are not to be confident in your own opinion that a cause is bad, but to say all you can for your client, and then hear the Judge's opinion." BOSWELL. "But, Sir, does not affecting a warmth when you have no warmth, and appearing to be clearly of one opinion when you are in reality of another opinion, does not such dissimulation impair one's honesty? Is there not some danger that a lawyer may put on the same mask in common life, in the intercourse with his friends?" JOHNSON. "Why no, Sir. Everybody knows you are paid for affecting warmth for your client; and it is, therefore, properly no dissimulation: the moment you come from the bar you resume your usual behaviour. Sir, a man will no more carry the artifice of the bar into the common intercourse of society, than a man who is paid for tumbling upon his hands will continue to tumble upon his hands when he should walk on his feet."

**James Boswell**

One law for the ox and the ass is oppression.

**William Blake**

The law, in its majestic equality, forbids the rich as well as the poor to sleep under bridges, to beg in the streets, and to steal bread.

**Anatole France**

Decency, security and liberty alike demand that government officials shall be subjected to the same rules of conduct that are commands to the citizen. In a government of laws, existence of the government will be imperilled if it fails to observe the law scrupulously. Our Government is the potent, the omnipresent teacher. For good or for ill, it teaches the whole people by its example. Crime is contagious. If the Government becomes a lawbreaker, it breeds contempt for law; it invites every man to become a law unto himself; it invites anarchy. To declare that in the administration of the criminal law the end justifies the means —to declare that the Government may commit crimes in order to secure the conviction of a private criminal—would bring terrible retribution. Against that pernicious doctrine this Court should resolutely set its face.

**Louis D. Brandeis**

Censorship upholds the dignity of the profession, know what I mean?

**Mae West**

## Martin Luther King, Jr.

# Nonviolent Resistance

Oppressed people deal with their oppression in three characteristic ways. One way is acquiescence: the oppressed resign themselves to their doom. They tacitly adjust themselves to oppression, and thereby become conditioned to it. In every movement toward freedom some of the oppressed prefer to remain oppressed. Almost 2800 years ago Moses set out to lead the children of Israel from the slavery of Egypt to the freedom of the promised land. He soon discovered that slaves do not always welcome their deliverers. They become accustomed to being slaves. They would rather bear those ills they have, as Shakespeare pointed out, then flee to others that they know not of. They prefer the "fleshpots of Egypt" to the ordeals of emancipation.

There is such a thing as the freedom of exhaustion. Some people are so worn down by the yoke of oppression that they give up. A few years ago in the slum areas of Atlanta, a Negro guitarist used to sing almost daily: "Ben down so long that down don't bother me." This

Martin Luther King Jr., (1929–1968), clergyman and civil rights leader, achieved national fame in 1955–1956 when he led the boycott against segregated bus lines in Montgomery, Alabama. His policy of passive resistance succeeded in Montgomery, and King then organized the Southern Christian Leadership Conference in order to extend his efforts. In 1964 he was awarded the Noble Peace Prize, but he continued to encounter strong opposition. On April 4, 1968, while in Memphis to support striking sanitation workers, he was shot and killed.

is the type of negative freedom and resignation that often engulfs the life of the oppressed.

But this is not the way out. To accept passively an unjust system is to cöoperate with that system; thereby the oppressed become as evil as the oppressor. Noncoöperation with evil is as much a moral obligation as is coöperation with good. The oppressed must never allow the conscience of the oppressor to slumber. Religion reminds every man that he is his brother's keeper. To accept injustice or segregation passively is to say to the oppressor that his actions are morally right. It is a way of allowing his conscience to fall asleep. At this moment the oppressed fails to be his brother's keeper. So acquiescence—while often the easier way—is not the moral way. It is the way of the coward. The Negro cannot win the respect of his oppressor by acquiescing; he merely increases the oppressor's arrogance and contempt. Acquiescence is interpreted as proof of the Negro's inferiority. The Negro cannot win the respect of the white people of the South or the peoples of the world if he is willing to sell the future of his children for his personal and immediate comfort and safety.

A second way that oppressed people sometimes deal with oppression is to resort to physical violence and corroding hatred. Violence often brings about momentary results. Nations have frequently won their independence in battle. But in spite of temporary victories, violence never brings permanent peace. It solves no social problem; it merely creates new and more complicated ones.

Violence as a way of achieving racial justice is both impractical and immoral. It is impractical because it is a descending spiral ending in destruction for all. The old law of an eye for an eye leaves everybody blind. It is immoral because it seeks to humiliate the opponent rather than win his understanding; it seeks to annihilate rather than to convert. Violence is immoral because it thrives on hatred rather than love. It destroys community and makes brotherhood impossible. It leaves society in monologue rather than dialogue. Violence ends by defeating itself. It creates bitterness in the survivors and brutality in the destroyers. A voice echoes through time saying to every potential Peter, "Put up your sword." History is cluttered with the wreckage of nations that failed to follow his command.

If the American Negro and other victims of oppression succumb to the temptation of using violence in the struggle for freedom, future generations will be the recipients of a desolate night of bitterness, and our chief legacy to them will be an endless reign of meaningless chaos. Violence is not the way.

The third way open to oppressed people in their quest for freedom is the way of nonviolent resistance. Like the synthesis in Hegelian philosophy, the principle of nonviolent resistance seeks to reconcile the truths of two opposites—acquiescence and violence—while avoiding the extremes and immoralities of both. The nonviolent resister agrees with the person who acquiesces that one should not be physically aggressive toward his opponent; but he balances the equation by agreeing with the person of violence that evil must be resisted. He avoids the nonresistance of the former and the violent resistance of the latter. With nonviolent resistance, no individual or group need submit to any wrong, nor need anyone resort to violence in order to right a wrong.

It seems to me that this is the method that must guide the actions of the Negro in the present crisis in race relations. Through nonviolent resistance the Negro will be able to rise to the noble height of opposing the unjust system while loving the perpetrators of the system. The Negro must work passionately and unrelentingly for full stature as a citizen, but he must not use inferior methods to gain it. He must never come to terms with falsehood, malice, hate, or destruction.

Nonviolent resistance makes it possible for the Negro to remain in the South and struggle for his rights. The Negro's problem will not be solved by running away. He cannot listen to the glib suggestion of those who would urge him to migrate en masse to other sections of the country. By grasping his great opportunity in the South he can make a lasting contribution to the moral strength of the nation and set a sublime example of courage for generations yet unborn.

By nonviolent resistance, the Negro can also enlist all men of good will in his struggle for equality. The problem is not a purely racial one, with Negroes set against whites. In the end, it is not a struggle between people at all, but a tension between justice and injustice. Nonviolent resistance is not aimed against oppressors but against oppression. Under its banner consciences, not racial groups, are enlisted.

If the Negro is to achieve the goal of integration, he must organize himself into a militant and nonviolent mass movement. All three elements are indispensable. The movement for equality and justice can only be a success if it has both a mass and militant character; the barriers to be overcome require both. Nonviolence is an imperative in order to bring about ultimate community.

A mass movement of militant quality that is not at the same time committed to nonviolence tends to generate conflict, which in turn breeds anarchy. The support of the participants and the sympathy of the uncommitted are both inhibited by the threat that bloodshed will engulf the community. This reaction in turn encourages the opposition to threaten and resort to force. When, however, the mass movement repudiates violence while moving resolutely toward its goal, its opponents are revealed as the instigators and practitioners of violence if it occurs. Then public support is magnetically attracted to the advocates of nonviolence, while those who employ violence are literally disarmed by overwhelming sentiment against their stand.

Only through a nonviolent approach can the fears of the white community be mitigated. A guilt-ridden white minority lives in fear that if the Negro should ever attain power, he would act without restraint or pity to revenge the injustices and brutality of the years. It is something like a parent who continually mistreats a son. One day that parent raises his hand to strike the son, only to discover that the son is now as tall as he is. The parent is suddenly afraid—fearful that the son will use his new physical power to repay his parent for all the blows of the past.

The Negro, once a helpless child, has now grown up politically, culturally, and economically. Many white men fear retaliation. The job of the Negro is to show them that they have nothing to fear, that the Negro understands and forgives and is ready to forget the past. He must convince the white man that all he seeks is justice, *for both himself and the white man.* A mass movement exercising nonviolence is an object lesson in power under discipline, a demonstration to the white community that if such a movement attained a degree of strength, it would use its power creatively and not vengefully.

Nonviolence can touch men where the law cannot reach them. When the law regulates behavior it plays an indirect part in molding public sentiment. The enforcement of the law is itself a form of peaceful persuasion. But the law needs help. The courts can order desegregation of the public schools. But what can be done to mitigate the fears, to disperse the hatred, violence, and irrationality gathered around school integration, to take the initiative out of the hands of racial demagogues, to release respect for the law? In the end, for laws to be obeyed, men must believe they are right.

Here nonviolence comes in as the ultimate form of persuasion. It is the method which seeks to implement the just law by appealing to the conscience of the great decent majority who through blindness, fear, pride, or irrationality have allowed their consciences to sleep.

The nonviolent resisters can summarize their message in the following simple terms: We will take direct action against injustice without waiting for other agencies to act. We will not obey unjust laws or submit to unjust practices. We will do this peacefully, openly, cheerfully because our aim is to persuade. We adopt the means of nonviolence because our end is a community at peace with itself. We will try to persuade with our words, but if our words fail, we will try to persuade with our acts. We will always be willing to talk and seek fair compromise, but we are ready to suffer when necessary and even risk our lives to become witnesses to the truth as we see it.

The way of nonviolence means a willingness to suffer and sacrifice. It may mean going to jail. If such is the case the resister must be willing to fill the jail houses of the South. It may even mean physical death. But if physical death is the price that a man must pay to free his children and his white brethren from a permanent death of the spirit, then nothing could be more redemptive.

## Questions

1. In the first paragraph, the passage about Moses and the children of Israel is not strictly necessary; the essential idea of the paragraph is stated in the previous sentence. Why, then, does King add this material? And why the quotation from Shakespeare?
2. Pick out two or three sentences that seem to you to be especially effective and analyze the sources of their power. You can choose either isolated sentences or (because King often effectively links sentences with repetition of words or of constructions) consecutive ones.
3. In a paragraph set forth your understanding of what nonviolent resistance is. Use whatever examples from your own experience or reading you find useful. In a second paragraph, explain how Maya Angelou's "Graduation" (page 201) offers an example of nonviolent resistance.

## Plato

# Crito

*Persons of the Dialogue: Socrates and Crito*
*Scene: The Prison of Socrates*

*Socrates.* Why have you come at this hour, Crito? it must be quite early?

*Crito.* Yes, certainly.

*Soc.* What is the exact time?

*Cr.* The dawn is breaking.

*Soc.* I wonder that the keeper of the prison would let you in.

*Cr.* He knows me, because I often come, Socrates; moreover, I have done him a kindness.

*Soc.* And are you only just arrived?

*Cr.* No, I came some time ago.

*Soc.* Then why did you sit and say nothing, instead of at once awakening me?

*Cr.* I should not have liked myself, Socrates, to be in such great trouble and unrest as you are—indeed I should not: I have been watching with amazement your peaceful slumbers; and for that reason I did not awake you, because I wished to minimize the pain. I have always thought you to be of a happy disposition; but never did I see anything like easy, tranquil manner in which you bear this calamity.

*Soc.* Why, Crito, when a man has reached my age he ought not to be repining at the approach of death.

---

Plato (427–347 B.C.) in his dialogues often uses the Athenian philosopher Socrates as a mouthpiece for ideas that scholars believe are Platonic, but in the dialogue called *Crito* he probably was fairly careful to represent Socrates' own ideas.

In 399 B.C. Socrates was convicted of impiety and was sentenced to death. Behind the charge of impiety was another, that Socrates had "corrupted the young." It seems clear, however, that the trial was a way of getting rid of a man considered by some to be a troublesome questioner of conventional opinions.

About a month intervened between the trial and Socrates' death because the law prohibited execution until a sacred ship had returned to Athens. Socrates could easily have escaped from prison but made no effort to leave, as we see in this dialogue reporting his decision to abide by the unjust decision of a duly constituted group of jurors.

---

*Cr.* And yet other old men find themselves in similar misfortunes, and age does not prevent them from repining.

*Soc.* That is true. But you have not told me why you come at this early hour.

*Cr.* I come to bring you a message which is sad and painful; not, as I believe, to yourself, but to all of us who are your friends, and saddest of all to me.

*Soc.* What? Has the ship come from Delos, on the arrival of which I am to die?

*Cr.* No, the ship has not actually arrived, but she will probably be here today, as persons who have come from Sunium tell me that they left her there; and therefore tomorrow, Socrates, will be the last day of your life.

*Soc.* Very well, Crito; if such is the will of God, I am willing; but my belief is that there will be a delay of a day.

*Cr.* Why do you think so?

*Soc.* I will tell you. I am to die on the day after the arrival of the ship.

*Cr.* Yes; that is what the authorities say.

*Soc.* But I do not think that the ship will be here until tomorrow; this I infer from a vision which I had last night, or rather only just now, when you fortunately allowed me to sleep.

*Cr.* And what was the nature of the vision?

*Soc.* There appeared to me the likeness of a woman, fair and comely, clothed in bright raiment, who called to me and said: O Socrates,

> The third day hence to fertile Phthia shalt thou go.[1]

*Cr.* What a singular dream, Socrates!

*Soc.* There can be no doubt about the meaning, Crito, I think.

*Cr.* Yes; the meaning is only too clear. But, oh! my beloved Socrates, let me entreat you once more to take my advice and escape. For if you die I shall not only lose a friend who can never be replaced, but there is another evil: people who do not know you and me will believe that I might have saved you if I had been willing to give money, but that I did not care. Now, can there be a worse disgrace than this—that I should be thought to value money more than the life of a friend? For the many will not be persuaded that I wanted you to escape, and that you refused.

[1]Homer, *Iliad,* ix. 363.

*Soc.* But why, my dear Crito, should we care about the opinion of the many? Good men, and they are the only persons who are worth considering, will think of these things truly as they occurred.

*Cr.* But you see, Socrates, that the opinion of the many must be regarded, for what is now happening shows that they can do the greatest evil to any one who has lost their good opinion.

*Soc.* I only wish it were so, Crito; and that the many could do the greatest evil; for then they would also be able to do the greatest good—and what a fine thing this would be! But in reality they can do neither; for they cannot make a man either wise or foolish; and whatever they do is the result of chance.

*Cr.* Well, I will not dispute with you; but please to tell me, Socrates, whether you are not acting out of regard to me and your other friends: are you not afraid that if you escape from prison we may get into trouble with the informers for having stolen you away, and lose either the whole or a great part of our property; or that even a worse evil may happen to us? Now, if you fear on our account, be at ease; for in order to save you, we ought surely to run this, or even a greater risk; be persuaded, then, and do as I say.

*Soc.* Yes, Crito, that is one fear which you mention, but by no means the only one.

*Cr.* Fear not—there are persons who are willing to get you out of prison at no great cost; and as for the informers, they are far from being exorbitant in their demands—a little money will satisfy them. My means, which are certainly ample, are at your service, and if you have a scruple about spending all mine, here are strangers who will give you the use of theirs; and one of them, Simmias the Theban, has brought a large sum of money for this very purpose; and Cebes and many others are prepared to spend their money in helping you to escape. I say, therefore, do not hesitate on our account, and do not say, as you did in the court, that you will have a difficulty in knowing what to do with yourself anywhere else. For men will love you in other places to which you may go, and not in Athens only; there are friends of mine in Thessaly, if you like to go to them, who will value and protect you, and no Thessalian will give you any trouble. Nor can I think that you are at all justified, Socrates, in betraying your own life when you might be saved; in acting thus you are playing into the hands of your enemies, who are hurrying on your destruction. And further I should say that you are deserting your own children; for you might bring them up and educate them; instead of which you go away and leave them, and they will have to take their chance; and if they do not meet with the usual fate of orphans, there will be small thanks to you. No man should bring children into the world who is unwilling to persevere to the end in their nurture and education. But you appear to be choosing the easier part, not the better and manlier, which would have been more becoming in one who professes to care for virtue in all his actions, like yourself. And indeed, I am ashamed not only of you, but of us who are your friends, when I reflect that the whole business will be attributed entirely to our want of courage. The trial need never have come on, or might have been managed differently; and this last act, or crowning folly, will seem to have occurred through our negligence and cowardice, who might have saved you, if we had been good for anything; and you might have saved yourself, for there was no difficulty at all. See now, Socrates, how sad and discreditable are the consequences, both to us and you. Make up your mind then, or rather have your mind already made up, for the time of deliberation is over, and there is only one thing to be done, which must be done this very night, and if we delay at all will be no longer practicable or possible; I beseech you therefore, Socrates, be persuaded by me, and do as I say.

*Soc.* Dear Crito, your zeal is invaluable, if a right one; but if wrong, the greater the zeal the greater the danger; and therefore we ought to consider whether I shall or shall not do as you say. For I am and always have been one of those natures who must be guided by reason, whatever the reason may be which upon reflection appears to me to be the best; and now that this chance has befallen me, I cannot repudiate my own words: the principles which I have hitherto honored and revered I still honor, and unless we can at once find other and better principles, I am certain not to agree with you; no, not even if the power of the multitude could inflict many more imprisonments, confiscations, deaths, frightening us like children with hobgoblin terrors. What will be the fairest way of considering the question? Shall I return to your old argument about the opinions of men?—we were saying that some of them are to be regarded, and others not. Now were we right in maintaining this before I was condemned? And has the argument which was once good now proved to be talk for the sake of talking—mere childish nonsense? That is what I want to consider with your help, Crito:—whether, under my present circumstances, the argument appears to be in any way different or not; and is to be allowed by me or disallowed. That argument, which, as I believe, is maintained by many persons of authority, was to the effect, as I was saying, that the opinions of some men are to be regarded, and of other men not to be regarded. Now you, Crito, are not going to die tomorrow—at least, there is no human probability of this—and therefore you are disinterested and not liable to be deceived by the circumstances in which you are placed. Tell me then, whether I am right in saying that some opinions, and the opinions of some men only, are to be valued, and that other opinions, and the opinions of other men, are not to be valued. I ask you whether I was right in maintaining this?

*Cr.* Certainly.

*Soc.* The good are to be regarded, and not the bad?

*Cr.* Yes.

*Soc.* And the opinions of the wise are good, and the opinions of the unwise are evil?

*Cr.* Certainly.

*Soc.* And what was said about another matter? Is the pupil who devotes himself to the practice of gymnastics supposed to attend to the praise and blame and opinion of every man, or of one man only—his physician or trainer, whoever he may be?

*Cr.* Of one man only.

*Soc.* And he ought to fear the censure and welcome the praise of that one only, and not of the many?

*Cr.* Clearly so.

*Soc.* And he ought to act and train, and eat and drink in the way which seems good to his single master who has understanding, rather than according to the opinion of all other men put together?

*Cr.* True.

*Soc.* And if he disobeys and disregards the opinion and approval of the one, and regards the opinion of the many who have no understanding, will he not suffer evil?

*Cr.* Certainly he will.

*Soc.* And what will the evil be, whither tending and what affecting, in the disobedient person?

*Cr.* Clearly, affecting the body; that is what is destroyed by the evil.

*Soc.* Very good; and is not this true, Crito, of other things which we need not separately enumerate? In questions of just and unjust, fair and foul, good and evil, which are the subjects of our present consultation, ought we to allow the opinion of the many and to fear them; or the opinion of the one man who has understanding? ought we not to fear and reverence him more than all the rest of the world: and if we desert him shall we not destroy and injure that principle in us which may be assumed to be improved by justice and deteriorated by injustice;—there is such a principle?

*Cr.* Certainly there is, Socrates.

*Soc.* Take a parallel instance—if, acting under the advice of those who have no understanding, we destroy that which is improved by health and is deteriorated by disease, would life be worth having? And that which has been destroyed is—the body?

*Cr.* Yes.

*Soc.* Could we live, having an evil and corrupted body?

*Cr.* Certainly not.

*Soc.* And will life be worth having, if that higher part of man be destroyed, which is improved by justice and depraved by injustice? Do we suppose that principle, whatever it may be in man, which has to do with justice and injustice, to be inferior to the body?

*Cr.* Certainly not.

*Soc.* More honorable than the body?

*Cr.* Far more.

*Soc.* Then, my friend, we must not regard what the many say of us: but what he, the one man who has understanding of just and unjust, will say, and what the truth will say. And therefore you begin in error when you advise that we should regard the opinion of the many about just and unjust, good and evil, honorable and dishonorable—"Well," some one will say, "but the many can kill us."

*Cr.* Yes, Socrates; that will clearly be the answer.

*Soc.* And it is true: but still I find with surprise that the old argument is unshaken as ever. And I should like to know whether I may say the same of another proposition—that not life, but a good life, is to be chiefly valued?

*Cr.* Yes, that also remains unshaken.

*Soc.* And a good life is equivalent to a just, honorable one—that holds also?

*Cr.* Yes, it does.

*Soc.* From these premises I proceed to argue the question whether I ought or ought not to try and escape without the consent of the Athenians: and if I am clearly right in escaping, then I will make the attempt; but if not, I will abstain. The other considerations which you mention, of money and loss of character and duty of educating one's children, are, I fear, only the doctrines of the multitude, who would be as ready to restore people to life, if they were able, as they are to put them to death—and with as little reason. But now, since the argument has thus far prevailed, the only question which remains to be considered is, whether we shall do rightly either in escaping or in suffering others to aid in our escape and paying them in money and thanks, or whether in reality we shall not do rightly; and if the latter, then death or any other calamity which may ensue on my remaining here must not be allowed to enter into the calculation.

*Cr.* I think that you are right, Socrates; how then shall we proceed?

*Soc.* Let us consider the matter together, and do you either refute me if you can, and I will be convinced; or else cease, my dear friend, from repeating to me that I ought to escape against the wishes of the Athenians: for I highly value your attempts to persuade me to do so, but I may not be persuaded against my own better judgment. And now please to consider my first position, and try how you can best answer me.

*Cr.* I will.

*Soc.* Are we to say that we are never intentionally to do wrong, or that in one way we ought and in another we ought not to do wrong, or is doing wrong always evil and dishonorable, as I was just now saying, and as has been already acknowledged by us? Are all our former admissions which were made within a few days to be thrown away? And have we, at our age, been earnestly discoursing with one another all our life long only to discover that we are no better than children? Or, in spite of the opinion of the many, and in spite of consequences whether better or worse, shall we insist on the truth of what was then said, that injustice is always an evil and dishonor to him who acts unjustly? Shall we say so or not?

*Cr.* Yes.

*Soc.* Then we must do no wrong?

*Cr.* Certainly not.

*Soc.* Nor when injured injure in return, as the many imagine; for we must injure no one at all?

*Cr.* Clearly not.

*Soc.* Again, Crito, may we do evil?

*Cr.* Surely not, Socrates.

*Soc.* And what of doing evil in return for evil, which is the morality of the many—is that just or not?

*Cr.* Not just.

*Soc.* For doing evil to another is the same as injuring him?

*Cr.* Very true.

*Soc.* Then we ought not to retaliate or render evil for evil to any one, whatever evil we may have suffered from him. But I would have you consider, Crito, whether you really mean what you are saying. For this opinion has never been held, and never will be held, by any considerable number of persons; and those who are agreed and those who are not agreed upon this point have no common ground, and can only despise one another when they see how widely they differ. Tell me, then, whether you agree with and assent to my first principle, that neither injury nor retaliation nor warding off evil by evil is ever right. And shall that be the premise of our argument? Or do you decline and dissent from this? For so I have ever thought, and continue to think; but, if you are of another opinion, let me hear what you have to say. If, however, you remain of the same mind as formerly, I will proceed to the next step.

*Cr.* You may proceed, for I have not changed my mind.

*Soc.* Then I will go on to the next point, which may be put in the form of a question:—Ought a man to do what he admits to be right, or ought he to betray the right?

*Cr.* He ought to do what he thinks right.

*Soc.* But if this is true, what is the application? In leaving the prison against the will of the Athenians, do I wrong any? or rather do I not wrong those whom I ought least to wrong? Do I not desert the principles which were acknowledged by us to be just—what do you say?

*Cr.* I cannot tell, Socrates; for I do not know.

*Soc.* Then consider the matter in this way:—Imagine that I am about to play truant (you may call the proceeding by any name which you like), and the laws and the government come and interrogate me: "Tell us, Socrates," they say; "what are you about? are you not going by an act of yours to overturn us—the laws, and the whole state, as far as in you lies? Do you imagine that a state can subsist and not be overthrown, in which the decisions of law have no power, but are set aside and trampled upon by individuals?" What will be our answer, Crito, to these and the like words? Any one, and especially a rhetorician, will have a good deal to say on behalf of the law which requires a sentence to be carried out. He will argue that this law should not be set aside; and shall we reply, "Yes; but the state has injured us and given an unjust sentence." Suppose I say that?

*Cr.* Very good, Socrates.

*Soc.* "And was that our agreement with you?" the law would answer; "or were you to abide by the sentence of the state?" And if I were to express my astonishment at their words, the law would probably add: "Answer, Socrates, instead of opening your eyes—you are in the habit of asking and answering questions. Tell us—What complaint have you to make against us which justifies you in attempting to destroy us and the state? In the first place did we not bring you into existence? Your father married your mother by our aid and begat you. Say whether you bave any objection to urge against those of us who regulate marriage?" None, I should reply. "Or against those of us who after birth regulate the nurture and education of children, in which you also were trained? Were not the laws, which have the charge of education, right in commanding your father to train you in music and gymnastic?" Right, I should reply. "Well then, since you were brought into the world and nurtured and educated by us, can you deny in the first place that you are our child and slave, as your fathers were before you? And if this is true you are not on equal terms with us; nor can you think that you have a right to do to us what we are doing to you. Would you have any right to strike or revile or do any other evil to your father or your master, if you had one, because you have been struck or reviled by him, or received some other evil at his hands?—you would not say this? And because we think right to destroy you, do you think that you have any right to destroy us in return, and your country as far as in you lies? Will you, O professor of true virtue, pretend that you are justified in this? Has a philosopher like you failed to discover that our country is more to be valued and higher and holier far than mother or father or any ancestor, and more to be regarded in the eyes of the gods and of men of understanding? also to be soothed, and gently and reverently entreated when angry, even more than a father, and either to be persuaded, or if not persuaded, to be obeyed? And when we are punished by her, whether with imprisonment or stripes, the punishment is to be endured in silence; and if she leads us to wounds or death in battle, thither we follow as is right; neither may any one yield or retreat or leave his rank, but whether in battle or in a court of law, or in any other place, he must do what his city and his country order him; or he must change their view of what is just: and if he may do no violence to his father or mother, much less may he do violence to his country." What answer shall we make to this, Crito? Do the laws speak truly, or do they not?

*Cr.* I think that they do.

*Soc.* Then the laws will say, "Consider, Socrates, if we are speaking truly that in your present attempt you are going to do us an injury. For, having brought you into the world, and nurtured and educated you, and given you and every other citizen a share in every good which we had to give, we further proclaim to any Athenian by the liberty which we allow him, that if he does not like us when he has become of age and has seen the ways of the city, and made our acquaintance, he may go where he pleases and take his goods with him. None of us laws will forbid him or interfere with him. Any one who does not like us and the city, and who wants to emigrate to a colony or to any other city, may go where he likes, retaining his property. But he who has experience of the manner in which we order justice and administer the state, and still remains, has entered into an implied contract that he will do as we command him. And he who disobeys us is, as we maintain, thrice wrong; first, because in disobeying us he is disobeying his parents; secondly, because we are the authors of his education; thirdly, because he has made an agreement with us that he will duly obey our commands; and he neither obeys them nor convinces us that our commands are unjust; and we do not rudely impose them, but give him the alternative of obeying or convincing us;—that is what we offer, and he does neither.

"These are the sort of accusations to which, as we were saying, you, Socrates, will be exposed if you accomplish your intentions; you, above all other Athenians." Suppose now I ask, why I rather than anybody else? they will justly retort upon me that I above all other men have acknowledged the agreement. "There is clear proof," they will say, "Socrates, that we and the city were not displeasing to you. Of all Athenians you have been the most constant resident in the city, which, as you never leave, you may be supposed to love. For you never went out of the city either to see the games, except once when you went to the Isthmus, or to any other place unless when you were on military service; nor did you travel as other men do. Nor had you any curiosity to know other states or their laws: your affections did not go beyond us and our state; we were your special favorites, and you acquiesced in our government of you; and here in this city you begat your children, which is a proof of your satisfaction. Moreover, you might in the course of the trial, if you had liked, have fixed the penalty at banishment; the state which refuses to let you go now would have let you go then. But you pretended that you preferred death to exile, and that you were unwilling to die. And now you have forgotten these fine sentiments, and pay no respect to us the laws, of whom you are the destroyer; and are doing what only a miserable slave would do, running away and turning your back upon the compacts and agreements which you made as a citizen. And first of all answer this very question: Are we right in saying that you agreed to be governed according to us in deed, and not in word only? Is that true or not?" How shall we answer, Crito? Must we not assent?

*Cr.* We cannot help it, Socrates.

*Soc.* Then will they not say: "You, Socrates, are breaking the covenants and agreements which you made with us at your leisure, not in any haste or under any compulsion or deception, but after you have had seventy years to think of them, during which time you were at liberty to leave the city, if we were not to your mind, or if our covenants appeared to you to be unfair. You had your choice, and might have gone either to Lacedaemon or Crete, both which states are often praised by you for their good government, or to some other Hellenic or foreign state. Whereas you, above all other Athenians, seemed to be so fond of the state, or, in other words, of us her laws (and who would care about a state which has no laws?), that you never stirred out of her; the halt, the blind, the maimed were not more stationary in her than you were. And now you run away and forsake your agreements. Not so, Socrates, if you will take our advice; do not make yourself ridiculous by escaping out of the city.

"For just consider, if you transgress and err in this sort of way, what good will you do either to yourself or to your friends? That your friends will be driven into exile and deprived of citizenship, or will lose their property, is tolerably certain; and you yourself, if you fly to one of the neighboring cities, as, for example, Thebes or Megara, both of which are well governed, will come to them as an enemy, Socrates, and their government will be against you, and all patriotic citizens will cast an evil eye upon you as a subverter of the laws, and you will confirm in the minds of the judges the justice of their own condemnation of you. For he who is a corrupter of the laws is more than likely to be a corrupter of the young and foolish portion of mankind. Will you then flee from well-ordered cities and virtuous men? and is existence worth having on these terms? Or will you go to them without shame, and talk to them, Socrates? And what will you say to them? What you say here about virtue and justice and institutions and laws being the best things among men? Would that be decent of you? Surely not. But if you go away from well-governed states to Crito's friends in Thessaly, where there is great disorder and license, they will be charmed to hear the tale of your escape from prison, set off with ludicrous particulars of the manner in which you were wrapped in a goatskin or some other disguise, and metamorphosed as the manner is of runaways; but will there be no one to remind you that in your old age you were not ashamed to violate the most sacred laws for a miserable desire of a little more life? Perhaps not, if you keep them in a good temper; but if they are out of temper you will hear many degrading things; you will live, but how?—as the flatterer of all men, and the servant of all men; and doing what?—eating and drinking in Thessaly, having gone abroad in order that you may get a dinner. And where will be your fine sentiments about justice and virtue? Say that you wish to live for the sake of your children—you want to bring them up and educate them—will you take them into Thessaly and deprive them of Athenian citizenship? Is this the benefit which you will confer upon them? Or are you under the impression that they will be better cared for and educated here if you are still alive, although absent from them; for your friends will take care of them? Do you fancy that if you are an inhabitant of Thessaly they will take care of them, and if you are an inhabitant of the other world that they will not take care of them? Nay; but if they who call themselves friends are good for anything, they will—to be sure they will.

"Listen, then, Socrates, to us who have brought you up. Think not of life and children first, and of justice afterward, but of justice first, that you may be justified before the princes of the world below. For neither will you nor any that belong to you be happier or holier or juster in this life, or happier in another, if you do as Crito bids. Now you depart in innocence, a sufferer and not a doer of evil; a victim, not of the laws but of men. But if you go forth, returning evil for evil, and injury for injury, breaking the covenants and agreements which you have made with us, and wronging those whom you ought least of all to wrong, that is to say, yourself, your friends, your country, and us, we shall be angry with you while you live, and our brethren, the laws in the world below, will receive you as an enemy; for they will know that you have done your best to destroy us. Listen, then, to us and not to Crito."

This, dear Crito, is the voice which I seem to hear murmuring in my ears, like the sound of the flute in the ears of the mystic; that voice, I say, is humming in my ears, and prevents me from hearing any other. And I know that anything more which you may say will be vain. Yet speak, if you have anything to say.

*Cr.* I have nothing to say, Socrates.

*Soc.* Leave me then, Crito, to fulfill the will of God, and to follow whither he leads.

## Questions

1. Socrates argues that because throughout his life he lived in Athens, in effect he established a compact with the city to live by its laws and must therefore now accept the judgment—however mistaken—of a duly constituted court. How convincing is this argument? Suppose this argument were omitted. Would Socrates' conclusion be affected?
2. Socrates argues that just as in matters of caring for the body we heed only experts and not the multitude, so in moral matters we should heed the expert, not the multitude. How convincing is this analogy between bodily health and moral goodness? Socrates sometimes compared himself to an athletic coach, saying he trained people to think. Judging from the dialogue, how did he train a student to think?
3. The personified figure of the laws does not add much to the essential argument. Why, then, is the passage included?
4. The ancient Chinese teacher Confucius asked one of his pupils, "Do you think of me as a man who knows about things as the result of wide study?" When the pupil replied "Yes," Confucius disagreed: "I have one thing, and upon it all the rest is rooted." Exactly what did Confucius mean? If Socrates had been asked the question, would he have given Confucius's answer?

## Luke, John, and an Anonymous Japanese

# Four Short Narratives

### 1. Luke *Parable of the Prodigal Son*

Then drew near unto [Jesus] all the publicans and sinners for to hear him. And the Pharisees and scribes murmured, saying "This man receiveth sinners, and eateth with them." And he said, "A certain man had two sons: and the younger of them said to his father, 'Father, give me the portion of goods that falleth to me.' And he divided unto them his living. And not many days after, the younger son gathered all together, and took his journey into a far country, and there wasted his substance with riotous living. And when he had spent all, there arose a mighty famine in that land, and he began to be in want. And he went and joined himself to a citizen of that country, and he sent him into his fields to feed swine. And he would fain have filled his belly with the husks that the swine did eat: and no man gave unto him. And when he came to himself, he said, 'How many hired servants of my father's have bread enough and to spare, and I perish with hunger? I will arise and go to my father, and will say unto him, "Father, I have sinned against heaven, and before thee. And am no more worthy to be called thy son: make me as one of thy hired servants." ' And he arose, and came to his father. But when he was yet a great way off, his father saw him, and had compassion, and ran, and fell on his neck, and kissed him. And the son said unto him, 'Father, I have sinned against heaven, and in thy sight, and am no more worthy to be called thy son.' But the father said to his servants, 'Bring forth the best robe, and put it on him, and put a ring on his hand, and shoes on his feet. And bring hither the fatted calf, and kill

---

Luke, the author of the third of the four Gospels, was a second-generation Christian. He probably was a Roman, though some early accounts refer to him as a Syrian; in any case, he wrote in Greek. John, the author of the fourth Gospel, is traditionally said to be John, son of Zebedee, one of the twelve apostles of Jesus. Tradition also holds that John is the author of three epistles and of Revelation, though much modern scholarship doubts that the same man could have written these works, which differ in matters of style and doctrine. Our two selections from Luke and our one selection from John are all from the King James Version (1611). The author of the Japanese anecdote called "Muddy Road" is not known.

---

it, and let us eat, and be merry. For this my son was dead, and is alive again; he was lost, and is found.' And they began to be merry. Now his elder son was in the field, and as he came and drew nigh to the house, he heard music and dancing. And he called one of the servants, and asked what these things meant. And he said unto him, 'Thy brother is come, and thy father hath killed the fatted calf, because he hath received him safe and sound.' And he was angry, and would not go in: therefore came his father out, and entreated him. And he answering said to his father, 'Lo, these many years do I serve thee, neither transgressed I at any time thy commandment, and yet thou never gavest me a kid, that I might make merry with my friends: but as soon as this thy son was come, which hath devoured thy living with harlots, thou hast killed for him the fatted calf.' And he said unto him, 'Son, thou art ever with me, and all that I have is thine. It was meet that we should make merry, and be glad: for this thy brother was dead, and is alive again: and was lost, and is found.' "

## 2. Luke *Parable of the Good Samaritan*

But [a certain lawyer], willing to justify himself, said unto Jesus, and who is my neighbor?

And Jesus answering said, "A certain man went down from Jerusalem to Jericho, and fell among thieves, which stripped him of his raiment, and wounded him, and departed, leaving him half dead. And by chance there came down a certain priest that way: and when he saw him, he passed by on the other side. And likewise a Levite.[1] when he was at the place, came and looked on him, and passed by on the other side. But a certain Samaritan, as he journeyed, came where he was: and when he saw him, he had compassion on him, and went to him, and bound up his wounds, pouring in oil and wine, and set him on his own beast, and brought him to an inn, and took care of him. And on the morrow when he departed, he took out two pence, and gave them to the host, and said unto him, "Take care of him; and whatsoever thou spendest more, when I come again, I will repay thee.' Which now of these three, thinkest thou, was neighbor unto him that fell among the thieves?"

And he said, "He that shewed mercy on him."

Then said Jesus unto him, "Go, and do thou likewise."

[1]The Levites were assistants to the temple priests. The Samaritans (referred to in the next sentence) claimed to be Israelites but were regarded by the Jews as transplanted Assyrians. (Editors' note)

### 3. John *The Woman Taken in Adultery*

Jesus went unto the mount of Olives. And early in the morning he came again into the temple, and all the people came unto him; and he sat down, and taught them.

And the scribes and Pharisees brought unto him a woman taken in adultery; and when they had set her in the midst, they say unto him, "Master, this woman was taken in adultery, in the very act. Now Moses in the law commanded us that such should be stoned: but what sayest thou?" This they said, tempting him, that they might have to accuse him. But Jesus stooped down, and with his finger wrote on the ground, as though he heard them not. So when they continued asking him, he lifted up himself, and said unto them, "He that is without sin among you, let him first cast a stone at her." And again he stooped down, and wrote on the ground. And they which heard it, being convicted by their own conscience, went out one by one, beginning at the eldest, even unto the last: and Jesus was left alone, and the woman standing in the midst.

When Jesus had lifted up himself, and saw none but the woman, he said unto her, "Woman, where are those thine accusers? Hath no man condemned thee?" She said, "No man, Lord." And Jesus said unto her, "Neither do I condemn thee; go, and sin no more."

### 4. Anonymous Japanese *Muddy Road*

Tanzan and Ekido were once traveling together down a muddy road. A heavy rain was still falling.

Coming around a bend, they met a lovely girl in a silk kimono and sash, unable to cross the intersection.

"Come on, girl," said Tanzan at once. Lifting her in his arms, he carried her over the mud.

Ekido did not speak again until that night when they reached a lodging temple. Then he no longer could restrain himself. "We monks don't go near females," he told Tanzan, "especially not young and lovely ones. It is dangerous. Why did you do that?"

"I left the girl there," said Tanzan. "Are you still carrying her?"

## Questions

1. What is the function of the older brother in the Parable of the Prodigal Son? Characterize him, and compare him with the younger brother.

2. Is the father foolish and sentimental? Do we approve or disapprove of his behavior at the end? Explain.
3. The biblical command is to love one's neighbor. The question put to Jesus, before he recounts the Parable of the Good Samaritan, is, "Who is my neighbor?" In the parable, what is Jesus' interpretation of the question and of the commandment?
4. Do you interpret the episode of the Woman Taken in Adultery to say that crime should go unpunished? Or that a judge cannot punish a crime if he himself is guilty of it? Or what?
5. What is the moral of the Japanese story? Does it bear any resemblance to the moral of the Parable of the Good Samaritan? Explain.

## Thomas Jefferson

# The Declaration of Independence

In CONGRESS, July 4, 1776.

*The Unanimous Declaration of the Thirteen United States of America.*

When in the Course of human events, it becomes necessary for one people to dissolve the political bands which have connected them with another, and to assume among the powers of the earth, the separate and equal station to which the Laws of Nature and of Nature's God entitle them, a decent respect to the opinions of mankind requires that they should declare the causes which impel them to the separation.

We hold these truths to be self-evident, that all men are created equal, that they are endowed by their Creator with certain unalienable Rights, that among these are Life, Liberty and the pursuit of Happiness.

That to secure these rights, Governments are instituted among Men, deriving their just powers from the consent of the governed.

---

Thomas Jefferson (1743–1826), governor of Virginia and the third president of the United States, devoted most of his adult life, until his retirement, to the service of Virginia and of the nation. The spirit and the wording of the Declaration are almost entirely Jefferson's.

That whenever any Form of Government becomes destructive of these ends, it is the Right of the People to alter or to abolish it, and to institute new Government, laying its foundation on such principles and organizing its powers in such form, as to them shall seem most likely to effect their Safety and Happiness. Prudence, indeed, will dictate that Governments long established should not be changed for light and transient causes; and accordingly all experience hath shewn, that mankind are more disposed to suffer, while evils are sufferable, than to right themselves by abolishing the forms to which they are accustomed. But when a long train of abuses and usurpations, pursuing invariably the same Object evinces a design to reduce them under absolute Despotism, it is their right, it is their duty, to throw off such Government, and to provide new Guards for their future security.

Such has been the patient sufferance of these Colonies; and such is now the necessity which constrains them to alter their former Systems of Government. The history of the present King of Great Britain is a history of repeated injuries and usurpations, all having in direct object the establishment of an absolute Tyranny over these States. To prove this, let Facts be submitted to a candid world.

He has refused his Assent to Laws, the most wholesome and necessary for the public good.

He has forbidden his Governors to pass Laws of immediate and pressing importance, unless suspended in their operation till his Assent should be obtained; and when so suspended, he has utterly neglected to attend to them.

He has refused to pass other Laws for the accommodation of large districts of people, unless those people would relinquish the right of Representation in the Legislature, a right inestimable to them and formidable to tyrants only.

He has called together legislative bodies at places unusual, uncomfortable, and distant from the depository of their public Records, for the sole purpose of fatiguing them into compliance with his measures.

He has dissolved Representative Houses repeatedly, for opposing with manly firmness his invasions on the rights of people.

He has refused for a long time, after such dissolutions, to cause others to be elected; whereby the Legislative powers, incapable of Annihilation, have returned to the People at large for their exercise; the State remaining in the mean time exposed to all the dangers of invasion from without, and convulsions within.

He has endeavoured to prevent the population of these States; for that purpose obstructing the Laws for Naturalization of Foreigners; refusing to pass others to encourage their migrations hither, and raising the conditions of new Appropriations of Lands.

He has obstructed the Administration of Justice, by refusing his Assent to Laws for establishing Judiciary powers.

He has made Judges dependent on his Will alone, for the tenure of their offices, and the amount and payment of their salaries.

He has erected a multitude of New Offices, and sent hither swarms of Officers to harass our people, and eat out their substance.

He has kept among us, in times of peace, Standing Armies without the Consent of our legislatures.

He has affected to render the Military independent of and superior to the Civil power.

He has combined with others to subject us to a jurisdiction foreign to our constitution, and unacknowledged by our laws; giving his Assent to their Acts of pretended Legislation:

For Quartering large bodies of armed troops among us:

For Protecting them, by a mock Trial, from punishment for any Murders which they should commit on the Inhabitants of these States:

For cutting off our Trade with all parts of the world:

For imposing Taxes on us without our Consent:

For depriving us in many cases, of the benefits of Trial by Jury:

For transporting us beyond Seas to be tried for pretended offenses:

For abolishing the free System of English Laws in a neighbouring Province, establishing therein an Arbitrary government, and enlarging its Boundaries so as to render it at once an example and fit instrument for introducing the same absolute rule into these Colonies:

For taking away our Charters, abolishing our most valuable Laws, and altering fundamentally the Forms of our Governments:

For suspending our own Legislatures, and declaring themselves invested with power to legislate for us in all cases whatsoever.

He has abdicated Government here, by declaring us out of his Protection and waging War against us:

He has plundered our seas, ravaged our Coasts, burnt our towns, and destroyed the lives of our people.

He is at this time transporting large Armies of foreign Mercenaries to compleat the works of death, desolation and tyranny, already begun with circumstances of Cruelty & perfidy scarcely paralleled in the most barbarous ages, and totally unworthy the Head of a civilized nation.

He has constrained our fellow Citizens taken Captive on the high Seas to bear Arms against their Country, to become the executioners of their friends and Brethren, or to fall themselves by their Hands.

He has excited domestic insurrections amongst us, and has endeavoured to bring on the inhabitants of our frontiers, the merciless Indian Savages, whose known rule of warfare, is an undistinguished destruction of all ages, sexes and conditions. In every stage of these Oppressions We have Petitioned for Redress in the most humble terms: Our repeated Petitions have been answered only by repeated injury. A Prince, whose character is thus marked by every act which may define a Tyrant, is unfit to be the ruler of a free people. Nor have We been wanting in attentions to our British brethren. We have warned them from time to time of attempts by their legislature to extend an unwarrantable jurisdiction over us. We have reminded them of the circumstances of of our emigration and settlement here. We have appealed to their native justice and magnanimity, and we have conjured them by the ties of our common kindred to disavow these usurpations, which, would inevitably interrupt our connections and correspondence. They too have been deaf to the voice of justice and of consanguinity. We must, therefore, acquiesce in the necessity, which denounces our Separation, and bold them, as we hold the rest of mankind, Enemies in War, in Peace Friends.

We, THEREFORE the Representatives of the UNITED STATES OF AMERICA, in General Congress Assembled, appealing to the Supreme Judge of the world for the rectitude of our intentions, do, in the Name and by Authority of the good People of these Colonies, solemnly publish and declare, That these United Colonies are, and of Right ought to be FREE AND INDEPENDENT STATES: that they are Absolved from all Allegiance to the British Crown, and that all political connection between them and the State of Great Britain, is and ought to be totally dissolved; and that as Free and Independent States, they have full Power to levy War, conclude Peace, contract Alliances, establish Commerce, and to do all other Acts and Things which Independent States may of right do.

And for the support of this Declaration, with a firm reliance on the protection of divine Providence, we mutually pledge to each other our Lives, our Fortunes and our sacred Honor.

# Questions

1. What assumptions lie behind the numerous specific reasons that are given to justify the rebellion? Set forth the gist of that argument of the Declaration using the form of reasoning known as a syllogism, which consists of a major premise (such as "All men are mortal"), a minor premise ("Socrates is a man"), and a conclusion ("Therefore, Socrates is mortal"). For a brief discussion of syllogisms, see pages 637–38.
2. What audience is being addressed in the Declaration of Independence? Cite passages in the text that support your answer.
3. The Library of Congress has the original manuscript of the rough draft of the Declaration. This manuscript itself includes revisions that are indicated below, but it was later further revised. We print the first part of the second paragraph of the draft, and after it the corresponding part of the final version. Try to account for the changes within the draft, and from the revised draft to the final version.

> We hold these truths to be *self-evident* ~~sacred & undeniable;~~ that all men are created equal ~~& independent;~~ that *they are endowed by their creator wit* ~~from that equal creation they derive equal rights some of which are~~ ~~in rights~~ inherent & inalienable *rights; that* among ~~which~~ *these* are ~~the preservation of~~ life, ~~&~~ liberty, & the pursuit of happiness.

> We hold these Truths to be self-evident, that all Men are created equal, that they are endowed by their Creator with certain unalienable Rights, that among these are Life, Liberty, and the Pursuit of Happiness.

   In a paragraph evaluate the changes. Try to put yourself into Jefferson's mind and see if you can sense why Jefferson made the changes.
4. In a paragraph define *happiness,* and then in a second paragraph explain why, in your opinion, Jefferson spoke of "the pursuit of happiness" rather than of "happiness."
5. In "We Have No 'Right to Happiness' " (page 589) C. S. Lewis discusses the meaning of "the pursuit of happiness" in the Declaration, and a current misinterpretation of the phrase. How does he explain and define the phrase? How does his interpretation differ from what he considers an erroneous interpretation?
6. In a paragraph argue that the assertion that "all Men are created equal" is nonsense, or, on the other hand, that it makes sense.
7. If every person has an unalienable right to life, how can capital punishment be reconciled with the Declaration of Independence? (You need not in fact be a supporter of capital punishment; simply offer the best defense you can think of, in an effort to make it harmonious with the Declaration.)

Rosika Schwimmer

# Court Record of Petition for Naturalization

Rosika Schwimmer, the petitioner herein, called as a witness in her own behalf, having been first duly sworn, was examined by Mr. Jordan, and testified as follows:

Q. What is your full name, please?
A. Rosika Schwimmer.
Q. You were born in Hungary?
A. Hungary, Budapest. . . .
Q. Is it your intention to remain in the United States permamently?
A. It is.
Q. Is there anything in our form of government that you are not in sympathy with?
A. Nothing.
Q. You have read the oath of allegiance?
A. I did.
Q. Are you able to take that oath without any reservations?
A. I am.
Q. I would like for you to inform the court that this is the information sheet you filled out in connection with your application for citizenship (*handing document to the witness*).
A. Yes.
Q. And in answer to question 22, "If necessary, are you willing to take up arms in defense of this country?" You have answered, "I would not take up arms personally."

---

Rosika Schwimmer (1877–1948), a Hungarian feminist and pacifist, achieved international fame during the First World War, when she persuaded Henry Ford to support the Ford Peace Ship. In 1921 she moved to the United States, and 6 years later she applied for citizenship. The court denied her request, as we see in the transcript given here, because she refused to swear that she would bear arms in the defense of the country. The case was appealed, but the Supreme Court upheld the decision, though Justices Holmes, Brandeis, and Sanford dissented. We print Holmes's dissent on page 546.

A. Yes.

Q. And that is correct, is it?

A. Yes.

Q. Now, on January 11, 1927, Mr. Schlotfeldt wrote you a letter, didn't he?

A. Yes.

Q. About some statement you had made to Colonel Stone?

A. Well, it wasn't a statement. It was part of a letter. It wasn't a statement at all.

Q. And in that you also reiterated to Mr. Schlotfeldt to this effect: "I am an uncompromising pacifist for whom even Jane Addams is not enough of a pacifist. I am an absolute atheist. I have no sense of nationalism."

A. Yes.

Q. Is that correct?

A. Yes, that is correct.

THE COURT: What do you mean by "no sense of nationalism?"

A. I mean that if I had a sense of nationalism I could not want to leave the Hungarian nationality into which I was born.

Q. This has nothing to do with war. I am asking you what you mean when you say you have no sense of nationalism, because nationalism is a very comprehensive term and includes more than war.

A. I didn't speak now of war. Perhaps I didn't express myself well enough, Your Honor. I say I meant when I said this, if I had a feeling of nationalism, then being born a Hungarian, I would have such a feeling of Hungarian nationality that I would not want to leave that nationality, whatever the things are that are displeasing me.

Q. In other words, if something came up between Hungary and the United States, your sympathies would still be with Hungary?

A. No, to the contrary they would not be. I said I have no sense of nationality that would bind me to Hungary.

Q. Of course, I do not believe that time is ever coming when this country, this government is going to send its women to fight. We have not as yet a regiment of Amazons.

A. I hope you don't have.

Q. But we may have to send them as nurses to look after our fighters. We may have to send them in the various religious organizations, like the Y.M.C.A. or the Knights of Columbus, to give succor and aid to our fighters. Now, are you willing to be sent on missions of that sort by this government to look after the boys that are fighting for this country?

A. I am willing to do everything that an American citizen has to do, except fighting.

Q. Well, our women do not fight. We do not expect you to shoulder a musket.

A. Oh, I am willing to obey every law that the American government compels its citizens to do.

Q. Are you willing to do anything that an American woman is called upon to do? I mean an American citizen, a woman of this country.

A. Yes, I am, because I have not found that anything was asked that was against—I mean it is only the fighting question. That is, if American women would be compelled to do that, I would not do that.

Q. You say you are an uncompromising pacifist?

A. Yes.

Q. How far does that go? Does it refer only to yourself?

A. Yes.

Q. That you are not going to use your fists on somebody?

A. Yes.

Q. Or that you disapprove of the government fighting?

A. It means that I disapprove of the government asking me to fight.

Q. You mean fight personally?

A. Yes, physically.

Q. Carrying a gun?

A. Yes.

Q. Is that as far as it goes?

A. That is as far as it goes.

Q. Or is it more deep-seated?

A. No.

Q. Really, of course, none of us wants war—

A. Yes.

Q. But there are a great many of us when war comes and our country is in danger who get our backs to the wall—

A. Yes.

Q. And we fight until there is nothing but the wall left.

A. Yes.

Q. Now, are you willing to do that?

A. I am afraid, Your Honor, I did not catch the point of the question. I am awfully sorry.

Q. I don't mean to bear arms for the country.

A. Yes.

Q. The time will never come, I venture to say, when the women of the United States will have to bear arms.

A. Well, I am not willing to bear arms. In every other single way, civic way, I am ready to follow the law and do everything that the law compels American citizens to do. I am willing to do that. That is why I say I can take the oath of allegiance because as far as I, with the able help of my lawyers, could find out there is nothing that I could be compelled to do that I could not do.

Q. Your lawyer can't search into your heart any more than I can. You are the only one that can answer these questions.

A. I am opening my heart very frankly because there is nothing to hide. As I said when the question came up, if it is a question of fighting, as much as I desire American citizenship I would not seek the citizenship.

Q. Now, is it a question of fighting personally?

A. Yes.

Q. You yourself?

A. Myself.

Q. You do not care how many other women fight?

A. I don't care because I consider it a question of conscience. If there are women fighters, it is their business.

Q. Do you expect to spread this propaganda throughout this country with other women?

A. Which propaganda, may I ask?

Q. That you are an uncompromising pacifist and will not fight.

A. Oh, of course, I am always ready to tell that to anyone who wants to hear it.

Q. What is your occupation, madam?

A. I am a writer and lecturer.

Q. And in your writings and in your lectures you take up this question of war and pacifism?

A. If I am asked for that, I do.

Q. You know we have a great deal to give—at least we think so—

A. I think so, too.

Q. —when we confer citizenship upon people of other countries.

A. I think so, too.

Q. And we expect when we do that they come in on an equal footing, and out of regard to the other stockholders in this great united corporation we have to see to it that any partners or stockholders coming in are willing to do what those who are already here are willing to do. Now, it seems that your general views—

Now, I am not at all against people writing. There are a great many American citizens who are now decrying the possibility of the occurrence of war. They are against it. We have a great many pacifists in this country, but when the time comes, and they are called out for the country, they forget all their views, all of the things they have been talking about, and start in on the defense of the home.

Now, you can't come in halfway. You must come in the whole distance, because there you are and under that flag is our country, and you can't get under that flag unless you promise to do every single thing that the citizens of this country not only have permission to do, but are willing to do.

A. Well, I can only repeat what I said: that I am willing to do everything that, to my knowledge to this day, American women are asked to do.

THE COURT: Well, can we ask anything more than that?

MR. JORDAN: I would just like, Your Honor, to bring out a few things in Madame Schwimmer's letter to Mr. Schlotfeldt, and also excerpts from one of her radio speeches.

In the letter here, "My answer to question 22 in my petition for final examination demonstrated that I am an uncompromising pacifist." A little further down: "Highly as I prize the privilege of American citizenship, I could not compromise my way into it by giving an untrue answer to question 22, though for all practical purposes I might have done so."

Then there are a few little excerpts here from the radio talks I would like the court to hear: "I cannot see that a woman's refusal to take up arms is a contradiction to the oath of allegiance, promising to support and defend the Constitution and laws of the United States of America. I have for the fulfillment of this duty other ways and means in mind."

MRS. RABE: Would you mind reading the rest of that statement right there?

MR. JORDAN: That finishes that paragraph, I believe.

MRS. RABE: Oh, does it? I thought she spoke about having written in favor of our Constitution.

THE COURT: Let me ask you this one question—

A. Yes, sir.

Q. If you were called to the service, and the kind of work that women usually can perform better than the men can—say as a nurse or as someone to give cheer to the soldiers—and you were at some place in a war, which I hope never will come, and you saw someone coming in the headquarters or the barracks, wherever it was, with a pistol in his hand to shoot the back of an officer of our country, and you had a pistol handy by, would you kill him?

A. No, I would not.

THE COURT: The application is denied.

MR. GEMMILL: Just a moment, Your Honor. We would like to perfect our record. We expect to go up on this case, Your Honor. . . .

MR. GEMMILL: I would like to ask Mrs. Schwimmer one question.

Q. What do you mean, Mrs. Schwimmer, when you say you can take the oath and you are willing to support and defend the Constitution and the laws of the United States?

A. I mean the things that I have practically already done; that I was in many meetings in which it was said that it would be far better to have a Soviet regime—"that is a far better kind of regime" —and myself having lived under Soviet regime in Hungary, I could get up and tell the people—as I have practically done—"Don't think you change to something better." To this day there is no better form of government than that of the United States, which is by the people, for the people, as the great saying is, and that Sovietism is nothing but tyranny under another name—old fashioned tyranny under a new name; and I wrote these things and I said these things, and I can prove it by writings which I can get from Hungary; so that is what I meant; that there are other means to defend the Constitution and the institutions of this country.

Q. Is it your belief, Mrs. Schwimmer, your own personal belief, that you would not take the life of anyone?

A. Yes.

Q. Of any animal?

A. Animals, no. I have no objections against taking the life of animals. I personally wouldn't shoot, but I have no objections against that; but I would not shoot. Even if a pistol was pointed to me, I would not shoot.

Q. Is that what you had in mind when you answered the court's last question—

A. Yes.

Q. —relative to the shooting of the officer?

A. Yes, of course, I couldn't.

THE COURT: What do you mean by that?

Mr. Gemmill: I mean to say, Your Honor, I am trying to explain her answer. It wasn't the cold-blooded murder of the United States officer that Mrs. Schwimmer had in mind. It was her feeling against the killing of anyone.

The Witness: Yes.

Mr. Gemmill: May I ask one or two more questions?

The Court: Yes.

Mr. Gemmill: Under the same case, Mrs. Schwimmer, would you have given the officer any warning, if it was possible?

A. Certainly.

Q. So that he could defend himself?

A. Certainly.

The Court: That is, you would have given him—

A. I would try to hit the pistol out of the man's hand who tries to shoot. That is what I would try to do.

Q. Let me ask you this: Would you have thrown yourself on the assailant?

A. Yes, I might do that.

Q. And run the risk of being shot yourself?

A. Yes, I might do that. Yes.

Mr. Jordan: You say you might do that?

A. Well, I speak of a possibility. I can't say I would do that. We speak of hypothetical things. I can't say I "will" do that, because there is no occasion for it.

The Court: One never can tell until the occasion arises what will be done.

The Witness: If it would happen this moment I would do it.

The Court: But my first question referred not to your trying to stop the man from reaching the American soldier.

The Witness: I understand.

The Court:—because he may have been ten feet off—

The Witness: I understand.

The Court:—and the American soldier would have been killed before you could have reached his assailant.

The Witness: Yes.

The Court: I am asking if you had the weapon, if it were handy by—

The Witness: Yes.

The Court:—would you have killed the assailant—

The Witness: No.

The Court:—before he reached the American soldier?

THE WITNESS: No.

THE COURT: Then I am of the same opinion.

MR. GEMMILL: Supposing that pistol had been pointed at you and you had a pistol?

A. I would not defend myself. I mean I wouldn't take a pistol to defend myself even if you handed it to me; under no circumstances.

THE COURT: That question is not involved at all. This is a very close question, gentlemen, and I am really refusing this because the government, I think, has no appeal, but it is an attitude—the attitude of the applicant—that I think is not common with the women of this country.

Is there anything more, gentlemen?

MR. GEMMILL: I just want to be a little careful about this record.

THE COURT: Suppose it is written up and then we will reduce it to an agreed statement of facts?

MR. GEMMILL: That is satisfactory.

MR. JORDAN: Do you care, Your Honor, to take the statements of the witnesses so that they will not be required further?

THE COURT: Oh, yes. Let both witnesses step forward, please. . . .

THE COURT: Both of the witnesses believe that the applicant is a thoroughly good woman.

MR. BIRD: Yes.

MISS HOLBROOK: Yes, I do.

THE COURT: That is all. That is what we want to know.

MR. JORDAN: The witnesses may be excused then.

MR. GEMMILL: I suppose in this kind of a case a motion for a new trial first should be made.

THE COURT: No, I think not.

MR. GEMMILL: Motion in arrest, or pray an appeal then. . . .

THE COURT: . . . You understand, madam, that while the court may have said some things that shock, perhaps, your views of nationalism, we are here to administer the law as we see it. We have taken an oath for that purpose and we try to live up to it. There is nothing personal about it all.

MADAME SCHWIMMER: I realize that, Your Honor.

## Questions

1. Summarize, as briefly as possible, but covering all of the essentials, Rosika Schwimmer's beliefs.
2. Although women volunteers serve in the armed forces of the United States, the government has not drafted women and has not sent women into combat. What arguments can you offer for and against this position?

Pierce Butler

# Opinion of the Supreme Court, in *The United States of America, Petitioner,* v. *Rosika Schwimmer*

Respondent filed a petition for naturalization in the District Court for the Northern District of Illinois. The court found her unable, without mental reservation, to take the prescribed oath of allegiance and not attached to the principles of the Constitution of the United States and not well disposed to the good order and happiness of the same; and it denied her application. The Circuit Court of Appeals reversed the decree and directed the District Court to grant respondent's petition 27 F. (2d) 742.

The Naturalization Act of June 16, 1906 requires:

"He [the applicant for naturalization] shall, before he is admitted to citizenship, declare an oath in open court . . . that he will support and defend the Constitution and laws of the United States against all

---

Pierce Butler (1866–1939) practiced law in Minnesota until President Harding appointed him to the Supreme Court in 1923. Butler, who was generally regarded as a conservative, delivered the majority opinion in the Schwimmer case.

enemies, foreign and domestic, and bear true faith and allegiance to the same." U.S.C., Tit. 8, § 381.

"It shall be made to appear to the satisfaction of the court . . . that during that time [at least 5 years preceding the application] he has behaved as a man of good moral character, attached to the principles of the Constitution of the United States, and well disposed to the good order and happiness of the same. . . ." § 382.

Respondent was born in Hungary in 1877 and is a citizen of that country. She came to the United States in August, 1921, to visit and lecture, has resided in Illinois since the latter part of that month, declared her intention to become a citizen the following November, and filed petition for naturalization in September, 1926. On a preliminary form, she stated that she understood the principles of and fully believed in our form of government and that she had read, and in becoming a citizen was willing to take, the oath of allegiance. Question 22 was this: "If necessary, are you willing to take up arms in defense of this country?" She answered: "I would not take up arms personally."

She testified that she did not want to remain subject to Hungary, found the United States nearest her ideals of a democratic republic, and that she could whole-heartedly take the oath of allegiance. She said: "I cannot see that a woman's refusal to take up arms is a contradiction to the oath of allegiance." For the fulfillment of the duty to support and defend the Constitution and laws, she had in mind other ways and means. She referred to her interest in civic life, to her wide reading and attendance at lectures and meetings, mentioned her knowledge of foreign languages and that she occasionally glanced through Hungarian, French, German, Dutch, Scandinavian, and Italian publications and said that she could imagine finding in meetings and publications attacks on the American form of government and she would conceive it her duty to uphold it against such attacks. She expressed steadfast opposition to any undemocratic form of government like proletariat, fascist, white terror, or military dictatorships. "All my past work proves that I have always served democratic ideals and fought—though not with arms—against undemocratic institutions." She stated that before coming to this country she had defended American ideals and had defended America in 1924 during an international pacifist congress in Washington.

She also testified: "If . . . the United States can compel its women citizens to take up arms in the defense of the country—something that no other civilized government has ever attempted—I would not be able to comply with this requirement of American citizenship. In this case I would recognize the right of the Government to deal with me as it is dealing with its male citizens who for conscientious reasons refuse to take up arms."

The district director of naturalization by letter called her attention to a statement made by her in private correspondence: "I am an uncompromising pacifist . . . I have no sense of nationalism, only a cosmic consciousness of belonging to the human family." She answered that the statement in her petition demonstrated that she was an uncompromising pacifist. "Highly as I prize the privilege of American citizenship I could not compromise my way into it by giving an untrue answer to question 22, though for all practical purposes I might have done so, as even men of my age—I was 49 years old last September—are not called to take up arms. . . . That 'I have no nationalistic feeling' is evident from the fact that I wish to give up the nationality of my birth and to adopt a country which is based on principles and institutions more in harmony with my ideals. My 'cosmic consciousness of belonging to the human family' is shared by all those who believe that all human beings are the children of God."

And at the hearing she reiterated her ability and willingness to take the oath of allegiance without reservation and added: "I am willing to do everything that an American citizen has to do except fighting. If American women would be compelled to do that, I would not do that. I am an uncompromising pacifist. . . . I do not care how many other women fight, because I consider it a question of conscience. I am not willing to bear arms. In every other single way I am ready to follow the law and do everything that the law compels American citizens to do. That is why I can take the oath of allegiance, because, as far as I can find out, there is nothing that I could be compelled to do that I can not do. . . . With reference to spreading propaganda among the women throughout the country about my being an uncompromising pacifist and not willing to fight, I am always ready to tell anyone who wants to hear it that I am an uncompromising pacifist and will not fight. In my writings and in my lectures I take up the question of war and pacifism if I am asked for that."

Except for eligibility to the Presidency, naturalized citizens stand on the same footing as do native born citizens. All alike owe allegiance to the Government, and the Government owes to them the duty of protection. These are reciprocal obligations and each is a consideration for the other. *Luria v. United States,* 231 U.S. 9, 22. But aliens can acquire such equality only by naturalization according to the uniform rules prescribed by the Congress. They have no natural right to become citizens, but only that which is by statute conferred upon them. Because of the great value of the privileges conferred by naturalization, the statutes prescribing qualifications and governing procedure for admission are to be construed with definite purpose to favor and support the Government. And, in order to safeguard against admission of those who are unworthy or who for any reason fail to measure up to required standards, the law puts the burden upon every applicant to show by satisfactory evidence that he has the specified qualifications. *Tutun* v. *United States,* 270 U.S. 568, 578. And see *United States* v. *Ginsberg,* 243. U.S. 472, 475.

Every alien claiming citizenship is given the right to submit his petition and evidence in support of it. And, if the requisite facts are established, he is entitled as of right to admission. On applications for naturalization, the court's function is "to receive the testimony, to compare it with the law, and to judge on both law and fact." *Spratt* v. *Spratt,* 4 Pet. 393, 408. We quite recently declared that: "Citizenship is a high privilege and when doubts exist concerning a grant of it, generally at least, they should be resolved it favor of the United States and against the claimant." *United States* v. *Manzi,* 276 U.S. 463, 467. And when, upon a fair consideration of the evidence adduced upon an application for citizenship, doubt remains in the mind of the court as to any essential matter of fact, the United States is entitled to the benefit of such doubt and the application should be denied.

That it is the duty of citizens by force of arms to defend our government against all enemies whenever necessity arises is a fundamental principle of the Constitution.

The common defense was one of the purposes for which the people ordained and established the Constitution. It empowers Congress to provide for such defense, to declare war, to raise and support armies, to maintain a navy, to makes rules for the government and regulation of the land and naval forces, to provide for organizing, arming and disciplining the militia, and for calling it forth to execute the laws of the Union, suppress insurrections and repel invasions; it makes the President commander in chief of the army and navy and of the militia of the several States when called into the service of the United States; it declares that a well regulated militia, being necessary to the security of a free State, the right of the people to keep and bear arms, shall not be infringed. We need not refer to the numerous statutes that contemplate defense of the United States, its Constitution and laws by armed citizens. This Court, in the *Selective Draft Laws Cases,* 245 U.S. 366, speaking through Chief Justice White, said (p. 378) that "the very conception of a just government and its duty to the citizen includes the reciprocal obligation of the citizen to render military service in case of need. . . ."

Whatever tends to lessen the willingness of citizens to discharge their duty to bear arms in the country's defense detracts from the strength and safety of the Government. And their opinions and beliefs as well as their behavior indicating a disposition to hinder in the performance of that duty are subjects of inquiry under the statutory provisions governing naturalization and are of vital importance, for if all or a large number of citizens oppose such defense the "good order and happiness" of the United States can not long endure. And it is evident that the views of applicants for naturalization in respect of such matters may not be disregarded. The influence of conscientious objectors against the use of military force in defense of the principles of our Government is apt to be more detrimental than their mere refusal to bear arms. The fact that, by reason of sex, age or other cause, they may be unfit to serve does not lessen their purpose or power to influence others. It is clear from her own statements that the declared opinions of respondent as to armed defense by citizens against enemies of the country were directly pertinent to the investigation of her application.

The record shows that respondent strongly desires to become a citizen. She is a linguist, lecturer and writer; she is well educated and accustomed to discuss governments and civic affairs. Her testimony should be considered having regard to her interest and disclosed ability correctly to express herself. Her claim at the hearing that she possessed the required qualifications and was willing to take the oath was much impaired by other parts of her testimony. Taken as a whole it shows that her objection to military service rests on reasons other than mere inability because of her sex and age personally to bear arms. Her expressed willingness to be treated as the Government dealt with conscientious objectors who refused to take up arms in the recent war indicates that she deemed herself to belong to that class. The fact that she is an uncompromising pacifist with no sense of nationalism but only a cosmic sense of belonging to the human family justifies belief that she may be opposed to the use of military force as contemplated by our Constitution and laws. And her testimony clearly suggests that she is disposed to exert her power to influence others to such opposition.

A pacifist in the general sense of the word is one who seeks to maintain peace and to abolish war. Such purposes are in harmony with the Constitution and policy of our Government. But the word is also used and understood to mean one who refuses or is unwilling for any purpose to bear arms because of conscientious considerations and who is disposed to encourage others in such refusal. And one who is without any sense of nationalism is not well bound or held by the ties of affection to any nation or government. Such persons are liable to be incapable of the attachment for and devotion to the principles of our Constitution that is required for aliens seeking naturalization.

It is shown by official records and everywhere well known that during the recent war there were found among those who described themselves as pacifists and conscientious objectors many citizens—though happily a minute part of all—who were unwilling to bear arms in that crisis and who refused to obey the laws of the United States and the lawful commands of its officers and encouraged such disobedience in others. Local boards found it necessary to issue a great number of noncombatant certificates, and several thousand who were called to camp made claim because of conscience for exemption from any form of military service. Several hundred were convicted and sentenced to imprisonment for offenses involving disobedience, desertion, propaganda and sedition. It is obvious that the acts of such offenders evidence a want of that attachment to the principles of the Constitution of which the applicant is required to give affirmative evidence by the Naturalization Act.

The language used by respondent to describe her attitude in respect of the principles of the Constitution was vague and ambiguous; the burden was upon her to show what she meant and that her pacifism and lack of nationalistic sense did not oppose the principle that it is a duty of citizenship by force of arms when necessary to defend the country against all enemies, and that her opinions and beliefs would not prevent or impair the true faith and allegiance required by the Act. She failed to do so. The District Court was bound by the law to deny her application.

*The decree of the Circuit Court of Appeals is reversed.*
*The decree of the District Court is affirmed.*

## Oliver Wendell Holmes

# Dissent in the Rosika Schwimmer Case

The applicant seems to be a woman of superior character and intelligence, obviously more than ordinarily desirable as a citizen of the United States. It is agreed that she is qualified for citizenship except so far as the views set forth in a statement of facts "may show that the applicant is not attached to the principles of the Constitution of the United States and well disposed to the good order and happiness of the same, and except in so far as the same may show that she cannot take the oath of allegiance without a mental reservation." The views referred to are an extreme opinion in favor of pacifism and a statement that she would not bear arms to defend the Constitution. So far as the adequacy of her oath is concerned, I hardly can see how it is affected by the statement, inasmuch as she is a woman over fifty years of age, and would not be allowed to bear arms if she wanted to. And as to the opinion the whole examination of the applicant shows that she holds none of the now-dreaded creeds, but thoroughly believes in organized government and prefers that of the United States to any other in the world. Surely it cannot show lack of attachment to the principles of the Constitution that she thinks it can be improved. I suppose that most intelligent people think that it might be. Her particular improvement looking to the abolition of war seems to me not materially different in its bearing on this case from a wish to establish cabinet government as in England, or a single house, or one term of seven years for the President. To touch a more

---

Oliver Wendell Holmes (1841–1935) was the son of a distinguished Boston writer with the same name. After serving with distinction as a soldier in the Civil War, the younger Holmes began practicing law in 1867. In 1870 he began to teach law at Harvard, and he soon achieved fame by his lectures and his publications. In 1882 he was appointed to the Massachusetts supreme judicial court; in 1902 he was appointed to the United States Supreme Court. Holmes preached "judicial restraint"; that is, he frequently dissented from the "strict constructionists," who, in his opinion, capriciously thwarted the will of the people as it was expressed in the actions of their elected representatives.

We give here his dissent in the Schwimmer case. For a transcript of part of the earlier proceedings in this case, see page 532.

burning question, only a judge mad with partisanship would exclude because the applicant thought that the Eighteenth Amendment should be repealed.

Of course the fear is that if a war came the applicant would exert activities such as were dealt with in *Schenck* v. *United States,* 249 U.S. 47. But that seems to me unfounded. Her position and motives are wholly different from those of Schenck. She is an optimist and states in strong and, I do not doubt, sincere words her belief that war will disappear and that the impending destiny of mankind is to unite in peaceful leagues. I do not share that optimism nor do I think that a philosophic view of the world would regard war as absurd. But most people who have known it regard it with horror, as a last resort, and, even if not yet ready for cosmopolitan efforts, would welcome any practicable combination that would increase the power on the side of peace. The notion that the applicant's optimistic anticipations would make her a worse citizen is sufficiently answered by her examination, which seems to me a better argument for her admission than any I can offer. Some of her answers might excite popular prejudice, but if there is any principle of the Constitution that more imperatively calls for attachment than any other it is the principle of free thought—not free thought for those who agree with us but freedom for the thought that we hate. I think that we should adhere to that principle with regard to admission into, as well as to life within, this country. And, recurring to the opinion that bars this applicant's way, I would suggest that the Quakers have done their share to make the country what it is, that many citizens agree with the applicant's belief, and that I had not supposed hitherto that we regretted our inability to expel them because they believe more than some of us do in the teachings of the Sermon on the Mount.

## Questions

1. Summarize, as briefly as possible but covering all of the essentials, Rosika Schwimmer's beliefs.
2. In Dickens's *Oliver Twist* an irate character exclaims, "The law is a ass." Given Mr. Jordans's questions, in the Schwimmer case, and given the majority decision of the Supreme Court, can we say that at least in this case the law was "a ass"? Explain.
3. In a sentence or two summarize Holmes's views of war.
4. Pick out the one sentence in Holmes's dissent that you think is the most memorable, perhaps for *what* is said, perhaps for the *way* it is said, or perhaps for both.

5. If you found Holmes's opinion easier and more enjoyable to read than Butler's, try to account for the difference.

## Jacques Barzun

# In Favor of Capital Punishment

A passing remark of mine in the *Mid-Century* magazine has brought me a number of letters and a sheaf of pamphlets against capital punishment. The letters, sad and reproachful, offer me the choice of pleading ignorance or being proved insensitive. I am asked whether I know that there exists a worldwide movement for the abolition of capital punishment which has everywhere enlisted able men of every profession, including the law. I am told that the death penalty is not only inhuman but also unscientific, for rapists and murderers are really sick people who should be cured, not killed. I am invited to use my imagination and acknowledge the unbearable horror of every form of execution.

I am indeed aware that the movement for abolition is widespread and articulate, especially in England. It is headed there by my old friend and publisher, Mr. Victor Gollancz, and it numbers such well-known writers as Arthur Koestler, C. H. Rolph, James Avery Joyce and Sir John Barry. Abroad as at home the profession of psychiatry tends to support the cure principle, and many liberal newspapers, such as the *Observer,* are committed to abolition. In the United States there are at least twenty-five state leagues working to the same end, plus a national league and several church councils, notably the Quaker and the Episcopal.

---

Jacques Barzun, born in France in 1907, came to the United States in 1920. He did his college and graduate work at Columbia University, and in 1927 he began to teach history at Columbia. Later he served as dean and as provost there. He has written not only about history and law, but about art, philosophy, and music.

The assemblage of so much talent and enlightened goodwill behind a single proposal must give pause to anyone who supports the other side, and in the attempt to make clear my views, which are now close to unpopular, I start out by granting that my conclusion is arguable; that is, I am still open to conviction, *provided* some fallacies and frivolities in the abolitionist argument are first disposed of and the difficulties not ignored but overcome. I should be glad to see this happen, not only because there is pleasure in the spectacle of an airtight case, but also because I am not more sanguinary than my neighbor and I should welcome the discovery of safeguards—for society *and* the criminal—other than killing. But I say it again, these safeguards must really meet, not evade or postpone, the difficulties I am about to describe. Let me add before I begin that I shall probably not answer any more letters on this arousing subject. If this printed exposition does not do justice to my cause, it is not likely that I can do better in the hurry of private correspondence.

I readily concede at the outset that present ways of dealing out capital punishment are as revolting as Mr. Koestler says in his harrowing volume, *Hanged by the Neck.* Like many of our prisons, our modes of execution should change. But this objection to barbarity does not mean that capital punishment—or rather, judicial homicide —should not go on. The illicit jump we find here, on the thresbold of the inquiry, is characteristic of the abolitionist and must be disallowed at every point. Let us bear in mind the possibility of devising a painless, sudden and dignified death, and see whether its administration is justifiable.

The four main arguments advanced against the death penalty are: *1.* punishment for a crime is a primitive idea rooted in revenge; *2.* capital punishment does not deter; *3.* judicial error being possible, taking life is an appalling risk; *4.* a civilized state, to deserve its name, must uphold, not violate, the sanctity of human life.

I entirely agree with the first pair of propositions, which is why, a moment ago, I replaced the term capital punishment with "judicial homicide." The uncontrollable brute whom I want put out of the way is not to be punished for his misdeeds, nor used as an example or a warning; he is to be killed for the protection of others, like the wolf that escaped not long ago in a Connecticut suburb. No anger, vindictiveness or moral conceit need preside over the removal of such dangers. But a man's inability to control his violent impulses or to imagine the fatal consequences of his acts should be a presumptive reason for his elimination from society. This generality covers drunken driving and teen-age racing on public highways, as well as incurable obsessive violence; it might be extended (as I shall suggest later) to other acts that destroy, precisely, the moral basis of civilization.

But why kill? I am ready to believe the statistics tending to show that the prospect of his own death does not stop the murderer. For one thing he is often a blind egotist, who cannot conceive the possibility of his own death. For another, detection would have to be infallible to deter the more imaginative who, although afraid, think they can escape discovery. Lastly, as Shaw long ago pointed out, hanging the wrong man will deter as effectively as hanging the right one. So, once again, why kill? If I agree that moral progress means an increasing respect for human life, how can I oppose abolition?

I do so because on this subject of human life, which is to me the heart of the controversy, I find the abolitionist inconsistent, narrow or blind. The propaganda for abolition speaks in hushed tones of the sanctity of human life, as if the mere statement of it as an absolute should silence all opponents who have any moral sense. But most of the abolitionists belong to nations that spend half their annual income on weapons of war and that honor research to perfect means of killing. These good people vote without a qualm for the political parties that quite sensibly arm their country to the teeth. The West today does not seem to be the time or place to invoke the absolute sanctity of human life. As for the clergymen in the movement, we may be sure from the experience of two previous world wars that they will bless our arms and pray for victory when called upon, the sixth commandment notwithstanding.

"Oh, but we mean the sanctity of life *within* the nation!" Very well: is the movement then campaigning also against the principle of self-defense? Absolute sanctity means letting the cutthroat have his sweet will of you, even if you have a poker handy to bash him with, for you might kill. And again, do we hear any protest against the police firing at criminals on the street—mere bank robbers usually—and doing this, often enough, with an excited marksmanship that misses the artist and hits the bystander? The absolute sanctity of human life is, for the abolitionist, a slogan rather than a considered proposition.

Yet it deserves examination, for upon our acceptance or rejection of it depend such other highly civilized possibilities as euthanasia and seemly suicide. The inquiring mind also wants to know, why the sanctity of *human* life alone? My tastes do not run to household pets, but I find something less than admirable in the uses to which we put animals—in zoos, laboratories and space machines—without the excuse of the ancient law. "Eat or be eaten."

It should moreover be borne in mind that this argument about sanctity applies—or would apply—to about ten persons a year in Great Britain and to between fifty and seventy-five in the United States. These are the average numbers of those excuted in recent years. The count by itself should not, of course, affect our judgment of the principle: one life spared or forfeited is as important, morally, as a hundred thousand. But it should inspire a comparative judgment: there are hundreds and indeed thousands whom, in our concern with the horrors of execution, we forget: on the one hand, the victims of violence; on the other, the prisoners in our jails.

The victims are easy to forget. Social science tends steadily to mark a preference for the troubled, the abnormal, the problem case. Whether it is poverty, mental disorder, delinquency or crime, the "patient material" monopolizes the interest of increasing groups of people among the most generous and learned. Psychiatry and moral liberalism go together; the application of law as we have known it is thus coming to be regarded as an historic prelude to social work, which may replace it entirely. Modern literature makes the most of this same outlook, caring only for the disturbed spirit, scorning as bourgeois those who pay their way and do *not* stab their friends. All the while the determinism of natural science reinforces the assumption that society causes its own evils. A French jurist, for example, says that in order to understand crime we must first brush aside all ideas of Responsibility. He means the criminal's and takes for granted that of society. The murderer kills because reared in a broken home or, conversely, because at an early age he witnessed his parents making love. Out of such cases, which make pathetic reading in the literature of modern criminology, is born the abolitionist's state of mind: we dare not kill those we are beginning to understand so well.

If, moreover, we turn to the accounts of the crimes committed by these unfortunates, who are the victims? Only dull ordinary people going about their business. We are sorry, of course, but they do not interest science on its march. Balancing, for example, the sixty to seventy criminals executed annually in the United States, there were the seventy to eighty housewives whom George Cvek robbed, raped and usually killed during the months of a career devoted to proving his virility. "It is too bad." Cvek alone seems instructive, even though one of the law officers who helped track him down quietly remarks:

"As to the extent that his villainies disturbed family relationships, or how many women are still haunted by the specter of an experience they have never disclosed to another living soul, these questions can only lend themselves to sterile conjecture."

The remote results are beyond our ken, but it is not idle to speculate about those whose death by violence fills the daily two inches at the back of respectable newspapers—the old man sunning himself on a park bench and beaten to death by four hoodlums, the small children abused and strangled, the middle-aged ladies on a hike assaulted and killed, the family terrorized by a released or escaped lunatic, the half-dozen working people massacred by the sudden maniac, the boatload of persons dispatched by the skipper, the mindless assaults upon schoolteachers and shopkeepers by the increasing horde of dedicated killers in our great cities. Where does the sanctity of life begin?

It is all very well to say that many of these killers are themselves "children," that is, minors. Doubtless a nine-year-old mind is housed in that 150 pounds of unguided muscle. Grant, for argument's sake, that the misdeed is "the fault of society," trot out the broken home and the slum environment. The question then is, What shall we do, not in the Utopian city of tomorrow, but here and now? The "scientific" means of cure are more than uncertain. The apparatus of detention only increases the killer's antisocial animus. Reformatories and mental hospitals are full and have an understandable bias toward discharging their inmates. Some of these are indeed "cured"—so long as they stay under a rule. The stress of the social free-for-all throws them back on their violent modes of self-expression. At that point I agree that society has failed—twice: it has twice failed the victims, whatever may be its guilt toward the killer.

As in all great questions, the moralist must choose, and choosing has a price. I happen to think that if a person of adult body has not been endowed with adequate controls against irrationally taking the life of another, that person must be judicially, painlessly, regretfully killed before that mindless body's horrible automation repeats.

I say "irrationally" taking life, because it is often possible to feel great sympathy with a murderer. Certain *crimes passionnels* can be forgiven without being condoned. Blackmailers invite direct retribution. Long provocation can be an excuse, as in that engaging case of some years ago, in which a respectable carpenter of seventy found that he could no longer stand the incessant nagging of his wife. While she excoriated him from her throne in the kitchen—a daily exercise for fifty years—the husband went to his bench and came back with a hammer in each hand to settle the score. The testimony to his character, coupled with the sincerity implied by the two hammers, was enough to have him sent into quiet and brief seclusion.

But what are we to say of the type of motive disclosed in a journal published by the inmates of one of our Federal penitentiaries? The author is a bank robber who confesses that money is not his object:

> My mania for power, socially, sexually, and otherwise can feel no degree of satisfaction until I feel sure I have struck the ultimate of submission and terror in the minds and bodies of my victims. . . . It's very difficult to explain all the queer fascinating sensations pounding and surging through me while I'm holding a gun on a victim, watching his body tremble and sweat. . . . This is the moment when all the rationalized hypocrisies of civilization are suddenly swept away and two men stand there facing each other morally and ethically naked, and right and wrong are the absolute commands of the man behind the gun.

This confused echo of modern literature and modern science defines the choice before us. Anything deserving the name of cure for such a man presupposes not only a laborious individual psychoanalysis, with the means to conduct and to sustain it, socially and economically, but also re-education of the mind, so as to throw into correct perspective the garbled ideas of Freud and Nietzsche, Gide and Dostoevski, which this power-seeker and his fellows have derived from the culture and temper of our times. Ideas are tenacious and give continuity to emotion. Failing a second birth of heart and mind, we must ask: How soon will this sufferer sacrifice a bank clerk in the interests of making civilization less hypocritical? And we must certainly question the wisdom of affording him more than one chance. The abolitionists' advocacy of an unconditional "let live" is in truth part of the same cultural tendency that animates the killer. The Western peoples' revulsion from power in domestic and foreign policy has made of the state a sort of counterpart of the bank robber: both having power and neither knowing how to use it. Both waste lives because hypnotized by irrelevant ideas and crippled by contradictory emotions. If psychiatry were sure of its ground in diagnosing the individual case, a philosopher might consider whether such dangerous obsessions should not be guarded against by judicial homicide *before* the shooting starts.

I raise the question not indeed to recommend the prophylactic execution of potential murderers but to introduce the last two perplexities that the abolitionists dwarf or obscure by their concentration on changing an isolated penalty. One of these is the scale by which to judge the offenses society wants to repress. I can for example imagine a truly democratic state in which it would be deemed a form of treason punishable by death to create a disturbance in any court or deliberative assembly. The aim would be to recognize the sanctity of orderly discourse in arriving at justice, assessing criticism and defining policy. Under such a law, a natural selection would operate to remove permanently from the scene persons who, let us say, neglect argument in favor of banging on the desk with their shoe. Similarly, a bullying minority in a diet, parliament or skupshtina would be prosecuted for treason to the most sacred institutions when fists or flying inkwells replace rhetoric. That the mere suggestion of such a law sounds ludicrous shows how remote we are from civilized institutions, and hence how gradual should be our departure from the severity of judicial homicide.

I say gradual and I do not mean standing still. For there is one form of barbarity in our law that I want to see mitigated before any other. I mean imprisonment. The enemies of capital punishment—and liberals generally—seem to be satisfied with any legal outcome so long as they themselves avoid the vicarious guilt of shedding blood. They speak of the sanctity of life, but have no concern with its quality. They give no impression of ever having read what it is certain they have read, from Wilde's *De Profundis* to the latest account of prison life by a convicted homosexual. Despite the infamy of concentration camps, despite Mr. Charles Burney's remarkable work, *Solitary Confinement,* despite riots in prisons, despite the round of escape, recapture and return in chains, the abolitionists' imagination tells them nothing about the reality of being caged. They read without a qualm, indeed they read with rejoicing, the hideous irony of "Killer Gets Life"; they sigh with relief instead of horror. They do not see and suffer the cell, the drill, the clothes, the stench, the food; they do not feel the sexual racking of young and old bodies, the hateful promiscuity, the insane monotony, the mass degradation, the impotent hatred. They do not remember from Silvio Pellico that only a strong political faith, with a hope of final victory, can steel a man to endure long detention. They forget that Joan of Arc, when offered "life," preferred burning at the stake. Quite of another mind, the abolitionists point with pride to the "model prisoners" that murderers often turn out to be. As if a model prisoner were not, first, a contradiction in terms, and second, an exemplar of what a free society should not want.

I said a moment ago that the happy advocates of the life sentence appear not to have understood what we know they have read. No more do they appear to read what they themselves write. In the preface to his useful volume of cases, *Hanged in Error,* Mr. Leslie Hale, M. P., refers to the tardy recognition of a minor miscarriage of justice—one year in jail: "The prisoner emerged to find that his wife had died and that his children and his aged parents had been removed to the workhouse. By the time a small payment had been assessed as 'compensation' the victim was incurably insane." So far we are as indignant with the law as Mr. Hale. But what comes next? He cites the famous Evans case, in which it is very probable that the wrong man was hanged, and he exclaims: "While such mistakes are possible, should society impose an irrevocable sentence?" Does Mr. Hale really ask us to believe that the sentence passed on the first man, whose wife died and who went insane, was in any sense *revocable?* Would not any man rather be Evans dead than that other wretch "emerging" with his small compensation and his reasons for living gone?

Nothing is revocable here below, imprisonment least of all. The agony of a trial itself is punishment, and acquittal wipes out nothing. Read the heart-rending diary of William Wallace, accused quite implausibly of having murdered his wife and "saved" by the Court of Criminal Appeals—but saved for what? Brutish ostracism by everyone and a few years of solitary despair. The cases of Adolf Beck, of Oscar Slater, of the unhappy Brooklyn bank teller who vaguely resembled a forger and spent eight years in Sing Sing only to "emerge" a broken, friendless, useless, "compensated" man—all these, if the dignity of the individual has any meaning, had better have been dead before the prison door ever opened for them. This is what counsel always says to the jury in the course of a murder trial and counsel is right: far better hang this man than "give him life." For my part, I would choose death without hesitation. If that option is abolished, a demand will one day be heard to claim it as a privilege in the name of human dignity. I shall believe in the abolitionist's present views only after he has emerged from twelve months in a convict cell.

The detached observer may want to interrupt here and say that the argument has now passed from reasoning to emotional preference. Whereas the objector to capital punishment *feels* that death is the greatest of evils, I *feel* that imprisonment is worse than death. A moment's thought will show that feeling is the appropriate arbiter. All reasoning about what is right, civilized and moral rests upon sentiment, like mathematics. Only, in trying to persuade others, it is important to single out the fundamental feeling, the prime intuition, and from it to reason justly. In my view, to profess respect for human life and be willing to see it spent in a penitentiary is to entertain liberal feelings frivolously. To oppose the death penalty because, unlike a prison term, it is irrevocable is to argue fallaciously.

In the propaganda for abolishing the death sentence the recital of numerous miscarriages of justice commits the same error and implies the same callousness: what is at fault in our present system is not the sentence but the fallible procedure. Capital cases being one in a thousand or more, who can be cheerful at the thought of all the "revocable" errors? What the miscarriages point to is the need for reforming the jury system, the rules of evidence, the customs of prosecution, the machinery of appeal. The failure to see that this is the great task reflects the sentimentality I spoke of earlier, that which responds chiefly to the excitement of the unusual. A writer on Death and the Supreme Court is at pains to point out that when the tribunal reviews a capital case, the judges are particularly anxious and careful. What a left-handed compliment to the highest judicial conscience of the country! Fortunately, some of the champions of the misjudged see the issue more clearly. Many of those who are thought wrongly convicted now languish in jail because the jury was uncertain or because a doubting governor commuted the death sentence. Thus Dr. Samuel H. Sheppard, Jr., convicted of his wife's murder in the second degree is serving a sentence that is supposed to run for the term of his natural life. The story of his numerous trials, as told by Mr. Paul Holmes, suggests that police incompetence, newspaper demagogy, public envy of affluence and the mischances of legal procedure fashioned the result. But Dr. Sheppard's vindicator is under no illusion as to the conditions that this "lucky" evader of the electric chair will face if he is granted parole after ten years: "It will carry with it no right to resume his life as a physician. His privilege to practice medicine was blotted out with his conviction. He must all his life bear the stigma of a parolee, subject to unceremonious return to confinement for life for the slightest misstep. More than this, he must live out his life as a convicted murderer."

What does the moral conscience of today think it is doing? If such a man is a dangerous repeater of violent acts, what right has the state to let him loose after ten years? What is, in fact, the meaning of a "life sentence" that peters out long before life? Paroling looks suspiciously like an expression of social remorse for the pain of incarceration, coupled with a wish to avoid "unfavorable publicity" by freeing a suspect. The man is let out when the fuss has died down, which would mean that he was not under lock and key for our protection at all. He *was* being punished, just a little—for so prison seems in the abolitionist's distorted view, and in the jury's and the prosecutor's, whose "second-degree" murder suggests killing someone "just a little."[1]

If, on the other hand, execution and life imprisonment are judged too severe and the accused is expected to be harmless hereafter—punishment being ruled out as illiberal—what has society gained by wrecking his life and damaging that of his family?

What we accept, and what the abolitionist will clamp upon us all the more firmly if he succeeds, is an incoherence which is not remedied by the belief that second-degree murder merits a kind of second-degree death; that a doubt as to the identity of a killer is resolved by commuting real death into intolerable life; and that our ignorance whether a maniac will strike again can be hedged against by measuring "good behavior" within the gates and then releasing the subject upon the public in the true spirit of experimentation.

These are some of the thoughts I find I cannot escape when I read and reflect upon this grave subject. If, as I think, they are relevant to any discussion of change and reform, resting as they do on the direct and concrete perception of what happens, then the simple meliorists who expect to breathe a purer air by abolishing the death penalty are deceiving themselves and us. The issue is for the public to judge; but I for one shall not sleep easier for knowing that in England and America and the West generally a hundred more human beings are kept alive in degrading conditions to face a hopeless future; while others—possibly less conscious, certainly less controlled—benefit from a premature freedom dangerous alike to themselves and society. In short, I derive no comfort from the illusion that in giving up one manifest protection of the law-abiding, we who might well be in any of these three roles—victim, prisoner, licensed killer—have struck a blow for the sanctity of human life.

[1]The British Homicide Act of 1957, Section 2, implies the same reasoning in its definition of "diminished responsibility" for certain forms of mental abnormality. The whole question of irrationality and crime is in utter confusion, on both sides of the Atlantic.

# Questions

1. What is Barzun up to (as the writer of a persuasive essay) in his second and third paragraphs?
2. Jot down a sort of summary-outline of Barzun's chief arguments for capital punishment. Take one argument and do what you can to strengthen it. Take another and do what you can to refute it.
3. If you have read Schwarzschild's "In Opposition to Death Penalty Legislation" (page 559), indicate which of Schwartzschild's arguments, if any, Barzun does not face.
4. Barzun says (page 549) that "the uncontrollable brute whom I want put out of the way . . . is to be killed for the protection of others, like the wolf that escaped not long ago in a Connecticut suburb." Is the analogy effective? And can one adequately reply to Barzun: "If that's your reason, life imprisonment will serve your purpose"? Barzun later in his essay addresses life imprisonment, but are his remarks adequate?
5. If you have read Schwarzschild's remarks opposing capital punishment (page 559), write an essay indicating which essay you think is a better piece of persuasive writing. Note that it is not a matter of which position you subscribe to; in your essay you are concerned only with the essays as examples of persuasive writing.

Henry Schwarzschild

# In Opposition to Death Penalty Legislation

You know the classic arguments about the merits of the death penalty:

Its dubious and unproved value as a deterrent to violent crime;
The arbitrariness and mistakes inevitable in any system of justice instituted and administered by fallible human beings;
The persistent and ineradicable discrimination on grounds of race, class, and sex in its administration in our country's history (including the present time);
The degrading and hurtful impulse toward retribution and revenge that it expresses;
The barbarousness of its process (whether by burning at the stake, by hanging from the gallows, by frying in the electric chair, by suffocating in the gas chamber, by shooting at the hands of a firing squad, or by lethal injection with a technology designed to heal and save lives);
Even the deeply distorting and costly effect the death penalty has upon the administration of the courts, upon law enforcement, and upon the penal institutions of the country.

Let me therefore concentrate my remarks upon a few selected issues about which much unclarity exists in the public mind, in the media, and even in many legislative chambers.

I want to discuss these issues in the context of the evident support of public opinion for the reintroduction of capital punishment in the country. Let me be candid: For the past few years, public opinion polls, whether national or regional, have tended to reflect a substantial majority of the American people affirming their support

---

Henry Schwarzschild is the director of the National Coalition Against the Death Penalty. The material that we print is an excerpt from his statement submitted at the hearing in 1978 before the Subcommittee on Criminal Justice of the Committee on the Judiciary, House of Representatives, 95th Congress, 2nd Session.

for the death penalty, to the level of between 65 percent and 75 percent—enough to make many an elected official surrender his or her religious or moral principles against capital punishment. As little as twenty years ago, the polls reflected almost precisely the opposite distribution of views in the country. It is not hard to infer what has turned the American people back toward support of so atavistic and demonstrably useless a criminal sanction. The causes are (a) the rising rate of violent crime in the past two decades, (b) the increasing panic about the rising crime rate, together with a justified (as well as exaggerated) fear for the safety of lives and property, (c) the understandable reaction to a terrible series of assassinations and attempted assassinations of our national leaders and other prominent personalities (President John Kennedy, Senator Robert Kennedy, the Rev. Dr. Martin Luther King Jr., Governor George Wallace, Malcolm X, Medger Evers, and others), (d) the rise of international terrorism, including aircraft hijackings and the murder of prominent political and business leaders as well as the random political killings of innocent victims, (e) many years of the effective discontinuation of capital punishment and the remoteness from actual experience of its horrors, and finally (f) a largely subliminal but sometimes almost articulated racism that attributes most violent criminality to the minority community, that knows quite well that the poor and the black are most often the subjects of the death penalty, and that thinks that's just the way it ought to be.

What, then, are the rational answers to this series of partly understandable and partly impermissible misconceptions in the American public?

True, violent crime has risen sharply in the past two decades, but to begin with it has been abundantly demonstrated by social research that the availability of the death penalty has no effect whatsoever upon the rate of violent crime; to the contrary, there is some scientific evidence that death sentences imposed and carried out may, for peculiar reasons of social and psychic pathology, be an incentive to further acts of violence in the society. Furthermore, while the rates of most major, violent felonies have been rising—most probably by reason of increased urbanization, social mobility, economic distress, and the like—the rate of non-negligent homicide has been rising at a rate *slower* than the other major felonies, and non-negligent homicide is, of course, the only crime for which the death penalty has been declared constitutionally permissible by the Supreme Court. The crisis in violent crime, such as it is, has therefore been least acute in the area of homicide. Indeed, in the past three years, the murder rate in this country has actually been declining. Thirdly, there is an appalling number of about 20,000 non-negligent homicides in this country per year. But we would have to return to the condition of the mid-1950s to execute as many as one hundred persons per year, and even that would constitute only one in every two hundred murderers. In other words, we have always picked quite arbitrarily a tiny handful of people among those convicted of murder to be executed, not those who have committed the most heinous, the most revolting, the most destructive murders, but always the poor, the black, the friendless, the life's losers, those without competent, private attorneys, the illiterate, those despised or ignored by the community for reasons having nothing to do with their crime. Ninety-nine and one-half percent of all murderers were never executed—and the deterrent value (which very likely does not exist at all in any case) is reduced to invisibility by the overwhelming likelihood that one will not be caught, or not be prosecuted, or not be tried on a capital charge, or not be convicted, or not be sentenced to death, or have the conviction or sentence reversed on appeal, or have one's sentence commuted.

And if we took the other course and eliminated those high chances of not being executed, but rather carried out the death penalty for every murder, then we should be executing 400 persons per week, every week of the month, every month of the year—and that, Mr. Chairman, should strike even the most ardent supporters of the death penalty as a bloodbath, not as a civilized system of criminal justice.

Assassinations and terrorism are well known to be undeterrable by the threat of the death penalty. They are acts of political desperation or political insanity, always committed by people who are at least willing, if not eager, to be martyrs to their cause. Nor would executing terrorists be a preventive against the subsequent taking of hostages for the purpose of setting political assassins or terrorists free. There would of course be a considerable interval of time between arrest and execution, at least for the purpose of trial and the accompanying processes of law, and during that time their fellow activists would have a far more urgent incentive for taking hostages, since not only the freedom but the very lives of their arrested and sentenced colleagues would be at stake. Let me only respectfully add that distinguished fellow citizens of ours such as Senator Edward Kennedy and Ms. Coretta King, who have suffered terrible sadness in their lives at the hands of assassins, are committed opponents of the death penalty.

There has been only one execution in the United States since 1967, that of Gary Mark Gilmore, by a volunteer firing squad in Utah on January 17, 1977. Gilmore's execution troubled the public conscience less than it might have otherwise because of his own determination to die. The public and perhaps the legislators of our states and in the Congress have forgotten in a decade that was virtually without executions what sort of demoralizing and brutalizing spectacle executions are. There are now enough people on death row in the country to stage one execution each and every single day for more than a year, to say nothing of the other people who are liable to be sentenced to death during that time. We will again know the details of men crazed with fear, screaming like wounded animals, being dragged from the cell, against their desperate resistance, strapped into the electric chair, voiding their bowels and bladder, being burned alive, almost breaking the restraints from the impact of the high voltage, with their eyeballs popping out of their sockets, the smell of their burning flesh in the nostrils of the witnesses. The ghastly experience of men being hanged, their heads half torn off their bodies, or of the slow strangulation in the gas chamber, or of the press sticking their fingers into the bloody bullet holes of the chair in which Gilmore sat to be executed by rifles, or the use of forcible injection by a paralyzing agent—these reports will not ennoble the image of the United States of America that wants to be the defender of human rights and decency in a world that has largely given up the death penalty as archaic.

No one in this Committee surely is guilty of that shoddiest of all impulses toward capital punishment, namely the sense that white, middle-class people, irrespective of their crime, in fact hardly ever get sentenced to death and in such an extremely rare case are virtually never executed. You, Mr. Chairman and Members, and I and probably everyone in this hearing room are in fact absolutely immune, no matter what ghastly crime we might commit, from the likelihood of being executed for it. The penalty of death is imposed almost entirely upon members of what the distinguished social psychologist Kenneth B. Clark has referred to as "the lower status elements of American society."

Blacks have always constituted a dramatically disproportionate number of persons executed in the United States, far beyond their share of capital crimes, and even as we sit here today they represent half of the more than 500 persons on the death rows of our state prisons. Indeed, not only the race of the criminal is directly proportional to the likelihood of his being sentenced to death and executed but the race of the victim of the crime as well. The large majority of criminal homicides are still disasters between people who have some previous connection with each other (as husband and wife, parent and child, lovers, business associates, and the like), and murder is therefore still largely an intra-racial event, i.e. black on black or white on white. Yet while half the people under sentence of death right now are black (showing egregious discrimination on the grounds of the race of the murderer), about 85 percent of their victims were white.

In other words, it is far more likely to get the murderer into the electric chair or the gas chamber if he has killed a white person than if he had killed a black person, quite irrespective of his own race. (I say "he" in this context for good reason: the death penalty is also highly discriminatory on grounds of sex. Of the 380 death-row inmates in the country today, only two are women, and even they are far more likely objects of executive commutation of their death sentences than their male counterparts.)

Let me add here that, to the extent to which fear of crime and greater exposure to it, combined with inadequate police protection and more callous jurisprudence, has made the minority communities also voice increasing support for the death penalty, they have not yet fully realized that the death penalty will not protect them from what they (and all of us) rightly fear but that their support of capital punishment will only put their brothers and husbands and sons in jeopardy of being killed by the same state that has been unable properly to protect their lives, their rights, or their property to begin with.

In sum: The public is deeply uninformed about the real social facts of the death penalty and is responding to the seemingly insoluble problem of crime by a retreat to the hope that an even more severe criminal penalty will stem the tide of violence. But it will not. We do not know what will. Judges and lawyers do not know, philosophers and criminologists don't, not even civil libertarians or legislators know the answer—if any of us did, we would have long since accomplished our purpose of reducing crime to the irreducible minimum. But legislators are not therefore entitled to suborn illusory solutions merely because they would garner widespread though uninformed public approval, in order to signal to the electorate that they are "tough on crime." Capital punishment does not deal with crime in any useful fashion and in fact deludes the public into an entirely false sense of greater security about that complex social problem. The death penalty is a legislative way of avoiding rather than dealing with the problem of crime, and the American public will come to learn this very dramatically and tragically if the Congress should unwisely enact the bill before you today.

Two final words about public support for the death penalty.

There are strong indications that the public in great numbers answers in the affirmative when asked whether they support capital punishment because they want a death penalty law on the books in the hope that this threat will deter criminals from committing violent crimes. Many, perhaps most, of the people who support the enactment of the death penalty do not want executions and would be horrified at being asked to sentence a living human being to a premeditated, ceremonial, legally sanctioned killing. They want deterrence, not electrocutions; prevention, not lethal injections; safety, not firing squads. But a re-enactment by this Congress of a federal death penalty statute will give them at best only electrocutions or lethal injections or firing squads, but neither deterrence nor crime prevention nor safety from violence.

The last stand of supporters for the death penalty, when all the other arguments have been rebutted or met, is that of retribution or revenge, the proposition that a murderer has forfeited his life and that we should kill him as an act of abstract equity, irrespective of whether executions serve any social purpose whatsoever. We do not need to preach to each other here this morning, but it is important to have it said once more that civilized societies have instituted systems of justice precisely in order to overcome private acts of retribution and revenge and that they have done so with the understanding that social necessity and social usefulness will be the guideposts of their punishments. Since there has never been and cannot be a showing of social usefulness or social necessity for capital punishment, the virtually unanimous voices of the religious community of our land, our leading thinkers and social analysts, in unison with enlightened opinion for hundreds, perhaps thousands, of years should guide your actions on this matter. Whatever the understandable, bitter, vengeful impulses might be of any of us who suffer the disastrous tragedy of having someone we love or respect murdered by pathological or cruel killers, the society's laws are written not to gratify those impulses but to channel them into helpful, healing, and life-sustaining directions. Gratifying the impulse for revenge is not the business of a government that espouses the humane and liberating ideas expressed in our Declaration of Independence and Constitution. It would be rather a return to the darkest instincts of mankind. It would be arrogating unto the state, unto government, either the god-like wisdom to judge who shall live and who shall die or else the totalitarian arrogance to make that judgment. We, as a nation, have foresworn that idolatry of the state that would justify either of these grounds for the legally sanctioned killing of our fellow citizens, of any human being, except perhaps in personal or national self-defense.

Mr. Chairman: The question before the country and before the Congress ultimately is whether it is the right of the state, with premeditation, with the long foreknowledge of the victim, under color of law, in the name of all of us, with great ceremony, and to the approval of many angry people in our land, to kill a fellow citizen, a fellow human being, to do that which we utterly condemn, which we utterly abhor in him for having done. What does the penalty, after all, say to the American people and to our children? That killing is all right if the right people do it and think they have a good enough reason for doing it! That is the rationale of every pathological murderer walking the street: he thinks he is the right person to do it and has a good reason for doing his destructive deed. How can a thoughtful and sensible person justify killing people who kill people to teach that killing is wrong? How can you avert your eyes from the obvious: that the death penalty and that executions in all their bloody and terrible reality only aggravate the deplorable atmosphere of violence, the disrespect for life, and brutalization of ourselves that we need to overcome?

If the death penalty were shown, or even could be shown, to be socially necessary or even useful, I would personally still have a deep objection to it. But those who argue for its re-enactment have not and cannot meet the burden of proving its necessity or usefulness. At the very least, before you kill a human being under law, do you not have to be absolutely certain that you are doing the right thing? But how can you be sure that the criminal justice system has worked with absolute accuracy in designating this single person to be the guilty one, that this single person is the one that should be killed, that killing him is the absolutely right thing to do? You cannot be sure, because human judgment and human institutions are demonstrably fallible. And you cannot kill a man when you are not absolutely sure.

You can (indeed sometimes you must) make sure that he is incapacitated from repeating his crime, and we obviously accomplish that by ways other than killing him. And while there is fallibility there also, death is different: it is final, irreversible, barbarous, brutalizing to all who come into contact with it. That is a very hurtful model for the United States to play in the world, it is a very hurtful model for a democratic and free government to play for its people.

# Questions

1. In the first paragraph, what is Schwarzschild getting at when he says that administration of the death penalty has been discriminatory?
2. In the paragraph beginning, "True, violent crime has risen sharply" (page 560), Schwarzschild points out that even when capital punishment was relatively common, "ninety-nine and one-half percent of all murderers were never executed." Assuming the truth of this statement, is it inherently unjust to execute the remaining half of one percent? Would it be adequate to reply thus, by way of analogy: Most of the people who steal are not caught, but those who *are* caught should be punished; the law cannot excuse known wrongdoers simply on the ground that other wrongdoers escape undetected.
3. In the paragraph beginning "There has been only one execution" (page 562), Schwarzschild briefly describes some of the horrible physical responses of persons about to be executed. If one believes that the death penalty serves a useful purpose as a deterrent, should one argue (against Schwarzschild) that executions ought to be televised, so that they would have a maximum effect as deterrents?
4. Can it be argued that in the paragraph beginning "The last stand" (page 564) Schwarzschild distorts an important point: Capital punishment partly satisfies society's sense of justice; that is, certain crimes are so outrageous that a moral society must exact capital punishment—for instance, to satisfy the legitimate outrage of the friends and family of the murderer's victim?
5. What is Schwartzschild's strategy in his next-to-last paragraph?
6. Evaluate Schwartzschild's final paragraph as a piece of persuasion.
7. If you have read Barzun's "In Favor of Capital Punishment" (page 548), indicate which of Barzun's arguments, if any, Schwartzschild does not face.

## Arthur Hugh Clough

# The Latest Decalogue

Thou shalt have one God only; who
Would be at the expense of two?
No graven images may be
Worshiped, except the currency.
Swear not at all; for, for thy curse
Thine enemy is none the worse.
At church on Sunday to attend
Will serve to keep the world thy friend.
Honor thy parents; that is, all
From whom advancement may befall.
Thou shalt not kill; but need'st not strive
Officiously to keep alive.
Do not adultery commit;
Advantage rarely comes of it.
Thou shalt not steal; an empty feat,
When it's so lucrative to cheat.
Bear not false witness; let the lie
Have time on its own wings to fly.
Thou shalt not covet, but tradition
Approves all forms of competition.

The sum of all is, thou shalt love,
If anybody, God above:
At any rate shall never labor
*More* than thyself to love thy neighbor.

Arthur Hugh Clough (1819–1861), whose name rhymes with "rough," was born into a family of English cotton merchants. He spent 5 years of his early childhood in South Carolina, but was educated in England, where his teachers and friends, recognizing him as a gifted student and a talented poet, expected him to go on to a promising career. But Clough, deeply troubled both by doubts about the authenticity of the teachings of the Christian church and by the materialism of his age, never fulfilled those expectations.

# Questions

1. Explain the title.
2. The commandments in this poem (e.g., "Thou shalt have one god only," "Thou shalt not kill") are ancient (see page 502) and they are widely accepted as a guide to our moral life. What is new in the poem?
3. The poem was written in 1849. On the basis of this poem, how would you characterize the period? Does the poem speak to our own period also?

# 9

# THE DEEP HEART'S CORE

*At the Lapin Agile*
**Pablo Picasso, 1905**

*Self-Portrait with a Palette*
**Pablo Picasso, 1906**

Philadelphia Museum of Art, A. E. Gallatin Collection

*The Sculptor and His Statue*
**Pablo Picasso, 1933**

*Picasso*
**René Burri**

Magnum Photos Inc.

# Short Views

The heart has its reasons which reason knows nothing of.
**Blaise Pascal**

The Masai when they were moved from their old country, north of the railway line, to the present reserve, took with them the names of their hills, plains, and rivers, and gave them to the hills, plains, and rivers in the new country. It is a bewildering thing to the traveler. The Masai were carrying their cut roots with them as a medicine.
**Isak Dinesen, *Out of Africa***

Man is the only animal that laughs and weeps; for he is the only animal that is struck by the difference between what things are and what they might have been.
**William Hazlitt**

We are not only gregarious animals, liking to be in sight of our fellows, but we have an innate propensity to get ourselves noticed, and noticed favorably, by our kind. No more fiendish punishment could be devised, were such a thing physically possible, than that one should be turned loose in society and remain absolutely unnoticed by all the members thereof.
**William James**

My life is spent in a perpetual alternation between two rhythms, the rhythm of attracting people for fear I may be lonely and the rhythm of trying to get rid of them because I know that I am bored.
**C. E. M. Joad**

The eye is not satisfied with seeing, nor the ear filled with hearing.
**Ecclesiastes 1:8**

*London, December 5, 1749*

Dear Boy: Those who suppose that men in general act rationally, because they are called rational creatures, know very little of the world, and if they act themselves upon that supposition, will nine times in ten find themselves grossly mistaken. . . . Thus, the speculative, cloistered pedant, in his solitary cell, forms systems of things as they should be, not as they are; and writes as decisively and absurdly upon war, politics, manners, and characters, as that pedant talked, who was so kind as to instruct Hannibal in the art of war. Such closet politicians never fail to assign the deepest motives for the most trifling actions: instead of often ascribing the greatest actions to the most trifling causes, in which they would be much seldomer mistaken. They read and write of kings, heroes, and statesmen, as never doing anything but upon the deepest principles of sound policy. But those who see and observe kings, heroes, and statesmen, discover that they have headaches, indigestions, humors, and passions, just like other people; everyone of which, in their turns, determine their wills, in defiance of their reason. Had we only read in the "Life of Alexander," that he burned Persepolis, it would doubtless have been accounted for from deep policy: we should have been told, that his new conquest could not have been secured without the destruction of that capital, which would have been the constant seat of cabals, conspiracies, and revolts. But, luckily, we are informed at the same time, that this hero, this demi-god, this son and heir of Jupiter Ammon, happened to get extremely drunk with his w—e; and, by way of frolic, destroyed one of the finest cities in the world. Read men, therefore, yourself, not in books but in nature. Adopt no systems, but study them yourself. Observe their weaknesses, their passions, their humors, of all which their understanding are, nine times in ten, the dupes. You will then know that they are to be gained, influenced, or led, much oftener by little things than by great ones; and, consequently, you will no longer think those things little, which tend to such great purposes.

**Lord Chesterfield**

The changing wisdom of successive generations discards ideas, questions facts, demolishes theories. But the artist appeals to that part of our being which is not dependent on wisdom: to that in us which is a gift and not an acquisition—and, therefore, more permanently enduring. He speaks to our capacity for delight and wonder, to the sense of mystery surrounding our lives; to our sense of pity, and beauty, and pain; to the latent feeling of fellowship with all creation—and to the subtle but invincible conviction of solidarity that knits together the loneliness of innumerable hearts, to the solidarity in dreams, in joy, in sorrow, in aspirations, in illusions, in hope, in fear, which binds men to each other, which binds together all humanity—the dead to the living and the living to the unborn.

**Joseph Conrad**

The storyteller's own experience of men and things, whether for good or ill—not only what he has passed through himself, but even events which he has only witnessed or been told of—has moved him to an emotion so passionate that he can no longer keep it shut up in his heart. Again and again something in his own life or in that around him will seem to the writer so important that he cannot bear to let it pass into oblivion. There must never come a time, he feels, when men do not know about it.

**Lady Murasaki, *The Tale of Genji***

In seed time learn, in harvest teach, in winter enjoy.
Drive your cart and your plow over the bones of the dead.
The road of excess leads to the palace of wisdom.
Prudence is a rich ugly old maid courted by incapacity.
He who desires but acts not, breeds pestilence.
The cut worm forgives the plow.
Dip him in the river who loves water.
A fool sees not the same tree that a wise man sees.
He whose face gives no light, shall never become a star.
Eternity is in love with the productions of time.
The busy bee has no time for sorrow.
The hours of folly are measured by the clock; but of wisdom, no clock can measure.
All wholesome food is caught without a net or a trap.
Bring out number, weight, and measure in a year of dearth.
No bird soars too high, if he soars with his own wings.
A dead body revenges not injuries.
The most sublime act is to set another before you.
If the fool would persist in his folly he would become wise.
Folly is the cloak of knavery.
Shame is Pride's cloak.

**William Blake**

Before his death, Rabbi Zusya said, "In the coming world, they will not ask me: 'Why were you not Moses?' They will ask me: 'Why were you not Zusya?' "

**Hasidic Tale**

William Butler Yeats

# The Lake Isle of Innisfree

I will arise and go now, and go to Innisfree,
And a small cabin build there, of clay and wattles made:
Nine bean-rows will I have there, a hive for the honey-bee,
And live alone in the bee-loud glade.

And I shall have some peace there, for peace comes dropping slow,
Dropping from the veils of the morning to where the cricket sings;
There midnight's all a glimmer, and noon a purple glow,
And evening full of the linnet's wings.

I will arise and go now, for always night and day
I hear lake water lapping with low sounds by the shore;
While I stand on the roadway, or on the pavements gray,
I hear it in the deep heart's core.

William Butler Yeats (1865–1939), born in Ireland, became one of the leading forces both in the Irish Literary Renaissance and in English literature of the first half of the twentieth century. He wrote plays, prose fiction, and essays, but he is best known for his poetry. In 1924 he was awarded the Nobel Prize for literature. We give one of his early poems, then a comment on it from his *Autobiographies.*

## William Butler Yeats

# Remembering "The Lake Isle of Innisfree"

I had various women friends on whom I would call toward five o'clock mainly to discuss my thoughts that I could not bring to a man without meeting some competing thought, but partly because their tea and toast saved my pennies for the 'bus ride home; but with women, apart from their intimate exchanges of thought, I was timid and abashed. I was sitting on a seat in front of the British Museum feeding pigeons when a couple of girls sat near and began enticing my pigeons away, laughing and whispering to one another, and I looked straight in front of me, very indignant, and presently went into the Museum without turning my head toward them. Since then I have often wondered if they were pretty or merely very young. Sometimes I told myself very adventurous love-stories with myself for hero, and at other times I planned out a life of lonely austerity, and at other times mixed the ideals and planned a life of lonely austerity mitigated by periodical lapses. I had still the ambition, formed in Sligo in my teens, of living in imitation of Thoreau on Innisfree, a little island in Lough Gill, and when walking through Fleet Street very homesick I heard a little tinkle of water and saw a fountain in a shop-window which balanced a little ball upon its jet, and began to remember lake water. From the sudden remembrance came my poem *Innisfree,* my first lyric with anything in its rhythm of my own music. I had begun to loosen rhythm as an escape from rhetoric and from that emotion of the crowd that rhetoric brings, but I only understood vaguely and occasionally that I must for my special purpose use nothing but the common syntax. A couple of years later I would not have written that first line with its conventional archaism —"Arise and go"—nor the inversion in the last stanza. Passing another day by the new Law Courts, a building that I admired because it was Gothic—"It is not very good," Morris had said, "but it is better than anything else they have got and so they hate it"—I grew suddenly oppressed by the great weight of stone, and thought, "There are miles and miles of stone and brick all round me," and presently added, "If John the Baptist or his like were to come again and had his mind set upon it, he could make all these people go out into some wilderness leaving their buildings empty," and that thought, which does not seem very valuable now, so enlightened the day that it is still vivid in the memory.

## Questions

1. In his autobiographical account Yeats describes himself as "very homesick" at the time that the idea for "The Lake Isle of Innisfree" came to him. If "homesick" strikes you, as it does us, as inadequate to describe the speaker's mood in the poem, how would you describe it?
2. What other discrepancies do you find between Yeats's account of writing the poem and the poem itself? How do you explain the differences?

### Vladimir Nabokov

# Speak, Memory

Few things indeed have I known in the way of emotion or appetite, ambition or achievement, that could surpass in richness and strength the excitement of entomological exploration. From the very first it had a great many intertwinkling facets. One of them was the acute desire to be alone, since any companion, no matter how quiet, interfered with the concentrated enjoyment of my mania. Its gratification admitted of no compromise or exception. Already when I was ten, tutors and governesses knew that the morning was mine and cautiously kept away.

Vladimir Nabokov (pronounced VlaDEEmir NaBOHKoff) was born in Russia in 1899, the son of rich aristocrats. In the 1920s and 1930s he lived in Berlin and Paris. In 1940 he came to the United States, where *Lolita* (1955), a novel, brought him fame. Among Nabokov's other works are novels, stories, critical studies, translations, and *Speak, Memory* (from which we give a selection), a memoir of childhood in Czarist Russia and of college years in England. Nabokov died in 1977.

In this connection, I remember the visit of a schoolmate, a boy of whom I was very fond and with whom I had excellent fun. He arrived one summer night from a town some fifty miles away. His father had recently perished in an accident, the family was ruined and the stouthearted lad, not being able to afford the price of a railway ticket, had bicycled all those miles to spend a few days with me.

On the morning following his arrival, I did everything I could to get out of the house for my morning hike without his knowing where I had gone. Breakfastless, with hysterical haste, I gathered my net, pillboxes, sailor cap, and escaped through the window. Once in the forest, I was safe; but still I walked on, my calves quaking, my eyes full of scalding tears, the whole of me twitching with shame and self-disgust, as I visualized my poor friend, with his long pale face and black tie, moping in the hot garden—patting the panting dogs for want of something better to do, and trying hard to justify my absence to himself.

Let me look at my demon objectively. With the exception of my parents, no one really understood my obsession, and it was many years before I met a fellow-sufferer. One of the first things I learned was not to depend on others for the growth of my collection. Aunts, however, kept making me ridiculous presents—such as Denton mounts of resplendent but really quite ordinary insects. Our country doctor, with whom I had left the pupae of a rare moth when I went on a journey abroad, wrote me that everything had hatched finely; but in reality a mouse had got at the precious pupae, and upon my return the deceitful old man produced some common Tortoise-shell butterflies, which, I presume, he had hurriedly caught in his garden and popped into the breeding cage as plausible substitutes (so *he* thought). Better than he, was an enthusiastic kitchen boy who would sometimes borrow my equipment and come back two hours later in triumph with a bagful of seething invertebrate life and several additional items. Loosening the mouth of the net which he had tied up with a string, he would pour out his cornucopian spoil—a mass of grasshoppers, some sand, the two parts of a mushroom he had thriftily plucked on the way home, more grasshoppers, more sand, and one battered Cabbage butterfly.

I also found out very soon that an entomologist indulging in his quiet quest was apt to provoke strange reactions in other creatures. How often, when a picnic had been arranged, and I would be self-consciously trying to get my humble implements unnoticed into the tar-smelling charabanc (a tar preparation was used to keep flies away from the horses) or the tea-smelling Opel convertible (benzine forty years ago smelled that way), some cousin or aunt of mine would remark: "Must you *really* take that net with you? Can't you enjoy yourself like a normal boy? Don't you think you are spoiling everybody's pleasure?" Near a sign *Nach Bodenlaube,* at Bad Kissingen, Bavaria, just as I was about to join for a long walk my father and majestic old Muromtsev (who, four years before, in 1906, had been President of the first Russian Parliament), the latter turned his marble head toward me, a vulnerable boy of eleven, and said with his famous solemnity: "Come with us by all means, but do not chase butterflies, child. It mars the rhythm of the walk." On a path above the Black Sea, in the Crimea, among shrubs in waxy bloom, in March, 1919, a bow-legged Bolshevik sentry attempted to arrest me for signaling (with my net, he said) to a British warship. In the summer of 1929, every time I walked through a village in the Eastern Pyrenees, which I was exploring lepidopterologically, and happened to look back, I would see in my wake the villagers frozen in the various attitudes my passage had caught them in, as if I were Sodom and they Lot's wife. A decade later, in the Maritime Alps, I once noticed the grass undulate in a serpentine way behind me because a fat rural policeman was wriggling after me on his belly to find out if I were not trapping song birds. America has shown even more of this morbid interest in my doings than other countries have—perhaps because I was in my forties when I came here to live, and the older the man, the queerer he looks with a butterfly net in his hand. Stern farmers have drawn my attention to *No Fishing* signs; from cars passing me on the highway have come wild howls of derision; sleepy dogs, though unmindful of the worst bum, have perked up and come at me, snarling; tiny tots have pointed me out to their puzzled mammas; broadminded vacationists have asked me whether I was catching bugs for bait; and one morning on a wasteland, lit by tall yuccas in bloom, near Santa Fé, a big, black mare followed me for more than a mile.

## Questions

1. In the first paragraph, what devices does Nabokov use to suggest that his hobby is special, something precious?
2. Nabokov begins his fourth paragraph (page 580) thus: "Let me look at my demon objectively." Check a dictionary to see how many meanings of "demon" might fit. How objective *is* the rest of the paragraph?

3. Nabokov's passion does not prevent him from being amusing—not only about others but also about himself. Point out some examples of self-irony. How do we know that he is nevertheless serious?

E. M. Forster

# My Wood

A few years ago I wrote a book which dealt in part with the difficulties of the English in India. Feeling that they would have had no difficulties in India themselves, the Americans read the book freely. The more they read it the better it made them feel, and a cheque to the author was the result. I bought a wood with the cheque. It is not a large wood—it contains scarcely any trees, and it is intersected, blast it, by a public footpath. Still, it is the first property that I have owned, so it is right that other people should participate in my shame, and should ask themselves, in accents that will vary in horror, this very important question: What is the effect of property upon the character? Don't let's touch economics; the effect of private ownership upon the community as a whole is another question—a more important question, perhaps, but another one. Let's keep to psychology. If you own things, what's their effect on you? What's the effect on me of my wood?

In the first place, it makes me feel heavy. Property does have this effect. Property produces men of weight, and it was a man of weight who failed to get into the Kingdom of Heaven. He was not wicked, that unfortunate millionaire in the parable, he was only stout; he stuck out in front, not to mention behind, and as he wedged himself this way and that in the crystalline entrance and bruised his well-fed flanks, he saw beneath him a comparatively slim camel passing

E[dward] M[organ] Forster (1879–1970) was born in London and was graduated from King's College, Cambridge. He traveled widely and lived for a while in India, but most of his life was spent back at King's College. His best-known novel, *A Passage to India* (1926), is alluded to in the first line of the essay that we reprint.

through the eye of a needle and being woven into the robe of God. The Gospels all through couple stoutness and slowness. They point out what is perfectly obvious, yet seldom realized: that if you have a lot of things you cannot move about a lot, that furniture requires dusting, dusters require servants, servants require insurance stamps, and the whole tangle of them makes you think twice before you accept an invitation to dinner or go for a bathe in the Jordan. Sometimes the Gospels proceed further and say with Tolstoy that property is sinful; they approach the difficult ground of asceticism here, where I cannot follow them. But as to the immediate effects of property on people, they just show straightforward logic. It produces men of weight. Men of weight cannot, by definition, move like the lightning from the East unto the West, and the ascent of a fourteen-stone[1] bishop into a pulpit is thus the exact antithesis of the coming of the Son of Man. My wood makes me feel heavy.

In the second place, it makes me feel it ought to be larger.

The other day I heard a twig snap in it. I was annoyed at first, for I thought that someone was blackberrying, and depreciating the value of the undergrowth. On coming nearer, I saw it was not a man who had trodden on the twig and snapped it, but a bird, and I felt pleased. My bird. The bird was not equally pleased. Ignoring the relation between us, it took fright as soon as it saw the shape of my face, and flew straight over the boundary hedge into a field, the property of Mrs. Henessy, where it sat down with a loud squawk. It had become Mrs. Henessy's bird. Something seemed grossly amiss here, something that would not have occurred had the wood been larger. I could not afford to buy Mrs. Henessy out, I dared not murder her, and limitations of this sort beset me on every side. Ahab did not want that vineyard—he only needed it to round off his property, preparatory to plotting a new curve—and all the land around my wood has become necessary to me in order to round off the wood. A boundary protects. But—poor little thing—the boundary ought in its turn to be protected. Noises on the edge of it. Children throw stones. A little more, and then a little more, until we reach the sea. Happy Canute! Happier Alexander! And after all, why should even the world be the limit of possession? A rocket containing a Union Jack, will, it is hoped, be shortly fired at the moon. Mars. Sirius. Beyond which . . . But these immensities ended by saddening me. I could not suppose that my wood was the destined nucleus of univer-

[1]196-pound. (Editors' note)

sal dominion—it is so very small and contains no mineral wealth beyond the blackberries. Nor was I comforted when Mrs. Henessy's bird took alarm for the second time and flew clean away from us all, under the belief that it belonged to itself.

In the third place, property makes its owner feel that he ought to do something to it. Yet he isn't sure what. A restlessness comes over him, a vague sense that he has a personality to express—the same sense which, without any vagueness, leads the artist to an act of creation. Sometimes I think I will cut down such trees as remain in the wood, at other times I want to fill up the gaps between them with new trees. Both impulses are pretentious and empty. They are not honest movements towards money-making or beauty. They spring from a foolish desire to express myself and from an inability to enjoy what I have got. Creation, property, enjoyment form a sinister trinity in the human mind. Creation and enjoyment are both very very good, yet they are often unattainable without a material basis, and at such moments property pushes itself in as a substitute, saying, "Accept me instead—I'm good enough for all three." It is not enough. It is, as Shakespeare said of lust, "The expense of spirit in a waste of shame": it is "Before, a joy proposed; behind, a dream." Yet we don't know how to shun it. It is forced on us by our economic system as the alternative to starvation. It is also forced on us by an internal defect in the soul, by the feeling that in property may lie the germs of self-development and of exquisite or heroic deeds. Our life on earth is, and ought to be, material and carnal. But we have not yet learned to manage our materialism and carnality properly; they are still entangled with the desire for ownership, where (in the words of Dante) "Possession is one with loss."

And this brings us to our fourth and final point: the blackberries.

Blackberries are not plentiful in this meagre grove, but they are easily seen from the public footpath which traverses it, and all too easily gathered. Foxgloves, too—people will pull up the foxgloves, and ladies of an educational tendency even grub for toadstools to show them on the Monday in class. Other ladies, less educated, roll down the bracken in the arms of their gentlemen friends. There is paper, there are tins. Pray, does my wood belong to me or doesn't it? And, if it does, should I not own it best by allowing no one else to walk there? There is a wood near Lyme Regis, also cursed by a public footpath, where the owner has not hesitated on this point. He has built high stone walls each side of the path, and has spanned it by bridges, so that the public circulate like termites while he gorges on the blackberries unseen. He really does own his wood, this able chap. Dives in Hell did pretty well, but the gulf dividing him from Lazarus could be traversed by vision, and nothing traverses it here.[2] And perhaps I shall come to this in time. I shall wall in and fence out until I really taste the sweets of property. Enormously stout, endlessly avaricious, pseudo-creative, intensely selfish, I shall weave upon my forehead the quadruple crown of possession until those nasty Bolshies come and take it off again and thrust me aside into the outer darkness.

## Question

Much of the strength of the essay lies in its concrete presentation of generalities. Note, for example, that the essay is called "My Wood," but we might say that the general idea of the essay is "The Effect of Property on Owners." Forster gives four effects, chiefly through concrete statements. Put these four effects into four general statements.

[2]According to Christ's parable in Luke 16:19–26, the rich man (unnamed, but traditionally known as Dives) at whose gate the poor man Lazarus had begged was sent to hell, from where he could see Lazarus in heaven. (Editors' note)

## Joan Didion

# On Going Home

I am home for my daughter's first birthday. By "home" I do not mean the house in Los Angeles where my husband and I and the baby live, but the place where my family is, in the Central Valley of California. It is a vital although troublesome distinction. My husband likes my family but is uneasy in their house, because once there I fall into their ways, which are difficult, oblique, deliberately inarticulate, not my husband's ways. We live in dusty houses ("D-U-S-T," he once wrote with his finger on surfaces all over the house, but no one noticed it) filled with mementos quite without value to him (what could the Canton dessert plates mean to him? how could he have known about the assay scales, why should he care if he did know?), and we appear to talk exclusively about people we know who have been committed to mental hospitals, about people we know who have been booked on drunk-driving charges, and about property, particularly about property, land, price per acre and C-2 zoning and assessments and freeway access. My brother does not understand my husband's inability to perceive the advantage in the rather common real-estate transaction known as "sale-leaseback," and my husband in turn does not understand why so many of the people he hears about in my father's house have recently been committed to mental hospitals or booked on drunk-driving charges. Nor does he understand that when we talk about sale-leasebacks and right-of-way condemnations we are talking in code about the things we like best, the yellow fields and the cottonwoods and the rivers rising and falling and the mountain roads closing when the heavy snow comes in. We miss each other's points, have another drink and regard the fire. My brother refers to my husband, in his presence, as "Joan's husband." Marriage is the classic betrayal.

Or perhaps it is not any more. Sometimes I think that those of us who are now in our thirties were born into the last generation to carry the burden of "home," to find in family life the source of all tension and drama. I had by all objective accounts a "normal" and

Joan Didion was born in Sacramento in 1934, and she was educated at the University of California, Berkeley. She has written essays, stories, screenplays, and novels.

a "happy" family situation, and yet I was almost thirty years old before I could talk to my family on the telephone without crying after I had hung up. We did not fight. Nothing was wrong. And yet some nameless anxiety colored the emotional charges between me and the place that I came from. The question of whether or not you could go home again was a very real part of the sentimental and largely literary baggage with which we left home in the fifties; I suspect that it is irrelevant to the children born of the fragmentation after World War II. A few weeks ago in a San Francisco bar I saw a pretty young girl on crystal take off her clothes and dance for the cash prize in an "amateur-topless" contest. There was no particular sense of moment about this, none of the effect of romantic degradation, of "dark journey," for which my generation strived so assiduously. What sense could that girl possibly make of, say, *Long Day's Journey into Night*? Who is beside the point?

That I am trapped in this particular irrelevancy is never more apparent to me than when I am home. Paralyzed by the neurotic lassitude engendered by meeting one's past at every turn, around every corner, inside every cupboard, I go aimlessly from room to room. I decide to meet it head-on and clean out a drawer, and I spread the contents on the bed. A bathing suit I wore the summer I was seventeen. A letter of rejection from *The Nation,* an aerial photograph of the site for a shopping center my father did not build in 1954. Three teacups hand-painted with cabbage roses and signed "E.M.," my grandmother's initials. There is no final solution for letters of rejection from *The Nation* and teacups hand-painted in 1900. Nor is there any answer to snapshots of one's grandfather as a young man on skis, surveying around Donner Pass in the year 1910. I smooth out the snapshot and look into his face, and do and do not see my own. I close the drawer, and have another cup of coffee with my mother. We get along very well, veterans of a guerrilla war we never understood.

Days pass. I see no one. I come to dread my husband's evening call, not only because he is full of news of what by now seems to me our remote life in Los Angeles, people he has seen, letters which require attention, but because he asks what I have been doing, suggests uneasily that I get out, drive to San Francisco or Berkeley. Instead I drive across the river to a family graveyard. It has been vandalized since my last visit and the monuments are broken, overturned in the dry grass. Because I once saw a rattlesnake in the grass I stay in the car and listen to a country-and-Western station. Later

I drive with my father to a ranch he has in the foothills. The man who runs his cattle on it asks us to the roundup, a week from Sunday, and although I know that I will be in Los Angeles I say, in the oblique way my family talks, that I will come. Once home I mention the broken monuments in the graveyard. My mother shrugs.

I go to visit my great-aunts. A few of them think now that I am my cousin, or their daughter who died young. We recall an anecdote about a relative last seen in 1948, and they ask if I still like living in New York City. I have lived in Los Angeles for three years, but I say that I do. The baby is offered a horehound drop, and I am slipped a dollar bill "to buy a treat." Questions trail off, answers are abandoned, the baby plays with the dust motes in a shaft of afternoon sun.

It is time for the baby's birthday party: a white cake, strawberry-marshmallow ice cream, a bottle of champagne saved from another party. In the evening, after she has gone to sleep, I kneel beside the crib and touch her face, where it is pressed against the slats, with mine. She is an open and trusting child, unprepared for and unaccustomed to the ambushes of family life, and perhaps it is just as well that I can offer her little of that life. I would like to give her more. I would like to promise her that she will grow up with a sense of her cousins and of rivers and of her great-grandmother's teacups, would like to pledge her a picnic on a river with fried chicken and her hair uncombed, would like to give her *home* for her birthday, but we live differently now and I can promise her nothing like that. I give her a xylophone and a sundress from Madeira, and promise to tell her a funny story.

## Questions

1. Didion reveals that members of her family are difficult, inarticulate, poor housekeepers, and so forth. Do you find these revelations about her family distasteful? Would you mind seeing in print similarly unflattering things you had written about your own family? How might such revelations be justified? Are they justified in this essay?
2. Summarize the point of the second paragraph. Do you find Didion's speculations about the difference between her generation and succeeding generations meaningful? Are they accurate for your generation?
3. Do you think that growing up necessarily involves estrangement from one's family?

C. S. Lewis

# We Have No "Right to Happiness"

"After all," said Clare, "they had a right to happiness."

We were discussing something that once happened in our own neighborhood. Mr. A. had deserted Mrs. A. and got his divorce in order to marry Mrs. B., who had likewise got her divorce in order to marry Mr. A. And there was certainly no doubt that Mr. A. and Mrs. B. were very much in love with one another. If they continued to be in love, and if nothing went wrong with their health or their income, they might reasonably expect to be very happy.

It was equally clear that they were not happy with their old partners. Mrs. B. had adored her husband at the outset. But then he got smashed up in the war. It was thought he had lost his virility, and it was known that he had lost his job. Life with him was no longer what Mrs. B. had bargained for. Poor Mrs. A., too. She had lost her looks—and all her liveliness. It might be true, as some said, that she consumed herself by bearing his children and nursing him through the long illness that overshadowed their earlier married life.

You mustn't, by the way, imagine that A. was the sort of man who nonchalantly threw a wife away like the peel of an orange he'd sucked dry. Her suicide was a terrible shock to him. We all knew this, for he told us so himself. "But what could I do?" he said. "A man has a right to happiness. I had to take my one chance when it came."

I went away thinking about the concept of a "right to happiness."

At first this sounds to me as odd as a right to good luck. For I believe—whatever one school of moralists may say—that we depend for a very great deal of our happiness or misery on circumstances outside all human control. A right to happiness doesn't, for me, make much more sense than a right to be six feet tall, or to have a millionaire for your father, or to get good weather whenever you want to have a picnic.

For a biographical note on Lewis, see page 362.

I can understand a right as a freedom guaranteed me by the laws of the society I live in. Thus, I have a right to travel along the public roads because society gives me that freedom; that's what we mean by calling the roads "public." I can also understand a right as a claim guaranteed me by the laws, and correlative to an obligation on someone else's part. If I have a right to receive £100 from you, this is another way of saying that you have a duty to pay me £100. If the laws allow Mr. A. to desert his wife and seduce his neighbor's wife, then, by definition, Mr. A. has a legal right to do so, and we need bring in no talk about "happiness."

But of course that was not what Clare meant. She meant that he had not only a legal but a moral right to act as he did. In other words, Clare is—or would be if she thought it out—a classical moralist after the style of Thomas Aquinas, Grotius, Hooker and Locke. She believes that behind the laws of the state there is a Natural Law.

I agree with her. I hold this conception to be basic to all civilization. Without it, the actual laws of the state become an absolute, as in Hegel. They cannot be criticized because there is no norm against which they should be judged.

The ancestry of Clare's maxim, "They have a right to happiness," is august. In words that are cherished by all civilized men, but especially by Americans, it has been laid down that one of the rights of man is a right to "the pursuit of happiness." And now we get to the real point.

What did the writers of that august declaration mean?

It is quite certain what they did not mean. They did not mean that man was entitled to pursue happiness by any and every means—including, say, murder, rape, robbery, treason and fraud. No society could be built on such a basis.

They meant "to pursue happiness by all lawful means"; that is, by all means which the Law of Nature eternally sanctions and which the laws of the nation shall sanction.

Admittedly this seems at first to reduce their maxim to the tautology that men (in pursuit of happiness) have a right to do whatever they have a right to do. But tautologies, seen against their proper historical context, are not always barren tautologies. The declaration is primarily a denial of the political principles which long governed Europe: a challenge flung down to the Austrian and Russian empires, to England before the Reform Bills, to Bourbon France. It demands that whatever means of pursuing happiness are lawful for any should be lawful for all; that "man," not men of some particular caste, class, status or religion, should be free to use them. In a century when this is being unsaid by nation after nation and party after party, let us not call it a barren tautology.

But the question as to what means are "lawful"—what methods of pursuing happiness are either morally permissible by the Law of Nature or should be declared legally permissible by the legislature of a particular nation—remains exactly where it did. And on that question I disagree with Clare. I don't think it is obvious that people have the unlimited "right to happiness" which she suggests.

For one thing, I believe that Clare, when she says "happiness," means simply and solely "sexual happiness." Partly because women like Clare never use the word "happiness" in any other sense. But also because I never heard Clare talk about the "right" to any other kind. She was rather leftist in her politics, and would have been scandalized if anyone had defended the actions of a ruthless man-eating tycoon on the ground that his happiness consisted in making money and he was pursuing his happiness. She was also a rabid teetotaler; I never heard her excuse an alcoholic because he was happy when he was drunk.

A good many of Clare's friends, and especially her female friends, often felt—I've heard them say so—that their own happiness would be perceptibly increased by boxing her ears. I very much doubt if this would have brought her theory of a right to happiness into play.

Clare, in fact, is doing what the whole western world seems to me to have been doing for the last forty-odd years. When I was a youngster, all the progressive people were saying, "Why all this prudery? Let us treat sex just as we treat all our other impulses." I was simple-minded enough to believe they meant what they said. I have since discovered that they meant exactly the opposite. They meant that sex was to be treated as no other impulse in our nature has ever been treated by civilized people. All the others, we admit, have to be bridled. Absolute obedience to your instinct for self-preservation is what we call cowardice; to your acquisitive impulse, avarice. Even sleep must be resisted if you're a sentry. But every unkindness and breach of faith seems to be condoned provided that the object aimed at is "four bare legs in a bed."

It is like having a morality in which stealing fruit is considered wrong—unless you steal nectarines.

And if you protest against this view you are usually met with chatter about the legitimacy and beauty and sanctity of "sex" and accused of harboring some Puritan prejudice against it as something disreputable or shameful. I deny the charge. Foam-born Venus . . . golden Aphrodite . . . Our Lady of Cyprus . . . I never breathed a word against you. If I object to boys who steal my nectarines, must I be supposed to disapprove of nectarines in general? Or even of boys in general? It might, you know, be stealing that I disapproved of.

The real situation is skillfully concealed by saying that the question of Mr. A.'s "right" to desert his wife is one of "sexual morality." Robbing an orchard is not an offense against some special morality called "fruit morality." It is an offense against honesty. Mr. A.'s action is an offense against good faith (to solemn promises), against gratitude (toward one to whom he was deeply indebted) and against common humanity.

Our sexual impulses are thus being put in a position of preposterous privilege. The sexual motive is taken to condone all sorts of behavior which, if it had any other end in view, would be condemned as merciless, treacherous and unjust.

Now though I see no good reason for giving sex this privilege, I think I see a strong cause. It is this.

It is part of the nature of a strong erotic passion—as distinct from a transient fit of appetite—that it makes more towering promises than any other emotion. No doubt all our desires make promises, but not so impressively. To be in love involves the almost irresistible conviction that one will go on being in love until one dies, and that possession of the beloved will confer, not merely frequent ecstasies, but settled, fruitful, deep-rooted, lifelong happiness. Hence *all* seems to be at stake. If we miss this chance we shall have lived in vain. At the very thought of such a doom we sink into fathomless depths of self-pity.

Unfortunately these promises are found often to be quite untrue. Every experienced adult knows this to be so as regards all erotic passions (except the one he himself is feeling at the moment). We discount the world-without-end pretensions of our friends' amours easily enough. We know that such things sometimes last—and sometimes don't . And when they do last, this is not because they promised at the outset to do so. When two people achieve lasting happiness, this is not solely because they are great lovers but because they are also—I must put it crudely—good people; controlled, loyal, fairminded, mutually adaptable people.

If we establish a "right to (sexual) happiness" which supersedes all the ordinary rules of behavior, we do so not because of what our passion shows itself to be in experience but because of what it professes to be while we are in the grip of it. Hence, while the bad behavior is real and works miseries and degradations, the happiness which was the object of the behavior turns out again and again to be illusory. Everyone (except Mr. A. and Mrs. B.) knows that Mr. A. in a year or so may have the same reason for deserting his new wife as for deserting his old. He will feel again that all is at stake. He will see himself again as the great lover, and his pity for himself will exclude all pity for the woman.

Two further points remain.

One is this. A society in which conjugal infidelity is tolerated must always be in the long run a society adverse to women. Women, whatever a few male songs and satires may say to the contrary, are more naturally monogamous than men; it is a biological necessity. Where promiscuity prevails, they will therefore always be more often the victims than the culprits. Also, domestic happiness is more necessary to them than to us. And the quality by which they most easily hold a man, their beauty, decreases every year after they have come to maturity, but this does not happen to those qualities of personality—women don't really care twopence about our *looks*—by which we hold women. Thus in the ruthless war of promiscuity women are at a double disadvantage. They play for higher stakes and are also more likely to lose. I have no sympathy with moralists who frown at the increasing crudity of female provocativeness. These signs of desperate competition fill me with pity.

Secondly, though the "right to happiness" is chiefly claimed for the sexual impulse, it seems to me impossible that the matter should stay there. The fatal principle, once allowed in that department, must sooner or later seep through our whole lives. We thus advance toward a state of society in which not only each man but every impulse in each man claims *carte blanche.* And then, though our technological skill may help us survive a little longer, our civilization will have died at heart, and will—one dare not even add "unfortunately"—be swept away.

## Questions

1. Having read the entire essay, look back at Lewis's first five paragraphs and point out the ways in which he is not merely recounting an episode but is already conveying his attitude and seeking to persuade.

2. Lewis argues that we do not have a "right to (sexual) happiness." What *duty* or *duties* do we have, according to Lewis?
3. Evaluate Lewis's comment, in his next-to-last paragraph, on the differences between men and women.

## May Sarton

# The Rewards of Living a Solitary Life

The other day an acquaintance of mine, a gregarious and charming man, told me he had found himself unexpectedly alone in New York for an hour or two between appointments. He went to the Whitney and spent the "empty" time looking at things in solitary bliss. For him it proved to be a shock nearly as great as falling in love to discover that he could enjoy himself so much alone.

What had he been afraid of, I asked myself? That, suddenly alone, he would discover that he bored himself, or that there was, quite simply, no self there to meet? But having taken the plunge, he is now on the brink of adventure; he is about to be launched into his own inner space, space as immense, unexplored and sometimes frightening as outer space to the astronaut. His every perception will come to him with a new freshness and, for a time, seem startlingly original. For anyone who can see things for himself with a naked eye becomes, for a moment or two, something of a genius. With another human being present vision becomes double vision, inevitably. We are busy wondering, what does my companion see or think of this, and what do I think of it? The original impact gets lost, or diffused.

"Music I heard with you was more than music." Exactly. And therefore music *itself* can only be heard alone. Solitude is the salt of personhood. It brings out the authentic flavor of every experience.

May Sarton, born in Belgium in 1912, was brought to the United States in 1916; in 1924 she became a citizen. A teacher of writing and a distinguished writer herself, she has received numerous awards for her fiction, poetry, and essays.

"Alone one is never lonely: the spirit adventures, walking/In a quiet garden, in a cool house, abiding single there."

Loneliness is most acutely felt with other people, for with others, even with a lover sometimes, we suffer from our differences of taste, temperament, mood. Human intercourse often demands that we soften the edge of perception, or withdraw at the very instant of personal truth for fear of hurting, or of being inappropriately present, which is to say naked, in a social situation. Alone we can afford to be wholly whatever we are, and to feel whatever we feel absolutely. That is a great luxury!

For me the most interesting thing about a solitary life, and mine has been that for the last twenty years, is that it becomes increasingly rewarding. When I can wake up and watch the sun rise over the ocean, as I do most days, and know that I have an entire day ahead, uninterrupted, in which to write a few pages, take a walk with my dog, lie down in the afternoon for a long think (why does one think better in a horizontal position?), read and listen to music, I am flooded with happiness.

I am lonely only when I am overtired, when I have worked too long without a break, when for the time being I feel empty and need filling up. And I am lonely sometimes when I come back home after a lecture trip, when I have seen a lot of people and talked a lot, and am full to the brim with experience that needs to be sorted out.

Then for a little while the house feels huge and empty, and I wonder where my self is hiding. It has to be recaptured slowly by watering the plants, perhaps, and looking again at each one as though it were a person, by feeding the two cats, by cooking a meal.

It takes a while, as I watch the surf blowing up in fountains at the end of the field, but the moment comes when the world falls away, and the self emerges again from the deep unconscious, bringing back all I have recently experienced to be explored and slowly understood, when I can converse again with my hidden powers, and so grow, and so be renewed, till death do us part.

## Questions

1. What does Sarton mean when she says: "Anyone who can see things for himself with a naked eye becomes, for a moment or two, something of a genius"? Does your own experience confirm her comment?
2. Drawing on Sarton's essay, explain the distinction between being "alone" and being "lonely."
3. What phrase in the last paragraph connects the ending with the first paragraph?

**Albert Camus**

# The Myth of Sisyphus

The gods had condemned Sisyphus to ceaselessly rolling a rock to the top of a mountain, whence the stone would fall back of its own weight. They had thought with some reason that there is no more dreadful punishment than futile and hopeless labor.

If one believes Homer, Sisyphus was the wisest and most prudent of mortals. According to another tradition, however, he was disposed to practice the profession of highwayman. I see no contradiction in this. Opinions differ as to the reasons why he became the futile laborer of the underworld. To begin with, he is accused of a certain levity in regard to the gods. He stole their secrets. Aegina, the daughter of Aesopus, was carried off by Jupiter. The father was shocked by that disappearance and complained to Sisyphus. He, who knew of the abduction, offered to tell about it on condition that Aesopus would give water to the citadel of Corinth. To the celestial thunderbolts he preferred the benediction of water. He was punished for this in the underworld. Homer tells us also that Sisyphus had put Death in chains. Pluto could not endure the sight of his deserted, silent empire. He dispatched the god of war, who liberated Death from the hands of her conqueror.

It is said also that Sisyphus, being near to death, rashly wanted to test his wife's love. He ordered her to cast his unburied body into the middle of the public square. Sisyphus woke up in the underworld. And there, annoyed by an obedience so contrary to human love, he obtained from Pluto permission to return to earth in order to chastise his wife. But when he had seen again the face of this world, enjoyed water and sun, warm stones and the sea, he no longer wanted to go back to the infernal darkness. Recalls, signs of anger, warnings were of no avail. Many years more he lived facing the curve of the gulf, the sparkling sea, and the smiles of earth. A decree of the gods was necessary. Mercury came and seized the impudent man by the collar and, snatching him from his joys, led him forcibly back to the underworld, where his rock was ready for him.

For a biographical note on Camus, see page 483.

You have already grasped that Sisyphus is the absurd hero. He *is,* as much through his passions as through his torture. His scorn of the gods, his hatred of death, and his passion for life won him that unspeakable penalty in which the whole being is exerted toward accomplishing nothing. This is the price that must be paid for the passions of this earth. Nothing is told us about Sisyphus in the underworld. Myths are made for the imagination to breathe life into them. As for this myth, one sees merely the whole effort of a body straining to raise the huge stone, to roll it and push it up a slope a hundred times over; one sees the face screwed up, the cheek tight against the stone, the shoulder bracing the clay-covered mass, the foot wedging it, the fresh start with arms outstretched, the wholly human security of two earth-clotted hands. At the very end of his long effort measured by skyless space and time without depth, the purpose is achieved. Then Sisyphus watches the stone rush down in a few moments toward that lower world whence he will have to push it up again toward the summit. He goes back down to the plain.

It is during that return, that pause, that Sisyphus interests me. A face that toils so close to stones is already stone itself! I see that man going back down with a heavy yet measured step toward the torment of which he will never know the end. That hour like a breathing-space which returns as surely as his suffering, that is the hour of consciousness. At each of those moments when he leaves the heights and gradually sinks toward the lairs of the gods, he is superior to his fate. He is stronger than his rock.

If this myth is tragic, that is because its hero is conscious. Where would his torture be, indeed, if at every step the hope of succeeding upheld him? The workman of today works every day in his life at the same tasks, and this fate is no less absurd. But it is tragic only at the rare moments when it becomes conscious. Sisyphus, proletarian of the gods, powerless and rebellious, knows the whole extent of his wretched condition: it is what he thinks of during his descent. The lucidity that was to constitute his torture at the same time crowns his victory. There is no fate that cannot be surmounted by scorn.

If the descent is thus sometimes performed in sorrow, it can also take place in joy. This word is not too much. Again I fancy Sisyphus returning toward his rock, and the sorrow was in the beginning. When the images of earth cling too tightly to memory, when the call of happiness becomes too insistent, it happens that melancholy rises in man's heart: this is the rock's victory, this is the rock itself. The boundless grief is too heavy to bear. These are our nights of Gethsemane. But crushing truths perish from being acknowledged. Thus, Oedipus at the outset obeys fate without knowing it. But from the moment he knows, his tragedy begins. Yet at the same moment, blind and desperate, he realizes that the only bond linking him to the world is the cool hand of a girl. Then a tremendous remark rings out: "Despite so many ordeals, my advanced age and the nobility of my soul make me conclude that all is well." Sophocles' Oedipus, like Dostoevsky's Kirilov, thus gives the recipe for the absurd victory. Ancient wisdom confirms modern heroism.

One does not discover the absurd without being tempted to write a manual of happiness. "What! by such narrow ways—?" There is but one world, however. Happiness and the absurd are two sons of the same earth. They are inseparable. It would be a mistake to say that happiness necessarily springs from the absurd discovery. It happens as well that the feeling of the absurd springs from happiness. "I conclude that all is well," says Oedipus, and that remark is sacred. It echoes in the wild and limited universe of man. It teaches that all is not, has not been, exhausted. It drives out of this world a god who had come into it with dissatisfaction and a preference for futile sufferings. It makes of fate a human matter, which must be settled among men.

All Sisyphus' silent joy is contained therein. His fate belongs to him. His rock is his thing. Likewise, the absurd man, when he contemplates his torment, silences all the idols. In the universe suddenly restored to its silence, the myriad wondering little voices of the earth rise up. Unconscious, secret calls, invitations from all the faces, they are the necessary reverse and price of victory. There is no sun without shadow, and it is essential to know the night. The absurd man says yes and his effort will henceforth be unceasing. If there is a personal fate, there is no higher destiny, or at least there is but one which he concludes is inevitable and despicable. For the rest, he knows himself to be the master of his days. At that subtle moment when man glances backward over his life, Sisyphus returning toward his rock, in that slight pivoting he contemplates that series of unrelated actions which becomes his fate, created by him, combined under his memory's eye and soon sealed by his death. Thus, convinced of the wholly human origin of all that is human, a blind man eager to see who knows that the night has no end, he is still on the go. The rock is still rolling.

I leave Sisyphus at the foot of the mountain! One always finds one's burden again. But Sisyphus teaches the higher fidelity that negates the gods and raises rocks. He too concludes that all is well. This universe henceforth without a master seems to him neither sterile nor futile. Each atom of that stone, each mineral flake of that night-filled mountain, in itself forms a world. The struggle itself toward the heights is enough to fill a man's heart. One must imagine Sisyphus happy.

## Questions

1. Philosophers of the absurd hold that there is a disparity between the mind's need for coherence and the incoherence that the mind perceives in the world around it. The absurdist longs for clarity and is confronted by irrationality. It is this confrontation—not merely the irrationality of the surroundings—that makes for the absurd. How is Camus's Sisyphus an absurdist in his life on earth as well as in his life in the underworld?
2. Camus says that Sisyphus's consciousness of his torment makes him superior to the torment. Does this make sense? Camus goes even further and says that Sisyphus is happy. Presumably Camus is telling us something about how *we* ought to respond to life, but exactly *what* ought we to do?
3. If you have read Camus's "The Guest" (pages 483–494), see if "The Myth of Sisyphus" helps explain the story. Is Daru a rational man who finds irrationality around him?

Nakajima Atushi

# The Expert

There lived in the city of Hantan, the capital of the ancient Chinese state of Chao, a man called Chi Ch'ang who aspired to be the greatest archer in the world. After many enquiries, he ascertained that the best teacher in the country was one Wei Fei. So great was this Master's skill in archery that he was able, by repute, to shoot a quiverful of arrows into a single willow-leaf at the distance of a hundred paces. Chi Ch'ang journeyed to the far-away province where Wei Fei lived and became his pupil.

First Wei Fei ordered him to learn not to blink. Chi Ch'ang returned home and as soon as he entered his house, crept under his wife's loom and lay there on his back. It was his plan to stare without blinking at the treadle as it rushed up and down directly before his eyes. His wife was amazed to see him in this posture and said that she could not weave with a man, albeit her husband, watching from this strange angle. She was, however, constrained to work the treadle despite her embarrassment.

Day after day Chi Ch'ang took up his peculiar station under the loom and practised staring. After two years he had reached the point of not blinking even if one of his eye-lashes was caught in the treadle. When Chi Ch'ang finally crawled out for the last time from under the machine, he realised that his lengthy discipline had been effective. Nothing now could make him blink—not a blow on the eyelid, nor a spark from the fire, nor a cloud of dust raised suddenly before his

---

Nakajima Atushi (1909–1942) was a Japanese writer of essays and stories. (We give the name in Japanese style, family name first.)

In Chinese thinking, the Tao (the Way) is the underlying harmony of the universe. For the Taoist, the trick is to participate in this harmony, and this is best done by "inaction." Thus, a drunkard falling from a horse is less likely to be injured than a sober person, because the drunkard does not act to interrupt the fall; the sober person thrusts out an arm and the action produces a broken arm. Similarly, the best swimmers know how to use the currents, and the best craftsmen know how to submit themselves to the properties of their material—for instance, the grain of the wood. In this story, note Chi Ch'ang's teaching that "the ultimate stage of activity is inactivity."

eyes. So thoroughly had he trained his eye-muscles to inactivity that even when he slept his eyes remained wide open. One day as he sat staring ahead of him, a small spider wove its web between his eyelashes. Now at last he felt sufficiently confident to report to his teacher.

"To know how not to blink is only the first step," said Wei Fei when Chi Ch'ang had eagerly recounted the story of his progress. "Next you must learn to look. Practise looking at things, and if the time comes when what is minute seems conspicuous, and what is small seems huge, visit me once more."

Again Chi Ch'ang returned home. This time he went to the garden and searched for a tiny insect. When he had found one barely visible to the naked eye, he placed it on a blade of grass and hung this by the window of his study. Now he took up his post at the end of the room and sat there day after day staring at the insect. At first he could barely see it, but after ten days, he began to fancy that it was slightly bigger. At the end of the third month it seemed to have grown to the size of a silk-worm and he could now clearly make out the details of its body.

As Chi Ch'ang sat staring at the insect, he scarcely noticed the changing of the seasons—how the glittering spring sun changed to the fierce glare of summer; how before long the geese were flying through a limpid autumn sky; and how autumn in turn gave way to the sleety grey winter. Nothing seemed to exist now but the little animal on the blade of grass. As each insect died or disappeared, he had his servant replace it by another one equally minute. But in his eyes they were constantly becoming larger.

For three years he hardly left his study. Then one day he perceived that the insect by the window was as big as a horse. "I've done it!" he exclaimed, striking his knee, and so saying he hurried out of the house. He could scarcely believe his eyes. Horses seemed as big as mountains; pigs looked like great hills, and chickens like castle-towers. Bounding with joy, he ran back to his house and immediately noticed a slender Shuo P'êng arrow on a Swallow bow. He took aim and shot the insect straight through the heart without so much as touching the blade of grass on which it rested.

He lost no time in reporting to Wei Fei. This time his teacher was sufficiently impressed to say, "Well done!"

It was five years since Chi Ch'ang had embarked on the mysteries of archery and he felt that his rigorous training had indeed borne fruit. No feat of bowmanship now seemed beyond his powers. To confirm this, he set himself a series of exacting tests before returning home.

First he decided to emulate Wei Fei's own accomplishment, and at the distance of a hundred yards he succeeded in shooting every arrow through a willow-leaf. A few days later he undertook the same task, using his heaviest bow and balancing on his right elbow a cup filled to the brim with water; not a drop was spilt and again every arrow found its mark.

The following week he took a hundred light arrows and shot them in rapid succession at a distant target. The first one hit the bull's-eye; the second one pierced the first arrow straight in the notch; the third arrow lodged itself in the notch of the second; and so it continued until in a twinkling all hundred arrows were joined in a single straight line extending from the target to the bow itself. So true had he aimed that even after he had finished, the long line of arrows did not fall to the ground but remained quivering in mid-air. At this, even the Master Wei Fei, who had watched from the side, could not help clapping and shouting, "Bravo!"

When after two months Chi Ch'ang finally returned home, his wife, chafing at his long neglect, started to rail at him. Thinking to correct her shrewishness, Chi Ch'ang quickly notched a Ch'i Wei arrow on a Raven bow, drew the string to its fullest extension and fired just above her eye. The arrow removed three of her lashes, but so great was its speed and so sure the aim that she was not even aware that anything had happened, and without so much as blinking, continued to nag at her husband.

There was nothing more for Chi Ch'ang to learn from his teacher Wei Fei. He seemed close to the achievement of his ambition. Yet one obstacle remained, he realised with an unpleasant jolt: that obstacle was Wei Fei himself. So long as the Master lived, Chi Ch'ang could never call himself the greatest archer in the world. Though he now equalled Wei Fei in bowmanship, he felt sure that he could never excel him. The man's life was a constant denial of his own great purpose.

Walking through the fields one day, Chi Ch'ang caught sight of Wei Fei far in the distance. Without a moment's hesitation, he raised his bow, fixed an arrow and took aim. His old master, however, had sensed what was happening and in a flash had also notched an arrow on his bow. Both men fired at the same moment. Their arrows collided half way and fell together to the ground. Chi Ch'ang immediately shot another arrow, but this was stopped in mid-air by a second unerring arrow from Wei Fei's bow. So the strange duel continued until the Master's quiver was empty but one arrow still remained to the pupil. "Now's my chance!" muttered Chi Ch'ang and at once aimed the final arrow. Seeing this, Wei Fei broke off a twig from the thorn-bush beside him. As the arrow whistled towards his heart, he flicked the point sharply with the tip of one of the thorns and brought it to the ground at his feet.

Realising that his evil design had been thwarted, Chi Ch'ang was filled with a fine sense of remorse, which, to be sure, he would have been far from feeling had any of his arrows lodged where he intended. Wei Fei, on his side, was so relieved at his escape and so satisfied with this latest example of his own virtuosity that he could feel no anger for his would-be assassin. The two men ran up to each other and embraced with tears of devotion. (Strange indeed were the ways of ancient times! Would not such conduct be unthinkable today? The hearts of the men of old must have differed utterly from our own. How else explain that when the Duke Huan one evening demanded a new delicacy, the Director of the Imperial Kitchen, by name I Ya, baked his own son and begged the Duke to sample it; or that the fifteen-year-old youth, who was to be the first Emperor of the Shin Dynasty, did not scruple on the very night his father died to make love three times to the old man's favorite concubine?)

Even as he embraced his head-strong pupil in forgiveness, Wei Fei was aware that his life might any day be threatened again. The only way to rid himself of this constant menace was to divert Chi Ch'ang's mind to some new goal.

"My friend," he said, standing aside, "I have now, as you realise, transmitted to you all the knowledge of archery that I possess. If you wish to delve further into these mysteries, cross the lofty Ta Hsing Pass in the western country and climb to the summit of Mount Ho. There you may find the aged Master Kan Ying, who in the art of archery knows no equal in this or any age. Compared to his skill, our bowmanship is as the puny fumbling of children. There is no man in the world but the Master Kan Ying to whom you can now look for instruction. Seek him out, if indeed he be still alive, and become his pupil."

Chi Ch'ang immediately set out for the West. To hear his achievements described as child's play had pricked his pride and made him fear that he might still be far from realising his great ambition. He must lose no time in climbing Mount Ho and matching his own achievements against those of this old Master.

He crossed the Ta Hsing Pass and made his way up the rugged mountain. His shoes were soon worn out and his feet and legs were cut and bleeding. Quite undaunted, he clambered up perilous precipices and traversed narrow planks set over huge chasms. After a month he reached the summit of Mount Ho and burst impetuously into the cave where dwelt Kan Ying. He proved to be an aged man with eyes as gentle as a sheep's. He was, indeed, quite frighteningly old—far older than anyone Chi Ch'ang had ever seen. His back was bent, and as he walked his white hair trailed along the ground.

Thinking that anyone of such an age must needs be deaf, Chi Ch'ang announced in a loud voice, "I have come to find out if I am indeed as great an archer as I believe." Without waiting for Kan Ying's reply, he took the great poplar bow, which he was carrying on his back, notched a Tsu Chieh arrow and aimed at a flock of migrating birds which were passing by high overhead. Instantly five birds came hurtling down through the clear blue sky.

The old man smiled tolerantly and said, "But my dear Sir, this is mere shooting with bow and arrow. Have you not yet learned to shoot without shooting? Come with me."

Ruffled by his failure to impress the old hermit, Chi Ch'ang followed him in silence to the edge of a great precipice some two hundred paces from the cave. When he glanced down, he thought that he must indeed have come into the presence of "the great screen three thousand cubits high" described of old by Chang Tsai. Far below he saw a mountain-stream winding its way like a shining thread over the rocks. His eyes became blurred and his head began to spin. Meanwhile the Master Kan Ying ran lightly on to a narrow ledge which jutted straight out over the precipice and, turning round, said, "Now show me your real skill. Come where I am standing and let me see your bowmanship."

Chi Ch'ang was too proud to decline the challenge, and without hesitation changed places with the old man. No sooner had he stepped on to the ledge, however, than it began to sway slightly to and fro. Assuming a boldness that he was far from feeling, Chi Ch'ang took his bow and with trembling fingers tried to notch an arrow. Just then a pebble rolled off the ledge and began to fall thousands of feet through space. Following it with his eye, Chi Ch'ang felt that he was going to lose his balance. He lay down on the ledge, clutching its edges firmly with his fingers. His legs shook and the perspiration flowed from his whole body.

The old man laughed, reached out his hand and helped Chi Ch'ang down off the ledge. Jumping on to it himself, he said, "Allow me, Sir, to show you what archery really is."

Though Chi Ch'ang's heart was pounding and his face was deadly white, he still had sufficient presence of mind to notice that the Master was emptyhanded.

"What about your bow?" he asked in a sepulchral voice.

"My bow?" said the old man. "My bow?" he repeated laughing. "So long as one requires bow and arrow, one is still at the periphery of the art. Real archery dispenses with both bow and arrow!"

Directly above their heads a single kite was wheeling in the sky. The hermit looked up at it and Chi Ch'ang followed his gaze. So high was the bird that even to his sharp eyes it looked like a tiny sesame seed. Kan Ying notched an invisible arrow on an incorporeal bow, drew the string to its full extension and released it. Chi Ch'ang seemed to hear a swishing sound; the next moment the kite stopped flapping its wings and fell like a stone to the ground.

Chi Ch'ang was aghast. He felt that now for the first time he had glimpsed the limit of the art which he had so glibly undertaken to master.

For nine years he stayed in the mountains with the old hermit. What disciplines he underwent during this time, none ever knew. When in the tenth year he descended from the mountains and returned home, all were amazed at the change in him. His former resolute and arrogant countenance had disappeared; in its place had come the expressionless, wooden look of a simpleton. His old teacher, Wei Fei, come to visit him, said after a single glance, "Now I can see that you have indeed become an expert! Such as I are no longer worthy ever to touch your feet."

The inhabitants of Hantan hailed Chi Ch'ang as the greatest archer in the land and impatiently awaited the wonderful feats which he no doubt would soon display. But Chi Ch'ang did nothing to satisfy their expectations. Not once did he put his hands to a bow or arrow. The great poplar bow which he had taken with him on his journey he evidently had left behind. When someone asked him to explain, he answered in a languid tone, "The ultimate stage of activity is inactivity; the ultimate stage of speaking is to refrain from speech; the ultimate in shooting is not to shoot."

The more perceptive citizens of Hantan at once understood his meaning and stood in awe before this great expert archer who declined to touch a bow. It was his very refusal to shoot that now caused his reputation to grow.

All sorts of rumours and tales were bruited abroad about Chi Ch'ang. It was reported that always after midnight one could hear the sound of someone pulling an invisible bow-string on the roof of his house. Some said that this was the god of archery, who dwelt each day within the Master's soul and at night escaped to protect him from all evil spirits. A merchant who lived nearby circulated a rumour that one night he had clearly seen Chi Ch'ang riding on a cloud directly above his own house; for once he was carrying his bow, and he was matching his accomplishments against those of Hou I and Yang Yu-chi, the famous archers of legendary times. According to the merchant's story, the arrows fired by the three Masters disappeared in the distance between Orion and Sirius, trailing bright blue lights in the black sky.

There was also a thief who confessed that, as he had been about to climb into Chi Ch'ang's house, a sudden blast of air had rushed through the window and struck him so forcefully on the forehead that he had been knocked off the wall. Thenceforth all those who harboured evil designs avoided the precincts of Chi Ch'ang's house, and it was said that even flocks of migrating birds kept clear of the air above his roof.

As his renown spread through the land, reaching to the very clouds, Chi Ch'ang grew old. More and more he seemed to have entered the state in which both mind and body look no longer to things outside but exist by themselves in restful and elegant simplicity. His stolid face divested itself of every vestige of expression; no outside force could disturb his complete impassiveness. It was rare now for him to speak, and presently one could no longer tell whether or not he still breathed. Often his limbs seemed stark and lifeless as a withered tree. So attuned had he become to the underlying laws of the universe, so far removed from the insecurities and contradictions of things apparent, that in the evening of his life he no longer knew the difference between "I" and "he," between "this" and "that." The kaleidoscope of sensory impressions no longer concerned him; for all he cared, his eye might have been an ear, his ear a nose, his nose a mouth.

Forty years after he had come down from the mountains, Chi Ch'ang peacefully left the world, like smoke disappearing in the sky. During these forty years he had never once mentioned the subject of archery, let alone taken up a bow and arrow.

Of his last year, the story is told that one day he visited a friend's house and saw lying on a table a vaguely familiar utensil whose name and use he could, however, not recall. After vainly searching his memory, he turned to his friend and said, "Pray tell me: that object on your table—what is it called and for what is it used?" His host laughed as if Chi Ch'ang was joking. The old man pressed his question but his friend laughed again, though this time somewhat uncertainly. When he was questioned seriously for a third time, a look of consternation appeared on the friend's face. He gazed intently at Chi Ch'ang and, having made sure that he had heard correctly and also that the old man was neither mad nor speaking in jest, he stammered out in an awe-struck tone, "Oh, Master. You must indeed be the greatest Master of all times. Only so can you have forgotten the bow—both its name and its use!"

It was said that for some time after this in the city of Hantan painters threw away their brushes, musicians broke the strings of their instruments, and carpenters were ashamed to be seen with their rules.

## Question

If you enjoyed this story, try to account for your pleasure. Consider not only the story as a whole, but its parts. Are there certain passages, or even certain sentences, that are especially delightful?

## Chewing Blackbones

# Old Man and Old Woman

### A Blackfoot Indian Myth Retold

Long, long ago, there were only two persons in the world: Old Man and Old Woman. One time when they were traveling about the earth, Old Woman said to Old Man, "Now let us come to an agreement of some kind. Let us decide how the people shall live when they shall be on the earth."

"Well," replied Old Man, "I am to have the first say in everything."

"I agree with you," said Old Woman. "That is—if I may have the second say."

Then Old Man began his plans. "The women will have the duty of tanning the hides. They will rub animals' brains on the hides to make them soft and scrape them with scraping tools. All this they will do very quickly, for it will not be hard work."

"No," said Old Woman, "I will not agree to this. They must tan hides in the way you say; but it must be very hard work, so that the good workers may be found out."

"Well," said Old Man, "we will let the people have eyes and mouths, straight up and down in their faces."

"No," replied Old Woman, "let us not have them that way. We will have the eyes and mouths in the faces, as you say, but they shall be set crosswise."

"Well," said Old Man, "the people shall have ten fingers on each hand."

"Oh, no!" replied Old Woman. "That will be too many. They will be in the way. There will be four fingers and one thumb on each hand."

So the two went on until they had provided for everything in the lives of the people who were to be.

---

Nothing is known about Chewing Blackbones except that he was a Blackfoot Indian described in 1953 as "an elderly grandfather . . . [who] could tell the old tales only in the old Blackfoot language." Ella E. Clark collected this tale in 1953, and published it in her 1966 collection, *Indian Legends from the Northern Rockies.*

"What shall we do about life and death?" asked Old Woman. "Should the people live forever, or should they die?"

Old Woman and Old Man had difficulty agreeing about this. Finally Old Man said, "I will tell you what we will do. I will throw a buffalo chip into the water. If it floats, the people will die for four days and then come to life again; if it sinks, they will die forever."

So he threw a buffalo chip into the water, and it floated.

"No," said Old Woman, "we will not decide in that way. I will throw this rock into the water. If it floats, the people will die for four days; if it sinks, they will die forever."

Then Old Woman threw the rock into the water, and it sank to the bottom.

"There," said she. "It is better for the people to die forever. If they did not, they would not feel sorry for each other, and there would be no sympathy in the world."

"Well," said Old Man, "let it be that way."

After a time, Old Woman had a daughter, who soon became sick and died. The mother was very sorry then that they had agreed that people should die forever. "Let us have our say over again," she said.

"No," replied Old Man. "Let us not change what we have agreed upon."

And so people have died ever since.

## Questions

1. Do we think of Old Man and Old Woman as people or as gods? Explain.
2. Though briefly sketched, Old Man and Old Woman are distinct characters. What are the important differences between them?
3. The dialogue helps to characterize Old Man and Old Woman. What other function does it serve?
4. If the story ended six sentences earlier (after Old Man says: "Well . . . let it be that way"), the myth would still provide an explanation of why people die. What would be lost?

## William Shakespeare

# Sonnet 29

When, in disgrace with Fortune and men's eyes,
I all alone beweep my outcast state,
And trouble deaf heaven with my bootless[1] cries,
And look upon myself and curse my fate,
Wishing me like to one more rich in hope,
Featured like him, like him[2] with friends possessed,
Desiring this man's art, and that man's scope,
With what I most enjoy contented least;
Yet in these thoughts myself almost despising,
Haply[3] I think on thee, and then my state,
Like to the lark at break of day arising
From sullen earth, sings hymns at heaven's gate;
  For thy sweet love rememb'red such wealth brings,
  That then I scorn to change my state with kings.

## Questions

1. Disregarding for the moment the last two lines (or *couplet*), where does the sharpest turn or shift occur? In a sentence, summarize the state of mind before this turn, and in another sentence, the state of mind after it.
2. In the last two lines of a sonnet Shakespeare often summarizes the lines that preceded. In this sonnet, how does the structure of the summary differ from that of the statement in the first twelve lines? Why?

---

William Shakespeare (1564–1616) probably wrote most of his 154 sonnets between 1593 and 1600, at about the same time that he wrote such plays as *Romeo and Juliet, A Midsummer Night's Dream, The Merchant of Venice,* and *As You Like It.* The sonnets were not published, however, until 1609.

---

[1]Useless.
[2]Like this man, like that man.
[3]Perchance.

# APPENDIX A

## Reading (and Writing About) Essays

### Getting Started: Reading Closely

"Some books are to be tasted, others to be swallowed, and some few to be chewed and digested." You may already have encountered this wise remark by Francis Bacon, a very good reader (and a good writer too, though he did not write Shakespeare's plays). Bacon puts his finger on an important truth: not all books (or essays) are to be read in the same way. We daily see advertisements for courses in speed reading; one ad claimed that President Kennedy took such a course and learned to read a couple of hundred pages in an hour. That's about the right speed for most of the stuff that crossed his desk. But (despite the advertisements) he wasn't reading, he was skimming. The art of skimming is essential if we are to survive the daily deluge of paper loosed upon us, and most of us develop the art satisfactorily: we get through junk mail in a matter of seconds, the newspaper and *Time* or *Newsweek* in a matter of minutes. We skim, perhaps taking in only the captions, and then, when an item catches our interest, we stop skimming and really read; possibly we even go back and reread the opening paragraphs that we had skimmed.

Skimming has its place in academic life too; in studying for an examination or in doing a research paper you probably will skim many pages to find the material that is relevant and that will require close reading. Even if you know at the outset that an article or book is important, you may skim it first, to get the gist, so that you can then more easily read it a second time (really a first time) and take notes on it. Skimming may reveal, for instance, that each chapter ends with a summary, and so even before you begin to read closely you know that you will not have to take very general notes later when you inch through each page.

Inevitably, however, and especially in a composition course, much of the assigned reading and every essay that you intend to write about must be read slowly and with all of your powers of attention. Only by reading attentively do we hear in the mind's ear the writer's *tone*—whether it is ironic or earnestly straightforward, indignant or genial. Perhaps you know the line from Owen Wister's novel *The Virginian:* "When you call me that, smile." Words spoken with a smile mean something different from the same words forced through clenched teeth. But while speakers can communicate by body language and by gestures, by facial expressions and by changes in tone of voice, writers have only words in ink on paper. As writers, you are learning control of tone as you learn to take pains in your choice of words, in the way you arrange sentences, and even in the punctuation marks you may find yourself changing in your final draft. These skills will pay off doubly if you apply them to your reading, by putting yourself in the place of the writer whose work you are reading. As a reader, to be attentive you must also make some effort to "hear" the writer's tone as part of the meaning the words communicate. Skimming is not adequate to that task.

Close reading begins with reading and thinking, at least briefly, about the title. If we pick up an essay called "Do-It-Yourself Brain Surgery" we ought to know at once that we can prepare to be amused. Such a title must be ironic; it simply cannot be taken straight by a thoughtful reader. What about Judy Syfers's "Why I Want a Wife"?: That title on an essay by a woman demands at least a double take and, very likely, a glance at the biographical note at the bottom of the page. There, as it happens (page 40 in this book), you'll find the information that the essay first appeared in the premier issue of *Ms.* magazine. If that means nothing to you, reading the first paragraph, just three brief sentences, should confirm your hunch that Syfers's title is not exactly straightforward and it should prepare you for the essay's ironic content. We say "should" because a surprising number of college students persist, despite these clues, in reading this and other essays containing irony as if the essays were perfectly straightforward or even solemn. Perhaps such students have been conditioned to expect only "fact" in a printed text, and thus miss what is more usually there—a particular writer's opinions, beliefs, and attitudes, which may or may not be based on facts or supported by facts. Or, it may be that such students, whose own conversation and even writing are often richly ironic, fail to detect irony in what they read because they have come to expect that anything in a textbook, certainly anything in a textbook for an English class, is solemn and boring, and that a safe tack is to fake a kind of pious interest in it, whatever it is. If you have fallen into that trap yourself, we recommend three remedies: first, look at the entries on "Irony," "Satire," and "Persona" in "A Writer's Glossary" (page 638); second, consciously question your own assumptions about what you read;

and finally, at least in reading this book, be prepared for some surprises.

Many titles in this anthology *are* perfectly straightforward and informative. Paul Goodman's "A Proposal to Abolish Grading" is one, and Paul Robinson's "TV Can't Educate" is a terse summary of the essay's argument, or thesis. But some titles convey very little: E. B. White's "Education" hardly prepares us for his rather genial comparison of a public elementary school with a private school, or for the argumentive edge of the comparison. We will have to read further to get even the faintest idea of what he is up to. Orwell's "Shooting an Elephant" deliberately misleads us, for the title suggests some sort of hunting tale, though if we know that Orwell is fundamentally a social critic we suspect he is not really going to give us a yarn about an Englishman's pleasure in shooting big game. "Animal Liberation," which sounds like a spoof, as its author is well aware, sets forth a serious, closely reasoned analysis of our treatment of nonhumans. But what of "Zen and the Art of Burglary"? Is the coupling of Zen Buddhism with burglary—or, for that matter, is suggesting that burglary is an art—intended to be funny? You will have to read the essay and think about it to settle that question. Even then you might find yourself disagreeing with an equally attentive reader.

## Identifying the Topic and Thesis

If the writer's *thesis* is not stated or implied in the title, it ought to become increasingly evident as you work your way into the essay. This thesis is a point, an argument; and a point or argument implies an *attitude* toward a *topic.* In reading, then, try to identify the topic (not really do-it-yourself brain surgery, but do-it-yourself books) and the attitude (amused contempt for such books). Even an essay that is largely narrative, recounting a personal experience or a bit of history, will usually include an attitude toward the event being narrated, and it is the attitude—the interpretation of the event—rather than the event itself that is usually the richest part of the essay. "Shooting an Elephant" does in fact recount an episode in which Orwell shot an elephant, but the essay is really about *why* he shot the elephant, and what the experience revealed. His analysis of the episode brought him, he says, to an understanding of the "the real nature of imperialism—the real motives for which despotic governments act."

## Analyzing and Evaluating

When you read, try to read sympathetically, opening yourself to the writer's vision of things. But when you have finished an attentive reading, and an attentive rereading, you are ready consciously to *analyze* the writer's methods and to *evaluate* the piece. In analyzing, you will examine the relationships between the parts; that is, you will ask such questions as What does the title do? What speaker or persona does the writer create, and how does the writer create it? Is it created, for example, by using colloquial diction or, on the other hand, by using formal diction? By figurative language? Does the tone shift as the essay progresses? If so, why? How is the argument set forth? By logic? By drawing on personal experience? How does the author support the argument? If the thesis is never explicitly stated (as in E. B. White's "Education"), why is it not?

In evaluating, you will ask such questions as, Is the essay as clear as it can be, given the complexity of the material? (Again, the "material" includes not only the topic but the attitude and argument that make up the thesis.) If the thesis is not explicitly stated, is the essay unclear or is it perhaps better because of its indirectness? Is the argument (if the essay is chiefly an argument) convincing, or is it marred by faulty thinking? Is the essay interesting? If so, in what ways, and if not, why not?—which gets us back to analysis. If there are passages of undisguised argument, for instance, are they clear without being repetitious and boring? Is the writer's tone appropriate to the topic, and does it engage rather than alienate the reader? Exactly what devices does the writer use to make the persona engaging? If the essay includes narrative or descriptive passages, are they pertinent? Should they have been amplified, or should they have been reduced or perhaps even deleted?

Another way of thinking about the criteria for evaluating an essay is this: Is the essay persuasive (whether because of its logic or because of the power of the speaker's personality), and does the essay give pleasure? Don't hesitate to demand that an essay give you pleasure. The author probably thought that he or she was writing well, and certainly hoped to hold your interest throughout the essay and to make you feel that you were learning something of interest. In short, the author hoped that you would like the essay. You have every right to evaluate the essay partly by considering the degree of pleasure that it affords. Of course, in *your* essay you cannot simply say that you enjoyed an essay or that you were bored by it. You will have to support your assertions with reasons based on evidence. To support your assertions you must have read the writer's words carefully, so we are back to an earlier point: the first thing to do if you are going to write about a piece of writing is to read it attentively.

As you read and reread the material that you are writing about, subjecting it to the kinds of questions we have mentioned, your understanding of it will almost surely deepen. You will probably come to feel that it is better—or worse—than you had thought at first, or in any case somewhat different. As you prepare to write your own essay, and as you draft it, you are learning, feeling your way toward a considered analysis. All writers are in the position of the little girl who, told by an adult that she should think before she spoke, replied, "How do I know what I think until I say it?" But once having said something—whether in a mental question to yourself or in a note or a draft—you have to evaluate your thought, and improve it if it doesn't fit the facts.

## Taking Notes, Writing Drafts

"It is thinking," the philosopher John Locke wrote, "that makes what we read ours." But when do you start writing about what you have read? And how do you begin? The answer is that if you have been reading closely you have already begun writing. You have had a pen or pencil in your hand, a notebook or sheets of paper beside your book, a dictionary within arm's reach, perhaps a handbook, and, of course, a wastebasket. You have read with pen in hand not simply to record what you think, but to help you think. Assuming that you are reading a book that you own, as you read begin making discreet marks in the margins of the text. Not broad yellow lines through every other sentence—those will only distract you later and impede thoughtful rereading—but little checks, or brackets, or question marks next to passages that you find especially interesting, or puzzling, or quotable. On rereading, paying special attention to those passages, you may begin to detect a pattern that will disclose a topic and may eventually lead you to formulate a thesis.

Suppose you are going to write on George Orwell's "Shooting an Elephant" (page 476). Possibly at this stage of the course your instructor is concerned with teaching a particular topic—let's say organization, or narration, or description, or the creation of a persona —and therefore he or she limits the scope of your study of Orwell's essay to an examination of this topic. Perhaps the topic is organization. In reading or rereading the essay you notice that from the third paragraph through the next-to-last paragraph, Orwell is telling a story, but in the middle—not the end—he tells us the significance of the story. And so you mark the passage, perhaps with a question mark, perhaps with a pair of square brackets:

> [ And it was at this moment, as I stood there with the rifle in my hands, that I first grasped the hollowness, the futility of the white man's ? dominion in the East. . . . I perceived in this moment that when the white man turns tyrant it is his own freedom that he destroys. He becomes a sort of hollow, posing dummy, the conventionalized figure of a sahib. ]

You might even jot down some questions in your notebook. Why does Orwell spill the beans here, and why—pages later—does he describe at length the death throes of the elephant, since even without the elephant's lingering death he had come to his insight? Answers will vary (perhaps good reasons can be offered, or perhaps Orwell bungled the essay), but in noting and questioning this apparently unusual organization you may come to a fuller understanding of Orwell's essay (and you may also learn something about strategies of organization that you can apply to your own writing in other courses and after you leave college).

Let's say, however, that the instructor has not assigned a topic but has left the choice up to you. Again, your marginal notes should suggest various possibilities. Perhaps you were puzzled by Orwell's depiction of the Burmese, which doesn't seem terribly sympathetic for someone who claims to be on their side. "Sneering yellow faces," "no one had the guts to raise a riot"—such passages may be worth thinking about and writing about. Looking at the essay again you notice that although Orwell begins with more or less the conventional attitudes of the white oppressor, he increasingly reveals his sympathy for the Burmese without sentimentalizing them. An essay on Orwell's way of depicting the Burmese (and therefore to some extent on his way of depicting his own changing attitudes) as it develops in the essay is a possibility. At this point you might try writing a few sentences in your notebook.

Let's assume that on thinking further about "Shooting an Elephant" you come to feel that your greatest interest is in Orwell's political interpretation of his action. Now, in other words, you are *settling on a topic.* You keep coming back to that passage, in the middle, about his recognition of the nature of imperialism, and somehow you don't quite feel that Orwell has correctly interpreted his own experience. For one thing, you are bothered by what seems to you to be an act of cowardice on his part. Yes, the pressure on him was great—that mob at his back, his fear of losing face—and you see that Orwell has from the beginning of the essay carefully depicted the plight of the white man in Burma. But you still think that a person of greater moral fiber would have resisted the pressure and would not have shot the elephant. That is to say (and this is crucial in feeling your way toward your essay) you are *formulating a thesis statement.* Orwell, you come to feel, is explaining away his own failure by giving it a grand significance, by inflating it with political meaning. (And so now you are *refining the thesis.*)

The step after this will be to work out, at least tentatively, *strategies for putting forth this thesis.* How will you begin? With a quotation from Orwell? With a statement of your initial reaction to the essay? Which passages will you quote? What tone will you adopt? Will a comparison be useful? How personal should you get? You can't hope to settle all of these questions at once, and it will almost certainly be impossible for you to write an introductory paragraph. Fortunately, the only thing you need to do at this point is to start writing. With a topic in mind, an idea about it (your thesis), and some rough notes, you start getting as many of your ideas on paper as you can. It might be useful to sketch a very rough outline, a sort of shopping list of the points you want to make. Here is the outline with which one student began.

```
Sympathy for Orwell—how he creates it
His interpretation of shooting ("the system")
Why I don't buy it
Was he a "tyrant"?
  "   "  "  "dummy"?
Maybe a coward? ——————→
How I interpret shooting: Guilt
Why he misinterprets: Guilt
(End with something good?)
```

With some such outline in front of you, simply begin writing sentences. Don't worry about mechanical matters, such as spelling, or getting every word exactly right. Leave gaps in your sentences if you need to. What you are doing is writing a *rough draft* that no one else need ever see and that even you must not regard as sacred. You can always add or delete, or change a word, or even your mind. If you have written a rough outline you will probably tinker with that too as your ideas take clearer shape because you find more and more evidence to support or to modify the thesis.

When you reach this point, you are probably ready to try writing your introductory paragraph. Take a fresh sheet of paper for this job. If you find that your first effort is a false start, crumple the page and throw it away. Your next attempt, or your next after your next, will be better and will show you what parts of your draft can be used, what must be added, or deleted, or rearranged.

And finally, of course, you revise (preferably after giving the manuscript a day's rest) and revise again, copying out the most suitable quotations, choosing a title, deleting unnecessary repetitions, adding necessary transitions, such as "but," "furthermore," and "on the other hand," and finally checking spellings of words you're not sure of in a dictionary and checking doubtful constructions in a handbook. In short, you are laboriously doing all of the things (including typing or writing legibly and proofreading) that will make your essay seem effortless to your reader.

## Sample Essay

We have just described (partly by imagining them) the thought processes and the work of a student who wrote the following essay. We suggest that first you read Orwell's essay on pages 476–82. Then read the student's essay. Finally, reread her essay, this time glancing back at her rough outline and our marginal notes.

Title is provocative, and implies the thesis

IS ORWELL'S ELEPHANT BIG ENOUGH TO HOLD ORWELL'S INTERPRETATION?

Essay begins by showing appreciation of Orwell, i.e. shows fair-mindedness

George Orwell's "Shooting an Elephant" is a memorable essay and almost the exciting story the title seems to promise. The beginning of the first sentence compels our attention: "In Moulmein, in Lower Burma, I was hated by large numbers of people." And, so that on second thought this will not seem egotistical to the reader, Orwell wryly adds that this was "the only

Reference to note citing source

Brief relevant quotations let us hear Orwell's voice

Transition ("But") lets us know that essayist will now take a somewhat different view

Thesis statement

Repetition of "interpretation" provides transition

Citation of source, and explanation of subsequent references

time in my life that I have been important enough for this to happen to me."[1] We can hardly fail to like the writer of this sentence. The next paragraph, too, with its sympathy for "the wretched prisoners huddling in the stinking cages of the lock-ups" presents us with a man who, because of his sympathy for the oppressed and because of his "intolerable sense of guilt," gains our sympathy. But to say that we sympathize with Orwell is not to say that we have to share all of his opinions. Although we have to take his word for what happened when he shot the elephant, and we recognize that he has first-hand experience of imperialism, we do not have to believe that his interpretation of his experience gives us the truth about the nature of imperialism.

He first presents his interpretation just beyond the middle of the essay—just as Orwell is about to shoot the elephant (page 479). He explains not one but two things. He explains why he shot the elephant, and he also explains, or claims to explain, the contradiction of imperialism: "When the white man turns tyrant it is his own freedom that he destroys. He becomes a sort of hollow, posing dummy." Now, in

[1]In The Little, Brown Reader, 3rd ed., Marcia Stubbs and Sylvan Barnet, eds.. (Boston: Little, Brown, 1983), p. 476. Subsequent references will be made parenthetically within the text.

"Shooting an Elephant" Orwell admits that <u>he</u> became a sort of dummy. He felt that he was forced to shoot the elephant because the Burmese wanted him to shoot it, and he was afraid not to live up to their expectations. He was afraid, he says, that if he didn't shoot the elephant "some of them would laugh" (p. 480). Orwell has effectively prepared us for the terrible power of contemptuous laughter when, in his first paragraph, he says, "The crowd yelled with hideous laughter." Nevertheless the generalization about what happens "when the white man turns tyrant" is not really supported. In the first place, Orwell does not give us any reason to believe that he was a tyrant. True, he was a British police officer in Burma, and thus he was a representative of imperial England, but nothing in the essay suggests that he was cruel or even unfair. We do know, however, that his work as a policeman produced in him "an intolerable sense of guilt" (page 476), and this, I think, is a clue to Orwell's interpretation of his act.

First sentence of new paragraph offers a clear transition

What was his act? Under pressure from a crowd, he needlessly killed an elephant. He certainly <u>should</u> feel guilt for killing a harmless beast, and also for depriving the owner of valuable property. And he should feel guilt, I think, for yielding to the pressure of the crowd. I am not saying that I wouldn't have yielded too, but I am saying that

Essayist's criticism of Orwell is not smug

it was wrong to yield and that a stronger person would have said to himself or herself, "Never mind what all of these people think; the elephant is harmless and I won't shoot it." Perhaps if he had refused to shoot the elephant the malicious jeers would soon have turned into cheers for the brave sahib who dared to face a crazy elephant and then walked calmly away.

Clarification of thesis

But Orwell did yield to the mob, and he felt guilty for doing so. It is probably this guilt, this awareness of his weakness, rather than the guilt about being a policeman in Burma, that is at the heart of the essay. But apparently he couldn't face it. Despite his modesty and his no doubt genuine sympathy for the victims of imperialism, he shifts the blame from himself to, as we now say, "the system." It isn't really his fault, Orwell says in effect, that he was a coward; it is the nature of imperialism to turn the imperialist into a coward, a "dummy."

Again essayist tries to be fair and not seem superior to author she is analyzing; good tone

Let me say again that, judging from this essay, Orwell was in many ways a decent person, and we can admire his honesty when he admits, in the last line, that he killed the elephant "solely to avoid looking a fool." This humble confession certainly gains our sympathy, and if the essay were entirely about his deed and his awareness of his weakness there would be nothing to complain about. But Orwell tries to explain away his failure by seeing himself as (no less than the Burmese) the victim of imperialism, and so, finally, for all of his good nature and his modesty and his confession of weakness, he presents himself as innocent. He _had_ to shoot the elephant, he wants us to believe, because imperialists _have_ to do what their victims want them to do. His comments about the nature of imperialism may or may not be true, but it seems clear, even from his own essay, that Orwell's action in the last analysis resulted not from "the nature of imperialism," as he claims, but from Orwell's own failure of nerve.

Forceful ending

Restatement of thesis

Our marginal comments offer our chief views, but a brief restatement and amplification may be useful:

1. Although the title may be a trifle strained, it at least provides the reader with a focus, and thus it is far better than such an unhelpful title as "George Orwell's 'Shooting an Elephant' " or "On 'Shooting an Elephant.' "
2. The writer's tone is satisfactory. She is critical of Orwell, but she avoids condescending to him.

## Using Quotations

Our marginal comments call your attention to some of the essay's strengths as well as to some of the conventions of editing your final draft. Here we remind you of procedures for using quotations (covered in detail in most handbooks). These procedures are not noteworthy when handled properly, but they become noticeable and even ruinous to your essay when bungled. Read the following reminders over, check them against the student's essay you just read, and consult them again the first few times you write about an essay.

1. Quote. Quotations from the work under discussion provide indispensable support for your thesis.

2. Quote briefly. Use quotations as evidence, not as padding.
3. Comment on what you quote, immediately before or immediately after the quotation. Make sure your reader understands why you find the quotation relevant. Don't count on the quotation to make your point for you.
4. Take care with embedded quotations (quotations within a sentence of your own). A quotation must fit grammatically into the sentence of which it is a part.

Incorrect:

> The first sentence does not sound egotistical because "the only time in my life that I have been important enough for this to happen to me."

Correct:

> The first sentence does not sound egotistical because Orwell adds that this was "the only time in my life that I have been important enough for this to happen to me."

Don't try to fit a long quotation into one of your own sentences. It is almost impossible for the reader to come out of the quotation and pick up the thread of your sentence. It is better to lead into a long quotation with "Orwell says," and then, after quoting, to begin a new sentence of your own.

5. Quote exactly. Any material that you add (to make the quotation coherent with your sentence) must be in square brackets. Thus:

> Orwell says the torture of prisoners "oppressed [him] with an intolerable sense of guilt."

Any material that you omit from within a quotation must be indicated by three spaced periods:

> He knew that "a sahib has got to . . . know his own mind and do definite things."

If a quotation ends before the end of the author's sentence, add a period and then three spaced periods to indicate the omission:

> As Orwell claims, "it was a tiny incident in itself. . . ."

(Orwell's sentence followed the word "itself" with "but it gave me a better glimpse than I had had before of the real nature of imperialism—the real motives for which despotic governments act.")

6. Quote fairly. It would not be fair, for example, to say "Orwell claims he 'had done the right thing' " when in fact he says "legally I had done the right thing." His qualification "legally" is important, and it would be unfair to omit it.
7. Identify the quotation clearly for your reader. Notice in this essay such helpful expressions as "Orwell . . . adds," and "The next paragraph . . . represents," as well as references to pages.

# APPENDIX B

## Reading (and Writing About) Pictures

Let's begin by talking about pictures that most of us would agree are "art"—paintings and drawings rather than photographs, though we shall go on to argue that most of what we say from the outset is also true of photography.

Until the twentieth century most pictures were representational, showing gods and goddesses and kings and saints and landscapes and dishes of fruit, but they were also expressive, revealing the artist's feelings toward the subject, the artist's (or society's) particular vision. An object is seen, but not only with the eye; the mind interprets it, and when the object ends up on canvas, it has been shaped by an idea. As the painter Degas said, "The artist does not draw what he sees, but what he must make others see." Van Gogh put it thus, when he heard that a painter complained that his figures were distorted:

> I don't want them to be "correct." Real artists paint things not as they are, in a dry analytical way, but as *they* feel them. I adore Michelangelo's figures, though the legs are too long and the hips and backsides too large. What I most want to do is to make these incorrectnesses, deviations, remodelings, or adjustments of reality something that may be "untrue" but is at the same time more true than literal truth.

The proportion of accurate optical representation to distortion introduced by the expression of an idea of course varies from age to age and from painter to painter, but even in periods when individuality was not highly valued we may speak of an expressive content; the expression is that of the age. After all, it is entirely possible that innumerable nameless and almost indistinguishable twelfth-century painters expressed their religious ideals while working comfortably within the established traditions of medieval art. In twelfth-century art Christ is regularly shown seated on the heavens with the earth as a footstool; he holds the Bible in his left hand and gives a benediction with his right hand. The pose and setting, and even the rendering of stylized details, are traditional; the difference between one rendition and another is chiefly a matter of the painter's technical competence. But all the renditions, similar though they are, may express what the artists wanted to express about Christ. Don't we often express ourselves in thoroughly traditional ways? We applaud at the end of a performance that has impressed us; we feel no need to find a personal way (throwing white mice into the air?) of expressing our pleasure and approval. We are content to express ourselves in the traditional way.

The artist of course often works within bounds that severely limit personal expression. If a court painter, obliged to represent the splendor of his king, did not share the king's opinions, he might very well have had to suppress his feelings. Then again, he might have been able to smuggle something subversive into his painting, so that the royal sitter might see the painting as the image of kingliness, though the painter and the perceptive viewer saw it as the image of arrogance. A painter might even, with a splendid painting and a sitter endowed with taste, persuade the king that arrogance was more interesting and attractive than kingliness.

Even artists working under tight control, then, may—and do—endow their paintings with a life beyond optical representation of the apparent subject. In ordinary language we recognize that a painting is not simply *of* something but *by* someone; we may say, "That's a painting of a Dutch merchant," but more often we say, "That's a painting by Rembrandt," or, more tellingly, "Look at that Rembrandt." For when we look at the picture we experience Rembrandt—his way of seeing—quite as much as a merchant-sitter.

Although many of the world's greatest artists have had to please their royal or ecclesiastical or bourgeois patrons by representing certain subjects in certain ways, we know that often another subject lies on the canvas: the paintings give visible form to the artist's mind. A picture, then, is a sort of utterance, an "outterance," a sending out of attitudes, an outer report of feelings. The picture conveys meaning (as well as phenomena) in visual form, and it may intensify or newly shape the spectator's perception of any aspect of life.

Speaking metaphorically, we can say that this meaning is conveyed in the *language* of painting. Just as a succession of short sentences "says" something different from a succession of long ones (probably if it doesn't convey mere childishness it tells of tight-lipped assurance, authority, or at least self-restraint), so too a picture with short, choppy, angular lines will "say" something different from a picture with gentle curves, even though the object represented (let's say a man sitting at a table) is about the same. Similarly, a painting with a rough surface built up with vigorous or agitated brushstrokes will not say the same thing as a painting with a smooth polished surface that gives no evidence of the brush. And a soft pencil drawing on pale gray paper will say something different from a pen drawing made with a broad nib on bright white paper; at the very least, the medium and the subdued contrast of one is "quieter" or "less active" than the other.

What are some of the basic things to look for in understanding the language of pictures? One can begin almost anywhere, but let's begin with the relationship among the parts:

Do the figures share the space evenly, or does one figure overpower another, taking most of the space or the light?

Are the figures harmoniously related, perhaps by a similar stance or shared action, or are they opposed, perhaps by diagonals thrusting at each other? (Speaking generally, diagonals may suggest instability, except when they form a triangle resting on its base. Horizontal lines suggest stability, as do vertical lines when connected by a horizontal line. Circular lines are often associated with motion, and sometimes—especially by men—with the female body and with fertility. These simple formulas, however, must be applied cautiously, for they are not always appropriate.)

In a landscape, what is the relation between humans and nature? Are the figures at ease in nature, or are they dwarfed by it? Are they earthbound, beneath the horizon, or (because the viewpoint is low) do they stand out against the horizon and perhaps seem in touch with the heavens, or at least with open air. If there are woods, are these woods threatening or are they an inviting place of refuge? If there is a clearing, is the clearing a vulnerable place or is it a place of refuge from threatening woods? Do the natural objects in the landscape somehow reflect the emotions of the figures in it?

If the picture is a portrait, how do the furnishings and the background and the angle of the head or the posture of the head and body (as well, of course, as the facial expression) contribute to our sense of the person portrayed?

What is the effect of light in the picture? Does it produce sharp contrasts, brightly illuminating some parts and throwing others into darkness, or does it, by means of gentle gradations, unify most or all of the parts? Does the light seem theatrical or natural, disturbing or comforting? If the picture is in color, is the color realistic or is it expressive, or both?

We believe that you can stimulate responses by asking yourself two kinds of questions:

1. *What is this doing?* Why is this figure here and not there, why is this tree so brightly illuminated, why are shadows omitted, why is this seated figure leaning forward like that?
2. *Why do I have this response?* Why do I find this figure pathetic, this landscape oppressive, this child revoltingly sentimental but that child fascinating?

The first of these questions, "What is this doing?" requires you to identify yourself with the artist, wondering perhaps whether pen is better than pencil for this drawing, or watercolor better than oil paint for this painting? The second question, "Why do I have this response?," requires you to trust your feelings. If you are amused or repelled or unnerved or soothed, assume that these responses are appropriate and follow them up, at least until further study of the work provides other responses.

Let's turn to a specific painting, Velázquez's *The Water Seller,* painted about 1620. Velázquez painted it while he lived in Seville, but the precise locale and the time are unimportant, because even if we didn't realize until now that in the seventeenth century people required the services of a water carrier, the pictures tells us so. Velázquez reproduces appearances with careful fidelity to nature. But what is Velázquez saying, and how does he say it?

We'll begin with the largest figure, the old man who, in full light, dominates the center of the picture and who seems to stand closest to us, his hand on the great jar that appears easily within our reach. His clothes are tattered, but he has immense dignity, partly because he seems almost a central pillar, partly because his hand rests assuredly on the big globular vessel of life-sustaining water, partly because his facial expression is serious, and partly because we see his face in profile. If we think of the profile of Lincoln on a penny, of Jefferson on a nickel, of Roosevelt on a dime, of Washington on a quarter or in the painting *Washington Crossing the Delaware,* we notice that a face in profile is in no immediate relation to us. It stares off, ignoring us, looking at something that exists only in the flat world of the picture plane. Because a profile avoids contact with the space or world between the picture and the viewer, it usually strikes us as independent, even aloof. If a profile has a personality or inner life, it is probably not jovial or confiding or anguished; it is probably

*The Water Seller of Seville*
**Diego Velázquez, c. 1620**

The Victoria and Albert Museum, London

solemn, poised, self-sufficient. And there is another important thing about a profile: it can be very interesting, for we are attracted to, say, that high forehead, long nose, downturned mouth. The line that defines the profile is sharply arresting, in a way that the lines of a frontal view usually are not. In any case, if we ask ourselves which figure in Velázquez's painting is the center of interest, the answer must be evident. But the other figures are not mere contrasts to set off the water carrier. The old water seller is giving a glass to a boy, and we notice that between the two figures, to the rear, is a third person, apparently older than the boy and younger than the old man. And so we have the ages of man: youth, maturity, old age. The man in the middle, whose glass is tipped in front of his face, has already drunk substantially—even in this frozen action he is in mid-career, so to speak—but the boy is about to receive a full glass, for his life is all ahead of him. The figure in the middle, mostly obscured, although the least important, is not unimportant; he is represented because Velázquez wants more than the obvious contrast of youth and age. The painter, however, concentrates his vision on the old man passing the life-sustaining water to the young man. We see the renewal of life.

And what of the vessels, so prominent in the picture? Of course they belong in the picture; a water seller must have a jar of water, and his customers must have jars or glasses to receive the water. These vessels are handsome ones, interesting shapes beautifully painted. Still, realism would have been satisfied with a glass and perhaps the top of the large pot. The painter must have had not only a perceptive eye for things of the real world, but an idea for a picture. (This is not to say that an artist's idea precedes visual stimulus. Quite the reverse: almost surely the artist first sees something, something he feels he wants to capture and to show to others, and this initial perception stimulates whatever idea he develops. Velázquez perhaps was first moved by the face of the water carrier, or by the way the old man poured water into a glass, or even by the gleaming droplets on the shoulder of a great earthenware jar; this, he may have felt, glows with such an inner life that it must be recorded for others to see, forever. Perhaps with some such thought the picture began, but it did not stop there.) Velázquez's utensils, beautiful though they are in themselves, contribute to the whole picture and take their fullest life from the whole picture. What do they contribute? For one thing, although the three figures are closely bound by their physical positions and (even more important) by participating in a unified action, the vessels help to bring them still closer to one another, for our eye makes a sort of wheeling motion as it goes from one bright patch to another, from the water carrier's face to his shoulder and arm, perhaps then to the large vessel and then to the smaller one, then to the boy's illuminated hand and up along the glass to the boy's face, and finally to the shadowy face of the man in the middle. But there may be more. What is the effect of that great bulging jar at the bottom of the canvas? Why should earthenware receive so much space and be painted so much more illusionistically than the rather flat face of the mature man drinking from the glass? Our own response—and the picture has long exerted a spell on us—is that this vessel, the thing nearest to us, almost bulging into the space we occupy, and made of the substance to which we return, is given prominence and exerts its appeal because it contains not only the stuff that sustains life but the stuff out of which life came. First, water; then, nourished by water, life. In fact, impressive though the figures are, it seems to us that it is to this pregnant jar with unseen precious contents that the eye (or at least the mind's eye) returns after it surveys the figures.

After we have admired the astounding technical skill that can render people and objects so convincingly and interestingly, what can we say about the meaning of the picture? The painter, in pictorial language, perhaps is saying something like this. Our lives may seem poor battered things, as the water carrier's torn smock and wrinkled face indicate, but a source whose bottom we cannot see has given us the gift of life, and we can live with dignity and nourish succeeding generations. Of course Velázquez probably never said anything like this in words, but he did say it in paint. Our summary is crudely put and takes no account of the sheer sensuous appeal of the lines and colors (mostly earthy colors), but anything that we say about a great picture is crude compared with the richness of the picture itself. We realize too that our commentary has come close to turning the picture into an allegory. We hope that we have not quite said that the three men stand for three parts of a life span, that the water stands for life, that the rip in the carrier's sleeve stands for the hardships of this world. When we look at this painting, we never forget that it is a representation of men engaged in a specific commonplace action. Still, the more we respond to this representation, the more we feel that it adds up to something; and the more we feel that the whole is greater than the sum of its parts, the more we want to account for its mysterious appeal. By asking ourselves questions and trying to answer them, we may heighten our understanding of the picture and of life.

We have banged this picture around a good deal, but it can

withstand anything we do to it, and we want to spend another minute on it, setting forth what we might write if we were asked to write a paragraph about it, perhaps as a caption in a picture-book or a label on a museum wall. Up to now we have tried to show, in some detail, how we came to our understanding of the picture, but of course in writing a finished piece one does not reproduce all the byways of thought. Here is what we would say.

> Velázquez's *The Water Seller* was painted in Seville, and doubtless it represents a common enough sight, people receiving the carrier's services. But we sense more than mere realism here, more than an optically convincing report of what happened at a particular moment. Velázquez has turned the disorder of daily experience into a pattern and a meaning. We see three people closely joined; an old man of enormous gravity (despite his tattered apppearance) hands a glassful of water to a youth; between them, and between them in years, too, a mature man drinks a glass, and so we see a cycle of life, a cycle reinforced as our eyes move from the great water jar in the foreground up to the glass, to the boy's attentive face, across the adult's face to the water seller's solemn profile, and down again to the jar that is the source of nourishment for all ages.

In 1839, more than two hundred years after Velázquez painted *The Water Seller,* Louis Jacques Mandé Daguerre made public the daguerreotype, an early photographic process. "From this moment," the painter Paul Delaroche is supposed to have said, "painting is dead." This remark implies, of course, that painting seeks to render external appearances and that it cannot compete with a camera. But another and far greater painter of the period took a different view. Honoré Daumier said that photography describes everything and explains nothing. The implication is that photography offers optical realism but cannot offer the idea, the vision, which a work of art embodies. Daumier's statement, it turned out, was as inadequate as Delaroche's, as we shall try to show in a capsule historical analysis of photography.

In the middle of the nineteenth century, after a few years of intoxication with machines that could produce a permanent image that was neither drawn nor painted, photographers began to divide into two schools, which we can call pictorialists and reporters. (Of course we are simplifying; the labels are overstatements, and some photographers occupied a middle ground, or shifted allegiance from one school to the other.) The pictorialists had artistic ambitions. They posed their subjects carefully into compositions resembling those of the old master painters, and they often used religious or literary motifs, as painting had done. Julia Margaret Cameron (1815–1879) pressed her friends and servants to dress up like King Arthur's knights so that she might photograph scenes from Tennyson's *Idylls of the King,* or she arranged a woman and children into a composition that she called "Madonna with Children." She also did portrait photography, and although it might at first be thought that this at least was tied to reportage, her subjects were such notables as Tennyson, Browning, Longfellow, and Darwin, and she did not at all wish to present them as ordinary men caught in some trivial act of daily living:

> When I have had such men before my camera my whole soul has endeavored to do its duty towards them in recording faithfully the greatness of the inner as well as the features of the outer man. The photograph thus taken has been almost the embodiment of a prayer.

Moreover, because early photography required a long exposure during which the subject could not move, almost all the pictures of people—even of ordinary people, say a man supposedly sawing wood or a middle-class family dining—have a studied, posed, pictorial effect.

In Julia Cameron's time, however, other photographers (we are calling them reporters) specialized in a technique that was supposed to be the mere reproduction of anything the eye might see. Many of these concentrated on exotic sights—the Nile, American Indians, Greek architecture. The idea was that the folks back home could see exactly what these strange places and people looked like. These photographs were documents, it was claimed, showing what you would see if you were able to take the long, expensive, arduous trip. Supposedly, the photograph offered the facts—not the Ideal Truth of the pictorialists but the truth of the fleeting moment. This tradition of recording the passing scene was fostered by technical developments that greatly decreased the time required for the exposure, allowing shots of moving objects; the development of easily portable cameras, too, was essential to the documentary or reportorial tradition. The result was photo-journalism, which implicitly offers the facts without comment, and also the run-of-the-mill snapshot, which tells us what Aunt Julie looks like, standing on the porch of her new house.

Still speaking broadly, we can say that the pictorialists usually emphasize an obviously studied composition; they often use a soft focus to suppress details, they alter the negative by underdeveloping or by overdeveloping it, and they print their pictures (often retouched) on warm, soft, matte (dully finished) paper. On the other hand, the reporters value pictures with seemingly unplanned compositions (a figure cut at the side, or the top of a head cut off); they also prefer a sharp focus and prints on cold, hard, glossy paper. The effect, they might claim, is that of the moment, not that of the ages; truth, not beauty.

Now, a newspaper photograph or an amateur's snapshot does not in fact record the object-as-it-really-is. It records what you would see if you had only one eye and stood at a particular place at a particular time of day, and if what you saw was printed on a particular kind of paper. Besides, except for a few pictures taken in desperation—a picture of a parade taken by a photographer who, unable to see over the heads of a crowd, simply holds the camera as high as he can and snaps at random—the pictures of the reporters (and we include the amateur who takes snapshots) are, like those of the pictorialists, at least somewhat composed. After all, one backs up a little, shifts the lens to the right a bit, bends the knees, waits for someone to get out of the way, or, conversely, waits for a dog to come along and sniff the garbage. A Victorian reportorial photographer went up in a balloon so that he could get an interesting shot of the entrance to a cave in India, and today there is scarcely a serious photographer who has not gone to great pains to get a shot that seems "natural," "inevitable," "spontaneous." There is, of course, a visible difference between pictures at either extreme, but most of the reporters as well as the pictorialists will have to say with the late Minor White, "I don't take pictures, I make them."

What we said about reading paintings, then, applies to reading photographs too, whether they are conspicuously pictorial or allegedly reportorial. The relationships between one object and another (of one figure to another, or figures to background) are revealing, and so too is the angle of vision. And the focus—soft, or precise and hard—and the degree of contrast—gentle gradations suggesting harmony, or unity, or sharp contrasts of black and white suggesting dislocations or conflict or at least harshness—contribute to the meaning of a photograph. Because photographers make these and many other choices, they might agree with the painter Cézanne, who said that pictures are "the means of making the public feel what we feel ourselves."

Let's look at a photograph from Robert Frank's book, *The Ameri-*

*Drugstore—Detroit*
**Robert Frank**

*cans* (1969), "Drugstore—Detroit." If he had to choose from our categories, Frank would unhesitatingly call himself a reporter, so his photograph will be a severe but fair test of a method of analysis derived from studying painting.

As we look at Frank's photograph, here are some of the things we see. (We see them partly because we have asked ourselves questions, as suggested on page 627.)

1. A line of crowded people. Possibly the seating really is ample, but the angle from which the picture was taken gives us the impression that the eaters are crowded.
2. Most of these people, though in an eating place, are in fact waiting, not eating. Each is waiting by himself. Although there is a crowd, no one seems to be conversing with a neighbor. It's a lonely crowd. Those who are not staring blankly are looking curiously at the photographer, but even the unusual experience of seeing a photographer taking a picture at a lunch counter does not seem to break through to most of the men here.
3. The counter serves a useful purpose in the eatery, but in the picture it gives the effect of a barrier, separating all the customers (white males) from the women (apparently black) who serve them. Moreover, the angle from which the picture was taken (relatively high) produces a swift foreshortening; the rear of the picture seems eerily tilted up, giving a slightly surrealistic effect.
4. A good deal of machinery (apparently mini-jukeboxes) is evident along the counter, further dehumanizing the place.
5. Advertisements for Orange Whip, Orange Whip, Orange Whip, hang over the heads of the customers, almost threateningly. If the man in the foreground is indeed drinking Orange Whip, he shows no sign of enjoying it.

If we were to write a short paragraph on this picture, then, trying to report not only what it says but also *how* it says it, we might write:

> Robert Frank's photograph shows us people at mealtime, but this occasion is not a time of relaxed and friendly renewal of body or of spirit. The picture shows clutter, machine after machine, boredom, and isolation. Men sit, for the most part not dining but staring into space, each avoiding eye-contact with his neighbor, and separated by a counter from the women who serve them. Apparently not even two of the dozen or so are friends with a word to exchange. In the foreground,

> perhaps submitting to the aggressive advertisements for Orange Whip that dangle overhead, a man sips a beverage. He shows no sign of pleasure. The steep perspective unsettles us as we look at this picture of people who seem almost as dehumanized as the counter they sit at.

The Chinese aphorism says that a picture is worth a thousand words; but sometimes it takes that many words (well, a couple of dozen, anyway) to bring the picture home to us.

# APPENDIX C

## A Writer's Glossary

**analogy.** An analogy (from the Greek *analogos,* proportionate, resembling) is a kind of comparison. Normally an analogy compares substantially different kinds of things and reports several points of resemblance. A comparison of one city with another ("New York is like Chicago in several ways") does not involve an analogy because the two things are not substantially different. And a comparison giving only one resemblance is usually not considered an analogy, "Some people, like olives, are an acquired taste." But if we claim that a state is like a human body, and we find in the state equivalents for the brain, heart, and limbs, we are offering an analogy. Similarly, one might construct an analogy between feeding the body with food and supplying the mind with ideas: the diet must be balanced, taken at approximately regular intervals, in proper amounts, and digested. An analogy may be useful in explaining the unfamiliar by comparing it to the familiar ("The heart is like a pump . . . "), but of course the things compared are different, and the points of resemblance can go only so far. For this reason, analogies cannot prove anything, though they are sometimes offered as proof. "Slave plantations resembled Nazi concentration camps in some ways; it is reasonable to assume that slaves suffered the same dehumanization observed in victims of concentration camps." But it is not reasonable to make this assumption. The plantations and camps resembled each other in some ways but they differed in many others.

**analysis.** Examination of the parts and their relation to the whole. To take a simple brief example, an analysis of a sentence from Hollander's essay (page 122)—"Hair, once carefully prevented from exhibing wayward traits, was given its head"—might point out that "wayward traits" is playful, for we hardly attribute immorality to hair, and this playfulness is reinforced in the pun, "was given its head."

**argument.** Discourse in which some statements are offered as *reasons* for other statements. Argument, then, like emotional appeal and wit, is a form of persuasion, but argument seeks to persuade by appealing to reason. (See *deduction,* page 639.)

**audience.** The writer's imagined readers. An essay on inflation written for the general public—say, for readers of *Newsweek*—will assume less specialized knowledge than will an essay written for professional economists—say, the readers of *Journal of Economic History.* In general, the imagined audience in a composition course is *not* the instructor (though in fact the instructor may be the only reader of the essay); the imagined audience usually is the class, or, to put it a little differently, someone rather like the writer but without the writer's specialized knowledge of the topic.

**cliché.** Literally, a *cliché* was originally (in French) a stereotype or an electrotype plate for printing; in English the word has come to mean an oft-repeated expression such as "a sight for sore eyes," "a heartwarming experience," "the acid test," "a meaningful relationship," "last but not least." Because these expressions implicitly claim to be impressive or forceful, they can be distinguished from such unpretentious common expressions as "good morning," "thank you," and "see you tomorrow." Clichés in fact are not impressive or forceful; they strike the hearer as tired, vague, and unimaginative.

**compare/contrast.** Strictly speaking, to compare is to examine in order to show similarities. (It comes from the Latin *comparare,* "to pair," "to match.") To contrast is to set into opposition in order to show differences. (It comes from the Latin *contra,* "against," and *stare,* "to stand.") But in ordinary usage a comparison may include not only similarities but also differences. (For a particular kind of comparison, emphasizing similarities, see *analogy.*) In comparing and contrasting, a writer usually means not simply to list similarities or differences but to reveal something clearly, by calling attention either to its resemblances to something we might not think it resembles, or to its differences from something we might think it does resemble.

**connotation.** The associations that cluster around a word. "Mother" has connotations that "female parent" does not have, yet both words have the same denotation or explicit meaning.

**convention.** An agreed-on usage. Beginning each sentence with a capital letter is a convention.

**deduction.** Deduction is the process of reasoning from premises to a logical conclusion. Here is the classic example: "All men are mortal" (the major premise); "Socrates is a man" (the minor premise); "therefore Socrates is mortal" (the conclusion). Such an argument, which takes two truths and joins them to produce a third truth, is called a syllogism (from Greek for "a reckoning together"). Deduction (Latin for "lead down from") moves from a general statement to a specific application; it is, therefore, the opposite of induction, which moves from specific instances to a general conclusion.

Notice that if a premise of a syllogism is not true, one can reason logically yet can come to a false conclusion. Example: "All teachers are members of a union"; "Jones is a teacher"; "therefore Jones is a member of a union." Although the process of reasoning is correct here, the major premise is false and so the conclusion is worthless—Jones may or may not be a member of the union. Another point: some arguments superficially appear logical but are not. Let's take this attempt at a syllogism: "All teachers of Spanish know that in Spanish *hoy* means 'today'" (major premise); "John knows that in Spanish *hoy* means 'today'" (minor premise); "therefore John is a teacher of Spanish" (conclusion). Both of the premises are correct, but the conclusion does not follow. What's wrong? Valid deduction requires that the subject or condition of the major premise (in this case, teachers of Spanish) appear also in the minor premise, but here it does not. The minor premise should be "John is a teacher of Spanish," and the valid conclusion, of course, would be "Therefore John knows that *hoy* means 'today.'"

**denotation.** The explicit meaning of a word, as given in a dictionary, without its associations. "Horse doctor" and "veterinarian" have the same denotation, though veterinarian probably has a more favorable connotation (see connotation).

**description.** Discourse that aims chiefly at producing a sensory response (usually a mental image) to, for example, a person, object, scene, taste, smell, and so on. A descriptive essay, or passage in an essay, uses concrete words (words that denote observable qualities such as "hair" and "stickiness") and it uses specific language (words such as "basketball" rather than "game," and "steak, potatoes, and salad" rather than "hearty meal").

**diction.** Choice of words. Examples: between "car," "auto," and "automobile," between "lie" and "falsehood," between "can't" and "cannot."

**euphemism.** An expression such as "passed away" for "died," used to avoid realities that the writer finds unpleasant. Thus, oppressive governments "relocate people" (instead of putting then in concentration camps).

**evaluation.** Whereas an interpretation seeks to explain the meaning, an evaluation judges worth. After we interpret a difficult piece of writing we may evaluate it as not worth the effort.

**explication.** An attempt to reveal the meaning by calling attention to implications, such as the connotations of words and the tone conveyed by the brevity or length of a sentence. Unlike a paraphrase, which is a rewording or rephrasing in order to set forth the gist of the meaning, an explication is a commentary that makes explicit what is implicit. If we paraphrased the beginning of the Gettysburg Address (page 337), we might turn "Four score and seven years ago our fathers brought forth" into "Eighty-seven years ago our ancestors established," or some such statement. In an explication, however, we would mention that "four score" evokes the language of the Bible, and that the biblical echo helps to establish the solemnity and holiness of the occasion. In an explication we would also mention that "fathers" initiates a chain of images of birth, continued in "conceived in liberty," "any nation so conceived," and "a new birth." (See Highet's explication of the Gettysburg Address, page 338.)

**exposition.** An expository essay is chiefly concerned with giving information—how to register for classes, the causes of the French Revolution, or the tenets of Zen Buddhism. The writer of exposition must, of course, have a point of view (an attitude or a thesis), but because exposition—unlike persuasion—does not assume that the reader's opinion differs from the writer's, the point of view in exposition often is implicit rather than explicit.

**general** and **specific** (or **particular**). A general word refers to a class or group: a specific (particular) word refers to a member of the class or group. Example: "vehicle" is general compared with "automobile" or with "motorcycle." But "general" and "specific" are relative. "Vehicle" is general when compared to "automobile," but "vehicle" is specific when compared to "machine," for "machine" refers to a class or group that includes not only vehicles but clocks, typewriters, and dynamos. Similarly, although "automobile" is specific in comparison with "vehicle," "automobile" is general in comparison with "Volkswagen" or "sportscar."

**generalization.** A statement relating to every member of a class or category, or, more loosely, to most members of a class or category. Example: "Students from Medford High are well prepared." Compare: (1) "Janet Kuo is well prepared" (a report of a specific condition); (2) "Students from Medford High are well prepared" (a low-level generalization, because it is limited to one school); (3) "Students today are well prepared" (a high-level generalization, covering many people in many places).

**imagery** and **symbolism.** When we read "rose," we may more or less call to mind a picture of a rose, or perhaps we are reminded of the odor or texture of a rose. Whatever in a piece of writing appeals to any of our senses (including sensations of heat and pressure as well as of sight, smell, taste, touch, sound) is an image. In short, images are the sensory content of a work, whether literal (the roses discussed in an essay on rose-growing) or figurative (a comparison, in a poem, of a girl to a rose). It is usually easy to notice images in literature, particularly in poems, which often include comparisons such as "I wandered lonely as a cloud," "a fiery eye," and "seems he a dove? His feathers are but borrowed." In literature, imagery (again, literal as well as figurative) plays a large part in communicating the meaning of the work. For instance, in *Romeo and Juliet* abundant imagery of light and dark reenforces the conflict between life and death. Juliet especially is associated with light (Romeo says, "What light through yonder window breaks? It is the east and Juliet is the sun"), and at the end of the play, when the lovers have died, we are told that the morning is dark: "The sun for sorrow will not show his head."

If we turn from imaginative literature to the essay, we find, of course, that descriptive essays are rich in images. But other kinds of essays, too, may make use of imagery—and not only by literal references to real people or things. Such essays may use figures of speech, as Thoreau does when he says that the imagination as well as the body should "both sit down at the same table." The imagination, after all, does not literally sit down at a table—but Thoreau personifies the imagination, seeing it as no less concrete than the body.

The distinction between an image and a symbol is partly a matter of emphasis and partly a matter of a view of reality. If an image is so insisted on that we feel that the writer sees it as highly significant in itself and also as a way of representing something else, we can call it a symbol. In Henry James's words, symbolism is the presentation "of objects casting . . . far behind them a shadow more curious . . . than the apparent figure." A symbol is what it is, and yet it is also much more. We may feel that a passage about the railroad, emphasizing its steel tracks and its steel cars, its speed and its noise, may be not only about the railroad but also about industrialism and, even further, about an entire way of life—a way of thinking and feeling —that came into being in the nineteenth century. But, again, such a passage is not just a simile or metaphor, using the railroad as a way of pointing at something else; it is very much about the railroad itself. A simile such as "My love is like a red, red rose" is not about roses, but about a lovely woman. A symbol, then, is an image so loaded with significance that it is not simply literal, and it does not simply stand as a figure for something else; it is both itself *and* something else that it richly suggests, a kind of manifestation of something too complex or too elusive to be otherwise revealed. In a symbol, Thomas Carlyle wrote, "the Infinite is made to blend with the Finite, to stand visible, and as it were, attainable there." Still, having said all of this, one must add that the distinction between image and symbol is not sharp, and usage allows us even to say such things as, "The imagery of light symbolizes love," meaning that the imagery stands for or represents or is in part about love.

**induction.** Reasoning from the particular to the general, or drawing a conclusion about all members of a class from a study of some members of the class. Every elephant I have seen is grayish, so by induction (from Latin, "lead into," "lead up to") I conclude that all elephants are grayish. Another example: I have met ten graduates of Vassar College and all are females, so I conclude that all Vassar graduates are females. This conclusion, however, happens to be incorrect; a few years ago Vassar began to admit males, and so although male graduates are few they do exist. Induction is valid only if the sample is representative. Because one can rarely be certain that it *is* representative, induced conclusions are usually open to doubt. Still, we live our lives largely by induction; we have dinner with a friend, we walk the dog, we write home for money—all because these actions have produced certain results in the past and we assume that actions of the same sort will produce results consistent with our earlier findings. Nelson Algren's excellent advice must have been arrived at inductively: "Never eat at a place called Mom's, and never play cards with a man called Doc."

**interpretation.** An explanation of the meaning. If we see someone clench his fist and tighten his mouth, we may interpret these signs as revealing anger. When we say that in the New Testament the passage alluding to the separation of sheep from goats is to be understood as referring to the saved and the damned, we are offering an interpretation.

**irony.** In *verbal irony,* the meaning of the words intentionally contradicts the literal meaning, as in "that's not a very good idea," where the intended meaning is "that's a terrible idea." Irony, in distinction from sarcasm, employs at least some degree of wit or wryness. Sarcasm reveals contempt obviously and heavily, usually by asserting the opposite of what is meant: "You're a great guy" (if said sarcastically) means "It's awful of you to do this to me." Notice that the example of irony we began with was at least a trifle more ingenious than this sarcastic remark, for the sarcasm here simply is the opposite of what is meant, whereas our example of verbal irony is not quite the opposite. The opposite of "that's not a very good idea" is "that is a very good idea," but clearly (in our example) the speaker's meaning is something else. Put it this way: sarcasm is irony at its crudest, and finer irony commonly uses overstatement or especially understatement, rather than a simple opposite. (For a brief discussion of the use of irony in satire, see the entry on satire.)

If the speaker's words have an *un*intentional double meaning, the irony may be called *dramatic irony:* a character, about to go to bed, says, "I think I'll have a sound sleep," and dies in his sleep. Similarly, an action can turn dramatically ironic: a character seeks to help a friend and unintentionally harms him. Finally, a situation can be ironic: thirsty sailors are surrounded by water that cannot be drunk.

All these meanings of irony are held together, then, by the sense of a somewhat bitter contrast.

**jargon.** Technical language used inappropriately or inexactly. "Viable" means "able to survive." To speak of "a viable building" is to use jargon. "A primary factor in my participation in the dance" is jargon if what is meant is "I dance because. . . ."

**metaphor.** Words have literal meanings: a lemon is a yellow, egg-shaped citrus fruit; to drown is to suffocate in water or other fluid. But words can also have metaphoric meanings: we can call an unsatisfactory automobile a lemon, and we can say that we are drowning in paperwork. Metaphoric language is literally absurd; if we heed only the denotation it is clearly untrue, for an automobile cannot be a kind of citrus fruit, and we cannot drown in paperwork. (Even if the paper literally suffocated someone, the death could not be called a drowning.) Metaphor, then, uses not the denotation of the word but the associations, the connotations. Because we know that the speaker is not crazy, we turn from the literal meaning (which is clearly untrue) to the association.

**myth.** (1) A traditional story dealing with supernatural beings or with heroes, often accounting for why things are as they are. Myths tell of the creation of the world, the creation of man, the changes of the season, the achievements of heroes. A Zulu myth, for example, explains that rain is the tears of a god weeping for a beloved slain bird. *Mythology* is a system or group of such stories, and so we speak of Zulu mythology, or Greek mythology, or Norse mythology. (2) Mark Schorer, in *William Blake,* defines myth as "a large controlling image that gives philosophic meaning to the facts of ordinary life. . . . All real convictions involve a mythology. . . . Wars may be described as the clash of mythologies." In this sense, then, a myth is not a traditional story we do not believe, but any idea, true or false, to which people subscribe. Thus, one can speak of the "myth" of democracy or of communism.

**narration.** Discourse that recounts a real or a fictional happening. An anecdote is a narrative, and so is a history of the decline and fall of the Roman Empire. Narration may, of course, include substantial exposition ("four possible motives must be considered") and description ("the horse was an old gray mare"), but the emphasis is on a sequence of happenings ("and then she says to me, . . . ").

**parable.** A parable is a short narrative from which a moral or a lesson can be drawn. Christ's tale of the prodigal son (page 524) is told in order to reveal the blindness of the Pharisees who blame Christ for receiving sinners. A parable may, but need not, be an allegory wherein, say, each character stands for an abstraction that otherwise would be hard to grasp. Usually the parable lacks the *detailed* correspondence of an allegory.

**paradox.** An apparent self-contradiction, such as "He was happiest when miserable."

**paraphrase.** A rewording of a passage, usually in order to clarify the meaning. A paraphrase is a sort of translating within the same language; it can help to make clear the gist of the passage. But one must recognize the truth of Robert Frost's charge that when one paraphrases a line of good writing one puts it "in other and worse English." Paraphrase should not be confused with explication.

**parody.** A parody (from the Greek "counter song") seeks to amuse by imitating the style—the diction, the sentence structure—of another work, but normally the parody substitutes a very different subject. Thus, it might use tough-guy Hemingway talk to describe not a bullfighter but a butterfly catcher. Often a parody of a writer's style is a good-natured criticism of it.

**persona.** The writer or speaker in a role adopted for a specific audience. When Abraham Lincoln wrote or spoke, he sometimes did so in the persona of commander in chief of the Union Army, but at other times he did so in the persona of the simple man from Springfield, Illinois. The persona is a mask put on for a performance (*persona* is the Latin word for mask). If mask suggests insincerity, we should remember that whenever we speak or write we do so in a specific role —as friend, or parent, or teacher, or applicant for a job, or whatever. Although Lincoln was a husband, a father, a politician, a president, and many other things, when he wrote a letter or speech he might write solely as one of these; in a letter to his son, the persona (or, we might say, personality) is that of father, not that of commander in chief. The distinction between the writer (who necessarily fills many roles) and the persona who writes or speaks a work is especially useful in talking about satire, because the satirist often invents a mouthpiece very different from himself. The satirist—say Jonathan Swift—may be strongly opposed to a view, but his persona (his invented essayist) may favor the view; the reader must perceive that the real writer is ridiculing the invented essayist.

**persuasion.** Discourse that seeks to change a reader's mind. Persuasion usually assumes that the writer and the reader do not agree, or do not fully agree, at the outset. Persuasion may use logical argument (appeal to reason), but it may also try to win the reader over by other means—by appeal to the emotions, by wit, by geniality.

**rhetoric.** Although in much contemporary usage the word's meaning has sadly decayed to "inflated talk or writing," it can still mean "the study of elements such as content, structure, and cadence in writing or in speech." In short, in the best sense rhetoric is the study of the art of communicating with words.

**satire.** A work ridiculing identifiable objects in real life, meant to arouse in the reader contempt for its object. Satire is sometimes distinguished from comedy in that comedy aims simply to evoke amusement whereas satire aims to bring about moral reform by ridicule. According to Alexander Pope, satire "heals with morals what it hurts with wit." Satire sometimes uses invective (direct abuse), but if the invective is to entertain the reader it must be witty, as in a piling up of ingenious accusations. Invective, however, is probably less common in satire than is irony, a device in which the tone somehow contradicts the words. For instance, a speaker may seem to praise ("well, that's certainly an original idea that you have"), but we perceive that he is ridiculing a crackpot idea. Or the satirist may invent a naive speaker (a persona) who praises, but the praise is really dispraise because a simpleton offers it; the persona is sincere but the writer is ironic and satiric. Or, adopting another strategy, the writer may use an apparently naive persona to represent the voice of reason; the persona dispassionately describes actions that we take for granted (a political campaign), and through this simple, accurate, rational description we see the irrationality of our behavior. (For further comments on irony, see page 644.)

**style.** A distinctive way of expression. If we see a picture of a man sitting on a chair, we may say that it looks like a drawing for a comic book, or, we may say that it looks like a drawing by Rembrandt or Van Gogh or Andrew Wyeth. We have come to recognize certain ways of expression—independent of the content—as characteristic of certain minds. The content, it can be said, is the same—a man sitting in a chair—but the creator's way of expressing the content is individual. Similarly, "Four score and seven years ago" and "Eighty-seven years ago" are the same in content; but the style differs, because "Four score and seven years ago" distinctively reflects a mind familiar with the Bible and an orator speaking solemnly. Many people (we include ourselves) believe that the content is *not* the same if the expression is not the same. The "content" of "Four score and seven years ago" includes suggestions of the Bible and of God-fearing people not present in "eighty-seven years ago." In this view, a difference in style is a difference in content and therefore a difference in meaning. Surely it is true that in the work of the most competent writers, those who make every word count, one cannot separate style and content. Let C. S. Lewis have the next-to-last word: "The way for a person to develop a style is (a) to know exactly what he wants to say, and (b) to be sure he is saying exactly that. The reader, we must remember, does not start by knowing what we mean. If our words are ambiguous, our meaning will escape him. I sometimes think that writing is like driving sheep down a road. If there is any gate open to the left or the right the readers will most certainly go into it." And let the Austrian writer Karl Kraus have the last word: "There are two kinds of writers, those who are and those who aren't. With the first, content and form belong together like soul and body; with the second, they match each other like body and clothes."

**summary.** The word "summary" is related to "sum," to the total something adds up to. (The Greeks and Romans counted upward, and wrote the total at the top.) A summary is a condensation or abridgment briefly giving the reader the gist of a longer work. Here are a few principles that govern summaries: (1) A summary is much briefer than the original. It is *not* a paraphrase—a word-by-word translation of someone's words into your own—for a paraphrase is usually at least as long as the original, whereas a summary is rarely longer than one-fourth the original, and may even be much briefer, perhaps giving in a sentence or two an entire essay. (2) A summary usually achieves its brevity by omitting almost all the concrete details of the original, presenting only the sum that the details add up to. (3) A summary is accurate; it has no value if it misrepresents the point of the original. (4) The writer of a summary need not make the points in the same order as that of the original. In fact, a reader is occasionally driven to write a summary because the original author does not present the argument in an orderly sequence; the summary is an attempt to disengage the author's argument from the confusing presentation. (5) A summary normally is written in the present tense, because the writer assumes that although the author *wrote* the piece last year or a hundred years ago, the piece speaks to us today. (In other words, the summary is explicitly or implicitly prefaced by "He says," and all that follows is in the present tense. (6) Because a summary is openly based on someone else's views, not your own, you need not use quotation marks around any words that you take from the original. Here is a summary of this entry on "summary":

> A summary is a condensation or abridgment. These are some characteristics: (1) it is rarely more than one-fourth as long as the original; (2) its brevity is usually achieved by leaving out most of the concrete details of the original; (3) it is accurate; (4) it may rearrange the organization of the original, especially if a rearrangement will make things clearer; (5) it normally is in the present tense; (6) quoted words need not be enclosed in quotation marks.

**thesis.** The writer's position or attitude; the proposition advanced.

**thesis statement.** A sentence or two summarizing the writer's position or attitude. An essay may or may not have an explicit thesis statement. (See page 617.)

**tone.** The prevailing spirit of an utterance. The tone may be angry or bitter or joyful or solemn, or expressive of any similar mood or emotion. Tone usually reflects the writer's attitude toward the subject, the audience, and the self. (For further comments on tone, see pages 611–12.)

## ACKNOWLEDGMENTS (*continued from page iv*)


Michael J. Arlen, "Ode to Thanksgiving" reprinted by permission of Farrar, Straus and Giroux, Inc. from *The Camera Age* by Michael J. Arlen. Copyright © 1978, 1981 by Michael J. Arlen.

Nakashima Atushi, "The Expert," translated by Ivan Morris, *Encounter,* May 1958. Reprinted by permission of *Encounter* magazine. [Originally appeared under the pseudonym Nakashima Ton.]

W. H. Auden, "Work, Labor, and Play" from *A Certain World.* Copyright © 1970 by W. H. Auden. Reprinted by permission of Viking Penguin Inc.

James Baldwin, "Stranger in the Village" from *Notes of a Native Son* by James Baldwin. Copyright © 1955 by James Baldwin. Reprinted by permission of Beacon Press.

Toni Cade Bambara, "The Lesson" from *Gorilla, My Love,* by Toni Cade Bambara. Copyright © 1972 by Toni Cade Bambara. Reprinted by permission of Random House, Inc.

Jacques Barzun, "In Favor of Capital Punishment" reprinted from *The American Scholar,* Volume 31, Number 2, Spring, 1962. Copyright © 1962 by the United Chapters of Phi Beta Kappa. By permission of the publishers.

Black Elk, "High Horse's Courting" from John G. Neihardt, *Black Elk Speaks,* pp. 67–76. Copyright © 1932, 1959, 1972 by John G. Neihardt. Reprinted by permission of the John G. Neihardt Trust.

Black Elk, "War Games," from John G. Neihardt, *Black Elk Speaks,* pp. 14–15, 59–60. Copyright © 1932, 1959, 1972 by John G. Neihardt. Reprinted by permission of the John G. Neihardt Trust.

Albert Camus, "The Guest" from *Exile and the Kingdom,* by Albert Camus, translated by Justin O'Brien. Copyright © 1957, 1958 by Alfred A. Knopf, Inc. Reprinted by permission of the publisher.

Albert Camus, "The Myth of Sisyphus" from *The Myth of Sisyphus and Other Essays,* by Albert Camus, translated by Justin O'Brien. Copyright © 1955 by Alfred A. Knopf, Inc. Reprinted by permission of the publisher.

Chewing Blackbones, "Old Man and Old Woman" from Ella B. Clark, *Indian Legends from the Northern Rockies,* pp. 239–241. Copyright 1966 by the University of Oklahoma Press, Publishing Division of the University. Reprinted by permission.

John R. Coleman, "Blue-Collar Journal," excerpts from pages 182–185, 195–196, 216–218 of *Blue-Collar Journal: A College President's Sabbatical* (J. B. Lippincott Company). Copyright © 1974 by John R. Coleman. Reprinted by permission of Harper & Row, Publishers, Inc.

Gregory Corso, "Marriage" from *The Happy Birthday of Death.* Copyright © 1960 by New Directions Publishing Corporation. Reprinted by permission of New Directions Publishing Corporation.

Lewis A. Coser, "The Family" from *Sociology Through Literature,* © 1963, pp. 250–251. Reprinted by permission of Prentice-Hall, Inc., Englewood Cliffs, New Jersey.

Laura Cunningham, "The Girls' Room" reprinted by permission of William Morris Agency, Inc. on behalf of the author. Copyright © 1981 Laura Cunningham.

Joan Didion, "On Going Home" from *Slouching Towards Bethlehem* by Joan Didion. Copyright © 1961, 1964, 1965, 1966, 1967, 1968 by Joan Didion. Reprinted with the permission of Farrar, Straus & Giroux, Inc.

Excerpt on pp. 156–157 from pp. 21–22 of *Measuring Growth in English* by Paul Diederich. Copyright © 1974 by National Council of Teachers of English. Reprinted by permission of National Council of Teachers of English.

Peter Farb and George Armelagos, "The Patterns of Eating" from *Consuming Passions* by Peter Farb and George Armelagos. Copyright © 1980 by the Estate of Peter Farb. Reprinted by permission of Houghton Mifflin Company.

E. M. Forster, "My Wood" from *Abinger Harvest,* copyright © 1936, 1964 by E. M. Forster. Reprinted by permission of Harcourt Brace Jovanovich, Inc. and Edward Arnold (Publishers) Ltd.

Ernesto Galarza, "Growing into Manhood" from *Barrio Boy,* pp. 51–59. Copyright © 1971 University of Notre Dame Press, Notre Dame, Indiana 46556. Reprinted with permission.

Ruth Gay, "Fear of Food" reprinted from *The American Scholar,* Volume 45, Number 3, Summer, 1976. Copyright © 1976 by the United Chapters of Phi Beta Kappa. By permission of the publishers.

Paul Goldberger, "Quick! Before It Crumbles!" This article first appeared in *Esquire* magazine (September, 1975). Copyright © 1975 by Paul Goldberger. Permission granted by International Creative Management. Photographs copyright © 1975 by Esquire Publishing Inc. Reprinted by permission.

Paul Goodman, "A Proposal to Abolish Grading" reprinted from *Compulsory Mis-Education* by Paul Goodman, copyright 1964, by permission of the publisher, Horizon Press, New York.

Jeff Greenfield, "The Black and White Truth About Basketball" reprinted from *Esquire* (October 1975). Copyright © 1975 by Esquire Publishing Inc. Used by permission.

Edward T. Hall, "Proxemics in the Arab World" excerpted from *The Hidden Dimension* by Edward T. Hall. Copyright © 1966 by Edward T. Hall. Reprinted by permission of Doubleday & Company, Inc.

Thomas Hardy, "The Man He Killed" from *Collected Poems of Thomas Hardy* (New York: Macmillan, 1953).

Richard Hawley, "Television and Adolescents" from *American Film,* Vol. 4, No. 1, October 1978, pp. 53–56. Reprinted by permission of the author.

Gilbert Highet, "The Gettysburg Address" from *A Clerk of Oxenford,* pp. 84–91, reprinted by permission of Curtis Brown, Ltd. Copyright © 1954 by Gilbert Highet.

Anne Hollander, "Clothes Make the Man—Uneasy" from *The New Republic,* September 7, 1974. Reprinted by permission of *The New Republic,* © 1974 The New Republic, Inc.

John Holt, "The Right To Control One's Learning" from *Escape from Childhood* by John Holt. Copyright, © 1974, by John Holt. Reprinted by permission of the publisher, E. P. Dutton, Inc.

Jane Howard, "All Happy Clans are Alike: In Search of the Good Family" from *Families.* Copyright © 1978 by Jane Howard. Reprinted by permission of Simon & Schuster, a Division of Gulf & Western Corporation.

Jane Jacobs, "A Good Neighborhood" from *The Death and Life of Great American Cities,* by Jane Jacobs. Copyright © 1961 by Jane Jacobs. Reprinted by permission of Random House, Inc.

Oliver Jensen, "The Gettysburg Address in Eisenhowese" previously published in *The Territorial Enterprise* and *The New Republic* (June 17, 1957). Copyright 1957 by Oliver Jensen, then Editor of *American Heritage,* the magazine of history. Reprinted by permission.

James Weldon Johnson, "Lift Ev'ry Voice and Sing." © Copyright: Edward B. Marks Music Corporation. Used by Permission.

Pauline Kael, "High School and Other Forms of Madness" from *Deeper Into Movies* by Pauline Kael. Copyright © 1969 by Pauline Kael. First appeared in *The New Yorker.* By permission of Little, Brown and Company in association with the Atlantic Monthly Press.

X. J. Kennedy, "Who Killed King Kong?" from *Dissent* (Spring, 1960). Reprinted by permission of *Dissent* and the author.

Jamaica Kincaid, "Girl" from *The New Yorker,* June 26, 1978. Reprinted by permission; © 1978 The New Yorker Magazine, Inc.

Martin Luther King, Jr., "Nonviolent Resistance" (editors' title) from pp. 211–216 in *Stride Toward Freedom* by Martin Luther King, Jr. Copyright © 1958 by Martin Luther King, Jr. Reprinted by permission of Harper & Row, Publishers, Inc.

Excerpt on pp. 403–404 from *More Lives Than One* by Joseph Wood Krutch. Copyright © 1962 by Joseph Wood Krutch. By permission of William Morrow & Co.

Barbara Lawrence, "Four-Letter Words Can Hurt You," from *The New York Times,* October 27, 1973. © 1973 by The New York Times Company. Reprinted by permission.

C. S. Lewis, "We have No 'Right to Happiness' " from *God In The Dock,* copyright © 1970 by the Trustees of the Estate of C. S. Lewis. British title *Undeceptions,* © 1971, The Trustees of the Estate of C. S. Lewis. Reproduced by permission of Curtis Brown, Ltd., London, and William Collins Sons & Co., Ltd., London.

C. S. Lewis, "Xmas and Christmas" from *God In The Dock* copyright © 1970 by the Trustees of the Estate of C. S. Lewis. British title *Undeceptions,* © 1971, The Trustees of the Estate of C. S. Lewis. Reproduced by permission of Curtis Brown, Ltd., London, and William Collins Sons & Co., Ltd., London.

Lin Yutang, "Art as Play and Personality" from *The Importance of Living,* copyright © 1937 by Reynal and Hitchcock. Reprinted by permission of Tsuifeng Lin.

Malcolm X, "The Shoeshine Boy" from *The Autobiography of Malcolm X,* by Malcolm X with Alex Haley. Copyright © 1964 by Alex Haley and Malcolm X, © 1965 by Alex Haley and Betty Shabazz. Reprinted by permission of Random House, Inc.

Marya Mannes, "Television Advertising," original title "The Splitting Image," from *The Saturday Review,* November 4, 1970. Copyright © 1970 by Marya Mannes. Reprinted by permission.

W. S. Merwin, "Make this Simple Test," in *The Miner's Pale Children.* Copyright © 1969, 1970 W. S. Merwin. Reprinted with the permission of Atheneum Publishers.

Stanley Milgram, "Reflections on News." Copyright 1977 by the Antioch Review, Inc. First published in *The Antioch Review,* Volume 35, Numbers 2–3. Reprinted by permission.

Marianne Moore, "The Student" from *What Are Years.* Copyright © 1941 by Marianne Moore, renewed 1969 by Marianne Moore. Reprinted with permission of Macmillan Publishing Co., Inc.

Sir Thomas More, "Work and Play in Utopia" reprinted from *Utopia* by Sir Thomas More, Translated and Edited by Robert M. Adams, A Norton Critical Edition. With the permission of W. W. Norton & Company, Inc. Copyright © 1975 by W. W. Norton & Company, Inc.

Desmond Morris, "Altruistic Behavior," reprinted from *Manwatching: A Field Guide to Human Behavior* by Desmond Morris. Text © 1977 by Desmond Morris, published by Harry N. Abrams, Inc., New York. Reprinted by permission.

Vladimir Nabokov, "Speak, Memory" from *Speak, Memory,* pp. 126–131 of the Putnam edition. Copyright 1948, © 1960, 1966 by Vladimir Nabokov. Reprinted by permission of Vera Nabokov.

Flannery O'Connor, "Revelation" from *Everything That Rises Must Converge* by Flannery O'Connor. Copyright © 1964, 1965 by the Estate of Mary Flannery O'Connor. Reprinted with the permission of Farrar, Straus & Giroux, Inc.

George Orwell, "Politics and the English Language" from *Shooting an Elephant and Other Essays,* copyright 1945, 1946, 1949, 1950 by Sonia Brownell Orwell, renewed 1973, 1974, 1977 by Sonia Orwell; renewed 1978 by Sonia Pitt-Rivers. Reprinted by permission of Harcourt Brace Jovanovich, Inc., the estate of the late Sonia Brownell Orwell, and Martin Secker & Warburg Ltd.

George Orwell, "Shooting an Elephant" from *Shooting an Elephant and Other Essays,* copyright 1945, 1946, 1949, 1950 by Sonia Brownell Orwell; renewed 1973, 1974, 1977 by Sonia Orwell; renewed 1978 by Sonia Pitt-Rivers. Reprinted by permission of Harcourt Brace Jovanovich, Inc., the estate of the late Sonia Brownell Orwell, and Martin Secker & Warburg Ltd.

J. H. Plumb, "The Dying Family" from *In the Light of History* by J. H. Plumb. The Penguin Press, 1972. Copyright © 1972 by J. H. Plumb. Reprinted by permission of Houghton Mifflin Company and Penguin Books Ltd.

Neil Postman, "Order in the Classroom," original title "Teaching As a Conserving Activity," excerpted from the book *Teaching As a Conserving Activity* by Neil Postman. Copyright © 1979 by Neil Postman. Reprinted by permission of Delacorte Press.

Paul Robinson, "TV Can't Educate" from *The New Republic,* August 12, 1978. Reprinted by permission of *The New Republic,* © 1978, The New Republic, Inc.

Theodore Roethke, "My Papa's Waltz" from *The Collected Poems of Theodore Roethke.* Copyright 1942 by Hearst Magazines, Inc. Reprinted by permission of Doubleday & Company, Inc.

Theodore Roethke, "Child on Top of a Greenhouse" from *The Collected Poems of Theodore Roethke.* Copyright 1946 by Editorial Publications, Inc. Reprinted by permission of Doubleday & Company, Inc.

Bertrand Russell, "Work" from *The Conquest of Happiness,* pp. 209–219. Reprinted from *The Conquest of Happiness* by Bertrand Russell, with the permission of Liveright Publishing Corporation. Copyright 1930 by Horace Liveright, Inc. Copyright renewed 1958 by Bertrand Russell. Reprinted also by permission of George Allen & Unwin (Publishers) Ltd.

Excerpt on p. 7 reprinted from *The Conquest of Happiness* by Bertrand Russell, with the permission of Liveright Publishing Corporation. Copyright 1930 by Horace Liveright, Inc. Copyright renewed 1958 by Bertrand Russell. Reprinted also by permission of George Allen & Unwin (Publishers) Ltd.

May Sarton, "The Rewards of Living a Solitary Life," from *The New York Times*, April 6, 1974. © 1974 by The New York Times Company. Reprinted by permission.

Peter Singer, "Animal Liberation" from *The New York Review of Books,* April 5, 1973, pp. 17–21. Copyright © 1973 by Peter Singer. Reprinted by permission of the author.

Stevie Smith, "Not Waving But Drowning" from *Selected Poems.* Copyright © 1964 by Stevie Smith. Reprinted by permission of New Directions Publishers and agents for the estate of Stevie Smith.

Robert Sommer, "Hard Architecture" from *Tight Spaces: Hard Architecture and How to Humanize It,* pp. 1–3, 7–19, 111–114, copyright 1974 Prentice-Hall, Inc., Englewood Cliffs, New Jersey. Reprinted by permission of the author.

Mark Stevens, "Goya's Third of May, 1802," *Travel and Leisure,* 1982. Reprinted by permission of the author.

Judy Syfers, "Why I Want a Wife" from *Ms.,* Vol. 1 (December 31, 1971). Reprinted by permission of the author.

Studs Terkel, "Three Workers: Terry Mason, Airline Stewardess; Roberta Victor, Hooker; Maggie Holmes, Domestic" from *Working: People Talk About What They Do All Day And How They Feel About What They Do,* by Studs Terkel. Copyright © 1972, 1974 by Studs Terkel. Reprinted by permission of Pantheon Books, a Division of Random House, Inc.

Lewis Thomas, "On Committees" from *The Medusa and The Snail: More Notes of A Biology Watcher* by Lewis Thomas. Copyright © 1976 by Lewis Thomas. Originally published in the New England Journal of Medicine. Reprinted by permission of Viking Penguin Inc.

Lewis Thomas, "The Iks" from *The Lives of a Cell.* Copyright © 1973 by The Massachusetts Medical Society. Reprinted by permission of The Viking Press.

James Thurber, "The Secret Life of Walter Mitty" from *My World—And Welcome To It,* published by Harcourt Brace Jovanovich. Originally printed in *The New Yorker.* Copyright © 1942 James Thurber. Copyright © 1970 Helen Thurber. Reprinted by permission of Mrs. James Thurber.

Lionel Tiger, "Omnigamy: The New Kinship System" from *Psychology Today,* July 1978, pp. 14 and 17. Reprinted by permission of International Creative Management. Copyright © 1978 by Lionel
Tiger.

John Updike, "The Playground," from *Five Boyhoods,* Martin Levin, ed., published by Doubleday & Co. Copyright © 1962 by Martin Levin. Reprinted by permission of Martin Levin.

Excerpt on p. 87 from *Assorted Prose,* by John Updike. Copyright © 1964 by John Updike. Reprinted by permission of Alfred A. Knopf, Inc. First appeared in *The New Yorker.*

Arturo Vivante, "The Orchard," (Copyright © 1968 Arturo Vivante) in *Run to the Waterfall.* Copyright © 1979 Arturo Vivante. Reprinted with the permission of Charles Scribner's Sons. "The Orchard" was first published in *The New Yorker.*

Excerpt on p. 160 from *In My Own Way,* by Alan Watts. Copyright © 1972 by Alan Watts. Reprinted by permission of Pantheon Books, a Division of Random House, Inc.

E. B. White, "The Door" from *Poems and Sketches of E. B. White* by E. B. White. Copyright 1939 by E. B. White. Originally appeared in *The New Yorker.* Reprinted by permission of Harper & Row, Publishers, Inc.

E. B. White, "Education" from pp. 52–54 in "Education—March, 1939" in *One Man's Meat* by E. B. White. Copyright 1939 by E. B. White. Reprinted by permission of Harper & Row, Publishers, Inc.

William Carlos Williams, "The Poor" from *Collected Earlier Poems.* Copyright 1938 by New Directions Publishing Corporation. Reprinted by permission of New Directions Publishing Corporation.

Virginia Woolf, "Professions for Women" from *The Death of the Moth and Other Essays.* Copyright 1942 by Harcourt Brace Jovanovich, Inc.; copyright 1970 by Marjorie T. Parsons, executrix. Reprinted by permission of the author's literary estate, The Hogarth Press, Ltd. and Harcourt Brace Jovanovich, Inc.

Wu-tsu Fa-yen, "Zen and the Art of Burglary" from Diasetz T. Suzuki, *Zen and Japanese Culture,* Bollingen Series LXIV, copyright 1959. Excerpt reprinted by permission of Princeton University Press.

Laurence Wylie, "Having a Good Time in Peyrane, 1950" (editors' title) reprinted by permission of the publishers from *Village in the Vaucluse,* Third Edition, by Laurence Wylie, Cambridge, Mass.: Harvard University Press. Copyright © 1957, 1964, 1974 by the President and Fellows of Harvard College.

William Butler Yeats, "The Lake Isle of Innisfree" from *Collected Poems* by William Butler Yeats. Copyright 1906 by Macmillan Publishing Co., Inc., renewed 1934 by William Butler Yeats. Reprinted with permission of M. B. Yeats, Miss Anne Yeats, Macmillan Company of London & Basingstoke, and Macmillan Publishing Co., Inc.

William Butler Yeats, "Remembering 'The Lake Isle of Innisfree,' " excerpt from *Autobiography* by William Butler Yeats. Copyright 1916, 1935 by Macmillan Publishing Co., Inc., renewed 1944, 1963 by Bertha Georgie Yeats. Reprinted by permission of M. B. Yeats, Miss Anne Yeats, the Macmillan Company of London & Basingstoke, and Macmillan Publishing Co., Inc.

# Index

# To the Student

Part of our job as educational publishers is to try to improve the textbooks we publish. Thus, when revising a book, we take into account the experience of both instructors and students with the previous edition. At some time your instructor will be asked to comment extensively on *The Little, Brown Reader,* Third Edition, but right now we want to hear from you. After all, though your instructor assigned this book, you are the one who paid for it.

Please help us by completing this questionnaire and returning it to College English Developmental Group, Little, Brown & Company, 34 Beacon Street, Boston, Massachusetts 02106.

School ________________ Course title ________________

Instructor's Name ______________________________________

Please rate the selections:

| 1. ALL IN THE FAMILY | *Liked best* | | | | *Liked least* | *Didn't read* |
|---|---|---|---|---|---|---|
| Lewis Coser, The Family | 5 | 4 | 3 | 2 | 1 | — |
| J. H. Plumb, The Dying Family | 5 | 4 | 3 | 2 | 1 | — |
| Laura Cunningham, The Girls' Room | 5 | 4 | 3 | 2 | 1 | — |
| Lionel Tiger, Omnigamy: The New Kinship System | 5 | 4 | 3 | 2 | 1 | — |
| Jane Howard, All Happy Clans Are Alike | 5 | 4 | 3 | 2 | 1 | — |
| Black Elk, High Horse's Courting | 5 | 4 | 3 | 2 | 1 | — |
| Judy Syfers, Why I Want a Wife | 5 | 4 | 3 | 2 | 1 | — |
| Anonymous, Confessions of an Erstwhile Child | 5 | 4 | 3 | 2 | 1 | — |
| Jonathan Swift, A Modest Proposal | 5 | 4 | 3 | 2 | 1 | — |
| Peter Singer, Animal Liberation | 5 | 4 | 3 | 2 | 1 | — |
| Jamaica Kincaid, Girl | 5 | 4 | 3 | 2 | 1 | — |
| Theodore Roethke, My Papa's Waltz | 5 | 4 | 3 | 2 | 1 | — |
| Gregory Corso, Marriage | 5 | 4 | 3 | 2 | 1 | — |

| 2. FOOD, CLOTHING, SHELTER | | | | | | |
|---|---|---|---|---|---|---|
| Peter Farb & George Armelagos, The Patterns of Eating | 5 | 4 | 3 | 2 | 1 | — |
| Ruth Gay, Fear of Food | 5 | 4 | 3 | 2 | 1 | — |
| Michael J. Arlen, Ode to Thanksgiving | 5 | 4 | 3 | 2 | 1 | — |
| W. S. Merwin, Make This Simple Test | 5 | 4 | 3 | 2 | 1 | — |

| | *Liked best* | | | | *Liked least* | *Didn't read* |
|---|---|---|---|---|---|---|
| Paul Goldberger, Quick! Before It Crumbles! | 5 | 4 | 3 | 2 | 1 | — |
| Henry David Thoreau, As for Clothing | 5 | 4 | 3 | 2 | 1 | — |
| Anne Hollander, Clothes Make the Man — Uneasy | 5 | 4 | 3 | 2 | 1 | — |
| Robert Sommer, Hard Architecture | 5 | 4 | 3 | 2 | 1 | — |
| Jane Jacobs, A Good Neighborhood | 5 | 4 | 3 | 2 | 1 | — |
| E. B. White, The Door | 5 | 4 | 3 | 2 | 1 | — |
| William Carlos Williams, The Poor | 5 | 4 | 3 | 2 | 1 | — |
| **3. TEACHING AND LEARNING** | | | | | | |
| Plato, The Myth of the Cave | 5 | 4 | 3 | 2 | 1 | — |
| Ernesto Galarza, Growing into Manhood | 5 | 4 | 3 | 2 | 1 | — |
| E. B. White, Education | 5 | 4 | 3 | 2 | 1 | — |
| Pauline Kael, High School and Other Forms of Madness | 5 | 4 | 3 | 2 | 1 | — |
| Neil Postman, Order in the Classroom | 5 | 4 | 3 | 2 | 1 | — |
| John Holt, The Right to Control One's Learning | 5 | 4 | 3 | 2 | 1 | — |
| Maya Angelou, Graduation | 5 | 4 | 3 | 2 | 1 | — |
| Paul Goodman, A Proposal to Abolish Grading | 5 | 4 | 3 | 2 | 1 | — |
| Paul Robinson, TV Can't Educate | 5 | 4 | 3 | 2 | 1 | — |
| Toni Cade Bambara, The Lesson | 5 | 4 | 3 | 2 | 1 | — |
| Wu-tsu Fa-yen, Zen and the Art of Burglary | 5 | 4 | 3 | 2 | 1 | — |
| Marianne Moore, The Student | 5 | 4 | 3 | 2 | 1 | — |
| **4. WORK AND PLAY** | | | | | | |
| Bertrand Russell, Work | 5 | 4 | 3 | 2 | 1 | — |
| W. H. Auden, Work, Labor, and Play | 5 | 4 | 3 | 2 | 1 | — |
| Arturo Vivante, The Orchard | 5 | 4 | 3 | 2 | 1 | — |
| John R. Coleman, Blue-Collar Journal | 5 | 4 | 3 | 2 | 1 | — |
| Malcolm X, The Shoeshine Boy | 5 | 4 | 3 | 2 | 1 | — |
| Studs Terkel, Three Workers | 5 | 4 | 3 | 2 | 1 | — |
| Virginia Woolf, Professions for Women | 5 | 4 | 3 | 2 | 1 | — |
| Thomas More, Work and Play in Utopia | 5 | 4 | 3 | 2 | 1 | — |
| Lin Yutang, Art as Play and Personality | 5 | 4 | 3 | 2 | 1 | — |
| Jeff Greenfield, The Black and White Truth About Basketball | 5 | 4 | 3 | 2 | 1 | — |
| Black Elk, War Games | 5 | 4 | 3 | 2 | 1 | — |
| John Updike, The Playground | 5 | 4 | 3 | 2 | 1 | — |
| Laurence Wylie, Having a Good Time in Peyrane, 1950 | 5 | 4 | 3 | 2 | 1 | — |
| Theodore Roethke, Child on Top of a Greenhouse | 5 | 4 | 3 | 2 | 1 | — |

| | *Liked best* | | | | *Liked least* | *Didn't read* |
|---|---|---|---|---|---|---|
| **5. MESSAGES** | | | | | | |
| Abraham Lincoln, Address at the Dedication of the Gettysburg National Cemetery | 5 | 4 | 3 | 2 | 1 | — |
| Gilbert Highet, The Gettysburg Address | 5 | 4 | 3 | 2 | 1 | — |
| Oliver Jensen, The Gettysburg Address in Eisenhowese | 5 | 4 | 3 | 2 | 1 | — |
| George Orwell, Politics and the English Language | 5 | 4 | 3 | 2 | 1 | — |
| Barbara Lawrence, Four-Letter Words Can Hurt You | 5 | 4 | 3 | 2 | 1 | — |
| C. S. Lewis, Xmas and Christmas | 5 | 4 | 3 | 2 | 1 | — |
| Edward T. Hall, Proxemics in the Arab World | 5 | 4 | 3 | 2 | 1 | — |
| Flannery O'Connor, Revelation | 5 | 4 | 3 | 2 | 1 | — |
| Stevie Smith, Not Waving but Drowning | 5 | 4 | 3 | 2 | 1 | — |
| **6. NETWORKS** | | | | | | |
| Richard A. Hawley, Television and Adolescents: A Teacher's View | 5 | 4 | 3 | 2 | 1 | — |
| Marya Mannes, Television Advertising: The Splitting Image | 5 | 4 | 3 | 2 | 1 | — |
| X. J. Kennedy, Who Killed King Kong? | 5 | 4 | 3 | 2 | 1 | — |
| Stanley Milgram, Confessions of a News Addict | 5 | 4 | 3 | 2 | 1 | — |
| Lewis Thomas, On Committees | 5 | 4 | 3 | 2 | 1 | — |
| James Thurber, The Secret Life of Walter Mitty | 5 | 4 | 3 | 2 | 1 | — |
| **7. RIVALS AND ENEMIES** | | | | | | |
| Thomas Hobbes, Of the Natural Condition of Mankind, as Concerning Their Felicity, and Misery | 5 | 4 | 3 | 2 | 1 | — |
| Mark Stevens, Goya's *Third of May, 1808* | 5 | 4 | 3 | 2 | 1 | — |
| Lewis Thomas, The Iks | 5 | 4 | 3 | 2 | 1 | — |
| Desmond Morris, Altruistic Behavior: How Do We Help Others at Our Own Expense? | 5 | 4 | 3 | 2 | 1 | — |
| James Baldwin, Stranger in the Village | 5 | 4 | 3 | 2 | 1 | — |
| George Orwell, Shooting an Elephant | 5 | 4 | 3 | 2 | 1 | — |
| Albert Camus, The Guest | 5 | 4 | 3 | 2 | 1 | — |
| Thomas Hardy, The Man He Killed | 5 | 4 | 3 | 2 | 1 | — |
| **8. LAW AND ORDER** | | | | | | |
| Martin Luther King, Jr., Nonviolent Resistance | 5 | 4 | 3 | 2 | 1 | — |
| Plato, Crito | 5 | 4 | 3 | 2 | 1 | — |

| | *Liked best* | | | | *Liked least* | *Didn't read* |
|---|---|---|---|---|---|---|
| Luke, John, and an Anonymous Japanese, Four Short Narratives | 5 | 4 | 3 | 2 | 1 | — |
| Thomas Jefferson, The Declaration of Independence | 5 | 4 | 3 | 2 | 1 | — |
| Rosika Schwimmer, Court Record of Petition for Naturalization | 5 | 4 | 3 | 2 | 1 | — |
| Pierce Butler, Opinion of the Supreme Court, in *The United States of America, Petitioner,* v. *Rosika Schwimmer* | 5 | 4 | 3 | 2 | 1 | — |
| Oliver Wendell Holmes, Dissent in the Rosika Schwimmer Case | 5 | 4 | 3 | 2 | 1 | — |
| Jacques Barzun, In Favor of Capital Punishment | 5 | 4 | 3 | 2 | 1 | — |
| Henry Schwarzschild, In Opposition to Death Penalty Legislation | 5 | 4 | 3 | 2 | 1 | — |
| Arthur Hugh Clough, The Latest Decalogue | 5 | 4 | 3 | 2 | 1 | — |

9. THE DEEP HEART'S CORE

| | | | | | | |
|---|---|---|---|---|---|---|
| William Butler Yeats, The Lake Isle of Innisfree | 5 | 4 | 3 | 2 | 1 | — |
| William Butler Yeats, Remembering the Lake Isle of Innisfree | 5 | 4 | 3 | 2 | 1 | — |
| Vladimir Nabokov, Speak, Memory | 5 | 4 | 3 | 2 | 1 | — |
| E. M. Forster, My Wood | 5 | 4 | 3 | 2 | 1 | — |
| Joan Didion, On Going Home | 5 | 4 | 3 | 2 | 1 | — |
| C. S. Lewis, We Have No "Right to Happiness" | 5 | 4 | 3 | 2 | 1 | — |
| May Sarton, The Rewards of Living a Solitary Life | 5 | 4 | 3 | 2 | 1 | — |
| Albert Camus, The Myth of Sisyphus | 5 | 4 | 3 | 2 | 1 | — |
| Nakajima Atushi, The Expert | 5 | 4 | 3 | 2 | 1 | — |
| Chewing Blackbones, Old Man and Old Woman | 5 | 4 | 3 | 2 | 1 | — |
| William Shakespeare, Sonnet 29 ("When, in disgrace with Fortune and men's eyes") | 5 | 4 | 3 | 2 | 1 | — |
| Appendix A: Reading (and Writing About) Essays | 5 | 4 | 3 | 2 | 1 | — |
| Appendix B: Reading (and Writing About) Pictures | 5 | 4 | 3 | 2 | 1 | — |
| Appendix C: A Writer's Glossary | 5 | 4 | 3 | 2 | 1 | — |

What did you think of the *Short Views?* Did you discuss them in class?

____________________________________________________

____________________________________________________

Did you like the idea of discussing and writing about pictures?

___

Please add any comments or suggestions on how we might improve this book. ___

___

___

___

___

Your Name ___ Date ___

Mailing address ___

May we quote you either in promotion for this book or in future publishing ventures?

Yes___ No___

Thank you.